"Information through Innovation"

SYSTEMS ANALYSIS AND DESIGN

A COMPREHENSIVE METHODOLOGY WITH CASE

MICHAEL L. GIBSON
AUBURN UNIVERSITY

CARY T. HUGHES
MIDDLE TENNESSEE STATE UNIVERSITY

boyd & fraser publishing company

Executive Editor: James H. Edwards
Developmental Editor: Jill Pisoni
Production Editor: Barbara Worth
Project Management: Laurie K. Stewart, ex libris
Production Services and Layout: Marian Hartsough Associates
Developmental and Copy Editor: Judith Brown
Proofreaders: Judith Abrahms and Linda Hartsough
Illustrations: Valerie Winemiller and Edwin Smith
Interior and Cover Design: Vargas/Williams Design
Cover Art Special Effects: Iikka Valli
Index: Katherine Stimson
Manufacturing Coordinator: Tracy Megison

© 1994 by boyd & fraser publishing company
One Corporate Place • Ferncroft Village
Danvers, Massachusetts 01923

International Thomson Publishing
boyd & fraser publishing company is an ITP company.
The ITP trademark is used under license.

This book is printed on recycled, acid-free paper that meets Environmental Protection Agency standards.

All rights reserved. No part of this work may be reproduced or used in any form or by any means—graphic, electronic, or mechanical, including photocopying, recording, taping, or information storage and retrieval systems—without written permission from the publisher.

Names of all products mentioned herein are used for identification purposes only and may be trademarks and/or registered trademarks of their respective owners. boyd & fraser publishing company disclaims any affiliation, association, or connection with, or sponsorship or endorsement by such owners.

Manufactured in the United States of America

Library of Congress Cataloging-in-Publication Data

Gibson, Michael L.
    Systems analysis and design : a comprehensive methodology
with CASE / Michael L. Gibson, Cary T. Hughes.
        p. cm.
    Includes index.
    ISBN 0-87709-247-8
    1. Management information systems. 2. System design.
3. Computer-aided software engineering.   I. Hughes, Cary T.
II. Title.
T58.6.G494 1994
658.4'038'011—dc20   93-39103
                                                          CIP

2 3 4 5 6 7 8 9 10 D 8 7 6 5

Brief Contents

Contents

PART VI   # MAINTAINING AND SECURING THE SYSTEM   717

CHAPTER 16   ## Post-Implementation Review and Maintenance   718

Preface

Systems analysis and design has seen the growth of various methods for analyzing and designing computer systems for business applications, as well as the advent of a number of tools to assist people in the use of these methods. As a result, systems professionals are able to create and maintain computer systems and to perform analysis and design functions more efficiently and consistently. However, the advent of these methodologies and their associated tools does not guarantee that better business systems will be created and maintained. Business systems development and maintenance depends a great deal on the individual ability of the systems professional to clearly understand the business and devise a system to supply the firm with its information needs.

To better understand the business and its systems, analysts build models of the business and its information systems. The use of various methodologies and tools provides a framework within which these systems craftsmen create these models. By having a recognized framework, systems professionals can now spend more of their time actually designing systems rather than searching through the sea of clerical work that accompanies the analysis and design of business systems. As a result, systems analysis and design has become more of a complete art form, with different methods of "crafting" business systems.

The emergence of recognized methodologies has created a need to train persons interested in analysis and design more fully. This text has a system project orientation, explaining the process of analyzing and designing systems and the various methods and tools that aid in developing and maintaining information systems based on business and system models. These methods and tools are employed in manual as well as automated forms. Methods and tools are discussed in reference to how, when, and where they are employed in the investigation and design of business information systems. Discussions of many of the most prominent methods relate their use to various phases of the life span of systems.

HOW THIS TEXT IS ORGANIZED

This text is designed to be used as the basis for courses in analysis and design (A&D) and as a reference for various methods and tools of A&D. The book is divided into seven parts.

In **Part I**, Chapter 1 presents a general introduction to systems analysis and design, while Chapters 2 and 3 explain methodology and the system life cycle. Chapter 2 explains and illustrates various methods and tools that can be used during analysis and design, explains methodology, and describes the methodology used in this text. Chapter 3 presents an overview of the system development life cycle and describes what is done in each phase. Many chapters in the remaining sections of the text expand upon portions of Chapters 2 and 3.

Part II, which includes Chapters 4, 5, and 6, deals with problem investigation and methods for documenting the results of systems analysis with a data and process modeling orientation. These chapters explain how to acquire data on user requirements, how to use a methodology to document them, and how to conduct a review of the analysis phase of the project.

Part III covers prototyping, logical design, and physical design in Chapters 7, 8, and 9, respectively. These chapters illustrate how prototyping influences the logical and physical design, how to logically design what is desired, and how to convert the logical design into the physical design.

In **Part IV**, Chapter 10 explains what a database is and its influence on systems projects. Chapter 11 explains the activities involved in physically developing the system. Chapter 12 describes file organization and system testing, and Chapter 13 covers training, system implementation, and review.

Part V contains Chapters 14 and 15, which describe project feasibility and project management. Although these topics should be considered throughout a project, they are discussed here so as not to interrupt the flow of material in Chapters 1 through 13. We believe that familiarity with the topics in the first thirteen chapters will better prepare aspiring analysts for understanding and applying the principles of feasibility analysis and project management. Chapter 14 describes the different types of feasibility and focuses on the methods used in economic feasibility analysis. Chapter 15 discusses the principles of project management and how to use them to control a system project.

Part VI contains Chapters 16 and 17, which deal with maintaining and securing business systems. Chapter 16 describes maintenance and the application of its principles in maintaining the business model and information system. Chapter 17 describes methods of securing the system and ethical issues regarding information systems.

Part VII contains two appendixes with additional information of interest to the aspiring analyst. Appendix A describes database data structures that aid in efficient access of data retained in a database. Appendix B provides an example list of COBOL programming rules that may be used to create structured programs in the information system.

WHY WE WROTE THIS BOOK

We undertook this book project because no other book on systems analysis and design provides a comprehensive methodological view of the topic or takes a project completion approach. This book takes a consultant's approach to systems analysis and design and can be used to follow an A&D project from start to finish.

Intended Audience

This book is intended for college and trade school students and business personnel who wish to learn how to perform systems analysis and design. The book assumes no familiarity with analysis and design. For undergraduate college and trade school students, the book can be used in either one or two courses. For a one-quarter or semester A&D course, we suggest assigning Chapters 1 through 9, which cover the process of systems analysis and design. For a two-quarter or semester A&D course, we suggest Chapters 1 through 6, 14, and 15 for the first course. The second course should begin with Chapter 7 and continue to the end of the book.

For business personnel, the book can be used independently or in a formal training program. Whether used in a school or business setting, the ancillary materials that supplement the book are useful aids in learning the principles of A&D and completing the exercises at the end of each chapter.

SUPPLEMENTS TO THIS BOOK

The following supplements can be obtained by schools that adopt this textbook:

- Instructor's Manual and accompanying transparency masters
- Lecture Presentation System
- Study Guide and ClassNotes
- Instructor's Resource Disk Package
- Test Item File

INSTRUCTOR'S MANUAL   The Instructor's Manual contains transparency masters and provides guidance on how to use this book in teaching systems analysis and design. Topics include:

- Planning, designing, and scheduling one-quarter, two-quarter, or semester courses
- Lesson planning for particular topics
- Integrating the example project in classroom lectures

LECTURE PRESENTATION SYSTEM A complete electronic slide presentation of all course material has been prepared for use in classroom lectures. The presentation is separated relative to the chapters in the book. The slide show was created in WordPerfect Presentation Manager. The run-time version of the slide show can be used for automatic display of all transparencies on an LCD projection panel connected to a desktop computer. If you have Presentation Manager, the files used to create the run-time slide show can be obtained for more customized lectures. The slide show can also be used as a tutorial for students to review in computer laboratories.

STUDY GUIDE AND CLASSNOTES The student Study Guide and ClassNotes includes tear-out pages of all slides and transparencies in reduced form for better, more organized note taking during classroom lectures. The Study Guide and ClassNotes also contains tear-out forms to complete chapter exercises using various modeling methods and dictionary entries to accompany the models created while completing exercises. These tear-out pages contain dictionary layouts similar to those used by various CASE tools to familiarize students with this type of documentation, even when CASE tools are not present.

INSTRUCTOR'S RESOURCE DISK PACKAGE The Instructor's Resource Disk Package includes the National Golf & Tennis example CASE project that appears throughout the book. The example CASE project was completed in Intersolv's Excelerator and Knowledgeware's Information Engineering Workbench (IEW). Copies of the CASE projects can be obtained in either Excelerator or IEW. These CASE projects can be used in class lectures or laboratory demonstrations. They can also be used by students in completing the exercises at the end of various chapters.

TEST ITEM FILE The Test Item File includes approximately 3000 questions in either true/false, matching, multiple choice, or short answer format. The answers to the questions are also included for grading purposes. The Test Item File is available in MicroExam 4.0.

ACKNOWLEDGMENTS

We are indebted to many persons for their help in the creation of this manuscript. Our most important thank you goes to our wives, Krystal L. Gibson and Constance Hughes, who aided us in many ways regarding the development of this manuscript. We also owe a debt of thanks to a number of different reviewers whose suggestions added immensely to the comprehensiveness and integration of the manuscript. In particular, we thank

Thomas Case
Georgia Southern University

C. Brian Honess
University of South Carolina

Robert Keim
Arizona State University

John Melrose
University of Wisconsin-Eau Claire

William Myers
Belmont Abbey College

Jerry Peters
Lambuth University

Layne Wallace
University of North Florida

We especially thank all of those who helped with the editing and production of this book. The following persons are responsible for much of the quality of this effort: Jim Edwards, Barb Worth, and Jill Pisoni from boyd & fraser; Laurie Stewart, Judith Brown, Marian Hartsough, Judith Abrahms, Linda Hartsough, Juan Vargas, and Katherine Stimson. Thank you all.

We also thank Michael Whitman and Marc Miller, who helped construct the ancillary materials that accompany this textbook. Finally, we dedicate this book to our families, Krystal Gibson and Jason G. Gibson, Connie Hughes, and Timothy Hughes, who encourage us and make us proud.

PART I

Establishing a Framework for Systems Analysis and Design

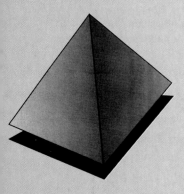 The field of systems analysis and design has seen the growth of various methodologies and techniques for analyzing and designing computer systems for business applications, which has made it possible for systems professionals to more effectively create and maintain computer systems. Part I describes systems analysis and design and emphasizes the need to establish an environment in which systems from various areas in the business are designed using standard methodologies.

The system life cycle provides a framework for designing systems. Even though a financial information system will look different from a personnel information system, the analyst goes through the same steps in the system development life cycle to design both of the systems. The final chapter in Part I, Chapter 3, emphasizes the importance of properly defining the problem and collecting the data necessary to complete analysis and design. If the problem is not accurately defined, an effective information system will not be built.

CHAPTER 1

Introduction to Systems Analysis and Design

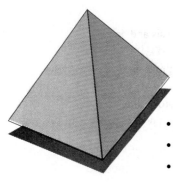

OVERVIEW

This chapter presents definitions and explanations of systems analysis and design that provide the necessary groundwork for understanding material in later chapters. It also describes qualifications and job opportunities for the systems analyst. To get you started, this chapter:

- Defines pertinent topics in analysis and design (A&D)
- Describes the general systems theory and provides a model of the firm
- Explains the relationship among management information systems (MISs), decision support systems (DSSs), management support systems (MSSs), and transaction processing systems (TPSs)
- Identifies and describes the different levels of management in the firm
- Lists attributes of systems
- Defines and describes information resource management (IRM)
- Discusses the evolution of the microprocessor and the growing importance of systems spanning computer architectures
- Identifies environmental and database considerations that affect systems analysis and design
- Describes the attributes and qualifications of a systems analyst

KEY TERMS

Analysis

Batch processing

Compatibility

Constraints

Data

Data querying

Database

Database management system (DBMS)

Decision support system (DSS)

Design

Detail reports

End-user

Exception reports

Fourth generation languages (4GLs)

General systems theory

Information

Information system (IS)

Information resource management
 (IRM)

Inputs

Management by exception (MBE)

Management information system (MIS)

Management support system (MSS)

Mathematical models

Model

On-line processing

Open systems architecture

Operational management

Operational personnel

Outputs

Periodic reports

Physical firm

Planning and control

Programmer/analysts

Ripple effect

Semistructured problem

Spanned system architecture

Standards

Strategic management

Structured problem

Summary reports

Suprasystem

Synergism

System

Systems analysis

Systems analysis and design

Systems analyst

Systems design

Tactical management

Transaction processing system (TPS)

Transformation processes

Transparency

Unstructured problem

Users

The computer revolution allows business people to be better informed about conditions in the business environment. Businesses gather *data* (facts) about operations and external circumstances that affect operations. When this data is recorded, transmitted, and processed, it provides business personnel (**users**) with the *information* they need to do their jobs. People from all levels of the organization use computer-processed data to help them work more effectively. Although the term **end-user** often identifies these people, they are referred to as users throughout this text.

The classical distinction between data and information defines information as processed data. In this text **information** is viewed as data that is presented in its proper context. The term **data** usually means facts about something—for example, a customer's name, address, and so on. These facts need not be processed to be useful for business personnel; they may require processing; or they may simply be used as raw data at the appropriate time within the proper setting. Figure 1-1 illustrates how the data on a mail-order form from a company called National Golf & Tennis (NG&T) becomes the information depicting the sale and shipment of a golf putter.

Information is the lifeblood of a business organization, and every part of an organization depends on the availability of information to ensure that its personnel are correctly informed. Because the business environment changes rapidly, information

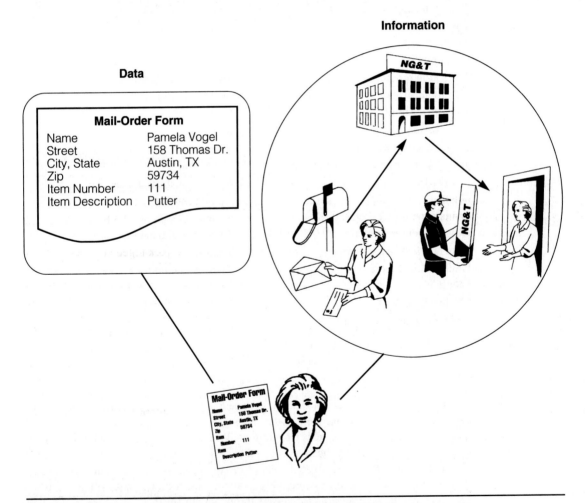

Information

Data

Mail-Order Form

Name	Pamela Vogel
Street	158 Thomas Dr.
City, State	Austin, TX
Zip	59734
Item Number	111
Item Description	Putter

Figure 1-1. Data versus information in the NG&T mail-order example

necessary for proper interpretation of the business climate must be constantly updated. In general, modern business personnel require ever-increasing amounts of information for correct and efficient performance. As a result, information systems need to be continuously created or "overhauled" in order to supply information that is both comprehensive and current.

Before you begin to understand how systems are created or overhauled, you must first understand and become familiar with the terms and methodology used in systems analysis and design, as described in this chapter. You will also learn who is responsible for performing analysis and design (A&D), how they become proficient in A&D activities, and various methods and tools they use to work more quickly and effectively. Unlike some introductory chapters in textbooks, this one is not to be taken lightly; it presents the basic premises of A&D. The terms defined and the premises described form the "language" of systems analysis and design. When you can speak this language fluently, you may be able to call yourself a systems analyst.

DEFINITION OF SYSTEMS ANALYSIS AND DESIGN

By defining system, analysis, and design individually and then together as a unit, we arrive at a definition of systems analysis and design.

First, a **system** is a set of interrelated and interactive elements that work together to accomplish specific purposes. The system may be physical or conceptual, animate or inanimate, static or dynamic, formal or informal, and so on; the basic concept is extremely general. The human body is a good example of a system; one in which the skeletal, muscular, circulatory, and nervous systems all work together to accomplish the purpose of keeping the body alive. Continuing the NG&T example introduced in Figure 1-1, Figure 1-2 illustrates NG&T's mail-order fulfillment system, which is made up of a data entry department that processes the order, a warehouse where the order is filled, and a shipping department where the order is packaged and sent out.

An **information system (IS)** consists of various sets of computer hardware, software, procedures, and personnel, each performing different functions that interrelate and interact to meet user information needs. These different functions are performed on data — data collected on hardware peripheral devices such as tapes and disks, which act as eyes and ears for the IS. People perform operational tasks for the system, such as loading tapes and disks, and they also guide and interact with the system. In many ways, an IS functions just like people. This should not be a surprise, because information systems are developed by people to perform tasks previously performed by them, or to support people during the performance of their tasks.

An important characteristic of a system is that the outcome of the whole is greater than the sum of the outcomes of the individual parts. Computer hardware is useless without the software to make it run, and both are unimportant without the people who

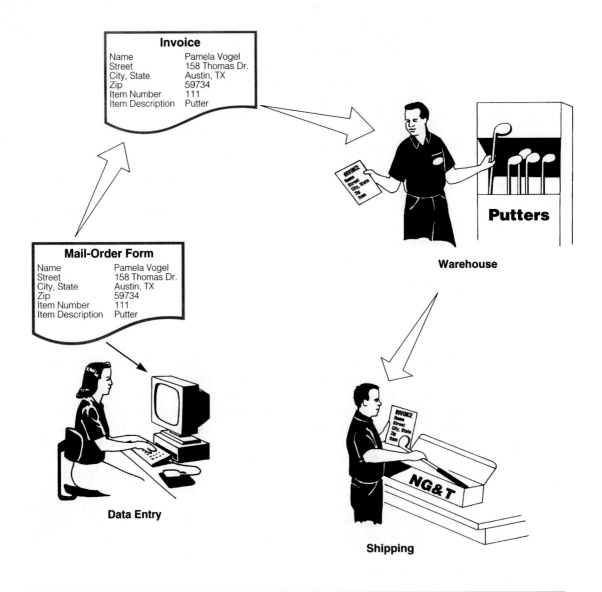

Figure 1-2. A system for getting products to the customer

use the system. Figure 1-3 illustrates the combination of elements that make up an IS. **Synergism** is a term used to express the way something consisting of harmonious integrated parts accomplishes more as a whole than as a collection of its individual parts. Therefore, systems are synergistic in relation to the purpose for which they exist.

Analysis is the decomposition of an item of interest into its constituent parts for investigative purposes. By decomposing something into its separate parts, analysts

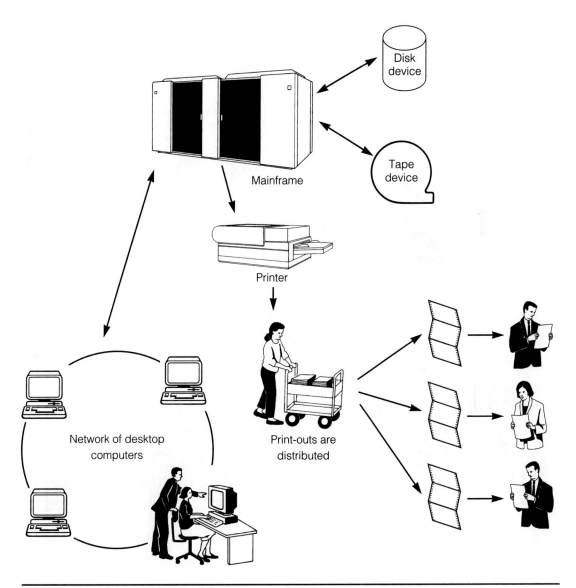

Figure 1-3. Elements of an information system

gain a better understanding of the way the whole functions, and they can do a more thorough investigation of its operations and the problems associated with its use. Figure 1-4 shows an analyst decomposing the NG&T order fulfillment system into its separate parts, taking the first step in determining how to get products out to the customer faster — the business problem or objective.

Systems analysis is the investigation of a system to decide what needs to be done to make it more efficient and effective. It involves decomposing the system into its components to allow closer investigation of how it functions. Studying the operation of each part provides a comprehensive understanding of the whole. This analysis allows the investigator to decide whether the components are functioning properly and whether they are properly integrated.

Systems analysis is usually undertaken because problems are observed in the operation of a system or in the results it produces. The systems analysis usually leads

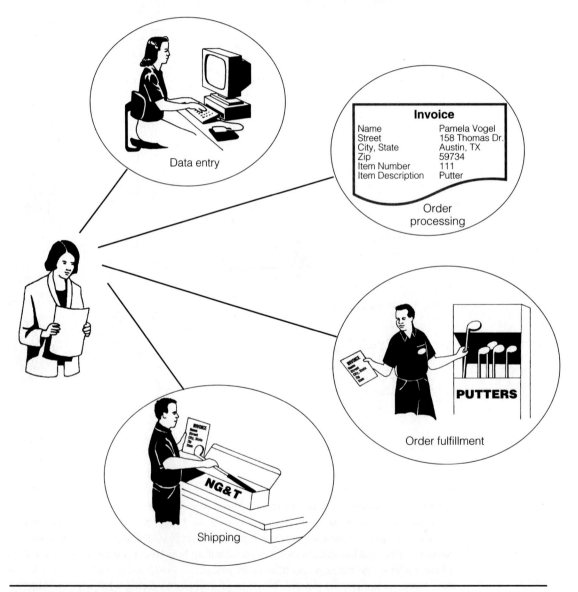

Figure 1-4. Analysis of a problem or objective

to modifications in an existing system or to the creation or purchase of a replacement system designed to eliminate the observed problem. For example, a user might make the following observations:

- Some amounts are missing on a sales report.
- Sales reports do not reflect a recent change in commission rates.
- Hiring dates for salespeople are not provided, so analyzing the relationship between longevity and productivity is impossible.
- Outlawed state taxes still appear on the sales report.

The systems analyst needs to investigate these observations to determine their origins and possible solutions. Chapter 4 explains how to obtain information about users' concerns in order to analyze them.

Design is the formulation of the requirements that provide the basis for creating or modifying something. For instance, blueprints that an architect creates provide the requirements for constructing a building. When designing information systems, the person conducting the analysis performs functions similar to those of an architect.

Systems design interprets and compiles the requirements that provide the basis for creating computer-related systems. Designs are the blueprints for developing information systems. They identify the components of a system and specify their operation and interaction. The aim is to create a design that allows independence between components while controlling for proper interaction. Figure 1-5 depicts a person performing a systems design of the NG&T order fulfillment system.

Systems analysis and design is the investigation of a system and the subsequent design of a replacement system or a modification to the existing system. The person who performs systems analysis and design is normally called a **systems analyst**. Frequently, firms employ people who perform systems analysis and design as well as programming. These employees are often called **programmer/analysts**. Figure 1-6 illustrates a person performing systems analysis and design activities for the NG&T order fulfillment system.

GENERAL SYSTEMS THEORY

Many systems professionals view the total environment of the firm as a **suprasystem**, of which industries, individual firms, and functional areas of a given firm are subsystems. This view represents the general systems theory, which often appears in business literature. Those who believe in the **general systems theory** view everything as a system that consists of many integrated components.

General systems theory is a universal science that attempts to unite many splintered disciplines with laws common to all. Aristotle was one of the first philosophers to understand that all systems are related. Basically, he said that every system is a part of a larger system and can itself be broken down into smaller systems. He believed that it was possible to understand a system only by looking at the whole, or taking the *holistic* view. This is the synergistic view discussed earlier.

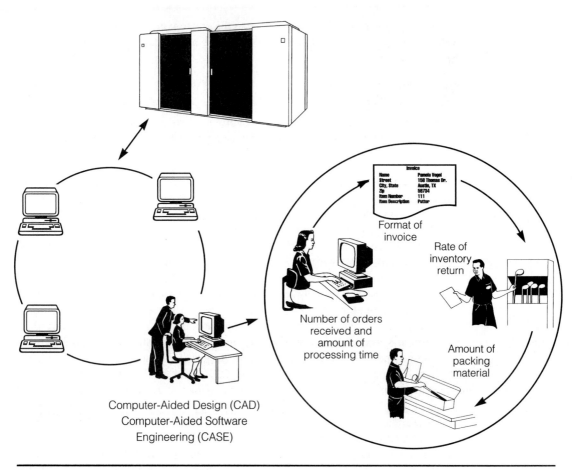

Invoice

Name	Pamela Vogel
Street	158 Thomas Dr.
City, State	Austin, TX
Zip	58734
Item Number	111
Item Description	Putter

Format of invoice

Rate of inventory return

Number of orders received and amount of processing time

Amount of packing material

Computer-Aided Design (CAD)
Computer-Aided Software
Engineering (CASE)

Figure 1-5. Systems design activities

Aristotle's view was later refuted and expanded by the French philosopher René Descartes. Descartes believed that because the human mind was finite, it could not possibly grasp a large system of any complexity. He believed that a system must be viewed by examining its constituent parts; it must be broken down into manageable elements and then reassembled. Only then could humans, with their limited reasoning ability, understand it. He referred to this procedure as the *analytic* view of systems.

The main drawback of Descartes' theory was that it did not consider the interactions between the parts. Clearly, a theory somewhere between Aristotle's holistic approach and Descartes' analytic approach was needed. The systems approach is a compromise between the two. It uses the analytic method of Descartes, but it also focuses on the system interactions deemed so necessary by Aristotle. The difference is that not all possible interactions are not considered, only the major ones that affect the

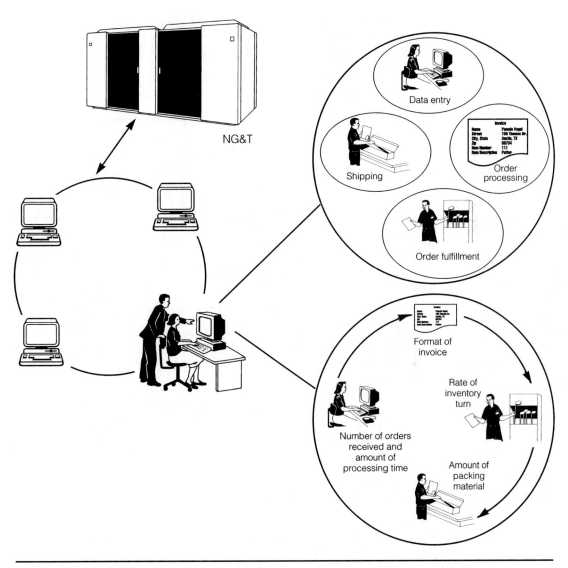

Figure 1-6. Systems analysis and design activities

way the system will operate. The trick is to determine which interactions are important.

Figure 1-7 portrays the systems approach in a business context. It shows how each industry, firm, functional area of the firm, and agent of the external environment is considered a subsystem within the suprasystem of the business world.

Business is composed of many industries. As an example, Figure 1-7 depicts Industry$_1$, computer manufacturers, and Industry$_2$, chip manufacturers. In business,

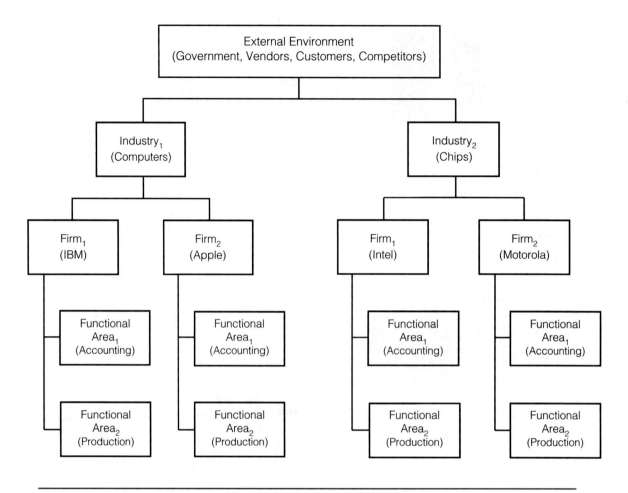

Figure 1-7. General systems theory representation of the business environment

each industry is composed of many firms. Figure 1-7 represents a number of firms in a particular industry by using IBM to represent Firm$_1$ and Apple to represent Firm$_2$. Each firm in a particular industry is in turn composed of several functional areas for the computer industry. Figure 1-7 represents a number of functional areas in a particular firm for a particular industry by using Accounting to represent Functional Area$_1$ and Production to represent Functional Area$_2$. The external environment in Figure 1-7 consists of subsystems including government, vendors, customers, competitors, and so on.

The environment of information systems includes hardware and software components, procedures, and personnel to assist the system in accomplishing its tasks. Figure 1-8 lists common hardware and software components of the system environment.

HARDWARE COMPONENTS	SOFTWARE COMPONENTS
Terminals/Computers	**Operating Systems and**
Standalone single-function terminal	**Computing Environments**
Integrated voice/data terminal (IVDT)	DOS, Windows, Windows/NT, OS/2, UNIX
PC, XT, AT, PS/2, or equivalent computer	Editors
Workstation computer	Utilities (sort, documentation software,
Mini or mainframe computer	for example)
Peripherals	Management information system
Monitor	Decision support system
Keyboard	Management support system
Mouse or trackball	Database management system
Printer	Knowledge-based system
Scanner	User interfaces
Plotter	**Network/Communication Software**
Storage Devices	Protocol conversion
Hard drive	Computer conferencing
Floppy disk drive and 3 1/2- or 5 1/4-inch	Electronic mail
floppy disks	Bulletin boards
CD-ROM drive and disks	**Application Software**
Tape backup unit and tapes	Project management software
Optical drive and disks	Planning software
Communication and Network Devices	Word processing software
Modem or fax/modem	Spreadsheets
Network card and cables	Designer/developer software
Network server	Third generation languages (3GLs)
Network switching box	Fourth generation languages (4GLs)
Furniture	Desktop publishing software
Terminal/computer desk and hutch	Utilities
Terminal/computer chair	Screen windowing software
Cabinets and covers for securing electronic	Desk organizer
devices	Electronic notepads
Auxiliary storage filing cabinets	Reference services
Accessories	Fast backup
Disk holder and labels	
Mouse pad	
Surge or spike protector, power bar	
Uninterruptible power supply unit	
Antistatic mats	

Figure 1-8. System hardware and software components

Systems Theory Model of the Firm

The general systems approach is often used to present a model of the firm. A **model** is a physical, graphical (pictorial), narrative (descriptive), and/or mathematical representation of something in the real world. The analyst often creates a conceptual, scaled-down model or replica of something before actually designing it. For instance, automobile manufacturers build scaled-down and exact replicas of cars before mass-producing them. The design of a system may be considered a conceptual model of a system to be developed. Often the object being modeled already exists, and the model allows you to study the object while avoiding operational or financial difficulties or intervention by external sources. Figure 1-9 shows a model of a firm based on the general systems theory.

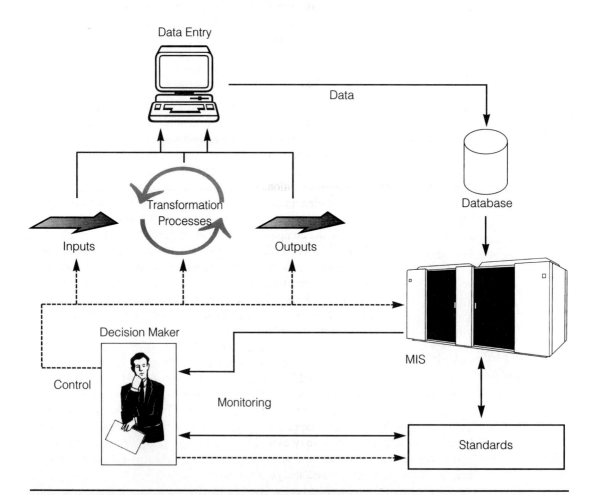

Figure 1-9. Model of a firm based on the general systems theory

The Physical Firm

Figure 1-9 models the physical and the conceptual firm. The **physical firm** is represented by the inputs, transformation processes, and outputs, which are the actual business operations of the firm. All functional areas of the firm contain transformation processes that transform inputs into outputs through normal business operations. For example, a system that aids sales and marketing may collect and process all sales of a new product for a particular geographical area. This system may also analyze how well the product sells in that market segment and make projections for the population as a whole. A marketing manager may then use this market analysis to make decisions regarding ways to better market the product to the general population.

The **inputs** in Figure 1-9 represent resources used to produce the outputs of the **transformation processes**. They include raw materials, finances, and personnel. The transformation processes include manufacturing processes, financial analysis, personnel procedures, and so on. Examples of **outputs** are finished goods or goods in process, budgetary functions, personnel placement, and services.

The Conceptual Firm

Data is gathered and recorded about inputs used in transformation processes, the operation of those processes, and their outputs. The **management information system** (MIS) consists of all systems within the organization that classify, aggregate, segregate, and process data to inform personnel of past, present, and future conditions concerning the operation of the physical firm. This information is a conceptual representation of the business conditions faced by the firm's personnel.

The MIS operates in on-line and batch-processing modes to convey a conceptual representation of conditions being faced. **On-line processing** allows immediate interaction between the user and the computer system through some form of terminal. As a result, employees of the firm have direct and rapid access to pertinent data. In **batch processing**, business transaction data is accumulated and processed in groups on a regularly scheduled basis, such as once a day, a week, or a month. Batch processing is very useful when it is not necessary to immediately process records of transactions as they occur. For example, many businesses accumulate warehouse receipts and shipments during the day to be processed in the evening, when the computer system has less traffic. Batch processing programs are typically easier to create, and serve applications in which the intensity of activities performed by machines outweighs the intensity of activities performed by humans regarding how current data actually is. Figure 1-10 illustrates the differences between on-line and batch processing.

Standards are expected operational performances. They are usually set by assessing what is expected to happen given that nothing unusual occurs. For example, based on past history, a firm may expect a certain amount of product sales within a given period. When sales are dramatically below or above this standard, it is important for someone to know it and analyze the reasons it occurred.

The information transmitted to decision makers (DMs) within the firm often compares actual conditions in the operation of the physical firm and expected conditions

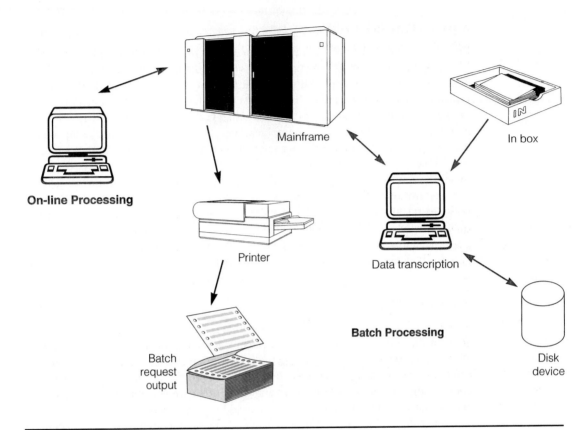

On-line Processing

Mainframe

In box

Printer

Data transcription

Batch Processing

Batch
request
output

Disk
device

Figure 1-10. On-line versus batch processing

(standards). The MIS either performs the comparisons and transmits the results, or provides information that DMs use in comparing actual and expected operational performance. The transmitted information represents monitoring operations: a management function that has been designed into the MIS. For example, the computer monitor provides a window through which the manager can view data representing the firm's actual performance. Using the MIS to monitor operations allows the firm's personnel to be quickly informed of exceptional situations. The phrase **management by exception (MBE)** is often used to describe the process in which only exceptional (both good and bad) situations are reported to management. DMs respond by making decisions (the dotted lines in Figure 1-9) that maintain the control necessary for efficient and correct operation of the firm. These decisions result in adjustments to components of the physical firm (inputs, processes, and outputs), the conceptual firm (data, information, MIS, and standards), or to both. The data acquired by the MIS, the procedures it uses to convert data into information, and the standards that are set for organizational performance provide a conceptual view of the firm. The firm's management hopes that this conceptual view provides an accurate and comprehensive picture of what really happens over a given period of time.

THE MANAGEMENT INFORMATION SYSTEM (MIS)

The two main functions that managers perform in the organization are **planning and control**. Most of the operations for which management is responsible fall within one or both of these two main functions. For example, traditional management activities, such as staffing, coordinating, and scheduling, all fall within the categories of either planning or control. Thus most of the information acquired for management is ultimately used for one of these two purposes. Planning and control activities occur in both structured and semistructured business situations, which are described in the "Mathematical Modeling" section, below.

In order for managers to make informed decisions, the MIS is created and maintained by systems analysts to supply information that accurately portrays the conditions facing the firm. Characteristics of the real world are collected, categorized, processed, and analyzed to determine what conditions the firm faces and what stance it should take on these conditions. The MIS provides information about these conditions through various data delivery methods, including periodic reporting, data querying, and mathematical modeling.

Methods of Supplying Information

Two main methods of supplying data are periodic reporting and data querying. Both of these methods provide information important to understanding the business environment and the operation and position of the firm in the environment. Periodic reporting provides information on a previously set cycle, whereas data querying provides more immediate access to the information. Mathematical modeling, a third source of data, provides scientific evaluation of business conditions to help determine an appropriate course of action.

Periodic Reporting

Periodic reports are produced by the MIS in cycles (daily, weekly, or monthly, for example). Over the years, business personnel have gradually gained confidence in the data maintained in computer files. Consequently, periodic reports of all conditions affecting the business are generally being replaced with periodic exception reporting. The MIS is designed to produce three types of reports: detail, summary, and exception.

DETAIL REPORTS These are usually produced from the day-to-day operations of the business. An example of a detail report would be a complete list of all customer transactions for the day, or of all inventory items in stock. These reports are normally used at the operational level of the business.

SUMMARY REPORTS These are often produced at predetermined times with predefined information to summarize what the data conveys about the organization. Financial statements, such as balance sheets or profit-and-loss statements, are examples of summary reports. A variety of other summary reports can also be produced, depending on the manager's needs. Midlevel managers normally use these reports. For example, a sales manager might request a daily, weekly, monthly, or quarterly sales summary.

EXCEPTION REPORTS These are designed to show deviations from some established policy or guideline. A credit manager might need to approve all credit sales over a certain amount and receive a listing of all of these transactions. A personnel manager might want only a report of all employees who have called in sick more than a certain number of days over the last six months. Exception reports are designed to report only situations that are outside established norms.

Data Querying

The MIS also allows the firm's personnel to obtain special reports containing more timely information than normal operation cycles provide. The system often does such reporting through the function of **data querying**, or direct access by personnel to current data maintained in computer files. On-line processing is usually necessary to carry out data querying functions. Figure 1-11 illustrates the difference between periodic reporting and data querying.

Mathematical Modeling

The design of the systems that compose a MIS often includes mathematical models from the fields of management science, finance, and operations management. Researchers in these areas have developed a variety of **mathematical models** that provide scientific evaluation of business conditions to help determine an appropriate course of action. Many of these mathematical models are too advanced for discussion in this textbook, but an example should help you understand how businesses use them.

The *transportation algorithm* is one of the mathematical models of management science. It can be used to decide how to strategically locate warehouses, determining how many should be built and where they should be located, between factories and retail outlets that produce and sell items for a company with a number of factories and retail outlets at different locations. The problem is complicated by the demand for the product at the retail outlets. The number of warehouses must be sufficient, and the warehouses positioned appropriately, so that the factories do not run out of internal

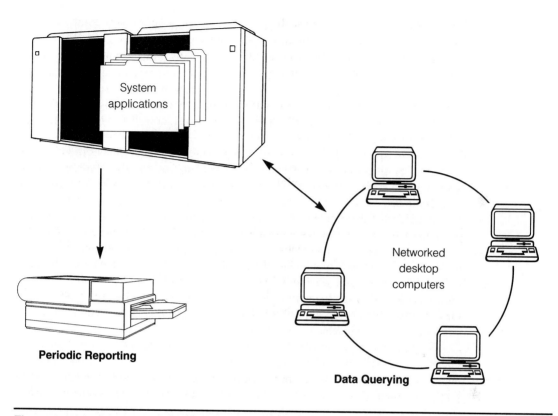

Figure 1-11. Periodic reporting versus data querying

storage space while waiting to ship products to the warehouse. Conversely, the warehouses must be sufficient in number, and positioned appropriately, so that requests for more products by the retail stores can be met. In addition, the company needs enough warehouses, positioned appropriately, so that individual warehouses do not become too full.

Many other mathematical models exist that can be used to support the functions of a business and its information system. These mathematical models are used for analysis of fully structured and semistructured problems. A **structured problem** or decision occurs when all important characteristics of the situation can be modeled, and the decision depends only upon mathematical analysis. Courses of action are known, and possible outcomes can be determined and automated. Examples of a structured decision include the decision to reorder a particular inventory item when only a certain number remain in stock and the decision to automatically grant someone credit if the purchase is less than a certain amount. Both of these decisions can be made by the system without human intervention. Typical transaction processing systems, like systems used to record and process product sales, often perform many, if not all, activities associated with structured problems.

An **unstructured problem** is one in which a large amount of uncertainty exists. So much uncertainty exists in many problem areas that no technique or tool can help resolve very much of the problem. These types of problems require subjective evaluation by someone with the expertise to analyze them. Artificial intelligence and expert systems can help narrow down the decision to be made; however, it remains largely a subjective evaluation by the DM.

A **semistructured problem** or decision provides the characteristics of a situation, similar to those provided for a structured problem, but not all characteristics are known, and a subjective evaluation must be made by a DM. As part of the MIS, the models use data values to formulate sets of mathematical expressions that represent the characteristics of the problem facing the firm's personnel. The model then presents possible alternatives so that a decision can be made about the best course of action.

Stated another way, a semistructured decision requires human judgment as a critical element. Examples of semistructured decisions include decisions on where to build a new warehouse, whether to introduce a new product, or whether it is a good idea to acquire a competing company. These decisions cannot be fully programmed; they require a human decision. A decision support system, discussed in the next section, aids the DM in reaching a better decision.

A systems analyst need not be proficient in management science, finance, or operations management; other personnel usually help the analyst to include appropriate mathematical models in the design of the firm's systems. The following steps outline the procedure for including such models as part of the design of the firm's MIS:

1. A user requests a certain investigative procedure as part of the requirements to be built into the MIS.

2. The analyst consults with personnel familiar with management science, finance, or operations management to determine whether a mathematical model already exists to accomplish this investigative purpose.

3. These persons help the analyst install an existing model or develop a new model for this investigative purpose.

Subsystems of the Management Information System

Information supplied by periodic reports, data queries, and mathematical models allows managers and operational personnel to better understand the business environment and their firm. To this purpose, the MIS embodies many different systems for many different business applications. These applications assume three primary perspectives: planning, control, and retaining data on daily operations. The three different types of systems that support these perspectives are the decision support system (DSS), the management support system (MSS), and the transaction processing system (TPS). These systems support the three different levels of management and operational personnel in understanding what is happening in business and making choices that help the firm.

Decision Support System (DSS)

A **decision support system (DSS)** incorporates the mathematical models just discussed to provide mathematical analysis of business conditions, as well as application of other techniques and tools in semistructured problem analysis. Traditionally, a DSS consists of a database, a set of rules to apply to the data in the database, and a user interface for interaction between the DSS and the user. For example, the area of finance provides certain financial algorithms to be used in assessing how well the firm is doing. One of these algorithms is the current ratio, which equals current assets divided by current liabilities. To determine this ratio, a firm might elect to place this formula in a spreadsheet and use data on current assets and current liabilities to obtain a total to use in the current ratio formula. This spreadsheet could also apply the algorithms for the remaining financial ratios—for liquidity, activity, leverage, profitability, and market measures—to current data regarding the firm's operations. All you need to add is a user-friendly interface, and the spreadsheet would embody a comprehensive financial-analysis DSS.

A DSS is used primarily to provide information to managers for planning. Although the MIS also provides this information, it usually does so on a scheduled basis. A DSS allows a manager to become informed and resolve "what if" questions in a more timely way. A DSS is generally used to support decision making in a semistructured problem situation. The mathematical models embedded in the DSS are used to represent the effects of various strategies on the condition of the firm. A manager provides information on strategies to be used in various scenarios and receives information on their probable effects. A DSS may be defined as a subsystem of the MIS that supports managerial planning and decision making in a more timely fashion for a semistructured problem. The DSS has rapidly emerged as an intricate component of the information engine of the firm, and it must also be developed and revised as the climate of the business environment evolves.

Management Support System (MSS)

The MIS usually includes a system known as the **management support system (MSS)**, an outgrowth of systems for exercising control. The purpose of the MIS is to provide information about actual and expected conditions, thereby allowing management to improve these conditions through better control of operations. The MSS is composed of systems for investigating the ways in which control is exercised and conceptually conceived in semistructured problem situations. To work effectively, the firm's personnel must have the means to exercise direct control over operations. They are aided in this by the MSS—a subsystem of the MIS that supports decisions and operations. For example, an organization may employ a system that records and processes product defects to aid the manager in determining who may need to be retrained, reprimanded, or fired because of poor on-the-job performance.

Each level of management performs both planning and control functions. Therefore, they all have access to information through systems designed to support these functions. The primary information for planning purposes is provided by the DSS, and the primary information for control purposes is provided by the MSS. Figure 1-12 depicts the relationship between the MIS and its subsystems, and indicates how they

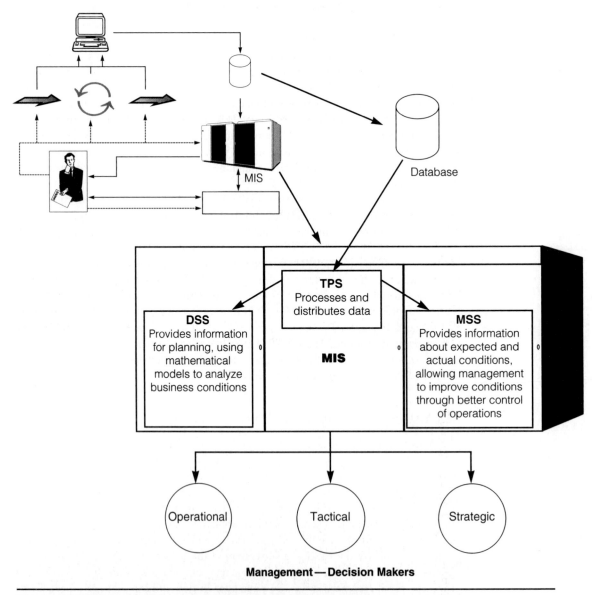

Figure 1-12. The management information system and its subsystems

supply information needed by the three levels of management (operational, tactical, and strategic), which you will learn about shortly.

The DSS and MSS, as presented in Figure 1-12, represent a continuum of planning and control, which are obviously interrelated within an organization. The transaction processing system (TPS), another subsystem of the MIS, supports planning and control functions by providing necessary processing of transactions.

Transaction Processing System (TPS)

The **transaction processing system (TPS)** consists of a variety of activities an organization must undertake to support its day-to-day operations. The TPS processes all transaction data used for all of the firm's purposes. These systems gather, record, aggregate, segregate, batch together, and process normal everyday data that forms the basis for determining the actual performance of the physical firm. The TPS is usually driven by the occurrence of events in the course of daily operations, such as completing a product sale, receiving payment for products, or registering a complaint about service.

The TPS is designed to answer routine questions and to track the flow of activities (transactions) throughout the organization. What happened to Mrs. Smith's order? How many of a particular part do we have left in inventory? Was Joan issued a paycheck last week? The kinds of problems solved by such systems are usually structured short-term issues. A firm's standard operating procedures usually provide a basis for the transaction processing system. The output of these systems is critical for the day-to-day survival of the company.

The TPS is the main supplier of information to operational management, but it serves management at higher levels as well. For example, a vice-president of manufacturing at an automobile plant might want current detailed information on completed cars rolling off the production line. Transaction processing is also required for mandatory reporting to external agencies such as the government.

Management Levels and Operational Personnel

Traditionally, organizations maintain three different levels of management, with corresponding levels of responsibility: strategic, tactical, and operational. These managers use information from the MIS to help them understand what they face in their areas of responsibility and how their areas fit into the organization as a whole. With this information they can make more informed decisions that should lead to better planning and control. Although each level of management performs some planning and control functions, the amount of time devoted to each differs among managerial levels.

Operational personnel, also called procedural personnel, need information to help them better perform the day-to-day tasks of the firm. They also aid in acquiring, transcribing, transmitting, and processing pertinent information regarding daily activities.

Strategic Management

Strategic management is mainly concerned with determining the direction in which the firm is headed. This is the responsibility of managers at the top level of the organization, such as the chief executive officer, president, and vice-presidents.

Top managers identify the mission of the firm and construct strategies and plans to accomplish this mission. They spend most of their time performing planning functions and devote smaller amounts of time to control. The MIS must provide sufficient information of sufficient quality to help top-level managers map out these strategic plans. The control functions relevant to strategic management usually consist of broad, comprehensive instructions carried out by tactical and operational managers.

Tactical Management

Tactical management is concerned with formulating the plans to carry out the strategies of top-level management. Tactical managers include regional managers, division heads, and directors. They establish a procedural framework for accomplishing the objectives of strategic management. The MIS must provide tactical managers with sufficient information concerning the firm, its resources, and other factors, to help them accomplish their tasks.

Tactical managers also perform tactical control functions. They monitor the progress of the firm's operations and make necessary adjustments (controlling operations) to ensure that these operations are consistent with the firm's goals and mission. They also establish policies for various courses of action consistent with the firm's mission and identify personnel needed to accomplish those goals. For example, a strategic manager might wish to decrease the warehouse shelf life, in the company warehouse, of various products the firm manufactures. To accomplish this, a tactical manager might establish a policy that requires that the first unit of a product to arrive in the warehouse be the first out on any truck being loaded for distribution. (This is commonly called FIFO—first in/first out.)

Tactical managers usually devote equal amounts of time to planning and control functions. Therefore, the MIS must provide aggregated information that supports tactical managers in both functions.

Operational Management

Operational management is concerned with the everyday operations of the firm: the detailed operations required by tactical plans. Managers at this level include department heads, project leaders, and foremen. Operational managers typically spend more time on control functions than on planning activities. As a result, the MIS usually provides information to these managers that aids in controlling everyday operations.

The following table summarizes the differences among strategic, tactical, and operational management.

Management Level	Time Frame	Scope	Detail
Strategic	Long-term	Broad	Low
Tactical	Short-term	Focused	Medium
Operational	Immediate	Narrow	High

Operational Personnel

Operational personnel are responsible for carrying out the functional operations of the firm. Without them, the firm could not complete its tasks and fulfill its mission. Typical operational personnel are sales clerks, factory workers, administrative assistants, and secretaries. Operational personnel are usually supervised by operational managers.

Different systems typically serve the three levels of management and operational personnel. Although they serve different personnel, these systems all have the same major attributes. Frequently, the specifics of the attributes are what distinguishes one system from another.

ATTRIBUTES OF SYSTEMS

All systems in the firm's MIS have certain attributes that describe and distinguish them. The five major attributes of systems are:

- Central purpose
- System structure
- System dependence
- System integration
- System interaction

Figure 1-13 illustrates the attributes of a system.

Central Purpose

Each system (and subsystem) has a central purpose for which it is designed. A system may do many things, but it must have a central purpose. For example, systems exist for payroll purposes, account posting, personnel management, and so forth. It is often said that 10 to 20 percent of system components do 80 to 90 percent of the work. Therefore, concentrating on that 10 to 20 percent in the design of systems ensures that the analyst will be focusing on the more important aspects of the system: those parts that usually accomplish the strategic aspects of its central purpose.

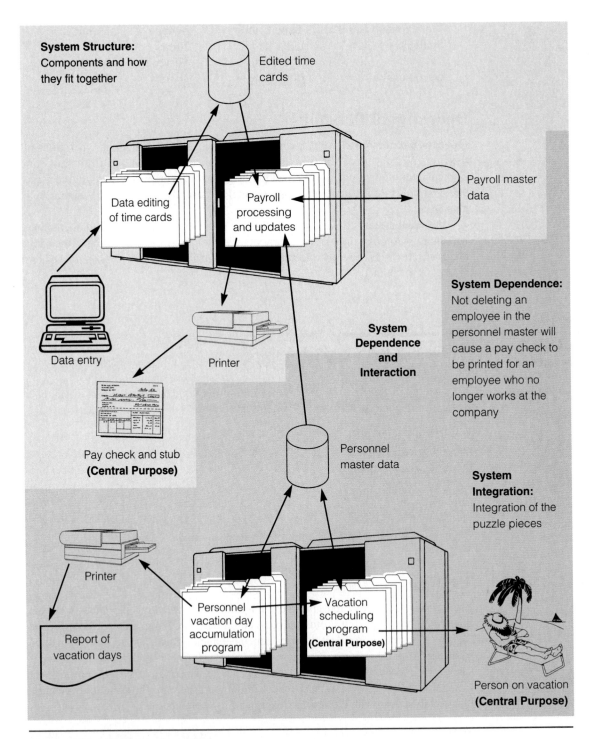

System Structure:
Components and how they fit together

Edited time cards

Data editing of time cards

Payroll processing and updates

Payroll master data

Data entry

Printer

System Dependence and Interaction

System Dependence:
Not deleting an employee in the personnel master will cause a pay check to be printed for an employee who no longer works at the company

Pay check and stub
(Central Purpose)

Personnel master data

System Integration:
Integration of the puzzle pieces

Printer

Report of vacation days

Personnel vacation day accumulation program

Vacation scheduling program
(Central Purpose)

Person on vacation
(Central Purpose)

Figure 1-13. Attributes of a system

System Structure

Every system has some underlying structure. The structure of most systems is based on the model of the physical firm shown in Figure 1-9. The data gathered concerning the operation of the firm is the input for the system, and the transformation processes use this data in processing operations to produce information as output. The output is either transformed input data or data that directly informs management of conditions existing in the firm. For example, the structure of many transaction processing systems is based on the way data is acquired and processed as real-world events occur. If real-time interaction is required, the system structure will be significantly different than if the system requires batch processing.

System Dependence

Systems are designed to perform independently of other systems. Each system is designed to accomplish its central purpose with the least possible intervention by outside sources. Systems that have greater degrees of dependence on other systems often suffer from the **ripple effect** — disturbances in one of several dependent systems cause disturbances in other systems, just as a stone dropped into water causes ripples on the entire surface. You will see how this can be a significant factor in the maintenance of systems in Chapter 16.

System Integration

Systems are designed for a central purpose, as previously mentioned, but they are integrated to meet the information needs of the entire firm. For instance, financial systems have the central purpose of tracking the use of the firm's monetary resources. Yet financial systems must be integrated with systems for the other functional areas, such as manufacturing systems, for proper planning in all functional areas. Each system is designed to stand alone in accomplishing its central purpose, but the accomplishment of each purpose is just one piece in the firm's operational jigsaw puzzle. The pieces are integrated so that the entire organization accomplishes its central purpose: to survive and prosper. To accomplish this central purpose, the firm must continue to produce profits or to provide its service, attempt to establish rapport with its personnel, improve its manufacturing operations, and accomplish a host of related objectives through the operation of its subsystems. Well-integrated functional area subsystems ensure the complete success of the firm. Also, well-integrated and successful information subsystems ensure the complete success of the entire collection of the firm's systems.

System Interaction

Most systems interact with other systems. Information maintained and produced in one system often helps meet the information needs of other systems, and interaction allows the sharing of this information across system lines; that is, data used by one system is also used by another system. As a result, all systems in the firm's MIS operate independently, but must harmoniously provide for the integrated information needs of functional areas within the firm.

Many organizational managers who help acquire and maintain the firm's systems and information have begun to consider them an important organizational resource—as important as financial, operational, and other more traditional resources. Consequently, a whole new area of management has emerged, called information resource management (IRM).

INFORMATION RESOURCE MANAGEMENT (IRM)

Each level of management and associated personnel in each firm's functional areas depends on information to keep it informed of relevant conditions. As a result, business people are realizing that information is an important resource and that its acquisition and use should be properly managed.

A new type of manager is emerging in many corporations who functions as an information consultant to the rest of the firm's personnel. **Information resource management (IRM)** is concerned with the executive management of the firm's information resources. Information has become a competitive weapon that gives a firm advantages over others that are not aware of certain information. Many information professionals believe that information management is now important enough to require a vice-president for information management. They believe that a strategic manager of information systems will ensure proper management of the corporate information resource and that appropriate systems design for top-level management will result.

Elements of Information Resource Management

One key element of IRM is the realization that information is a resource and must be planned for and managed, just like the more traditional resources of land, labor, and capital. Information systems planning should be a part of the firm's long-range strategic plan. This long-term philosophy is in contrast to the typical short-range focus prevalent in many organizations.

Another element of IRM is the need to standardize data across many different departments and even companies. For example, by standardizing data across systems, it is easier for senior executives to compare operational data regarding business units under their authority.

When a firm adopts the IRM concept, user departments must take a much more active role in planning for their future information needs. A department might become responsible for obtaining needed data, maintaining the accuracy of the data, and making the data available to the appropriate manager. This added user responsibility should be a team effort, made in conjunction with the IS department.

IRM seeks to manage all systems in the firm's MIS as a corporate resource. These systems can be DSS, MSS, or TPS. Being responsible for the systems that affect all management levels and operational personnel is one of the most important jobs to emerge in the 1990s.

Many companies have been moving away from central mainframe computer systems. This is called downsizing the computer installation. Other companies have replaced existing mainframe computers with either a new central mainframe or a faster minicomputer, an action sometimes called rehosting the computer installation. Changing computer architectures also causes information to be spread out among storage media connected to these computers, which complicates the job of managing information resources. Still other companies are determined to develop applications that execute in the same way on different computers. This is sometimes called cross-system architectures, referring to the different internal architectures of the computers. In this text, it is called spanned system architecture. All these changes in computer architectures are made to place the power of computing closer to the source of business activities. However, managing installation of computer architectures has also become more complicated.

SYSTEMS SPANNING COMPUTER ARCHITECTURES

The evolution of the microprocessor in the past few years has placed an incredible amount of processing power on the desks of the firm's personnel. The proliferation of desktop computers and the decentralization of the firm's systems are altering the manner in which businesses store, retrieve, and process data. This has led firms to provide communication links between desktop computers and mainframes or minicomputers, so that they can share data and software. The term *host computer* will be used throughout this book to represent either a mainframe or a minicomputer. Connecting these two (and sometimes three) different computer architectures allows a firm to take advantage of the desktop computer's versatility and ease of use, and the host computer's power. The migration of the desktop computer has taken the following path:

1. Installing the desktop computer as a standalone processor
2. Configuring the desktop computer as a terminal emulator
3. Sharing data across host and desktop computer architectures
4. Networking desktop computers
5. Connecting desktop computer networks with host networks
6. Connecting desktop/host computers with wide area networks, such as Internet

7. Sharing processing responsibilities between host and desktop computers as the distinction between them diminishes

8. Using host computer servers for centrally stored data and desktop client computers for processing the data retrieved through the server (called client/server processing)

This migration of desktop computers into previously uncharted areas of computing has not taken place in all firms. In some businesses, departments and personnel have migrated to the desktop computer at different rates of acceptance and use. This varying rate of desktop computer experience creates what many people call "islands of technology," meaning that small areas of the business have a much higher utility of technology.

Connecting desktop and host computers has caused compatibility problems to surface, such as problems that arise when you attempt to connect the host computers of different manufacturers. Software and data usually must undergo some conversion before they can be used by two different architectures. **Compatibility** means the ability of two different computing devices to share data, software, and hardware without having to provide unusual conversion of the shared resource. Desktop and host computers have historically had compatibility problems related to their different internal architectures.

Differences in Computer Architectures

Desktop computers are moving into information processing areas previously occupied only by host computers. Currently, some applications are better suited to host or to desktop computers. For example, large data files are best maintained on a host computer, with its accompanying high-speed, large-capacity storage devices. Conversely, it seems absurd to run a word processing software system on a $3 million host computer. Yet as information becomes more valued as a resource distributed throughout the firm, and as the differences between the processing capabilities of host computers and desktop computers decrease, many applications must be shared across computer architectures. Recent technological developments have produced a family of upwardly compatible computer architectures. The current major movement in compatibility among computer architectures is normally called open systems architecture. The main premise of **open systems architecture** is that data and software are readily available and completely compatible. Therefore, the systems developed in the next decade must be capable of spanning the architectures of different computers.

Spanned System Architecture

A method called **spanned system architecture** is emerging as a way to develop systems that will be usable on different computers. Thus business personnel can take advantage of the freedom that desktop computers offer, as well as the external storage capacity offered by host computers. Systems designed this way permit the sharing of data and software between architectures in a form that is transparent to users.

Transparency means that users can make requests, receive answers to questions, and view the results of processing without knowing where the data is located, which computer is actually performing the processing, or whether communication transfers are occurring. The need for transparency of operations between computers requires that systems designers and developers consider how new systems can be designed and implemented to span various architectures.

ENVIRONMENTAL CONSIDERATIONS IN SYSTEMS DESIGN

Figure 1-7 illustrated how a firm and its functional areas are all part of a larger suprasystem that comprises the business environment. Being a part of this suprasystem implies that environmental aspects external to the firm can affect the firm, and vice versa. Each new system design or maintenance project is also affected by the characteristics of the firm's environment. The particular characteristics of a firm are referred to as **constraints**. Some constraints are long-standing and others are temporary. Attributes of the environment affecting the analysis and design of systems include the following:

- Constraints involving governmental agencies and their requests and regulations
- Constraints involving the firm's industry
- Constraints involving the firm's individual attributes
- Functional constraints
- Technical constraints
- Financial constraints
- Operational constraints
- Personnel constraints

The analyst must consider all of these constraints when designing and developing a system to satisfy users' requirements. Figure 1-14 illustrates the environmental considerations involved in analysis and design.

Businesses must respond to requests and regulations established by governmental agencies. The MIS may respond directly or provide information to support a response. For example, many payroll systems need modifications because of income tax revisions that are made on a regular basis by federal, state, and local governments. Each firm must also stay abreast of developments in its industry. The information system of every firm must gather, process, and transmit information to the regulatory agencies for the firm's industry. The design of the MIS is therefore affected by the information needs of these regulatory agencies. For instance, the practices of doctors and their MIS are influenced by the American Medical Association.

In addition, the climate in each industry affects the operations of all firms in that industry. For example, as a result of the move from mainframes to decentralized pro-

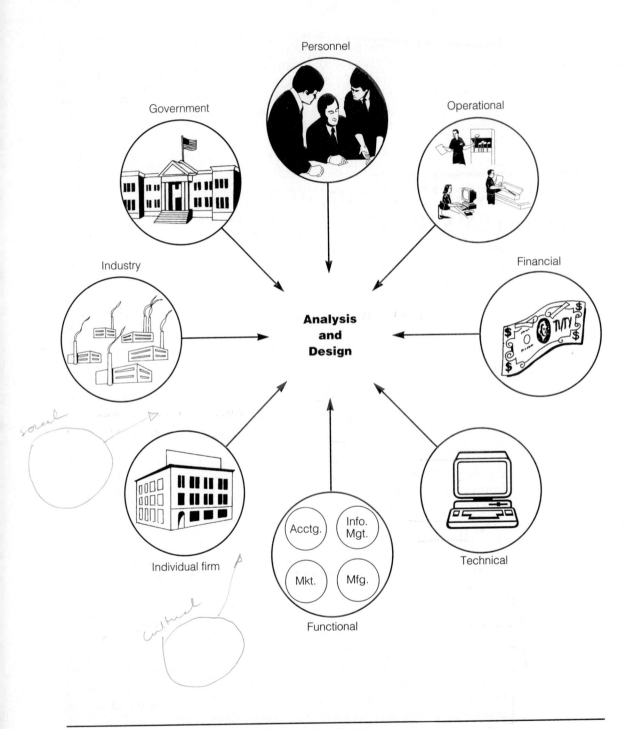

Figure 1-14. Environmental considerations involved in A&D

cessing systems, which took place in industry as a whole during the late 1980s, few computer hardware and software manufacturers in the early and middle 1990s have experienced the successes they knew in the 1980s. The MIS must be designed to gather information necessary for forecasting conditions that might affect the industry.

The attributes of an individual firm influence the design of the firm's systems. Depending on a firm's particular attributes, its systems may or may not be able to provide certain facilities desired by its personnel.

Certain functional constraints must also be mapped into the design of the MIS. System design is influenced by what functions a firm does or does not perform. For example, the MIS for a firm with a manufacturing component must track manufacturing activities, such as parts creation, resource usage, and product assembly.

The technology of either the industry or the individual firm also influences the design of the firm's systems. Technological development frequently occurs when someone observes that a desirable action is not possible because the right tool, method, or concept does not exist. The state of technology in an industry or a firm determines whether its systems can or cannot include certain desired features. For example, the use of sophisticated detection devices by many manufacturing firms decides certain quality-related characteristics. A firm without these detection devices cannot have a portion of its MIS tracking these quality conditions. Many steel mills use a detection device that checks the temperature in the melted-steel vats to make sure that it does not get outside certain tolerance ranges — a temperature that is too hot results in brittle steel; one that is too cold does not properly melt the iron ore. These firms may have a computer system that uses the temperature gauge as input and the delivery of fuel at the firing points as output. Thus, the computer system maintains the proper level of fuel at the firing points to ensure that the temperature inside the vat stays within prescribed tolerances.

Financial constraints also limit the design of the firm's systems. The cost of designing, developing, maintaining, and using portions of the firm's MIS is always an important factor in determining how sophisticated the MIS can be. The financial outlook of the firm, its industry, or the entire business environment may influence the design of the firm's MIS. For instance, startup firms with insufficient initial cash flows often postpone computerizing some of their record keeping to a later date when better cash flows exist.

Operational constraints are often directly related to technical constraints and also may affect the design of the firm's systems. Many desirable features may not be operationally possible, and thus cannot be included in the design of the firm's MIS. Often the sharing of data and software between computer architectures must wait until communication networks become operational. The technology is available, but is not yet available within the specific firm.

Finally, personnel constraints influence the design of the firm's systems. Without an appropriate number of specifically qualified personnel, many desirable characteristics may not be possible as part of the MIS design. For example, firms that have no personnel familiar with mathematical modeling must often forego including important mathematical models in the design of their MIS.

DATABASE CONSIDERATIONS IN SYSTEMS DESIGN

A **database** is a central collection of data needed by the firm. This central collection of data is a shared resource because all of the firm's systems and personnel share the data in the database. The major characteristics of a database are as follows:

- A data item is typically stored in a single location in the computer's auxiliary storage and is made available to all appropriate systems and personnel from that single location.

- A separate system, known as the **database management system (DBMS)**, is responsible for performing all operations necessary for physically accessing data.

As a result of storing a particular data item in a single storage location, all accesses to that data item will obtain the same values, with the access actually performed by the DBMS. The use of a database and a DBMS for data retrieval provides better support for the capabilities required in on-line data querying. Special query languages usually accompany the DBMS to allow more immediate access to the firm's data. These **fourth generation languages (4GLs)** typically require only that users specify what they wish to access, not how to retrieve the desired data. Figure 1-15 illustrates the database considerations for analysis and design. Chapter 10 covers database technologies and how they influence systems design in detail.

Many businesses use 4GLs exclusively in the development of their MIS. Through the use of 4GLs, the design of the MIS takes on many characteristics that are not available with third generation systems. These characteristics are intrinsic to the particular 4GL; therefore, they will not be discussed here. Yet these intrinsic differences should be known before a 4GL is used for MIS development. The following table presents a set of characteristics for the different generations of computing relative to the computer languages used. Note that for fifth generation languages, you use English-like statements, such as GROUP DATA ON STATE, which the system uses to generate a set of procedural instructions to carry out that task. In sixth generation languages, the system draws on a knowledge base of data and rules to generate procedural instructions that carry out the tasks indicated by the user.

Computer Generation	Language Characteristics
First generation	Machine binary code instructions
Second generation	Symbolic machine code command structure
Third generation	Macro procedural command structure
Fourth generation	High-level procedural command structure
Fifth generation	Specification-driven command structure
Sixth generation	Knowledge-based command structure

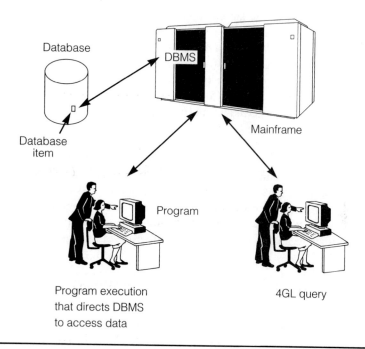

Database

DBMS

Mainframe

Database
item

Program

Program execution
that directs DBMS
to access data

4GL query

Figure 1-15. Database considerations for A&D

Because many systems in the firm's MIS have survived transitions to different generations of computing, the design of the MIS is often influenced by the characteristics of several generations. The strategy adopted in this text attempts to bridge the gaps between the generations and between computer architectures. This is an ambitious undertaking, but one that is necessary in order to keep the material in this text fresh.

ATTRIBUTES AND QUALIFICATIONS OF A SYSTEMS ANALYST

An analyst must be proficient in many skills to effectively understand user needs, investigate requests for assistance, design solutions to identified problems, oversee the development and implementation of these solutions, and understand the operations of the firm that are incorporated in the design of the information system. Some say that analysts need the skills of a snake-oil salesman and the virtues of a messiah. Analysts must be skilled in both written and oral communication to ensure clear understanding of users' needs. Investigative skills are also required for examining problems in an orderly and productive manner. Analysts need evaluation skills to assess the direction in which the design is to proceed. They must have the architectural skills to design an operationally efficient and valid system. They must be capable of organizing and overseeing projects and solving problems.

The world is rapidly becoming more technically oriented, and the analyst must have sufficient technical proficiency to meet the challenge. Functional business skills are also required for the analysis and design of systems that will be used by personnel in functional areas of the firm. Finally, analysts must have strong interpersonal and political skills to deal effectively with the diverse population of people who can influence the outcome of a systems analysis and design project. Among the many roles that the analyst plays during the life cycle of business systems are:

Investigator	Architect
Engineer	Supervisor
Monitor	Motivator
Moderator	Psychologist
Sociologist	Salesperson
Politician	Technical consultant
Agent for change	

To put it another way, an analyst must be an investigator with the acuity of Sherlock Holmes, an architect on a par with Frank Lloyd Wright, a supervisor in the style of Bill Gates, a motivator equal to Martin Luther King, a moderator on the lines of Daniel Webster, a psychologist à la Sigmund Freud, a salesman comparable to P. T. Barnum, a politician with the skills of Margaret Thatcher, a technical consultant with the imagination of Thomas Edison, an agent for change akin to Mikhail Gorbachev, and Big Brother, all rolled into one.

A systems analyst's many skills and abilities must be acquired through both education and experience. A person may be trained in many skills required for analysis and design, but only experience and a willingness to listen and learn make someone a *good* analyst. The qualifications for a career in A&D are acquired through:

- Formal education
- Professional education
- Manufacturers' training seminars
- In-house training courses
- Experience
- Development of good interpersonal skills

Educational Requirements

Formal education in A&D is acquired through either a four-year college or university or a two-year technical school. Analysts need a wide variety of courses to prepare them for the many different situations they will face in their jobs. They will need not only courses in programming, database use, systems analysis, and data communication, but an understanding of all business disciplines. It is difficult to design a markeing information system, a production information system, or an accounting information system without knowledge of these fields.

Professional education is available from organizations such as the Association for Systems Management (ASM), the Data Processing Management Association (DPMA), the Institute of Industrial Engineers (IIE), the Association for Computing Machinery (ACM), and a host of other professional and academic associations. These seminars keep those interested in A&D abreast of advances in the methods used for analyzing and designing systems. These courses will often provide credit needed to either acquire or maintain professional certification within the various sponsoring organizations. For example, the certification of Certified System Professional (CSP) can be obtained through the Association for Systems Management, that of Certified Data Processor (CDP) through the Data Processing Management Association, and that of Certified Computer Programmer from the Association for Computer Machinery.

Manufacturers' training courses provide training in the use of their products. In-house training is often provided by individual firms so that personnel can understand and use those firms' systems and related software and hardware. Finally, analysts become qualified through personal experience with business applications, products, methodologies, and so on. Candidates for A&D careers often have inquisitive minds. Since every day brings new and different experiences, analysts must be able to enjoy the constant state of flux offered by the dynamically changing world of A&D.

Job Opportunities

Entry-level positions in the IS area include classifications such as junior systems analyst, junior applications programmer, junior systems analyst/programmer, and computer marketing representative. Regardless of the job title, most graduates will work on developing and writing business applications programs during their first few years. After one or more years in an entry-level position, an individual can move up to a variety of positions such as these:

Title	Position Description
Senior systems analyst	Confers with users to define and formulate logical statements of business problems and devise procedures for solutions.
Database administrator	Analyzes an application's computerized dataneeds; coordinates data collection and storage needs.

Title	Position Description
Computer security specialist	Establishes and supervises systems for the protection of hardware, software, and data.
Training specialist	Organizes, prepares, and conducts training sessions for IS personnel and users.
Telecommunications manager	Designs data communications networks and organizes the installation and operation of data links.
Vice-president of MIS	Oversees all corporate information systems functions; sometimes called the chief information officer (CIO). Responsible for long-range planning, budgeting, and operations.

Current information regarding these and other positions in management information systems and business is available in articles from trade publications such as *Datamation*, *Software Magazine*, *ComputerWorld*, and the *Journal of Information Systems Management*. Trade publications also report on current system practices and the results of practical research projects. Information regarding theoretical as well as practical research can be found in academic journals such as *Communications of the ACM*, *MIS Quarterly*, and the *Journal of Management Information Systems*.

REVIEW

Systems analysis and design can be defined by separately defining systems, analysis, and design, what they entail, and who performs the activities associated with them. The general systems theory is an approach to understanding systems that combines the holistic approach of Aristotle and the analytic approach of Descartes. It shows how each industry, firm, functional area of the firm, and agent of the external environment is considered a subsystem within the suprasystem of the business world.

The management information system (MIS), which is created and maintained by systems analysts to supply information to users, is made up of subsystems that contribute to planning, control, and retaining data concerning daily operations. The three main subsystems are the decision support system (DSS), the management support system (MSS), and the transaction processing system (TPS). The MIS and its subsystems provide information for management at the tactical, strategic, and operational levels. Business people are beginning to realize that information itself is an important resource of the firm, which has resulted in the emergence of information resource management as a new branch of executive management.

The evolution of computer systems from mainframes to desktop computers has contributed to another new development in systems design: spanned system architecture. The aspiring analyst must be capable of designing systems that will be able to cross computer architectures now and in the future. The analyst must also understand the impact of environmental and database considerations on analysis and design projects. Environmental constraints on A&D projects can come from the firm's industry, governmental regulations, finances, and personnel. The firm's database, or central repository of data, determines which generation of computer language can be used in system design, or whether the design can cross several generations.

Finally, to become a systems analyst, formal education may be pursued at four-year colleges and two-year technical schools. Several organizations, such as the Association for Systems Management and the Data Processing Management Association, provide professional education; manufacturers' training courses provide training in system practices, methodologies, and the use of specific products. Job titles range from junior systems analyst to vice-president of MIS. The qualifications for a systems analyst include the talents of a brilliant investigator, a patient motivator, a gifted engineer, a sympathetic supervisor — in short, the ability to be all things to all people.

QUESTIONS

1. Clearly distinguish between data and information.
2. Define a system.
3. Describe a system that you use in your personal life.
4. Define analysis.
5. Define systems analysis.
6. Define design.
7. Define systems design.
8. Define systems analysis and design.
9. Explain the general systems theory approach by describing its origin and its major premises.
10. What is a model, and what is its purpose?
11. Describe a model that you may have encountered in your life.
12. Clearly distinguish between the conceptual and the physical firm, identifying the components of each and the purpose of each component.
13. Distinguish between batch and on-line processing.
14. For a company in your vicinity, describe both a batch and an on-line system that it might use.
15. What purpose does information serve for decision makers in the firm?
16. Identify the three ways in which information is supplied to decision makers.
17. Distinguish among the three different types of periodic reports.
18. For a company in your vicinity, obtain examples of the three different types of periodic reports.

19. Clearly distinguish between periodic reports and data querying.

20. Distinguish between structured and semistructured problems.

21. For a company in your vicinity, describe both a structured and a semistructured problem that it has.

22. Define a decision support system, identifying its purpose and describing what it is usually based on.

23. Distinguish among a decision support system, a management support system, and a management information system.

24. For a company in your vicinity, describe a decision support system, a management support system, and a management information system that it has.

25. Define a transaction processing system, identifying its purpose and describing what it is usually based on.

26. For a company in your vicinity, describe one of its transaction processing systems.

27. Distinguish among the three areas of management, identifying the main function each performs and the type of information that is usually required by each.

28. Define information resource management, identifying its purpose, the person who should be the ultimate authority, and its major premises.

29. List and explain the five major attributes of a system.

30. Why is it said that a system must have a central purpose?

31. For a company in your vicinity, describe a central purpose for one of its main systems (be sure to identify the system by name).

32. Define the characteristic of a system identified as system dependence.

33. Explain what is meant by *ripple effect*.

34. For a company in your vicinity, explain a ripple effect it may have created during an A&D project.

35. Distinguish between the system characteristics of integration and interaction.

36. Define compatibility.

37. Define spanned system architecture, its purpose, its relationship with the goal of transparency, and what development leads to its existence.

38. Why must environmental conditions be considered in systems development efforts?

39. For a company in your vicinity, describe environmental considerations important to it. Explain why those considerations are important to the company.

40. What are the two central characteristics of a database?

41. What is a database management system and what is its purpose?

42. For a company in your vicinity, identify and describe its database management system.

43. Distinguish between third and fourth generation languages.

44. For a company in your vicinity, identify and describe the fourth generation language it uses.

45. Identify the attributes associated with a systems analyst and explain why they are important.

46. How does a person become qualified as a systems analyst?

47. Distinguish among the different positions that a systems professional may aspire to occupy.

48. Search the IS literature for characteristics of the different jobs a system professional may hold. List the characteristics of the position you wish to hold. Explain why you would like to have this job. For example, what does a person in this job do that sounds like your area of interest?

CHAPTER 2

Business and Information Systems Modeling Using A&D Modeling Methods and Methodology

OVERVIEW

This chapter discusses the process of developing systems. It explains business modeling, various methods used to model business and information systems to support the business, and the methodology that consolidates these topics.

Topics are discussed individually and interwoven to show how they are related. The material here and in Chapter 3 provides the basis for understanding the use of methodology and the system development life cycle used during analysis and design. It also introduces computer-aided software engineering (CASE)—the technology that uses electronic tools to automate portions of A&D methodology—and specifies the methodology that will be used throughout this text. This chapter provides the building blocks you need to understand the use of modeling methods, methodology, and technology during analysis and design, by:

- Describing how the three facets of business—business objects, activities, and associations—are presented in models of the business and information system

- Describing methodology and its components

- Describing the various graphical and textual modeling methods—the techniques of methodology

- Describing principles and practices of methodology
- Describing the text methodology
- Describing computer-aided software engineering (CASE)

KEY TERMS

Action diagram
Analyst workbench software
Architecture
Association
Business activities
Business functions
Business objects
Business processes
Computer-aided software engineering
  (CASE)
Data flow diagram (DFD)
Data flows
Data model
Data modeling
Data store
Decision table
Detail diagram
Entity
Entity/relationship diagram (E/RD)
Entity type description
HIPO diagrams
Information engineering (IE)
Information systems procedures
Infrastructure
Iteration
Lower CASE
Methodology
Methodology philosophy
Middle CASE
Modeling method

Nassi-Schneiderman chart
Object-oriented modeling methods
Object services
Policy
Procedure model
Process dependency diagram (PDD)
Process model
Program flow charts
Program logic
Prototype
Pseudocode
Rapid application development (RAD)
Relationship cardinality
Repository
Rule
Selection
Sequence
Standards
Structure chart (STC)
Structured methodology
Structured programs
System development life cycle (SDLC)
System flow chart
Technique
Tool
Top-down design
Upper CASE
User requirements
Warnier/Orr (W/O) diagram

Systems are designed and maintained to provide information for business personnel, whose needs constantly change because of the dynamic nature of the business environment. In addition, existing systems in the MIS often neglect certain information needs. The ability to supply more information often increases the demand for additional information. When critical information needs are not being met satisfactorily by systems in the MIS, a system development project begins. During its life span, a system is developed and maintained to meet neglected or newly emerging information needs.

To understand and develop appropriate requirements for an information system, the analyst must understand the firm and its business. To acquire a complete understanding, the analyst gathers information abut the business and often creates models of it. These models aid communication between the analyst and users by ensuring that they have a comparable knowledge of the business. This chapter discusses business and information system modeling, various modeling methods used to create the models, and the full methodology used to create and integrate the business and information system models. Chapter 3 describes the system development life cycle; Chapter 4 describes how to gather the data needed to create the models described here.

Systems development methodology specifies how to build business and system models, and how to create and maintain the information system to support the business. Systems development/maintenance methodology consists of a combination of graphical and textual methods used by modelers and system developers to develop and maintain business models, information system models, and actual information systems. Hereafter in this text, the term *methodology* is synonymous with *system development/maintenance methodology*.

To fully understand methodology, the aspiring systems analyst needs to clearly distinguish among three often-confused sets of terms:

- Methodology
- System development life cycle
- Logical and physical design

MODELING THE BUSINESS

Designers must understand the business and its activities in order to develop information systems. They do this by acquiring a complete understanding of three facets of business: business objects, business activities, and associations. In this book, the terms *business* and *enterprise* will be used interchangeably.

Business Objects

Business objects are those objects internal or external to the business, including people (or organizations), places, things, events, and concepts, about which it is important to retain information. Internal objects may be departments, types of personnel, organizational resources, records of transactions, and a host of other people, places, things, events, or concepts. External objects may be clientele, suppliers, competitors, governmental agencies, or industry agencies. Figure 2-1 illustrates the general types of business objects.

You analyze a business to identify the many different object types that exist for the business. For example, "people" may encompass customers, employees, business contacts, and governmental agents. These different types of people may affect the business; therefore, it is important to know various facts about them. To know these facts, the business information systems department sets up information systems to gather, categorize, and process the properties (characteristics) of these business object types. An individual real-world business object, such as a particular customer, will be a single object in the collection of objects characterized by the object type. Or, to use file-processing phraseology, a single customer is a single record in a file of customers.

Figure 2-1. General types of business objects

Business Activities

Business activities are what the business does in terms of major functions, processes within those functions, and procedures that implement the business processes. Business functions, business processes, and information systems procedures, respectively, represent three different levels of abstraction for the activities of the business: conceptual/strategic, logical/functional, and physical/operational.

Business Functions

Business functions are those ongoing actions performed by organizational personnel that further the mission of the firm. Business functions specify the highest level of abstraction for organizational actions, but may be decomposed into subfunctions. Business functions typically cross normal organization chart positions. For example, a person from production and another from marketing may both be part of, or contribute to, a particular business function. Functions may include advertising products, distributing products, maintaining inventories, or a host of other major activities of the firm. A business function is ongoing, whereas a business process relates to a specific act that has definable start and stop points.

Business Processes

Business processes are the set of actions supporting business functions or subfunctions that transform inputs into outputs and have time-oriented start and stop points. A business process specifies only *what* action to perform, not *how* to perform the action. This definition also implies that when analysts identify and describe a business process, only the logical side of understanding the process is addressed, not the physical side. An example would be *what* manufacturing processes are used in manufacturing a particular product. For example, manufacturing automobiles might be one of the major functions of General Motors. Creating a part for a particular automobile might be a process that supports that general function. Figure 2-2 illustrates the differences between functions and processes. The functions of finance, manufacturing, and marketing represent the more abstract business activities, whereas the process of selling a golf club or recording a production total is a finite activity.

Decomposing business functions and processes should be done independently of decomposing the business into departments. Also, business functions and processes are concerned with what has to be done to operate a business and why, rather than how it is done. Procedures are concerned with how it is done, and these procedures change as technology and business practices change.

Information Systems Procedures

Information systems procedures are action statements specifying *how* an information system implements a business process or helps someone perform an organizational

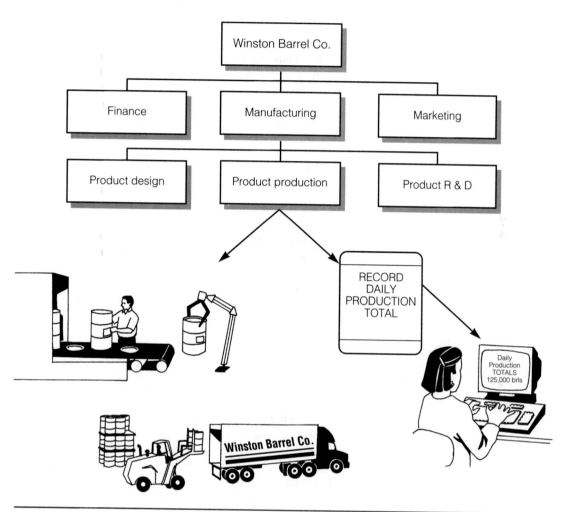

Figure 2-2. Functions versus processes

task. This definition implies that the logical process is accomplished through the physical nature of the term *procedure*. An example would be a procedure that specifies *how* to calculate payroll deductions, followed by computing the net pay from gross pay. In this text, *procedure* should be interpreted as *information systems procedure*.

Associations

Associations are connections between business objects and other business objects, connections between business activities and other activities, and connections between business objects and activities. An **association** can be a relationship, dependency, shared characteristics, or other connection. Associations are often illustrated by using a table to show the connections between row items and column items. For example, the well-known CRUD (create, read, update, delete) table, consisting of process rows and data object columns, illustrates the association between processes and data objects. Intersecting cells of the matrix indicate how the data objects are used (the association) by the processes. Figure 2-3 shows a CRUD table for management of inventory (supplier item ordering and receiving).

Another way to show an association is with a **decision table**. A decision table indicates various conditions (or states) that may exist and responses (actions) for those conditions. A decision table might result in a set of IF-THEN instructions in a proce-

Logical Data Object

Process	SUPPLIER	ITEM	QUANTITY	ORDER	RECEIPT	BILL	PAYMENT	SUPPLIER PAYABLE	RETURN
ADD SUPPLIER	C							C	
IDENTIFY SUPPLIER	R								
CHANGE SUPPLIER	U								
DELETE SUPPLIER	D								
ADD ITEM		C	C						
CHANGE ITEM		U							
DELETE ITEM		D							
CREATE SUPPLIER ORDER	R		U	C					
RECEIVE SUPPLIER ORDER	R			R	C				
COMPARE RECEIPT/ORDER				R	R				
UPDATE ITEM INVENTORY			U						
RECEIVE SUPPLIER BILL						C		U	
RETURN DEFECTIVE ITEMS						U	U	U	
PAY SUPPLIER							C	U	

Figure 2-3. CRUD table for inventory management shows associations between data objects and processes

	Sales Level Amounts		
Commission Rate	1.00–100.00	100.01–1000.00	1000.01+
5%	*		
10%		*	
15%			*

Figure 2-4. Decision table to determine commission rate

dure model for a program. An example illustrates this better than an elaborate explanation. Figure 2-4 shows a decision table that could be used to determine the amount of commission to pay a salesperson for a sale, based on different commission rates for different levels of sales.

Analysts and programmers use associations to create or change certain portions of the business and information system models, and the system. For example, from the decision table in Figure 2-4, a programmer could use the following COBOL IF-THEN instructions to compute the commission for a particular sale:

IF SALE_AMOUNT LESS THAN OR EQUAL TO 100.00
    COMPUTE COMMISSION = SALE_AMOUNT * .05.

IF SALE_AMOUNT > 100.00 AND
    SALE_AMOUNT < 1000.01
    COMPUTE COMMISSION = SALE_AMOUNT * .10.
IF SALE_AMOUNT GREATER THAN 1000.00
    COMPUTE COMMISSION = SALE_AMOUNT * .15.

Associations are also depicted by using various graphical methods that employ symbols to represent data objects and activities. For example, entity/relationship diagrams, described in greater detail in Chapter 5, not only identify data objects important to the organization, but also portray the relationship between the objects.

Figure 2-5 illustrates the elements of the business and information system models. These models consist of objects, activities, and associations used to provide analysts with a deeper understanding of the business. For example, an important object to a retail sales store like Sears might be the customer, the process of recording a charge sale for a customer might be one of its important activities, and connecting the customer sale with a customer billing statement might be an important association.

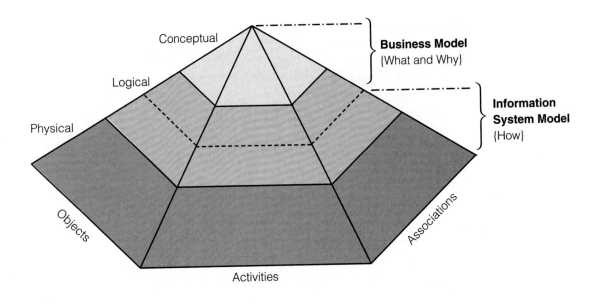

Figure 2-5. Business/information system model

Through knowledge of these things about business objects, activities, and associations, an understanding of a business is gained from a conceptual, logical, and physical perspective.

The conceptual and logical perspectives provide information about the three business elements in order to determine why they are part of the business and what they are, do, and/or provide for the business. For example, just knowing that a customer is important to the business and depicting it on the model as either a graphical symbol or a text entry represents a conceptualization of the real-world object as a part of the model. Furthermore, a list of the object's properties (characteristics) that are important to know represents a logical view of that object.

The physical perspective introduces the aspect of how objects are used, how activities are performed, and how associations are facilitated; in other words, what the system comprises. Equivalent terms for *conceptual*, *logical*, and *physical* perspectives could be *strategic*, *functional*, and *operational*. Systems analysis and design projects require that systems analysts understand the three facets from all three perspectives. They do this by gathering information about these facets from all three perspectives and using this information to create a model of the business (or the portion of the business of interest to their project) and a model of the system needed by the business.

A comprehensive business model shows all business objects and their relationships, all business activities, associations between business activities and other activities, and associations between business activities and objects. This information is captured by applying the principles of a comprehensive methodology. Establishing and applying the principles of the firm's methodology requires a thorough understanding of methodology and of all of its components.

The information system model prescribes a way to develop computer-based systems to support the business. This part of the model describes:

- The way to more effectively store data about the properties of objects
- How to develop procedure models that implement and support business processes
- How those procedures use the properties of data objects to satisfy the information needs of business personnel

Business personnel need to know about business objects and have actions available to manipulate those data objects in order to identify, categorize, compare, group, and summarize them. What users want to know about and have manipulated by the information system is collectively known as **user requirements**. These requirements specify the criteria that make up the information system model in Figure 2-5. Users want facts about business objects, and they want to be able to manipulate those facts to produce the information they need. Having these facts and this information helps users make better decisions and perform their jobs better.

METHODOLOGY

Practicing analysts have devised successful methods for performing certain steps in developing systems that have become recognized as proven methodologies. In general, a methodology is an assortment of capabilities and rules that the practitioners of a science or discipline follow in order to perform some task. More specifically, a methodology consists of the life cycle steps and the methods used to complete those steps. For example, the modeling methods, techniques, and tools used in some steps that focus on the logical and physical design actions are part of the methodology of systems analysis and design. SA&D methodology prescribes a particular style in creating either diagrams, text (or both), or system simulations to represent the design specifications. Methodology specifies how analysts model the business so that they can understand it and develop information systems appropriate for meeting its information needs.

Many methodologies have emerged in systems analysis and design. They generally represent the different stylistic methods of highly successful systems analysts. Using these accepted methodologies ensures that other analysts will more easily understand the system, and will aid them in maintaining the system after installation. The important point is that a standard for methodology should be adopted so that system specifications will be consistent for all the firm's systems. Following a standard methodology allows others to emulate the practices of innovative systems analysts.

Structured Methodology

The need to standardize and simplify design and development methodology has resulted in what is known as **structured methodology**, an approach in which A&D and programming activities are broken down into small, easily managed parts. By virtue of their size, many systems and programs appear complex, but if they are broken down into smaller, cohesive units, they become much easier to design and develop. An additional feature of this approach is that it helps prevent reinventing the wheel. Many components of one system can fit into other systems. Thus using a structured methodology induces reusing some units of one system as units of other systems, increasing the volume of reusable specifications.

Larry Constantine and Edward Yourdon are often credited with originating the concept of structured A&D in the early and mid-1970s. Structured A&D is a set of methods to follow in designing a system. Its premise is that major problems are broken down into small problems (the modular approach). The resulting modules are then hierarchically organized and related to one another in some manner, usually by sequence, selection, or iteration. These basic logic structures refer to the order (sequence) of instruction execution, various selection instructions, and repetition of instructions. **Sequence** is the order of the execution of commands (instructions) in a program. **Selection** is the way one of several actions is taken based on one or more conditions, such as the results of an IF statement in many programming languages. **Iteration** (or loop instruction) is the way programs repeat the execution of a sequence of instructions, such as iterative branching instructions (for example, PERFORM, DO, and so forth).

Tom DeMarco summarized the structured methodology strategy in the late 1970s as a methodology for producing a highly maintainable, easily tested, **top-down design**. By top-down design, DeMarco means producing an overview set of descriptions that systematically decompose into more detailed specifications for small units of the system. In the early to mid-1980s, Kathleen Dolan further summarized the goals of structured design as follows:

- To produce software on time and within budget
- To write program modules that easily and correctly interface with other related modules
- To make software easy to modify
- To simplify the debugging process

Methodology Components

The literature describing the methodologies of successful analysts generates confusion about methodology. This confusion stems from the lack of a recognized definition of methodology and its domain of terms. As a result, many terms pertaining to methodology have been misused, incorrectly used, or interchangeably used in an incorrect manner. For example, a noted methodologist calls a data flow diagram a modeling method, tool, technique, and procedure, all within a 30-page interval. In a rigorous, comprehensive methodology, these terms are not interchangeable. To understand methodology, you should understand the following key terms:

Business objects	Logical and physical design
Business activities	Modeling method
Business functions	Rule
Business processes	Entity
Information systems procedures	Technique
Associations	Standards
Architecture	Policy
Infrastructure	Tool
Life cycle	

The first six terms are defined in the "Modeling the Business" section, earlier in this chapter, and pertain to the three facets of the business about which the analyst must be familiar. In terms of activities, this text will be concerned with modeling business processes and procedures. Functions usually aid in higher-level modeling that supports strategic planning—not the normal subject of A&D projects.

The definition of process implies that identifying and describing processes involves only a conceptual and logical understanding of the process, not a physical understanding. In contrast, the definition of procedure is more physical in nature; it specifies how something is accomplished, often a transformation of a logical process. For example, portions of computer programs execute procedures to perform or serve business processes. To produce models of business objects, activities, and associations, the analyst must understand the company's overall architecture, used in modeling them, and the infrastructure that comprises the concrete aspects of the business.

Architecture and Infrastructure

Architecture defines and interrelates data, hardware, software, and communications resources to support the organization's conceptual, logical, and physical structure. Architecture specifies the way certain organizational aspects relate for a subject of interest.

The basic framework or features of a system or organization, including data, applications, and the underlying technology (for example, the hardware, system software, and network) make up its **infrastructure**. Infrastructure differs from architecture in that architecture is the design of the way the aspects relate (logical), whereas the infrastructure comprises those aspects (physical). For example, creating the specifications for the walls, ceiling, floors, and equipment to be included (built-in kitchen

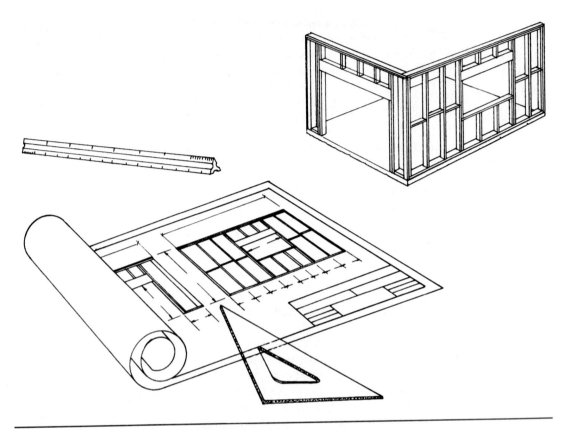

Figure 2-6. Architecture versus infrastructure

appliances, vacuum systems, and so on), for a house, represents architecture. Once the house is built, the walls, ceilings, floors, and amenities represent the living capacity that comprises the infrastructure for those living in the house. Figure 2-6 illustrates the difference between architecture and infrastructure.

System Development Life Cycle

Systems analysis and design projects usually follow a standard set of steps to complete the project. A **system development life cycle (SDLC)** is a recognized set of steps to complete a development or maintenance project, or the life span of a system. In information systems literature, *life cycle* frequently refers to the life span of systems and projects to develop or maintain systems. Every creature, place, and thing has a life cycle. In organizational modeling, the life cycles of all facets of the organization should be recorded.

Logical and physical design are covered in more detail in Chapter 3, where their relationship to the logical and physical design portions of the SDLC is discussed. For now, logical design implies developing desirable requirements for what is being developed or maintained in a project. Physical design implies the physical implementation of the desired logical requirements. An example of logical design for a career in MIS is the creation of a plan of study to follow while enrolled in a college or university; physical design is the completion of courses in the plan of study. During both logical and physical design, the analyst typically uses different modeling methods to model business objects, activities, and associations.

Modeling Methods and Rules

A **modeling method** is a protocol (set of rules) for modeling organizational objects, activities, and associations. It may be graphical or textual in nature. The rules provide guidance concerning the way to employ the modeling method.

To better understand what constitutes a modeling method, it is important to understand how the term *rule* applies. A **rule** is a guide used to describe business objects, activities, associations, and ways to perform procedures or use a modeling method. The following are examples of rules:

- **Description of objects**—Only inherent properties of an object need to be identified.
- **Processes**—Processes do not produce output without input.
- **Procedures**—Only the steps sufficient to complete the procedure need to be identified.
- **Modeling method**—Freestanding objects are not allowed in most graphical modeling methods.

A collection of rules actually constitutes a particular modeling method.

Most analysts identify and describe business objects and associations between objects by using a data model. **Data modeling** is a form of modeling in which diagrams and text entries are used to identify and provide facts about business objects. The entity/relationship models of Peter Chen and other pioneers in modeling data are examples of data modeling methods. Data modeling methods are discussed in detail in the following sections.

Most analysts illustrate business activities by using what they term a process model. A **process model** is a decomposition of business activities into functions, categories of processes within functions, and subcategories of major processes. For many years, practicing analysts referred to these collective activities as the *process model* or *process modeling*. Since processes constitute only part of the activities of the business in a logical (or functional) level of abstraction, the phrase *process model* can be confusing. For clarity, this text refers to these modeling methods as *activity modeling* methods. Remember that in the literature of different authors, *process model* and the term used here, *activity model*, are functionally equivalent.

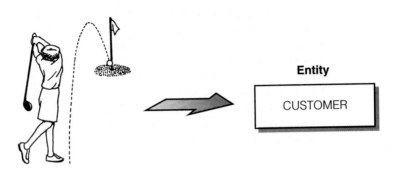

Figure 2-7. Object versus entity

Various modeling methods that analysts may use are described in this chapter. The descriptions are based on what is modeled by the modeling method—that is, business objects, activities, and associations. An entity/relationship diagram (E/RD) is used to model business data objects, for example. A function decomposition diagram is an example of a modeling method used for function modeling. The data flow diagram (DFD) and process dependency diagram (PDD) are examples of modeling methods used for process modeling. The structure chart (STC) and action diagram (AD) are examples of modeling methods used to model information system procedures. Although some of these modeling methods may not be used in very many businesses today, it is useful to review them for their historical significance and for some of their traits. This text focuses on certain modeling methods, identified in "The Text Methodology," at the end of this chapter.

Many data and process modeling methods use the term *entities* to describe business object types. An **entity** *abstractly represents* a business object type that may consist of people, places, things, events, or concepts. The business object type exists in the real world; the entity does not, as Figure 2-7 illustrates. An entity symbolically represents the object type; it is not the object type, as frequent misuse of the term implies.

Techniques

In addition to the normal rules for a modeling method, customs can be established for a particular modeling method or between modeling methods. Within a modeling method you can apply rules in a certain way, use principles in a conventional way, draw the diagram in a common way, or establish a customary way to use the symbols of the modeling method. A **technique** is a way of following a procedure or employing a modeling method to complete or portray organizational objects, activities, or associations. Here, *technique* implies a particular style to follow in accomplishing or using something. For example, a technique to construct an organization chart would be to connect organizational positions by specifying supraordinate and subordinate positions in the organization's chain of command. The term *technique* has also become synonymous with *modeling method* when a particular modeling method, such as DFDs (a method described later in this chapter), is referred to. The plural of the term, *techniques*, implies all modeling methods and ways to complete or portray approaches and organizational objects, activities, and associations. The goal of a methodology is to establish common use of techniques that all personnel apply in the same ways, to maintain consistency with what is being modeled regardless of who does the modeling. This represents the standards of a methodology.

Standards and Policies

Chapter 1 defined standards as expected operational performances or levels of performance. In methodology, *standards* means that and much more. **Standards** are expected methods and/or levels of performance for modeling objects, activities, or associations, or for using procedures, modeling methods, or techniques. Standards imply that there is a conventional way of doing or using something. For example, an organization may select Peter Chen's data modeling method as the standard for modeling objects and associations. Another example would be using a structured programming format for program procedure modeling. A business that requires all analysts to create a context-level DFD (as described in Chapter 6) has made this technique a standard within the use of that modeling method.

For a methodology, you need a term to enumerate or to collectively refer to all of the standards established for using that methodology. A **policy** is a collection of standards regarding major facets of an organization. *Policy* implies a group of standards that formally identify recognized ways of doing or using something. An example related to information systems could be adopting a policy of using Peter Chen's data modeling, Edward Yourdon's DFDs for process modeling, and James Martin's action diagrams for procedure modeling. A business policy could be cash customers only, delivery within two days, and back orders filled within ten days.

Tools

A **tool** is an instrument for implementing the procedures, modeling methods, and techniques of a methodology. You use tools to actually draw a diagram using a particular modeling method while applying all of the rules and techniques of the method. In the strictest sense, a tool can be almost any instrument, from a pencil to a large, complex machine. An example of an A&D tool is a programming language to make computer procedures operational. Computer-aided design (CAD), computer-aided manufacturing (CAM), and computer-aided software engineering (CASE) are examples of software used as tools to apply various modeling methods and techniques of a methodology.

CAD and CAM software systems are used to model the design of a product and the manufacturing assembly of that product, respectively. Product engineers use CAD software to draw pictures of products and specify their various features. Manufacturing engineers use CAM software to design the assembly of newly designed products for effective manufacturing of the products. They draw pictures that correspond to off-line creation of parts and then on-line assembly of those parts into the finished product. Systems analysts use CASE software to create models of the business and information systems during an analysis and design project. CASE systems are described in more detail later in this chapter, in the section "Computer-Aided Software Engineering (CASE)."

A Methodology for Systems Analysis and Design

A rigorous definition of methodology can be constructed from the definitions of the vocabulary of which it is composed. **Methodology** is an *architectural* framework grounded in an organization's *infrastructure* that is based on a common philosophy to use various *tools* that support *techniques* and *rules* of various *modeling methods* and/or procedures in *standard* ways within companywide *policies*. Its goal is to complete and/or portray organizational *objects*, *activities*, and *associations* within a framework of a particular *life cycle*. You might say that methodology is everything; it is all-important, and it incorporates all facets of business modeling.

The statement that "methodology is an architectural framework grounded in the organization's infrastructure that is based on a common philosophy" implies that it supports modeling of the conceptual, logical, and physical aspects of the organization. The architectural framework guides all aspects of modeling and design within the available organizational foundation (infrastructure) of capabilities, resources, equipment, structures, and culture. It also implies that the people who employ the methodology have a common **methodology philosophy** regarding the business and business modeling: an understanding that it is important to model the business, and that information systems are important to it.

To comprehensively model a business, the conceptual view of the organization must be reflected in the logical view, which is in turn reflected in the physical view. Most of what businesses do begins with a concept that is logically administered and physically implemented. The conceptual or strategic view is the direction in which management intends the business to go. To administer and implement the conceptual view, all logical and physical aspects of the organization must be known. Carrying the strategic view of the organization into the logical and physical aspects requires that the conceptual philosophy of the organization be shared with those involved in the logical and physical aspects of the organization.

A rigorous definition of methodology does not imply that there is only one *type* of methodology that can satisfy the methodological needs of all organizations. The choice of modeling methods, procedures, techniques, and tools to use is left to the discretion of those governing the methodology of the organization.

TWO APPROACHES TO DESIGNING INFORMATION SYSTEMS

A significant part of any SA&D methodology is the means of diagramming or recording the data and processes of the business that are essential to the design of the system. The two major approaches to this are the data-oriented and process-oriented approaches. Both are structured approaches in that they decompose the problem into smaller, easily managed parts, and both define data and processes. The main difference is that the data-oriented approach focuses on the data during decomposition, whereas the process-oriented approach focuses on the processes during decomposition. Most modern analysts use both data-oriented and process-oriented methods, since it is important to emphasize both data objects and activities during A&D projects. The following sections describe many of the modeling methods you may encounter in your work as an analyst. Some can be used in conjunction with one another; some are alternatives to one another; some are not commonly used any more, but are presented here so that you will recognize them.

DATA MODELING METHODS

Chapter 4 covers the various methods for gathering data during the analysis phase of the development life cycle. Recording the findings of this system investigation often involves using a modeling method to produce a data model. A **data model** consists of diagrams and text entries that:

- Identify and describe data types for various business objects
- Indicate and describe the importance of the relationships among these data types
- Indicate how many of one type of object can relate to another type of object (called cardinality of relationships)

Many problems that users experience result from not knowing key facts about types of objects in the business environment that may affect them. For example, not knowing that a customer is already financially overextended can add to an already burgeoning assortment of uncollectible accounts for a firm. A data modeling method helps to identify business object types and their key characteristics (properties or attributes). The relationships between business objects, and the relative importance of those relationships, also aid in understanding problem areas. For example, knowing which type of employee creates or uses the data about a business object helps to understand problem areas, since that person can be questioned about his or her involvement. **Relationship cardinality** defines how many of one type of business object can be related to another type of business object. The three main types of cardinality are one-to-one (1:1), one-to-many (1:M), and many-to-many (M:N). For example, you can usually represent wife-to-husband as a 1:1 relationship, since most wives and husbands have only one spouse; manager-to-employee as a 1:M relationship, since most employees have only one manager and a manager may manage many employees; and student-to-class/enrollment as a M:N relationship, since students may enroll in many classes and a class may have many students.

Entity/Relationship (E/R) Modeling Method

Two frequently used data modeling methods are the semantic data model (SDM) and the entity/relationship diagram (E/RD). The SDM method will not be discussed here, but its usefulness is very similar to that of the E/R modeling method. If you understand the ways the analyst uses the E/R modeling method, studying the SDM method will add very little to the discussion. The main difference between these two methods is that the SDM uses mainly text entries to identify and describe business objects, whereas the E/R modeling method primarily uses graphics for these purposes. The modern use of the **entity/relationship diagram (E/RD)** employs graphical symbols accompanied by text descriptions to depict business object types and relationships between them. Businesses typically use a single type of data modeling method, rather than different methods at different times.

The use of E/RDs as data modeling methods originated in the literature of database technologies, especially in the work of Peter Chen. This modeling method is very useful for producing diagrams that illustrate the relationships among various business objects that are internal and external to the firm. Internal and external objects are often the sources or destinations of data about other business objects.

Assembling a large volume of information into a logical representation of the system under study is not an easy task, and the E/R modeling method can be used to organize some of this information in a meaningful way. E/RDs are used only to *identify* user requirements within the information assembled at the start of the analysis phase. Much of what satisfies the user's need to know consists of knowing the characteristics of various business objects. For example, to assess daily sales, a sales manager might want to know the characteristics of sales (events) that occurred in a certain time period; who (persons) participated in those sales; the departments (places) that participated in those sales; what items (things) were sold; and what marketing strategies (concepts) contributed to those sales.

Entity/relationship diagrams are advantageous because they are simple, yet they can illustrate complicated business relationships. The classical use of the E/RD is to identify entities that represent files and data items and then to diagram the relationships between them. Another valuable use for these diagrams is to categorize business relationships between real-world entities, such as departments, personnel, and clientele, and to include narrative descriptions of these relationships and the objects within the relationships.

Figure 2-8 illustrates the different types of symbols and formats used to create E/R models. Figure 2-9 illustrates the use of the three primary E/RD formats. A more

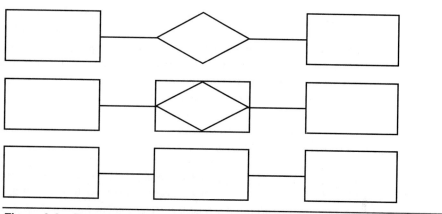

Figure 2-8. Entity/relationship model basic formats

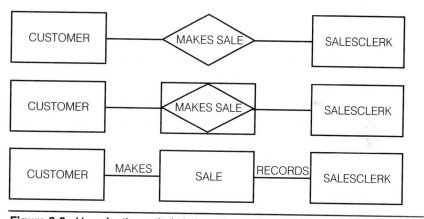

Figure 2-9. Uses for the entity/relationship model basic formats

complete explanation of the E/R modeling method appears in Chapter 5. Suffice it to say here that the entity/relationship modeling method helps document objects in the business environment to aid in determining where problems exist.

By creating E/RDs, systems analysts seek to conduct three important actions in modeling the business objects of the firm. They seek to:

- Identify all of the different types of business objects important to the firm for which data must be retained and the relationships between those objects

- Describe each business object type completely by identifying and recording the properties that are used to retain data about those types of objects

- Specify the cardinality of relationships between business object types depicted as entities on E/RDs

The analyst completes the first activity by creating separate E/RDs for different areas of the business in order to identify all of the types of objects that are important to all of the areas of the business. The analyst completes the second activity by creating a description of each entity (business object type), known as an entity type description. An **entity type description** specifies and describes the properties (attributes) of the business object type about which the firm needs to retain data. (Note that the terms *properties* and *attributes* are used interchangeably in this text.) Figure 2-10 shows a generic entity type description for a customer automobile retail sale, which an automobile dealership might retain.

An important feature of using E/RDs to record user requirements is that they do not impose a fixed structure. A fixed structure often causes salient features of the modeled object to be misinterpreted because of recording restrictions. Since E/RDs are somewhat free-form, individual user requirement specifications are less likely to be overlooked or misinterpreted. A top-down approach from more general to more specific can still be accomplished with E/RDs, as examples in Chapter 5 will illustrate.

ACTIVITY MODELING METHODS

Different modeling methods exist to model different types of activities, as well as different levels of abstraction for organizational activities. Over the years, activity modeling methods have changed from merely having an information systems orientation to having different orientations for different types of activities and different levels of abstraction for activities.

CUSTOMER_SALE
ORDER_NUMBER
CUSTOMER_NUMBER
AUTOMOBILE_REGISTRATION_NUMBER
ENGINE_BLOCK_NUMBER
LICENSE_TAG_NUMBER
AUTOMOBILE_MAKE
AUTOMOBILE_MODEL
PRICE
DATE

Figure 2-10. Customer sale entity type description

Some activity modeling methods are used in conjunction with each other by the analyst, whereas other modeling methods represent alternative ways to do similar activity modeling. For example, the function decomposition modeling method is often used in combination with one of the process modeling methods (process dependency diagrams or data flow diagrams). Process dependency diagrams and data flow diagrams are considered alternative process modeling methods. Alternative procedure modeling methods are also described.

Practicing analysts who work in a company that has a standard A&D methodology do not need to decide which modeling methods to use between different levels of abstraction (conceptual, logical, and physical), nor do they need to decide on alternative modeling methods for these levels of abstraction. They use the company's standard modeling methods. As an aspiring analyst seeking a systems analyst position in a company, however, you must be familiar with different modeling methods that accomplish similar tasks. You need to be able to say that you understand many modeling methods.

System Flow Charts

The system flow chart was a prominent modeling method of a previous era of computing; some businesses continue to use it. However, it has been largely replaced by the methods explained in the remainder of this chapter. Most of this chapter is devoted to the more current activity modeling methods.

A **system flow chart** is a modeling method that analysts may use to provide a graphic overview of the relationships between inputs, processing, and outputs for the whole system. Although it gives a broad overview of processing operations, it does not provide details concerning how inputs are converted into outputs. Businesses that still use system flow charts largely use them to document the overall system and as a guide for computer operators that outlines operating procedures for executing systems. Figure 2-11 illustrates the symbols used in system flow charting.

The symbols in Figure 2-11 show that a system flow chart can be used to diagram both electronic and manual operations that are necessary to prepare, process, and transmit data. Appropriate symbols are assigned names and inserted in the diagram in particular locations to symbolize the necessary preparation, processing, and transmission. These symbols are then connected by lines to show the sequence in which events should occur for correct execution. The key to appreciating the use and value of a system flow chart is to understand that it only portrays the preparation, processing, or transmission that occurs and the sequence of these operations. The way each of these operations is to be accomplished is left to additional design specifications. For example, a process symbol on a system flow chart only shows the point at which an application or utility program executes and *what* are its inputs and outputs. A program flow chart or a pseudocode expression of the logical procedures of the program is often created later in the development life cycle, specifically at the physical design phase, to show *how* program inputs are transformed into outputs.

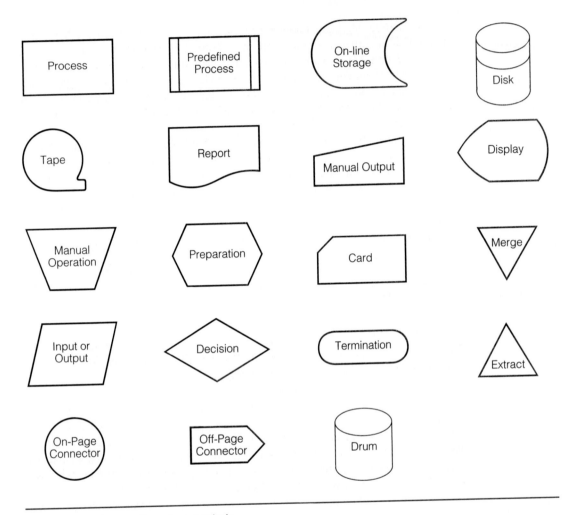

Figure 2-11. System flow chart symbols

System flow charts can represent either proposed or existing systems, but they have traditionally been used as graphic portrayals of existing systems. Figure 2-12 shows a system flow chart for a small component of an inventory system. Notice that the system flow chart in Figure 2-12 shows what input files to use, what outputs to create, what storage media to use for both inputs and outputs, and where preparation and processing occur in the sequence of events. It does not, however, show the details of preparation or processing that must occur.

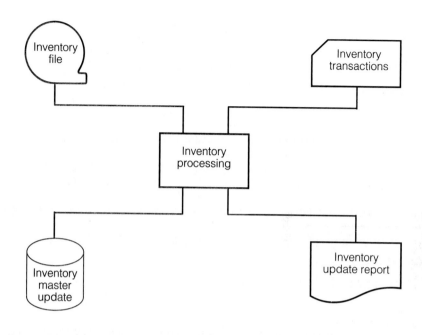

Figure 2-12. System flow chart of an inventory update

Function Decomposition Modeling Method

Functions were previously defined as the ongoing activities a business performs to further its mission. Most firms have five to ten major functions that define what they do and help characterize them. Each of these functions usually decomposes into sets of subfunctions, which are also ongoing actions that further the firm's mission.

A function decomposition provides a conceptual overview of all the activities an organization performs in support of its overall purpose. For example, a product manu-facturing company might have a function called manufacturing that decomposes into three subfunctions called product research and development, product production, and product distribution.

For personnel in the company who are responsible for major portions of the firm's activities, a function decomposition diagram helps them understand the rela-tionships between their functions and those other functions that support the firm's mission. For systems personnel, a function decomposition diagram provides a bird's-eye view of the activities of the entire organization.

The function decomposition modeling method is the simplest of the structured methods used in many methodologies. A function decomposition diagram begins with a single function placed at the top of the diagram that characterizes all of the firm's

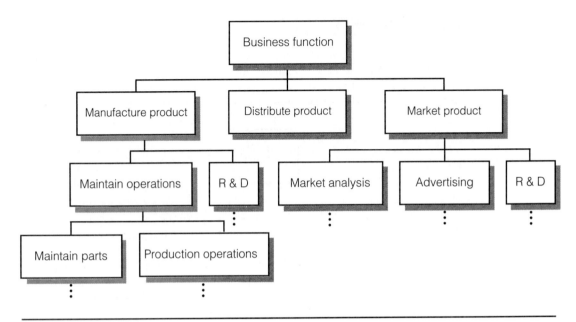

Figure 2-13. Example function decomposition diagram of a manufacturing business

functions. Below this function, and connected via lines, are the firm's five to ten major functions. Each one of these functions is connected to a set of subfunctions below it. The subfunctions may in turn decompose into even more detailed subfunctions below and connected to them. Function decomposition continues until further decomposition of a subfunction leads to identifying major processes that support the subfunction.

Figure 2-13 illustrates a function decomposition for a generic manufacturing business. For the sake of brevity, only a portion of this function decomposition appears. The ellipsis (. . .) signify other portions of this model that could be decomposed. It is unnecessary for these missing portions to be included in order to understand how to use this modeling method.

Process Modeling Methods

Data flow diagrams (DFDs), process dependency diagrams (PDDs), and Warnier/Orr diagrams represent alternative modeling methods for modeling the same thing—business processes. (Warnier/Orr diagrams can also be used to model an information system procedure.) A business typically uses only one of these three methods for business process modeling.

Data Flow Diagrams

A **data flow diagram (DFD)** is another structured modeling method often used during the A&D phases to model business processes. DFDs graphically depict business processes and the logical flows of data through those processes. This modeling method is largely viewed as a process-oriented method; however, it does include aspects of a data-oriented method. DFDs are considered process decomposition diagrams because they decompose business processes into smaller, more easily understood units. The processes that appear on a DFD may be processes that are completed in parallel, completed in a particular sequence, or both. The ability to show parallel as well as sequential processes distinguishes DFDs from other structured modeling methods. This characteristic allows you to use a DFD to show totally unrelated business actions performed in concert, with the same business objects (for example, customers and governmental agents) or with processes that share some of the same data objects (for example, customer orders and order payments). The input and output to DFD processes represent logical business objects. The processes on a DFD can also take place at totally different time intervals. For example, a DFD may have certain processes performed by clerks on a daily basis, as well as others performed on a monthly, quarterly, and yearly basis. The important thing to consider in creating a DFD is that you are modeling real-world processes in a business system and the data objects that flow through that business system.

Several different versions of symbols are used to construct DFDs. Two major

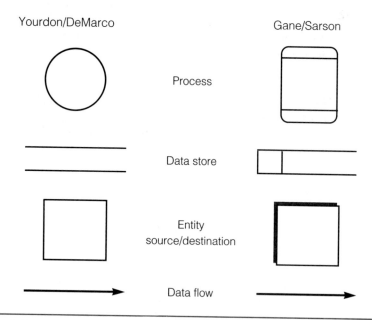

Figure 2-14. Data flow diagram symbols

versions—that of Yourdan/DeMarco and that of Gane/Sarson—are shown in Figure 2-14. Both versions are based on work begun by Larry Constantine and Edward Yourdon. The major difference between the versions is simply the symbols used to draw the diagram; the concepts and the usefulness of DFDs produced by the different versions are essentially the same.

DFDs are particularly useful for communication between the analyst and the user. They allow the analyst to present a graphic interpretation of the way data flows throughout the business, and of where and how processing occurs. Because DFDs are easy to understand, the analyst can present them to users and ask the users to suggest changes for omissions, additions, or corrections. These modifications can be incorporated during analysis and logical design rather than later, in the physical phases of the project, when suggestions for changes could result in significant reworking.

DATA SOURCES AND DESTINATIONS (ENTITIES)   In DFDs, entities represent initial sources and final destinations of data for DFD processes. The basic definition of entities on a DFD is similar to that for E/RDs: they represent organizations, agents, or people, inside and outside the system under study, that are sources or destinations of data. They either provide inputs to or receive outputs from processes of the business application under investigation. They are considered to be external to the application processes (not a part of them), yet necessarily related to them. The analyst must determine whether the entity is being controlled by the system or whether it is a part of the system's processes. Many entities internal to the business may become part of the processes, rather than sources of data for the processes.

Each entity symbol is assigned a label that names the real-world object it represents. A specification at the top of the symbol is often used as an identifier for the entity. Figure 2-15 shows a general form of the entity symbol and a specific entity, its dictionary ID, and the name of the object it represents. Dictionary IDs and dictionaries are explained in Chapter 5.

PROCESSES IN DFDS   Processes represent the transformation of data as it flows through the firm: data flows into a process, is changed (processed), and then flows out. Processes may be either manual or electronic. A DFD shows the logical operations performed for a business and how they are related to other processes. Figure 2-16

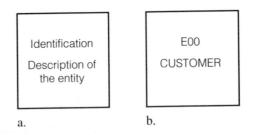

Figure 2-15. Entity symbols: *a.* general form and *b.* DFD entity example

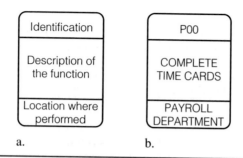

Figure 2-16. Process symbol: *a.* general form and *b.* DFD process example

shows a general process symbol, with explanations of the designations that usually appear on the symbol, and an example DFD process. The process symbol example in Figure 2-16 might be used to indicate the creation of payroll checks in an organizational payroll function. Note that the payroll department is optionally inserted as the location specification.

The label in the center of the process symbol designates the purpose and/or type of process to occur at the designated point in the DFD. The label should be a unique and easily understood phrase expressing a strong statement of action, such as COMPLETE TIME CARDS or UPDATE INVENTORY. The ID at the top of the symbol is a dictionary reference. The location specification at the bottom of the symbol is optional; it is used strictly as documentation, to show either where the process occurs or who is responsible for it.

DATA STORES IN DFDS A process either stores or accesses data. A **data store** is a temporary or permanent holding area for data—a stockpile where data is stored between processes. Data stores do not show the types of storage media used to hold the data. They represent data objects at rest. An easy way of conceptually viewing a data store is to realize that data used by an application is normally stored somewhere in a database (or in a manual medium such as a filing cabinet) that holds the data objects depicted as the data store. Thus it makes no sense to show the data objects leaving one data store and entering another data store without including a process symbol between the data stores. Data stores are assigned unique and descriptive names for reference purposes.

Data stores are not "black holes," from which data miraculously appears or into which data finally descends. Logical data objects that enter a store from one process should also exit the store, either to the same process or to some other process. A DFD models the real world of business processes. A data store is drawn to depict data objects being set aside for future use by a process. Analysts create a data store on a DFD when they are told that data is laid aside or is extracted from a place where it was previously laid aside. Figure 2-17 shows a general data store symbol and an example of a data store that represents CUSTOMER DATA, which could be accessed by processes on a DFD.

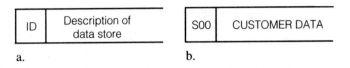

Figure 2-17. Data store symbol: *a.* general form and *b.* DFD data store example

DATA FLOWS IN DFDS **Data flows** are connections between processes and other DFD symbols along which individual logical objects and collections (sometimes called packets) of logical objects pass. Data flows depict logical data objects that pass between a process and another process, a data store, or an entity. When a data flow is directed to or from a data store, it should be viewed conceptually as entering or exiting a data holding area. For example, a data flow may be viewed as a database access that is performed to retrieve data from or send data to the database. Data flows are represented on a DFD by connecting arrows that show the path of the data through the

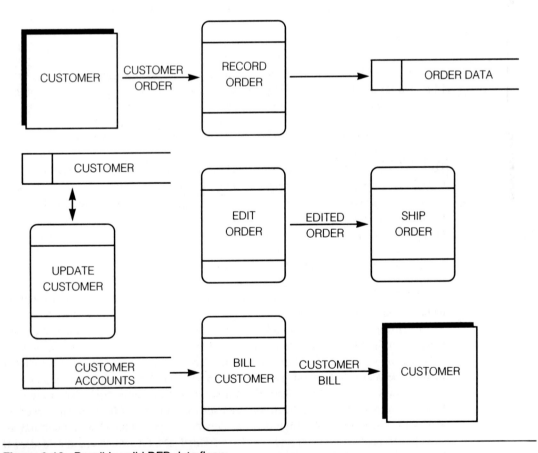

Figure 2-18. Possible valid DFD data flows

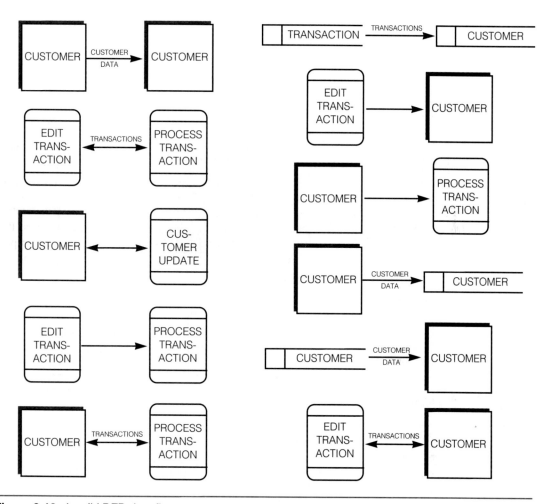

Figure 2-19. Invalid DFD data flows

application. Figure 2-18 shows examples of valid types of data flows that may occur on a DFD. Notice that the arrows can be one-way or two-way and that all possible combinations of flows between objects are represented. Figure 2-19 illustrates invalid data flows that should not be allowed on DFDs. Note that one of the symbols must be a process, that two-way flows are not permitted between processes, and that flows between processes and to, or from, entities must be labeled.

Figures 2-20 through 2-22 illustrate a set of decomposing DFDs to manufacture products and maintain inventory used in those products. These DFDs include progressively greater detail about business processes, as process decomposition occurs from level to level. This set of diagrams is used here to emphasize that a DFD represents a process decomposition modeling method. It is important to recognize that DFDs

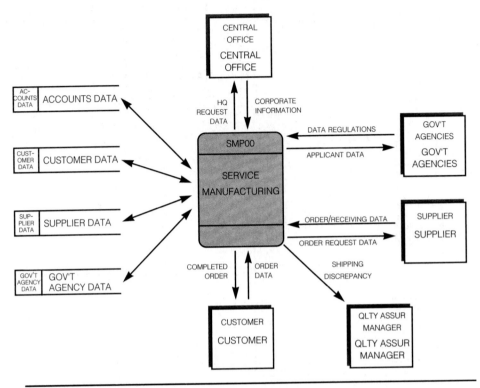

Figure 2-20. Top-level (0) DFD for service manufacturing

decompose a process on one DFD into multiple processes on a lower-level DFD. A process from an upper-level DFD decomposes into whatever degree of detail is necessary to ensure better understanding of business processes by the analyst and better communication between analyst and user. For example, the single process labeled SERVICE MANUFACTURING on the DFD in Figure 2-20 decomposes to the DFD in Figure 2-21. The DFD in Figure 2-21 decomposes the SERVICE MANUFAC-TURING process on the upper-level DFD into five processes. The MANAGE INVENTORY process on the DFD in Figure 2-21 then decomposes into the 11 processes on the DFD in Figure 2-22.

Process Dependency Diagrams

A **process dependency diagram (PDD)** decomposes business processes, but also shows dependencies that exist between processes and other processes, entities, and events. The dependencies are shown by a connecting line with an arrowhead indicating the direction. Perhaps it is best to use an example to illustrate the basic premises of this modeling method. Figure 2-23 illustrates a PDD equivalent to the DFD for managing inventory that was illustrated in Figure 2-22.

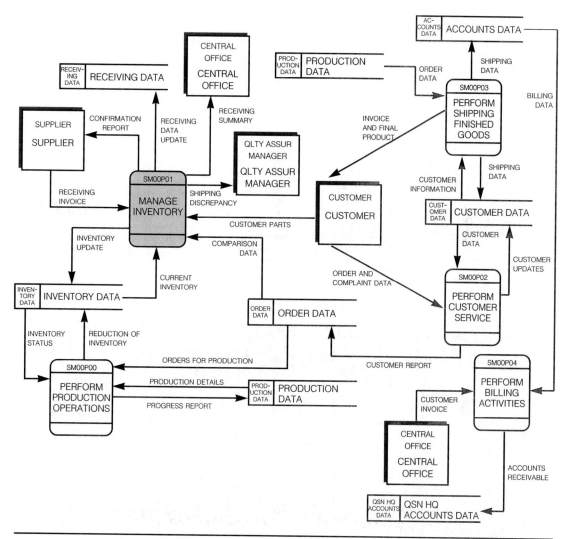

Figure 2-21. Level-1 DFD for manufacturing major processes

Notice that Figure 2-23 illustrates both the ordering of items from suppliers and their receipt. The event LOW ITEM AMOUNT triggers CREATE SUPPLIER ORDER, which leads to SEND SUPPLIER ORDER. SEND SUPPLIER ORDER is dependent on the CREATE SUPPLIER ORDER process. The SUPPLIER entity receives SUPPLIER ORDER from the SEND SUPPLIER ORDER process. The SUPPLIER entity at some time sends the ITEM ORDER to the RECEIVE SUPPLIER ORDER process. RECEIVE SUPPLIER ORDER leads to the CHECK ITEMS RECEIVED process. This process checks the items for defects and either returns them to the supplier or compares them with the original order for correctness.

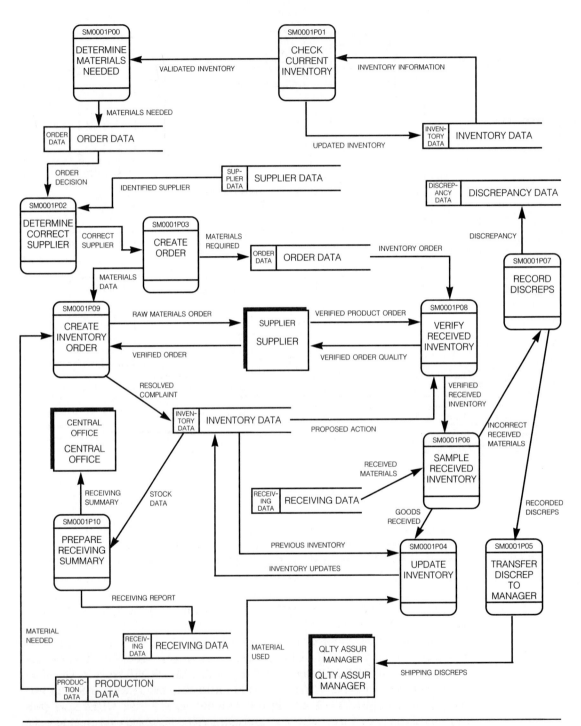

Figure 2-22. Level-2 DFD for managing inventory

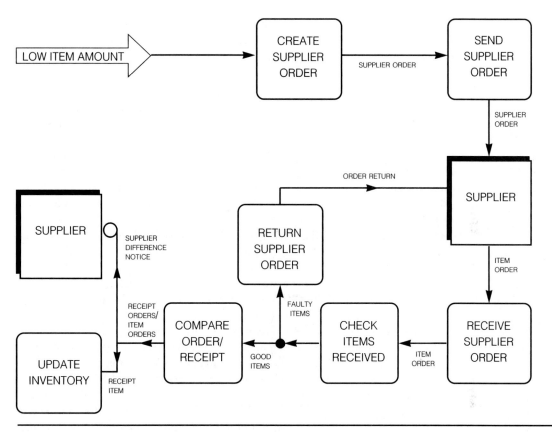

Figure 2-23. Process dependency diagram example

The dot (•) between the RETURN SUPPLIER ORDER and COMPARE ORDER/RECEIPT processes means that only one of these processes will occur—an either/or dependency. Completion of the RETURN SUPPLIER ORDER process leads to the ORDER RETURN being sent to the SUPPLIER entity. Completion of the COMPARE ORDER/RECEIPT process leads to the optional information flow labeled SUPPLIER DIFFERENCE NOTICE and the mandatory UPDATE INVENTORY process.

The flows of data objects between DFD processes can also be considered as dependencies; however, they are not considered as strict dependencies. The text that accompanies DFD processes can be used to explain strict dependencies that occur in the business process model. DFD text entries can also describe events that occur that may trigger the performance of a process. Entities and data flows that appear on DFDs and PDDs are essentially the same. PDDs can also model parallel areas of processes similarly to the way they appear on DFDs. PDD processes can also take place at different time intervals, like those found on DFDs. Considering these factors, you can conclude that PDDs and DFDs are essentially the same types of modeling methods for the same purpose.

Warnier-Orr Modeling Method

The Warnier-Orr modeling method represents a cross between business process modeling and information systems procedure modeling, although its final output more closely resembles a procedure model. The **Warnier-Orr (W/O) diagram**, often called a structure diagram, can represent the logical structure of data in outline form, as well as what must take place to produce data. The initial work on this modeling method was done by Jean-Dominique Warnier of France, in the mid- to late 1970s. Kenneth Orr, an American, expanded and introduced the modeling method in the United States in the early 1980s (see *Structured Systems Development* and *Structured Requirements Definition* by Orr, in the reference list at the end of this chapter).

As strictly a process or data decomposition modeling method, either the data or the process is decomposed in a sideways fashion, from left to right, using braces ({ }) to delineate portions of decomposition. For example, Figures 2-24 and 2-25 illustrate the use of a W/O diagram for decomposing data and processes into their constituent parts, respectively.

The W/O diagram is a modeling method sometimes used for the modular design of systems. Figure 2-26 illustrates the basic format of a W/O diagram, using an hourly wage payroll example. The diagram begins with the result (PAY_CHECK), and then works backward through the activities needed to produce that result, using the inputs required for it and the actions to be performed. Each input required for the result at the left of the first brace is also a result of applying transformation actions to other inputs. For example, GROSS_WAGE may result from applying the transformation

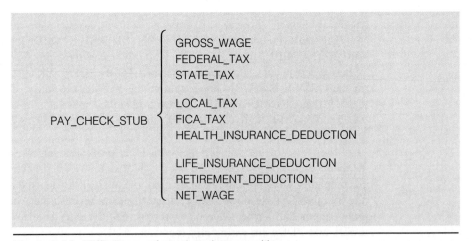

Figure 2-24. W/O diagram for a data decomposition

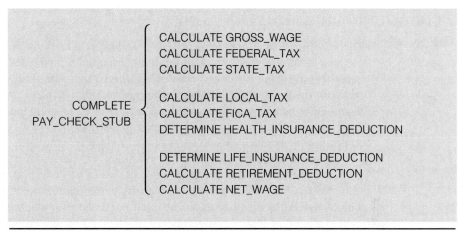

Figure 2-25. W/O diagram for a process decomposition

process to HOURS_WORKED and RATE_OF_PAY in the first set of braces on the right or using a base salary amount. Decomposition continues to the right until inputs required to assemble something else cannot be decomposed further. This will occur when basic inputs, such as transaction origination, have been reached.

The W/O diagram is a top-down approach, which means that general specifications appear to the left of the brace, and the details are progressively constructed by the items in the braces on the right. Detailed descriptions of the component items in the braces, such as the structure of the data acted on within a bracket, are usually provided later. A further understanding of this modeling method may be gained by reading the books written by Kirk Hansen and Ken Orr (see the reference list at the end of this chapter).

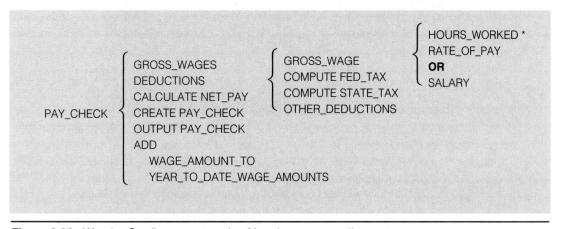

Figure 2-26. Warnier-Orr diagram example of hourly wage payroll

Procedure Modeling Methods

The remaining modeling methods in this section are all strictly procedure modeling methods. These methods can be used to help model the information system procedures that eventually become instructions that make up program logic. Again, the modeling methods described here represent alternative ways to model the same thing—information system procedures. Most businesses require that analysts and programmers use only one type of procedure modeling method so that all procedure models look very much alike in terms of their modeling framework.

Program logic refers to the way programs execute, sometimes called a program's **procedure model**. Program logic consists of procedures that include instructions for the three basic program constructs of sequence, selection, and iteration, which were defined earlier in this chapter. A number of modeling methods can be used to model the logic of programs. Six prominent ones are HIPO diagrams, Nassi-Schneiderman charts, program flow charts, pseudocode (structured English), action diagrams, and structure charts.

HIPO Diagram Modeling Method

HIPO is an acronym for **h**ierarchy plus **i**nput-**p**rocess-**o**utput. **HIPO diagrams** are used to hierarchically show the inputs, processing, and outputs of each processing module. These diagrams are sometimes used as supplements to structure charts. A HIPO diagram usually consists of three separate and interrelated sets of diagrams: a visual table of contents (VTOC) diagram, an overview diagram, and one or more detail diagrams.

HIPO VTOC DIAGRAMS You read the VTOC from left to right and top to bottom; the top-level symbol on the VTOC identifies the system. The second level of the VTOC identifies the major procedures performed by the system. The third and subsequent levels of the VTOC identify subordinate procedures necessary to successfully complete the major procedures—those that eventually identify the times when input and output occur. An example of a VTOC for creating a payroll record resulting from hiring a new employee is shown in Figure 2-27. Notice that each module has been numbered.

HIPO OVERVIEW DIAGRAMS Each level of processing within the VTOC is usually described in greater detail in the HIPO overview diagram. In some cases, an overview diagram can be created for each module in the VTOC. Figure 2-28 shows a HIPO overview diagram for the module labeled EMPLOYEE APPLICATION PROCESSING in Figure 2-27.

One of the benefits of HIPO charts is that any level of detail can be included. After appropriate overview diagrams are created, the analyst can use the VTOC and this single overview diagram as the specifications for the physical design. However, if more detailed design documentation is needed, Figure 2-28 can be expanded into a detail diagram.

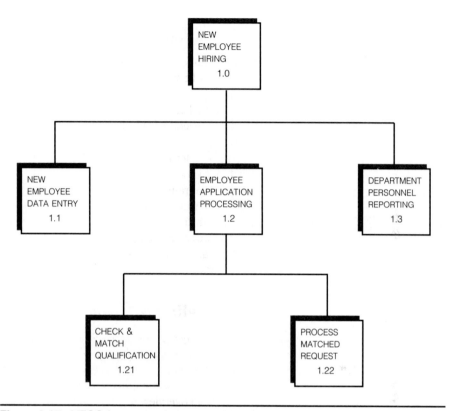

Figure 2-27. VTOC for processing a payroll application

HIPO DETAIL DIAGRAMS   The detail diagram represents the third possible diagram used as part of a HIPO physical design specification. The **detail diagram** contains the specific steps involved in procedures identified in the overview diagram. Figure 2-29 shows a detail diagram for the overview diagram in Figure 2-28. This diagram contains the specific details involved in processing personnel applications. The detail needs for the particular application determine the level of detail that is used by the analyst while using HIPO diagrams. Thus any level of detail required by the analyst is possible with a HIPO diagram.

The three different types of HIPO diagrams help you visualize system procedures from an overview perspective down to a more specific set of procedure specifications for portions of that overview. Some analysts and programmers find this helpful; others maintain that it encourages a choppy view of what may constitute a single program. A more detailed description of the HIPO modeling method can be found in Katzan's book (see the reference list at the end of this chapter).

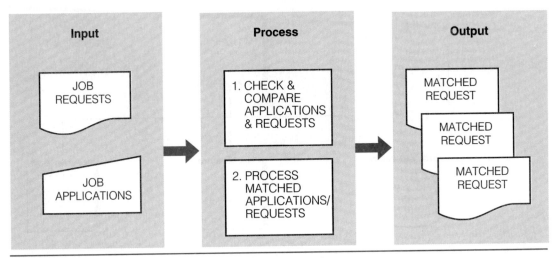

Figure 2-28. HIPO overview diagram for application processing

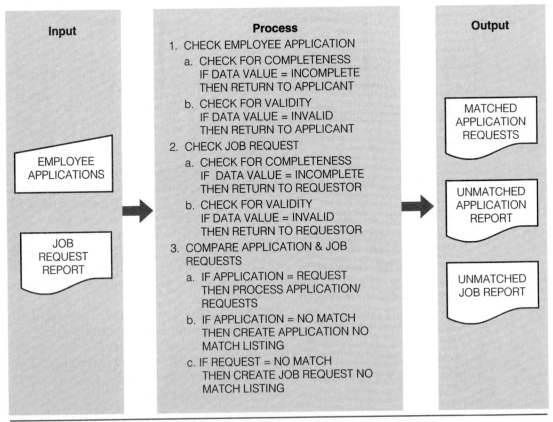

Figure 2-29. HIPO detail diagram for EMPLOYEE APPLICATION PROCESSING

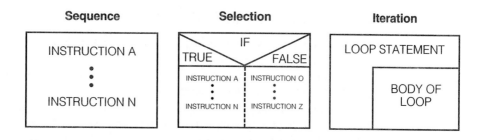

Figure 2-30. Control structures of Nassi-Schneiderman chart

Nassi-Schneiderman Charts

Another procedure modeling method is the **Nassi-Schneiderman chart**, sometimes called a Chapin chart because it can easily be changed to such a chart in spite of their using different symbols. Each type of control structure in Nassi-Schneiderman charts is used to specify the set of procedures required for a particular application using the three basic principles of good programming: sequence, selection, and iteration. The basic forms of the three control structures are shown in Figure 2-30.

The main advantages of the Nassi-Schneiderman chart are that it is relatively easy to draw and that it uses the three control structures of structured programming. Its main disadvantage is that it is difficult to change; changing requirements usually means completely redrawing the chart. An additional disadvantage is the difficulty of rendering the diagram using a standard graphic software system. Nassi-Schneiderman charts have seen only limited use by practicing analysts and programmers. Figure 2-31 shows a Nassi-Schneiderman chart for a repetitive procedure to input a set of records, determine whether each record is valid, and print either a valid record or an error record, depending on whether the input record is valid or not.

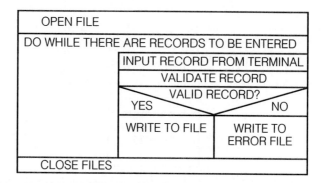

Figure 2-31. Example of Nassi-Schneiderman chart

Program Flow Charts

Program flow charts were more popular in the past than they are today, though practicing analysts and programmers may still use them. Primarily used before the 1980s, **program flow charts** use graphical symbols to specify the logic of programming procedures that express sequence, selection, and iteration. Figures 2-32 and 2-33 show, respectively, the basic symbols of program flow charts and a program flow chart for a simple routine to process college bookstore purchases.

Notice that the program flow chart in Figure 2-33 is constructed in a structured programming format. It inputs the first bookstore purchase, processes it, and inputs the next purchase record. This program framework exemplifies the prime-the-pump and iterative processing of the input data that is typical of a structured programming style recommended for serial data processing. The logic of the flow chart computes a total for non-textbook purchases, computes a total for textbook purchases, identifies the purchaser as faculty or student, computes and deducts a faculty discount, computes a total for the entire sale, calculates the sales tax, prints the sales information for individual purchases, adds sales amounts to accumulate totals for various sales amounts, inputs the next purchase, and returns to COMPUTE NON-TEXTBOOK SALES or prints out a final total sales amount for all daily purchases after processing the last purchase record.

Pseudocode and Structured English Routines

Pseudocode consists of instructions written in broken-English statements that are fundamentally equivalent to their counterparts in a particular computer language. For most businesses, pseudocode routines gradually replaced program flow charts as the program procedure modeling method of choice in the mid- to late 1970s. A pseudocode procedure is equivalent to a program flow chart, but in place of graphical symbols, pseudocode uses short, cryptic English-like statements corresponding to instructions that specify sequence, selection, and iteration.

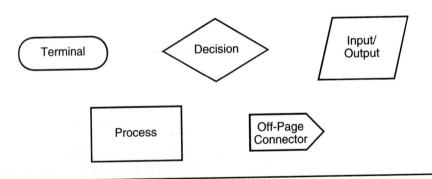

Figure 2-32. Program flow chart symbols

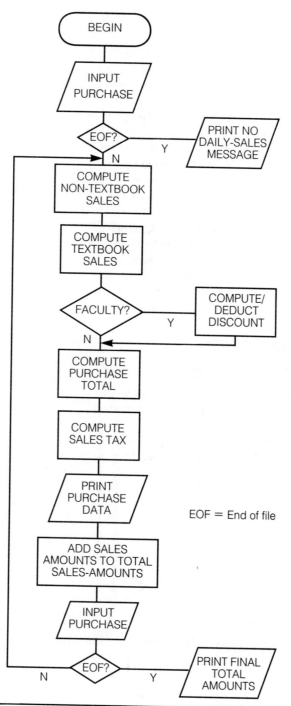

Figure 2-33. Program flow chart example

A procedure modeling method emerged later that was similar in use to pseudocode, but less cryptic in its statements. This modeling method is commonly called structured English. The main difference between pseudocode and structured English is that pseudocode is more closely related to programming structure—it uses statements similar to programming languages, such as DOWHILE, PERFORM, and so on. Figure 2-34 illustrates side-by-side pseudocode and structured English routines equivalent to the Warnier/Orr diagram in Figure 2-26.

The pseudocode routine in Figure 2-34 executes the following sequence of instructions: Data is input; check for premature end of data (selection) and message printing; check for hourly or salary status and calculation of wage or use of input salary; calculate deduction from gross pay; calculate net pay; create the pay check from input and calculated data; print out the pay check data; add wage amounts to total wage amounts; loop back (iteration) to input the next set of data. The sequence of instructions continues to execute until the end of data is reached, at which time total wages are output. Note that the pseudocode statements between the check for premature end of data and END_OF_DATA illustrate the sequence construct of good programming. The structured English statements perform the same actions, but have more English-like statements for them.

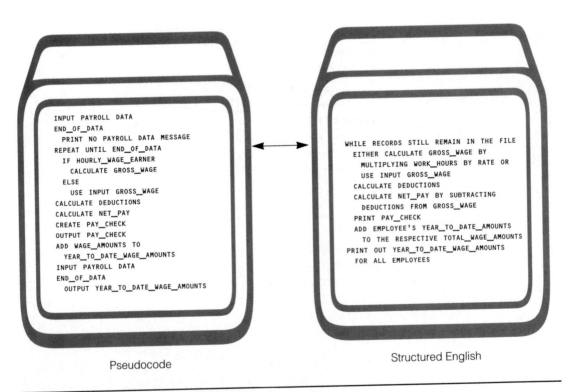

```
INPUT PAYROLL DATA
END_OF_DATA
    PRINT NO PAYROLL DATA MESSAGE
REPEAT UNTIL END_OF_DATA
    IF HOURLY_WAGE_EARNER
        CALCULATE GROSS_WAGE
    ELSE
        USE INPUT GROSS_WAGE
CALCULATE DEDUCTIONS
CALCULATE NET_PAY
CREATE PAY_CHECK
OUTPUT PAY_CHECK
ADD WAGE_AMOUNTS TO
    YEAR_TO_DATE_WAGE_AMOUNTS
INPUT PAYROLL DATA
END_OF_DATA
    OUTPUT YEAR_TO_DATE_WAGE_AMOUNTS
```

Pseudocode

```
WHILE RECORDS STILL REMAIN IN THE FILE
    EITHER CALCULATE GROSS_WAGE BY
        MULTIPLYING WORK_HOURS BY RATE OR
        USE INPUT GROSS_WAGE
    CALCULATE DEDUCTIONS
    CALCULATE NET_PAY BY SUBTRACTING
        DEDUCTIONS FROM GROSS_WAGE
    PRINT PAY_CHECK
    ADD EMPLOYEE'S YEAR_TO_DATE_AMOUNTS
        TO THE RESPECTIVE TOTAL_WAGE_AMOUNTS
PRINT OUT YEAR_TO_DATE_WAGE_AMOUNTS
    FOR ALL EMPLOYEES
```

Structured English

Figure 2-34. Pseudocode and structured English examples

```
INPUT PAYROLL DATA
REPEAT UNTIL END_OF_DATA

    WAGE_EARNER?

        CALCULATE GROSS_WAGE
        ELSE USE INPUT GROSS_WAGE

    CALCULATE DEDUCTIONS
    CALCULATE NET_PAY
    CREATE PAY_CHECK FROM INPUT DATA AND CALCULATED DATA
    OUTPUT PAY_CHECK DATA
    INPUT PAYROLL DATA
    ADD WAGE_AMOUNTS TO YEAR_TO_DATE_WAGE_AMOUNTS

    OUTPUT TOTAL YEAR_TO_DATE_WAGE_AMOUNTS
```

Figure 2-35. Example of an action diagram

The pseudocode and structured English examples in Figure 2-34 were purposely created in the most general form because not much standardization exists regarding what constitutes correct statements for either modeling method. IS departments that use these procedure modeling methods often develop their own standards regarding the format and statements to use. The purpose of describing these methods is to emphasize how to use them to derive a general layout of procedures on which to base program structure and content.

Action Diagrams

An **action diagram** resembles a pseudocode routine, but uses brackets ({ }) to specify the three constructs of good program design: sequence, selection, and iteration. Figure 2-35 illustrates an action diagram equivalent to the pseudocode routine in Figure 2-34. Note that the action diagram in Figure 2-35 treats the instructions INPUT PAYROLL DATA and REPEAT UNTIL END_OF_DATA as a sequence of instructions in the outer bracket. In addition, iterations of the sequence of instructions in the inner bracket will continue until END_OF_DATA occurs, at which time the instruction OUTPUT YEAR_TO_DATE_WAGE_AMOUNTS executes. The Martin and McClure book (1989) in the reference list at the end of this chapter provides the most comprehensive coverage of this topic to date.

Structure Charts

A **structure chart (STC)** is a graphical modeling method that depicts the procedure logic of programs in a basic format consistent with the layout of structured programs. Ideally, **structured programs** have a single control routine that calls on subordinate worker routines that actually perform the data manipulation procedures. Worker routines are typically small and easy to understand and maintain. A STC is drawn in the same format as a structured program, with rectangles to signify processing procedures and symbols to specify input/output data, iteration, and selection conditions. Figure 2-36 shows the basic symbols of a STC; Figure 2-37 shows a STC equivalent for the procedure models in Figures 2-34 and 2-35.

The STC in Figure 2-37 just illustrates the basic layout of the structured program. The procedure at the top, called the boss, represents the single control procedure for the entire STC, which is functionally equivalent to the control routine in a structured program. The boss procedure would actually contain a label name indicative of the overall STC, such as PREPARE PAYROLL CHECK REPORT. This module calls on the worker modules below it from left to right, with the exception of the calls encircled with the loop symbol. These calls will continue until the end-of-file (EOF) occurs and output of the wage total executes. Often the STC does not indicate all of the detailed actions indicated in program models. These details are written in text that accompanies the STC procedure symbol. Thus the STC graphically lays out the program procedures in a structured format and includes the detailed instructions in pseudocode statements that accompany the STC procedure symbols.

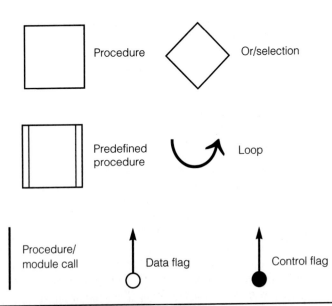

Figure 2-36. Basic symbols for structure charts

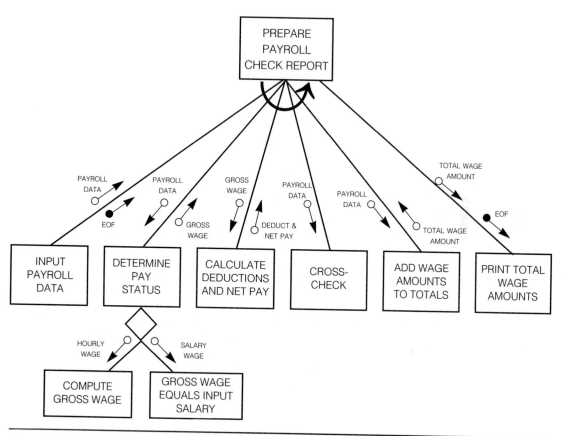

Figure 2-37. Structure chart example

OBJECT-ORIENTED MODELING METHODS

Object-oriented analysis and design (OOA&D) modeling methods are a relatively new way of modeling business objects and activities. **Object-oriented modeling methods** combine data modeling and procedure modeling into one modeling method. One main point of confusion exists between the OOA&D method and traditional data modeling using E/RDs. The terms *entity* and *object* reverse their meanings in the OOA&D method. In object-oriented analysis and design, an entity is considered the real-world person, place, thing, event, or concept, whereas an object represents an abstract representation of the real-world entity. If this fact is kept in mind, the OOA&D method is fairly easy to understand.

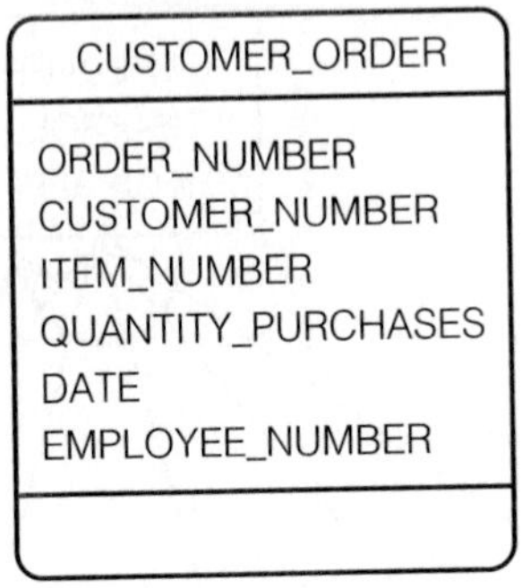

```
┌─────────────────────────────────┐
│        CUSTOMER_ORDER           │
├─────────────────────────────────┤
│   ORDER_NUMBER                  │
│   CUSTOMER_NUMBER               │
│   ITEM_NUMBER                   │
│   QUANTITY_PURCHASES            │
│   DATE                          │
│   EMPLOYEE_NUMBER               │
│                                 │
│                                 │
└─────────────────────────────────┘
```

Figure 2-38. An OOA&D customer order object

The basic principles of OOA&D methods combine the specifications of conceptual/logical data types and information systems procedures into a single modeling method. In this modeling method, the object used to depict the real-world entity type will also list its properties as part of the object; therefore, there is no separate entity type entry to list object properties. Figure 2-38 illustrates an OOA&D object for a CUSTOMER_ORDER real-world data entity. Notice that the CUSTOMER_ORDER object lists the properties of a customer order as part of the object.

The objects in OOA&D also list the procedures to be performed on a particular object. These procedures are known as object services in OOA&D. **Object services** include all the different actions to be performed on the individual data properties, as well as the actions to be performed on collections of these properties.

The OOA&D method has three main advantages:

- Inheritance of properties and services between generalized data types and data types within them
- Combined data modeling and procedure modeling in a single modeling method
- Elimination of redundancy in specifying procedures to perform on data objects

Figure 2-39 illustrates a set of OOA&D objects for customers and clerical personnel who service product ordering for one of many stores owned by a firm.

The OOA&D method uses what are known as *classes* for what normally constitutes a generalized data type. For example, the SALES&MKT object in Figure 2-39 is a generalized object representing all sales and marketing departments, divisions, and personnel. The objects beneath and connected to this object represent data types (or other data classes) within the SALES&MKT data class. These objects inherit the properties of the SALES&MKT data class—that is, these properties also apply to the two department data classes beneath it (MKTG_DEPT and SALES_DEPT), as well as to data types and classes below these two data classes. This means that the vice-president of sales and

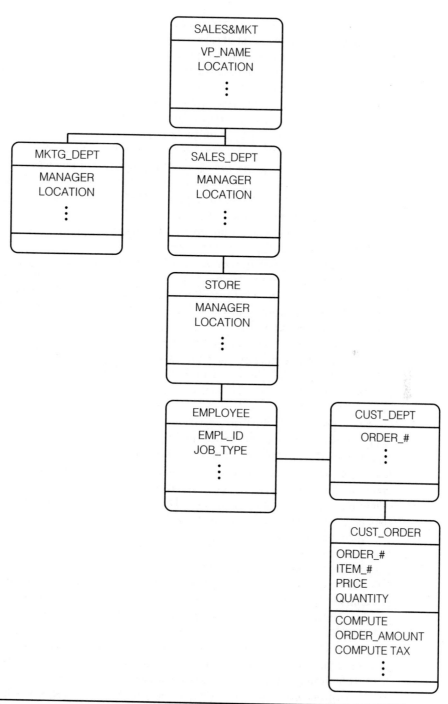

Figure 2-39. Customer/salesclerk OOA&D example

marketing is also the vice-president for the marketing department and sales department. Furthermore, the vice-president of sales and marketing is also the vice-president for the manager of the sales department, for the manager of a store, and for an employee in a store. Since the objects beneath and connected to another object inherit the properties of the class object, redundancy of data entry specifications is virtually eliminated. There is no need to indicate who is the vice-president, the manager of the sales department, or the store manager for a retail salesclerk employee while defining it.

Each data class and data type object in Figure 2-39 should have all its properties listed in one area beneath its class or data type name. Beneath the list of properties for the object are listed the *unique* services for the properties of that object. For the sake of brevity, only the property and service entries for the CUST_ORDER object are shown in Figure 2-39. The PRICE and QUANTITY properties listed in the CUST_ORDER object are used in the COMPUTE ORDER_AMOUNT service to obtain the total amount due for the order. This amount, in turn, is used in the COMPUTE TAX service for that customer order.

Note that not all properties or services for a data class or type object are listed in Figure 2-39. Completion of these is indicated by an ellipsis beneath a property or a service. The intention here is to explain the major premises of the OOA&D method, not to make you an expert in it. The references at the end of this chapter include some of the prominent books on this very important topic.

When class object services are listed beneath their properties, it means that these services are also inherited by class and data type objects beneath them. This means that many procedures (services) that particular classes have will also apply to classes and data types within those class objects. Thus repeating many procedures for a class or data type is also eliminated.

Many programs in the firm's systems need to perform the same actions on a particular class or data type object. In traditionally developed systems, these routines are repeated in all programs that require the procedure to be executed. In OOA&D systems, when an object is referenced, all of its properties, as well as its services, are referenced. Thus the services of a class or data type object need only be described once, where the object is originally defined. The use (or reuse) of a particular service is implied by referring to the object in the system.

Many people who have been involved in the formulation of methodology believe that all methodologies will some day have the OOA&D method as their kernel. It is reasonable to assume that everyone will eventually see the three main advantages of OOA&D and will want to have systems that comply with them. However, recent research by Robert Fichman and Chris Kemerer (1993) found that the investment in existing methods and reinvestment in OOA&D methods create problems in changing to OOA&D.

Many people believe that OOA&D methods will completely replace traditional structured methods in the future. OOA&D methods have one main problem that may keep them from entirely replacing traditional methods: They only combine data modeling and *procedure modeling*. They do not currently provide a way to produce a model for conceptual and logical business functions and processes.

People using the OOA&D method typically do what analysts have done for many years regarding understanding business and information system models: they carry an understanding of these models in their heads. Thus OOA&D systems suffer from the same malady that has afflicted systems for many years—the analysts may understand the system, but they do not fully understand the business, or they have an incorrect understanding of the business. As a result, major portions of the business model are nonexistent and the system does not fully support the business, or is inconsistent with what an accurate and comprehensive business model would show regarding the business and its systems.

PROTOTYPING AS A MODELING METHOD

A working model of portions of a proposed system, called a **prototype**, is often created to show users what those portions will be like. As Chapter 7 will explain, prototyping is most appropriate for systems that include data querying, on-line data updating, and on-line data reporting functions. Prototyping is not normally used to develop full-blown transaction processing systems.

Prototyping can be either an array of techniques that constitute an entire methodology, or just one of a number of modeling methods used in a methodology. When prototyping is used as an entire methodology, most of the modeling methods illustrated in this chapter are not used. Specifically, the analyst and users create, re-create, and execute the prototype until the users are satisfied with the capabilities and data interfaces of the prototype.

In recent years, an approach to system development connected with this style of development, called **rapid application development (RAD)**, has emerged. Its basic process is to get systems personnel and users together in formal meetings, where they rapidly develop systems that provide users with their information needs. A prototype application is created and modified during and between RAD sessions, based on the interaction between systems personnel and users.

In this text, prototyping is considered one of the modeling methods that contribute to a comprehensive methodology. Prototyping is used in this capacity to create appropriate data access interfaces for users and to help identify the capabilities that the user wants in the system, such as the options on a menu used by a system.

Prototyping blends logical and physical design, which allows developers to present a model of the system to users for their evaluation. Prototyping permits more effective evaluation of the design by appropriate users. Since it involves simulation of the operations of the completed system, it permits subjective, hands-on evaluation of the design before the heavy expenses of development are incurred.

The prototype provides information concerning what is provided by the system and how it will work from the user's perspective. Feedback from users regarding prototype execution helps the analyst make changes to better satisfy user interaction requirements. Furthermore, by using the prototype to elicit recommendations, the analyst can clarify specifications during design activities, rather than during the development phase, when corrections to the system design are much more costly. Chapter 7 deals exclusively with this modeling method and provides a detailed discussion of its principles and uses.

COMPUTER-AIDED SOFTWARE ENGINEERING (CASE)

The last few years have produced exciting results in the development of computer tools used to support the analysis and design of business systems. Electronic tools to automate portions of the methodology of A&D are affecting all phases of the system life cycle and will continue to do so. This technology is called **computer-aided software engineering**, or **CASE**.

The Philosophy Behind Using CASE

As Daniel Cougar observed in 1973, "It is simply amazing that the system professional delayed so long in using the computer as an aid in system analysis." He further states, "Within the next year there should be sufficient results in each of these research efforts to evaluate their impact upon the computing community." The research efforts Cougar was referring to were fourth generation A&D methods. Although his prediction of one year for fruition was premature, it remains prophetic about the use of the computer as a tool during the A&D process. Cougar's statements are also the first to herald the basic premise of the philosophy behind CASE: Systems analysts should use the computer as a tool during development or maintenance projects. CASE is not just about a new software system catching the fancy of industry designers; it is about tools supporting the philosophy behind a comprehensive methodology for information system development and maintenance.

The key concept of the philosophy behind CASE is using the computer as a *development tool* at each phase, from planning through the development of computer systems and documentation. Traditionally, corporations have not used the computer as a development tool. It has largely been relegated to performing transaction processing tasks and supplying limited managerial information. With CASE, system user requirements are entered into a CASE software system by corporate planners, systems designers, and systems developers. Strategic planners use a CASE software system to create specifications for business plans. Systems designers use it to create A&D specifications. Finally, systems developers use it to create SA&D specifications from which CASE systems generate the program code.

The use of CASE bridges the wide gap between the immediacy of the need for information that reflects changing corporate plans and the time required for computer system development. In addition, the use of CASE addresses the comprehensive integration of functional planning and computer system development.

Components of CASE

Most articles on CASE suggest that there are two components of CASE: an A&D component, labeled upper CASE, and a development component labeled lower CASE. In reality, there are upper, middle, and lower CASE components. **Upper CASE** includes a computer-aided component for planning purposes; **middle CASE** includes components for A&D; **lower CASE** includes components for actual system development. These designations for CASE components are intended to be analogous to the strategic, tactical, and operational levels of management.

Upper CASE

Corporate management spends a large percentage of time in planning. Corporate plans prescribe goals, generate blueprints for achieving these goals, establish policies to control the operations that move the firm toward these goals, and establish standards for acceptable levels of operational performance. Unfortunately, such elaborate plans frequently become information-bound because so much information is required to maintain policies and stay within the standards for operations.

Every plan depends on the timely transmission of information to ensure its success, but corporate life is often violently dynamic. Conditions facing the corporation continually change, yet the traditional development of computer systems to supply needed information is often a slow and arduous task. A computer system of any size may take more than two years to develop. By the time it is complete, corporate plans have often changed to meet new challenges in the business environment. As a result, newly developed computer systems are often immediately obsolete because the information they supply to corporate management is insufficient or inappropriate.

The upper CASE planning software system is a special-purpose database management system (DBMS) or dictionary system with a built-in ability to show the relationship between the components of a plan and the accouterments required for its completion. More thorough explanations of dictionary systems and a DBMS will be provided in Chapters 5 and 10, respectively. This built-in ability is related to the basic functioning of a DBMS or dictionary system. Corporate managers use the CASE planning tool to create specifications for functional area and IS plans to ensure that strategic information will be supplied as the functional area plans are carried out.

During brainstorming sessions, the attributes of corporate plans may be assigned names and stored in a planning database. These planning specifications represent the resources (including information) and task completions needed to complete the plan.

These planning attributes are entered into the structure of the upper CASE system. For different plans, the structural relationship of the components and their requirements remains the same. Only planning attribute values change for different corporate plans. What this means is that the way analysts or managers describe and decompose important aspects of corporate strategy remains the same; the specific values they specify for these strategic aspects change over time.

One of the earliest upper CASE systems, called PC Prism, was originated by a company named Delta-Com and purchased by Index Technology, an early leader in CASE products. Other upper CASE products are part of a suite of CASE products offered by a single CASE vendor, such as the planning workstations of Arthur Andersen, Texas Instruments, and KnowledgeWare.

Middle CASE

Middle CASE involves using a software component to create a set of A&D specifications. CASE A&D software has a special-purpose dictionary very much like the data dictionary used in combination with the firm's DBMS. A dictionary software system allows the entry of specifications concerning something being developed or already developed. A system designer can use middle CASE to enter specifications for the design of a computer system that conforms to corporate IS planning specifications. Once the IS planning specifications are mapped into the CASE system, designers can enhance them to provide a more comprehensive set of A&D specifications for particular computer systems.

Just as structured programming changed the programming function in the 1970s, the use of analyst workbenches changed the way the methodology of A&D is used in the 1980s and 1990s. Enhancing a design with middle CASE involves using a software system known as an analyst workbench, a tool developed in the early 1980s. These systems are frequently called front-end CASE systems; however, front-end CASE can also include upper CASE systems. **Analyst workbench software** provides an on-line way to perform the following tasks:

- Identify user requirements via on-line data modeling
- Diagram the logical processing and flow of data using on-line data and process modeling methods
- Document program procedures using on-line physical design modeling methods
- Document diagram components via design dictionary entries

One of the earliest middle CASE systems, called Excelerator, was originated by Index Technology, which merged with Sage to become InterSolve. Like upper CASE products, other middle CASE products are part of a suite of CASE products offered by a single CASE vendor, such as analysis and design workstations provided by Arthur Andersen, Texas Instruments, and KnowledgeWare.

Lower CASE

Lower CASE involves using development software to create a set of system development specifications. Like the other CASE systems, the development software system is also a dictionary system. Mapping of A&D specifications into the CASE development software system amounts to interfacing the CASE A&D dictionary with the CASE development dictionary. A system developer enhances the physical design and development specifications for a particular computer system and their accompanying documentation. The CASE development system then uses these specifications to generate the system's programs and documentation. Lower CASE systems are commonly called back-end CASE.

One of the earliest lower CASE systems, called Telon, was originated by PAN-SOPHIC, which later merged with Computer Associates. Other lower CASE products are often a part of a suite of CASE products offered by a single CASE vendor, such as development features in design and construction workstations provided by Arthur Andersen, Texas Instruments, and KnowledgeWare.

Integrated CASE Systems

Some CASE vendors provide a suite of CASE systems for planning, analysis and design, and construction of systems. These CASE products usually share specifications among the various workstations, although the output of one CASE product can sometimes be converted to a format that can be input to a subsequent CASE product. The latter type of CASE integration is often called conversion CASE, and is the less desirable form of integrating CASE specifications because of the potential for the loss of data during conversion.

The more desirable form of integrated CASE (ICASE) requires the use of either a single dictionary system or a special-purpose dictionary-type system known as a repository to store the specifications from the three different types of CASE systems. In either form, the specifications become truly integrated, because they are stored in the same unit by the dictionary system and made available to each of the different CASE systems.

A dictionary system stores only specifications that describe conceptually, logically, or physically modeled phenomena. A dictionary does not typically contain intelligence; it simply documents or describes something. A **repository** is much more than a dictionary; it contains all of the same types of information as a dictionary, as well as rules that permit cross-checking, correlation analysis, and validation. It is endowed with a certain amount of intelligence that allows it to understand the design and enforce consistency across the business and information system models. The repository not only stores information; it aids in controlling accuracy, completeness, integrity, and validity of plans, models, and designs. Figure 2-40 illustrates the concept of ICASE from the standpoint of using a repository.

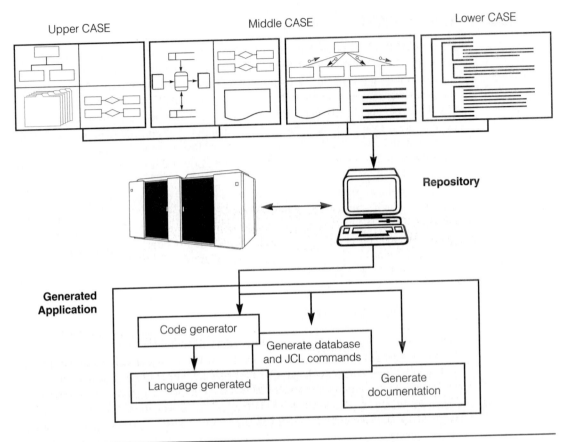

Figure 2-40. ICASE using a repository for integration (adapted from J. Martin, 1988)

The Benefits of Using CASE

CASE software manufacturers propose that using their products substantially reduces the time required for normal project life cycles. This is certainly important, but the major benefits gained by employing these systems are:

- Documentation of the information that is in the minds of business personnel
- Computer support for corporate planning
- Integration of corporate planning with IS planning
- Integration of IS planning and A&D
- Standardization of the methodology of A&D
- Facilitation of prototype design

- On-line creation and maintenance of A&D specifications
- Increased control during A&D projects through project management support
- Integration of A&D specifications with systems development
- Computer code generation
- On-line storage of the basis for thoroughly testing newly developed or modified systems
- Increased productivity
- Increased quality of the results of system design and development
- Reusability of planning, A&D, and development specifications

CASE systems avoid the pain associated with manual development of structured diagrams. Frequently the analyst must redraw a diagram when there is one small change. Cyclical A&D activities prescribe the modification of specifications, and CASE systems allow easy modification of the corresponding diagrams as the need arises. Software systems already exist that analysts use to electronically produce E/RDs, DFDs, and other diagrams on desktop computers.

These tools permit the entering of A&D specifications in several formats using modeling methods. For example, analyst workbench systems commonly allow the use of either DeMarco or Gane and Sarson versions for creating DFDs. They also often make several modeling methods available that share common entries, such as data structure entries.

Because the types of symbols used within an IS department should be standardized, it is often wise to set a policy of adopting a single methodology for system development and maintenance projects. For example, a particular set of DFD symbols should be the standard for all DFDs created within a particular installation. If everyone is using the Gane and Sarson DFD version of the symbols, no one can become confused because someone entered a DFD in the DeMarco format. Since many CASE systems can limit the types of models available after they are installed, only the modeling methods recommended as the methodological standards for the firm may be available to the analyst. This prevents a firm with fifty analysts from having fifty different methodologies for designing systems.

The Importance of Using CASE

The importance of using CASE systems cannot be overemphasized. By using CASE systems to describe entities in the organization, user responsibilities and information needs, business processes within the organization, data structures that support relationships between entities and processing, and procedures to implement processes, documentation that, in the past, existed only in the minds of company personnel is stored on computers. When documentation is stored on-line, companies ensure that expertise gained from employees' experiences does not leave the company along with departing employees. The company protects its investment by storing information about the employees' experiences as part of the documentation created and maintained while using CASE systems. Since new employees (novice or experienced) can navigate through CASE-produced A&D documentation, they can obtain an understanding of the organization that only years of experience in the organization would otherwise provide. Thus personnel can come and go without causing major disturbances in the activities of the organization.

Most CASE tools that currently exist use the structured modeling methods outlined in this chapter, although some OOA&D CASE systems have recently emerged for both middle and lower CASE. Future CASE systems will most likely combine these methods, or use newly emerging modeling methods to replace some of the methods described here. In any event, the era of CASE does provide an advantage over previous eras, when all or most specifications regarding the business and its information systems were carried in the minds of the firm's analysts and programmers.

You should understand that these tools do not, by themselves, ensure that the quality and comprehensiveness of A&D specifications will increase. The tools simply provide electronic assistance for much of the clerical work involved. CASE systems do not automate analysis and design; they automate a portion of the methodology used by the organization to develop systems. These systems can enhance the existing good work of a skilled analyst, but they only permit a bad analyst to do poor work, faster and more comprehensively. The use of CASE is discussed throughout this text; many chapters have a section at the end relating CASE to the topics discussed in the chapter.

THE TEXT METHODOLOGY

This text adapts the structured A&D approach to establish an integrated, comprehensive methodology that includes both a data-oriented and a process-oriented inclination. Yet, rather than only one modeling method, a variety of modeling methods are used. The modeling method used in any instance depends on its suitability in a particular phase of the life cycle and its use in modeling either business objects or activities, or both. In general, this text uses the following modeling methods to integrate and broaden design specifications:

E/RDs — DFDs — Prototyping — Structure charts

Table 2-1 indicates how each modeling method is used in the text methodology.

Using these modeling methods in the text methodology allows for the efficient, effective, and comprehensive design of information systems. Figure 2-41 illustrates the way these modeling methods are related in the methodology of this text.

Understanding the implications of Figure 2-41 provides great insight into how methodology will be used in this text. The E/RD graphic in the upper-left corner of Figure 2-41 shows that E/RDs are used to identify the objects of interest to the business—objects described in entity type descriptions that specify the properties of the

Table 2-1	Uses of modeling methods in the text methodology	
Modeling Method	**Use**	
E/RDs	To identify and describe business objects and *identify* user requirements	
DFDs	To identify and describe business processes and where data objects flow between processes	
Prototyping	To simulate the actions (capabilities) of the system, the format of the user interface, and the interaction with the user	
Structure charts	To create a procedure model required to physically accom-plish the processing necessary for the desired flows of data As an *outline* to derive specifications for structured programs to physically implement processing procedures	

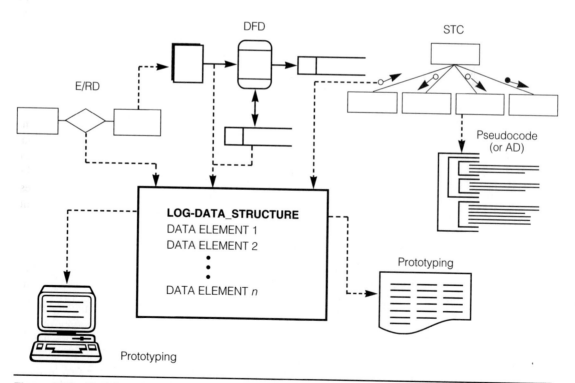

Figure 2-41. Modeling methods of the text methodology

object types. The logical data structure in the center of Figure 2-41 represents the entity type description specification used to indicate the properties (data elements) of those objects.

The DFD graphic in the upper middle of Figure 2-41 depicts a DFD created to portray business processes in the project area. The logical objects identified by using the E/RDs and described in the entity type description are depicted as data flows and stores on the DFD—the logical objects on which the DFD processes act.

The STC graphic in the upper-right corner of Figure 2-41 represents a structure chart created by converting the DFD into its procedure model equivalent. The data flag passed among the procedures of the STC represents the same logical object depicted as either a DFD data flow or store, and originally identified and described while creating E/RDs.

The Pseudocode graphic in the middle of the right side of Figure 2-41 illustrates the pseudocode statements that accompany the STC procedures. These pseudocode statements provide the detailed instructions that make the STC a more complete program procedure model. They are functionally equivalent to some of the statements in a portion of an action diagram that could be created in place of a STC, as depicted by the AD graphic on the right side of Figure 2-41.

The Prototyping graphics in the bottom-left and -right corners of Figure 2-41 represent screens and business forms created while prototyping. These screens and forms are used to display the logical objects that satisfy certain user information requirements. Note that these interfaces may be used to display the same logical objects identified in E/RDs, used as DFD data flows and stores, and passed among the STC logical procedures.

Figure 2-41 depicts a methodology known as **information engineering (IE)**, which is an approach as well as a methodology. As its name implies, it is an engineering-style approach to business and information systems modeling and system development. It is also a set of rigorous methods used individually and collectively to create and maintain business models and information systems.

In the brand of IE used in this text, E/RDs, DFDs, STCs, and prototyping are the primary methods for data modeling, process modeling, procedure modeling, and information system modeling, respectively. Although these methods are currently the most prominent methods, our intention is not to establish or further an existing "religion" regarding the continuing use of these methods. This methodology could just as easily use other modeling methods, such as OOA&D methods, to replace the E/RDs, DFDs, STCs, and prototyping, and still be a version of IE. The point is to have a methodology that helps model the objects, activities, and associations that make up the business and its information systems. Which particular modeling methods are used for this purpose are relatively unimportant. Figure 2-42 shows which modeling methods are used in the text methodology for different levels of abstraction for business objects, business functions, business processes, information systems procedures, and associations between objects and activities.

For the "Objects" portion of the pyramid in Figure 2-42, the top two levels of abstraction (conceptual and logical) indicate how E/RDs and entity type descriptions are used to:

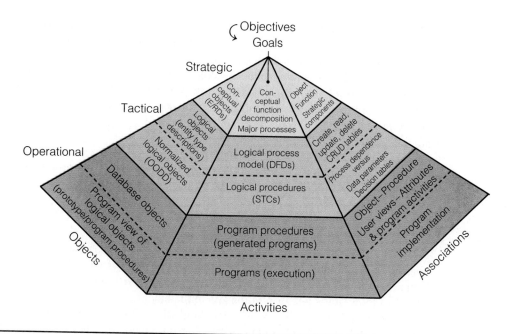

Figure 2-42. Business model and modeling methods

- Identify all of the objects of importance to the business about which it retains data
- Specify the relationships between those objects
- Describe the entities on the E/RDs by specifying the properties of the objects of importance to the business

Chapters 5 and 8 will explain how E/RDs and entity type descriptions can be used to meet these three goals.

The next two levels of abstraction for objects specify the activities needed to create more usable data structures, which are required for database design. These activities are explained in Chapter 10. The bottom of the "Objects" portion of the pyramid illustrates the way portions of programs reconstruct the logical objects of the business from the database objects and make that logical object available for users to see. Chapters 7, 10, and 11 explain how the logical objects are reconstructed and displayed to the user.

The middle portion of the pyramid, "Activities," illustrates the different levels of abstraction for businesses' activities and various modeling methods in the methodology used to model them. The top activity level indicates how functional decomposition is used to model business functions. The second abstraction level indicates how DFDs are used to model the business processes that support the business functions. Chapters 6 and 8 explain function and process modeling using functional decomposition and

DFDs. The third abstraction level indicates how STCs are used to model the information systems procedures that implement the business processes. Chapter 9 explains how STCs are used to model the logical procedures. The fourth abstraction level indicates how the STC procedure models become the code of the system's programs. The very bottom level of abstraction indicates how program execution acts on data objects to provide information users need to perform their jobs. Chapter 11 explains how the logical procedures of STCs become part of the system's program code for execution purposes.

The "Associations" side of the pyramid in Figure 2-42 indicates the different levels of abstraction for the associations between data objects and activities that help to understand them better. No specific chapters in this text are dedicated to association modeling. Explanations of the different abstractions of associations are included as part of the descriptions and illustrations in Chapters 5 through 11.

More detailed descriptions of this methodology and of the methods used are given in subsequent chapters, where you will learn to create the models depicting the objects, activities, and associations of a business and its systems. Chapters 5 and 6 explain using E/RDs and DFDs during systems analysis, respectively. Chapter 7 describes prototyping and its relationship to the other modeling methods. Chapter 8 describes and illustrates the use of E/RDs and DFDs during logical system design. Chapters 9 and 11 cover physical design, procedure modeling, and system development; they also explain the two uses of structure charts. Chapter 10 explains databases and how to create them.

DFDs appear in the analysis and logical design, whereas the physical design and development uses STCs to convert logical design specifications from the DFD to a format consistent with the way programmers write programs. Prototyping activities depicted in Figure 2-41 actually involve creating the specifications for a computer program or a set of related programs that form the system. Besides the primary approach to the structured methodology, the text discusses alternate modeling methods, to provide a well-rounded understanding of how components of methodology are used during A&D projects.

REVIEW

By thoroughly analyzing and identifying the objects, activities, and associations in a business, analysts develop models of the business that help them design an effective information system. Many methodologies exist that specify how to model the business, as well as the steps in the system development life cycle and the steps that focus on logical and physical design actions. Methodology is a complex structure of rules and capabilities involving business objects, activities (functions, processes, and information systems procedures), the life cycle, logical and physical design, modeling methods, and tools that provides the framework for systems development.

It is best to use a standard methodology and a standard set of modeling methods in the design of information systems. There are two major approaches in these methods: data-oriented and process-oriented. Most analysts use a combination of these, from the various methods available:

- Entity/relationship diagrams
- System flow charts
- Data flow diagrams
- Process dependency diagrams
- Warnier-Orr diagrams
- HIPO diagrams
- Pseudocode routines
- Action diagrams
- Structure charts

Object-oriented analysis and design modeling methods are a relatively new way of modeling businesses, and they have some advantages over traditional methods. Many people believe they will completely replace traditional methods in the future. Prototyping is an important modeling method in the methodology of this text. It is used to present a model of the system to users for their evaluation. The text methodology uses E/RDs, DFDs, prototyping, and structure charts with accompanying pseudocode to integrate and broaden design specifications.

Computer-aided software engineering, or CASE, tools make it easier to create structured diagrams, and they allow analysts to enter A&D specifications in several formats using modeling methods. CASE is affecting all phases of the system life cycle. It is no longer relegated to minor tasks, but is being used as a development tool in planning and on through development of systems and documentation.

QUESTIONS

1. Explain the relationship between understanding the firm and its business and developing information systems.
2. What is the purpose of a systems analysis and design methodology and what are its elements?
3. Search IS literature to identify three prominent methodologies not listed in this chapter; describe their basic premises.
4. Define *business object* and explain the various types of business objects that need to be identified and described.
5. Select a company in your vicinity and identify one of each of the five different types of business objects for that company.
6. Define *business activities* and explain what they include.

7. Define and distinguish among *functions*, *processes*, and *procedures*.

8. For the company you selected in question 5, identify one of its functions, processes, and information systems procedures.

9. Define *association* and explain the various associations used in business modeling. Also, explain the various association methods used in business modeling.

10. For the company you selected in questions 5 and 8, identify associations that occur between two business objects, two functions, two processes, two procedures, business objects and functions, business objects and processes, and business objects and information systems procedures.

11. For the company you selected in questions 5, 8, and 10, create a CRUD table similar in format to the one in Figure 2-3.

12. Explain what constitutes the business and systems models by explaining the different abstraction levels of the models and how the components of the models are related.

13. Define user requirements by explaining what they are, how they are obtained, their purpose, and the two main methods for recording them.

14. For the company selected in questions 5, 8, 10, and 11, list some of its user requirements regarding data and actions to be performed on that data.

15. Define and explain *structured methodology*.

16. List and define the terms important to understanding a methodology.

17. Identify companies in your vicinity that use an information engineering methodology.

18. Search the IS literature to identify companies that use the three methodologies you identified in question 3.

19. Define methodology in a way that indicates all of its aspects.

20. Distinguish between data-oriented and process-oriented modeling methods. Explain why a methodology should contain both orientations.

21. List and explain the modeling methods available to the analyst for analysis and design.

22. Describe the purpose of a system flow chart and what it normally shows.

23. Obtain a system flow chart from a company in your vicinity and explain what system it describes in terms that indicate how it serves the business.

24. Define *data model*. Explain the three major aspects of modeling business objects that it comprises.

25. Define and distinguish between the semantic data modeling method and the E/RD data modeling method.

26. For a company in your vicinity, obtain a copy of an E/RD.

27. What are the three important actions that an analyst seeks to complete while

creating E/RDs to create a data model? To which levels of abstraction do these actions contribute?

28. Define *entity type description* and explain what abstraction level it is on relative to modeling business objects.

29. For the company in question 26, show an entity type description for one of the entities on the E/RD.

30. Define *entity* and give real-world examples for objects that entities represent.

31. For the company selected in questions 26 and 29, identify some of the business objects represented as entities.

32. Define *relationships* and identify relationships that might exist in the real world.

33. For the company selected in questions 26, 29, and 31, identify at least one of each of the three different relationship cardinalities. For those relationships, identify the business objects, as well as the cardinality of the relationships between them.

34. Explain the purpose of function decomposition and what it contributes to business modeling.

35. For a company in your vicinity, obtain a function decomposition diagram.

36. What do data flow diagrams represent? Describe the symbols used in creating a DFD.

37. For a company in your vicinity, obtain a top-level DFD.

38. Define and distinguish between the following DFD components:
    a. Entity
    b. Process
    c. Data store
    d. Data flow

39. For the DFD obtained for question 37, use the label to identify one of each of the following: entity, process, data flow, and data store (data store may be omitted if one does not appear on the DFD).

40. Explain the purpose of decomposition paths of DFDs as they relate to processes on the DFDs.

41. For the company selected in question 37, obtain two DFDs along one decomposition path from the top-level DFD (not including the top-level DFD).

42. Explain what the process dependency modeling method models. Distinguish between the DFD and process dependency modeling methods by identifying similarities and differences.

43. Search the IS literature to obtain a copy of a process dependency diagram. Explain the purpose of this diagram and how it accomplishes this purpose.

44. What is the purpose of a Warnier-Orr diagram? Why can using such diagrams be considered a top-down approach?

45. Search the IS literature to obtain a copy of a W/O diagram. Explain the purpose of this W/O diagram and how it accomplishes this purpose.

46. Distinguish between the use of W/O diagrams during the logical and physical design portions of the detailed design phase.

47. Identify and distinguish among the three types of HIPO diagrams.

48. Search the IS literature to obtain a copy of a HIPO diagram. Explain the purpose of HIPO diagrams and how they accomplish this purpose.

49. Identify and distinguish between the different control structures used within Nassi-Schneiderman charts.

50. Search the IS literature to obtain a copy of a Nassi-Schneiderman chart. Explain the purpose of this diagram and how it accomplishes this purpose.

51. Distinguish among program flow charts, pseudocode routines, and action diagrams.

52. Search the IS literature to obtain a copy of a program flow chart. Explain the purpose of this diagram and how it accomplishes this purpose.

53. Search the IS literature to obtain a copy of a pseudocode routine. Explain the purpose of this routine and how it accomplishes this purpose.

54. Search the IS literature to obtain a copy of an action diagram. Explain the purpose of this diagram and how it accomplishes this purpose.

55. Distinguish among the three basic constructs of program logic contained in a procedure model.

56. For the diagram obtained for question 52, indicate where the three basic constructs of program logic are illustrated.

57. For the diagram obtained for question 53, indicate where the three basic constructs of program logic are illustrated.

58. For the diagram obtained for question 54, indicate where the three basic constructs of program logic are illustrated.

59. Define and explain *structured programming*.

60. Define and explain *prototyping*. Explain of what it consists.

61. What are the main places in the SDLC where prototyping is employed?

62. For a company in your vicinity, obtain a copy of prototype user interfaces of the following types:

    a. A menu

    b. Screen data entry form

    c. Screen data display form

    d. Data entry paper business form

    e. Data display business form or report

63. What are the types of applications for which prototyping is appropriate?

64. Explain the methodology of this book in textual and graphical ways.

65. Explain in textual and graphical ways how the components of the text methodology are related to modeling the objects, activities, and associations of the business.

66. Explain what *standards* refers to in an A&D project.

67. Define *structured methodology* and *structured analysis and design* and the advantage of using this approach.

68. Define *computer-aided software engineering* and distinguish between its components (their purpose, what are they used for, what is created by using them, how output is integrated).

69. Search the IS literature to identify middle and lower CASE tools.

70. Explain what ICASE means and how the integration is accomplished.

71. Search the IS literature to identify at least two ICASE systems.

EXERCISES

Chapter 2 of *Systems Analysis and Design: A Comprehensive Methodology with CASE Student Workbook* contains blank documentation forms to use in the exercises for this chapter.

1. Create a DFD for an explosion on the PERFORM PRODUCTION OPERATIONS process on the DFD in Figure 2-21. (*Hint:* A visit to a local manufacturing company would help you to identify the processes and other symbols needed to complete this diagram.)

2. Create a process dependency diagram equivalent to the DFD completed for exercise 1.

3. Create a system flow chart for an employment application in which employees use time cards to clock in their daily work time, new employees can start work at any time during a month, and each employee gets a check when the time card and employee master update programs execute. (*Hint:* The system should have two major process symbols for system programs.)

4. Create a program flow chart equivalent to the pseudocode example that appears in Figure 2-34.

5. Create a Nassi-Schneiderman chart equivalent to the program flow chart that appears in Figure 2-33.

6. Create a complete set of HIPO diagrams equivalent to the program flow chart that appears in Figure 2-33.

7. Create a W/O diagram equivalent to the program flow chart that appears in Figure 2-33.

8. Create a STC diagram equivalent to the program flow chart that appears in Figure 2-33.

SELECTED REFERENCES BY TOPIC

Structured Modeling Methods

Boar, B. H. 1985. *Application Prototyping*. New York: John Wiley and Sons, Inc.

Chen, P. 1976. "The Entity-Relationship Model—Toward a Unified View of Data." *ACM Transactions on Database Systems* 1:9–36.

Constantine, L. L. and E. Yourdon. 1975. *Structured Design: Fundamentals of a Discipline of Computer Program and Systems Design*. Englewood Cliffs, NJ: Prentice-Hall.

DeMarco, T. 1978. *Structured Analysis and System Specification*. Englewood Cliffs, NJ: Prentice-Hall.

Dolan, K. A. 1984. *Business Computer Systems Design*. Santa Cruz, CA: Mitchell Publishing Inc.

Gane, C. and T. Sarson. 1977. *Structured Systems Analysis: Tools and Techniques*. New York: Improved Systems Technologies.

Hansen, K. 1984. *Data Structured Program Design*. Topeka, KS: Ken Orr and Associates, Inc.

Katzan, H. 1976. *Systems Design and Documentation: An Introduction to the HIPO Method*. New York: Van Nostrand Reinhold.

Martin, J. and C. McClure. 1989. *Action Diagrams: Clearly Structured Program Design*. Englewood Cliffs, NJ: Prentice-Hall.

Orr, K. T. 1977. *Structured Systems Development*. Englewood Cliffs, NJ: Yourdon Press.

——. 1981. *Structured Requirements Definition*. Topeka, KS: Ken Orr and Associates, Inc.

Tsichritzis, D. C. and F. H. Lochovsky. 1982. *Data Models*. Englewood Cliffs, NJ: Prentice-Hall.

Vetter, M. 1987. *Strategy for Data Modelling*. Chichester, NY: John Wiley and Sons.

Warnier, J. D. 1981. *Logical Construction of Systems*. New York: Van Nostrand Reinhold.

——. 1976. *The Logical Construction of Programs*. New York: Van Nostrand Reinhold.

Yourdon, E. and L. Constantine. 1989. *Structured Design*, 2nd ed., Englewood Cliffs, NJ: Yourdon Press.

Yourdon, E. 1979. *Classics in Software Engineering*. Englewood Cliffs, NJ: Prentice-Hall.

——. 1976, *Techniques of Program Structure and Design*. Englewood Cliffs, NJ: Prentice-Hall.

——. 1989. *Modern Structured Methods*. Englewood Cliffs, NJ: Prentice-Hall.

Yourdon Inc. 1993. *Yourdon Systems Method: Model-Driven Systems Development*. Englewood Cliffs, NJ: Yourdon Press.

Object-Oriented Modeling Methods

Booch, G. 1991. *Object-Oriented Design with Applications.* Redwood City, CA: Benjamin/Cummings.

Coad, P. and E. Yourdon. 1991. *Object-Oriented Analysis*, 2nd ed. Englewood Cliffs, NJ: Prentice-Hall.

———. 1991. *Object-Oriented Design.* Englewood Cliffs, NJ: Prentice-Hall.

Fichman, R. G. and C. F. Kemerer. 1993. "Adoption of Software Engineering Process Innovations: The Case of Object Orientation." *Sloan Management Review* 34, no. 2.

Martin, J. and J. J. Odell. 1992. *Object-Oriented Analysis and Design.* Englewood Cliffs, NJ: Prentice-Hall.

Methodology and Information Engineering

Andersen, Arthur & Co. 1989. *Foundations of Business Systems.* Orlando, FL: The Dryden Press, Holt, Rinehart and Winston.

Finkelstein, C. 1989. *An Introduction to Information Engineering.* Reading, MA: Addison-Wesley.

Inmon, W. H. 1988. *Information Engineering for the Practitioner.* Englewood Cliffs, NJ: Prentice-Hall.

———. 1989, *Advanced Topics in Information Engineering.* Wellesley, MA: QED Information Sciences, Inc.

Martin, J. 1988. *Information Engineering: Book I, Introduction.* Englewood Cliffs, NJ: Prentice-Hall.

Orr, K., C. Gane, E. Yourdon, P. Chen, and L. Constantine. 1989. "Methodology: The Experts Speak." *BYTE* 14, no. 4.

Computer-Aided Software Engineering

Couger, J. D. 1973. "Evolution of Business System Analysis Techniques." *ACM Computing Surveys* 5, no. 3 (September).

Gane, C. 1990. *Computer-Aided Software Engineering.* Englewood Cliffs, NJ: Prentice-Hall.

Gibson, M. 1989. "The CASE Philosophy." *BYTE* 14, no. 4.

McClure, C. 1988. *CASE Is Software Automation.* Englewood Cliffs, NJ: Prentice-Hall.

McGauhey, R. and M. Gibson. March 1993. "The Encyclopedia/Repository: Essential to Information Engineering and Fully Integrated CASE." *Journal of Systems Management* 44, no. 3.

CHAPTER 3

The System Development Life Cycle

OVERVIEW

Proper development and installation of a system requires an understanding of the system development life cycle (SDLC) and the methodologies to use during life cycle steps. Taking you through the next step toward understanding the A&D process, this chapter:

- Describes the activities involved in each phase of the system development life cycle, from problem definition, design, development, and testing to implementation, review, modification, and maintenance
- Describes system development and user documentation
- Describes the logical and physical design portions of the SDLC
- Introduces project management
- Distinguishes between reactive and proactive projects
- Discusses the National Golf & Tennis case, which is used as an example throughout this book

KEY TERMS

Design dictionary

Documentation

Economic feasibility

Feasibility study

Immediate changeover

Life cycle

Logical design

Logical errors

Operational feasibility

Parallel execution

Path testing

Phased changeover

Physical design

Pilot execution

Proactive project

Problem definition

Project management

Project master schedule

Reactive project

Structured analysis and design

Syntactical errors

System analysis and design
documentation

System development life cycle
(SDLC)

System maintenance

System testing

User documentation

A system project goes through a recognized set of phases, beginning with a request and continuing through the creation or modification of a system. This is known as the **system development life cycle (SDLC)**: a series of steps completed over a period of time by analysts in the course of a system development or maintenance project. The main steps of the SDLC include analyzing how the current system meets users' information needs, providing a design for a new system or a modification of an existing system to meet these needs, developing a system based on the design, and implementing the system. This chapter briefly discusses each step of the SDLC to provide an overall view of the process, of how and why the process is begun, and of how it is managed. Succeeding chapters are devoted to the details of each of these topics.

SYSTEM DEVELOPMENT LIFE CYCLE PHASES

A system **life cycle** embodies the entire life span of a system. In this text, the term *life cycle* refers to project life cycle, unless otherwise indicated. The design phase of the SDLC is frequently divided into logical and physical design. The **logical design** provides the user's view of the system; it specifies the desired logical assembly of the system relative to what it will do and why. The **physical design** specifies the way to physically implement the logical design.

Many life cycles appear in the literature of systems analysis and design. Most SDLCs have a systems approach, rooted in Aristotle's view of the whole and Descartes' view of the parts and their integration, as described in Chapter 1. Most modern SDLCs are based on a systematic approach to solving problems called *scientific management*, originated by Frederick Taylor. Taylor recommended the following steps for solving problems:

1. Define the problem.
2. Identify alternative solutions.
3. Evaluate the alternatives.
4. Select an alternative to implement.
5. Implement the selected alternative solution.

Because most modern SDLCs are based on scientific management, good SDLCs usually only show a different way of doing the same thing. One way is not necessarily better than another, especially if a detailed explanation is provided for the functions performed in each step. A system undergoes many transitional operations during a system project. Although some disagreement exists regarding the initial and ending phases of the SDLC, different SDLCs essentially combine system development operations into different sets of steps that may vary both in the number of steps and the terms assigned to identify each step.

The following steps outline the SDLC that this book follows. They represent the stages viewed as necessary for successfully analyzing, designing, developing, and implementing information systems in a more detailed way than alternative SDLCs. This more detailed set of steps helps to clearly identify the best times to perform certain operations:

1. Problem definition
2. System analysis
3. System design
4. System development
5. System testing

6. System implementation
7. Formal review
8. System project modification and enhancement
9. System maintenance

Problem Definition

The analyst performs **problem definition** in order to identify the central purpose of the SA&D project. This phase often begins with a very quick initial analysis that determines the overall feasibility of the project. Without a quick analysis, many resources may be wasted chasing an unreachable target. This initial analysis provides a rule of thumb for how the project should proceed. Frequently a problem or objective that users identify in their requests can be addressed more easily by applying something that already exists; sometimes it does not require an A&D project at all.

Much time is wasted by analysts who do not clearly define the observed problem. An efficient approach to an appropriate solution depends on a full understanding of the problem. Attempting to solve problems that are not fully understood is as bad as providing a solution for which no problem exists. A legitimate problem usually involves one or a combination of the following:

- Omission
- Addition
- Modification
- Deletion

In general, something has been left out of a system and must be added, or something must be changed or deleted. The problem may be a long-standing one, or it may be a new one stemming from internal changes or changes in the environment.

The problem usually comes to the attention of the systems analysis staff either through a formal system request or through direct communication by affected users. In a small business with no formal channels between users and analysts, users may talk directly to the systems analyst, if there is one at all. In larger businesses, systems analysts or programmer/analysts are often assigned to certain types of users. Direct communication between developers and users usually occurs in both situations.

Larger organizations are likely to have formal channels for systems analysis requests. Individual users inform their supervisors of the need either to acquire more information or to modify information that is currently supplied. This supervisor, or a designated employee, writes a formal request explaining the observed problem, the importance of the problem relative to the operation of the business, and the details of how the problem surfaced. Figure 3-1 shows a hypothetical example of a formal request.

Hughes and Gibson Manufacturing Co.
2149 Industrial Lane
San Diego, California 97500

A&D Request

Requestor: Arnold U. Sire

Position: Billing Account Supervisor

Phone: 555-4148   Ext: 4149

Department: Billings and Collections

Definition of problem:
A discrepancy appears to exist between the amounts being
billed by vendors and the amounts recorded as maximum
amounts that are supposed to be paid for certain products.

Explanation of how the problem was discovered:
One of the auditors in our department noticed a difference
between prices being paid for a certain product and the
posted maximum allowable amount paid. The auditor then
backtracked all purchases of similar items and determined
that it was a recurring problem.

Seriousness of problem:
The overpayment is a large amount for a frequently purchased
item and could cost several thousand dollars a week. As a
result, the firm's financial status could be in serious jeopardy.

Importance code:
1 — Extremely serious
2 — Moderately serious
3 — Mildly serious   Code: 1

Figure 3-1. Typical user request

P 140

The user request is delivered to the appropriate A&D staff supervisor, who reads it, determines how important it is relative to existing system projects, sets priorities, and eventually assigns someone to respond to the request.

System Analysis

After a request is received and priorities are set, a system project begins. The analyst examines the details of the request and obtains a general understanding of the current system. This process includes a study to decide whether a systems analysis and design project is both operationally and economically feasible, and a study of all the components of the systems and their uses from the perspectives of both the designer/developer and the user.

Feasibility Study

The analyst performs an early, general study to decide whether the problem is important enough to warrant the money, time, and effort required to solve it. A more detailed operational/economic **feasibility study** is performed as more information is acquired concerning the project.

Operational feasibility refers to whether or not a project can be completed operationally or can be operationally supported by the company. A project may be operationally infeasible for several reasons. Many situations could create a need for a new system or for modification or replacement of an existing system. Yet current technology in the industry may not be advanced enough to fit recommendations concerning the project, or the technology of the particular firm may not be capable of accommodating the recommendations. Sources or destinations of data might be outside the realm of the firm's influence. For example, a company may be legally bound not to approach certain clients of other businesses, as in the legal and medical professions. In these cases, original sources of data may not be available. A variety of other situations can also make a system project impractical.

Economic feasibility refers to whether or not the financial costs of the project are justified by the benefits of completing the project. A system might be found to be economically infeasible by comparing development (or purchasing) costs, and the costs of operating and maintaining the system, with the benefits of developing and using the system. The costs associated with acquiring and creating the software and hardware that compose a business system must be recoverable for the expenditure to be justified. The analyst uses various cost/benefit analysis procedures to justify the expenditures involved in a system project. An economic feasibility study determines whether the benefits of a project justify its costs.

Justifying an A&D project is an intricate part of the project life cycle; Chapter 14 is devoted to this topic. It discusses ways to determine the costs and benefits associated with the analysis and design of a system and how to perform a cost/benefit analysis to justify the project. Automated cost-estimation software systems that help with this task, such as SPQR/20 (from Software Productivity Research) and Project Bridge (from Applied Business Technology), are also discussed.

After it is determined that a solution is generally feasible, both operationally and economically, analysis of the problem and its solution begins. This involves determining the cause and effect. The analyst gathers and evaluates data about the problem to find its source. The underlying source of problems in information systems is usually that some information is being incorrectly supplied, requires some enhancing, or is not being supplied at all.

Documentation

Documentation begins with the original request that initiates the project; it is the creation of detailed descriptions and explanations of all of the components of systems and of their use. Complete documentation explains the system from the perspectives of both a designer/developer and a user. It records the results of analyzing the identified problem and the requirements stated for the proposed system during the A&D phases of a project. It also defines the purpose of the system: what it does, how to make use of it, and how to interpret the results of its output.

SYSTEM ANALYSIS AND DESIGN DOCUMENTATION   Designer/developer documentation provides a bird's-eye view of the system that allows the project team to track the development of the project. This is called **system analysis and design documentation**; it becomes a permanent record of the development of the completed system. During the analysis phase, the analyst begins with the arduous task of documenting the information needs of users. All facts gathered and recorded become part of the development.

SA&D documentation should be continually updated throughout the SDLC; it should be considered a dynamically changing record of the system at all points of the life cycle. After development and installation, the documentation should be modified as the system is modified. As a result, the documentation remains current during the entire life span of the system. Failure to maintain proper documentation as a system is modified often causes a decline in system performance.

USER DOCUMENTATION   Documentation is also created from a user's perspective during the development project. **User documentation** consists of a general explanation of the system, detailed explanations of what is required of users in employing the system, and detailed explanations of the results of system executions. The general explanation allows users to become familiar with the system as a whole; the detailed explanations allow them to use the system correctly and to interpret the results of system executions.

Creating and maintaining working documentation during A&D is critical to successful systems analysis and design. Insufficient or incorrect user documentation is often the source of problems reported by users. Other problems may also result from incorrect use of the documentation in employing the system and interpreting its results. In addition, documentation updates resulting from system modification may not have been inserted in the user documentation manual. This last problem has led many businesses to store user documentation on-line, which helps to ensure that it is current. Since it is stored in a single place, any updates affect the documentation for all users. Because the source of reported problems may be improper use of the system or simply poor user documentation, the analyst should look at documentation first in evaluating the source of a problem.

USER REQUIREMENTS DOCUMENTATION   Documenting the information needs of people in the business produces the user requirements from which systems are constructed. Many methods for documenting user requirements appear in A&D literature. Chapters 5 and 6 cover in greater detail two modeling methods that compose major portions of the current overall methodology: the entity/relationship diagram (E/RD) and the data flow diagram (DFD) modeling methods. The E/RD method provides initial documentation of user requirements by documenting business objects and the relationships between objects. The DFD method is used to expand user requirements by documenting the processing performed and the data required for the processing. Consistent aspects of methodology are important in both completion and documentation of various phases of the SDLC.

Adopting E/RD and DFD modeling methods to enter user requirements is one way to standardize the creation of user requirements. As defined in Chapter 2, standards are guidelines that prescribe an accepted way of doing things or expected levels of performance. For example, structured programs written in COBOL are the standard for programs in many businesses. Using standard methods in all phases of the SDLC preserves consistency throughout the development of all systems. By standardizing the creation of user requirements documentation and other system documentation, a company makes it easier for someone with knowledge of one system to gain a working knowledge of another system.

The final output of the analysis phase includes a detailed problem definition, identification of the sources of the problem, alternative solutions to the problem, and estimations of the expense and effort of implementing a solution. Usually, simple problems imply simple solutions and complex problems imply complex solutions. Thorough documentation during the analysis phase of the life cycle provides a clear picture of the problem, which gets the project started on firm ground and allows it to move more swiftly toward a satisfactory solution.

Design Dictionary

All of the documentation gathered during the SDLC becomes part of a dictionary. The phrase *data dictionary* has long been used for this information, but its connotation is not as comprehensive as that of the term *design dictionary*. As its name implies, the **design dictionary** is a comprehensive collection of the design specifications used to define and describe all of the components of a system. The design dictionary may consist of written or typed specifications stored on paper, but it is also often stored on-line in special computer files.

Software systems are available for the explicit purpose of entering dictionary specifications for the design of a system. Such software allows the designer to enter and update design specifications with the help of a computer. The formats of design specifications either are already a part of the software package or may become a part of it. The designer can select and enter specifications from the computer screen and make them part of the dictionary for the proposed system. One great advantage of a dictionary system with preprogrammed screen formats is that it forces standardization of dictionary entries. Since the entry screens are preformatted, all entries conform to the same style, no matter who makes them.

The design dictionary becomes an extremely valuable source of information because it permits another analyst to gain a comprehensive knowledge of the system. It is an excellent source of data during the analysis of an existing system. When combined with other archival data, it is a primary source of information.

System Design

Although doing nothing is always a possibility, design usually implements one of three basic alternatives to solve the problem:

- Modify the existing system.
- Replace the existing system by developing a new system.
- Replace the existing system by purchasing a new system.

A system that usually performs satisfactorily but exhibits some problems is a candidate for the first option. The lack of a system, or a system that performs poorly, calls for the second or third option. Historically, the second option has been taken more often than the third option. However, the third option is being selected more frequently.

The existing system is replaced by purchasing an available vendor-supplied system when an existing vendor-supplied system provides a cost-effective way to meet the user's needs, and/or the firm does not have available staff to complete a development project. Many systems are the same from business to business—for example, payroll systems, personnel systems, and so on. Creating one of these systems from scratch can mean reinventing the wheel. Most vendor-supplied versions of these typical systems can easily be modified to meet the needs of the firm. Frequently the purchase or lease of these systems requires customization by the vendor or customization privileges for the firm's staff. Many small businesses do not have a systems personnel staff. For these firms, and for firms with an overtaxed systems staff, purchase or lease becomes either the only option or a better option.

A new system is developed to replace the existing system when no software vendor supplies a system of the type needed, an appropriate vendor-supplied system is deemed too costly, a vendor-supplied system would require far too much customization for it to match the needs of the users, or the firm does have the staff available to complete the system project. When any of these conditions exists, a new development project will be the selected alternative.

For each of the three alternative solutions, three perspectives can be taken:

- The pessimistic (conservative) solution
- The most likely (middle-of-the-road) solution
- The optimistic (liberal) solution

These solutions suggest answers to the "what if" questions that assume (1) the worst possible outcome, (2) the most likely outcome, or (3) the best possible outcome. The choice of an approach depends on the attributes of the designers and of interested users, and on the climate of the business environment.

The design of a system to solve a problem involves a twofold strategy. The user's documented information needs (sometimes called the requirements statement) are the basis for the logical design that is generated, with little regard for physical implementation. This requirements statement is constructed by describing a logical series of operations necessary to meet users' new or additional information needs.

User involvement is essential to a successful A&D project. Practicing analysts and programmers build systems for users, not for themselves. Getting users to open up regarding their jobs and what they need to know is usually the hardest part of an A&D project. Users know what they do and don't know; without their active involvement, a developed system cannot meet all of their information needs. Furthermore, their involvement helps ensure that the way a system performs is consistent with the way they want the system to interact with them personally.

Following the creation of the logical design, the analyst determines how to physically implement the logical solution. This results in the creation of the physical design, which includes the details of software and hardware that make the logical design a physical reality.

Logical Design

During logical design, the analyst often creates a model of the proposed system that shows the user what the system will look like, what it will do, and what outputs it will generate. User reactions to the model guide the analyst in modifying the logical design to conform more closely to the user's desires. Using a model thus allows the analyst to develop a design that will meet the user's information needs and also allows the user to evaluate the design effectively. Whereas analysis specifications show what already exists, logical design specifications show how the system should perform and, often, how the business could change to more effectively use the system.

Logical design focuses on *what* the user needs, with little if any consideration for *how* that need can be met through physical circumstances. This may seem presumptuous at first glance, since the physical environment may impose natural limitations on design. However, such limitations are considered later, during physical design. Basing a system design on current physical limitations often results in a design for what the analyst *believes* can be supplied, not necessarily what the user wants. Systems developed in the 1960s and early 1970s frequently suffered from this malady. Many designers during that era produced systems based solely on what the designer perceived could be physically delivered, not on what the user really wanted. In fact, the desires of the user may not even have been known before the development of the system.

The logical design ends with a review of the design. If users are satisfied, the managers involved sign forms stating their approval. Disapproval of the logical design means that the project is discarded or is returned to the analysis and logical design phases. With an approved logical design, the systems analyst and project team begin the physical design. Chapters 8 and 9 describe the activities of the logical design in greater detail.

Physical Design

Physical design is devoted to creating specifications that establish the working environment within which the system will operate, the physical characteristics of the system, and the way it will actually function. The completed logical design (what the user wants) is translated into the physical design (the way to fulfill the user's desires). For example, an architect commissioned for a custom-built house first obtains specifications of the features the client desires. First, second, and third drafts depicting the house may be necessary, but the house the client wants is finally drawn. This logical design is then drawn as a blueprint, identifying all the exact physical dimensions and types of materials to be used inside and outside the house. This blueprint is the physical design of the house. The projected costs of the physical design may force the client to modify her initial desires, but the architect has allowed the client to register her desires first and then to decide whether they should be modified. A development project should follow the same path.

The physical design includes diagrams and text descriptions of the data flows and physical data structures required, documentation of procedures for the processing to be done, and detailed program specifications. The physical design begins by developing a series of detailed specifications for the procedures required to implement processes that will meet the user's information needs. The physical design involves the following steps:

1. Identifying resources to meet user needs
2. Identifying procedures to meet user needs
3. Describing the procedures so that appropriate computer code can be developed or acquired
4. Describing data so that stored data can be created or modified
5. Identifying additional technology necessary for the new or modified system

The physical design ends with a review of the design, accompanied by the signing of approval documents by appropriate personnel. The output of the physical design phase is a set of clearly defined physical design specifications for the solution that is selected after the analysis phase. It also includes a detailed designation of resources, an identification of all tasks necessary for the development and implementation of the system, a detailed plan for completing those tasks, an estimate of the expense and effort needed to develop and implement the system, and an estimate of ongoing costs associated with using and maintaining the system. Chapters 8 through 11 provide a more comprehensive account of the operations performed in the logical and physical portions of the design, and examples of the results of this phase.

System Development

The system development phase of the SDLC, also known as *design implementation*, involves creating or acquiring the separate modules that compose the system and integrating them with other software into a harmonious system. Different analysts on the project team are sometimes assigned responsibility for separate components of the developing system. Each analyst may employ a staff of programmers to develop and test individual programs or to help modify acquired software. Businesses employing programmer/analysts use the same people to create the system design and to code the programs in their areas of responsibility.

In Chapter 2, we stated that **structured analysis and design** dictates that modules be designed and developed as separate components that are integrated to produce a harmoniously performing system. Integration is accomplished through the creation of various interfaces, the sharing of data, and limited task sharing. The output of the development phase is a completely developed set of programs that have been integrated to become a system.

System Testing

In **system testing**, each component is individually tested to ensure that its procedures produce correct output and that this output meets the requirements specified for the system. Project members test each portion of the system for syntactical and logical errors. **Syntactical errors** occur when programmers do not follow the rules (the grammar) of the specific software language, or when they misspell or misuse key words (the vocabulary) of the language. **Logical errors** occur if the output does not precisely conform to the requirements specified for a given component of the system, even though the program passes all syntactical checks. For example, the following set of COBOL instructions will not properly compute NET_PAY because the instructions are out of sequence, even though the COBOL instructions will pass syntactical checks:

```
COMPUTE FED_TAX = GROSS_WAGE * FED_TAX_RATE.
COMPUTE STATE_TAX = GROSS_WAGE * STATE_TAX_RATE.
COMPUTE GROSS_WAGE = HOURS_WORKED * RATE_OF_PAY.
COMPUTE NET_PAY = GROSS_WAGE - FED_TAX - STATE_TAX.
```

Logical testing involves testing each module of the program for individual correctness as well as **path testing** for all the paths of logic in the entire program. In path testing, key sequences of actions in the program are tested in a prescribed order as a path through the program.

After programmers complete the initial testing, team members responsible for that portion of the system review the results for accuracy. Any errors detected are used to guide modification of appropriate program modules. Successful testing of individual components is reported to the project leader for recording in the project master schedule.

After the testing of individual programs, the entire system is tested to find out whether it performs harmoniously. These tests determine whether the output of individual programs can be successfully integrated. Well-designed and -developed modules frequently fail because of poorly designed and developed integration. Any inaccuracy requires the modification of appropriate program modules to produce a well-integrated, coherent system.

The output of the testing phase of the life cycle is a system of thoroughly tested programs and interfaces. Documentation should show that each program has been thoroughly tested and that all outputs produced allow for complete integration of the programs into a harmoniously performing system.

System Implementation

System implementation consists of three main activities: installation, conversion, and training. These three activities all have a transitional nature, in that they also continue as the system goes into production; as data is converted, stored, and so on; and as training is conducted in the use of the new system and the accompanying practices and technology. This section provides a brief review of these topics; Chapter 13 covers installation, conversion, and training in detail.

Installation

System installation may be accomplished in four ways: immediately, gradually, through a series of simultaneous executions, or in a pilot environment.

- **Immediate changeover** occurs when there is no system or the current system is performing so badly that immediate installation of the newly developed system is warranted.
- **Phased changeover** occurs when the execution of components of the new system mirrors that of components of the old system so closely that portions of the old one may be individually replaced by portions of the new one.
- **Parallel execution** involves executing *both* the new and the old systems and comparing the results for accuracy and comprehensiveness.
- **Pilot execution** helps test the system by installing it in a small department or area of the business before broadcasting its use across the entire organization.

The output of the installation phase should be a completely installed system, ready for use. Documentation should show that all portions of the system have been successfully installed.

Conversion

Systems created for completely different purposes may include components that are so similar that they can be reused by other systems. This significantly reduces the effort and expense of installation. Reusable components usually need to be modified so that they work harmoniously. Conversion is the practice of modifying existing data, data storage, software, and hardware to fit a newly modified or developed system.

New or modified systems often use existing data and data storage in modified form, and much software can be reused from system to system. The term *reusable code* refers to existing software modules that can be reused in new or modified systems, although they often need conversion into a new format. Reusable code saves considerable amounts of time and money in software development or maintenance projects.

Installing new or modified software systems frequently requires the conversion and/or replacement of hardware. Additional purchases may be necessary to avoid an increased drain on hardware resources or to meet the need for special-purpose hardware.

Training

You have seen that newly installed systems often require both new hardware and software for increased operational performance, including additional memory, peripheral devices, communication hardware and software, database management systems, operating systems, and utility software. Proper training of personnel responsible for the performance of the new system is essential if they are to use these new acquisitions effectively. This training usually involves both in-house courses and external seminars.

Users also need training in the use of the new system and the interpretation of its output. The new system often requires users to become acquainted with screen-formatted data entry, responses to system-generated screen prompts, and new reporting methods. Also, on-line and preprogrammed data accessing methods require additional training for users—usually some form of in-house training.

Formal Review

Once installed and ready for production, the system enters a formal review by a committee of upper-level and lower-level management and staff personnel and systems professionals responsible for evaluation. They review the system on an operational and functional basis to identify any modifications and enhancements that it needs before formal release. Usually, the need for these changes is only evident after the system has been installed. In addition, a post-installation review should occur six months after the system is released, to ensure users' confidence both in the system and in the people responsible for its performance. The output of the formal review is a document showing that the system performs according to its intended purposes and that the review committee is satisfied with its performance. A more detailed discussion of the formal review is presented in Chapter 13.

System Project Modification and Enhancement

New or modified systems usually need some modifications and enhancements immediately after the formal review phase of the project. It is impossible to design and develop a system that meets all of the user's "hidden" needs, needs that only surface after the user becomes acquainted with the system. The analyst should establish a time limit within which to make modifications and enhancements to the original project. In standard practice, many changes that require little effort and time are performed as part of the original project at no extra charge. (Any modifications or enhancements that significantly depart from the original system specifications and require larger expenditures of effort and time are considered new projects and enter the normal maintenance request cycle. A time always arrives to "cut the cord" and allow the system to stand on its own.)

The duration of this phase, following the formal review, is very short. In fact, many installations consider this phase to be the beginning of the maintenance phase. In this book, it is considered to be the final phase of the actual development or maintenance project (especially if it is a development project), so that the specifications and results of a particular project become frozen for a given time interval. Actual maintenance may occur in an informal as well as a formal manner.

System Maintenance

System maintenance involves modifying the design of the system and the developed programs to provide for the needs of the users. The information needs of business personnel often change because of changes in the business environment, and systems must also change. (Chapter 16 is devoted to the details of system maintenance.) However, the need for maintenance should be continually considered during the project life cycle. Properly developed or modified systems are typically easier to maintain. The system design and development documentation should provide the information required for correct maintenance of the system after it is installed. After installation, the development documentation becomes maintenance documentation and should be updated whenever the system is modified. Proper maintenance of systems and documentation helps to extend the life span of systems.

Although some system professionals might not consider system maintenance a part of the SDLC, it is a part of the life cycle of a system. The SDLC covers the entire life span of the system, including its development, use, maintenance, decline in performance, and replacement. All systems go through development, are used, and are then modified to correct errors and to accommodate changing user needs. Generally, systems eventually decline in performance because of poor integration of modified components, or because superior technology becomes available. Finally, they are replaced when the integrity of their outputs is questionable or their performance is entirely too poor. Figure 3-2 illustrates the life span of systems from development through use, maintenance, decline, and ultimate replacement.

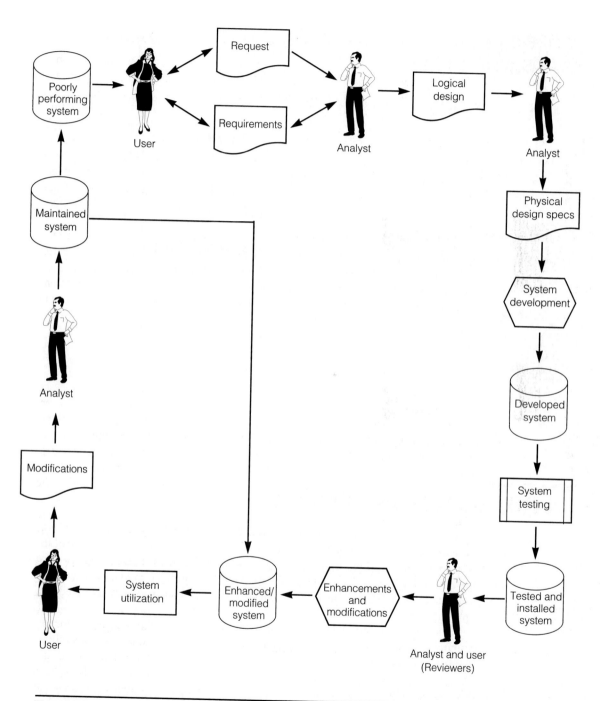

Figure 3-2. Life span of systems

Table 3-1	Relationships among the system life cycle, logical and physical representation, and modeling methods	

Life Cycle Phase	Logical/Physical	Modeling Methods
Problem definition	Logical	Analysis modeling methods
System analysis and feasibility study	Logical	Analysis modeling methods
Logical design	Logical	Logical modeling methods
Physical design	Physical	Physical modeling methods
Development	Physical	Physical modeling methods
System testing	Physical	Physical procedures
Installation, conversion, and training	Physical	Physical procedures
Formal review	Physical	Physical evaluation
System modification and enhancement	Logical, physical	Logical/physical modeling methods and procedures

Table 3-1 shows the relationships among the phases of the system life cycle, logical and physical representation, and components of the methodologies employed.

PROJECT MANAGEMENT

Before and during the activities of an A&D project, consideration must be given to the management of the project. An A&D project mobilizes a significant amount of the firm's resources, including personnel, materials, and facilities. These resources must be used in the most efficient and valid manner. This process is known as **project management**. Responsibility for the entire SA&D project is usually assigned to a project leader.

The project leader maps out a plan for the project, identifies and allocates resources, identifies the tasks to be completed, assigns individual task responsibilities to project team members, monitors progress, supervises the project team, and acts as a general liaison between the team and management. Tools and methods have been devised to help with project management. They help in monitoring the use of resources, monitoring the overall progress of the project, and assisting the project leader in producing a project master schedule. The **project master schedule** is used to track the actual completion of portions of the project. The project leader uses the information gained from monitoring the master schedule to adjust materials so that the project can be completed in a timely and logical fashion. The project master schedule is loosely based on the company's SDLC. Chapter 15 is devoted exclusively to project management.

REACTIVE AND PROACTIVE SYSTEM DEVELOPMENT

A review of the users' desires and stated objectives usually reveals the true nature of a development or maintenance project, which may be reactive or proactive. A **reactive project** originates as a reaction to changes in the business environment. Its purpose is to provide a proper response, within the firm and its systems, to a stimulus originating in the internal and/or the external environment. Such projects are performed in defense of the firm's well-being in the business community. For example, most payroll systems underwent modifications in the 1980s and 1990s in reaction to federal tax legislation that changed tax rates and allowable deductions.

A **proactive project** anticipates positive modifications in the operation of the firm and its systems that are planned by key personnel in the firm. Such projects show that people and systems are actively shaping the firm's direction. The firm is not responding to stimuli; it is more likely taking the offensive and generating stimuli to which the external environment must respond. The firm may also be attempting to use a system to proactively increase its competitive advantages over other firms. For example, major consulting firms in recent years have sought to develop software systems to automate many tasks performed in the analysis, design, development, and maintenance of application systems. These firms created the software packages in a positive and purposeful move to control the direction of systems analysis and design and to increase their advantages over other consulting firms. Both reactive and proactive projects must consider the scope of the project, its subjects, and its objects.

A system development or maintenance project may investigate areas that include or lack an existing computer system. The scope, subjects, and objects of these types of investigation would be different, but the methods would be very similar. The primary difference is that without an existing system, project objectives tend to include several specifications for what the user wishes to have designed into the proposed system. In addition, there is a discouraging difference between these two kinds of development projects in the list of subjects and the number and types of data sources. Existing computer systems usually offer more documentation concerning current operations than systems that have not been computerized.

Finally, the A&D project team must ensure that the scope and the objectives of the investigation are compatible. The objectives of the study should clarify what things, persons, and places need investigation. Conversely, the scope should prevent the investigation from stepping out into areas where additional objectives continue to surface. All computer systems can stand some modification. An analyst who continually moves outside the scope of investigation can stay busy addressing continually emerging objectives. Defining the boundaries prescribed by the problem domain and adhering to them prevent the analyst from being tied to the system by an electronic umbilical cord.

SAMPLE PROJECT PROFILE FOR NATIONAL GOLF & TENNIS (NG&T)

This section introduces a sample case that will be used to illustrate the A&D principles presented in most chapters of this book. This case is based on an actual project completed by one of the authors. The name of the company, location of the business, and names of the constituencies have been altered to preserve the privacy of all involved.

Tim and Jason Richardson opened National Golf & Tennis (NG&T) in an effort to combine their love of those sports and their business interests. NG&T started out as a small retail store in San Diego that sold only golf and tennis equipment. The business rapidly grew into a thriving chain, with stores located in shopping malls in San Diego, Los Angeles, and San Francisco. These stores provide sporting equipment of all types. As the company grew, so did the need to provide more timely and comprehensive information system services. Currently all the firm's computer services are centrally located in an office complex in Los Angeles. The brothers' wives, Connie and Crystal, became the chief controller and financial officer of the firm, respectively. About two years ago, NG&T started a mail-order business. Mail orders now account for over one-third of total sales and are expected to exceed $30 million this year. In addition, the company expects to open ten new stores in the next five years. Jason will relocate and manage five of them, to be located in the Northeast.

The brothers realize that the old manual and minicomputer-based system is no longer adequate to handle the volume of paperwork demanded by the rapid expansion of the business. The order processing system especially needs overhauling. As Christine Slice, divisional manager of the San Diego stores, observes, "Back when we were handling 50 orders per week, our system was fine. Now that we exceed 500 orders per day, a new system is desperately needed."

The company has just hired George Serve as the new director of information systems (IS) at NG&T. Based on Mr. Serve's experience in his previous job at a large national sporting goods supplier, he believes the primary need is for a new order processing system to handle the rapid growth expected for the company. At the same time, cash flow is a problem, and any new system development must be thoroughly justified. Mr. Serve is also particularly concerned that the new system provide faster stock updating and better management reporting. The following is a summary of the current situation at NG&T and the expectations for the needed system.

Present System Concerns

Mr. Serve's conversations with division and store managers have revealed the following major shortcomings of the present system:

- The sheer volume of paperwork is much too time-consuming and costly.
- Management feels it is losing control.
- If a customer calls to check on an order, much searching is required to determine the status of the order.
- Inventory is not updated as rapidly as necessary, and management does not know what they have or how much they have of it in a real-time mode.
- The managerial reports generated are very limited, and management has few reports to show exactly how much has been sold and what items are selling.
- Expansion and growth are already at their limits under the present system; a new system must be devised to allow the business to continue to grow at its present rate.

Systems personnel have interviewed management and store employees and have also personally observed retail sales, order placement, and order servicing. Order servicing has been observed for both customer and vendor orders. The systems personnel have also searched archival data concerning completed sales for quarterly periods over the last three years. Finally, a sampling of order servicing and retail sales has been conducted over a five-week period.

New System Requirements

From the data gathered and from his own experience, Mr. Serve expects the system to provide the following benefits:

- Less manual activity should provide more control.
- Daily transaction reports will be generated.
- Inventory will be updated as the sales are rung up on point-of-sale (POS) terminals.
- Invoices will be typed by a line printer as data is entered by data entry clerks.
- Mailing lists will be maintained and updated daily.
- More management reports will be generated, including reports on inventory turnover, high-sales items, and low-sales items. One particular concern of management is the assessment of the effectiveness of the firm's advertising programs.

Management Decisions

Before work begins on the new system, the following questions must be answered by management:

- When should an order be filled? Should large orders be given priority?
- Should retail sales have priority over phone/mail-order sales?
- How should an order be shipped? Options might include UPS, Greyhound, mail, and air freight.
- What methods of payment should be accepted? Options include C.O.D., Visa, house accounts, cash, and others.
- What should be the policy on returned merchandise?
- What should be the minimum and maximum inventory levels?
- Should volume discounts be allowed?
- Should more emphasis be placed on foreign mail-order sales?

The main questions management expects the systems analysis and design to answer are:

- How many POS terminals should there be in retail stores?
- How many 800 telephone lines should we have?
- How many people do we need to handle the phone orders?

Specific System Objectives

After considerable discussion with management, the following specific objectives for the new system were determined:

- The system should tally the number of retail sales orders processed daily, with processing time limited to a maximum of 10 minutes.
- Orders should be shipped within 48 hours of receipt.
- The percentage of orders with errors should be less than 5 percent of total orders received.
- The system should tally the number of customer complaints, broken down into incorrect merchandise shipped, delays in shipping, incorrect pricing, and other reasons.
- The processing cost per invoice should be tracked.
- Sales should be broken down by magazine advertisement and region of the country.
- Customer inquiries on the status of an order should be handled in a maximum of 3 minutes.

- The system should provide immediate look-up on the status of an order at the customer's request.

System Analysis and Design at NG&T

The methodology of analysis and design and a discussion of the system development life cycle have been presented in Chapters 2 and 3. The remainder of this book uses NG&T as a basis for further discussion of methodology, techniques, tools, and the SDLC. For example, Chapter 4 shows you how to gather the data; Chapter 5 discusses methods for recording and analyzing the data gathered concerning data objects during the analysis phase of a system project. Chapter 6 demonstrates how to use the DFD modeling method during the analysis phase of the NG&T example project.

Subsequent chapters continue the NG&T case throughout the remainder of its life cycle and use NG&T examples to demonstrate A&D principles, practices, methods, and deliverables.

REVIEW

Many versions of the system development life cycle (SDLC) exist, but this book covers a detailed set of steps that clearly identify the right times to perform certain operations:

1. Problem definition
2. System analysis
3. System design
4. System development
5. System testing
6. System implementation
7. Formal review
8. System project modification and enhancement
9. System maintenance

A primary responsibility of the analyst and the project team is management of all aspects of the SDLC. The rudiments of project management are introduced here, and an entire chapter (Chapter 15) is devoted to this topic. SA&D projects are begun either in reaction to changes in the business environment (reactive) or as specifically planned changes to actively shape the firm's direction (proactive). You will learn how to recognize these two types of projects and how they affect the way a system is designed.

Finally, the system needs of a growing business, National Golf & Tennis, are described in this chapter. They provide the case study for various aspects of systems development as the book progresses.

QUESTIONS

1. Define system development life cycle (SDLC) and explain what it comprises.
2. Explain the basic steps in any SDLC.
3. Why is it most important that the problem be clearly defined? Explain the four different types of problems encountered in a system project.
4. For a company in your vicinity, obtain documentation that demonstrates characteristics of each type of problem.
5. Distinguish between operational feasibility and economic feasibility. Identify instances of each.
6. What function does the project leader perform and why is it important?
7. What is the project master schedule and what purpose does it serve?
8. For a company in your vicinity, obtain a copy of a project master schedule. Explain the purpose of this schedule regarding the project it serves for that company.
9. Identify the sources of data used in investigating the source of the observed problem.
10. For a company in your vicinity, obtain a copy of archive data that could be used in an analysis and design project.
11. For a company in your vicinity, obtain a copy of a set of interview questions used during a user interview session for an A&D project.
12. For a company in your vicinity, obtain a copy of a questionnaire distributed to users for data gathering during an A&D project.
13. For a company in your vicinity, identify data obtained through personal observation that could be used for an A&D project.
14. Explain what documentation means in regard to an A&D project.
15. Distinguish between the two major forms of documentation for an A&D project.
16. For a company in your vicinity, obtain a copy of designer/development documentation. Explain the purpose of that documentation and what it describes.
17. For a company in your vicinity, obtain a copy of user documentation. Explain the purpose of that documentation and what it describes.
18. Distinguish between logical and physical design.
19. Distinguish among the three basic alternatives available for implementation and the three approaches to evaluating and implementing these alternatives.
20. For a company in your vicinity, obtain a description of different alternatives available for one of its A&D projects.
21. Distinguish among the four types of changeovers to the newly designed or modified system. Explain when each is appropriate.

22. For a company in your vicinity, identify and explain how it used the following changeover methods during one of its projects:

    a. Immediate changeover
    b. Phased changeover
    c. Parallel changeover
    d. Pilot changeover

23. What is the purpose of the formal review, and what part do each of the two major participants play?

24. For a company in your vicinity, obtain documentation from a formal review of one of their projects.

25. Why do modification and enhancement occur at the end of the project life cycle?

26. For a company in your vicinity, explain the modifications and enhancements performed on a system after the formal review of a project before the system was released for general use.

27. Clearly distinguish between reactive and proactive development projects and give examples of each.

28. What is the primary difference between development projects with previously existing systems and those without existing systems?

29. For a company in your vicinity, identify a development project to serve the business where no information system previously existed. Explain the purpose of this project and how it will support the business in ways in which it previously lacked support.

30. For a company in your vicinity, identify a development project to serve the business that replaces a previously existing information system. Explain the purpose of this project and how it will better support the business in ways that the previous system did not.

31. Why is compatibility between the scope and the objective of a project important?

32. For a company in your vicinity, explain how it ensured that compatibility between scope and objective were accomplished for one of its A&D projects.

33. Distinguish among the terms *methodology*, *system development life cycle*, and *logical and physical design*.

34. What is a design dictionary and what purpose does it serve for an A&D project?

35. What are the two main types of errors that must be corrected in programs created during the development phase of the project life cycle?

36. Explain what path testing involves.

37. Define the term reusable code and explain how it contributes to a systems analysis and design project and conversion to its newer forms.

EXERCISES

1. Search the IS literature to identify three different SDLCs that are different from the one described in this chapter. Identify the author of each SDLC and the publication in which it appears. Explain how each of these SDLCs is related to Frederick Taylor's steps in scientific management. Explain the differences and similarities among these SDLCs.

2. For a company in your vicinity, obtain a copy of a project management schedule based on its SDLC. Explain the tasks to be accomplished on that schedule.

SELECTED REFERENCES

Boehm, B. 1981. *Software Engineering Economics*. Englewood Cliffs, NJ: Prentice-Hall.

Canning, R. G. 1956. *Electronic Data Processing for Business and Industry; and Installing Electronic Data Processing Systems*. New York: John Wiley & Sons.

Engel, N. L. 1981. "Classical and Structured Systems Life Cycle Phases and Documentation." In *Systems Analysis and Design: A Foundation for the 1980s*. Edited by W. M. Cotterman, J. D. Couger, N. L. Engel, and F. Harold. North Holland, NY: Elsevier.

Taylor, F. 1912. *Scientific Management*. New York: Harper's.

PART II

Data Gathering and Analysis Using Data and Process Modeling Methods

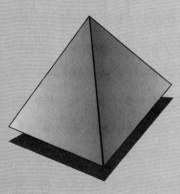

You have learned the role of proper problem definition in information systems design. Part II expands the area of problem definition by explaining two important modeling methods to use in modeling data objects and business processes. These aid in understanding the problem and creating a system design that helps solve it. A data modeling method, such as an entity/relationship diagram, is used to document the objects of importance to the business, which in turn become a part of user requirements for the system. Data flow diagrams help the analyst document and understand the business processes associated with the system. Taken together, data and process modeling provide an accurate description of the system under study, and they provide valuable insight into requirements for the new system.

CHAPTER 4

Defining the Problem and Collecting Data

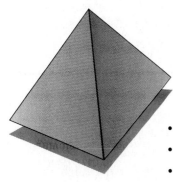

OVERVIEW

The analysis phase of the system development life cycle begins by clearly identifying the problem and describing the environment in which it exists. To present the procedures for investigating system problems during the analysis phase, this chapter covers the elements of:

- Identifying types of systems and associated problems
- Staffing and justifying a project
- Planning a project
- Detecting and defining the problem
- Identifying categories of problems
- Determining the domain of the problem
- Defining the various data collection methods
- Using joint application design (JAD) to identify user requirements and plan system design

KEY TERMS

Close-end questions

Executive sponsor

Facilitators

Hawthorne effect

JAD/CASE experts

Joint application design (JAD)

Objects

Open-end questions

Problem domain

Scope

Subjects

User interfaces

This book defines systems analysis as the decomposition of a system into its components for the purpose of investigating when and where problems occur. The business world is now far more complicated than ever before, and providing information that represents conditions in the business community has become more demanding. In addition, the technical advances in information systems themselves have created a complex arena of possibilities for the construction of systems. As a result, analyzing systems to improve their service is more involved.

Nothing can substitute for experience in most endeavors. The experience of the analyst contributes enormously to the validity, comprehensiveness, consistency, and completeness of A&D projects. All experienced analysts can attest that the A&D work they now perform is much better than that of previous years. Through contact with newer and better ways of performing their functions, analysts ensure that their work reflects the maturity required for the current business environment. As an analyst, you must stay informed concerning improvements and new developments in the field.

Topics in this chapter illustrate how to identify and analyze problems and gather more information about user requirements. The resulting information becomes the basis for completing problem investigation during the analysis phase.

TYPES OF SYSTEMS AND ASSOCIATED PROBLEMS

Systems may be arranged either in technical categories or in IS business support categories. The technical categories of systems, such as batch, time-sharing, interactive, and real-time, are discussed in Chapter 11. Analysis and design must first be performed on support categories in order to provide the basis for analysis of problems and design of solutions. The IS support categories explained in this text are management information systems, decision support systems, management support systems, and transaction processing systems, which were first introduced in Chapter 1.

The analysis of problem areas in business systems is complicated by the sheer number and magnitude of possible combinations of system types. The inexperienced reader is not expected to have a complete background in the different types of systems and problems. Only years of experience in systems analysis and design will properly acquaint you with the attributes of different systems and the ways to identify and correct problems in all types of systems.

Management Information Systems

As Chapter 1 explained, a management information system (MIS) provides information that enables managers to answer many questions concerning the operations of the firm. The questions that the MIS can answer are structured; that is, all important situational characteristics can be modeled, and the answers involve structured and fixed inputs, transformation procedures, and outputs. Many decisions facing business personnel, however, are not so highly structured; for these decisions, a decision support system (DSS) often provides the greatest benefits. Frequently, the combination of all functional business systems, special-purpose management reports, and inquiry systems is considered part of the MIS.

Decision Support Systems

Chapter 1 explained that a DSS is a system of decision-supporting tools that is part of the MIS and provides information for planning and forecasting in a semistructured environment. As noted in Chapter 1, the DSS works by incorporating mathematical models that allow exploration of the opportunities facing the firm in a semistructured setting—one in which not all situational characteristics are known, and a subjective evaluation must be made by a decision maker. These systems allow decision makers to answer "what if" questions about changes in certain conditions that the firm faces. A critical component of a DSS is the interface between the user and the mathematical foundation of the system. The most desirable interface facilitates the use of the mathematical algorithms of the DSS without taxing the user's patience and knowledge.

An example of a DSS is a system that forecasts the business climate in an unstable environment to aid the planning of product lines that will suit the whims of the buying public. The decision is semistructured because of uncertainties about the environment and the preferences of buyers.

The main problems associated with a DSS are as follows:

- Inadequate or invalid modeling of business conditions
- Inadequate or invalid data sources
- Poorly designed user interfaces
- Poorly designed user control paths
- Response-time difficulties and user impatience

In order to design a model that adequately portrays the real situation, all necessary variables and their correct relationships to the rest of the model must be considered. Inadequate modeling of business conditions occurs when critical conditions affecting the decision are not provided as parameters that influence the choices available. An attempt to build a sales forecasting model that fails to include price is a good example of inadequate modeling. In contrast, invalid modeling takes place when key components of the decision environment are incorrectly portrayed by the mathematical model of the DSS. A firm that includes price in the sales forecasting model, but assigns an incorrect relationship between price and sales, has made an invalid model of the situation.

Regardless of how appropriately the model is designed, if the data is incorrect or missing, the model will not yield valid results. Inadequate data sources exist when data critical to the decision is either unavailable, unknown, or incorrectly reported. In the case of NG&T, management does not know how many customers complain or what the status of an order is at any given time. The data sources are inadequate. On the other hand, invalid data sources occur when data that influences the decision-making process is incorrectly recorded and entered into the DSS. Incorrect information entered into the DSS is just as bad as (and often worse than) not having the information. For example, if NG&T's personnel believe that adequate inventory is available when in fact it is not, the invalid data will lead to a wrong decision; stock outages may occur.

Regardless of how appropriately the situation is modeled and how accurate the data is, if the system is not easy to use, it will not be helpful to the user. Poorly designed user interfaces take many forms, but the most prevalent problem is poor shielding of the user from the sophistication of the underlying mathematical model. Decision makers typically have no need to know how the mathematical model works. They just need to know the meaning behind the responses from the system that they direct.

Poorly designed user control paths occur when it is not clear what the user should do next or how the user should respond next to the DSS. Help screens should always be available so that the user never has to sit and stare at the screen, wondering what to do next. Function keys can also direct the user as to what options are available.

Managers are very busy people. They expect to receive information both quickly and accurately. If they must wait for a response from the system, a new source of information with quicker response time will be sought. Response-time difficulties frequently occur as the result of large amounts of number crunching and/or large input/output demands by the mathematical algorithm embedded in the DSS. With speed and convenience so important in the modern business community, a decision maker's patience can wane as the DSS takes a long time to go through the decision process.

Management Support Systems

A management support system (MSS) was defined in Chapter 1 as a system that is part of the MIS, the main purpose of which is to support managerial control functions. As such, the key characteristic of a MSS is to provide information that helps managers control operations and monitor the environment of the firm. MSS designers are knowledgeable about control approaches, the ways control is exercised, and what controlling interventions will produce the desired outcomes.

An example of a MSS is a system that helps production managers to control the allocation, use, and integration of resources used to manufacture products. A MSS helps make sure that the right part is at the right place at the right time.

A MSS may suffer from many of the same problems that affect a DSS. The most prevalent problems are:

- Inadequate data sources
- Poorly designed user interfaces
- Response-time difficulties resulting in user impatience
- Poorly designed user control paths
- Poorly designed control mechanisms

The first four problems are described under "Decision Support Systems," above. The last one, poorly designed control mechanisms, can assume many characteristics. Problems may occur with the control mechanism when the MSS is not properly designed. Often the MSS is not sophisticated enough to provide proper control information. In addition, the controlling influences generated by the MSS may not be specific enough to pinpoint the correct object of control without influencing objects that do not need control. The former problem occurs when the magnitude of the control object is underestimated or the MSS lacks the technical sophistication to control highly technical control objects. The latter problem occurs when the MSS control system is designed shotgun-fashion, with too much controlling "buckshot" penetrating areas that need no controlling adjustments. This same problem may exist when a complex object of control lacks the precision needed to adjust the target object without also affecting other factors.

Transaction Processing Systems

Chapter 1 defined a transaction processing system (TPS) as a system that performs a variety of activities to support an organization's day-to-day operations. TPSs process transactions that gather, record, aggregate, segregate, batch together, and process normal everyday transaction data. They also process and track data regarding the occurrence of events in daily operations, such as completing an order, sending a billing invoice, receiving payment for the order, and so on.

TPSs provide most of the data to operational management, but serve management at higher levels as well. Much of the data that originates externally or that is sent to external places is processed by a TPS. A TPS may suffer from many of the same problems that affect a DSS or MSS. The main problems associated with a TPS are:

- Inadequate or invalid data sources
- Poorly designed user interface
- Poorly designed control sequence paths

- Response-time difficulties resulting in user impatience
- Inadequate or invalidly depicted event data objects
- Poorly designed reports and report processing

The latter two problems are the only ones needing further explanation.

Inadequate or invalidly defined events raise questions concerning the entire integrity of the system. The main purpose of many TPSs is to process events and make data concerning them available to business personnel. Knowledge concerning events helps business personnel better understand conditions facing the business. If key facts concerning an event or knowledge concerning key events are not adequately known or are invalid, then organizational personnel will not understand what they need to know and on which facts to base their actions.

INVESTIGATING A PROJECT AND STUDYING ITS FEASIBILITY

Investigation of problems associated with information processing and the study of project feasibility should be considered a joint effort by people in the information systems department and users in the functional areas of the firm. Systems belong primarily to managers and staff personnel in the functional areas and should properly serve their information needs. However, information professionals have a stake in systems because they are primarily responsible for their smooth and comprehensive operation. Consequently, personnel in both areas have critical interests in ensuring that problems are properly addressed and resolved in A&D projects.

Authorization for Project Investigation

Because systems personnel must interact with appropriate users to investigate a problem, users must know that the systems personnel are empowered to investigate system problems. Users and managers affected by the project should be formally notified that the investigative team will be examining the current system and possibly developing a new one.

Formal recognition of the project team helps it to gain the acceptance and support of both workers in information systems and users in functional areas. Only when the team has the cooperation of everyone involved in or affected by the system can it expect to be successful. The team must have *serious* assistance from employees during the investigation. Formal recognition and authorization help assure that the team is taken seriously.

Determining the Feasibility of the Project

An analysis of the feasibility of a proposed system should occur at several strategic points in the development life cycle: the beginning of the life cycle, the end of the analysis phase, the end of the logical design, and the end of the physical design. The feasibility study evolves from preliminary justification of the project, with highly general feasibility estimates, to quite detailed estimates once physical design work is complete. Since less detailed information is usually known at the beginning of the project, preliminary estimates are often quite subjective. The preliminary feasibility study largely depends on the experience and judgment of the analyst and the manager involved. The power to terminate the project resides primarily in functional area managers, but they depend greatly on the recommendations of the project team.

Chapter 14 details the steps necessary to determine the feasibility of a proposed project. It also provides a cost/benefit methodology to determine which system alternative is the best.

PREPARING A PLAN OF INVESTIGATION

Planning is an integral part of all business functions. Only when projects are properly planned do they have a high probability of success. In a highly competitive business environment, a firm's functions must be properly planned to retain a competitive advantage. Proper planning can help to avoid the pitfalls of the competitive "rat race" and other events detrimental to the firm's well-being.

Since a major A&D project can mobilize a tremendous amount of the firm's resources, a plan should be made *before* the project begins, and should be monitored and modified as a benchmark to measure the project's progress. Chapter 15 is devoted to project management. This chapter elaborates on the creation and use of a plan to monitor and control projects. An overview of this material follows, to acquaint you with the plan's origin in the life cycle and its major components. General planning activities are as follows:

- Identify areas and systems to investigate.
- Estimate the resources available for use during the project phases.
- Identify project tasks.
- Sequence project tasks.
- Allocate responsibility for project tasks.
- Derive a schedule for the progress of the project.
- Identify measures for determining when tasks are completed.
- Diagram the phases of the project from a project management standpoint.

Planning is generally performed at the beginning of the project and at the beginning of each phase of the development life cycle. Planning begins by identifying the scope of the project. The team must initially determine and document which functional areas and systems are either involved in the system or affected by it. Furthermore, it is necessary to identify the major components of the systems and functional areas that must be studied in greater detail. The resources available are identified and their levels of usage are recorded during project activities. Identifying tasks should include explaining how and when they are to be completed. As task responsibilities are allocated and a schedule is derived, measures must be agreed on to determine when a task can be considered completed and when those responsible for it can move to the next task. Finally, a schematic diagram should prominently display the layout of the project as well as progress on the project. This helps the project manager to monitor and adjust task responsibilities and resource usage to ensure that the project is completed on schedule.

Objectives of the Project

Identifying the objectives implied by stated requests or direct communication from users is the major purpose of the investigation. The goals of the project can be derived from close scrutiny of the information needs conveyed in these requests. For example, a request may state that it takes too long to receive outputs after queries. The objectives implied by this request would be to decrease the response time for user queries and to increase the efficiency of the system.

Discussions with users during the preliminary investigation of their requests may lead to the identification of additional objectives. The original objectives and any that subsequently emerge should be used to create a set of formally stated goals to guide the project in the correct direction.

Types of objectives depend on a variety of factors, including:

- Characteristics of the firm's industry and of the firm itself; its functional areas and their components
- Personnel in the functional areas and on the project team
- Systems in the firm's MIS
- Available data sources
- Technological advances in the information systems community
- Available technology within the firm

There are a certain number of objectives that typically surface in various types of development projects. In the majority of cases, users want a system that:

- Provides more comprehensive and timely information
- Increases the validity of information
- Increases the reliability of the system and the data
- Increases the flow of data relative to system capacity and throughput

- Increases system efficiency
- Reduces data recording, transmission, and processing
- Reduces costs
- Improves service to external and internal sources
- Improves internal operations
- Increases internal control
- Improves the integration of data processing and data flows
- Responds to legal issues
- Complies with governmental proclamations and regulations
- Incorporates technological advances into the firm's operations
- Gains advantages over competitors

DETECTING AND DEFINING THE PROBLEM

Chapter 3 provided an overview of the problems that are most often discovered by people in functional areas of the firm. Figure 3-1 in Chapter 3 illustrated a typical user request notifying the information systems department of a perceived problem. The request is transmitted through the channels of command to the appropriate functional area manager. It then goes to the information systems professionals who are responsible for responding to the request.

In addition to problem signals from users in the functional area, the analyst can get an indication that something is wrong from a variety of other sources. The analyst may hear managers complaining over coffee, may get a call from the union representative, may be visited by an internal or external auditor, or may simply be made aware that customers are not happy with the service they are receiving. Whatever the actual source of the complaint, projects must be initiated by the functional area manager. Of course, there is nothing wrong with the analyst's diplomatically telling the manager about potential problems.

Determining Whether a Problem Actually Exists

The preliminary investigation may reveal that a problem does not actually exist in the information system. There are many reasons why users might think there is a problem when there is none. Some problems in the functional areas of a business may be caused by poorly trained users. Since businesses often experience high turnover rates among clerical personnel, new hires may not have the benefit of a person familiar enough with critical operations to provide proper training. This may result in insufficient user training in data entry, procedures required to run the system, interpretation of outputs, implications of the outputs for their functions in the firm, or the capabilities of the system. In addition, users may not use or maintain the system's documentation properly.

The preliminary investigation may reveal that users are providing the system with inadequate or erroneous data and are not running the system as intended. It may show that outputs are being incorrectly interpreted by users and that important implications of the outputs are being misunderstood or ignored. Users may simply be unaware that the system is already capable of providing the service listed in the formal request. The investigation may also show that user documentation is poor or is insufficiently used. Updates to user documentation may be missing or be ignored. Firms that use hard-copy documentation frequently distribute updates to the user documentation manual in the form of replacement or insertion pages. If these pages are not included, users are left with an invalid manual. The turnover of employees adds to the confusion, and new employees may receive invalid manuals. On-line storage and screen displays of user documentation help to ensure that user documentation always remains current and is not lost. Computer screen displays, data-entry-point help, and documentation access makes on-line documentation even more valuable.

Perceived problems with a firm's information processing systems are often caused by external influences that the firm's personnel or systems cannot control. For example, a few years ago one of the authors purchased, by check, a desktop computer at a price of $2,747.00. The next month, he received a bank statement indicating that his balance was $2,719.53 more than the balance in his own records. By comparing checks with recorded drafts on his bank statement, he discovered that the check for the desktop computer had been erroneously recorded by the payee's bank as $27.47. The amount had passed the scrutiny of the author's bank. An error initially perceived to be in the author's financial management system was found to originate in external sources beyond the control of his system. Fearing that computer goblins would visit him late some lonely night if he took advantage of the situation, the author notified his bank of the mistake, and the problem was corrected.

Problems typically caused by external influences are invalid data sources, invalid external processing of data, incorrect communication of data, invalid external interpretation of transmitted information, and invalid or inappropriate sources of input data or destinations of output data. Such problems are often difficult to identify because so many external sources may be involved. Firms often spend much time and energy, only to discover that problems perceived by users as being within the system are actually caused by external sources.

Separating Problems from Symptoms of Problems

Many things in this world exhibit a cause-and-effect relationship between some form of stimulus and some resultant outcome. The resultant outcome is often the only visible indication of the occurrence of the stimulus. The same relationship exists between problems and their symptoms. A cause-and-effect relationship exists between the sources of problems and their symptoms, but the true sources of problems are often buried among a variety of potential causes. Symptoms may appear to be problems in themselves. As a result, an investigator may expend effort and resources in treating

Not used as intended

the symptom instead of the actual problem. For example, an analyst may expend effort in speeding up a program's execution when in fact its slow response time may be the result of difficulties with communications software.

Systems and functional areas of the business are interrelated. Since problems in one may cause symptoms in the other (and vice versa), it is often difficult to distinguish between actual problems and their visible symptoms. Nevertheless, an analyst must find a way to do this. Identifying and correcting problems, whether they are in systems or functional areas, will correct the symptoms of those problems; treating symptoms, however, will not correct problems.

Major Types of System Problems

Chapter 3 identified and defined the major types of problems exhibited by business systems. The four main types of generic problems exhibited by business systems are problems of omission, modification, deletion, and addition. The following sections briefly describe how and why the problems may occur.

Problems of Omission

One of the most important objectives of any business system is to meet the requirements of the users, perform the business functions, and carry out the business operations. If they do not fulfill these vital needs, systems may suffer from the following problems:

- Inadequate provision for information needs
- Inadequate interfaces
- Inadequate processing
- Inadequate control of operations

A problem of omission can occur when a necessary piece of information is not available to the user. If a customer calls in and is granted credit, when in fact she already has bills overdue, the system is not reporting all of the necessary information. This information has been omitted from the system as it is currently designed. Another example might be the case in which a salesperson promises to deliver a particular inventory item within three days, only to find out later that the item is already back-ordered. In this case, the system interface between sales and inventory is inadequate. In both of these cases, the system may need to be redesigned to correct these omission errors.

Problems of Modification

The business is in a constant state of change. Even though the system may have met the user's needs when it was designed, these needs have probably changed. The following changes often signal a need for modifications to a system:

- Environmental changes (including governmental proclamations and regulations)
- Increased internal needs
- Modifications in information gathering, transmission, and processing in current systems

These changes may be necessary to increase efficiency; reduce cost; improve the validity of data recording, transmission, and processing; improve the reliability of the operations of current systems; provide better service to people inside and outside the firm; improve system response time; provide better controls within systems and functional areas; and improve the integration of processing and the flows of data throughout systems and functional areas.

Problems of Deletion

Business is dynamic; the information needed last month or last year may no longer be required. Therefore, the system needs changing. Deletions from an existing system may be required as a result of:

- Environmental changes
- Redundancy of data and effort
- Deletions in information gathering, transmission, and processing requirements in current systems and operations within functional areas

These deletions are often undertaken to improve efficiency, reduce cost, eliminate redundancy, and improve response time.

Problems of Addition

As you have seen, user needs are constantly changing. It is necessary to add new capabilities to existing systems to meet these changing needs. Needed additions come from a variety of sources, including:

- Environmental changes (including governmental proclamations and regulations)
- Greater expectations from users
- Additions to information gathering, transmission, and processing requirements

Additions may be necessary to meet increased information needs, increase the firm's knowledge base, improve efficiency, improve service, improve system response time, increase the validity of data and processing, increase system reliability, better integrate data processing and flows of data through systems and functional areas, and incorporate technological advances.

Problem Domains

The **problem domain** is the set of factors involved in the problem or affected by it that are either areas of data sources, actual data sources, actual data, and/or objectives of the investigation. These factors may be functional areas of the business or their components, systems used by functional areas or their components, data sources in sections of the functional areas, stored data, and/or objectives of the investigation. Another way of saying this is that the analyst must decide exactly which systems must be studied, then limit the project to those areas. For example, if you are designing a new inventory control system, you may not want to get involved with the purchasing or accounts-payable functions. You must limit the project to specific areas of concern.

Three terms—*scope*, *subjects*, and *objects*—have long been used to describe the domain of information problems. They are borrowed from other sciences, where they also serve to define the domain of problem areas.

- **Scope** is the breadth and depth of the problem area, which defines how far the investigation must extend to be sufficient.
- **Subjects** are sources that are either researched, polled, observed, or sampled for information that helps identify and solve problems.
- **Objects** are either the information that is gathered and processed or the stated objectives of the project.

Scope identifies the limits within which to perform the investigation; subjects identify what to explore within the scope; objects identify what to look for in the investigation.

Scope

The scope provides a framework for the investigation. Keeping in mind the cause-and-effect relationship of problems and symptoms, the project team must clearly delineate the systems, components of systems, functional areas, components of functional areas, and associated data sources that may lead to the sources of the detected problems. Doing so limits the depth and breadth of the investigation. The components of systems and functional areas constrain the depth of the investigation, and how widely each component is investigated constrains its breadth. The scope must be clearly defined to properly restrict the focus of the investigative team. Much effort and expenditure of resources may be wasted on interesting data that is totally unrelated to the problem. A clearly defined scope helps the team restrict the investigation to the areas that are most likely to produce information that is relevant to the sources of problems and their subsequent solution.

Subjects

The subjects of investigation in business information systems problems are as follows:

- Key sections within functional areas and components of these functional areas in which data is stored
- Key sections of these same areas and components in which developmental and maintenance documentation is stored

- Places in which user documentation is stored in these same sections
- Key personnel within these same sections

These subjects are the sources for data collection during the analysis stage of the problem.   Chapter 2

Objects

The objects of the investigation are the data obtained or the stated objectives of the project. Data is gathered concerning operations in order to answer questions that arise in the course of analyzing the problem. The answers to these questions either resolve conflicting perceptions or statements in documentation or provide background information needed to clearly identify and understand the problem. This data is captured in an organized form that is specifically designed to document the progress of the analysis and other phases of the development life cycle. The data is later connected to appropriate specifications in the design dictionary to provide a more formal representation of the progress and findings of the analysis phase.

METHODS OF DATA COLLECTION

Several methods may be used to collect data:

- User interviews and questionnaires
- Archival data searches
- Personal observation
- On-site work sampling

Since each of these data collection methods is equally important in most projects, the investigation team uses a combination of them to gather data. Chapters 5 and 6 discuss methods of recording collected data in a form that facilitates analysis.

Collecting Data from Users

Today, the users are considered to be a primary source of information. The interview and the questionnaire are two techniques commonly used to collect information from them. Both techniques permit the analyst to record users' reactions to questions. Through these forms of data collection, users can describe most shortcomings of the current information system and what the new system needs to do. The main purpose of these methods is to learn what the system actually does and how it actually performs from the user's perspective, rather than how it should perform according to the documentation.

Interviews and questionnaires, as well as personal observation by the analyst during data collection, may produce what is known as the **Hawthorne effect**. The Hawthorne effect was first evidenced in manufacturing studies conducted in the 1920s and 1930s that attempted to determine the effect on productivity of variations in working conditions. Both favorable and detrimental conditions were instituted in the workers' surroundings. Also, the measurement of production levels was introduced in the workers' surroundings, and these production levels were tracked as conditions changed. Initially, the findings seemed to indicate that productivity was not affected by changes in working conditions. It was later determined that productivity was affected more by the attention given to the workers.

The attention that users receive during the administration of interviews and questionnaires, and during personal observations, also has the potential of producing a Hawthorne effect. Consequently, the analyst should be aware of this possibility and closely monitor whether the Hawthorne effect occurs. This is usually accomplished by cross-checking similar information obtained from different users.

The interview and the questionnaire are similar in a number of ways. Both methods should be properly planned. The main differences in planning their administration are site and time selection for the interview and distribution and collection for the questionnaire. Both methods should be adjusted to suit the respondents. The questions should be restricted to areas familiar to respondents, and the level of the questions should match their level of sophistication. The types of information obtained through both of these methods are also very similar: both seek factual information, attitudinal information, and perceptual information as seen through the eyes of the user. Both methods should emphasize the confidentiality of the data collected. Punitive actions should not be implied for providing negative views. The more relaxed the respondent is, the more likely it is that the interview or questionnaire will produce candid responses.

The two main formats for the questions asked in either an interview or a questionnaire are close- and open-end questions. **Close-end questions** limit the possible responses; examples are yes/no questions, check-off questions, and range questions such as those in Figure 4-1. Note that the response of the participant is limited in all cases.

Open-end questions are useful when the analyst needs the respondent's opinions or recommendations about a specific problem. **Open-end questions** ask respondents for unstructured answers; the questions are merely asked without limiting the response. For example:

Do you feel that a new mail-order system is needed at NG&T?
Why or why not?

What are the most serious problems in the current mail-order
system at NG&T?

The main difference between interviews and questionnaires is that the interview provides data concerning user reactions that is only available through face-to-face contact. Body language often shows as much about users' attitudes and perceptions as

Yes/No

Do you agree that users need more than one
hour of training on the use of the new system?   _____ Yes

_____ No

Check-off

Check all of the professional degrees you have:
_____ Associate of Arts
_____ Bachelor's
_____ Master's
_____ Doctorate

Range

How many times each day must you use the
telephone to verify information on the invoice?   _____ 0

_____ 1–3

_____ 4–5

_____ 6–8

_____ Over 8

Figure 4-1. Examples of close-end questions

do the answers they give. In addition, the interview can be dynamically adjusted as
critical factors surface. The final difference between these two reactive forms of data
collection is that the questionnaire can be administered to a much larger population
simultaneously and results are more easily tabulated. (By reactive data collection, we
mean that data is collected based on reactions to the questions.) Apart from these
three major differences, the two methods are essentially the same. As a result, a study
of one of them provides insights about the other.

Personal Interviews

The personal interview can be used effectively when only a few people need to be
polled, and the analyst needs to be able to judge their answers as they are given and
to probe for additional information as needed. Personal interviews are particularly
useful at the beginning of an analysis project to gather initial information and views.

The main disadvantages of the personal interview are time and cost. It is often
difficult to schedule meetings with busy managers and users. Another problem is that
people may not be totally candid in a face-to-face interview, although with practice
the analyst can draw them out without putting them on the defensive.

WHO SHOULD BE INTERVIEWED Determining who should be interviewed is a very important part of the data-gathering process. Generally, the analyst will need to interview four different categories of users: clerical, supervisory, managerial, and executive.

Interviewing in each of these categories allows the analyst to gather particular types of information, but it also leads to some special concerns. Often it is best to interview higher levels of users last, because at that time the interviewer has a better understanding of the system and any discrepancies in system objectives can be presented to the person who is responsible for the final decision.

Clerical and supervisory personnel will often have the most detailed insights into how the system currently works and what its major problems are. They are often the ones who use it on a day-to-day basis. Since these are very detailed interviews, they will normally require more time than interviews of higher-level managers or executives. Interviews of clerical and supervisory personnel often require several hours, whereas thirty minutes to an hour is usually the maximum an analyst can expect from an executive and from most managers. In addition, the analyst will often find that it is necessary to interview the clerical and/or supervisory personnel several times.

The level of detail and the type of question to ask also vary with the person interviewed. The manager or executive will have a very broad view of the system and how it works. Do not embarrass the executive by asking questions about the details of specific functions.

Even though the analyst often starts with interviews at the clerical or supervisory level, it is important to clear these interviews with the interviewee's immediate supervisor. The last thing the analyst wants to do is make the supervisor feel that he or she is being bypassed.

One final caution is in order. The analyst must always take political issues into account. Personnel omitted from the interview process can be resentful and oppose the final implementation of the system. It is better to schedule too many interviews than to leave someone out who will cause problems in a later stage of project development.

Figure 4-2 shows who will be interviewed for the initial information gathered at NG&T. This decision was made for two main reasons. First, the number of employees to be interviewed is small. Second, initial discussions indicated that NG&T's record-keeping procedures would not provide the necessary information — that is, that the current documentation is inadequate or missing.

FACTORS CONTRIBUTING TO INTERVIEW SUCCESS Three factors often contribute to the success of an interview:

- Knowledge and confidence of the interviewer
- Attitude of the interviewee
- Atmosphere of the interview

The knowledge of the interviewer is critical to the success of the interview. The analyst should learn as much as possible about the system before scheduling the interview. The attitude of the interviewee often shows a bias toward the questions being

Titles	Personnel to Be Interviewed	Number to Interview
Executives	Tim and Jason Richardson Connie and Crystal Richardson	All executives
Managers	Christine Slice George Serve Each store manager Mail-order manager Accounting manager	All managers
Supervisors	Store assistant managers	Selected
Clerical	Sales personnel Shipping and receiving Mail-order clerks Accounting clerks	Selected

Figure 4-2. Possible interviewees at NG&T

asked and may bias the interviewer toward the interviewee. The atmosphere of the interview should be amiable enough to promote trust, and the interviewer should attempt to make the interviewee feel like a part of the investigation.

Various forms of data gathering may be used during and after the interview. Ideally, the interviewer should tape the interviews, but if taping is not possible, he or she should transcribe the responses of the interviewee in detail. If detailed transcription would interfere with the flow, the interviewer should use shorthand transcription. At the conclusion, the interviewer should briefly summarize the data collected so that the interviewee may validate the recorded responses. Afterwards, the interviewer should immediately add detail to the data collected. He or she should then create a detailed summary of the results of individual interviews, analyze the interview data, and create a summary of the results of collective interviews. A written summary of the interview should be sent to each interviewee for his or her verification or amplification.

Whenever possible, second and third interviews should be conducted to validate previous responses and gather additional data. Subsequent interviews should be planned to get answers to previously unanswered questions and to ask questions stemming from previous interviews and questions excluded from them. Figure 4-3 illustrates the interview process.

Questionnaires

Questionnaires are useful when data needs to be gathered from a large number of people in a short period of time. For example, if the analyst wants data from 100 clerks,

1. Determine information needed.
2. Identify people to interview.
3. Call and set up appointments.
4. Send each interviewee a set of the questions you will ask.
5. Verify appointment a day before actual interview.
6. Show up on time.
7. Conduct the interview.
8. Summarize results immediately.
9. Send interviewee a summary of results.
10. Follow up as needed.

Figure 4-3. The interview process

the best way to collect it is to use a standardized questionnaire with standardized wording. The standard form allows quantification of the data collected. In addition, this method allows respondents to be candid without worrying about the analyst's response.

The main disadvantages of questionnaires are possible low response rates, the time involved in preparation and testing, and the inability to adapt questions to the respondent in real time. The problem of low response rates can be overcome in a variety of ways: paying respondents, holding a prize drawing for all who respond, following up with phone calls or letters to nonrespondents, having management emphasize the importance of responding, and having managers or key employees distribute and collect responses from people in their areas.

QUESTION CONSTRUCTION   The actual construction of the questions often determines the amount of useful data gathered by the questionnaire. Two key concerns are question content and wording.

Question content deals with the actual structure of the question. Should it be asked? Is the question of the proper scope? Can and will the respondent answer adequately? Will responses provide the data needed to help with the analysis? The answers to these questions will determine the quality of the information obtained. Note that all of the preceding questions assume that the analyst has a good idea of what information is required. This is true only if a thorough analysis of what information is required has been performed.

Generally it is first necessary to decide what information is required, draft the questions to gather that information, arrange them in a logical order, and pretest the results. Figure 4-4 summarizes this process.

1. Determine required information.
2. Design questions to gather required information.
3. Arrange questions in logical order.
4. Pretest questions.
5. Make necessary changes.
6. Repeat process until satisfied with design.

Figure 4-4. Steps in question design

QUESTION WORDING   Just as important as question construction is question wording. It is important that questions be expressed clearly, not be misleading, not be biased, and be nonthreatening in nature. Consider the following questions:

> In order to introduce CASE technology into the company, should the company hire outside consultants or retrain current employees?

> Are you generally satisfied with the information systems department, or are there some things about it you don't like?

In the first question, if the respondents do not want the company to introduce CASE, they cannot respond. In the second question, the respondents may agree with both alternatives and have trouble choosing between them. It should not be possible to agree with more than one alternative in a question. The two sample questions could be reworded like this:

> Should we introduce CASE technology into our company? Why or why not? If we should, should we hire outside consultants or retrain current employees to help with CASE training?

> Are you generally satisfied with the information systems department? Why or why not? Though you may be satisfied, are there things about it that could be improved, and if so, why?

Disk-by-Mail (DBM) Surveys

A relatively new method of obtaining information from users is disk-by-mail (DBM) surveys. Instead of receiving the standard hard-copy questionnaire, respondents are sent a disk with the questionnaire on it. They are then able to sit down at their computers and answer the questions.

The main advantage of DBM surveys is their automatic electronic branching to the appropriate question that follows when an alternative is chosen. The respondent does not have to determine what question to answer next. Another advantage is that responses can be edited by the respondent on-line, resulting in cleaner data. Finally, DBM surveys minimize the data entry costs for large studies.

Of course, proper problem identification and good survey question design are still necessary. In addition, the analyst must be certain that respondents have computers and are receptive to using them.

The use of electronic mail (E-mail) in business makes DBM even more advantageous and useful during A&D. E-mail systems set up mailboxes for people on a network to receive messages from other people on the network. These messages could be the questions from an analyst to users regarding the system under investigation.

Archival Data Sources

Archival data is primarily used to obtain, at the origin, background information that influences the firm's operations. It also provides information about the maintenance of operations. Historical data is gathered and analyzed regarding the origins of the system, conditions and decisions affecting it, and modifications to it. The main problem with archival data is that it is often poorly updated and may reflect only what formerly existed, not what currently exists. As a result, the analyst should determine whether archival data does in fact reflect current conditions. For example, in 1973 one of the authors worked on a system in which archival data indicated that a certain file had 50-character logical records. The program that updated that file was modified, but the report generated from the file was a garbled mess. Further investigation revealed that the records in the file were actually 100 characters long. The problem was easy to correct, but the analyst's credibility had already been damaged. Project teams can look equally foolish if they do not validate the integrity of archival data. This data comes from the following sources:

- Source documents
- Reports
- File structures
- User interfaces
- System processing
- Communication channels

Source Documents

Data is gathered from archival sources such as source documents and data reporting. The data normally enters the business through a source document. A sales invoice is a good example of a source document. A customer places an order for given items on a sales invoice, the order is processed, and eventually the items are shipped. A clear understanding of the sources through which data enters the business gives the analyst insight into the origins of the firm's business operations and keeps the investigation well grounded in the ways data and operations are related.

Systems developed in recent years use new ways of capturing source data. Terminal and desktop computer screens are formatted to display video versions of earlier hard-copy source documents, and data is keyed to the same locations on the screen where it was previously written on hard-copy documents. In many systems, bar codes are scanned to give the system the needed information without the clerk's ever pressing a key.

Screen displays often allow users to select from a menu (list) of options for data entry. The data entered using these methods is immediately stored on external storage media such as tapes or disks, and may also be processed as the screen entry is transmitted to the computer system. Archival data sources also exist for screen-formatted source documents.

Reports

Archival data sources also describe the origins and purposes of both hard-copy reports and screen-formatted reports. Hard-copy reports typically result from batch processing, whereas screen-formatted reporting is associated with more interactive systems such as on-line transaction processing, decision support systems, and expert systems. Data reports provide a "snapshot" of the stored data at a given instant and reflect conditions that are current at that instant.

Archival data on a report typically specifies the purpose of the report, how often it is generated, what it contains, and who receives it. It may also specify the source of the data that a report contains. Archival records regarding reports give the analyst an understanding of the user's expectations about output that is critical to correcting problems in the system.

File Structures

The company's file structures are usually available from archival data. These file layouts usually contain information indicating the names of the files, the storage media, the file organization, the field on which the records in a file are sequenced, operating command specifications necessary for system programs, field arrangements, and field descriptions. A careful scrutiny of archival data about file layouts helps the analyst understand how data is stored for processing by the system.

User Interfaces

Archival data also exists for **user interfaces**, sometimes called human/machine interfaces, which are the means provided for user access to software systems and stored data. The user interface is often the most important part of the system from the user's standpoint. Often an entire system is judged by the quality of this interface. The interface should be flexible enough to allow users the freedom of the interaction they desire. It should also be convenient to use and easy to understand. Archival data about user interfaces helps the analyst to understand the many ways in which users employ the system.

System Processing

One of the most important kinds of archival data concerns the processing performed by the system. This information usually includes what the system does, how it performs those operations, what the procedures act upon, and the possible results of processing. It also often includes written documentation concerning the procedural steps performed in system processing. The analyst must have a thorough understanding of system processing in order to design valid solutions to problems. A walk through the archival data about processing operations is a good way to obtain this understanding.

Data retained in archives from the original development of the system under scrutiny, along with a properly updated maintenance log, is also extremely important to the analyst. This data provides an understanding of the characteristics that the system is *supposed* to have and what it is *supposed* to do. Bear in mind that the archival documentation does not necessarily paint a true picture of the system. If it is not properly updated, it may convey an entirely different picture from the one that actually exists.

Communication Channels

The final piece of archival information that may be available is documentation concerning communication channels used by personnel and by the system. These records typically identify the components of systems that use communication channels, the hardware and software required to employ these channels, and the procedures for employing them. The problems observed in distributed, remote job-entry, time-sharing, and interactive systems often involve the performance of the communication channels. As a result, the investigation team should acquire as much information about these channels as security permits.

Personal Observation

Data collection by personal observation means that the analyst directly watches the situation under study. This can range from watching a clerk check an invoice to physically following the work flow through the office. It may often be useful for the analyst to do the actual work. Personal observation is advantageous in that the analyst can see firsthand how a document is handled, how data flows through the system, and where bottlenecks occur. This is an especially useful method when existing documentation does not actually represent the work flow or the processing of documents.

The main disadvantage of the observation technique is the reaction of people to being observed: they often do not behave in the same manner as when no one is watching (remember the Hawthorne effect). The analyst's experience in working with people and putting them at ease can help prevent this problem.

Personal observation of the work at NG&T is essential. Documentation is virtually nonexistent, so the analyst must observe the work as it is being done. Possible areas to observe include mail-order entry, shipping, and handling customer inquiries.

On-Site Work Sampling

The final method of data collection, on-site work sampling, is the process of gathering information about the whole operation by studying only a subset of it. For example, if the analyst needs to know the approximate error rate on customer bills, instead of looking at all the bills, he or she can select a certain percentage to examine and make an inference from the sample about the error rate for the entire set.

Work sampling is particularly appropriate when a large amount of data is present. It would be impossible to look at all the data, so only a portion of it is analyzed. This method requires statistical sampling. Most analysts have been introduced to the appropriate formulas in their college statistics courses. A quick review should refresh their memories. In addition, numerous microcomputer statistical packages, such as SPSS, SAS, and MINITAB, are available to help with the formulas and calculations.

JOINT APPLICATION DESIGN (JAD)

Joint application design (JAD) consists of joint interactive sessions between users and IS personnel for the purpose of identifying user requirements through modeling the business and information systems. A JAD session may cover a single day or several days. The need for the interactions between the many participants and the availability of participants dictate the duration of the session. A JAD session involves a detailed agenda, with visual aids (often technology-based), a facilitator who moderates the session, a scribe who records pertinent information, and users who supply the information and review the specifications entered by the scribe. Companies that use JAD sessions (JADs) typically conduct a number of JADs on a periodic basis over the life span of a project. For long projects, a JAD session may be conducted every two to three months. These sessions produce a final document that includes definitions of data objects and properties, activity work flow, and user interfaces and reports, and a clear picture of business activities and support provided by information systems.

JADs help acquire the information that would normally be gathered through interviews with users or questionnaires distributed to them. JADs may replace or supplement individual interviews and questionnaires as a way to acquire information during analysis. They can also be used to create and review the business and information systems models that are required for the development of a system that will satisfy user information needs. Thus JADs aid in identification of user requirements, agreement on the requirements, and agreement on a system design that satisfies them.

Between JADs, the project team refines the graphs drawn and the text descriptions that conform to previous suggestions by the users for presentation at the next JAD session. At the end of the final JAD session, participants sign a document that confirms their agreement with the requirements and supporting documentation resulting from the JAD sessions. Striving to achieve these objectives improves the entire A&D process and contributes to the overall quality of project completion and developed systems.

Benefits of JADs

JADs provide a simple, structured technique that saves time in accumulating data from users, depicting the business and information system, and arriving at a set of collective user requirements. It helps consolidate months of A&D meetings, follow-up meetings, data acquisition and review meetings, individual and collective interviews, and telephone-call meetings into individual structured workshops.

JADs help users feel that they have more impact on the project. They get users involved in A&D projects and encourage ongoing involvement throughout the process. This participation often leads to users assuming ownership of the project and becoming more committed to its success. JADs help analysts understand what users face in the business and how an information system can aid them within that scenario. Capturing and documenting information in joint sessions improves communication between users and analysts, and increases their joint understanding of the business and information system. JADs inspire users with a greater sense of belonging to the project and help make them and IS personnel into a more cohesive team.

JADs help identify important issues and the people responsible for resolving them. They offer a way to collectively answer questions and address issues that require decisions or further investigation. The process of setting up a JAD session also helps identify the people who have the knowledge that is needed as input to the A&D project.

JADs facilitate the evolutionary process of defining the business and information systems models of the firm. They provide systematic ways to track user requirements as the analyst progresses through the phases of the project life cycle. The sessions facilitate the transition between project life cycle phases. JADs help to better integrate the outputs from project phases, where output from one phase often constitutes input to the next phase.

JAD Participants

The nature of JADs requires participation by users as well as IS personnel. Participants come from different parts of the organization and hold different positions, but they should all be considered equal participants. Some systems personnel find it difficult to accept users as equal participants in system development. These IS personnel often have a very narrow view regarding user expertise—a view that prevents them from obtaining all of the data needed during analysis and design. IS personnel should view user participation as a way of sharing the responsibility for accuracy in requirements, and, more than likely, a way to reduce errors. Users with a more progressive orientation toward using information systems readily adapt to becoming JAD participants; others require more coaxing to become participants and more coaching during initial sessions.

JAD participants are typically involved in building the application from the start of the project to its finish. Those who need to make decisions should be active participants in the JAD sessions. They are needed to help define work flow, data objects, and their properties, processes that act on those data objects, user interfaces, and actions they want the system to perform on data. Participants should work together in an organized forum until everyone arrives at a consensus or compromise agreement regarding topics of investigation and review. Responsibility should be shared among the different participants to produce consensus regarding the deliverables from JADs; that is, the business and IS models on which to base the information system. The major participants in JADs are functional area managers (including the executive sponsor), functional area clerical personnel, key functional area technical personnel, the facilitator, JAD/CASE specialists, scribes, IS managers, and systems personnel.

The Role of Functional Area Managers in JADs

Managers from functional areas who affect or are affected by the A&D project are often chosen to participate in JADs because of their wider perspective on the organization. They may be strategic, tactical, or operational managers with responsibility for the competitive, functional, and operational health of the organization. Their perspective aids in identifying what is done in those areas of business, how those activities aid in the harmony of the organization, and what effect satisfying information needs may have on those areas. They help ensure that the results of JADs will support the long-term goals of the organization.

A particular functional area manager, often called the **executive sponsor**, provides the executive support that is needed for any major organization change. The executive sponsor must have the authority to mandate participation and be willing to make or enforce policies that ensure greater success during JADs. Though the executive sponsor often participates only minimally in the actual JAD sessions, he or she provides crucial support and commitment to the whole process. The endorsement of the JAD process by the executive sponsor encourages the participation and commitment of the appropriate business personnel. Their encouragement, in turn, helps sustain the momentum provided by JADs to ensure complete attendance at all JADs and implementation of the results of the sessions. The executive sponsor often appears at the kickoff session to enumerate the purposes of the JAD sessions and to motivate participants.

The Role of Clerical Personnel in JADs

Clerical personnel from the areas that affect the project become participants in JADs. These employees should be familiar with the area of business under study and the information systems that currently serve that area. They provide a staff person's view of the whole process, information about the functioning of the business, and suggestions regarding their information needs. They also review the accuracy and completeness of business and information systems models, as well as the accuracy and completeness of the ever-increasing set of user requirements. These participants must live with the results of the project on a daily basis; therefore, they should take an active interest in the specifications resulting from JADs.

The Role of Key Technical Personnel in JADs

The functional area technical personnel provide input on the technology in place or needed to aid the system. Many different types of technology are employed by users in fulfilling their job responsibilities. The way these technologies are used may influence the way to develop an IS. By having technical personnel from business as JAD participants, many clashes of information technology and these other technologies can be foreseen and addressed. A participant from this category may not be required if existing technologies that are well known to JAD participants are to be used.

The Role of Facilitators in JADs

Facilitators help maintain an atmosphere free of hostility or intimidation. They control the meeting, maintaining adherence to the agenda and keeping the focus on important issues (by not permitting issues outside of the project to interfere with the process). Facilitators lead people from different parts of the organization and of mixed rank to a consensus of thought regarding the business and the A&D project. They must draw everyone into becoming more active members during JAD sessions, and must be persistent in working toward consensus. They also act as consultants to project leaders and project team members. Facilitators also create the JAD workshop structure and set the atmosphere. Typically, they are not part of the project team. Their detachment from the project team helps them remain objective. Facilitators should be well trained in technical, organizational, and behavioral processes that contribute to the success of the JAD.

The Role of JAD/CASE Experts in JADs

JAD/CASE experts provide expert information on all aspects of the JAD process, CASE tools, and other technologies before and during JADs. They help those conducting the session before it begins, by compiling and distributing the agenda and related documentation. They aid in the smooth transition from one topic to the next during the JAD. They help with administration of the JAD when user contributions seem to falter. To help with the various technologies used in the JAD sessions, including CASE systems, they should be experts in these technologies, as well as being qualified analysts. As specialists, they are not actually involved in decision making during JADs, but are there to ensure that all knowledge and decisions become part of the documentation delivered by JADs.

The Role of Scribes in JADs

Scribes record the information acquired from users that composes the user requirements, business models, and information system models. Several scribes working on networked desktop computers provide the most comprehensive support. As a user responds to questions, makes comments, asks questions, reviews documentation, and approves certain portions of user requirements and models, scribes record the information and create drawings that depict various aspects of the business and information system described by the user. This information is often displayed over a large-screen video connected to the computer of the scribe and may include the display of various graphs created by using CASE systems.

The Role of IS Managers and Personnel in JADs

IS managers provide a show of support for the project team and contribute their expertise in areas covered during JADs. By being present at the kickoff meeting, they solidify managerial support and commitment to the JAD process for users and IS personnel. Their expertise and their more holistic view of the information systems contribute to the way IS will support current and future user information needs. Their role is one of quality assurance regarding the user requirements and the system that result from JAD sessions. They help keep the JAD facilitator apprised of organizational issues that may affect the A&D project. They also help with project feasibility analysis.

The IS personnel who participate during and between JAD sessions are the project team members. During JADs, they support the project leader in discussions regarding A&D documentation developed by them. They answer many questions during JADs, and also ask many questions that help clarify confusing areas of the business and system requirements requested by users. Between JADs, they help refine the documentation resulting from the JADs, and enhance certain aspects of the business and information systems models and user requirements. These activities help ensure the success of the next JAD session.

Preparing for and Conducting JADs

Companies that adopt the JAD technique often sponsor professional training for the participants who must manage the JADs. Upon receiving professional training and beginning to use JADs, these participants set up rules for conducting JAD sessions. The following general rules, which are adapted from Andrews and Leventhal (1993), help make JAD sessions more productive:

- The project leader and facilitator develop the JAD agenda.
- The agenda is distributed to all participants before the JAD session.
- Supporting documentation is gathered and distributed to participants before the JAD session.
- A facilitator controls the agenda.
- JADs are conducted from the perspective of the user.
- Functional area managers show endorsement of the JAD technique and encourage attendance by functional personnel.
- Everyone participates.
- One participant at a time speaks, without interruptions.
- Participant availability and the need for participant interaction dictate the length of the session.
- Technology is incorporated into JADs to produce more formal results and aid in review.
- Several JAD sessions may be required over the project life span.
- JAD sessions continue until a consensus is reached.

A JAD session consists of nontraditional meetings that extend over three to five days. Group dynamics provide constant feedback and stimulate creativity during this period. JADs make these meetings less frequent, more structured, and more productive than traditional meetings. An agenda provides structure for the JAD session under the direction of the JAD leader.

Andrews and Leventhal describe the JAD structure as having three different phases. The following three sections synopsize the activities they recommend.

Preworkshop Activities

Before the JAD session, the scope of the JAD should be identified, all background information accumulated, the structure of the JAD defined, the goals of the JAD defined, all documentation created, and the participants selected and educated regarding the process and their participation. The project leader should make sure appropriate documentation is distributed, usually three to five days before the JAD, to ensure that participants have time to prepare for the review. This documentation should include background information on the project, a concise statement of the results of the current phase, the importance of participation by users, the time and place of the session, and the agenda of the JAD.

Background information typically consists of archive data, but it may include responses to questionnaires and preliminary interviews, personal observations, and the knowledge and experience of the analysts—the data acquisition methods described earlier in this chapter. The actual JAD session may be used for collective verification of this information by all participants.

To prevent confusion, no technical jargon should be used in the distributed documentation. The documentation should also include statements indicating how the system may affect users.

Workshop Activities

Typically, bonds quickly form between participants as a result of isolating them from their normal work environments. The resulting social setting creates participant camaraderie. All participants in the JAD session typically become impelled to solve the problem or to achieve the objective of the project. The involvement of participants in the JAD process gives them a vested interest in the results, the source of true commitment.

The review should include time to respond to questions from participants in the review. The question-and-answer session permits users to express their concerns regarding any aspect of the project. Resolving user questions during the presentation greatly diminishes the likelihood of misinterpretations.

Question-and-answer periods during JADs should follow the guidelines specified in the sections of this chapter on personal interviews and questionnaires. During these periods, the analyst or facilitator should adopt the appropriate style and type of questions, encourage more knowledgeable participants to respond and generally to be open to sharing their knowledge, inspire an atmosphere of collaboration, keep respondents relaxed, and move swiftly through all the questions. Scribes should record all questions and responses, which should then be reviewed, checked for accuracy, and made more clear and comprehensive by the participants. The information obtained should be quickly transcribed into appropriate places in the ever-growing set of user requirements and system specifications. This transcription could be made to business and information system models, such as those described in Chapter 2.

During JADs, the models described in Chapter 2 can be built as participants describe their work environments and information needs. The entity/relationship diagram (E/RD) and data flow diagram (DFD) modeling methods can be used to create data and process models as participants interact. These models can be used as the focal points of communication between participants and verified for accuracy and completeness in real time. Prototypes can be built and reviewed by participants in real time to determine whether they provide the capabilities and data access desired by users. JADs can also be used to review and verify data models, process models, and prototypes that were created by analysts during preworkshop activities. Chapters 5, 6, and 7 describe the use of these methods during JADs in greater detail.

JAD ROOM LAYOUT AND TECHNOLOGY   The physical setting and technology are important ingredients in JAD sessions. A recent hardware development helps project teams display user requirement specifications more clearly to groups of users while creating and modifying them. This development is a color LCD screen panel attached to a desktop computer and placed on a standard overhead projector. When a computer is attached to this device, the information displayed on the computer screen is also displayed on the panel screen and projected on a white screen large enough for everyone to see. The project team can therefore navigate through analysis specifications while all JAD participants view an enlargement of the computer screen display.

CASE systems are often used during JADs to create data and process models using portions of the methodology. Using CASE systems to create these models helps obtain immediate feedback from users regarding their accuracy and completeness. The

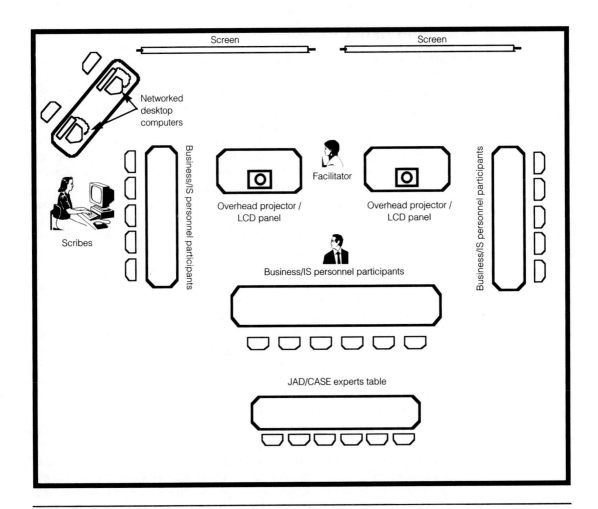

Figure 4-5. JAD room layout and participant positions

display of these models on an LCD panel helps participants review and analyze them.

The JAD meeting room should be laid out in a U-shape, with tables arranged in such a way that all participants can see the front of the room where the projector screen and possibly a drawing easel are located. Figure 4-5 illustrates the layout of the JAD room and the positions of various participants. The JAD room layout may also include rooms for breakout sessions for participants of like interests to meet in private during the JAD workshop. These rooms provide places for more informal communication and a change of scenery for participants confined for three to five days.

Postworkshop Activities

Postworkshop activities validate JAD results, construct the final documents that describe these results, and help with the transition to post-JAD activities. Complex user requirement specifications that result from JADs must be thoroughly validated for accuracy and completeness. During analysis of these requirements, better and better documentation of requirements is achieved.

The postworkshop verifies the results of the previous JAD session and sets the guidelines regarding what needs to be done to provide more complete specifications for the next JAD session. The process is then repeated for the next JAD session, and for any subsequent JAD sessions. Through this iterative process of pre/current/post-workshops, the project team steadily produces more accurate and comprehensive business and IS models and user requirements. The cyclical nature and the goal of continuous improvement instilled in JAD participants regarding these specifications help improve the entire A&D process.

JADs may continue at different intervals throughout the life cycle of an A&D project. Various modeling methods that are part of the methodology described at the end of Chapter 2 may be used during JAD sessions, with CASE systems used to make them operational during and between JADs. Keep in mind that the models created using the modeling methods described in the next few chapters may be created and reviewed in JAD sessions with IS personnel and users, with the help of CASE systems and visual-aid technology.

REVIEW

The procedures involved in identifying problems in the analysis phase include becoming familiar with the types of systems and their associated problems. Analysis begins with the IS business support systems: the management information system (MIS), the decision support system (DSS), the management support system (MSS), and the transaction processing system (TPS). Problems such as inadequate data, poorly designed user interfaces, and response-time difficulties are frequently associated with these systems, along with problems specific to the functions of particular systems. Investigation of these problems is a joint effort by the IS department and users in the functional area of the firm. The systems personnel must have authorization to conduct the project before they can determine its feasibility and plan for a thorough investigation. Several common objectives typically emerge from a study of system problems. Some of these are increasing the reliability of the system and the data, increasing the efficiency of the system, reducing costs, improving service, and gaining advantages over competitors.

Although the analyst should be aware that a perceived problem may not be a problem at all, or that the source of a problem can be camouflaged by misleading "symptoms," once it is determined that a problem exists, it can frequently be classified as one of four types: omission, modification, deletion, or addition. The problem domain must also be taken into account in deciding how to control the scope of the investigation. Once the investigation begins, the primary methods of data collection are user interviews and questionnaires, archival data searches, personal observation, and on-site work sampling.

Joint application development (JAD) is a modern technique for conducting problem identification, business modeling, and other phases of the system development life cycle in an intensive session involving participants from relevant areas of the firm. Functional area managers, clerical personnel, technical personnel, JAD/CASE specialists, and IS managers and personnel join with a facilitator and scribes to arrive at a consensus regarding topics under investigation and review.

Readers are encouraged to apply the principles of analysis presented in this chapter in the investigation of an actual system in order to gain experience with the method for analyzing system problems.

QUESTIONS

1. Clearly distinguish among MIS, DSS, MSS, and TPS.

2. Provide examples of inadequate or invalid modeling from the areas of marketing, production, and finance for a company in your vicinity.

3. Provide examples of inadequate or invalid data sources from three functional areas of your choice for a company in your vicinity.

4. Talk with a variety of users, either on campus or in the business community, then explain the importance of an adequately designed user interface; illustrate one and explain its effects on the business.

5. Why and how may it be found that a problem does not exist within the firm's information system?

6. Explain how the real problem may be camouflaged and not easily identified.

7. Identify the four major categories of problems associated with system projects and provide examples of each.

8. For a company in your vicinity, explain how it had problems of each of the four types.

9. Explain what the domain is and how the terms *scope*, *subjects*, and *objects* contribute to understanding the problem domain.

10. For a company in your vicinity, describe the domain of one of its projects; explain the scope, subjects, and objects of this project.

11. Provide examples of each of the major objectives of a typical project.

12. For a company in your vicinity, identify and explain the objectives of one of its projects.

13. List the six data collection methods and explain the advantages and disadvantages of each.

14. List all possible sources of archival data and the information that may be obtained from each source.

15. For a company in your vicinity, obtain copies of correct and incorrect archival data.

16. Define the user interface and explain why it is so important to users.

17. Explain why personal interviews and questionnaires are called reactive data sources.

18. List the similarities and differences between personal interviews and questionnaires as data sources.

19. Distinguish between close- and open-end questions and give examples of each.

20. For a company in your vicinity, obtain a copy of a questionnaire that contains both close- and open-end questions.

21. When is an interview an effective data-gathering tool?

22. What are the three major factors that contribute to the success of an interview and why are they important?

23. Why are proper question construction and wording so important in questionnaire design?

24. Select someone either on or off campus to interview about a computerized information system he or she is currently using. Prepare a report of your findings.

25. Explain the advantages and disadvantages of using personal observation for data collection.

26. For a company in your vicinity, collect data by the personal observation method concerning a problem it is currently experiencing. Prepare a report of your findings.

27. Explain what is involved in on-site work sampling and when it is appropriate for data collection.

28. For a company in your vicinity, obtain a copy of on-site work sampling data that either indicates a problem or shows that a suspected problem does not actually exist. Prepare a report of your findings.

29. Define JAD and explain the purpose for it, why it appears necessary, how it is conducted, who participates and why, and what should be the final deliverable.

30. List and explain the benefits of conducting JADs. Could these benefits be achieved by other methods?

31. Distinguish among all of the different types of JAD participants — who they are, why they are participants, what they contribute, how they could benefit from the experience, and what impact they have on user requirements gathered during JADs.

32. Explain how each item in the list of items to consider contributes to preparing and conducting JADs.

33. Distinguish between preworkshop, workshop, and postworkshop activities for conducting JADs.

34. Explain how the JAD room layout and various forms of technology contribute to JADs.

35. For a company in your vicinity, seek permission and become an observer during one of its JAD sessions. Prepare a report of your experience that explains what happened during the JAD session.

EXERCISES

1. Based on the summary of the NG&T case in Chapter 3, prepare a problem statement for NG&T management.

2. Prepare a list of constraints applicable to a systems development project at NG&T.

3. Prepare a list of specific objectives that a new system must satisfy at NG&T.

4. Design a questionnaire suitable for collecting the needed data for a systems development project at NG&T.

5. Determine who the design team will need to interview at NG&T, and design the questions that you will ask.

6. For the NG&T case, create a JAD prospectus that lists the participants and why they should attend, what you expect the JADs to produce, how and where to conduct the JAD, what preworkshop activities to perform, and what areas to discuss in the JADs.

7. Repeat exercise 6 for your class project.

SELECTED REFERENCES

Alreck, P. L. and R. B. Settle. 1993. *The Survey Research Handbook*. Homewood, IL: Richard Irwin.

Andrews, D. and S. Lind. 1985. "User-Driven Design: A New Way to Computer Creativity." *The Office* (May).

Andrews, D. C. and N. S. Leventhal. 1993. *Fusion Integrating IE, CASE and JAD: A Handbook for Reengineering the Systems Organization*. Englewood Cliffs, N.J.: Prentice-Hall.

Bardoudi, J. J., M. H. Olson, and B. Ives. 1986. "An Empirical Study of the Impact of User Involvement on System Usage and User Satisfaction." *Communications of the ACM* 29, no. 3 (March).

Barki, H. and J. Hartwick. 1989. "Rethinking the Concept of User Involvement." *MIS Quarterly* 13, no. 1 (March).

Baronas, A. K., M. R. Louis, and R. Merly. 1988. "Restoring a Sense of Control During Implementation: How User Involvement Leads to System Acceptance." *MIS Quarterly* 12, no. 1 (March).

"Developing High Quality Systems Faster." 1986. *EDP Analyzer* 24, no. 6 (June).

Emory, W. C. 1985. *Business Research Methods*. Homewood, IL: Richard Irwin.

Fowler, F. J. 1988. *Survey Research Methods*. Newbury Park, CA: Sage Publications.

Franz, C. and D. Robey. 1986. "Organizational Context, User Involvement, and the Usefulness of Information Systems." *Decision Sciences 17*, no. 3 (Summer).

Gill, A. 1987. "Setting Up Your Own Group Design Session." *Datamation* (November 15).

——. 1988. "Accelerated Design Techniques: Methods Without Madness." *Best's Review* (Life and Health) 88, no. 11 (March).

Horten, L. 1990. "Disk-Based Surveys: New Way to Pick Your Brain." *Software Magazine* 10, no. 2 (February): 76–77.

Ives, B. and M. H. Olson. 1984. "User Involvement and MIS Success: A Review of Research." *Management Science* 30, no. 5.

Kerr, J. 1989. "Systems Design: Users in the Hot Seat." *Computerworld* 23, no. 8 (February 27).

Leavitt, D. 1987. "Team Techniques in System Development." *Datamation* (November 15).

Rush, G. 1984. "JAD Project Aids Design." *Computerworld* (December 24).

——. 1985. "A Fast Way to Define Systems Requirements." *Computerworld* (October 7).

Sharpe, J. 1986. "Getting the User Involved in Systems Design." *National Underwriter* (February 21).

Tait, P. and I. Vessey. 1988. "The Effect of User Involvement on System Success: A Contingency Approach." *MIS Quarterly* 12, no. 1 (March).

White, K. B. and R. Leifer. 1986. "Information Systems Development Success: Perspectives from Project Team Participants." *MIS Quarterly* 10, no. 3 (September).

CHAPTER 5

Analyzing the Problem Using Data Modeling Methods

OVERVIEW

This chapter shows you how to use data modeling methods—in particular, the entity/relationship (E/R) modeling method—to document user requirements as they relate to business objects. It also explains how an analyst uses computer-aided software engineering (CASE) to employ this modeling method. Through discussions and real-world examples, this chapter gives you the working knowledge you need to model business objects effectively by:

- Defining the basic components of a data model: business objects and data types

- Describing the basic premises of business modeling and how they affect planning and maintenance of the models

- Explaining how the entity/relationship (E/R) modeling method is used to model business objects and data types

- Describing the components of an entity/relationship diagram (E/RD)

- Explaining how the design dictionary recording method works

- Modeling the NG&T case based on the text methodology

- Describing CASE data modeling and documentation

172

KEY TERMS

Abstraction

Alias

Application data view

Computer-Aided Planning (CAP)

Data classes

Data type

Design dictionary

Domain

Domain definition

Entity

Entity key property

Entity property

Entity type description

E/R expression

Functional primitive E/R expressions

Generalized data type

Graph explosion

Logical data structure (LDS)

Mass logical data structures (M-LDSs)

Mass physical data structure (M-PDS)

Naming conventions

Object type

Physical data structures (PDSs)

Relationship

Subject area

Sufficiency requirement

The business model and modeling methods shown in Figure 2-42 of Chapter 2 illustrated the relationships among life cycle phases, logical and physical design, and modeling methods. You learned in Chapter 3 that analysis and logical design involves developing design specifications that logically meet users' requirements for the proposed system. Chapter 4 explained how to gather information from users and other sources about the problems being faced in order to better understand them and to develop user requirements based on that understanding. Figure 5-1 shows the areas of the enterprise/methodology model on which this chapter focuses its attention. In this portion of the pyramid, the conceptual and logical levels indicate how entity/relationship diagrams (E/RDs) and entity type descriptions are used to identify and describe the types of business objects and their properties.

In the portion of the pyramid emphasized in Figure 5-1, objects of importance to the business are identified and described. Also described are the relationships between objects and the cardinality of those relationships. Remember that cardinality means how many of one type of business object are related to another type of business object, and vice versa.

MODELING BUSINESS OBJECTS

Users need information to understand what they face and how their jobs are affected by current conditions. This information can be obtained by knowing the characteris-

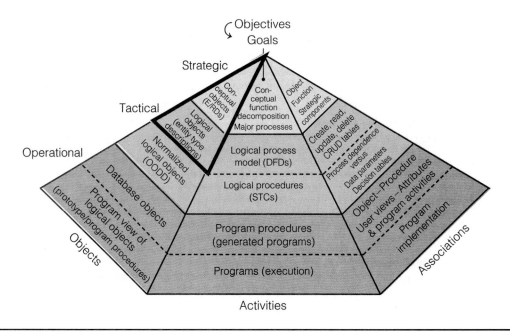

Figure 5-1. Enterprise/methodology model focus of Chapter 5

tics of business objects examined in their proper context. Users need to know the following about business objects:

- What they are
- What their characteristics are
- How they might affect user's job functions
- How they are related to other business objects

Users' "need to know" can frequently be satisfied just by making them aware of various characteristics (also known as properties or attributes) of business objects. For example, knowing a CUSTOMER object's current data values for its corresponding CREDIT_LIMIT and CREDIT_BALANCE properties and an ORDER_TOTAL property for a PURCHASE_ORDER can help a salesclerk determine whether the customer can actually purchase this order item. Other user information needs may require actions to be performed on the properties of these business objects. For example, the average purchase amount and the number of purchases for a particular customer may help an accounts clerk determine a customer rating for use within the firm. To determine this average and number of purchases, the accounts clerk would process all PURCHASE_ORDER objects for that customer for a given period.

In Chapter 2, business objects were defined as those objects internal or external to the business that are made up of the people (or organizations), places, things, events, and concepts about which it is important to retain information. For the purpose of brevity, this text uses *object* interchangeably with *business object* or *data object*. These objects represent something identifiable in the real world that is independent of other objects and possesses some property or set of properties that uniquely identifies it.

Businesses typically have hundreds, and sometimes thousands, of different types of business objects. Five different categories of object types exist that need to be identified and described in order to help satisfy users' information needs:

Object Type	Example
Person	An administrator, teacher, or student
Place	The location of agencies or departments
Thing	A building, machine, or production item
Event	Enrolling in a seminar or college course
Concept	A belief of some kind

For each category, many different types of business objects may exist. For example, an employee, a customer, and a supplier contact person are all examples of the person object type about which a business may want to retain data. Figure 5-2 illustrates the distinctions among the five categories of business objects. (This figure also appeared in Chapter 2 as Figure 2-1.)

People

Places

Things

Events

Concepts

Figure 5-2. Categories of business objects

Modeling real-world objects important to a business requires a sufficiently abstract and powerful method for understanding them and understanding the relationships between them and other business objects. As you learned in Chapter 2, a data model is an abstract model that symbolizes real-world data objects. Data modeling helps organize data about object types so that they more closely represent those real-world objects. Data models help us grasp part of the meaning of types of business objects and act as an aid to understanding real-world data objects. Data modeling is first performed during the analysis phase and then in the design phase of the project life cycle. Logical design specifications, produced using data modeling methods, form the basis for creating physical design specifications.

A **data type** or **object type** defines data objects together with their important properties and helps define the operations that can be performed on those objects and properties. A data type provides a general set of data values that help classify a particular collection of real-world objects. An example of a data type might be the EMPLOYEE data type for a collection of real-world employees at a company. Here, the EMPLOYEE data type would consist of various data values for particular employees. These data values correspond to the characteristics of the EMPLOYEE data type and help indicate what those characteristics are. For example, our names, Michael Gibson and Cary Hughes, are data values for the NAME characteristic that all EMPLOYEE data objects have in personnel data at our respective universities. Hereafter, the term *property* will be substituted for *characteristic* with regard to traits of a business object.

A business typically has many different data types for each category of business objects. To more completely understand the business, it is important to identify each different data type for each business object category (persons, places, things, events, concepts) and the properties of those data types important enough to retain data for. For the person category, for example, *customer, employee, business contact person,* and *governmental agent* are four different data types for which the firm may need to retain data. The data to be retained may be similar—the same properties, for example, such as name, address, and so on—or different, such as CREDIT_BALANCE for a customer, WAGE for an employee, and so on. Figure 5-3 shows how many different data types for a business object category can be identified as individually important to the business.

A data model for a business consists of the collection of all data types for all business object categories for that business, properties of those data types, and relationships between those data types consistent with the relationships between real-world business objects in the data type. A data model also defines the rules that govern the way to structure data in order to provide effective ways to collect and access it. However, data structures do not provide a way to specify how to use data or interpret its meaning. The meaning or interpretation is subjectively determined by users and by what the data values mean to them. Processing the data in structures helps provide the user with meaning concerning the data; defining data types as structures helps categorize different business objects for easier processing.

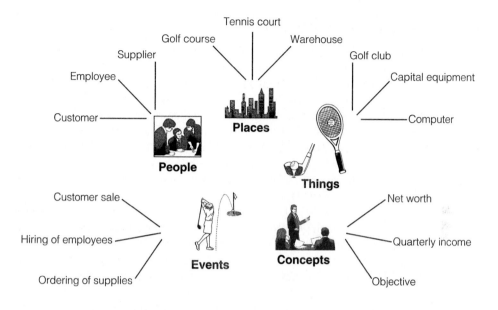

Figure 5-3. Multiple data types for business object categories

BASIC PREMISES OF BUSINESS MODELING

The logical representation of data types is a cornerstone of business modeling. The five basic premises of good business modeling are as follows:

- The center of modern information systems is data supported by data type identification.
- The types of business data objects do not change very much (data values change constantly, but not the types or structures of data objects).
- Business functions change more frequently than do data objects, but they still do not change much.
- Business processes change much more frequently than do functions, but even these activities may remain the same for long periods of time.
- Information systems procedures (*how* specifications) that use data objects change frequently.

Data Types Rarely Change

Companies that approach data modeling rigorously and correctly may not need to change their data models very much over the years. Business objects remain fairly stable for an organization that remains in the same business and undergoes few major external disturbances. Which data types exist and the important properties of those data types typically do not change for a firm that remains in the same business. For example, the EMPLOYEE data type is an important data type to retain data about, and its properties, such as NAME, ADDRESS, and NEXT_OF_KIN, are likely to remain the same. What changes are the different employees that the EMPLOYEE data type represents, and possibly different *values* for some of the properties of a particular employee, such as ADDRESS.

For the types of objects to change, something rather drastic must change in the business. For example, if a company switches from manufacturing products that are sold to distributors within a state to distributing products manufactured by other companies in other states, the data types with which the company interacts are likely to change. This company may have to interact with new governmental agencies that track interstate commerce, for example. It may have to deal with retailers directly, rather than with distributors of their products. It will probably also have to deal with manufacturers of the products it distributes. All of these new data types with which the company now interacts will lead to retaining data on additional data types; thus, its data model will change.

Since a firm's data types rarely change, the data types and properties can be used to represent the objects of importance to the business for many years. Furthermore, since much of the users' information needs can be satisfied by knowing the data values for various properties of real-world objects for a data type, data is central to satisfying user information needs. For example, just knowing that a customer has outstanding back-payments due and several delinquencies recorded in his CUSTOMER_STATUS business object may help a clerk to decide whether or not to permit that customer to purchase another item and charge it to his or her account.

Functions Rarely Change

Functions were defined in Chapter 2 as the major ongoing activities and subactivities that support the organization's overall mission. These functions indicate only *what* the organization does and *why*, not *how*. When organizational activities are modeled at a very high level with only an orientation of what ongoing activities the organization performs and why it performs them, that portion of the activity model is likely to remain the same for many years. Organizational functions include such activities as distributing products, researching product manufacturing, and researching new markets. Each of these major functions can be decomposed into subfunctions that will also be ongoing and stable.

A function decomposition is a relatively simple diagram to create, because the only objective is to determine what the ongoing activities of the organization are.

Most upper managers in the firm know what major functions the firm performs, as well as their subfunctions. Thus interviews with these managers can help the analyst create a function decomposition in a fairly short time. A function decomposition diagram was depicted in Figure 2-13 of Chapter 2.

When an organization makes major strategic directional changes, some of its functions and/or subfunctions are likely to change. For example, when an organization moves from having central warehousing of its manufacturing products to having warehouses in many locations across the country, some of its product distribution subfunctions will probably change.

Processes Change More than Functions

Business processes were defined in Chapter 2 as business actions with definite starting and stopping points, which transform input into output. The fact that these actions have start and stop times means that they do change from time to time, but they may remain the same for long periods of time. For example, the actions necessary to complete a retail customer order are likely to remain the same for long periods of time. However, if the company starts permitting credit sales, completing a retail sale will involve additional actions from a *what* and *why* perspective. For example, a person taking a credit sale will have to perform additional actions to identify the customer, check the credit rating, and update the accounts receivable for the amount of the sale.

For many other processes performed by the business, what they do and why may remain the same for long periods of time. What changes most frequently are the procedures that implement the business processes. Procedures specify the ways to perform the business activities.

Procedures Frequently Change

The action statements that specify *how* to implement business processes or perform organizational tasks make up the information systems procedures (as defined in Chapter 2). Note that throughout this text, *procedure* should be interpreted to mean *information systems procedure*, unless otherwise indicated. *How* business activities are performed changes frequently. Procedures change when changes occur in technology, governmental legislation and proclamations, areas in which a company competes (sometimes called competitive spaces or arenas), industry groups, the experience of personnel, business practices, and a host of other components of the business infrastructure.

For example, technology may be used to automate some business processes formerly performed by hand. Businesses that have replaced mechanical cash registers with computerized models provide an example. When standalone mechanical cash registers are replaced with computerized models, many actions previously performed by sales personnel are carried out automatically. Someone must create a program to accept sales data from the computerized cash register. In addition, each new automated feature, such as automatic updating of inventory on hand while completing sales, requires that new procedures be installed in the program that runs the cash register. Data models provide a foundation on which to more quickly create these procedures.

How These Rates of Change Affect Business Modeling

Since data types almost never change and functions rarely change, analysts should spend most of their time determining and making changes to processes and procedures—especially procedures. This observation assumes that an organization has in fact created a comprehensive model of all of its business objects and activities. Very few organizations now have such models. The lack of a comprehensive data model in most organizations has caused much redundancy in storing data values for many object properties, and missing data values for other object properties. In traditional file processing and in many database environments, many of the same properties of a given object are stored in different files or database objects. In addition, some important object properties, and some whole objects, tend to be missed unless a more systematic method is used to identify and describe objects important to the business. A comprehensive data model helps reduce the likelihood of these occurrences.

Since comprehensive data models generally do not exist, budding analysts will probably spend their time creating them rather than maintaining them. Business personnel have wanted accurate models of their businesses for years. Modelers have also wanted a standardized methodology to be used by all personnel in their businesses. Many of these desires are now being fulfilled in some organizations. However, most organizations are still building the basic models of their businesses and will be doing so for many years to come. The main reasons these models have not been created until now are the time required to complete data models and the lack of expertise in data modeling on the part of organizational personnel. The remainder of this chapter will help qualify you to fill this void.

MODELING BUSINESS OBJECTS AS DATA TYPES

Modeling business objects as data types consists of identifying and sufficiently describing all data types of the business. To do this properly, the data collected at the start of the analysis phase is reviewed in order to seek out data types. Data types appear on archive documents such as employee job application forms, customer complaint forms, credit check forms for customers, and so on. Users tell the analysts about data types during interviews and in questionnaire responses. For example, they may indicate that they interact with a governmental agent or use a list of suppliers for vendor product ordering. Analysts may also identify data types by watching people work.

For example, a shipping and receiving clerk makes a note of who shipped a particular collection of products, or a clerk looks at customer delinquencies on a computer screen; these both represent data types. Regardless of how the analyst acquires information on a data type, it becomes part of the data model for the business.

Individual and Generalized Data Type Abstractions

Abstraction is the ability to ignore detail and concentrate on general, common properties of a set of data types. For example, abstraction can be applied to a collection of employees by designating the term EMPLOYEE as a data type to abstractly represent the collection of employees. The EMPLOYEE data type represents each individual employee in the EMPLOYEE data type, as well as all of the employees.

Having a way to abstractly represent all employees by using the term EMPLOYEE helps diminish information overload. For example, the thousands of employees for a particular company can be abstractly symbolized by the EMPLOYEE data type. It is unnecessary to remember all the traits of each employee, such as their names, since EMPLOYEE represents all employees and the NAME property of EMPLOYEE can be used to find a particular employee.

Generalized Data Types

Higher-level categories of data types can also be defined for collections of individual data types. For example, the BUSINESS PEOPLE data type may refer to the EMPLOYEE, SUPPLIER, and CUSTOMER data types, and to a host of other data types that represent different groups of people important to the business about which data needs to be retained.

A high-level data type category, typically called a **generalized data type**, is one on which the firm also has to retain data that consists of a group of individual data types. For example, a DEPARTMENT generalized data type may be identified for all data types in a department of the business. The DEPARTMENT data type would also have important properties, such as NAME, CHAIRPERSON, TELEPHONE_NUMBER, and LOCATION, that would be used to retain data on the department to distinguish it from other departments. The DEPARTMENT data type would represent all data types in a particular department.

In general, all properties of a generalized data type are inherited downward by all of the data types that it comprises. For example, in the DEPARTMENT generalized data type, the CHAIRPERSON property would be used to designate the chairperson for a particular department. The person's name in the CHAIRPERSON property of a particular department is inherited as the chairperson of an employee type in that department. For example, if Jessica Lee were the data value in the CHAIRPERSON property in the Women's Clothing DEPARTMENT of a retail store, a SALESCLERK named Brenda Vogel who works in this department would also have Jessica Lee as her chairperson.

Identifying All Individual and Generalized Data Types

To produce a complete data model, the modeler should identify the entire collection of individual and generalized data types by searching archive data, interviewing personnel, and performing a host of other activities, as discussed in Chapter 4. This data is used by the analyst to:

- Identify all of the data types, individual and generalized, of importance to the business
- Identify the properties of those data types about which organizational personnel need information
- Identify relationships between those data types and the cardinality of those relationships

These are the activities important to creating and maintaining a comprehensive, accurate, conceptual, and logical data model.

Data Model Complexity

The more complex the data types are, and the greater their number, the more complex the data model will be. Increased numbers of real-world objects for data types also increase the complexity of dealing with the firm's data. Using a data name to refer to a data type and its properties is a useful way to represent the large collection of real-world business objects, and helps shield users from the complexity of considering all of the business objects in this collection.

MODELING DATA TYPES AS ENTITIES ON AN ENTITY/ RELATIONSHIP DIAGRAM (E/RD)

Modeling the business creates a high-level view of the data that portrays the data types important to the enterprise from a conceptual perspective. In Chapter 2, **entity** was defined as an abstract representation of a business object. Data types in the high-level view are modeled as entities on an entity/relationship diagram (E/RD). When an entity is used to model data types, the entity symbolizes the data type. A rectangular symbol is often used to abstractly represent a data type on an E/RD. Figure 5-4 illustrates the use of the entity symbol to represent an organizational data type.

The entity/relationship modeling method provides a convenient and descriptive way of portraying the conceptual view of data types in their subject areas. Each entity on the E/RD is described in what is known as an entity type description. The entity type description created for each entity in an E/RD describes the logical view of it.

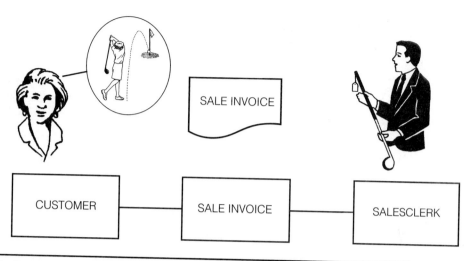

Figure 5-4. Data types modeled as entities

These conceptual and logical views of data types are depicted as the first and second portions of the object side of the pyramid in Figure 5-1.

Entities and Relationship Symbols Used to Model Data Types

Ensuring that you identify all data types, their properties, and the relationships among data types is best accomplished by using a modeling method to model enterprise data types. In the text methodology, the E/RD modeling method is used to identify the data types and the relationships among them; in the text E/RD modeling method, the entity symbol or relationship symbol is used to represent a data type.

A **relationship** is a connection between two entities that mutually associates them. These relationships are usually viewed as a set of binary relationships between two entities, although more complex relationships exist (three-way and higher). A particular relationship that has a particular value for a particular property also provides a fact worth retaining about that object. Figure 5-5 illustrates the connection between a real-world object, a data type, and an entity type or relationship type that represents the data type. Note that hereafter, *entity type* or *relationship type* should be considered an abstract synonym for *data type*.

Relationship Cardinality

A relationship can be just a line that connects entities, or it can be an object that exists because two entities have some relationship between them. The first type of relationship is called a *cardinality relationship*, and cardinality is demonstrated by the

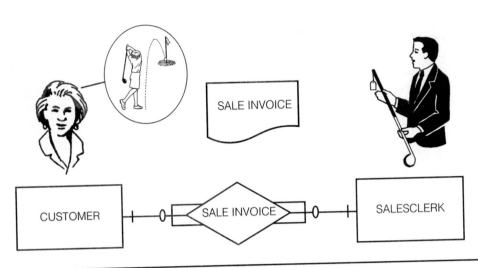

Figure 5-5. Business objects, data types, types of entities and relationships

appearance of the connection. (Relationship cardinality was defined in Chapter 2 as how many of one type of business object can be related to another type of business object.) For the second type of relationship, which embodies another data type, the term *relationship* is used alone. As an example, a CUSTOMER entity could be connected to a SALE INVOICE relationship data type that is also connected to a SALES-CLERK entity to show how a SALE INVOICE could embody a relationship between those two entities. Furthermore, the connection between the CUSTOMER entity and the SALE INVOICE relationship could be designated as 1:M (1-to-many) to show how a customer could make many sales but how a sale would be for a single customer. Figure 5-5 illustrates the use of both the relationship and the cardinality relationship designations for the CUSTOMER, SALE INVOICE, and SALESCLERK data types. Note that the cardinality indicator (———) connection between the entity and relationship symbols designates a 1:M cardinality relationship, meaning that customers can buy many items and salesclerks can sell many items.

For a cardinality relationship between two data types, either data type could be optional or mandatory, depending on what exists for the real-world business objects the data types represent. The optional or mandatory conditions are indicated by placing a "O" or an "I" on the cardinality relationship for each side of the connection. For example, the connection between the CUSTOMER entity and the SALE INVOICE relationship contains "I" and "O" to indicate that a CUSTOMER data type does not have to have a SALE INVOICE data type, but if a SALE INVOICE exists, a CUSTOMER is mandatory. A customer object may be added to the set of customers that compose the CUSTOMER data type, but that customer object may be retained in the CUSTOMER data type for a period prior to making its first SALE INVOICE. Conversely, for a SALE INVOICE object that exists, a CUSTOMER object must also exist: a sale does not exist without a customer.

Entity Type Descriptions

The text E/RD modeling method uses an **entity type description** to list and describe the properties of the data type that the entity represents. This entry provides the logical view of data types highlighted in Figure 5-1, at the beginning of this chapter.

Entity Properties

An entity is normally defined by properties. An **entity property** is a named attribute of an entity having a value that describes, characterizes, classifies, and identifies the characteristics of the data type that the entity symbolizes. An entity property comprises different facts, obtained by assigning attribute values to a collection of business objects represented as a data type. For example, the NAME property could serve this purpose for the SALESCLERK in the example used to explain a generalized data type, as well as for all salesclerks from that retail store. An entity property should correspond to the data type property for that type of business object. Throughout this book, *property* and *entity property* are synonymous. An entity property associates properties of an entity with attribute values from a domain of possible values. For example, there is a domain of possible values (1–12) for a MONTH entity property.

Domain Definitions

For entity properties, it is important to determine limits on the values for properties. This helps prevent erroneous data values from being assigned to particular business objects in the collection of business objects that the entity now represents. The term *domain* has become widely used as the mechanism to place limits on property values. A **domain** is a uniquely named collection of permissible values for a given property. By indicating these permissible values in a statement known as a **domain definition**, the value for an entity property associated with the domain definition is limited to those specifically stated values in the definition. For example, the values 1 through 31 could constitute the limitation for a domain definition for the number of days in a month; any values above 31 would be in error, as would the values 28, 29, 30, and 31 for certain months. This example illustrates that domain definitions can limit the value for an entity property individually, as in the case of limiting a DAY_OF_ MONTH entity property from being 32 or above; or a domain definition can limit the value of an entity property based on a value of another entity property, as in the case of limiting the values of the DAY_OF_MONTH for values between 28 and 31 depending on the value (1 through 12) of the MONTH_OF_YEAR entity property.

A domain limitation, or *constraint*, as it is typically called, can also be stated between permissible values of entity properties in different data types. For example, permitting a student to enroll in a graduate class could be constrained by whether that student was a graduate student—that is, STUDENT_STATUS of "G" (graduate status) rather than "U" (undergraduate status) in the STUDENT entity. Thus, the data value for a STUDENT_IDENTIFICATION_NUMBER property in a CLASS_ ENROLLMENT entity must be the student identification number for a student that also has a data value of "G" in the STUDENT_STATUS property of the STUDENT entity.

To prevent redundancy in domain definitions for different entity properties, the same domain definition can be associated with completely different entity properties. For example, the WAGE property of an EMPLOYEE entity could be associated with the same domain definition as an AMOUNT property of a SALE INVOICE relationship. This domain definition could limit the data values for both of these properties to being numeric and having a specified length that corresponds to both entity properties. Thus, the data modeler does not create a separate domain definition for each entity property; many domain definitions can be used to constrain the data values for multiple entity properties. Chapter 10 further explains how domain definitions affect the defining and maintaining of an organizational database.

Entity Keys

One entity property, normally called a key property, helps identify a particular object within that entity type. An **entity key property** is an entity property or collection of properties whose values uniquely identify objects belonging to the set of objects in the data type symbolized by the entity type. For example, the SOCIAL_SECURITY_NUMBER entity property could be used as a key property for the EMPLOYEE entity type described earlier in this chapter.

Creating Entity Type Descriptions

Figure 2-10 in Chapter 2 illustrated an entity type description for a CUSTOMER SALE data type. This entity type description listed all of the names assigned to all properties for the CUSTOMER SALE data type in this example. As defined in Chapter 2, an entity type description specifies and describes the properties (attributes) of the type of business object about which the firm needs to retain data. An entity type description defines an entity by listing its properties: those entity characteristics considered significant to understanding the entity and sufficient to model the real-world data type. A characteristic (property) is considered significant when it is related to a particular type of entity and generates a fact about that entity. Figure 5-6 illustrates an entity type description for a PATIENT data type that might be an entity on an E/RD for a hospital. This entity type description is similar in format to the entity type description for the CUSTOMER SALE entity of Figure 2-10. Note that some entity properties are properties that refer to other data types in which the PATIENT entity type has a relationship (for example, DOCTOR_ID_NUMBER).

For an entity type description used to describe data types, the text method uses a logical data structure. A **logical data structure (LDS)** is a list of data elements that correspond to entity properties that meet a reasonable need for data about a data type inside and outside a company. Depending on the technology used to create the E/RD models (graphics software or CASE tool, for example), you may need to use something other than a LDS to create entity type descriptions for data types appearing on

PATIENT
SOCIAL_SECURITY_NUMBER
NAME
STREET_ADDRESS
CITY
STATE
TELEPHONE_NUMBER
DOCTOR_ID_NUMBER
NEXT_OF_KIN
NEXT_OF_KIN_STREET
NEXT_OF_KIN_CITY
NEXT_OF_KIN_STATE
NEXT_OF_KIN_TELEPHONE

Figure 5-6. A PATIENT entity type description

E/RDs. For this situation, it should be relatively easy to determine what specification of that technology is functionally equivalent to the text LDS entity type description. For example, Figure 5-7 illustrates the PATIENT entity type description in a LDS format. The "DE" entry for the LDS stands for data element (as opposed to "DS" for data structure). The "SV" entry stands for single-valued (as opposed to "MV" for multivalued).

Because the individual data items are often stored in separate **physical data structures (PDSs)**, multiple physical accesses frequently occur to retrieve a combination of data items that has a logical meaning for users. For example, a hospital administrator may need to see the names of patients who died at the hospital, the types of treatments performed on them, the name of the doctor who performed the treatment on a specific date, and data on their next of kin. This data is likely to be stored in three physical data structures: PATIENT, TREATMENT, and DOCTOR. Therefore, each of these physical data structures must be accessed to obtain the string of data items meeting the administrator's logical need for data.

Subject Areas

To identify all of the data types important to the firm and model them as entities and relationships, the analyst should create separate E/RDs for business subject areas. Good data modeling divides the enterprise into manageable units called subject areas.

PATIENT				
No.	Ele/DS Name	DE/DS	SV/MV	Occurrences
01	SOCIAL_SECURITY_NUMBER	DE	SV	
02	NAME	DE	SV	
03	STREET_ADDRESS	DE	SV	
04	CITY	DE	SV	
05	STATE	DE	SV	
06	TELEPHONE_NUMBER	DE	SV	
07	DOCTOR_ID_NUMBER	DE	SV	
08	NEXT_OF_KIN	DE	SV	
09	NEXT_OF_KIN_STREET	DE	SV	
10	NEXT_OF_KIN_CITY	DE	SV	
11	NEXT_OF_KIN_STATE	DE	SV	
12	NEXT_OF_KIN_TELEPHONE	DE	SV	

Figure 5-7. PATIENT LDS used as an entity type description

Dividing the business into subject areas also divides the collection of data types that exist in the business. A **subject area** is a major topic of interest to the enterprise that helps it fulfill its mission—for example:

- Product distribution
- Project financing
- Products
- Customers
- Vendors
- Personnel
- Accounts

A subject area encompasses a manageable set of objects that support the overall mission of the enterprise from the perspective of that subject area. Subject areas (sometimes called **data classes**) relate to organizational subjects rather than to computer applications in the firm's MIS. So, to create a subject area E/RD, the analyst studies an organizational unit to identify all data types that affect that subject area, and models those data types as entities and relationships on that E/RD.

By approaching conceptual/logical data modeling through subject areas, *not* through applications, the likelihood of data type redundancy is somewhat minimized.

When applications are studied to identify and model data types as E/RD entities and relationships, it is easier to mistakenly identify two different sets of properties for the same data type as being two separate data types. For example, a hospital retains a medical history for each patient admitted to the hospital. An analyst studying a hospital application that uses a set of patient history properties related to previous operations or treatments administered to the patient might view these properties as a separate data type called PAST OPERATION/TREATMENTS. Another analyst studying another hospital application that uses a set of patient history properties related to various diseases previously contracted by a patient might view these properties as a separate data type called PAST DISEASES. Both of these data types would be separately identified in error. All of these properties should be properties of the PATIENT HISTORY data type. The erroneous identification of data types occurs more frequently when analysts study applications rather than subject areas during data modeling activities.

Subfunctions as Subject Areas

Many data modelers agree that using subject areas for modeling can produce superior results; however, no real systematic way of identifying subject areas currently exists in IS literature. One systematic way of identifying subject areas starts by producing a decomposition of functions. Remember that functions are the ongoing business activities combined to support one aspect of furthering the corporate mission.

In the text methodology, each subfunction of the functional decomposition, once constructed, is treated as a subject area, with an accompanying E/RD for that subject area created to identify and model the data types within the subfunction as E/RD entities and relationships. The basic premise behind using subfunctions as subject areas is that the essence of what constitutes an enterprise is its functions and the data types they comprise, use, serve, and are served by. Thus, by modeling the data types related to business functions and subfunctions as E/RD entities and relationships, most, if not all, of the data types representing real-world object types of importance to the business should be identified. Figure 5-8 builds on the function decomposition example that appeared in Figure 2-13 of Chapter 2 to illustrate using subfunctions as subject areas in data modeling activities.

Notice that the intent for the subject areas in Figure 5-8 is to identify all of the data types in each subject area for the five different categories of business objects. As previously stated, good data modeling seeks to:

- Identify the different data types for the business
- Produce entity type descriptions for those data types
- Specify the relationships among those data types, as well as their cardinality

These same three activities are performed for a particular subject area. Data modelers continue to perform these same three activities for each subject area until most, if not all, data types are identified and defined. To complete these activities, they use E/RDs, such as those described in Chapter 2, and entity type descriptions, as described in this chapter.

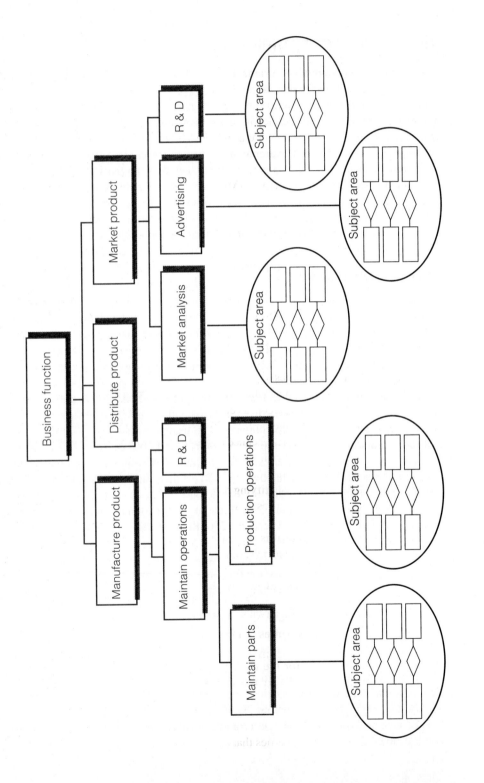

Figure 5-8. Subfunctions as subject areas

Data Types in Multiple Subject Areas

It should be understood that the same data type may be a part of several subject areas. However, care should be taken to not identify it as more than one data type. When a data type is part of more than one subject area, it provides a view of that data type from the context of its appearance in that subject area. This view may be the properties of the specific data type that are important to that area of the business or to a particular user in that area. For example, many companies retain hundreds of properties on individual EMPLOYEE objects. However, a receptionist who answers calls to employees only needs to see their NAME, JOB, and TELEPHONE_NUMBER properties on a computer screen to transfer an incoming call appropriately for a particular employee. For the receptionist, only those three properties are important within the context of being able to properly transfer an incoming call.

As another example, an EMPLOYEE data type may have many different properties; however, only certain properties, such as NAME, JOB_CLASSIFICATION, TELEPHONE_NUMBER, and LOCATION may be important to an employee questioned about this data type in the retail sales area of the business during systems analysis. These properties represent a view of the EMPLOYEE data type for the person interviewed, who often believes those properties to be the only ones that are retained for that data type. The E/RD created for the retail sales subject area would contain the EMPLOYEE entity with an accompanying entity type description that lists only those entity properties.

Information systems that aid the interviewed employee may print out only those entity properties for the EMPLOYEE data type. This print-out could also be part of the archive data, viewed during data collection, that the analyst uses to identify data types and their properties. The existence of this print-out also reflects the view of the EMPLOYEE data type for that information system application. This view is often called an **application data view** of a data type. Application views of data types are also an important source for identifying data types and their properties; however, take care to not consider their properties as separate data types, as previously explained.

The appearance of a data type in several subject areas is helpful in identifying all properties of the data type as it is viewed by all personnel and in all contexts of its use. For a data type identified as part of a subject area, the modeler should determine what properties of the data type are important to that contextual view of the data type. For a data type that is part of several subject areas, a list of its properties should be created for each subject area in which it belongs. This list of properties should appear in a *partial* entity type description for that data type in the context of that subject area. The aggregate list of the properties of the data type is determined by accumulating all of the properties assigned to it within each subject area in which it appears. The aggregation of properties for the data type should be defined in a *full* entity type description. Thus, to sufficiently define a data type, the data modeler should:

1. Determine all of the subject areas of which it is part.
2. Use a *partial* entity type description for *each* subject area in which it appears to list those of its properties that are important to the subject area.

3. Accumulate all of the properties listed in all of the separate entity type descriptions for the data type into a single *full* entity type description.

This set of actions helps determine the **sufficiency requirement** for the data type; that is, it ensures that the data type is adequately described relative to identifying all of its properties of importance to the business, in all contextual uses of the data type.

Figure 5-9 shows how a data type may appear on multiple subject area E/RDs with accompanying contextual entity type descriptions used to create the full entity type description. Together, they sufficiently define the data type that the E/RD entity or relationship represents. The STUDENT entity in Figure 5-9 is part of the E/RD created for the Class Enrollment subject area, as well as an entity on the E/RD for the Scholarship Evaluation subject area. An entity type description was created for the STUDENT entity for each subject area listing the properties of the STUDENT entity that are important for that subject. Notice that some of the same properties appear in both entity type descriptions, whereas each has other STUDENT entity properties unique to that description. For each entity type description, the data modeler could have obtained data from users in that subject area, as well as archive data, application data, and so on from the subject area. For example, a user involved with the subject may have told the modeler what properties were important, or a review of an application report or form may have indicated what properties were important.

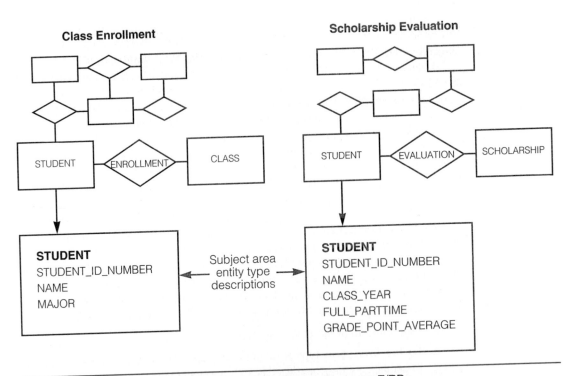

Figure 5-9. Defining data types that appear on multiple subject area E/RDs

STUDENT

No.	Ele/DS Name	DE/DS	SV/MV	Occurrences
01	STUDENT_ID_NUMBER	DE	SV	
02	NAME	DE	SV	
03	MAJOR	DE	SV	
04	CLASS_YEAR	DE	SV	
05	FULL_PARTTIME	DE	SV	
06	GRADE_POINT_AVERAGE	DE	SV	

Figure 5-10. STUDENT entity type description

Following the creation of entity type descriptions for the STUDENT entity in the context of these subject areas, the modeler would accumulate the properties listed in the entity type description for the STUDENT entity in the context of all of the subject areas in which the entity appears. Figure 5-10 illustrates the entity type description for the STUDENT entity that combines the properties of the two entity type descriptions of Figure 5-9. This entity type description should be considered a work in progress for the full entity type description of the STUDENT entity; other properties may need to be added to the list in Figure 5-10. Note that this entity type description is also in the text LDS entity type description format.

Basic Formats of Entity/ Relationship Diagrams

There are three basic formats used for E/R modeling that represent three different ways of doing the same thing: modeling the data types important to a subject area. (None of the three formats is particularly better than the others.) Figures 5-11 and 5-12 show the three basic formats of entity modeling methods and examples of each format. These same figures appeared in the section that provided an overview of the E/RD modeling method in Chapter 2.

The bottom format in Figures 5-11 and 5-12 uses only entity rectangles for the data types, and lines between the rectangles to represent the relationships between the entities. The top and middle formats use a diamond, or a rectangle with a diamond in it, to represent a data type that embodies the relationship between two other data types. The top two format examples in Figure 5-12 use the diamond or rectangle/diamond symbol to represent a sales order data type that embodies the relationship between the CUSTOMER and SALESCLERK data types. Note that the bottom format example also models these three data types; however, it uses the same symbol

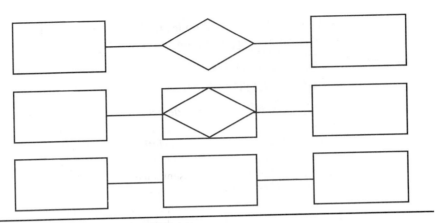

Figure 5-11. Basic entity model formats

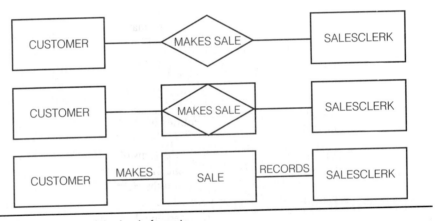

Figure 5-12. Uses of the basic formats

(the entity symbol) to represent all three data types. This text uses the top format for all E/RDs so that data types that embody the relationship between two other data types are clearly distinguished from the other data types. However, it is relatively unimportant which E/RD format is being used. What is important is that you consistently use a method and that by applying the method you correctly identify the data types of importance to the business. For example, in Figure 5-12, you need to identify three data types of importance.

Components of Entity/Relationship Diagrams

The E/RD modeling method first described in Chapter 2 can be used to categorize business relationships, real-world data types, and the data types that support the business relationship. A better understanding of the E/RD modeling method can be conveyed by describing its components used in this text.

E/R Expressions

An **E/R expression** is used to depict a business relationship; it has a left-side entity, followed by a middle relationship or associative entity, followed by a right-side entity. Note that hereafter the term *relationship* will be used to designate either the diamond or the associative entity symbol. The left-side and right-side entities in the text E/RD method abstractly represent a user or a category of users, such as a division, a department within a company, or external users such as clients, suppliers, and governmental agencies. These are the entities that enter into the business relationships. Data of a data type obtained from (or distributed because of) the relationship between left-side and right-side entity types also becomes an object about which the firm may retain data. The middle relationship represents the data type or data types that support the association a person entity type has with another person entity type, as illustrated by the diamond symbol in the top format in Figures 5-11 and 5-12.

The sample E/R expression in Figure 5-12 depicts three data types for the customer, sale, and salesclerk business objects. The interaction between the CUSTOMER and SALESCLERK entities creates the MAKES SALE data type. In other words, the MAKES SALE data type supports the business relationship between the CUSTOMER and SALESCLERK data types.

Notice that one of the entities on the left side or right side of the E/R expression is a data type external to the business: in this example, the CUSTOMER entity. E/R expressions often depict the interactions of users internal to the business with external persons or groups depicted as one of the entities participating in the business relationship. However, the two entities on the right and left sides of the E/R expression could both depict users internal to the business. This latter representation helps depict the interactions between internal personnel and groups that require data types to support the interactions.

In the text E/RD method, the relationship diamond symbol and the rectangle/diamond symbol in Figures 5-11 and 5-12 functionally correspond; however, either one of the top two formats in these figures could be used to depict an E/R expression, as previously stated. In the remainder of this text, references to the relationship diamond in an E/R expression mean the objects that support the business relationship, regardless of which symbol from Figures 5-11 and 5-12 appears in the middle of the E/R expression. In the remainder of this text, the diamond symbol will always be used to depict the middle symbol in an E/R expression.

Since entity symbols always represent people or group data types, and the diamond symbolizes the data types that support the business relationship between them, both the entity rectangle and the relationship diamond in the text method symbolize data types in the E/RD subject area. Thus, identifying all data types for the business consists of identifying those data types that enter into business relationships, as well as those that support the business relationships.

In the text E/RD method, a completely separate E/R expression is constructed for

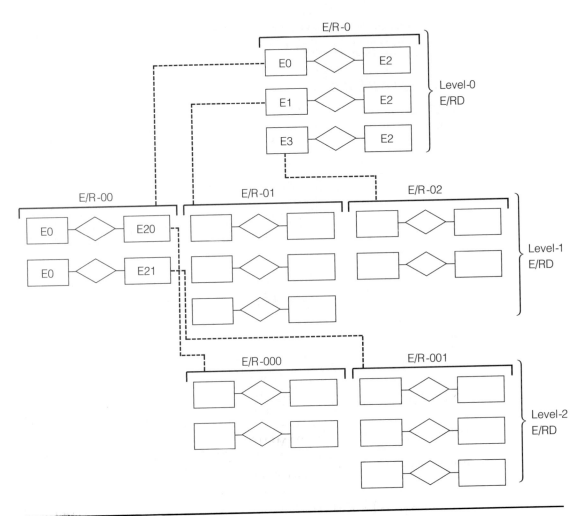

Figure 5-13. Progressive format of E/RDs

two entities having a business relationship. These separate E/R expressions categorize real-world data types from generalized user-type entities down to specific user-type entities in the business. Therefore, an E/RD is a combination of E/R expressions used to graphically portray all the business relationships that take place among various entities in a particular subject area. Figure 5-13 illustrates the progressive format used for E/RDs in this text.

Figure 5-13 displays the relationships between E/RDs within a set of E/RDs. The three E/R expressions boxed in at the top of the figure make up one complete E/RD. This E/RD, labeled "E/R-0," identifies the level-0 E/RD, which represents the top-level E/RD of the set of progressively related E/RDs. The E0, E1, E2, and E3 entities on E/R-0 represent four major categories of users (generalized data types) within or outside the firm that have business relationships supported by logical data structures (LDSs). For example, in the hospital example previously used, DOCTOR, PATIENT, HOSPITAL ADMINISTRATOR, and INSURANCE CARRIERS might be four entities that frequently interact. These interactions are considered business relationships, and can be modeled as separate E/R expressions on the top-level E/RD.

These major categories of users may embody many different types of users having relationships with the other types of users. For example, the HOSPITAL ADMINISTRATOR entity could represent different types of administrators who interact with other types of entities. An E/R expression could be created to represent those interactions between the HOSPITAL ADMINISTRATOR entity and the other entities.

In Figure 5-13, separate E/RDs need to be created to decompose the three E/R expressions on E/R-0 into subsets of business relationships depicted by E/R expressions on those separate E/RDs. The boxed E/RD labeled "E/R-00" is one of these E/RDs. On this diagram, the first E/R expression on the E/R-0 diagram decomposes into the two E/R expressions on the E/R-00 diagram. There could be more than two; the number of subsets of business relationships that actually exist in the real world dictates the number of E/R expressions. The E2 entity in the first E/R expression of E/R-0 decomposes into the E20 and E21 entities appearing in E/R-00. For example, if the E2 entity on the E/R-0 diagram was the HOSPITAL ADMINISTRATOR entity, this entity could decompose into two separate types of administrators, called EXECUTIVE ADMINISTRATOR and DEPARTMENT ADMINISTRATOR. The E0 entity on the E/R-00 diagram could be the INSURANCE CARRIER entity, illustrating that the two different types of hospital administrators interact with insurance carriers. This also illustrates why the E/R expressions on the E/R-00 diagram are subsets of the first E/R expression on the E/R-0 diagram. These E/R expressions are subsets because the two business relationships between the EXECUTIVE ADMINISTRATOR, INSURANCE CARRIER, and DEPARTMENT ADMINISTRATOR are subsets of the business relationship between the HOSPITAL ADMINISTRATOR and INSURANCE CARRIER entities represented on the E/R-0 diagram.

The decomposition of the E/R expression on the E/R-0 diagram also illustrates that the relationship diamond in the first E/R expression of E/R-0 has been decomposed into the two relationship diamonds in the E/R expressions of E/R-00. This means that the data types that support the relationship between the E0 and E2 entities have also been decomposed. Because the relationship diamond represents the data types that support the business relationship, this means that the group of data types supporting the business relationship depicted as the first E/R expression on the E/R-0 diagram has also been decomposed. For the hospital example, the relationship diamond on the E/R-0 diagram indicates that all the data types supporting the interaction between the HOSPITAL ADMINISTRATOR and the INSURANCE CARRIER have been decomposed into two subsets of that group of data types. These two subsets of data types are depicted as the two relationships on the E/R-00 diagram. What this means is that one of the relationships depicts only the data types supporting the relationship between the EXECUTIVE ADMINISTRATOR and INSURANCE CARRIER, while the other relationship depicts the data types that support the relationship between the DEPARTMENT ADMINISTRATOR and INSURANCE CARRIER.

Graph Explosion

Imagine that the E0 entity on the E/R-0 diagram has a button on it that automatically moves you to the E/R-00 diagram. By pushing this button, you migrate to the E/R-00 diagram, in which the E/R expression between the E0 and E2 entities on E/R-0 decomposes into the two E/R expressions on E/R-00. Pushing the button on the E0 entity and migrating to the E/R-00 diagram symbolizes an action known as graph explosion. For example, assuming that the E0 entity represents the INSURANCE CARRIER, exploding on the INSURANCE CARRIER entity would explode to the E/R-00 diagram, where the E2 entity decomposed into the E20 and E21 entities (EXECUTIVE ADMINISTRATOR and DEPARTMENT ADMINISTRATOR), and the first E/R expression on the E/R-0 diagram decomposed into the two E/R expressions on the E/R-00 diagram.

Graph explosion breaks the E/R expressions of a graph into E/R expressions that show more detail. Explosion from a symbol on one graph to another graph is called "exploding down" to the next graph level. Graph levels are numbered consecutively, starting from the top-level graph at level 0. For example, an explosion on the E0 entity on the level-0 E/RD of Figure 5-13 explodes down to the E/R-00 level-1 diagram, which provides a more detailed explanation for the E/R expression depicting the business relationship between the E0 and E2 entities on the E/R-0 diagram. The E1 and E3 entities on the E/R-0 diagram also explode down to separate level-1 E/RDs, which are boxed in and labeled "E/R-01" and "E/R-02" in Figure 5-13. Which entity (right-side or left-side) within an expression explodes is somewhat subjective, but will become clearer as examples are presented.

Entities on subsequent E/RD levels may also explode to lower-level E/RDs. For example, an explosion occurs on the E20 and E21 entities on the E/R-00 level-1 diagram down to the level-2 diagrams labeled E/R-000 and E/R-001. Explosions could also occur on the entities on the E/R-01 and E/R-02 level-1 diagrams. The need for further details regarding the business relationships dictates whether explosion occurs for an E/R expression. Figure 5-14 shows the overall concept of the E/RD modeling method used in this text.

The top portion of Figure 5-14 illustrates the E/R expression concept and the basic idea behind the text E/R modeling method. Beginning at the top-level E/RD, major categories of user data types (generalized data types) appear as either left-side or right-side entities in the individual E/R expressions, or as both. The lower portion of Figure 5-14, labeled "E/R-00," illustrates this concept. The E/R expressions on the top-level E/RD portray major business relationships supported by groups of data types. The relationship diamond in the middle of each E/R expression represents the group of data types that support the business relationships.

Decomposition of Generalized Data Types

When explosion occurs on the entities on the top-level E/RD down to E/RDs at the next level, the generalized entities on the top E/RD may decompose into types of entities or specific entities within the entity category. As entity explosion occurs on subsequent

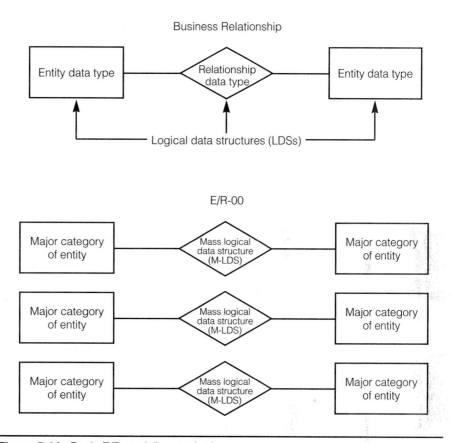

Figure 5-14. Basic E/R modeling method

E/RD levels, the types of entities may decompose into subtypes of the entity on the next E/RD. Entity explosion will continue until an E/RD level is reached in which the relationship diamond in the E/R expression denotes a single data type (a single LDS).

For example, an entity labeled CLERICAL PERSONNEL may appear on a top-level E/RD. An explosion on this entity may move to a level-1 E/RD in which different types of clerical personnel (for example, receptionists, salesclerks, secretaries, shipping/receiving clerks, or accounts clerks) appear as entities. An explosion on one of these clerk-type entities may progress down to a level-2 E/RD in which the E/RD portrays the relationships between that clerk-type entity and other types of entities. An explosion on one of these E/R expressions may then explode to a level-3 E/RD in which the relationship diamonds represent single LDSs. For example, an E/R expression may appear on the level-2 E/RD signifying the relationship between the salesclerk and customer entities. An explosion on the customer entity could explode down to the level-3 E/RD in which all the E/R expressions portray relationships between salesclerks and customers supported by single LDSs. The relationship diamonds on this level-3 E/RD might be labeled ORDER CREATION OBJECT, ITEM QUANTITY CHECKING OBJECT, and ORDER FILLING OBJECT, for example.

Mass Logical Data Structures (M-LDSs)

The relationship diamond between the user-type entities identifies the data types needed to support the business relationship between these entities. On the top-level E/RD, the relationship diamond symbolizes the group of data types (LDSs) needed to support the relationship between the major categories of entities. These groups of data types or LDSs are called **mass logical data structures (M-LDSs)**.

As entities explode down to more detailed E/RDs, diagrams on lower explosion levels continue to decompose business relationships and categories of entities and identify the information needed to support the relationship between the entities. Relationships on subsequent E/RD levels represent either subgroups of M-LDSs or individual LDSs. A subcategory of a M-LDS represents a portion of the M-LDS that is needed to support the business relationship between the subcategories of entities. Thus another M-LDS may be a subset of an original M-LDS portrayed as a relationship diamond on the top-level E/RD. Figure 5-15 illustrates an entity type description for an M-LDS that has subsets of M-LDSs; Figure 5-16 illustrates how one of those subset M-LDSs may contain the individual LDSs that support the relationship between the clerk-type and customer entities of the previous section.

As explosion continues to lower E/R levels, an E/RD level will be reached in which the relationship diamonds within each E/R expression symbolize individual LDSs. This typically occurs at the lowest E/RD levels. However, some E/R expressions along the explosion path may contain E/R expressions in which relationships symbolize individual LDSs. Frequently the lowest-level E/RDs display only relationships between two individual entities, with all relationships symbolizing individual LDSs. Figure 5-17 illustrates this concept.

Entry Type		Dictionary ID			
Data Structure		MLOG-CUSTOMER_ORDER_DATA			
Alias: CUSTOMER ORDER DATA					
Comment: A M-LDS for customer order data.					
Starting Volume: _____ Growth Potential: _____					
No.	**Ele/DS Name**		**DE/DS**	**SV/MV**	**Occurrences**
01	MLOG-CUSTOMER_ORDER		DS		
02	MLOG-CUSTOMER_ACCOUNTS		DS		

Figure 5-15. M-LDS with subsets of M-LDSs

Entry Type   **Dictionary ID**

Data Structure   MLOG-CUSTOMER_ORDER

Alias: _CUSTOMER ORDER__

Comment: _A M-LDS for customer orders._

Starting Volume: _____   Growth Potential: _____

No.	Ele/DS Name	DE/DS	SV/MV	Occurrences
01	LOG-ORDER	DS		
02	LOG-ITEM_QUANTITY	DS		
03	LOG-ORDER_INVOICE	DS		

Figure 5-16. M-LDS that contains LDSs

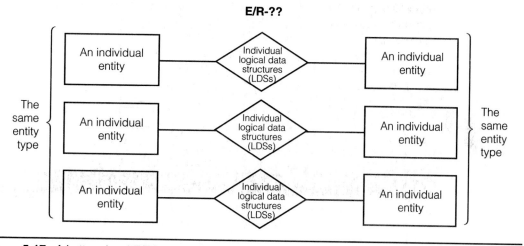

E/R-??

Figure 5-17. A bottom-level E/RD example

Summary of the Text Entity/ Relationship (E/R) Modeling Method

To summarize the text E/R modeling method, E/RDs are used to illustrate the business relationships existing between internal and external business objects (data types). E/R expressions depict the business relationships between categories, types, and individual business objects (data types). E/R expressions on a higher-level E/RD decompose into multiple E/R expressions on the next E/RD level. Decomposing the E/R expression causes the relationships in the expression to decompose into multiple relationships within the E/R expressions on the lower-level E/RD. Decomposing the relationship into multiple relationships on the lower-level E/RD causes the M-LDS depicted by the relationship diamond on the upper-level E/RD to decompose into multiple subsets of M-LDSs or individual LDSs depicted by the relationships within the expressions on the lower-level E/RD. Finally, decomposing an E/R expression on a higher-level E/RD may also cause the entities within the expression to decompose into subtypes of entities that appear in the E/R expressions on the lower-level E/RD. Thus, the complete set of E/RDs illustrates the categories and subcategories of business relationships, the categories and subcategories of business objects participating in those business relationships, and the groups and subgroups of business objects supporting those business relationships. Figure 5-18 shows more completely how to perform data modeling using the text methodology.

Several categories of business objects appear at the top of Figure 5-18. From these business object categories, data types are identified. These data types are modeled as entity and relationship symbols on E/RDs created for a subject area. Entity type descriptions are created for these data types in the context of the subject area: only properties of importance to that subject area are listed. The properties of data types that appear on multiple subject area E/RDs are accumulated into a single full data model entity type description to sufficiently model the data type for all contexts. This process is completed for all individual and generalized data types until the entire data model is complete.

DESIGN DICTIONARY RECORDING METHOD

Before continuing with data modeling methods, you should become familiar with the way text entries that accompany the graphical models are created. The text entries compose what is known as the dictionary of descriptions, or design dictionary, for the ways the graphical symbols and connections represent real-world objects, activities, and associations.

A **design dictionary** is a recording method that lists and defines users, processes, data, and relationships between users and other users (or users and data). The dictionary is often used to describe graphic models, what the symbols on the graphic models represent, and the purpose of connections between symbols. Later in this chapter, we will present several examples of dictionary entries. The analyst uses the design dictionary to keep track of details about users, data, and processes while developing a new system. Besides being useful in the analysis and design phases, the design dictionary should remain the main reference point for the system throughout its life. The design dictionary should include the following data description specifications:

- Name of the data element
- Description of the data element

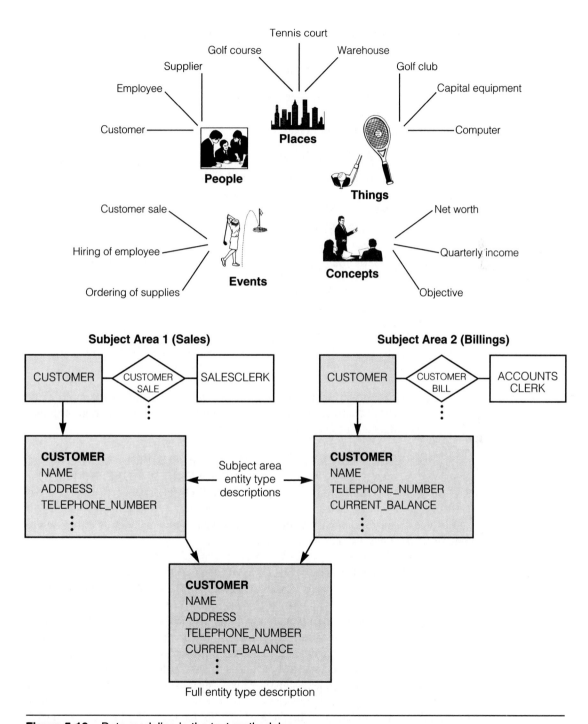

Figure 5-18. Data modeling in the text methodology

- Data structure in which the data element is found (which file)
- Synonyms (aliases) by which a data element is known
- Frequency with which data is used
- Cross-reference list of data and usages
- Source of the data
- Destination of the information
- Physical length of the data item

The following symbols are commonly used in dictionaries:

Symbol	Meaning
=	Equivalent to
+	And
{ }	Either/or; select from choices
*	Repetition
[ ]	Optional
* *	Comment
_	Key property designation (used to underscore the key property in an entity type description)

To illustrate the way dictionary entries are used, the following sample entry shows that a payroll transaction consists of an employee number, the regular hours worked, and (optionally) any overtime hours worked:

PAYROLL_TRANSACTION = EMPLOYEE_NUMBER + REGULAR_
HOURS_WORKED + [OVERTIME_
HOURS_WORKED]

The next entry illustrates the either/or structure. The employee is either newly hired or fired, or has had a change in status.

PAYROLL_CHANGE = {HIRE_EMPLOYEE, TERMINATE_
EMPLOYEE, CLASSIFICATION_CHANGE}

Many versions of design dictionary symbols exist, and their use may vary widely from organization to organization. Regardless of the diversity in usage, the purpose remains the same: to name and describe the various users, data elements, data structures, flows of data, and processing of data used in the developmental life cycle.

The task of developing the design dictionary entries and keeping them current is a formidable one. Commercial software systems have been developed to simplify entering, searching, and updating of the dictionaries. For example, design dictionaries for many CASE tools enable the analyst to generate a report that lists all of the programs that reference a particular data item. In addition, some dictionary software systems can generate the proper data structures for input to a database system (this is described in Chapter 10). Some systems actually change a design dictionary based on changes to the design of a system. This capability is particularly important in updating the documentation of an existing system when a change occurs.

The format and conventions of dictionary entries prescribe that narrative descriptions be included where possible, that diagrams appear where necessary, that definitions be inserted for all diagram components, that individual entries be integrated, that the conventions of punctuation be adhered to, and that summaries appear where appropriate.

EXAMPLE ENTITY/ RELATIONSHIP DIAGRAM FOR AN EMPLOYMENT SYSTEM

An example will show how to use the E/R modeling method and accompanying dictionary entries presented in this text. Figures 5-19, 5-21, and 5-22 illustrate the progressive decomposition of E/RDs for an employment application.

Level-0 Entity/Relationship Diagram (EMPLY)

The top-level E/RD (level-0) in Figure 5-19, labeled "EMPLY," contains four major categories of users: CLERICAL PERSONNEL, APPLICANT & EMPLOYEE, GOVERNMENTAL AGENCIES, and MANAGER. Each of the entities on the right sides of the E/R expressions explodes down to a lower-level E/RD that provides more detail regarding the E/R expression in which it appears. Each E/R expression in Figure 5-19 depicts a separate major business relationship within the employment application.

The relationship diamond between entities in each of the three E/R expressions symbolizes three separate mass logical data structures (M-LDSs) containing the logical data structures (LDSs) supporting those business relationships. For example, the APPLICANT/EMPLOYEE SERVICING OBJECTS relationship denotes a M-LDS called MLOG-APPLICANT_EMPLOYEE_DATA. Figure 5-20 shows that this M-LDS contains two separate M-LDSs, called MLOG-APPLICANT_DATA and MLOG-EMPLOYEE_DATA.

The diagram in Figure 5-19 shows how to determine which entity within an E/R expression explodes down to a lower-level diagram. Since the CLERICAL PERSONNEL entity appears in each of three expressions on this diagram, it could not explode to a lower-level E/RD that details an E/R expression. If graph explosion were tied to this entity, you could not know which of the three E/R expressions to decompose. Explosion on this graph occurs on the entities on the right side, because they are three different types of entities. The rule for exploding on an entity to a lower-level graph is to explode on the dissimilar entity (APPLICANT & EMPLOYEE, GOVERNMEN-

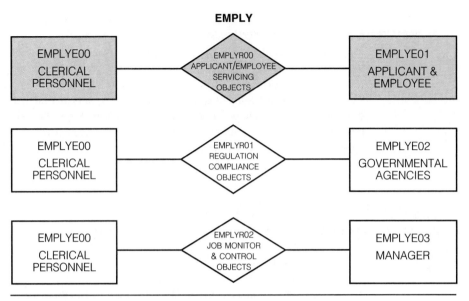

Figure 5-19. Level-0 employment system E/RD (EMPLY)

Entry Type   **Dictionary ID**

Data Structure   MLOG-APPLICANT_EMPLOYEE_DATA

Alias: _JOB APPLICATION EMPLOYEE DATA_

Comment: _A M-LDS for job application and employee data._

Starting Volume: _____   Growth Potential: _____

No.	Ele/DS Name	DE/DS	SV/MV	Occurrences
01	MLOG-APPLICANT_DATA	DS		
02	MLOG-EMPLOYEE_DATA	DS		

Figure 5-20. MLOG-APPLICANT_EMPLOYEE_DATA mass logical
             data structure (M-LDS)

TAL AGENCIES, and MANAGER here). In order to identify the entity on which explosions can occur, the analyst must be creative in constructing the E/R expressions so that dissimilar entities exist for each E/R expression. For example, the APPLI-CANT & EMPLOYEE entity depicts both applicants and employees. Entities sometimes embody multiple types of real-world objects in order to have dissimilar entities in the expressions. In this example it was not necessary; it was done simply to show how an entity that combines data types might be created.

Level-1 Entity/Relationship Diagram (EMPLY01)

The APPLICANT & EMPLOYEE entity in Figure 5-19 explodes to the E/RD in Figure 5-21 (the GOVERNMENTAL AGENCIES and MANAGER entities also explode to separate E/RDs). This diagram, labeled "EMPLY01," depicts the decomposition of the business relationship between the CLERICAL PERSONNEL and APPLICANT & EMPLOYEE business objects. The EMPLY01 E/RD decomposes the first E/R expression on the EMPLY E/RD into the two E/R expressions on the EMPLY01 E/RD. In addition, the APPLICANT & EMPLOYEE entity decomposes into two subcategories of this entity, namely the APPLICANT and EMPLOYEE entities. The relationship diamonds in the centers of the two E/R expressions on the EMPLY01 E/RD represent the decomposition of the APPLICANT/EMPLOYEE SERVICING OBJECTS relationship diamond in the first E/R expression on the EMPLY E/RD. These two relationships symbolize the logical data structures supporting the relationship between the CLERICAL PERSONNEL entity and the other two entities.

The relationship diamonds in the EMPLY01 E/RD in Figure 5-21 represent the MLOG-APPLICANT_DATA and MLOG-EMPLOYEE_DATA mass logical data structures. Note that these M-LDSs are subsets of the MLOG-APPLICANT_

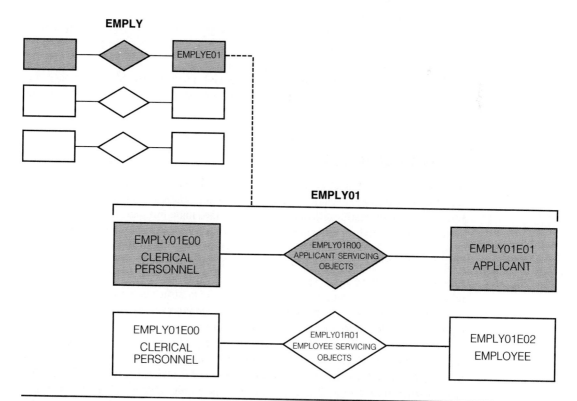

Figure 5-21. APPLICANT & EMPLOYEE explosion to level-1 E/RD (EMPLY01)

EMPLOYEE_DATA depicted as the APPLICANT/EMPLOYEE SERVICING OBJECTS relationship diamond on the EMPLY E/RD of Figure 5-19 and illustrated in the M-LDS entity type description in Figure 5-20. Thus, the APPLICANT & EMPLOYEE entity category and the MLOG-APPLICANT_EMPLOYEE_DATA M-LDS have both been decomposed on the level-1 E/RD of Figure 5-21.

Level-2 Entity/Relationship Diagram (EMPLY0101)

The APPLICANT entity in Figure 5-21 explodes down to the E/RD of Figure 5-22, causing the first E/R expression in Figure 5-21 to decompose into the three E/R expressions of the "EMPLY0101" level-2 E/RD in Figure 5-22. Notice that this diagram contains three subcategories of the CLERICAL PERSONNEL entity from Figure 5-21: EMPLOYMENT RECEPTIONIST, EMPLOYMENT CLERK, and PAYROLL CLERK.

The relationship diamonds within the three E/R expressions in Figure 5-22 symbolize decomposing the APPLICANT SERVICING OBJECTS relationship diamond in the first E/R expression on the EMPLY01 diagram. These three relationship diamonds portray the individual logical data structures supporting the relationship between the APPLICANT entity and the other three entities. These LDSs are the LOG-APPLICATION, LOG-POSITION_APPOINTMENT, and LOG-PAYROLL_ MASTER, respectively. These are the LDSs composing the MLOG-APPLICANT_ DATA M-LDS represented on the diagram in Figure 5-21 by the APPLICANT SER-VICING OBJECTS relationship diamond. Thus, both the CLERICAL PERSONNEL entity and the MLOG-APPLICANT M-LDS have been decomposed and portrayed on the diagram in Figure 5-22. Figure 5-23 illustrates the entity type description for the MLOG-APPLICANT_DATA M-LDS.

Cardinality Relationship

An important part of understanding the business objects and their meaning is understanding the cardinality relationship depicted by the relationship connection between E/RD entities and relationship diamonds (notice the single lines and branching lines on the right side of the relationship diamonds in the E/R expressions in Figure 5-22). These entries show how many of one data type have a relationship with another data type. In the E/RD modeling method used in this book, the cardinality only appears on **functional primitive E/R expressions**: the E/R expressions on an E/RD that have a relationship diamond depicting a single logical data structure and therefore do not decompose any further. The bottom E/RD for the employment example, EMPLY0101, represents an E/RD whose E/R expressions are all functional primitives.

The APPLICANT entity is in a 1:1 relationship with each of the three data types represented by the three relationship diamonds. These are the data types identified as the three LDSs in the entity type description for the MLOG-APPLICANT_DATA M-LDs structure in Figure 5-23. The three clerk-type entities (EMPLOYMENT RECEP-TIONIST, EMPLOYMENT CLERK, and PAYROLL CLERK) all maintain a 1:M

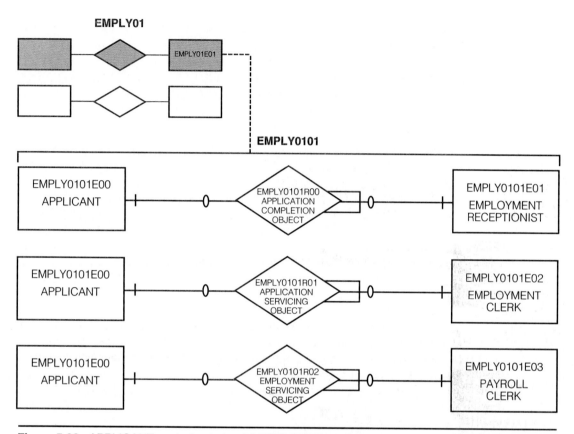

Figure 5-22. APPLICANT explosion to level-2 E/RD (EMPLY0101)

relationship with the three data types depicted as relationship diamonds.

All of the cardinality relationship connections of the three E/R expressions in the EMPLY0101 E/RD in Figure 5-22 indicate the optional ("O") or mandatory ("I") entries, as they should. Notice that for the APPLICANT, the APPLICATION COMPLETION OBJECT, APPLICATION SERVICING OBJECT, and EMPLOYMENT SERVICING OBJECT data types are all optional, and thus are denoted by the "O" entry. Furthermore, if those data types exist, an applicant must exist; hence the "I" entry. These designations signify that an applicant does not have to submit an application form, be selected for an employment servicing data type, or have a payroll data type created. However, if any one of the three data types exists, it must have an applicant associated with it. Although not explicitly designated, a cardinality relationship exists between the APPLICANT entity and the three relationship data types; namely, a 1:1 cardinality. When the cardinality relationship exists as a straight line, a 1:1 cardinality is assumed.

The cardinality relationships between the types of clerks and the three data types depicted by the relationship diamonds also show the optional and mandatory entries.

Entry Type	Dictionary ID			
Data Structure	MLOG-APPLICANT_DATA			

Alias: __JOB APPLICATION DATA__

Comment: __A M-LDS for job application form.__

Starting Volume: _____   Growth Potential: _____

No.	Ele/DS Name	DE/DS	SV/MV	Occurrences
01	LOG-APPLICATION	DS		
02	LOG-POSITION_APPOINTMENT	DS		
03	LOG-PAYROLL_MASTER	DS		

Figure 5-23. MLOG-APPLICANT_DATA entity type description

Each one of these types of clerks may not have an application object, employment object, or payroll object with which it is associated; that is, it may not exist yet. However, if any one of the data types depicted as relationship diamonds does exist, then the clerk-type data type must exist.

Explosion Paths on Entity/ Relationship Diagrams (E/RDs)

The explosion path from the top-level E/RD down to the E/RD in Figure 5-22 did not arrive at a bottom-level E/RD that contains just two individual user-type entities, as it might have. This happened because the relationship diamonds between the APPLICANT entity and the three different clerk-type entities are each fully supported by a single LDS. Had any of the relationship diamonds in Figure 5-22 symbolized a M-LDS, an explosion would have occurred on that clerk-type entity. Subsequently, the diagram on the next level would have only two entities, APPLICANT and that clerk-type entity. Thus, some explosion paths may not lead to an E/RD containing just two individual entities for each E/R expression on the E/RD. In addition, some E/R expressions on particular levels along a path may not have an entity that explodes to another diagram level. These E/R expressions would also have relationship diamonds symbolizing an individual LDS. Again, what signifies that the bottom of the decomposition has been reached is a *relationship in the E/R expression that signifies a single LDS.*

In the complete set of E/RDs for the employment application, each of the major entity categories on the right sides of the E/R expressions on the top-level diagram of Figure 5-19 explodes to its own E/RD. Successive explosions cause the categories and types of entities and M-LDSs to decompose on these lower-level diagrams.

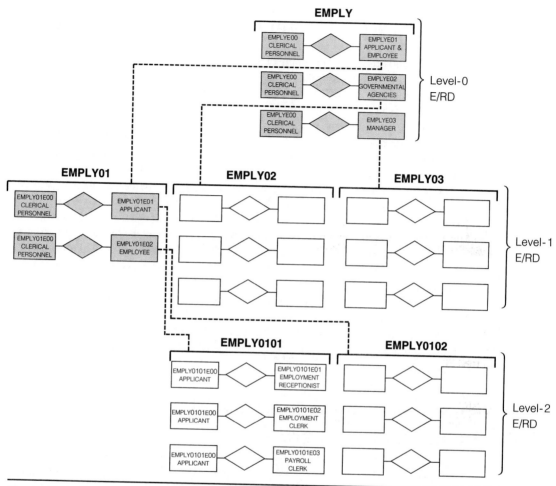

Figure 5-24. Tree illustration of employment E/RD explosions

Thus, the complete set of E/RDs theoretically forms the upside-down shape of a tree throughout successive explosions. Figure 5-24 illustrates this concept.

The collection of generalized and individual data types that enter into the business relationships and data types that support those business relationships in the tree of decomposed E/R expressions represents all of the data types for that subject area. Thus, the text E/RD modeling method performs the first important activity in good data modeling (identifying all of the data types for that subject area) through a system of purposeful decomposition of simple E/RDs. This differs significantly from other E/RD modeling methods. However, it delivers the same thing that other methods deliver: it identifies the data types important to a particular subject area, helps define them in entity type descriptions, and specifies the relationship between entities.

The text E/RD method has two main advantages. The first is the simplicity of each E/RD as created using the text E/RD modeling method. Each entity is connected to a single relationship, which in turn is connected to only one other entity. Most other E/RD methods have entities connected to many other entities and relationships for however many cardinality relationships exist between the entity and other data types. The fact that each entity is connected to many other entities often creates a jumbled mess of crossed connections among entities and relationships on the E/RD. These methods tend to defeat the purpose of using a picture to represent reality, which is to make it easier to understand.

The second advantage of the text E/RD modeling method is that business relationships are explicitly depicted. E/RDs created using other E/RD modeling methods contain business relationships, but they must be sought out in the jumble of cross-connections where three data types that have a business relationship are connected. In the text E/RD method, they are explicitly depicted, and can be used for verification with users. In most methodologies, E/RDs are used by data modelers only after discussions with users. The mess of crossed lines in an E/RD that depicts many data types makes it useless in interactions with users. Users understand the concepts of a business relationship, the objects that enter into the business relationship, and the objects that support the business relationship. Therefore, they not only help the analyst identify the objects of importance for the subject area for that E/RD decomposition; they also verify that the analyst has modeled the business relationships and objects of the business relationship properly. The simplicity of each E/RD makes it easy to teach the user how to interpret the diagrams.

Design Dictionary Specifications for Entity/Relationship Diagrams

E/RDs by themselves provide a simple method for categorizing data types for business objects, relationships between those data types, and the data types required to support those relationships. Yet the strength of this and of many other diagramming methods depends on the use of dictionary entries that describe the entities and relationships appearing on the diagrams and what they represent in the real business world. Design dictionary entries can be used to describe the components of business and information systems that appear as symbols on graph forms.

Naming Conventions

For some methodologies, every dictionary entry for a diagram symbol must be assigned a particular design dictionary identification (ID). Each dictionary ID for a symbol must be unique, but the same symbol, with the same dictionary ID, may appear more than once on a particular diagram or on subsequent levels of diagrams. For these methodologies, there is a fundamental difference between the symbol label and the accompanying dictionary ID. The symbol label (for example, CLERICAL PERSONNEL) identifies the symbol in terms easily understood by the reader of the diagram. The dictionary ID is used to index the symbol description in the design dictionary. During initial creation of the diagram, the analyst may choose to display the dictionary ID at the top or bottom of each symbol and the label in the middle of the symbol. Subsequently, the analyst will display only the labels while navigating through the set of diagrams with users; this is a way of clearing out trees in the system design forest to make it easier for users to understand.

According to established **naming convention**s for E/RDs in methodologies that use dictionary IDs, entity and relationship dictionary IDs are assigned using a combination of the E/RD name, an *E* or *R* for *entity* or *relationship*, and the entity or relationship number on the E/RD. For example, the ID for the CLERICAL PERSONNEL entity in Figure 5-19 would be EMPLYE00. The ID suggests that the symbol appears on the EMPLY diagram, that it is an entity (E), and that it is the 00 entity on this diagram. In the text E/RD modeling method, consecutive numbers are assigned to the entities from left to right and from top to bottom, beginning with 00. Relationship numbers are assigned from top to bottom, beginning with 00 in the text E/RD modeling method. Notice that the dictionary IDs for entities and relationships on the EMPLY E/RD in Figure 5-19 follow this convention, as they do on subsequent E/RDs.

Each software system that you use to create models has its own limitations on the maximum number of characters this name can have. In general, it is best to have a short acronym for the name of the top diagram, and to limit the number of explosions to between eight and ten for the sake of limiting the number of characters in the dictionary IDs to a reasonable length. A two-digit number is assigned to a symbol on a graph for dictionary IDs. This convention makes it possible to have more than nine symbols of a particular type on a single diagram. You may shorten these dictionary IDs even further by using alphabetical characters for numbers greater than 9—for example, 10 = A, 11 = B, 12 = C, and so on.

Related E/RDs are assigned names that show the navigational path from the top level down to any particular diagram. The top-level E/RD is assigned an acronym (symbolic name) signifying the subject area for which the diagrams are being constructed. Subsequent explosion E/RDs are assigned names composed of the initial acronym and numbers showing the E/R expressions from which the explosion occurred, starting from the top, down through the lower levels. This makes it possible to follow the explosion path for any set of business relationships.

The top-level diagram in Figure 5-19 is named EMPLY. Notice that an explosion on the top E/R expression that contains the entity APPLICANT & EMPLOYEE (EMPLYE01) navigates to the EMPLY01 E/RD, and that an explosion on the top E/R expression that contains the APPLICANT entity (EMPLY01E01) on the EMPLY01 diagram navigates to the EMPLY0101 E/RD. The name EMPLY0101 indicates that starting from EMPLY (the top-level E/RD), an explosion occurs on the top EMPLYE01 entity on the E/R expression down to an E/RD named EMPLY01. Subsequently, an explosion occurs on the EMPLY01E01 entity on the top E/R expression on the EMPLY01 E/RD down to the EMPLY0101 E/RD. The name of each lower-level E/RD suggests the explosion path from the E/R expression on the top E/RD down through E/R expressions on subsequent E/RD levels. Notice that the explosion path is specified by the entity in the E/R expression on which the explosion occurred, and that the E/RD level is shown by how many two-digit numbers follow the subject area acronym. Thus, the EMPLY0005 E/RD specifies that starting at the top (EMPLY, the level-0 E/RD), the 00 entity in an E/R expression was used to explode to the EMPLY00 level-1 E/RD. Subsequently, the 05 entity in an E/R expression on the EMPLY00 diagram was used to explode to the EMPLY0005 level-2 E/RD.

An additional naming convention involves the labels of the relationship diamonds on E/RDs. For relationship diamonds that depict a M-LDS (a group of objects), the plural "OBJECTS" is used in the label. For relationship diamonds that depict a single LDS, the singular "OBJECT" is used. This helps to show on the E/RD which E/R expression actually decomposes to another E/RD. The E/R expressions that have "OBJECTS" as part of their labels decompose to another E/RD; those that have "OBJECT" do not decompose. Maintaining this convention makes it easy to determine which E/R expressions on an E/RD decompose to another E/RD level.

To use the text methodology, you may decide to use a dictionary ID separate from the label of the graph symbol, especially when using the text methodology with particular CASE systems. When possible, it is preferred that the label be the dictionary ID for the graph symbols. However, the methodology will work for both choices. Examples in this text will include separate dictionary IDs so that those who prefer this method will have examples that conform to their wishes.

E/RD Dictionary Entries

Dictionary entries are created for all user-type entities and relationship diamonds that symbolize the LDSs that support the business relationship characterized by the E/R expression. These dictionary entries define the user-type entities, their relationships with other user-type entities, and the specific data supporting each relationship. The dictionary entries become progressively more specific as explosion to lower-level E/RDs occurs. The dictionary entries for top-level E/RDs define broad categories of users and the major groups of data types (M-LDSs) needed for the relationships between the categories of users. For lower-level E/RDs, the dictionary entries describe subcategories of user entities and subgroups of data types needed to support the relationships between the users. Figures 5-25, 5-26, and 5-27 illustrate dictionary entries for the CLERICAL PERSONNEL, APPLICANT/EMPLOYEE SERVICING OBJECTS, and APPLICANT & EMPLOYEE on the top E/R expression in Figure 5-19. Bear in mind that all the dictionary entry formats shown in this text are generic formats; they are not associated with any specific dictionary system.

The dictionary entries in Figures 5-25 and 5-27 are used to explain the major categories of users called CLERICAL PERSONNEL and APPLICANT & EMPLOYEE. For example, the dictionary entry in Figure 5-25 for the CLERICAL PERSONNEL entity provides textual information regarding this major category of entity. The first line of the dictionary entry in Figure 5-25 identifies it as the entry for an entity symbol labeled CLERICAL PERSONNEL, and gives the dictionary ID for this symbol as EMPLYE00. (Remember that many dictionaries do not require a separate dictionary ID.)

Exploding the E/R expression normally causes a decomposition of the E/R expression on a separate E/RD. However, for this example, the user-type entity in the

Entry Type   **Label**   **Dictionary ID**

Entity   CLERICAL PERSONNEL   EMPLYE00

Explodes to:

   E/RD: _____

   Data structure dictionary entry: _____

Text Description & Comments

This entity is used to represent clerical personnel involved with the employment system. They provide clerical assistance during the employment process and subsequent record keeping for persons hired. They require access to all relevant data needed to process applications for employment and subsequent employment history.

Figure 5-25. CLERICAL PERSONNEL entity dictionary entry

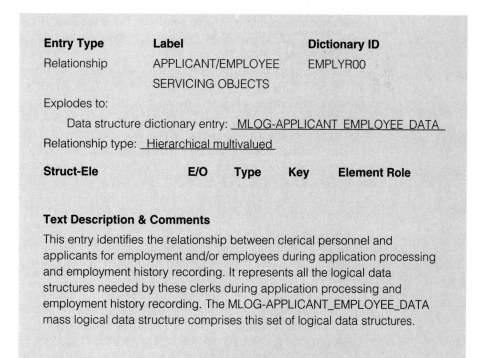

Entry Type   **Label**   **Dictionary ID**

Relationship   APPLICANT/EMPLOYEE   EMPLYR00
                        SERVICING OBJECTS

Explodes to:

   Data structure dictionary entry: _MLOG-APPLICANT_EMPLOYEE_DATA_

Relationship type: _Hierarchical multivalued_

Struct-Ele   **E/O**   **Type**   **Key**   **Element Role**

Text Description & Comments

This entry identifies the relationship between clerical personnel and applicants for employment and/or employees during application processing and employment history recording. It represents all the logical data structures needed by these clerks during application processing and employment history recording. The MLOG-APPLICANT_EMPLOYEE_DATA mass logical data structure comprises this set of logical data structures.

Figure 5-26. APPLICANT/EMPLOYEE SERVICING OBJECTS relationship
          dictionary entry

Entry Type   **Label**   **Dictionary ID**

Entity   APPLICANT & EMPLOYEE   EMPLYE01

Explodes to:

    E/RD: EMPLY01

    Data structure dictionary entry: _____

Text Description & Comments

This entity is used to represent applicants or existing employees having relationships with clerical personnel involved in the employment system.

Figure 5-27. APPLICANT & EMPLOYEE entity dictionary entry

E/R expression is used to cause explosion to a lower-level E/RD. This is used as the generic example because CASE systems may permit the application of the text E/RD method if the entity symbol dictionary entry is used for E/R expression explosion. Notice that the explosion could cause migration to an additional dictionary entry designated as a data structure. When an entity does not explode to another E/RD, it will explode to a LDS containing data elements used to identify the real-world data type that the entity represents.

The dictionary entry in Figure 5-26 provides textual information regarding the APPLICANT/EMPLOYEE SERVICING OBJECTS relationship. Figure 5-26 also contains blank entries, which will be explained in the discussion of database design issues in Chapter 10. Some entries here specify the symbol label (APPLICANT/ EMPLOYEE SERVICING OBJECTS) and the dictionary ID (EMPLYR00), which provides a textual explanation of the relationship. The "Explodes to:" entry suggests that exploding on this symbol causes migration to the data structure dictionary entry for the MLOG-APPLICANT_EMPLOYEE_DATA M-LDS. This M-LDS embodies the LDSs needed to support the business relationship between the CLERICAL PER-SONNEL and APPLICANT & EMPLOYEE entities.

The first line in Figure 5-27 specifies that this entry denotes an entity labeled APPLICANT & EMPLOYEE with a dictionary ID of EMPLYE01. The second line shows that this entity explodes to the EMPLY01 E/RD—the E/RD illustrated in Figure 5-21.

Dictionary entries for LDSs and M-LDSs provide formatting details for them. The dictionary entries for an individual LDS identify data elements that it comprises, whereas those for a M-LDS identify the LDSs or M-LDSs that it comprises. The dictionary entry for the MLOG-APPLICANT_EMPLOYEE_DATA data structure that accompanies the APPLICANT/EMPLOYEE SERVICING OBJECTS relationship appears in Figure 5-28.

The MLOG prefix shows that MLOG-APPLICANT_EMPLOYEE_DATA is a

Entry Type	Dictionary ID			
Data Structure	MLOG-APPLICANT_EMPLOYEE_DATA			

Alias: _JOB APPLICATION/NOTIFICATION EMPLOYEE SERVICING_

Comment: _MLOG-DS for job applicants and employees._

Starting Volume: _____ Growth Potential: _____

No.	Ele/DS Name	DE/DS	SV/MV	Occurrences
01	MLOG-APPLICANT_DATA	DS		
02	MLOG-EMPLOYEE_DATA	DS		

Figure 5-28. MLOG-APPLICANT_EMPLOYEE_DATA dictionary entry

mass logical data structure consisting of the two M-LDSs identified on separate lines of the entry. The line entries specify the name of each item, whether it represents a data element (DE) or a separate data structure (DS), whether it is single-valued (SV) or multivalued (MV), and the number of occurrences (if fixed) for MV items. The SV and MV entries will have more meaning in Chapter 10, especially in the discussion of a process called normalization. For now, these entries mean that only one (SV) or many (MV) instances of that line item are associated with the logical data structure.

Dictionary entries are created for the entity and relationship diamonds for each separate E/R expression on the top-level E/RD and subsequent levels, in order to provide the progressively more detailed documentation regarding users and data needed to support relationships between users.

At the lowest-level E/RD, the same user entity may appear either as the left side or as the right side of each E/R expression, or as both. Notice that APPLICANT appears on the left side of each E/R expression in Figure 5-22. Since all relationships on this E/RD depict single LDSs, it represents the lowest-level E/R explosion. The dictionary entry for APPLICANT at this level should explode to a LDS dictionary entry used as a data reference for the real-world data type the entity symbolizes. The relationship diamonds on this E/RD indicate that individual data items in the LDS provide the information needed to support the relationship between the users. Figures 5-29, 5-30, and 5-31 illustrate this idea with the dictionary entries for the APPLICANT and EMPLOYMENT RECEPTIONIST entities and the APPLICATION COMPLETION OBJECT relationship in the first E/R expression in Figure 5-22.

The dictionary entry in Figure 5-29 documents the APPLICANT symbols that appear in Figure 5-22. All have the same dictionary ID, EMPLY0101E00. Notice that this entry explodes to the data structure entry "LOG-APPLICANT." This shows how a user entity on the lowest E/RD level may explode to a LDS—in this case, LOG-APPLICANT describes the entity for reference purposes.

The dictionary entry in Figure 5-30 documents the relationship between the appli-

Entry Type	Label	Dictionary ID
Entity	APPLICANT	EMPLY0101E00

Explodes to:

E/RD: _____

Data structure dictionary entry: __LOG-APPLICANT__

Text Description & Comments

This entity represents an applicant for a job position in the employment system. Applicants require clerical assistance from the reception clerk to fill out the job application form for record keeping on persons applying for a job. The job application form becomes a permanent record for the applicant.

Figure 5-29. APPLICANT entity dictionary entry

Entry Type	Label	Dictionary ID
Relationship	APPLICATION COMPLETION OBJECT	EMPLY0101R00

Explodes to:

Data structure dictionary entry: __LOG-APPLICATION__

Relationship type: __Hierarchical multivalued__

Struct-Ele	E/O	Type	Key	Element Role
SSNUMBER	E	SV	PRI	Identification
NAME	E	SV	SEC	Person's name
ADDRESS	E	SV		Employee address
NEXT_OF_KIN	E	SV		Identify kin
NEXT_OF_KIN_TELEPHONE	E	SV		Kin phone number
DATE	E	MV		Application date

Text Description & Comments

This relationship identifies the data requested of a job applicant by the reception clerk for the employment system. This relationship explodes to the LOG-APPLICATION data structure that contains data items used by personnel employees to review applicants and fill positions. The LOG-APPLICATION data structure is also a permanent record for applicants.

Figure 5-30. APPLICATION COMPLETION OBJECT relationship dictionary entry

cant and the employment reception clerk entities. As stated previously, a business keeps records of data types that influence or are influenced by the business. LDSs are used to document these data types. The line items of the data structures contain either data elements or separate data types related to the data structures. For example, a data structure for a department within the business could contain a data element for the name of the department and a line item for personnel. Since personnel also represents a separate object, the line item represents a data type within a data type.

The main entries in Figure 5-30 identify line items of the data structure and describe how to use them. The "Struct-Ele" (Structure/Element) entry specifies the dictionary name for each line item in the data structure. The "E/O" entry specifies whether each line item represents a data element (E), referring to the data type, or an entirely separate but related object (O). The "Type" entry shows whether the line item is single-valued (SV) or multivalued (MV); that is, whether single or multiple values are required to document this line item accurately. For example, NAME is single-valued because the applicant only has one name, but since a person may fill out job applications on many different dates, DATE is multivalued.

The "Key" entry indicates which line item is used as a primary (PRI) key and which as a secondary (SEC) key for the particular set of data structure values. For example, a SSNUMBER value may be used to key on a particular applicant entry. The "Element Role" entry shows the role played by the data structure element in relation to the user entity's information needs.

Data Structure and Data Element Dictionary Entries

The dictionary also contains an entry for the LOG-APPLICATION like the one shown in Figure 5-32, which illustrates the format for this LDS. This LDS is depicted as the APPLICATION COMPLETION OBJECT relationship on the EMPLY0101 E/RD in Figure 5-22. The line items in Figure 5-32 first identify the elements of the data struc-

---

Entry Type	Label	Dictionary ID
Entity	EMPLOYMENT RECEPTIONIST	EMPLY0101E01
Explodes to:		

E/RD: _____

Data structure dictionary entry: LOG-EMPLOYEE MASTER

Text Description & Comments

This entity is used to represent the employment reception clerk who is responsible for securing job applications from applicants.

Figure 5-31. EMPLOYMENT RECEPTIONIST entity dictionary entry

ture under the heading "Ele/DS Name." The next column specifies whether they are data elements (DE) or separate data structures (DS) within this data structure. The last column specifies whether the line item is single-valued (SV) or multivalued (MV).

The "Alias" entry in Figure 5-32 provides a way to identify this data type by another name. Frequently, users from different areas of the business use different names for the same data type, usually names that describe their area of the business. The "Starting Volume" and "Growth Potential" entries provide a way of knowing how many objects to expect initially and how many to expect in the future. These two entries are particularly useful when the time comes to create ways of storing this type of data and to use the data in testing a new system.

Each data element identified in a data structure dictionary entry is also document-ed in data element dictionary entries. Figure 5-33 shows a data item dictionary entry for the SSNUMBER data element.

The first two entries—"Entry Type" and "Dictionary ID"—in Figure 5-33 speci-fy that this is a data element dictionary entry for an item called SSNUMBER. The "Alias" entry suggests additional names used in other functional areas of the business for a data element; some people in this firm refer to this data element by the name PERSON_ID or EMPLOYEE_NUMBER.

The next entries in Figure 5-33 specifies the type of data contained in this ele-ment, its length, and its input and output formats. The element type typically shows whether the item consists of characters or numbers; also, the type of numerical data (binary, decimal, packed-decimal, and other valid numerical types). "Length" shows the number of bytes, despite the element type. The input and output formats specify how the data is presented in input or output functions within different applications (remember that the same data element may serve many applications within the busi-ness). For example, the input format typically specifies only the digit positioning, except for the decimal position. The output format typically specifies digit positioning and appropriate editing of the data item—for example, adding hyphens.

The entries for "Data request prompt:" and "Columnar heading:" specify how users are to be prompted for data entry by the existing system and what column head-ing is to appear above the data element in reports. These entries ensure that system developers always consistently identify a data element on business forms, screen dis-plays, and reports.

Logical and Physical Data Structure Relationship

The final line item in Figure 5-33 illustrates a technique to connect logical data struc-tures with physical data structures. Typically, the files and databases of a business either already exist, or will exist shortly after the data model is created. A logical data structure represents the way a user wants data to be displayed, not necessarily the way the data is physically stored. In fact, a string of data that satisfies a user's information need typically causes more than one physical record to be retrieved. For example, the DATE and POSITION in Figure 5-32 are likely to be maintained in separate physical files with records for the social security number, date, and position regarding a partic-ular job classification.

Entry Type   **Dictionary ID**

Data Structure   LOG-APPLICATION

Alias: _JOB APPLICATION DATA_

Comment: _A LOG-DS for job application data._

Starting Volume: _____   Growth Potential: _____

No.	Ele/DS Name	DE/DS	SV/MV	Occurrences
01	SSNUMBER	DE	SV	
02	NAME	DE	SV	
03	ADDRESS	DE	SV	
04	TELEPHONE_NUMBER	DE	SV	
05	NEXT_OF_KIN	DE	SV	
06	NEXT_OF_KIN_TELEPHONE	DE	SV	
07	DATE	DE	MV	
08	POSITION	DE	MV	
09	MPHY-APPLICATION	DS		

Figure 5-32. LOG-APPLICATION dictionary entry

Entry Type   **Dictionary ID**

Data Element   SSNUMBER

Alias: _PERSON ID_
       EMPLOYEE NUMBER

Element Type	Length	Input Format	Output Format
Character	9	XXXXXXXXX	XXX-XX-XXXX

Data request prompt: _SOC. SEC. Number:_

Columnar heading: _SOC. SEC. Number_

Roles* portrayed by element: _Identify People_
                              Identify Applicant

Text Description & Comments

This data item is used to identify people within applicant, employment, and payroll data structures.

*This entry is not currently found in existing dictionary systems, but it can be simulated by including it at the beginning of the "Text Description & Comments" entry.

Figure 5-33. SSNUMBER dictionary entry

Entry Type   **Dictionary ID**

Data Structure   MPHY-APPLICATION

Alias: _JOB APPLICATION PHYSICAL DATA STRUCTURE_

Comment: _A MPHY-DS for job application data._

Starting Volume: _____   Growth Potential: _____

No.	Ele/DS Name	DE/DS	SV/MV	Occurrences
01	PHY-APPLICANT	DS		
02	PHY-APPLICATION	DS		

Figure 5-34. MPHY-APPLICATION dictionary entry

In the text methodology, the last line item in a LDS identifies a **mass physical data structure (M-PDS)** that identifies the physical data structures that contain the data elements of the LDS. The dictionary entry for the M-PDS specifies the physical data structures that must be accessed to make the elements of the LDS available to the user. Figure 5-34 illustrates the dictionary entry for the MPHY-APPLICATION, which has two physical data structures. Thus, the data needed in support of the relationship between the APPLICANT and EMPLOYMENT RECEPTIONIST entities, represented by LOG-APPLICATION, comes from two physical data structures: PHY-APPLICANT and PHY-APPLICATION. Physical data structures (PDSs) specify how data is physically stored, not necessarily how the data serves information needs. The importance of this entry will be clearer after you have studied the chapters on databases, prototyping, and system development.

The data elements identified in PDSs are typically the same as those specified in LDSs. The data element dictionary entries serve to define them for both LDSs and PDSs, thus avoiding redundant entries.

Entity/Relationship Modeling Method and the Logical Design Phase

The E/R data recording method is used to document business relationships in the application and to identify user requirements. Subsequently, data flow diagrams (DFDs) are used to document system processing and input and output data. This documentation is used to depict the findings of an investigation and to evaluate its results, as you will see in Chapter 6. Examples are presented for the types of information obtained through analyzing the data gathered during the analysis phase. Chapter 6 explains the process of review and evaluation of final results of the investigation, including identification of the participants, the content, and the structure of the review. Computer-aided methods for various portions of the analysis phase are also discussed, with examples of some of the types of assistance they provide. These are the combined set of activities that follow the information engineering activities. CASE systems help complete these activities, as the NG&T example illustrates.

DATA MODELING FOR THE NATIONAL GOLF & TENNIS (NG&T) PROJECT

The E/R modeling method discussed in previous sections will now be used to record and analyze the data obtained during data gathering, as described in Chapter 4, for the NG&T case introduced at the end of Chapter 3. (A short review of that case is recommended before proceeding.) First, the subject areas to use for E/R modeling must be identified. These subject areas embody business functions that appear on NG&T's function decomposition diagram. Figure 5-35 illustrates the part of this function decomposition that applies to the E/RDs created for servicing customer orders. This partial function decomposition is a part of the larger function decomposition comprising all NG&T functions. The function decomposition in Figure 5-35 identifies the major function, SERVICE ORDERS, which is used as the subject area for the NG&T entity/relationship diagrams that appear in the remaining portion of this chapter. The two boxes below the SERVICE ORDERS function, MAINTAIN INVENTORY and FILL ORDERS, could be either subfunctions or processes that support the SERVICE ORDERS function.

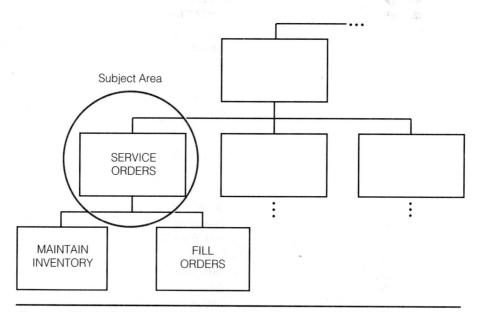

Figure 5-35. SERVICE ORDERS function as a subject area for the NG&T case

Interviews and personal observations by the project team reveal that specific data must be retained for five main participants who are involved in the order processing. The data is used in support of the business relationships between these participants:

- Clerical personnel to customers
- Clerical personnel to vendors
- Clerical personnel to carriers
- Clerical personnel to managers

National Golf & Tennis Entity/ Relationship Diagrams

Each set of expressions on respective E/RDs identifies business relationships between major categories of users with the data needed to support the relationships. For example, clerical personnel and customers have a number of relationships requiring data structures for support. Managers frequently study data gathered in support of clerical personnel and other participants. However, this data is usually gathered as a result of the relationships between clerical personnel and the other participants. Figures 5-36

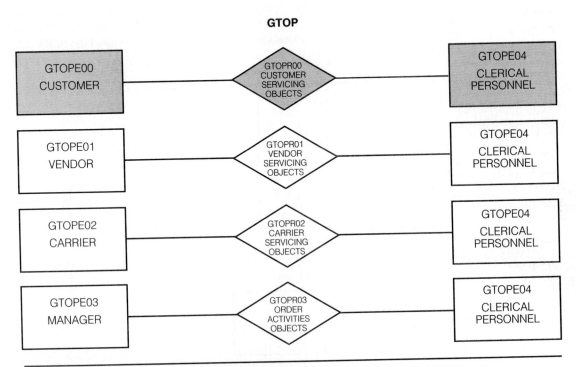

Figure 5-36. Order processing GTOP level-0 E/RD

through 5-39 contain three levels of E/RDs, showing some of the relationships between the participants in the SERVICE ORDERS subject area.

The set of E/RDs in Figures 5-36 through 5-39 starts with major categories of NG&T users on the GTOP level-0 E/RD. This E/RD contains four E/R expressions, depicting the four main business relationships for the SERVICE ORDERS subject

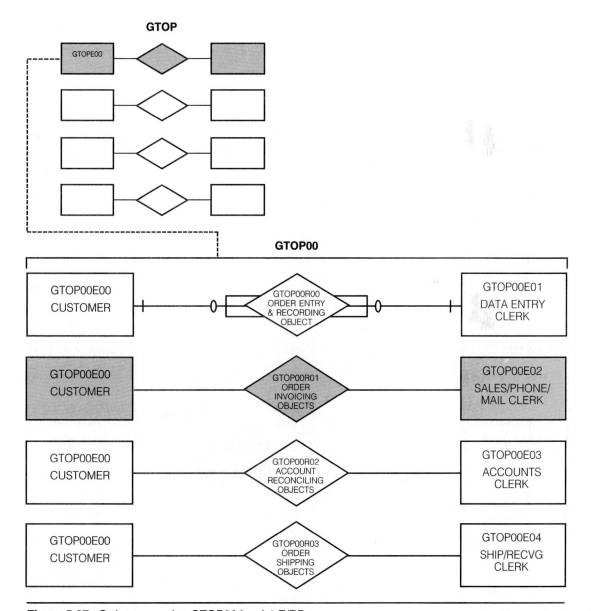

Figure 5-37. Order processing GTOP00 level-1 E/RD

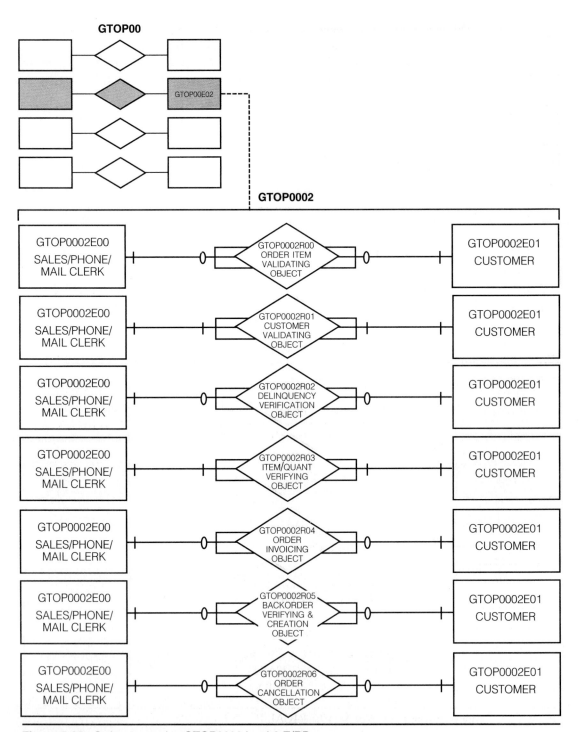

Figure 5-38. Order processing GTOP0002 level-2 E/RD

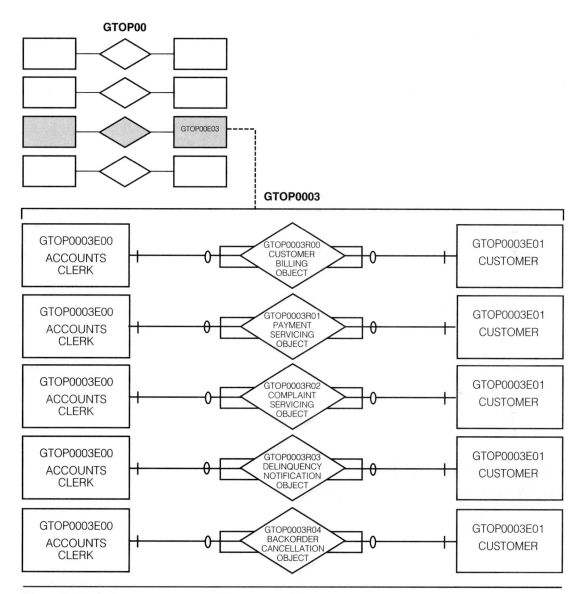

Figure 5-39. Order processing GTOP0003 level-2 E/RD

area. These business relationships exist between the CLERICAL PERSONNEL entity and the CUSTOMER, VENDOR, CARRIER, and MANAGER entities, respectively, from the top E/R expression to the bottom one.

The E/R expression at the top of the GTOP diagram in Figure 5-36 represents the relationship between the CLERICAL PERSONNEL and CUSTOMER entities. The CUSTOMER entity in this E/R expression is used to explode down to the GTOP00 level-1 E/RD in Figure 5-37. This E/RD decomposes the first E/R expression and also decomposes the CLERICAL PERSONNEL entity into types of clerks that have a relationship with the CUSTOMER entity, including the data types needed to support these relationships. Each of the entities (VENDOR, CARRIER, and MANAGER) that interacts with the CLERICAL PERSONNEL entity in the GTOP E/RD also explodes down to lower-level E/RDs (these explosions are not shown).

The GTOP00 level-1 E/RD in Figure 5-37 contains the major relationships between specific clerks and customers in the order processing application. Notice that the CLERICAL PERSONNEL entity has also been decomposed on this diagram. This E/RD indicates that there are four major relationships between these entities relative to the order-processing application:

- Order entry and recording
- Customer order invoicing
- Customer account reconciling
- Customer order shipping

The order is first entered by the DATA ENTRY CLERK and then serviced by the SALES/PHONE/MAIL CLERK. After a customer transaction is serviced by the SALES/PHONE/MAIL CLERK, data recorded during this relationship is used to reconcile the customer's account and fill the order. The respective relationships between the CUSTOMER entity and the SALES/PHONE/MAIL CLERK and ACCOUNTS CLERK entities are depicted in the GTOP0002 and GTOP0003 E/RDs in Figures 5-38 and 5-39. The SALES/PHONE/MAIL CLERK entity in Figure 5-37 explodes down to the E/RD in Figure 5-38; the ACCOUNTS CLERK entity in Figure 5-37 explodes down to the E/RD in Figure 5-39.

National Golf & Tennis Dictionary E/RD Entries

It is important to remember that without descriptive dictionary entries for each component of the E/RD, the use of E/RDs serves a very limited purpose. However, E/RDs accompanied by detailed dictionary entries for each component of the diagram can produce easily understood and factually based specifications for user requirements.

These dictionary entries help explain the components of E/RDs and related data structure and element descriptions. They provide narrative explanations for various entities, relationships, data structure descriptions, and data element descriptions.

Figures 5-40, 5-41, and 5-42 contain dictionary entries for the components and subcomponents of the E/R expression at the top of Figure 5-36. The entry in Figure 5-41 identifies a mass logical data structure (M-LDS) used to support this major business relationship. The dictionary entries correspond to the three symbols in Figure 5-36, reading from right to left at the top of the diagram, providing a general explanation for the relationship between clerical personnel and customers. Dictionary entries would also be recorded for the entities and relationships in the three remaining E/R expres-

Entry Type	Label	Dictionary ID
Entity	CLERICAL PERSONNEL	GTOPE04

Explodes to:

E/RD: _____

Data structure dictionary entry: _____

Text Description & Comments

This entity represents clerical personnel involved with order processing. These people are data entry, sales/phone/mail, accounts, and shipping/receiving clerks. These personnel are involved in securing customer orders, recording customer and vendor orders, validating customer orders, processing customer and vendor orders, recording customer and vendor shipments and receipts, recording accounts payment receipts, and expediting customer/ vendor complaints and delinquencies. They require access to all relevant data needed to service order filling.

Figure 5-40. CLERICAL PERSONNEL entity dictionary entry

Entry Type	Label	Dictionary ID
Relationship	CUSTOMER SERVICING OBJECTS	GTOPR00

Explodes to:

Data structure dictionary entry: _MLOG-CUSTOMER_DATA_

Relationship type: _Hierarchical multivalued_

Struct-Ele	E/O	Type	Key	Element Role

Text Description & Comments

This entry explains the relationship between clerical personnel and customers relative to their involvement in order processing. This relationship is supported by the mass logical data structure called MLOG-CUSTOMER_DATA, which contains other mass logical and individual logical data structures supporting the relationship between customers and clerical personnel.

Figure 5-41. CUSTOMER SERVICING OBJECTS relationship dictionary entry

Entry Type	Label	Dictionary ID
Entity	CUSTOMER	GTOPE00

Explodes to:

    E/RD: _GTOP00_____

    Data structure dictionary entry: _____

Text Description & Comments

This entity represents either phone/mail or retail customers who order goods, receive item shipments, receive billing notices, make payments, receive delinquency notices, or register complaints. Various clerical personnel are involved in servicing customers with respect to these activities.

Figure 5-42. CUSTOMER entity dictionary entry

Entry Type	Dictionary ID
Data Structure	MLOG-CUSTOMER_DATA

Alias: _CUSTOMER ORDER PROCESSING DATA_

Comment: _A MLOG-DS for customer ordering relationships._

Starting Volume: _____   Growth Potential: _____

No.	Ele/DS Name	DE/DS	SV/MV	Occurrences
01	LOG-CUSTTRNS	DS	SV	
02	MLOG-CUSTORDR	DS		
03	MLOG-CUSTACCOUNTS	DS		
04	MLOG-CUSTSHIP	DS		

Figure 5-43. MLOG-CUSTOMER_DATA M-LDS dictionary entry

sions on this E/RD. Figure 5-43 shows a dictionary entry for the MLOG-CUSTOMER_DATA data structure used to support the relationship between customers and clerical personnel.

The NG&T project team also creates data structure dictionary entries for each individual M-LDS contained in the MLOG-CUSTOMER_DATA M-LDS of Figure 5-43. These groups of logical data structures support relationships between different clerical personnel and customers. These relationships are exhibited in the GTOP00 E/RD of Figure 5-37.

Entry Type	Label		Dictionary ID
Relationship	ORDER ENTRY & RECORDING OBJECT		GTOP00R00

Explodes to:

Data structure dictionary entry: LOG-CUSTTRNS

Relationship type: Hierarchical multivalued

Struct-Ele	E/O	Type	Key	Element Role
CUSTNUM	E	SV	PRI	IDENTIFY CUSTOMER
CUSTNAME	E	SV	SEC	IDENTIFY CUSTOMER
STREET	E	SV		ADDRESS
CITY	E	SV		ADDRESS
STATE	E	SV		ADDRESS
ZIP	E	SV		ADDRESS
ORDER_NUMBER	E	SV		IDENTIFY ORDER
TRANTYPE	E	SV		RETAIL/PHONE/MAIL
SHIPSTREET	E	SV		SHIP ADDRESS
SHIPCITY	E	SV		SHIP ADDRESS
SHIPSTATE	E	SV		SHIP ADDRESS
SHIPZIP	E	SV		SHIP ADDRESS
ITEMNUM	E	MV		IDENTIFY ORD ITEM
QUANTITY	E	MV		ITEM ORD QUANT
DATE	E	SV		ORDER DATE
EMPNUM	E	SV		IDENTIFY ORD CLERK
MAGAZINE_SOURCE	E	SV		ADVERTISING SOURCE
REGION_SOURCE	E	SV		MAIL REGION

Text Description & Comments

This relationship represents the relationship between customers and sales/phone/mail clerks during initial recording and entry of customer orders. These clerks receive customer retail, phone, or mail orders and record them. This relationship is supported by the LOG-CUSTTRNS logical data structure.

Figure 5-44. ORDER ENTRY & RECORDING OBJECT relationship dictionary entry

Figures 5-44 and 5-45 are dictionary entries accompanying the relationship and CUSTOMER entity for the first E/R expression in Figure 5-37 (GTOP00). Notice that the relationship diamond has "OBJECT" as part of its label. The singular form signifies that this is a functional primitive E/R expression. This is the only E/R expression on this E/RD that is a functional primitive. This example shows how a functional primitive E/R expression may appear on an E/RD where other E/R expressions are not

Entry Type	Label	Dictionary ID
Entity	CUSTOMER	GTOP00E00

Explodes to:

    E/RD: _____

    Data structure dictionary entry: _LOG-CUSTMAST_

Text Description & Comments

This entity represents either phone/mail or retail customers who order goods, receive billing notices, make payments, accept back orders, receive delinque.ncy notices, register complaints, and/or cancel orders for goods. Various clerical personnel are responsible for servicing customers with respect to these activities.

Figure 5-45. CUSTOMER entity dictionary entry

functional primitives; that is, the relationship diamonds of the other expressions depict mass logical data structures. Also notice that the cardinality relationship entries appear on this E/R expression. Figure 5-46 shows the dictionary entry for the LOG-CUSTTRNS LDS to which the ORDER ENTRY & RECORDING OBJECT relationship diamond explodes.

Figures 5-47, 5-48, and 5-49 represent dictionary entries for the ORDER INVOICING OBJECTS relationship and the SALES/PHONE/MAIL CLERK entity appearing in the second E/R expression in the GTOP00 E/RD of Figure 5-37 and an entry for the MLOG-CUSTORDR M-LDS. This expression illustrates all data interaction between customers and sales/phone/mail clerks. Notice that the SALES/PHONE/MAIL CLERK entity explodes down to the GTOP0002 E/RD in Figure 5-38. Figure 5-49 illustrates the MLOG-CUSTORDR M-LDS supporting the relationship between customers and order clerks. This M-LDS contains a list of the individual LDSs needed during order servicing between customers and order clerks. Notice that the number of LDSs in this M-LDS corresponds to the number of business relationships on the lower-level E/RD (GTOP0002) to which the E/R expression that contains the ORDER INVOICING OBJECTS relationship explodes.

The relationship diamonds in the GTOP0002 E/RD of Figure 5-38 symbolize the individual LDSs identified as line items in Figure 5-49. Notice that the word "OBJECT" is included in all the labels. The GTOP0002 E/RD illustrates all relationships between the SALES/PHONE/MAIL CLERK and CUSTOMER entities during order processing. Notice that each E/R expression has a complete cardinality relationship entry.

Figures 5-50 and 5-51 show the dictionary entries for the ORDER INVOICING OBJECT relationship diamond and the LOG-CUSTORDR LDS for the GTOP0002

Entry Type   **Dictionary ID**

Data Structure   LOG-CUSTTRNS

Alias: __CUSTOMER ORDER DATA__

Comment: __A LOG-DS for a validated customer order.__

Starting Volume: _____   Growth Potential: _____

No.	Ele/DS Name	DE/DS	SV/MV	Occurrences
01	ORDER_NUMBER	DE	SV	
02	CUSTNUM	DE	SV	
03	CUSTNAME	DE	SV	
04	STREET	DE	SV	
05	CITY	DE	SV	
06	STATE	DE	SV	
07	ZIP	DE	SV	
08	SHIPSTREET	DE	SV	
09	SHIPCITY	DE	SV	
10	SHIPSTATE	DE	SV	
11	SHIPZIP	DE	SV	
12	ITEMNUM	DE	MV	
13	QUANTITY	DE	MV	
14	DATE	DE	SV	
15	EMPNUM	DE	SV	
16	MAGAZINE_SOURCE	DE	SV	
17	REGION_SOURCE	DE	SV	
18	MPHY-CUSTORDR	DS		

Figure 5-46. LOG-CUSTTRNS LDS dictionary entry

E/RD. Dictionary entries are also created for the entities, relationships, and data structures for this E/RD.

The entry in Figure 5-50 provides documentation concerning the data elements contained in the LDSs. The "Hierarchical multivalued" relationship type specification will be explained in Chapter 10. The heading line following this entry identifies specific information concerning the data elements in the LOG-CUSTORDR logical data structure. The first entry ("Struct-Ele") indicates the dictionary name for an individual data element or group of data elements. An example of a data item group might be CUST-NAME, which consists of the first and last name and the middle initial of a customer.

The "E/O" entry in Figure 5-50 specifies whether the line item is an element (individual data item) or a completely separate object that needs to be logically defined as a separate real-world data type. For example, the customer order is a real-

Entry Type	Label		Dictionary ID
Relationship	ORDER INVOICING OBJECTS		GTOP00R01

Explodes to:

    Data structure dictionary entry: <u>MLOG-CUSTORDR</u>

Relationship type: <u>Hierarchical multivalued</u>

Struct-Ele	E/O	Type	Key	Element Role

Text Description & Comments

This description identifies the relationship between customers and sales/phone/mail clerks. This relationship explains the association between these clerks and customers relative to their involvement in order processing. It is exhibited in the mass logical data structure called MLOG-CUSTORDR, which consists of individual logical data structures supporting the relationship between the order clerk and customers.

Figure 5-47. ORDER INVOICING OBJECTS relationship dictionary entry

Entry Type	Label	Dictionary ID
Entity	SALES/PHONE/MAIL CLERK	GTOP00E02

Explodes to:

    E/RD: <u>GTOP0002</u>

    Data structure dictionary entry: _____

Text Description & Comments

This entity represents sales/phone/mail clerks who record the customer order, validate the customer, check inventory levels for processing the order, create back orders, and cancel the order if necessary. These clerks pass the order to the accounts clerk for account reconciliation and to the shipping/receiving clerk for order filling. A vendor order and customer back order for stock outages is created for inventory falling short of the reorder point.

Figure 5-48. SALES/PHONE/MAIL CLERK entity dictionary entry

Entry Type   **Dictionary ID**

Data Structure   MLOG-CUSTORDR

Alias: CUSTOMER ORDERING DATA

Comment: A MLOG-DS for the order invoicing relationship.

Starting Volume: _____   Growth Potential: _____

No.	Ele/DS Name	DE/DS	SV/MV	Occurrences
01	LOG-ITEMMAST	DS		
02	LOG-CUSTMAST	DS		
03	LOG-CUST_DELINQUENCY	DS		
04	LOG-ITEMQUANTITY	DS		
05	LOG-CUSTORDR	DS		
06	LOG-CUST_BACKORDR	DS		
07	LOG-CUSTORDR_ CANCELLATION	DS		

Figure 5-49. MLOG-CUSTORDR M-LDS dictionary entry

world data type for NG&T. The data elements that describe the customer refer to a customer real-world data type. These data elements could have been separated out of the order invoice as a separate data structure and referenced as an object within the order invoice object. The object designation (O) will be explained in more detail in Chapter 10 during discussions of physical data structures used in database design.

The "Type" specification is used to indicate whether the data element is single-valued (SV) or multivalued (MV). For example, the data elements ORDER_NUMBER and CUSTNUM refer to data values used to identify orders and customers. A single data value can be used for these purposes. However, the data elements ITEMNUM and QUANTITY are correctly designated as multivalued. A customer order frequently contains several items being ordered in particular quantities.

A specification in the "Key" column for a data element indicates whether the data element is a primary (PRI) or secondary (SEC) key. A primary key is a principal data value used to distinguish between different data structures. For example, the data elements ORDER_NUMBER, CUSTNUM, CUSTNAME, ITEMNUM, and EMPNUM are all designated as keys. The ORDER_NUMBER data element is a primary key for the order invoice data structure itself. The CUSTNUM and CUSTNAME data elements are secondary keys that may both be used for customer identification. The ITEMNUM data element is a secondary key that may be used to identify inventory

Entry Type	Label		Dictionary ID
Relationship	ORDER INVOICING OBJECT		GTOP0002R04

Explodes to:

Data structure dictionary entry: <u>LOG-CUSTORDR</u>

Relationship type: <u>Hierarchical multivalued</u>

Struct-Ele	E/O	Type	Key	Element Role
ORDER_NUMBER	E	SV	PRI	IDENTIFY ORDER
CUSTNUM	E	SV	SEC	IDENTIFY CUSTOMER
CUSTNAME	E	SV	SEC	IDENTIFY CUSTOMER
STREET	E	SV		ADDRESS
CITY	E	SV		ADDRESS
STATE	E	SV		ADDRESS
ZIP	E	SV		ADDRESS
ITEMNUM	E	MV	SEC	IDENTIFY ORD ITEM
QUANTITY	E	MV		ITEM ORD QUANT
DATE	E	MV		ORDER DATE
EMPNUM	E	SV	SEC	IDENTIFY ORD CLERK

Text Description & Comments

This relationship represents the association between retail sales or sales/phone/mail clerks and customers during order invoicing. It involves creating customer order invoices for recording order filling or retail sales. This relationship is exhibited in the logical data structure called LOG-CUSTORDR.

Figure 5-50. ORDER INVOICING OBJECT relationship dictionary entry

items. The EMPNUM data element is a secondary key that may be used to identify the employee creating the order invoice. Figure 5-52 shows a dictionary entry for the ORDER_NUMBER data element. The NG&T project team also creates dictionary entries for the remaining data elements in the LOG-CUSTORDR data structure (as well as all other data structures).

The E/R expression containing the CUSTOMER and ACCOUNTS CLERK entities in the GTOP00 E/RD of Figure 5-37 decomposes down to the level-2 E/RD in Figure 5-39. Dictionary entries for the ACCOUNT RECONCILING OBJECTS relationship and ACCOUNTS CLERK entity appear in Figures 5-53 and 5-54, respectively. This business relationship is supported by the MLOG-CUSTACCOUNTS M-LDS. Figure 5-55

Entry Type	Dictionary ID			
Data Structure	LOG-CUSTORDR			

Alias: _CUSTOMER ORDER DATA_

Comment: _A LOG-DS for a validated customer order._

Starting Volume:_____ Growth Potential:_____

No.	Ele/DS Name	DE/DS	SV/MV	Occurrences
01	ORDER_NUMBER	DE	SV	
02	CUSTNUM	DE	SV	
03	CUSTNAME	DE	SV	
04	STREET	DE	SV	
05	CITY	DE	SV	
06	STATE	DE	SV	
07	ZIP	DE	SV	
08	ITEMNUM	DE	MV	
09	QUANTITY	DE	MV	
10	DATE	DE	SV	
11	EMPNUM	DE	SV	
12	PHY-CUSTORDR	DS		

Figure 5-51. LOG-CUSTORDR LDS dictionary entry

shows a dictionary entry for this M-LDS. This M-LDS contains a list of the individual LDSs needed during account servicing between customers and accounts clerks.

The GTOP0003 level-2 E/RD in Figure 5-39 provides the details of the business relationship between the accounts clerk and the customer. The E/R expressions in the GTOP0003 level-2 E/RD represent the decomposition of the E/R expression containing the ACCOUNT RECONCILING OBJECTS relationship diamond in the GTOP00 level-1 E/RD of Figure 5-37. The ACCOUNT RECONCILING OBJECTS relationship diamond in the GTOP00 E/RD represents a M-LDS containing the five individual LDSs listed in the M-LDS in Figure 5-55. Each relationship symbol on the GTOP0003 level-2 E/RD in Figure 5-39 represents one of these five LDSs.

The project team provides dictionary entries for each entity, relationship, and data structure for this explosion path for the order processing E/RDs. They also create dictionary entries for each data element appearing in these data structures that has not already been entered. Thus, the project team accumulates a large cache of information to analyze and then uses it to design a more acceptable method of servicing orders.

Entry Type   **Dictionary ID**

Data Element   ORDER _NUMBER

Alias: _CUSTOMER ORDER NUMBER_
         VENDOR ORDER NUMBER

Element Type	**Length**	**Input Format**	**Output Format**
Character	8	XXXXXXXX	XXXXXXXX

Data request prompt: _Order Number:_

Columnar heading: _Order Number_

Roles* portrayed by element: _Customer Order ID_
                                  Vendor Order ID

Text Description & Comments

This data item is either an order number for customer phone/mail orders or retail sales, or an order number for vendor orders to replenish inventory supplies. The order number is assigned by either an order or retail salesclerk while processing customer orders. An order number is assigned to a vendor order by the order clerk when inventory falls below the reorder level.

*This entry is not currently found in existing dictionary systems. However, it can be simulated by including it at the beginning of the "Text Description & Comments" entry.

Figure 5-52. ORDER_NUMBER data element dictionary entry

National Golf & Tennis E/RD Tree Format

As you can see in Figures 5-36 through 5-55, the design dictionary provides an elaborate means of entering specifications for user requirements. These entries give the NG&T project team a powerful method for documenting user requirements. Figure 5-56 depicts the collection of NG&T E/RDs in tree format, showing the explosion paths from top to bottom.

Maintaining Dictionary Entries

The task of keeping the design dictionary current is formidable, but commercial software systems have emerged that facilitate entering, retrieving, and updating dictionary entries. For example, a report could be produced listing all the programs that reference a particular data item. In addition, some dictionary systems can generate appropriate data structures for input into the database design. Finally, many dictionary

Entry Type	Label		Dictionary ID
Relationship	ACCOUNT RECONCILING OBJECTS		GTOP00R02

Explodes to:

   Data structure dictionary entry: _MLOG-CUSTACCOUNTS_

Relationship type: _Hierarchical multivalued_

Struct-Ele	E/O	Type	Key	Element Role

Text Description & Comments

This entry represents the relationship between customers and accounts clerks completed while reconciling customer accounts. In this relationship, the accounts clerks create bills to send to customers, record payments, send delinquency notices, record order returns and cancellations, and respond to customer complaints.

Figure 5-53. ACCOUNT RECONCILING OBJECTS relationship dictionary entry

Entry Type	Label	Dictionary ID
Entity	ACCOUNTS CLERK	GTOP00E03

Explodes to:

   E/RD: _GTOP0003_

   Data structure dictionary entry: _____

Text Description & Comments

This entity represents the accounts clerk who interacts with customers regarding their accounts receivable, order returns and cancellations, and complaints.

Figure 5-54. ACCOUNTS CLERK entity dictionary entry

systems can make changes in a design dictionary based on changes occurring in a graph, such as an E/RD. This capability is particularly important in updating the documentation for an existing system when a change occurs.

   The completion of the data model using E/RDs should be reviewed by the users

Entry Type		Dictionary ID			
Data Structure		MLOG-CUSTACCOUNTS			

Alias: _CUSTOMER ACCOUNTS DATA_

Comment: _A M-LDS for customer accounts data._

Starting Volume: _____   Growth Potential: _____

No.	Ele/DS Name	DE/DS	SV/MV	Occurrences
01	LOG-CUSTBILL	DS		
02	LOG-CUSTPYMT	DS		
03	LOG-CUSTCOMPLAINT	DS		
04	LOG-CUST_DELINQUENCY	DS		
05	LOG-CUSTBACKORDR	DS		

Figure 5-55. MLOG-CUSTACCOUNTS M-LDS dictionary entry

who were interviewed during data-gathering actions. These users should confirm that the analysts have accurately and completely depicted business relationships and identified the objects of importance to users. The analysis phase review will be discussed at the end of Chapter 6, the chapter that explains the use of process modeling during the analysis phase of the development life cycle.

COMPUTER-AIDED DATA MODELING METHODS AND DOCUMENTATION

Many computer-aided software engineering (CASE) systems exist to help the analyst using structured modeling methods accompanied by dictionary entries. In the definition of methodology and its components in Chapter 2, a tool was defined as an instrument used to make modeling methods, techniques, and procedures operational. CASE systems are merely tools for this purpose. Many CASE tools provide a framework from which analysts produce and store graphic models and accompanying dictionary entries in a form more easily created, retrieved, and modified. CASE systems used during the analysis and design phases of a project are often called analyst workbench software systems.

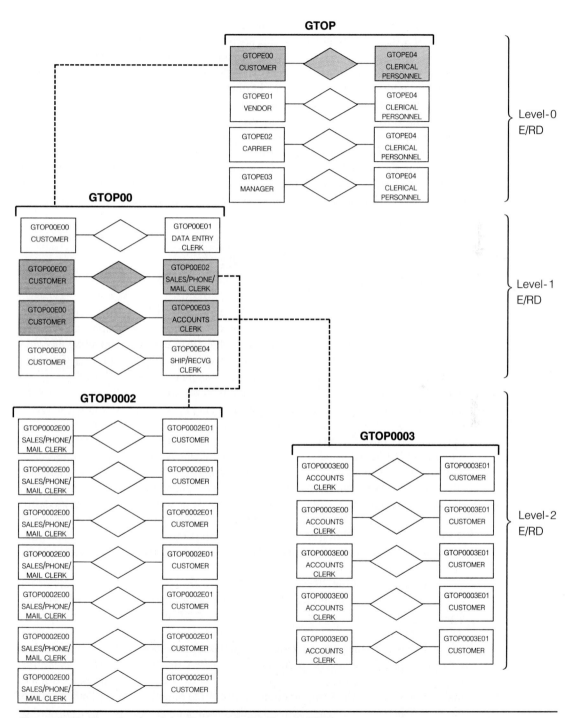

Figure 5-56. Tree format of the National Golf & Tennis E/RDs

CASE systems insert graphic symbols in appropriate locations on the graphic drawing screen. These symbols have the appropriate shapes for creating graphs to represent items of interest, such as the entity rectangles and relationship diamonds used in the text E/RD modeling method. Most CASE systems use a mouse cursor control device for more rapid entry or change of diagrams, and offer menus of commands to edit, display, and print the diagrams used in structured analysis and design.

All the E/RDs and accompanying dictionary entries that appear in this chapter were initially constructed using three of the leading analyst workbench systems currently available from commercial software vendors: Texas Instruments' Information Engineering Facility (IEF), KnowledgeWare's Information Engineering Workbench (IEW), and InterSolv's Excelerator. In addition, the generic format of the dictionary entries used throughout this text is modeled on the dictionary entries of several existing CASE systems.

Using Entity/Relationship Diagrams at the Start of System Projects

Systems analysts using structured methods have traditionally begun their investigations by employing some modeling method to show the decomposition of application activities. These modeling methods are a natural technique to use in documenting the ways in which the firm's personnel describe their job activities. For example, data flow diagrams (DFDs) can be used to help document statements such as "I send _____ to Sam," "Susie does _____," "The department forms are sent to the _____ department," and so on. These examples illustrate that people respond to questions in a fashion consistent either with data flow and process identification or with an outline of job function activities. Documenting these example statements is consistent with the premises of DFDs and of other process modeling methods. As a result, these modeling methods are sometimes considered to be the starting point for analysis documentation.

In the late 1980s and early 1990s, developments in methodology and in the tools that support it, such as CASE, have led many analysts to believe that data modeling methods, such as E/RDs, may be a more natural starting point for the analysis phase. Recently, some CASE tools have emerged as computer-aided tools for documenting corporate and departmental planning. These tools are formally called Computer-Aided Planning software systems.

A **Computer-Aided Planning (CAP)** software system defines aspects of the organization that are important to its strategic planning, such as its goals and the aspects of the organization related to those goals. CAP allows corporate managers to describe the company and plans for the company in a decomposition fashion. Just as sets of DFDs and other process modeling methods decompose A&D documentation, CAP tools permit managers to decompose portions of the organization as well as plans for the organization. For example, CAP systems often provide decomposition of managerial levels of the firm, functional units of the organization, and other areas of the firm. When CAP systems are used to document and decompose these portions of the organization, objects within the organization are also identified. These objects can be represented as entities on E/RDs. CAP systems typically have the capacity to produce E/RDs that show the relationship between these objects. As a result, E/RDs have become a part of many CASE planning activities, with many E/RDs completed prior to beginning A&D projects. E/R diagramming or a review of existing E/RDs is likely to conform to a natural starting point for A&D projects.

A second reason to use E/RDs at the start of projects is that database modification or design may be needed to facilitate gathering the additional data required by the newly modified or developed system. Traditionally, database design or modification has occurred at the conclusion of application design and development. Since database design or modification is a time-consuming set of activities, it is best to have these activities occurring in combination with other system design activities.

E/RDs are frequently used for data modeling in conjunction with database design or modification. Thus, it is important that both application design and database design or modification be performed concurrently. If not, the completion date for the application may have to be extended by the amount of time required for database design or modification. When E/R diagramming is employed at an early stage in the project life cycle, application and database design activities are more consistently coordinated, thus shortening the project completion time.

Using Entity/Relationship Diagrams During Joint Application Design (JAD) Sessions

Joint application design sessions (JADs), as described at the end of Chapter 4, are helpful for gathering and verifying the data in a collective setting of users and systems personnel. JADs can also be used to create, review, verify, and modify E/RDs.

During JADs, the use of CASE and visual aid technologies, such as the overhead LCD panels described in Chapter 4, provide an efficient way to create E/RDs quickly with most, if not all, of the parties who can provide information regarding data types that satisfy user information needs. A JAD may be set up with all of the users involved in a single subject area to create an E/RD and entity type descriptions for all data types appearing on that set of E/RDs. A JAD may also be arranged with users who are involved in multiple subject areas to take advantage of the quick interaction for developing multiple subject area E/RDs and accompanying entity type descriptions. As these users describe the people they interact with, the data types that aid those interactions, and the properties of those data types during JADs, scribes can record this data in E/RDs and entity type descriptions.

JADs can also be used to review and verify E/RDs and entity type descriptions created during preworkshop activities or between JAD workshops. As the E/RDs and entity type descriptions created prior to the JAD are reviewed and verified, changes may be made to the diagrams and entity type descriptions in real time. As users indicate variations in what is already included in these entries and what actually exists, scribes record changes to the E/RDs and entity type descriptions. Thus, JADs can contribute to the accuracy and completeness of the data model in a shorter period of time than more traditional approaches.

REVIEW

This chapter emphasizes the logical aspect of system analysis and design. Analysts collect data about the business in a variety of ways, all in an attempt to define user requirements. A data model is then produced, which consists of the collection of all data types for all business object categories for the business, properties of those data types, and relationships between those data types consistent with real-world business objects that the data types represent. The entity relationship (E/R) modeling method portrays the conceptual view of data types in their subject areas. The entity/relationship diagram (E/RD) identifies and describes the types of objects important to the business and the relationships among those objects. In the text E/RD method, an E/RD is a combination of E/R expressions used to graphically portray the business relationships that take place between various entities in a particular subject area. Design dictionaries are an important accompaniment to E/RDs; they track the objects, relationships between objects, processes, data structures, data items, and data flows described in the analysis and design phases. Several examples of design dictionary entries are given in this chapter to show how they can be used to describe graphic models, what the symbols on the graphic models represent, and the purpose for connections between symbols.

CASE systems are used during the analysis and design phases of a project to provide a framework for the production and storage of graphic models and accompanying dictionary entries. Recent developments in methodology and in CASE tools have led to the use of modeling methods, such as E/RDs, at the start of the analysis phase. One advantage of this is that planning, decomposition of the organization, documentation, and database design and/or modification can all take place concurrently. JADs are one way to bring all of the users together to describe the people they interact with, and the data types and properties that aid those interactions, in order to create E/RDs and entity type descriptions.

QUESTIONS

1. What do users need to know about business objects, and how does this knowledge relate to user requirements?
2. Define *object* and explain the purpose of business objects as they relate to understanding the real world of business.
3. List and distinguish among the five different types of business objects. Give examples of each type not listed in the text.
4. Define *data model* and explain what it is composed of.
5. Define *data type* and explain the meaning behind the term. Distinguish between *data type* and *business object*.
6. List and explain the five basic premises of good business modeling.

7. Explain why the statement "Data types rarely change" is true for most businesses.

8. Explain why the statement "Procedures frequently change" is true for most businesses.

9. Why should analysts spend most of their time modeling business processes and procedures?

10. Explain the purpose of a data model and what its data types correspond to in the real world of business objects.

11. Define *abstraction* and explain how it relates to modeling business objects.

12. Define *generalized data type* and explain what it means. Provide examples not in this text.

13. Explain the three most important actions of data modeling; explain how they are related to data model abstraction.

14. Define *subject area*. Explain how subject areas should be defined and how they are used to create E/RDs.

15. Explain why E/RDs should be created for subject areas.

16. Explain what is meant by the sufficiency requirement for data types in the data model.

17. Define *entity type description*; explain where it fits on the data model abstraction levels, and of what it consists.

18. For data types that appear in multiple subject areas, and therefore in multiple E/RDs, how does the entity type description for the data type help meet the sufficiency requirement?

19. Explain the relationship between entity type descriptions and logical data structures (LDSs).

20. Define *entity property* and *domain*; explain the relationship between them.

21. Define *entity key property* and explain its purpose.

22. Define *relationship* and explain the purpose it serves in modeling data types as entities on an E/RD.

23. Explain how E/RDs are used to model data types in the real world for a particular subject area.

24. Distinguish among the three basic E/RD formats; explain how each format can be used to create a model of the same real-world data types.

25. What is the purpose of the design dictionary? Explain its role in analysis and design.

26. At a minimum, what items should the design dictionary contain?

27. What other useful information is usually contained in the design dictionary?

28. List the data-describing specifications that may be recorded in the design dictionary.

29. What are the purposes of the symbols used in the design dictionary?

30. What is the purpose of the narrative entries in the design dictionary for entities and relationships?

31. Explain why it is important that dictionary entries accompany analysis diagram entries.

32. Explain what entities represent when E/RDs are used in the progressive format of this text.

33. Explain what the explosion paths for left-side or right-side entities represent when E/RDs are used in the progressive format of this text.

34. Explain why a relationship between managers and customers was not included as an E/R expression in the NG&T GTOP entity/relationship diagram.

35. Explain the naming conventions for dictionary IDs for the following:

    a. E/RD levels

    b. Entities on an E/RD

    c. Relationships on an E/RD

36. Illustrate how the NG&T project team conformed to the naming convention for symbols on E/RD levels for E/RD dictionary IDs.

37. What is a M-LDS and what does it represent in the progressive format of E/RDs?

38. What may the left-side and right-side entities represent on the lowest E/RD level?

39. What do the relationships represent on the lowest E/RD level?

40. Distinguish between a dictionary ID and a label.

41. What do *single-valued* and *multivalued* mean in relation to:

    a. Data structures

    b. Data elements

42. Distinguish between elements and objects.

43. What is the purpose of key dictionary entries for LDSs?

44. What is the purpose of element-role dictionary entries with respect to relationship diamonds on an E/RD?

45. What are aliases and why are they important?

46. Distinguish between logical and physical data structures.

47. How do CASE systems help keep the design dictionary current?

48. What are graphic symbols and what purpose do they serve?

49. What does the term *CASE* imply relative to diagramming methods and dictionary entries?

50. Thoroughly explain the relationship among E/R levels, M-LDSs, individual LDSs, and entities for the NG&T project.

EXERCISES

Chapter 4 of the student workbook contains blank documentation forms to use in the following exercises.

1. Create a level-1 E/RD for exploding on the GOVERNMENTAL AGENCIES entity in Figure 5-19. Create dictionary entries for *all* entities, relationships, data structures (mass logical/physical and individual logical/physical), and data elements relative to this level-1 E/R explosion.

2. Create a level-1 E/RD for explosion on the MANAGER entity in Figure 5-19. Create dictionary entries for *all* entities, relationships, data structures (mass logical/physical and individual logical/physical), and data elements relative to this level-2 E/R explosion.

3. Create a level-2 E/RD for exploding on the EMPLOYEE entity in Figure 5-21. Create dictionary entries for *all* entities, relationships, data structures (mass logical/physical and individual logical/physical), and data elements relative to this level-2 E/R explosion.

4. Create a lower level-1 detail E/RD and accompanying design dictionary entries for an explosion on the VENDOR entity of the GTOP E/RD in Figure 5-36.

5. Create a lower level-1 detail E/RD and accompanying design dictionary entries for an explosion on the CARRIER entity of the GTOP E/RD in Figure 5-36.

6. Create a lower level-1 detail E/RD and accompanying design dictionary entries for an explosion on the MANAGER entity of the GTOP E/RD in Figure 5-36.

7. For your class project, conduct a JAD with participants from the company used, during which E/RDs are reviewed, revised, created, and agreed upon. Prepare a report that describes all aspects of the JAD (remember to include preworkshop, workshop, and postworkshop activities).

SELECTED REFERENCES

Chen, P. 1976. "The Entity-Relationship Model—Toward a Unified View of Data." *ACM Transactions on Database Systems I.* 9–36.

Inmon, W. H. 1988. *Information Engineering for the Practitioner.* Englewood Cliffs, NJ: Prentice-Hall.

Martin, J. 1989. *Information Engineering, Book II: Planning and Analysis.* Englewood Cliffs, NJ: Prentice-Hall.

Tsichritzis, D. C. and F. H. Lochovsky. 1982. *Data Models.* Englewood Cliffs, NJ: Prentice-Hall.

Vetter, M. 1987. *Strategy for Data Modelling.* New York: John Wiley and Sons.

CHAPTER 6

Analyzing the Problem Using Business Process Modeling

OVERVIEW

This chapter illustrates how to document and analyze a business system using the data flow diagram (DFD) modeling method. Its thorough descriptions and examples of DFDs show how this method is used to depict business processes. It also describes the next stage of the analysis phase—the analysis of data and process models and the formal review of analysis results. Continuing the discussion of modeling methods and incorporating what you have learned in earlier chapters, this chapter emphasizes the importance of models in the analysis of a business system by:

- Explaining what is meant by the term *business process*, how processes act on data objects, and how the study of processes contributes to understanding user information needs

- Explaining how the data flow diagram (DFD) modeling method is used to model business processes

- Describing advantages and disadvantages of using DFDs

- Defining goals during construction of DFDs
- Illustrating how the DFD modeling method is used in this text
- Modeling the NG&T case based on the text methodology
- Describing the analysis and review of the NG&T study results based on findings from the E/RDs in Chapter 5 and on the DFDs in this chapter
- Introducing computer-aided analysis process modeling

KEY TERMS

Balanced input and output

Business processes

Computer-aided process modeling

Context-level diagram

Data flow diagram (DFD)

Data flow interface

Data store

Functional primitive

Input interface

Output interface

Reusable code

Semantic functional primitive DFD

Top-down approach

An analysis and design project should move from modeling the data objects and data types of the business system, as described in Chapter 5, to modeling the business processes of the business system. Although the more natural progression should be from data modeling to process modeling, sometimes the analyst models them together, while still taking advantage of the integration of these two models.

Business processes comprise actions with definite start and stop points that are performed to produce output from input. Remember that processes differ from functions in that functions are ongoing, and processes help implement functions. Processes typically support functions. They can be mechanical, computerized, or manual; periodic or on-demand; managerial or clerical. They can also come in a host of other forms. Business processes typically specify *what* actions to perform and *why*, but not *how* to perform those actions. The *how* portion of the business/system model equation comes when procedures are modeled to implement the processes.

Process modeling during the analysis phase provides additional information regarding user requirements; the information required through process modeling, in turn, provides the basis for the design phase of the project life cycle. Figure 6-1 shows the area of the enterprise/methodology model on which this chapter focuses its attention. In this portion of the pyramid, the major processes of the business are analyzed.

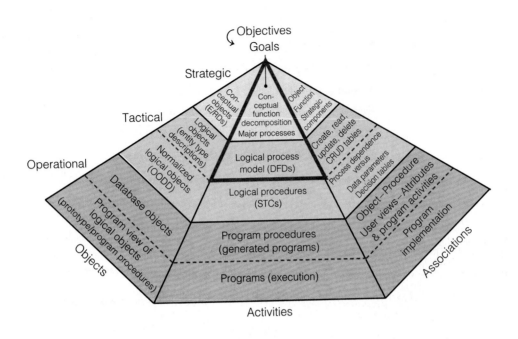

Figure 6-1. Enterprise/methodology model focus of Chapter 6

Once the business data and processes have been accurately and completely modeled, the next steps are *analyzing* the models, suggesting solutions to existing problems or directions toward achieving objectives, conducting a formal review of the analysis results, and then deciding on a plan of action—all of which will be described in this chapter.

Modeling business processes leads to a better understanding of the business and of its information needs. An information system could not be correctly defined and created without a thorough understanding of the processes performed in the business.

MODELING BUSINESS PROCESSES

A number of modeling methods have emerged over the years to model business processes. In recent years the most prominent of these methods are the process dependency diagram and data flow diagram (DFD) modeling methods. The DFD modeling method is used in this text to support modeling business processes. In the future, this modeling method could be replaced by other process modeling approaches; however, it is more important for you to know that business processes should be modeled; specific process modeling methods are less important. What is important concerning process modeling methods is that the company's methodology should include a process modeling method (or other way to model processes) and that all personnel should use this method.

Data Flow Diagram (DFD) Modeling Method

Chapter 2 introduced the **data flow diagram (DFD)** as a modeling method used to model business processes and the flow of data objects through those processes. The DFD is the most frequently used of the structured methods for modeling business processes. Other process modeling methods can be used to provide equally accurate models of business processes, but DFDs are used in the methodology of this text because of their frequency of use. Remember that having a standard way of modeling processes and constantly applying that method are considerably more important than the particular modeling method you use.

As initially described in Chapter 2, the DFD modeling method uses three basic symbols and a connector, called a data flow, to model business processes and the data objects that the processes use as input and produce as output. Figure 2-14 in Chapter 2 illustrated the two prominent sets of symbols used in creating DFDs. The symbols made popular by Gane and Sarson are used here, as shown in Figure 6-2. We could just as easily use those of Constantine and Yourdon, or of DeMarco; the type of symbols used does not change the model of business processes. Table 6-1 provides definitions for the symbols used in a DFD.

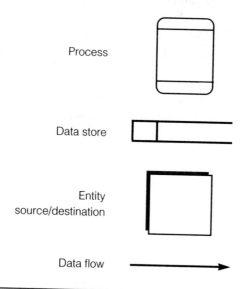

Process

Data store

Entity
source/destination

Data flow

Figure 6-2. Symbols used for DFDs throughout this text

Table 6-1	Definitions for DFD symbols
Symbol	**Definition**
Entity	A person or group that is an initial source or final destination of data objects
Process	An action that transforms input data objects into output data objects
Data store	A holding area for data, either permanent or temporary; a stockpile where data is stored between processes
Data flow	Connections between processes and other DFD symbols along which individual logical data objects and collections (sometimes called packets) of logical data objects pass

The DFD modeling method has certain rules regarding the use of the method to create a process model. These rules are summarized in Figure 6-3.

Rules Governing the Creation and Use of Data Flow Diagrams

General Rules

1. The DFD should model business processes and the flow of data through a business system (an application); it depicts the business system for further analysis of it.
2. DFDs should have no physical or time orientation; processes with totally different physical or time orientations often appear on the same DFD.
3. Entities should appear on DFDs as initial sources and final destinations of data.
4. No freestanding symbols (entities, processes, stores) or freestanding sections of symbols are permitted.
5. Balanced inputs and outputs should occur along decomposition (explosion) paths through DFD levels.
6. Complete dictionary entries should be created for all symbols and *labeled* data flows on the DFD.

Figure 6-3. DFD diagramming rules

Entity Rules

7. A source or destination entity does not directly connect to data stores or other entities.
8. All data leaving or entering an entity must be processed.
9. Entity names may be repeated only when they represent the same entity.

Data Flow Rules

10. Data flows depict a logical data object (LDS) or collection of logical data objects (M-LDSs) that flows into or out of a DFD process.
11. Data does not flow from one data store to another, or from a data store to an entity, or vice versa, without being processed.
12. A data flow into or out of a data store need not be labeled if it consists of the same data object or collection of data objects that the data store symbolizes.
13. Data flow labels are unique and nonrepeating.
14. Separate data flows on the same DFD may depict the same logical data object (LDS) or collection of logical data objects (M-LDSs).

Data Store Rules

15. A data store depicts a logical data object (LDS) or a collection of logical data objects (M-LDSs) at rest.
16. The physical nature of the storage media is not identified in logical DFDs.
17. Data stores are repeated as necessary.
18. In the design dictionary, data stores are classified as read-only, write-only, or read-write.

Process Rules

19. Processes do not produce output without input.
20. A process must be capable of producing the outputs exiting the process from the inputs entering it.
21. The names of processes are specified as active or passive.
22. Process names are unique and nonrepeating.
23. Process names for active processes should exhibit a strong statement of action.
24. DFD processes specify only *what* and *why*, not *how* to complete business processes.
25. A process on one DFD may decompose into multiple sub-processes on a lower-level DFD through the action known as explosion.

Figure 6-3. DFD diagramming rules *(continued)*

Explosion of Processes

Like the entity/relationship (E/R) expression in the text E/RD modeling method, processes on the DFD explode down (decompose) to a lower-level DFD to depict processes in greater detail. The DFD modeling method is a top-down analysis and design method similar in orientation to the E/RD general-to-detailed explosion diagram schematic presented in Chapter 5. It results in a hierarchy of DFDs that represent a general-to-detailed decomposition of processes. A top-level DFD (called the level-0 DFD) typically contains a single process or a small number of processes that explain the area of business under study from a contextual perspective; hence the name **context-level diagram**, which is often used to describe it.

The process on the top-level DFD usually represents a major business process of an application, or a complete self-contained application. Exploding the process on the level-0 DFD produces a level-1 DFD that provides greater detail for the level-0 process. Processes included on level-1 DFDs can then explode to separate level-2 DFDs, and so on. The explosion of processes to produce lower-level DFDs continues until the analyst obtains the desired amount of detail about the business processes. The desired level of detail is reached when further explosion of processes would not be necessary for the analyst and the user to understand the decomposition of processes. Figures 2-20, 2-21, and 2-22 in Chapter 2 illustrated a set of decomposing DFDs for a major process called SERVICE MANUFACTURING. These DFDs progressively included greater and greater detail as explosion occurred on processes from level to level. This set of diagrams only illustrated how to use the DFD modeling method to model a set of decomposed business processes, not how data types flow between those processes and the source of those data types. This chapter will describe the DFD modeling method in greater detail and will provide examples to illustrate how to use the method.

Advantages and Disadvantages of Using DFDs

One main advantage of using DFDs is that they allow the analyst to start with a complete view of the business application and then progressively decompose it into more detail. This is often called the **top-down approach**. It is beneficial for two main reasons:

- The analyst can take a large, complex business system or application and break it down into more manageable parts.
- The analyst can show each level to users and allow them to suggest modifications to the DFDs that result in a better or more accurate description of the business system or application at each level.

Another benefit of using DFDs for analysis and design is that they allow data to be tracked throughout the business application. Hereafter in this chapter, the terms *application, business system*, and *business application* should be considered synonymous. By properly constructing a DFD, the analyst can answer the following questions:

1. What data is needed by the application and what information is produced?
2. What are the processes that transform the data into information?

3. What is the basic flow of the data?

Another advantage is that users can more easily understand DFDs than E/RDs, since users deal with those business processes directly and are familiar with the data flowing in and out of those processes. Since users understand DFDs more easily, they may be helpful in refining E/RDs by identifying missing logical data types in the data model. For example, a user may specify an action performed on a data type that was not identified while creating E/RDs. Thus, the use of DFDs can help refine the data model.

The major drawback of using DFDs is that portions of the detailed logical analysis and design specifications typically reside on separate DFDs. This forces the analyst to navigate across several lower-level DFDs to obtain a deeper understanding of the logical details of the application.

Clarifying the Differences and Similarities Between E/RDs and DFDs

There are distinct differences between the use of E/RDs and the use of DFDs. E/RDs are used as initial documentation for user requirements. E/RDs model the decomposition of business relationships within the application to be documented: business objects, relationships between them, and data types needed to support the relationships. DFDs model the decomposition of processes and the flows of data types needed by the processes within a business application. DFDs may provide additional information regarding data objects. Thus, DFDs add the aspects of processing and flows of data types to the expanding model of the business and of user requirements. By this point in the development life cycle, many specifications for the logical aspects of the application have already been created and can be reused while creating other specifications. For example, many of the entities that appear on E/RDs and in their accompanying dictionary descriptions can be reused to indicate that the real-world person or group depicted as an E/RD entity can also be either the initial source or the final destination of a data object depicted on a DFD. Furthermore, many of the data types identified while creating E/RDs may appear as either data flows or data stores on a DFD. Since the data type is already described in an entity type description, it will not be necessary to describe it in a logical data structure (LDS) dictionary entry while creating the DFD. The existing entity type description will be used, with possibly a modification of the description based on additional information produced while creating DFDs.

Following the documentation of business relationships discovered during data gathering, information about entities and LDSs should be part of the design dictionary. The dictionary entries that document E/RDs provide much of this information. The analyst can capitalize on existing dictionary specifications and include them in the documentation of DFD components. Using existing specifications to develop additional specifications illustrates the reusability of these specifications. The important insight is that using DFDs permits greater integration of design dictionary specifications for the application.

DFD processes are also related to what E/RDs model. The information used to create a DFD comes from the same users who helped the analyst in creating E/RDs and entity type descriptions. The processes described by users are typically processes they perform either directly or with the help of a computer system or other technology. A DFD created from the information provided by the firm's clerks will depict the processes associated with the clerks; a DFD created from information provided by a manager will depict the processes associated with the manager. The clerks and managers will typically *not* appear on these DFDs as entities. For these DFDs, you may view the process on the DFD as actually representing the clerk or manager. In this way, a DFD may be used to model the processes of some people or groups internal to the business that appear as entities within E/R expressions on E/RDs.

Goals During Construction of DFDs

The main goal of creating DFDs is to obtain an accurate and complete picture of the processes of the business system under study. By modeling these processes and the data objects they act on, analysts can get verification from users that they correctly and more completely understand what those users face in terms of business processes. Once created, the model becomes a focal point for communication between the analyst and the user. It gives them something to point to and analyze in order to make sure that both the analyst and the user understand the user requirements being constructed for the system.

FUNCTIONAL PRIMITIVES DFDs start with overviews of the business application under study and break them down into smaller and smaller subcomponents. Many people who use DFDs recommend decomposing processes down to a DFD level at which each process has only one input and one output. They refer to this level as a **functional primitive**, similar in concept to the functional primitive E/R expressions in Chapter 5. While the general goal of drawing DFDs is to decompose an application into a series of functional primitives, this may not always be possible or desirable from an operational standpoint. Sometimes further decomposition would only create a lower-level DFD of trivial specifications that would not provide additional information necessary to document the processes and flows of data types in a manner understood by all. In this text, *functional primitive* means what is *semantically* a functional primitive: A **semantic functional primitive DFD** contains a decomposition of processes and accompanying dictionary text descriptions that thoroughly describe the set of processes in a way that both the analyst and the user completely understand.

BALANCED INPUTS AND OUTPUTS Another important concept in constructing DFDs is **balanced input and output**, which means that the same number of data objects used as inputs and outputs must be maintained for both the process on the upper-level DFD and the decomposition of that process on a lower-level DFD. For example, if an upper-level process has five input LDSs and eight output LDSs represented by data stores or data flows attached to it, the lower-level DFD must also have the same number of input and output LDSs represented by data stores or data flows. This is true even if the lower-level DFD includes processes that explode to additional lower-level DFDs.

Maintaining balanced inputs and outputs does not mean that an equal number of data stores or data flows appears on the upper-level and the lower-level DFD. Remember that a data store or data flow may comprise a collection of data types, called a mass logical data structure (M-LDS), which, in turn, contains a number of LDSs. Thus a single data store at the upper level that represents a M-LDS may become several data stores depicting individual LDSs at the lower level.

The concept of balanced inputs and outputs means that if an additional LDS is defined and introduced as a data flow or data store or part of them on a lower-level DFD, it should also be added as a new data flow or data store, or part of an existing data flow or data store, connected to the process on the upper-level DFD. If the analyst determines that a lower-level DFD needs additional LDSs that are not part of data stores or flows connected to the process on the upper-level DFD, he or she should backtrack through preceding levels and add these new LDSs either as new data stores or flows, or as part of a M-LDS for existing data stores and data flows on upper-level DFDs. The analyst is free to introduce new LDSs at lower explosion levels as long as the top-down orientation of upper- and lower-level DFDs is kept consistent.

The analyst should view each DFD level as a complete picture of the application. A process on an upper-level DFD should have the same number of LDSs entering and exiting it as enter and exit the processes it decomposes into on the lower-level DFD. The only exception to this rule is a LDS created by one process and passed directly to another process for a data object not retained any further. Some processes create a temporary or intermediate data object that is used to produce other data objects. These intermediate objects are often not retained and are just considered a part of the process. Upper-level DFDs provide a general picture of the business application; lower-level DFDs provide a more detailed picture of the application. Exploding down to semantic functional primitive levels and maintaining balanced inputs and outputs throughout the explosion levels ensure that this organization is maintained.

How the DFD Modeling Method Is Used in This Text

To summarize the use of data flow diagrams (DFDs) in this text, the main purpose is to create a model of business processes that shows the processes important to the business, data objects used by them, and their relationships. DFDs are also used to create the decomposition of these processes on separate diagrams for analysis and review. Processes on DFDs are related in several ways. They create and pass data objects as inputs and outputs between the processes, they share other data objects between them, and they serve the same and different entities that depict people external to the business system being modeled. Entities on DFDs are typically some of the same entities that appear on the left or right sides of entity/relationship (E/R) expressions. Many processes on DFDs depict actions performed by some of the entities on E/R expressions. These entities represent managers and staff personnel who are part of the business system being modeled with DFDs. Finally, the data types created using E/RDs are often the logical objects depicted as data flows and data stores on DFDs. Figure 6-4 depicts the general relationship that may exist between a DFD and an E/RD.

Data-Process Modeling

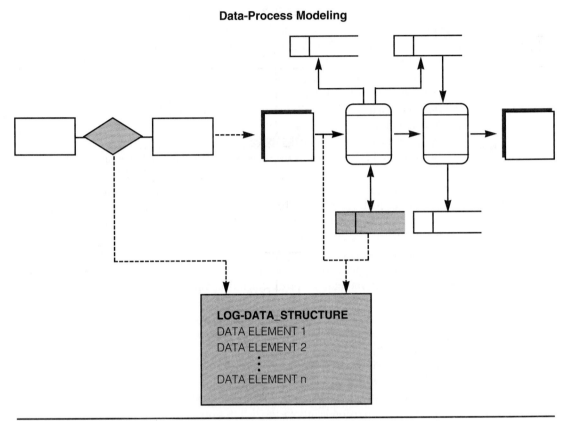

Figure 6-4. Relationship between a DFD and E/RD

Example Data Flow Diagram
for an Employment System

DFDs constructed for the employment application used to illustrate E/RDs in Chapter 5 are shown in Figures 6-5, 6-6, and 6-7. These examples show the basic principles for creating DFDs and the relationship between E/RDs and DFDs in the text methodology. Figure 6-5 is a level-0 overview, or context-level diagram that illustrates the general context of the application. The context-level DFD usually has only a single process on it, as shown by Figure 6-5. Figure 6-6 is a level-1 DFD that provides more detailed specifications through an explosion on the EMPLOYMENT SERVICES process in Figure 6-5. Figure 6-7 is a level-2 DFD providing the details of the level-1 process called COMPLETE EMPLOYMENT APPLICATION in Figure 6-6. Notice that each DFD level contains progressively more detail concerning processes and individual data flows.

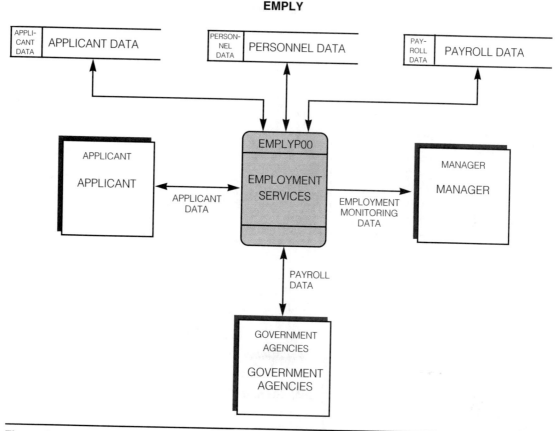

Figure 6-5. Level-0 employment system context-level DFD

Synopsis of Data Flow Diagram Levels

The three DFDs in Figures 6-5, 6-6, and 6-7 decompose processes along one path of process decomposition. The single process, EMPLOYMENT SERVICES, on the DFD in Figure 6-5 decomposes into the three processes on the DFD in Figure 6-6. The COMPLETE EMPLOYMENT APPLICATION process on the DFD in Figure 6-6 decomposes into the five processes on the DFD in Figure 6-7. The two other processes on the DFD in Figure 6-6 would also decompose on separate level-2 DFDs, not shown here. The decomposition of those two processes represents two other paths of decomposition for the complete set of DFDs.

LEVEL-0 DFD (EMPLY)   The context-level diagram (level-0 DFD) in Figure 6-5 has a single process, called EMPLOYMENT SERVICES. The data that it requires

EMPLY00

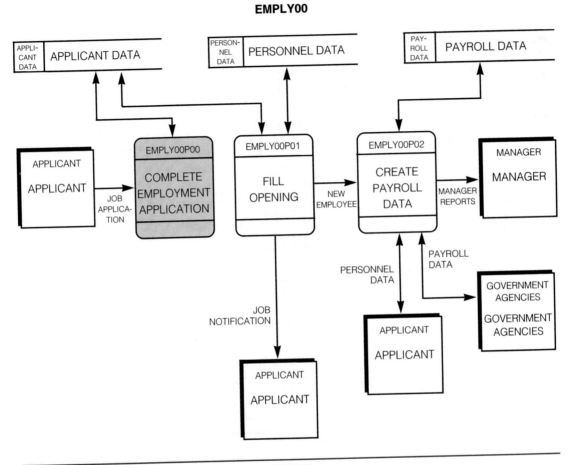

Figure 6-6. Level-1 DFD for EMPLOYMENT SERVICES

from the APPLICANT entity is processed to produce the data identified in the APPLICANT DATA, PERSONNEL DATA, and PAYROLL DATA data stores. The EMPLOYMENT SERVICES process uses this data to respond to requests by the GOVERNMENT AGENCIES and MANAGER entities, as well as the applicant.

LEVEL-1 DFD (EMPLY00) The level-1 DFD of Figure 6-6 provides details for the EMPLOYMENT SERVICES process. It shows three processes, COMPLETE EMPLOYMENT APPLICATION, FILL OPENING, and CREATE PAYROLL DATA, that use data from the APPLICANT entity to produce employment and payroll data identified by the APPLICANT DATA, PERSONNEL DATA, and PAYROLL DATA data stores. The actions are performed with assistance from data types entering and

EMPLY0000

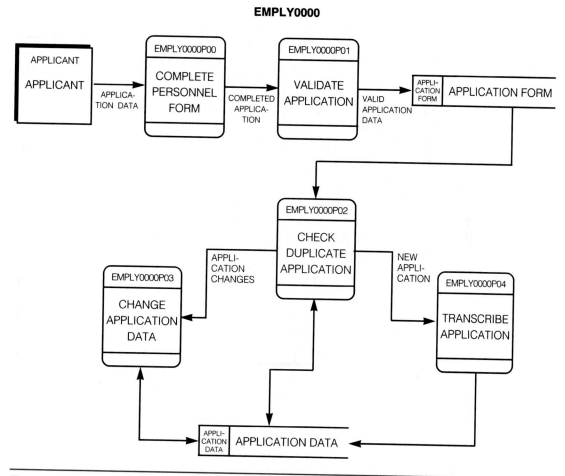

Figure 6-7. Level-2 DFD for COMPLETE EMPLOYMENT APPLICATION

exiting the processes from/to the GOVERNMENT AGENCIES and MANAGER entities. The following actions are symbolized by this DFD:

- Completion of applications by applicants
- Use of applicant data by employment clerks to fill job openings
- Use of employment data by payroll clerks
- Payroll processing and completion of governmental and managerial reports

LEVEL-2 DFD (EMPLY0000) The COMPLETE EMPLOYMENT APPLICATION process in Figure 6-6 explodes to the DFD in Figure 6-7, which provides the details for completing employment requests for the system. This DFD includes five process-es, COMPLETE PERSONNEL FORM, VALIDATE APPLICATION, CHECK DUPLICATE APPLICATION, CHANGE APPLICATION DATA, and TRAN-SCRIBE APPLICATION. These processes use data from the APPLICANT entity to create, validate, compare with existing applications, and either change an existing application or record a new application. Notice that most of the processes on the DFD in Figure 6-7 have only one input and one output; it is close to what many analysts would call a functional primitive. It is what we call a semantic functional primitive because no further decomposition is necessary for the analyst and the user to have a complete understanding of the processes.

The two data stores on this DFD represent a decomposition of the APPLICANT DATA data store on the level-1 and level-0 DFDs into subsets of the M-LDS it depicts. The two data stores, APPLICATION FORM and APPLICATION DATA, represent the handwritten application form and a computer record of the application, respectively. Both of these data stores depict individual logical data types, or individ-ual LDSs, that compose the APPLICANT DATA M-LDS. Thus, the two LDSs for the two data stores on the EMPLY0000 DFD in Figure 6-7 are balanced with the M-LDS depicted as the APPLICANT DATA data store on the upper-level DFDs.

Design Dictionary Specifications for Data Flow Diagrams

The modeling methods used in the analysis and design phases help to ensure that ana-lysts have a clear picture of the business application under investigation. However, drawing diagrams is not enough to get a system developed. What gives these dia-grams the power to influence the design of computer systems are the dictionary speci-fications that describe the components appearing on them.

NAMING CONVENTIONS In this text, the dictionary ID naming conventions for DFDs conform to those explained in Chapter 5 for E/RDs. Remember that not all method-ologies use a dictionary ID separate from the labels assigned to a symbol or connec-tion. For methodologies that use a separate dictionary ID, the main differences are that the ID contains the DFD name as a front-end prefix and the following DFD sym-bol indicators for the two symbols that should use a numbering system for specifying dictionary IDs:

- Process—P
- Data flow—F

Therefore, the EMPLYP00 dictionary ID for the process symbol in Figure 6-5 has the DFD name (EMPLY) followed by P for process and the process number (00) on this DFD level.

Each graph symbol of the same type is consecutively numbered from left to right, top to bottom in some logical sequence. A good rule of thumb is to assign consecutive

ID numbers to each logically related process beginning with 00. For example, the three processes on the EMPLY00 DFD in Figure 6-6 are assigned the dictionary IDs EMPLY00P00, EMPLY00P01, and EMPLY00P02. Consecutive ID numbers are also assigned to data flows on the DFD, beginning with 00 and continuing through the last data flow on the DFD.

Frequently, the same data store or entity may appear on an upper-level and a lower-level DFD. If these symbols are assigned different dictionary IDs depending on which DFD they are on, as is done for processes or data flows, two separate entries will be created for the same symbol, resulting in what most people call redundancy. To avoid this, use the same name for both the dictionary ID and the label for entities and data stores. Notice that dictionary IDs and labels correspond for all entities and data stores in Figures 6-5 through 6-7. By using the same dictionary ID for entities and data stores regardless of the DFD level, you avoid having to reenter the dictionary text descriptions that describe what these symbols represent in the real world, saving much time and effort.

The dictionary ID (or name) of the DFD comes from a combination of an acronym for the business application being modeled and the location of the DFD on the explosion path. For the context-level DFD, the acronym for the application should be its dictionary ID—for example, "EMPLY" for the context-level DFD for the employment application. The level-1 DFD dictionary ID is derived from the dictionary ID of the process from which it explodes. The dictionary ID of this process will be the application acronym plus P00, or "EMPLYP00." If you remove the *P* for *process* from its dictionary ID, you obtain the dictionary ID for the DFD to which it explodes; that is, "EMPLY00" for the level-1 DFD of the employment application for explosion from the EMPLOYMENT SERVICES (EMPLYP00) process on the level-0 DFD.

The dictionary ID for each succeeding DFD will come from the dictionary ID of the process from which it explodes on the upper-level DFD. For example, the COMPLETE EMPLOYMENT APPLICATION process on the EMPLY00 DFD in Figure 6-6 has a dictionary ID of EMPLY00P00. When you remove the *P* for *process*, you derive the dictionary ID of EMPLY0000 for the level-2 DFD shown in Figure 6-7. For methodologies that do not use dictionary IDs, the label of the process on which explosion occurs on the upper-level DFD becomes the name of the DFD to which it explodes.

DFD DICTIONARY ENTRIES   Design dictionary entries are also used to document the details of entities, processes, data stores, data flows, M-LDSs, LDSs, and data items. They are used to define the components of an E/RD as well as components that appear on DFD levels. Examples of design dictionary entries accompanying the DFDs of Figures 6-5 through 6-7 will illustrate the impact of using dictionary specifications and the power they give to analysts who use DFDs during the analysis and design phases. Figure 6-8 shows a design dictionary entry for the APPLICANT entity appearing on the three DFD levels. It provides enough detail to describe the entity and the purpose it serves in the business system under investigation. As with E/RDs, the dictionary entry formats for DFD symbols used in this text are generic formats; they are not associated with any particular dictionary system.

Entry Type	Label	Dictionary ID
Entity	APPLICANT	APPLICANT

Explodes to:

    Data structure dictionary entry: <u>LOG-APPLICANT DATA</u>

Text Description & Comments

This entity represents applicants in the employment system. These people provide the applicant data used to fill available positions in this system.

Figure 6-8. APPLICANT entity design dictionary entry

The first line of Figure 6-8 designates it as an *entity* entry with a label of "APPLI-CANT" and a dictionary ID of "APPLICANT." These entries serve the same purpose as they do in documenting E/RD symbols. The label is for human interpretation, and the dictionary ID identifies the symbol for reference purposes. The major difference in the dictionary entry for DFD entities lies in the explosion capability. An entity on a DFD can only explode to a LDS entry that provides important information concerning that entity. Thus, any further documentation concerning entities is found within the LDS dictionary entry.

Figure 6-9 shows the dictionary entry for the EMPLOYMENT SERVICES process in Figure 6-5. The first line in this entry specifies that this is an entry for a *process* symbol with a label of "EMPLOYMENT SERVICES" and a dictionary ID of "EMPLYP00." This process explodes to a level-1 DFD called "EMPLY00." Notice that the location is designated as the personnel/payroll departments. This designation documents the responsibility for this process, making it unnecessary to record this information on the process symbol in the DFD, as used on early DFDs.

The five entries below the "Explodes to:" entries help describe the process in terms of where it takes place (or who is responsible for it), whether it is a manual or computerized process (or both), whether it is a managerial or a clerical task, what triggers the process, and what it triggers. These entries help the process to more completely depict what it is intended to represent in the real world. By recording these entries, the analyst provides more thorough documentation for this business process.

The remainder of the dictionary specification in Figure 6-9 demonstrates how explicit narratives can be entered to provide a clear understanding of the process. These narrative entries include as much detail as desired and can be used to explain complicated relationships with other diagram components. Standard word processing and desktop publishing software systems can be used to provide professional-looking documentation that is easy to interpret and use when other technology is not available.

Figure 6-10 illustrates a design dictionary entry for the APPLICANT DATA data

Entry Type   **Label**   **Dictionary ID**

Process   EMPLOYMENT SERVICES   EMPLYP00

Explodes to:

     DFD: _EMPLY00_____

     Structure chart: _____

     E/RD: _____

Location: _Personnel/Payroll Departments_____

Type of process (manual or computerized): _____

Process level (managerial or clerical): _Clerical_____

Process triggered by: _____

_____

Process triggers: _____

_____

Text Description & Comments

This process incorporates all the actions involved in the employment system. It is an overview process for the entire system.

Figure 6-9. Design dictionary entry for EMPLOYMENT SERVICES process

Entry Type   **Label**   **Dictionary ID**

Data Store   APPLICANT DATA   APPLICANT_DATA

Explodes to:

     Data structure dictionary entry: _MLOG-APPLICANT DATA___

Text Description & Comments

This mass logical data structure (M-LDS) is used to represent data on applicants that is needed by personnel involved with the employment system. It represents all the logical data structures (LDSs) needed by these employees during job application processing and employment history recording.

Figure 6-10. APPLICANT DATA data store dictionary entry

store appearing on the level-0 DFD of Figure 6-5. The first line of Figure 6-10 indicates that this is a data store dictionary entry with the label "APPLICANT DATA" and a dictionary ID of "APPLICANT DATA." Notice that the data store explodes to a M-LDS called "MLOG-APPLICANT_DATA." This is the same M-LDS defined during creation of E/RDs; thus the text entry is similar to the text entry for the APPLICANT SERVICING OBJECTS relationship on the EMPLY01 E/RD in Figure 5-21.

Dictionary entries are created for each entity, process, data store, and appropriate data flow on every DFD level. When a data flow and the data store that it enters or exits represent the same LDS or M-LDS, no dictionary entry is required for the data flow. Undefined data flows leading to or away from a data store are assumed to be the same data. This prevents needless duplication of a dictionary entry for data associated with both the data flow and the data store. For example, the data flow between the EMPLOYMENT SERVICES process and the APPLICANT DATA data store in Figure 6-5 represents the same group of data structures, MLOG-APPLICANT_DATA. If you labeled this data flow, it would then be necessary to create a dictionary entry for the flow and explain that it explodes to the same M-LDS. By not labeling the flow, you are telling all who view this DFD that this data flow represents the same thing as the data store to which it is attached.

Balanced Inputs and Outputs in the Example DFD

As explained earlier, the concept of balanced inputs and outputs requires that all data structures referenced in lower-level DFDs be referenced in upper-level DFDs from which they exploded, with one exception noted earlier. Figures 6-11 through 6-14 illustrate balanced inputs and outputs for the APPLICANT DATA data flow of Figure 6-5 and the JOB APPLICATION and JOB NOTIFICATION data flows of Figure 6-6.

Figure 6-11 represents the dictionary entry for the APPLICANT DATA data flow

Entry Type	Label	Dictionary ID
Data Flow	APPLICANT DATA	EMPLYF00

Explodes to:

    Data structure dictionary entry: MLOG-APPLICANT_DATA

Timing (periodic or on-demand): _____

Text Description & Comments

This is a mass logical data structure used to represent application data provided by job applicants and job notifications sent to job applicants. This data represents all the logical data structures needed for this purpose.

Figure 6-11. APPLICATION DATA data flow dictionary entry

Entry Type	Dictionary ID			
Data Structure	MLOG-APPLICANT_DATA			

Alias: <u>JOB APPLICANT DATA</u>

Comment: <u> A M-LDS for job application notification. </u>

Starting Volume: _____   Growth Potential: _____

No.	Ele/DS Name	DE/DS	SV/MV	Occurrences
01	LOG-JOB_APPLICATION	DS		
02	LOG-JOB_NOTIFICATION	DS		

Figure 6-12. MLOG-APPLICANT_DATA data structure dictionary entry

on the DFD of Figure 6-5. Figure 6-12 is the dictionary entry for the MLOG-APPLI-CANT_DATA M-LDS to which the APPLICANT DATA data flow explodes. Notice that the line items of this M-LDS are the data structures LOG-JOB_APPLICATION and LOG-JOB_NOTIFICATION. Figures 6-13 and 6-14 illustrate the dictionary entries for the JOB APPLICATION and JOB NOTIFICATION data flows on the DFD in Figure 6-6, which explode to the LOG-JOB_APPLICATION and LOG-JOB_NOTIFICATION LDSs, respectively. Thus, these individually referenced LDSs on the level-1 DFD of Figure 6-6 are also referenced in the documentation accompanying the level-0 DFD of Figure 6-5. To be completely balanced, all LDSs associated with data flows and stores connected to processes on a lower-level DFD must also be associated with data flows and stores connected to the same processes on the upper level from which explosion occurred.

The dictionary entry "Timing (periodic or on-demand)" in Figures 6-11, 6-13, and 6-14 represents an entry to describe whether the data type flows to the process on a periodic basis or on demand by some triggering mechanism. Notice that only the flows that represent individual LDSs actually have entries here. This occurs because only flows at the detail DFD levels would be useful in documenting this trait. Flows that depict M-LDSs may have different LDSs that flow on-demand and periodic.

The dictionary entries accompanying diagram components allow for comprehensive descriptions of the design components depicted. These entries give life to the diagrams and provide a way to integrate many components of the developing system. Once analysts enter these specifications, they can more easily maintain the design documentation for the business system as changing conditions lead to modifications.

You can extrapolate from the examples in this chapter to understand how comprehensively the combined diagram and dictionary specifications describe the application. Every influence on the application may be included as part of text descriptions in dictionary entries. As the level of detail in these dictionary entries increases, the quality and comprehensiveness of analysis and design specifications increases.

Entry Type   **Label**   **Dictionary ID**

Data Flow   JOB APPLICATION   EMPLY00F00

Explodes to:

    Data structure dictionary entry: _LOG-JOB APPLICATION_

Timing (periodic or on-demand): _Periodic_

Text Description & Comments

This is a logical data structure used to represent application data provided by job applicants.

Figure 6-13. JOB APPLICATION data flow dictionary entry

Entry Type   **Label**   **Dictionary ID**

Data Flow   JOB NOTIFICATION   EMPLY00F01

Explodes to:

    Data structure dictionary entry: _LOG-JOB NOTIFICATION_

Timing (periodic or on-demand): _Periodic_

Text Description & Comments

This is a logical data structure used to represent job notifications sent to job applicants.

Figure 6-14. JOB NOTIFICATION data flow dictionary entry

The Relationships Among Entity/ Relationship Diagrams (E/RDs), Data Structures, and Data Flow Diagrams

The relationship between E/RD and DFD specifications is important. E/RD entries categorize business objects, business relationships, and data structures necessary to support those relationships. The data structures are documented using M-LDSs and individual LDSs. DFD modeling builds on the basic E/RD entries created for the business application. DFDs show the flow of these data structures through the firm's processing points and give logical explanations of the processing required for the flows within an application. Some of the E/RD entities appear on DFDs as sources and destinations of data flow LDSs. Some of the E/RD entities may also be what is being modeled as business processes. Some of the entities that enter into business relationships as depicted in E/R expressions provide information on what processes to perform. These processes often represent what these people do, as well as what processes are performed for them by a mechanized system.

All of the M-LDSs and LDSs identified and described while creating E/RDs and accompanying dictionary entries can be carried forward into DFDs, and they can also provide the basis for creating prototype screens and report forms. Chapter 7 illustrates the use of LDS and data dictionary entries for prototyping purposes. Figure 6-15 more completely illustrates the relationships among E/RDs, M-LDSs, LDSs, and DFDs.

A set of decomposition E/RDs appears at the top-left (ERD0) and middle-left (ERD?) sides of Figure 6-15. A set of decomposition DFDs appears at the middle-right (DFD0) and bottom-middle (DFD?) sides of Figure 6-15. These E/RDs and DFDs share M-LDSs and LDSs, symbolized by the E/RD relationship symbols and the DFD data flows and stores, respectively. Notice that M-LDS1 represents the mass logical data structure that supports a relationship between entities on the level-0 E/RD (ERD0); one of its logical data structures (LDS1) supports a subset business relationship for a lower decomposition of the E/R expression that M-LDS1 supports. Also notice that M-LDS1 appears as data flows and stores on the level-0 DFD (DFD0), and that the individual LDSs (LDS1) appear as data flows and stores on some lower-level DFD (DFD?). The M-LDSs and LDSs defined while creating the set of E/RDs need not be defined again while creating the set of DFDs. They will merely be referenced as needed. Figure 6-15 illustrates the reusability of specifications within a single project, reusability that becomes even more beneficial as analysts complete additional projects.

Figure 6-15 also shows how data models and process models should be fully integrated. Integration is natural in that data modeling seeks to identify the logical objects of the business, whereas process modeling seeks to describe the processes to be performed on those logical objects. In the text methodology, this integration is even more pronounced because both data modeling and process modeling begin at the same origin: function decomposition.

In the text methodology, a subfunction in the function decomposition diagram is used as the subject area for creating an E/RD. A subfunction also represents the starting point for process decomposition. The analyst recognizes the end of function decomposition when a subfunction decomposes into actions that have definite start and stop points—in other words, a process. In the text methodology, a set of E/RDs and a set of DFDs will both be created for a specific business subfunction and thus will be naturally integrated. Figure 6-16 illustrates the premise of this methodology: a subfunction represents both an E/RD subject area and the starting point for DFD process decomposition. Notice that subfunction F23 in Figure 6-16 represents both the E/RD subject area and the DFD decomposition starting point. The DFDs created for the NG&T case in the next section will further illustrate these principles. For the

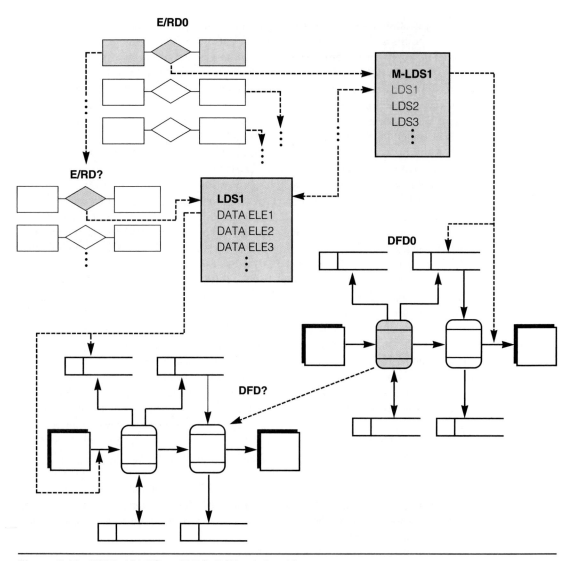

Figure 6-15. E/RD–M-LDS and LDS–DFD relationships

DFD, either the subfunction or one of the major processes that implements the sub-function may appear as the single process on the context-level DFD. If the subfunction appears as the single process on the context-level DFD, a single set of DFDs will depict the processes that implement the subfunction. If one of the major processes that implements the subfunction appears as the context-level process, then multiple sets of DFDs will be needed to depict the decomposition of processes that implement the

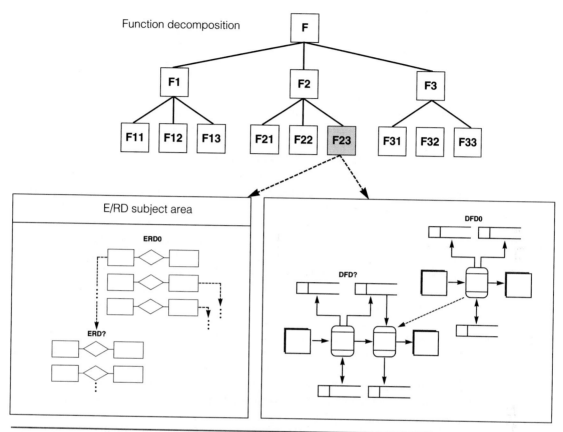

Figure 6-16. Function decomposition, E/RD–DFD entry relationships

subfunction. In any event, the same LDSs and M-LDSs will be specified for both the E/RD and the DFD(s) for the subfunction, since both are constructed to describe and act on the logical objects of that same subfunction.

PROCESS MODELING FOR THE NATIONAL GOLF & TENNIS (NG&T) PROJECT

The main contribution of DFD modeling during the analysis phase consists of describing business processes and data flows into those processes for an existing business system. If the project team begins with E/R diagramming, much of the underlying documentation for many DFD symbols should already exist. The entity and many M-LDS and LDS dictionary entries produced while creating E/RDs are carried forward while the project team creates DFDs.

A review of the E/RD entities in the E/RD levels of Figures 5-36 through 5-39 in Chapter 5 identifies most of the entities the project team will use as data sources and destinations on NG&T DFDs to service orders. In addition, a review of the M-LDSs associated with E/RD relationship symbols reveals many of the M-LDSs and LDSs to be used as data flows and data stores on these DFD levels. As a result of creating these E/RDs, the project team has less difficulty in creating the project DFDs.

Recall that the NG&T E/RDs were created for the subject area corresponding to the SERVICE ORDERS subfunction on NG&T's function decomposition diagram. This subfunction will be the starting point for creating the DFDs. Either it can be used as the central process on the context-level DFD, or the major processes in which this subfunction decomposes can be the central processes on context-level DFDs for different sets of DFDs. Using the subfunction as the central process on the context-level DFD, with its major processes as processes on the level-1 DFD to which this central process explodes, is the preferred method. When this approach is used, the level-1 DFD is sometimes called the system-level DFD. Figure 6-17 illustrates the top-level DFD for the SERVICE ORDERS subfunction; note the "SERVICE ORDERS" label on the central process.

The set of DFDs created by the project team specifies the processes that support the SERVICE ORDERS subfunction. These processes will use the M-LDSs and LDSs created for relationship and entity symbols in the set of E/RDs as data flows and stores on different DFD levels. Figure 6-17 illustrates the first of this set of DFDs, and it demonstrates the integration between data modeling and process modeling that exists in the text methodology.

Notice that the dictionary IDs for symbols and connections on the DFD of Figure 6-17 conform to the naming conventions explained earlier in this chapter. Each data flow and process is assigned a dictionary ID composed of the DFD name (GTOP), followed by *F* or *P*, and the number of the symbol or connection on that DFD level. Each entity and data store has a dictionary ID and a label that are the same. Also notice that the CUSTOMER, MANAGER, VENDOR, and CARRIER entities are the same entities appearing on the top-level E/RD for NG&T in Chapter 5.

The CUSTOMER DATA, INVENTORY DATA, VENDOR DATA, and CARRIER DATA data stores symbolize M-LDSs previously defined in the course of creating the E/RDs for NG&T. For example, Figure 6-18 shows the dictionary entry for the CUSTOMER DATA data store. Notice that the data store defined in Figure 6-18 explodes to the same MLOG-CUSTOMER_DATA M-LDS defined while creating the E/RDs for NG&T. Also notice that the dictionary ID and the label are the same, conforming to the text naming convention for data stores (and entities) that appear on multiple levels of DFDs.

The data flows to and from CUSTOMER, MANAGER, VENDOR, and CARRIER entities are previously defined M-LDSs, parts of these M-LDSs, or possibly additional M-LDS. For example, Figures 6-19, 6-20, and 6-21 are dictionary entries

GTOP

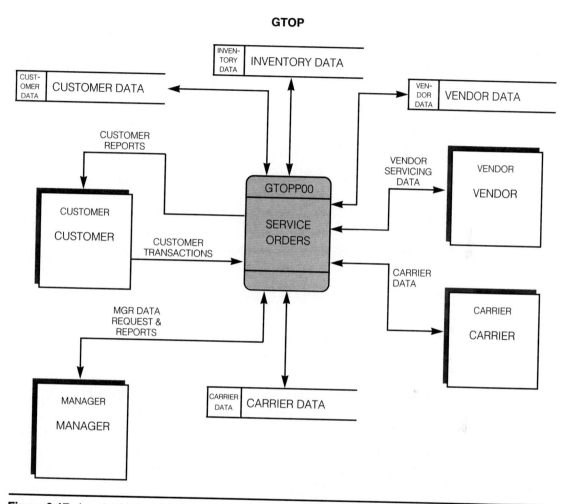

Figure 6-17. Level-0 National Golf & Tennis context-level DFD

created by the project team for the VENDOR SERVICING DATA, CUSTOMER TRANSACTIONS, and CUSTOMER REPORTS data flows in Figure 6-17. Note that the dictionary IDs conform to the naming convention for a data flow.

The data flow described in Figure 6-19 explodes to the MLOG-VENDOR_DATA data structure. This is the same M-LDS associated with the VENDOR SERVICING OBJECTS relationship in the GTOP E/RD of Figure 5-36. Thus, the previously defined M-LDS is carried into the DFDs by the project team.

The data flows described in Figures 6-20 and 6-21 explode to the MLOG-CUSTOMER_TRANS and MLOG-CUSTREPORTS M-LDSs, respectively. These are two new M-LDSs described here by the project team to show two new groups of data

Entry Type   **Label**   **Dictionary ID**

Data Store   CUSTOMER DATA   CUSTOMER_DATA

Explodes to:

   E/RD: _____

   Data structure dictionary entry: _MLOG-CUSTOMER_DATA_

Text Description & Comments

This is a mass logical data structure for all of the data retained in support of servicing customers. The primary data structures for customers are the customer master, order transactions, billings, payments, shipments, delinquencies, and complaints. This group of data structures is used in support of order processing for customers. A mass logical data structure called MLOG-CUSTOMER_DATA is defined for this purpose.

Figure 6-18. CUSTOMER DATA data store dictionary entry

Entry Type   **Label**   **Dictionary ID**

Data Flow   VENDOR SERVICING DATA   GTOPF03

Explodes to:

   E/RD: _____

   Data structure dictionary entry: _MLOG-VENDOR_DATA_

Timing (periodic or on-demand): _____

Text Description & Comments

This is a mass logical data structure for all of the data retained in support of servicing vendors. The primary data structures for vendors are the vendor master, vendor supply items, vendor orders, vendor receipts, vendor billings, vendor payments, vendor order delinquency notices, and vendor complaints. This group of data structures is used in support of inventory items for customer order processing. A mass logical data structure called MLOG-VENDOR_DATA is defined for this purpose.

Figure 6-19. VENDOR SERVICING DATA data flow dictionary entry

Entry Type   **Label**   **Dictionary ID**

Data Flow   CUSTOMER TRANSACTIONS   GTOPF00

Explodes to:

     E/RD: _____

     Data structure dictionary entry: _MLOG-CUSTOMER TRANS_

Timing (periodic or on-demand): _____

Text Description & Comments

This is a mass logical data structure for all of the data retained in support of servicing customers. The primary data structures for customers are the customer master, order transactions, billings, payments, shipments, delinquencies, and complaints. This group of data structures is used in support of order processing for customers. A mass logical data structure called MLOG-CUSTOMER_TRANS is defined for this purpose.

Figure 6-20. CUSTOMER TRANSACTIONS data flow dictionary entry

Entry Type   **Label**   **Dictionary ID**

Data Flow   CUSTOMER REPORTS   GTOPF01

Explodes to:

     E/RD: _____

     Data structure dictionary entry: _MLOG-CUSTREPORTS_

Timing (periodic or on-demand): _____

Text Description & Comments

This is a mass logical data structure for data retained to support data transmission to customers. The primary data structures for customer reports are the customer billings, shipment invoices, back order notices, delinquency notices, and order cancellation notices. A mass logical data structure called MLOG-CUSTREPORTS is defined for this purpose.

Figure 6-21. CUSTOMER REPORTS data flow dictionary entry

Entry Type	Label	Dictionary ID
Process	SERVICE ORDERS	GTOPP00

Explodes to:

    DFD: _GTOP00_

    Structure chart: _____

    E/RD: _____

Location: _Order Processing Department_

Type of process (manual or computerized): __Manual & computerized__

Process level (managerial or clerical): _Clerical_____

Process triggered by: _____

_____

Process triggers: _____

_____

Text Description & Comments

This is the central process for the level-0 context-level DFD for order processing. This process represents all of the actions performed while processing customer and vendor orders. These processes may be manual or computerized processes. This central process explodes down to a level-1 DFD called GTOP00. This level-1 DFD details the major actions performed during order processing. Processes on this level-1 DFD also explode to lower-level DFDs to provide increasingly more detailed diagrams of order processing actions.

Figure 6-22. SERVICE ORDERS process dictionary entry

types needed for the context-level DFD. However, the LDSs specified in these two M-LDSs actually represent some of the LDSs previously defined as part of the MLOG-CUSTOMER_DATA M-LDS, which was defined in the course of creating E/RDs. The project team uses these two new M-LDSs to illustrate the two types of data flows exiting and entering the CUSTOMER entity on the context-level DFD. They could have done the same thing with the VENDOR SERVICING DATA data flow and other data flows to/from entries on the GTOP DFD.

As previously noted, the main contribution of DFD modeling during the analysis phase consists of describing the processing that is performed to facilitate the flow of data. Figure 6-22 contains a dictionary entry for the SERVICE ORDERS process in the GTOP DFD of Figure 6-17.

National Golf & Tennis DFD Explosion Levels

The SERVICE ORDERS process explodes down to a DFD called GTOP00. The dictionary ID for this process is GTOPP00. Thus, the project team conforms to the naming convention for explosion of processes to lower-level DFDs. Remember that the names of explosion-level DFDs are formed by removing the *P* from the dictionary ID of the process from which they explode. Also recall that DFD dictionary ID names prescribe a navigational path throughout DFD levels. Figure 6-23 illustrates the GTOP00 DFD.

Starting from the lower-left side in the GTOP00 DFD, the customer issues either a phone/mail order or a retail sale, which is submitted to the RECEIVE CUSTOMER ORDERS process, which outputs the CUSTOMER TRANSACTION data flow to the CUSTOMER DATA data store. The VALIDATE ORDERS process then retrieves the CUSTOMER ORDER TRANSACTION data flow from the CUSTOMER DATA data store and validates it for correctness. A VALIDATED PHONE/MAIL INVOICE or a VALID RETAIL INVOICE data flow then goes to either the COMPLETE PHONE/MAIL INVOICES or the COMPLETE RETAIL INVOICES process, respectively. If the VALIDATE ORDERS process detects either insufficient inventory quantity for an order item or one that reaches its reorder point, vendor item ordering takes place. The VENDOR ORDER PROCESSING DATA data flow to the ORDER VENDOR ITEMS process indicates this activity. Customer account processing is performed within the RECONCILE CUSTOMER ACCOUNTS process (near the bottom right side of Figure 6-23). Management must monitor and control all of the order processing actions. Notice that all of the other major processes are connected to the PRODUCE MANAGER REPORTS process. This process represents all of the actions performed by management while overseeing all of the major order processing actions.

Dictionary entries are created by the project team for each one of the processes (RECEIVE CUSTOMER ORDERS, VALIDATE ORDERS, COMPLETE PHONE/MAIL INVOICES, COMPLETE RETAIL INVOICES, ORDER VENDOR ITEMS, RECONCILE CUSTOMER ACCOUNTS, and PRODUCE MANAGER REPORTS) for the GTOP00 DFD. Since each of these processes (except RECEIVE CUSTOMER ORDERS) involves many actions, the dictionary entries indicate that these processes all explode to lower-level DFDs. These lower-level DFDs provide greater detail for each of these major actions. Figure 6-24 illustrates the dictionary entry for the VALIDATE ORDERS process on the DFD in Figure 6-23. Dictionary entries are also created for all entities, data stores, and labeled data flows.

Balanced Inputs and Outputs on National Golf & Tennis DFDs

Remember that you must maintain balanced inputs and outputs on the DFDs. The data flow labeled CUSTOMER ORDER leading into the RECEIVE CUSTOMER ORDERS process represents the initial customer order transaction. This data flow explodes to the LOG-CUSTTRNS LDS. This LDS is one of the LDSs in the MLOG-CUSTOMER_TRANS M-LDS. Recall that the CUSTOMER TRANSACTIONS data

GTOP00

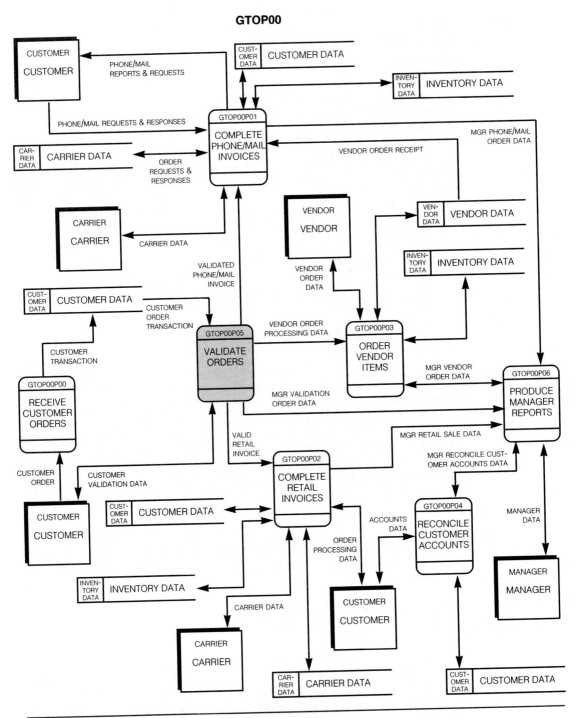

Figure 6-23. National Golf & Tennis GTOP00 level-1 DFD

Entry Type   **Label**   **Dictionary ID**

Process   VALIDATE ORDERS   GTOP00P05

Explodes to:

    DFD: _GTOP0005_

    Structure chart: _____

    E/RD: _____

Location: _Order Processing Department_____

Type of process (manual or computerized): _Manual & computerized_

Process level (managerial or clerical): _Clerical_____

Process triggered by: _Order receipt_____

_____

Process triggers: _Order servicing_____

_____

Text Description & Comments

This process represents all of the validating actions performed relative to customer orders or retail sales. The order invoice must first be checked for correctness, followed by validation of the customer's credit. The inventory level is then checked for sufficiency. If the order passes validation, it is processed normally as a phone/mail order or retail sale. If the inventory level is insufficient to fill the order, vendor order invoices will have to be completed and customers notified that a back order now exists for part or all of their order.

Figure 6-24. VALIDATE ORDERS process dictionary entry

flow on the GTOP DFD of Figure 6-17 exploded to this M-LDS. Thus, for the GTOP and GTOP00 DFDs, balanced data flows occur with respect to the LOG-CUSTTRNS LDS. The remaining LDSs in MLOG-CUSTOMER_TRANS are either individually or collectively associated with the remaining data flows on the GTOP00 level-1 DFD coming from the CUSTOMER entity. Figure 6-25 illustrates the dictionary entry accompanying the CUSTOMER ORDER data flow.

VALIDATE ORDERS Process Explosion Data Flow Diagram

Notice that the dictionary ID for the VALIDATE ORDERS process of Figure 6-24 is GTOP00P05, and that it explodes down to the GTOP0005 level-2 DFD. Note that the

Entry Type	Label	Dictionary ID
Data Flow	CUSTOMER ORDER	GTOP00F00

Explodes to:

    E/RD: _____

    Data structure dictionary entry: _LOG-CUSTTRNS_____

Timing (periodic or on-demand): _Periodic_____

Text Description & Comments

This data flow represents the data that flows when a customer issues either a phone/mail order or a retail sale. This data is dispatched to data entry in order to record the transaction for processing purposes. A logical data structure called LOG-CUSTTRNS is defined for this purpose.

Figure 6-25. CUSTOMER ORDER data flow dictionary entry

project team has again conformed to the standard naming convention for symbols on a DFD level and explosion-level DFD names. Figure 6-26 illustrates the GTOP0005 DFD.

The DFD in Figure 6-26 includes three processes indicating a portion of the validation process. The first process, VALIDATE ORDER ENTRIES, represents checking the order entries for correctness. The order is retrieved from the CUSTOMER TRANSACTION data store, and each entry on the recorded order or retail sale is checked for correctness. If any data item is incorrectly or insufficiently entered, valid information is requested from the customer. Notice the data flows between the CUSTOMER entity and the VALIDATE ORDER ENTRIES process; these data flows represent requests for changes and responses to those requests. The VERIFIED ORDER ENTRIES data flow then flow to the VERIFY CUSTOMER process from the VALIDATE ORDER ENTRIES process.

The VERIFY CUSTOMER process in Figure 6-26 compares the customer information on the customer order with information retained in the CUSTOMER MASTER (note the CUSTOMER INFO data flow). If differences from this recorded data are detected, the UNVERIFIED CUSTOMER INFO data flows to the CUSTOMER entity for correction, and the VERIFIED CUSTOMER INFO data flow returns to the VERIFY CUSTOMER process. During customer verification, it may be determined that the customer master is incorrect and must be updated (note the UPDATE INFO data flow leading to the CUSTOMER MASTER data store). If the customer is verified, the VERIFIED CUSTOMER data flow then flows to the VALIDATE ITEM

QUANTITY process, ELSE an ORDER CANCELLATION is created; note the flow to the ORDER CANCELLATION data store.

The VALIDATE ITEM QUANTITY process in Figure 6-26 determines whether sufficient inventory exists to fill the customer's order. The AVAILABLE INVENTORY data flow from the INVENTORY DATA data store indicates available inventory levels to be compared with the quantities of order items. If insufficient inventory quantities exist for filling the customer order, a back order is created, and a CUSTOMER BACKORDER STATEMENT data flow is sent to the customer. The customer then responds to the back-order statement by indicating whether he or she is willing to accept it. The CUSTOMER BACKORDER INFORMATION data flow coming from the CUSTOMER entity indicates the customer's acceptance or rejection

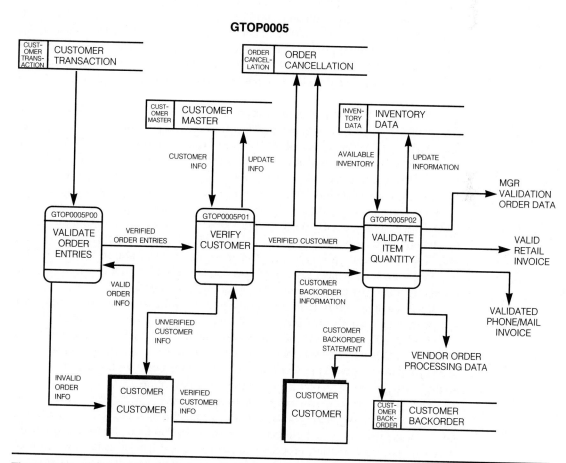

Figure 6-26. National Golf & Tennis GTOP0005 level-2 DFD

of the back order. If the back order is rejected, the customer order or a portion of the order is canceled.

If the customer consents to the back order, or the inventory reorder point is reached, then a customer back order is created (note the flow to the CUSTOMER BACKORDER data store) along with a vendor item order; again, note the data flow.

The VENDOR ORDER PROCESSING DATA data flow is a data flow interface. A **data flow interface** occurs on a lower-level DFD when the process on the upper-level DFD being exploded on is directly connected to another process on this upper-level DFD. For these cases, the analyst must show the flow, but the flow will be attached to only one process on the lower-level DFD. This occurs because the other process to which the flow should be attached resides on the upper-level DFD. In this case, the data flow interface represents an **output interface** because the flow is leading away from the process on which explosion occurs. For flows leading into the explosion process directly from another process on the upper-level DFD, the analyst would insert an **input interface**. For example, if the RECEIVE CUSTOMER ORDERS process on the GTOP00 DFD in Figure 6-23 were connected directly to the VALIDATE ORDERS process, rather than to the CUSTOMER DATA data store between them, then the VALIDATE ORDER ENTRIES process on the GTOP0005 DFD of Figure 6-26 would have an input interface, probably labeled "CUSTOMER ORDER TRANSACTION."

The VALIDATE ORDERS process on the GTOP00 level-1 DFD from which the GTOP0005 level-2 DFD exploded has data flows directly to four other processes on the GTOP00 DFD. The VENDOR ORDER PROCESSING DATA, MGR VALIDA-TION ORDER DATA, VALID RETAIL INVOICE, and VALIDATED PHONE/MAIL INVOICE are data flow interfaces indicating the data flows to these other processes on the GTOP00 DFD. These processes are outside the domain of the decomposition of the VALIDATE ORDERS process illustrated in the GTOP0005 DFD. They already appear on the GTOP00 DFD and would not be a part of the GTOP0005 DFD. However, since the VALIDATE ORDERS process on the GTOP00 DFD has flows leading away from it to these other processes on the GTOP00, a process (or processes) must have these flows on the GTOP0005 DFD, but must not be connected to the processes that already appear on the GTOP00 DFD.

If sufficient inventory exists for all or a portion of the customer order, the quanti-ty of that item in the INVENTORY DATA data store is updated (note the UPDATE INFORMATION data flow). Subsequently, either a VALID RETAIL INVOICE or a VALIDATED PHONE/MAIL INVOICE data flow occurs. Regardless of the outcome of the validation process, the MGR VALIDATION ORDER DATA data flow occurs so that management can monitor and control order validation.

The NG&T project team creates dictionary entries to accompany each symbol and labeled data flow on the GTOP0005 DFD. In addition, it creates separate level-2 DFDs for the remaining major processes on the GTOP00 DFD. It also creates dictio-nary entries for all entities, processes, data stores, and labeled data flows on these additional level-2 DFDs. As a result, the team has a comprehensive and systematic set of documentation for analyzing the information needs of NG&T order processing.

NATIONAL GOLF & TENNIS ANALYSIS AND REVIEW OF STUDY RESULTS

The NG&T project team uses the data and process modeling methods illustrated here and in Chapter 5 to organize its investigative findings. After it has organized its findings, it analyzes the results of its investigation to identify problems with the current order processing system. This process extends from an analysis of results and recommendations through a review of these results and a discussion of actions to take following the review. This review sets the stage for the design phase of the project.

Present Analysis Results and Make Recommendations

The main problem identified by the project team is that data passes through the hands of too many clerical personnel during processing. A great deal of labor and time is frequently expended between initial customer ordering and subsequent order completion, and a customer order cancellation may be the only result of all this effort.

The project team recommends three solutions to the main problem. The first solution is to install terminal devices at each retail and phone/mail ordering point. With real-time access to order validation, customers are serviced in a shorter period of time, with less effort expended. This solution requires installing a local area network for access to the company mainframe computer and the creation of mainframe executable programs.

The second solution is to install desktop computers at each retail and phone/mail ordering point. Real-time access to order validation again results, with the same benefits. This solution requires installing desktop computers at each ordering point, including a local area network, and either retaining the existing mainframe or acquiring a new minicomputer as a network server, or both. Network servers provide a larger variety and greater capacity of storage for all computers on the network. All executable programs for the system are to be created to run on desktop computers, with the network server providing access to the actual files of data.

The third option is to purchase a system to help service customer orders and manage inventory accordingly. This option was resoundingly declined in the analysis phase because Tim and Jason Richardson, the owners, want the system to provide for the more specialized needs of NG&T. In an initial review of commercially available systems, Tim, Jason, and George Serve (the director of IS) did not find a system that matched their needs well enough. Furthermore, Tim and Jason wanted the new director of information systems to feel that they had confidence in his ability to complete the project for NG&T.

The fourth option that could be considered is to do nothing; that is, to continue with the current system. This option is usually included, since the costs of alternatives may be prohibitive.

The first option recommended by the team requires either modifying the existing mainframe system or creating a new system. The second option might include modifying the existing mainframe system or creating a new system for the mainframe, and also acquiring the desktop computers. Modification is suitable if the existing system still provides most of the information needed, but modifications will meet some additional information needs. A new system is recommended if the current system is performing so poorly that it needs to be replaced.

Modifying the Existing System

The advantages of modifying the existing system are numerous. For example, if the present system can be modified to meet user requirements, many of the existing programs may be used. In addition, design and user documentation may be available for the system. Finally, a partial solution to the problem has already been defined, eliminating a large portion of the uncertainty in the design process.

There are also disadvantages in modifying the existing system. Frequently, the biggest problem is getting users to understand that the old system may not be as bad as they believe it is. For example, the old system may have features that users do not know about. Convincing dissatisfied users that the existing system can meet their needs with only minor modifications involves salesmanship on the part of the analyst.

An additional problem is that current documentation on the existing system often does not represent the actual system in use. It is common for documentation not to be updated as changes are made to the system. As a result, the documentation may be misleading for the user and the analyst.

The analyst must clearly understand the existing system to determine whether it can be updated and where changes need to be made. Identifying the places where changes need to be made is best accomplished by thorough evaluation of data gathered in the analysis phase of the development cycle.

Designing a New System

When no current system exists or when an existing system performs inadequately, the project results in the creation of an entirely new system. The main advantage of developing an entirely new system is that it can be designed specifically to meet current user requirements. In addition, weaknesses in the existing system need not be dealt with in the design phase. The old system was created for previous information needs, which may not coincide with current ones. Another advantage occurs when users have such a bad opinion of the old system that creating a new system is the only response capable of meeting their current needs. User acceptance and involvement in the development project are often increased when this action is taken. An analogy can be made to buying a used car or a new car: both cars get you where you want to go, but you feel much more confident about getting there in a new car.

The disadvantage of developing a new system is often the time frame and the resources involved. Many users are discouraged when they learn that development and implementation of a new system can take years and is very costly. The development cost is only one of the costs that must be considered. Lost opportunities and user dissatisfaction may far outweigh the cost of developing a new system. The analyst should be aware of "sticker shock," which is often experienced by managers when they are confronted with development costs. The analyst must encourage managers to compare the costs of dealing with an inadequate, old system while it is being modified and the costs of developing a new system.

One way to reduce costs and time spent developing a new application system is to reuse existing code. Portions of existing programs may be reused when developing new systems. Many procedures embedded in existing programs need not change over time and from application to application. As a result, those procedures may be included within procedures of newly developed systems as **reusable code**. Reusable code prevents the analysts from reinventing the wheel during the development life cycle.

Conduct a Formal Review of Analysis Results

The analyst is responsible for systematically recording and analyzing data concerning alternative courses of action, but functional area personnel are responsible for evaluating alternatives and determining which one they believe is the best. This evaluation often occurs in a formal review session at the conclusion of the current phase of the project life cycle.

Review is an essential part of any system project. It should be conducted continually throughout each phase of the development life cycle. However, there are four key points in the life cycle when a formal review is conducted: at the end of the analysis, logical design, and physical design phases, and at the conclusion of the entire project.

A properly presented set of results for the current phase of the project ensures that all parties agree with the results of the current phase, that cooperation can be expected for the next phase, and that the resultant system will be more readily accepted by users. A properly planned and prepared formal review can greatly influence all of these actions. In addition, users participating in the review feel that their involvement in the project adds to its success, which increases the acceptance of the system. Figure 6-27 lists the participants in the formal review, key considerations before and during the review, the formal content of review documentation, and formal review actions.

The distribution of documentation appropriate for the review should take place from three to five days before the presentation to ensure that participants have time to prepare for the review, but not enough time to forget the material. This documentation should include background information on the project, a concise statement of the results of the current phase, the importance of participation by users, and the time and place of the review.

Participants in the Formal Review

- Functional area supervisors
- Key functional area technical and clerical personnel
- IS managers responsible for the project
- Project leader and key IS participants

Key Considerations for the Formal Review

- Site selection and preparation for the review
- Date and time selection for the review
- Pre-presentation handouts
- Audio-visual presentation aids
- Use of computer conferencing
- Round-table Delphi response method in which everyone is given a turn to speak on each subject and no one is permitted to dominate the discussion
- Recording of evaluation responses (secretarial and tape support)
- Summary of evaluation responses
- Review analysis document signing
- Additional investigation where warranted by responses
- Follow-up summary of the results of the review derived and distributed to appropriate participants

Form and Content of Review Documentation

- Video and hard-copy documentation for collective and interactive as well as individual and isolated analysis and review

Figure 6-27. Elements of a formal review

In preparation for the review, the project team must remember that the presentation is being made to a group of users, not to fellow information systems professionals. The emphasis during the presentation should be on the way the system is going to affect the users.

The review should include time to respond to questions from participants in the review. The question and answer session permits users to express their concerns relative to any aspect of the project. User needs and expectations must be resolved before the project continues. Improperly interpreted analysis and design specifications produce a gloomy outlook for later phases of the project. Resolving user questions during the presentation greatly diminishes the likelihood of misinterpretations.

- Desktop-published documentation for quality review
- Table of contents and index of included material
- Copy of original request
- Print-out of all background documentation for the business area and system
- Print-out of all E/RDs in one section for easier review of all of them
- Print-out of each E/RD followed by the dictionary entries for all entities and relationships on the E/RD for easier review of E/RD graphic and accompanying dictionary entries for all symbols
- Print-out of all DFDs in one section for easier review of all of them
- Print-out of each DFD followed by the dictionary entries for all entities, processes, data stores, and data flows on the DFD in a separate section
- Print-out of each M-LDS, LDS, and data element

Formal Review Actions

1. Review general results of the analysis phase (true sources of the problem).
2. Review recorded data concerning viable alternatives.
3. Evaluate alternatives.
4. Select the best alternative.
5. Sign a formal review document indicating approval of the analysis results and agreement with evaluation and selection results.

Objectives of Formal Review

The main objective of a formal review in the analysis phase is to identify necessary changes to analysis specifications based on user responses during the review. If these specifications need further enhancements and/or modifications, the project team returns to the analysis phase to modify the specifications to conform to user suggestions. At the conclusions of these additional analysis actions, formal reviews should be held to present the changes to the users (even if two, three, or more reviews are required). Some firms simply send out a memo to all interested parties detailing the changes. These memos tend to be ignored, whereas when an actual review is conducted, user participation is guaranteed.

At the conclusion of the formal review, the formal review committee should sign a document stating that the analysis phase has been successfully completed. This document indicates that the review committee is in agreement with the analysis performed by the project team and has selected an alternative to implement. Figure 6-28 presents an example of this document.

The review does not always signify the end of the analysis phase. It may be discovered during review that more information is needed to understand the problem and evaluate alternatives. Consequently, the formal review may send the project team back to gather and analyze additional data on user requirements. Following these additional analysis actions, another formal review is scheduled and the actions enumerated in Figure 6-27 are once again performed.

You should always remember that analysis and design is an iterative activity: data is gathered and analyzed, results reviewed and evaluated, additional data is gathered and analyzed, and so on. If the evaluation is satisfactory, the project moves to the next phase. If the evaluation is not completely satisfactory, additional data is gathered for evaluation. All phases of the traditional project life cycle and actions in those phases exhibit the iterative nature of identification, review, and evaluation until the completion of the phase.

Analysis Phase Sign-off Document

I agree that the analysis specifications have been successfully completed by the project team directed by _____, Project Leader. I agree with the alternative action selected to resolve the problems identified during systems analysis.

SIGNED _____

DATE _____

Figure 6-28. Formal review agreement document

Following the analysis review, the project team should familiarize participants with the actions of the logical portion of the design phase. Doing this allows the analyst to define the purpose of the next phase, describe its contents, and identify participation in its actions. This provides a transition to the next phase and an opportunity for renewed commitment from participants who will be continuing the logical design. The introduction sets up the framework for the logical design phase—project team responsibility, functional area responsibility, and continuation of the work—and it provides an initial identification of participants in the review presentation for the next phase.

Results of National Golf & Tennis Analysis and Review

The NG&T project team makes a formal presentation of its findings. This presentation consists of a review of all E/RDs and DFDs, including dictionary descriptions of all entities, relationships, processes, data flows, data stores, and logical data structures (LDSs). The project team also provides various estimates for the three options to compare the costs and benefits of the alternatives.

The review committee immediately discounted the third option (purchase of a system to help service customer orders and manage inventory), since this option excludes providing the information needed for the intended expansion of the company. The current system has already been found to be inadequate for current operations. Consequently, continuing with the current system is even less desirable in light of the expansion strategy of the company.

The real decision for the review committee is to determine whether the current system can be enhanced to meet NG&T's increasing needs or whether a new system is required. Following a presentation by the project team on these two options, it is determined that it would be too difficult to enhance the current system to meet the more dynamic information needs of NG&T. Since the current system largely consists of batch processing actions, the review participants decide that NG&T personnel need on-line access to support the dynamic nature of both retail and phone/mail order sales.

A further consideration for the review committee is whether desktop computers or terminals better serve the information needs of the expanding company. The costs for installing terminals and those for desktop computers are roughly equivalent. However, costs for networking desktop computers are determined to be much higher; desktop computers need to be networked together, with the network server also networked to the mainframe computer.

Tom Ingram, the director of marketing, states that having desktop computers at order points provides the greatest benefit relative to customer servicing. By using desktop computers, order clerks can more rapidly service customers since mainframe transmission is not necessary for most ordering actions. The network server periodically updates or retrieves data retained on the mainframe without personnel intervention. Thus, a frequent bottleneck for data access is avoided without loss of access to current data.

Paul Hensel, a marketing supervisor, also supports the selection of desktop computers. He states that the use of desktop computers makes it easier for future expansion of NG&T operations. Connecting new order points in existing stores only involves installing additional desktop computers (and possibly expanding the storage in the network server and/or increasing the number of servers). However, he recognizes that connecting new stores is considerably more complicated, since it requires a desktop network and an extension of the mainframe.

George Serve, the director of IS, states that desktop computers also provide less costly system execution. However, he adds, in some ordering situations current data may not be available during the ordering actions of order/sales clerks. This occurs when periodic network server activity to update or access mainframe data does not have access to mainframe data updates from other sites. However, this situation occurs only in a small percentage of order servicing situations. Therefore, he too favors using desktop computers at order points.

The review committee decides that the desktop computer option is the preferred option for phone/mail orders, but terminals are preferred for retail sales. George Serve and Tom Ingram are designated by the committee to prepare a report for Tim and Jason Richardson.

Another major requirement recommended by the review committee is that retail and phone/mail clerks perform all validating actions. This results in on-line access during order/customer validation and back-order creation. It is determined that this feature causes order processing to be more judiciously performed, with fewer personnel involved. By having on-line access capabilities, the clerk taking the customer order can perform all validation actions and know immediately if errors need correction, if the customer status affects the order, if the order can be filled, and/or if a back order needs to be created. Thus, less time is required to correct or cancel orders because of poor customer delinquency records or customer dissatisfaction with a back order.

A final major requirement recommended by the review committee is to retain a separate group of data structures on which to base managerial reporting. For this, appropriate DFD levels should be modified to include a separate data store for this data, rather than have flows leading directly to the PRODUCE MANAGER REPORTS process.

A number of modifications to the analysis diagrams and the accompanying dictionary entries are also recommended during the course of the meeting. Since these changes have no effect on the committee's decision, the project team is commissioned to make these changes without the need for an additional review meeting.

The project team distributes a sign-off form to the review committee members to ensure their commitment to the selected alternative. Each member signs the review document with his or her attention directed to the modifications the project team will make.

The project team concludes the meeting by outlining the actions to be taken in the design phase of the project. This is important in order to provide a smooth transition to the next phase of the project life cycle.

COMPUTER-AIDED PROCESS MODELING DURING SYSTEMS ANALYSIS

Analyst workbench and dictionary software, as described in Chapters 2 and 5, includes **computer-aided process modeling** methods that provide automation for creating and storing specifications resulting from analysis, design, and development actions. These specifications are usually stored in files on desktop and mainframe computers, using software systems to enter them. During the analysis phase, these tools provide:

- Computer-aided archival searches for specific dictionary entries through the use of a "WHERE-USED" search for references to specific dictionary entries
- Computer-aided recording of questionnaire responses, observations made by the analyst, sampling of on-site data, and operations using modeling methods and dictionary entries for diagram components

The advantages of using these tools to aid process modeling are:

- More comprehensive and integrated recording of investigation results
- Uniform recording of analysis results for all systems
- Display of analysis results in a form easily explained to users—DFDs, E/RDs, etc.
- Easy navigation through analysis DFD specifications
- Easily modified DFD entries during the iterative actions of analysis
- CASE system checking for compliance with specific rules for the DFD modeling method, such as balanced input and output checks for DFD levels
- CASE system identification of inconsistent entries for the same or similar items in the dictionary, such as the same logical object defined differently on E/RDs and on DFDs
- Facilities for better maintenance of analysis specifications

CASE systems include A&D workbench software components to create DFDs to illustrate analysis findings, and dictionary software components to enter detailed descriptions for diagram elements. These dictionary descriptions usually involve:

- Preformatted screen data entry and reporting specifications
- More elaborate narrative explanations of analysis results
- Reductions in redundancy of analysis specifications
- Better integrated analysis specifications

- A central repository for analysis documentation
- More easily maintained documentation

The NG&T project team used one of the leading analyst workbench systems to create all of their diagrams and to enter their dictionary entries. Most of the examples in this chapter represent facsimiles of specifications that could have been entered on either an analyst workbench system or a dictionary software system. A careful look at the E/RD, DFD, and dictionary entry examples should illustrate the value of using these software systems.

Using Data Flow Diagrams During Joint Application Design (JAD) Sessions

Chapters 4 and 5 described the purpose and practice of joint application design sessions (JADs) and how E/RDs may be used during these sessions. In much the same way as they are used to gather and verify data and build E/RD models, JADs can be used to create, review, verify, and modify DFDs.

Using CASE and visual-aid technologies, users can provide immediate feedback regarding the process model at the same time as DFDs are being created or in review sessions for them. JADs can include only those users involved in a single subfunction and the creation of a DFD that depicts its business processes, or they can include users involved in multiple subfunctions to develop or review multiple DFDs that share data types depicted as data flows and data stores. As users describe the processes that they perform or for which they are responsible, scribes can record this data in DFDs and accompanying dictionary entries. The DFDs and the dictionary entries for their symbols and connections can be displayed on a large white screen, and the LCD panels can be used to get immediate feedback from JAD participants.

For review and verification of DFDs, JADs allow real-time changes to be made as users suggest modifications to DFDs and dictionary entries, and scribes record those changes. Thus, JADs can contribute to the accuracy and completeness of the process model in a shorter period of time than more traditional approaches.

REVIEW

Business processes are modeled during the analysis phase to provide additional information about user requirements. The data flow diagram (DFD) modeling method is currently the most frequently used of the structured methods for modeling business processes, and is the one used in this text. There are a number of very specific rules governing the use of DFDs. As with the entity/relationship (E/R) modeling method detailed in Chapter 5, DFDs are constructed on levels, which explode down to increasingly more detailed diagrams of business processes and their relationships. A DFD example for the employment application used to illustrate E/RDs in Chapter 5 was shown in this chapter, along with related design dictionary entries.

This chapter also showed how to use this portion of the methodology to investigate the problem during the analysis phase of the system development life cycle of the NG&T project. The DFD modeling method used for process decomposition during the analysis phase was demonstrated with regard to the NG&T case, and four alternative solutions were presented.

The results of the investigation should be reviewed throughout the system development life cycle, but especially at the ends of the analysis, logical design, and physical design phases, and at the conclusion of the entire project. A formal review, with its participants and purposes identified, was set up for the NG&T case, and the review committee made its recommendations.

The use of CASE systems and joint application development sessions (JADs) can make the mechanics of process modeling easier and more efficient. Readers are encouraged to apply the principles of analysis presented in this chapter to the investigation of an actual system in order to ensure that they have learned how analysis is performed.

QUESTIONS

1. Explain the DFD rules associated with the following:
   a. Entity
   b. Process
   c. Data store
   d. Data flow
2. What are the advantages of using the DFD method?
3. What questions does a well-constructed DFD answer?
4. What is the major drawback of using DFDs?
5. Distinguish between the use of E/RDs and the use of DFDs during analysis and design; explain the relationship between them.
6. What is the goal of the DFD modeling method?
7. Describe how different levels of a DFD work.
8. What is the purpose of the context-level diagram?
9. What is a semantic functional primitive DFD?
10. Explain what the phrase "balanced inputs and outputs" means in relation to DFD explosion levels.

11. Explain the dictionary ID naming conventions for the following:

    a. DFD diagram levels

    b. Entities on a DFD diagram

    c. Processes on a DFD diagram

    d. Data flows on a DFD diagram

    e. Data stores on a DFD diagram

12. Explain how mass and individual LDSs help integrate E/RD and DFD specifications.

13. Illustrate how the NG&T project team conformed to the naming convention for symbols on DFD levels for DFD dictionary IDs.

14. Explain the relationship between E/RDs, M-LDSs, individual LDSs, and DFDs for the NG&T project.

15. Explain the NG&T GTOP DFD in Figure 6-17 in relation to its use as a context-level diagram.

16. Explain the six main processes (not RECEIVE CUSTOMER ORDERS) and the relationships among them appearing on the GTOP00 DFD of Figure 6-23.

17. Explain why the PRODUCE MANAGER REPORTS process on the GTOP00 DFD in Figure 6-23 is connected to five of the six remaining DFD processes.

18. Explain the three main processes and the relationships between them appearing on the GTOP0005 DFD of Figure 6-26.

19. Explain the purpose for the four data flow interfaces connected to the VALIDATE ITEM QUANTITY process appearing on the GTOP0005 DFD of Figure 6-26.

20. Explain how the three processes on the GTOP0005 DFD in Figure 6-26 could explode to additional DFD levels.

21. Explain how the DFDs of this chapter assisted the NG&T project team in analyzing the problems with order processing.

22. Explain the purpose of the review conducted at the conclusion of the analysis phase; identify the participants and their involvement in the review process.

23. What are key considerations before and during the review meeting?

24. List and explain the formal review actions.

25. Explain the option selected by the NG&T review committee and why it was selected.

26. Explain why it is important that the review committee sign the formal review document at the conclusion of the review meeting.

27. Explain why the review meeting may not signify the end of the analysis phase of a project life cycle.

28. What is analyst workbench software and why is it useful for analysts?

29. Explain the two main purposes for using analyst workbenches and dictionary systems during the analysis phase.

30. List and explain the advantages of using CASE systems in creating and maintaining analysis specifications.

31. Explain the two major specification components of analyst workbenches and dictionary systems.

32. Explain what is involved in using CASE systems to create dictionary specifications.

33. Explain the advantage of using LCD display panels with projectors during JADs and the review meeting.

EXERCISES

Chapter 6 of the student workbook contains blank documentation forms and additional information to use in the following exercises.

1. Create a functional primitive level-2 explosion DFD for the process called FILL OPENING on the level-1 DFD in Figure 6-6 for the employment system example. Create dictionary entries for *all* entities, processes, data flows, data stores, data structures, and data elements relative to this level-2 DFD explosion.

2. Create a level-2 explosion DFD for the process called CREATE PAYROLL DATA on the level-1 DFD in Figure 6-6. Create dictionary entries for *all* entities, processes, data flows, data stores, data structures, and data elements relative to this level-2 DFD explosion.

3. Create a lower-level detail DFD and accompanying design dictionary entries for an explosion on the COMPLETE RETAIL INVOICES process of the GTOP00 DFD of Figure 6-23. Create dictionary entries for *all* entities, processes, data flows, data stores, data structures, and data elements relative to this level-2 DFD explosion.

4. Create a lower-level detail DFD and accompanying design dictionary entries for an explosion on the COMPLETE PHONE/MAIL INVOICES process of the GTOP00 DFD of Figure 6-23. Create dictionary entries for *all* entities, processes, data flows, data stores, data structures, and data elements relative to this level-2 DFD explosion.

5. Create a lower-level detail DFD and accompanying design dictionary entries for an explosion on the ORDER VENDOR ITEMS process of the GTOP00 DFD of Figure 6-23. Create dictionary entries for *all* entities, processes, data flows, data stores, data structures, and data elements relative to this level-2 DFD explosion.

6. Create a lower-level detail DFD and accompanying design dictionary entries for

an explosion on the PRODUCE MANAGER REPORTS process of the GTOP00 DFD of Figure 6-23. Create dictionary entries for *all* entities, processes, data flows, data stores, data structures, and data elements relative to this level-2 DFD explosion.

7. Create a lower-level detail DFD and accompanying design dictionary entries for an explosion on the RECONCILE CUSTOMER ACCOUNTS process of the GTOP00 DFD of Figure 6-23. Create dictionary entries for *all* entities, processes, data flows, data stores, data structures, and data elements relative to this level-2 DFD explosion.

8. For your class project, conduct a JAD with participants from the company used, during which DFDs are reviewed, revised, created, and agreed upon. Prepare a report that describes all aspects of the JAD (remember to include preworkshop, workshop, and postworkshop activities).

SELECTED REFERENCES

Andersen, Arthur & Co. 1989. *Foundations of Business Systems*. Orlando, FL: The Dryden Press, Holt, Rinehart and Winston.

Constantine, L. L. and E. Yourdon. 1975. *Structured Design: Fundamentals of a Discipline of Computer Program and Systems Design*. Englewood Cliffs, NJ: Prentice-Hall.

DeMarco, T. 1978. *Structured Analysis and System Specification*. Englewood Cliffs, NJ: Prentice-Hall.

Dolan, K. A. 1984. *Business Computer Systems Design*. Santa Cruz, CA: Mitchell Publishing Inc.

Gane, C. and T. Sarson. 1977. *Structured Systems Analysis: Tools and Techniques*. New York: Improved Systems Technologies.

Martin, J. and C. McClure. 1988. *Structured Techniques: The Basis for CASE*. Englewood Cliffs, NJ: Prentice-Hall.

Yourdon, E. 1989. *Modern Structured Analysis*. Englewood Cliffs, NJ: Yourdon Press, Prentice-Hall.

PART III

Logical and Physical Design

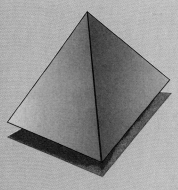

The need to correctly identify user needs and to accurately model the system is so important that it continues from the analysis phase into the design phase of the system life cycle. Prototyping is a useful modeling method to refine user requirements. For example, input screens are prototyped, and the users are allowed to enter data to determine if the screen design needs changing. User interfaces developed during prototyping display the data objects that were defined while completing the conceptual and logical data model using the entity/relationship modeling method. Once the analyst feels certain that user requirements have been accurately defined, a logical business solution is designed to meet user needs. This business solution appears as modifications to the entity/relationship diagrams and data flow diagrams that represent the data models and process models of the business. After the logical design of the business solution is complete, a physical design is created to implement the logical design. In other words, the logical business design represents what the user wants the system to do, and the physical design indicates how it will be accomplished. The physical design is created using the structure chart modeling method to create a procedure model for the information system.

CHAPTER 7

Prototyping and
the User Interface

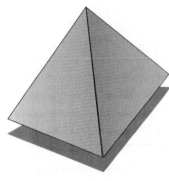

OVERVIEW

Prototyping is a modeling method that has been around for many years but is just now beginning to get the recognition it deserves. The pressure to get a working system model into the hands of the user is the main reason for the rise of interest in prototyping. Prototyping also helps refine user requirements regarding portions of the design and decreases the time and costs associated with designing an information system. This chapter shows how prototyping contributes to the full set of business and information system modeling methods by describing:

- Uses of prototyping
- Prototyping methods
- Design of user interfaces using prototyping
- Special considerations in screen design
- Prototyping for the National Golf & Tennis case
- Computer-aided prototyping

KEY TERMS

Graphical user interface (GUI)
Hard copy
Information hiding
Menu screens
Prototyping
Rapid application development (RAD)
Screen masks
Soft copy
User transparency

Prototyping is a modeling method that has been used by businesses for many purposes, but has only recently been recognized for its ability to produce a working system model for users to review. A prototype represents a proposed way of meeting some new need or refining an existing information need in the business. It can be conceptual or physical, theoretical or practical. For instance, auto manufacturers create a physical prototype model of a new car long before developing manufacturing operations to produce the car. The prototype is a hand-tooled car that may eventually be mass-produced. Prototyping in information systems analysis and design involves creating a model to simulate the operations of a new or modified system. Developing a prototype permits persons responsible for evaluating design activities to determine whether the design is progressing in the correct direction. Although prototyping can be used to develop a new system or modify an existing system, it is best suited for new system development. Figure 7-1 illustrates the part of the enterprise/methodology model on which this chapter focuses its attention. In this section of the model, logical data objects are made available to the user through the view of data by programs; in other words, how data is accepted from or delivered to the user.

Prototyping contributes to the full set of business and information modeling methods by focusing attention on the way the user interacts with the system and what it does for the user. This interaction consists of the way data is accepted from or delivered to the user and the operations the system permits the user to request to process the data, represented in the "Program view of logical objects" section of the enterprise/methodology model in Figure 7-1. A prototype simulates this interaction by using computer display screens, business forms, menus, and other means to accept data from and deliver data to the user.

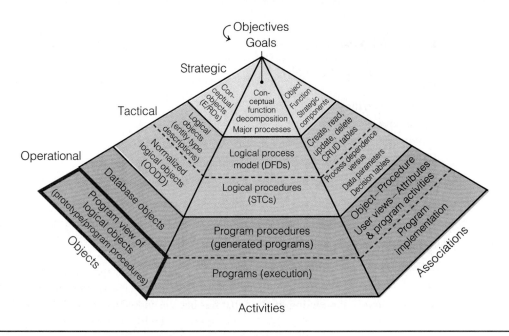

Figure 7-1. Enterprise/methodology model focus of Chapter 7

USES OF PROTOTYPING

System **prototyping** can be done either by developing a conceptual representation of the proposed system or by constructing a scaled-down working version of single or multiple alternatives. Either way, users can simulate operations that the completed system will eventually include. Except in cases in which a methodology is centered around prototyping, a prototype is normally created for selected portions of the proposed system; *it is not meant to be a fully functioning system that can go on line when finished.* Creating interfaces for input and output and simulating their operations are the primary objectives of prototyping activities.

One of the main problems with prototyping is that many companies have allowed it to become a de facto methodology because of their extensive and exclusive use of it. It can be very helpful as a standalone modeling method when systems must be built quickly because of circumstances internal or external to the business. However, when used alone, it keeps the important documentation of the business (business and system models) hidden away in the minds of business personnel. When used alone, prototyping makes for an informal "create, code, and continuous correction" life cycle that many firms practiced in earlier periods, and some still do.

Another problem with prototyping is that its ability to offer a solution to a business problem relatively quickly makes it even more prone to providing a solution to the wrong problem. By not having the more complete understanding of the business and system that the use of entity/relationship diagrams (E/RDs) and data flow diagrams (DFDs) provides, the analyst can readily miss the actual (or better) solution to the problem. Less knowledgeable users may accept the system without having a clear understanding of how it will help them perform their jobs. Many employees of large bureaucratic organizations tend to accept what is delivered to them regardless of its appropriateness for helping them perform their jobs.

Creating prototypes without graphic and textual models is tantamount to trying to build a car from scratch without the elaborate design of each part that goes into the car. No engineer would attempt to construct a bridge over a waterway without creating an elaborate set of architectural guidelines. Similarly, software engineers should not attempt to construct software systems without elaborate descriptions of the business and system the software needs to support.

Prototyping helps users see more clearly where design is heading. Users have greater difficulty in seeing what the final system will be as they review data and process models created by using E/RDs and DFDs. Including a prototype as part of analysis and design specifications helps ensure that the A&D project is progressing in the correct direction before actual system development is begun. It is considerably easier to correct misunderstandings in the analysis and design phases than in the development phase. Having a concrete system example for the user to test helps the analyst and the user to identify some of these misunderstandings.

Entity/Relationship Diagrams (E/RDs), Data Flow Diagrams (DFDs), and Prototype Specifications

Figure 7-2 shows the relationships among specifications created by using E/RDs, DFDs, and prototyping. The primary relationship is that the data values used on prototype screens and forms correspond to the properties (data elements) of the data types or logical data structures (LDSs) identified and described while creating E/RDs and DFDs. An additional relationship is that some prototype menu screens may have menu options that correspond to processes on a DFD.

Figure 7-2 illustrates how the LDSs are defined while creating E/RDs, and then referenced as the LDSs on which DFD processes act. The LDSs as depicted are the same logical objects used by the analyst to create various user interfaces. Recall that the analyst derives the E/RDs and LDSs by interviewing users and investigating the data types users need to access. Prototype data entry and report forms are represented in Figure 7-2 by the terminal screen and report form. Data elements appearing on these prototype models compose a LDS, which is used to support the relationships between entities on lower-level E/RDs. The LDSs are also depicted as data stores and/or data flows on

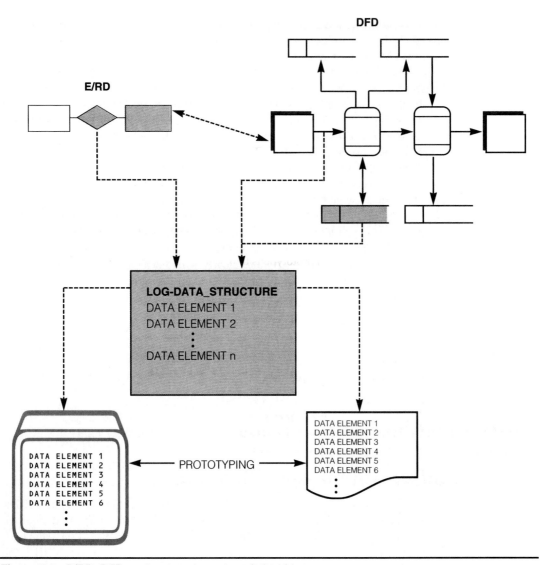

Figure 7-2. E/RD, DFD, and prototyping entry relationships

lower-level DFDs. Thus, prototyping activities may influence data structure dictionary entries associated with E/RD relationships and DFD data stores and data flows.

The information and data acquisition methods that analysts use during data modeling are the same information and data acquisition methods that they use to identify the types of user interfaces for the system under investigation. When analysts use E/RDs, DFDs, and prototyping in combination with each other, they should not be deciding what data elements (properties) to position on the user interface; they should simply be deciding where to position each data element of the LDS on the user interface.

As you will see in "Prototyping for the National Golf & Tennis (NG&T) Application," later in this chapter, the different modeling methods of the text methodology each contribute different facets to the ever-growing set of user requirements. Prototyping should not be the only method to model these logical data requirements. In fact, prototyping should be viewed as a way to verify many of the requirements that have been gathered and modeled using other methods. Although prototypes often help users to better articulate their information needs, in a comprehensive methodology as proposed by this text, the main purpose of prototyping is to validate most requirements, *not* to create them. The main user requirements obtained through prototyping are the layout of the data on the user interface, not what appears on it, and the list of options (capabilities) on a menu screen. The data properties that appear on the interface should have been identified during the creation of either E/RDs or DFDs or both.

Although some portions of the prototype may become part of a designed system, the purpose of creating a prototype is to determine whether the system design:

- Includes the specific data acquisition desired by the user
- Specifies how that data is made available to the user
- Indicates the format of the user interface
- Supports the capabilities the user desires

The prototype screens and reports should display the specific types of data that the user needs to access. The specific forms, reports, and on-line data acquisition methods used during prototyping specify how the data will be made available to the user. The specific layouts of forms, reports, and on-line screens indicate the format of the user interface. The lists of options on menu screens indicate what capabilities the system will provide for users—that is, what they can do.

Once the prototype is created, it is reviewed by users to determine whether the proposed design correctly meets their information needs. Hence, a prototype is viewed as a modeling method for fine-tuning the user requirements and the resultant design. For example, a prototype screen or business form used to display a customer order should contain the data elements (attributes) described as the CUSTOMER ORDER logical object on an E/RD and depicted as a data flow for a logical data object flowing into the order-filling process on a DFD. If users indicate that a data element is missing from the interface, the logical data object may not be correct, and the description of the logical data object may need to be changed.

Once reviewed and modified, the prototype may have little additional influence on the project. However, it can influence initial database design, various input and output screens, and hard-copy form designs. The database design will need expansion in a later phase of the development life cycle, but initial design specifications from the prototype can provide a starting point for the top-down design of the system's database.

Including prototyping as one of a set of modeling methods helps unite analysis and design activities. While performing analysis activities to create E/RDs and DFDs, some project team members may produce portions of the prototype for user evaluation. This avoids long periods of analysis activities without practical results for the user to review.

Observations on Prototyping

The following generalizations can be made about prototyping:

- It is particularly useful in situations in which user needs are hard to define or in which users have difficulty articulating their needs.
- It is an iterative exercise. The analyst should expect to change the prototype and, subsequently, design specifications, as needs are clarified.
- It identifies changes in the project at an early stage, when they are less costly to correct.
- It encourages user involvement in system development.
- It increases the probability of user acceptance.
- It encourages the use of new technology available to the analyst, such as workbench software systems and application generators.

The key aspect of prototyping is the encouragement of the involvement of users. Users can frequently specify their information and processing needs more easily and accurately when a prototype is created and made operational. By running the prototype, they see *what* capabilities are being built into the system and get a feel for *how* the system will function. When users iteratively use the prototype and express the ways it can be changed, analysts have dependable evidence that their design is progressing in the correct direction. Because the prototype becomes concrete to users and gets them more involved in the project, it usually leads them to more readily accept the completed system.

Prototypes are most beneficial when they are made operational. To do this, analysts must use software technology such as desktop database management systems, analyst workbenches, prototyping systems, and application generators to create them. Each of these systems displays input and output forms on computer screens to accept data entry from users or display data output to users. These systems use either actual data from the firm's data files or test data that simulates actual data. A desktop database management system usually provides a facility to create screen or paper forms for use in the prototype to simulate system execution. Prototyping is just another modeling method supported by the analyst workbenches of CASE systems. The analyst uses CASE systems to create input and output user interfaces for the user to interact with the system or view output it produces. Application generators are software systems that generate software to act on data. These systems generate standalone executable programs to display and accept data from either actual files or test files.

The analyst may be more successful in getting the user involved in design activities and in creating E/RDs and DFDs by using prototypes. Prototypes help users see how the system will interact with them, what the final output of the system project will be, and how it will help them perform their jobs better. From a practical standpoint, data and process models are often less meaningful to users than a prototype that they can get their hands on and test-drive.

PROTOTYPING METHODS

The primary methods for prototyping the design of a proposed system are:

- Creating screen formats for simulating reports, on-line data entry, inquiries, and updates
- Creating menu screens that indicate the capabilities the emerging system will provide to the user
- Creating user-oriented overview process models
- Creating graphic diagrams that indicate the functionality of the activities involved in interaction with the proposed system
- Using software systems to make the prototype operational

Data Entry, Inquiry, Update, and Report Screen Formats

Many software systems are currently available to aid in producing prototypes—for example, desktop database management systems and accompanying 4GLs, standalone prototyping software systems, prototyping components of CASE tools, and application generators, as previously mentioned. These systems frequently help analysts create screen formats to simulate on-line data entry and on-line queries, and to generate reports in both on-line and hard-copy form. These systems permit analysts to "paint" screens to represent both input and output forms. Screen formats for prototyping the design represent that portion of a prototype that may be retained for future development of the actual system. These screen formats are often called **screen masks**, and they will be described in more detail later, when the user interface and data entry are discussed.

Figures 7-3 and 7-4 show examples of on-line data entry and reporting screens created as part of a prototype. These figures simulate screens that were originally painted using one of the leading software systems with a prototyping capability, called MAGEC, from Al Lee and Associates, Inc., dba MAGEC.

At the beginning of the analysis and design phases, only examples of major data entry and reporting interfaces are created as part of the prototype. The remaining data entry and reporting interfaces become part of the prototype as these phases progress. Showing the user examples of interfaces early helps the analyst determine whether

```
                      CUSTOMER CREDIT LIMIT
      CUSTOMER NUMBER  _____
      CUSTOMER NAME    _____
      STREET           _____
      CITY             _____
      STATE            _____
      CREDIT LIMIT     _____
              PRESS ESC KEY TO SAVE AND EXIT DATA ENTRY
```

Figure 7-3. Prototype of a data entry screen

```
  CUSTOMER TRANSACTION REPORT
  ORDER NUMBER     TRANSACTION TYPE    ITEM NUMBER    ORDER QUANTITY
    XXXXXXXX              X              XXXXXXX          ZZZZZZ
```

Figure 7-4. Prototype of a data reporting screen

user requirements are being met by the proposed solution. (Note that hereafter *user interface* can mean either the screen or a form.)

Menu Screens

Menu screens have a more far-reaching impact on the progress of a system project than any other single type of user interface because they help establish the capabilities of the system: through them, users decide what the system should do. **Menu screens** provide a list of actions that users may ask the system to perform for them. When a user selects an option on a menu screen, it is a request for the system to perform that action—for example, to display data, to perform some action on data, and so forth. Once the program that displays the menu actually exists, each option listed on the menu will have a set of program commands that perform the action when the menu item is selected. Figure 7-5 illustrates a menu screen to support an accounts clerk dealing with customers either in person or by telephone. Each option on the menu specifies some action the clerk may need to perform to support his or her interaction with a customer.

```
                    SERVICE CUSTOMER
        1. CREATE/DISPLAY CUSTOMER BILL.

        2. RECORD PAYMENT.

        3. CREATE/DISPLAY CUSTOMER DELINQUENCY NOTICE.

        4. RECORD CUSTOMER COMPLAINT.

        5. CANCEL CUSTOMER CREDIT PRIVILEGES.
              ENTER OPTION HERE: ___

              PRESS ESC KEY TO RETURN TO MAIN MENU
```

Figure 7-5. Accounts clerk menu screen example

The actual use of the menu by users helps the analyst uncover practical information about system design. Users' reactions to the functioning of the prototype reveal specific changes the analyst can make to user requirements. Better communication between the analyst and the user leads to greater success for the project. The iterative nature of prototyping helps solidify better communication through the continuing actions of creating, using, and modifying the prototype.

The list of menu items indicates the actions that the system will perform for the user, or, put another way, the capabilities that the system bestows on the user. It is important for the reader to realize the importance of having users review the list of menu items. Their review and acceptance of the menu list embodies acceptance of the capabilities that the system will provide. Thus, reviewing and accepting the menu options support the fourth of the major purposes of prototyping: verifying that the system design supports the capabilities the user wants.

Using Menu Screens to Combine a System's User Interfaces

Users need many different interfaces to interact with the system and gain access to appropriate data. Most systems today have a set of menus that unite different types of interactions and data accesses that the user needs. These menus and submenus provide a systematic way for the user to interact with the system. The user selects an option from an opening menu, causing a new menu to display options within that broader option from the first menu. The options on the submenu may lead to display of additional submenus. Eventually, the options on a submenu will lead to the display of reports, screen masks, prompting data entry screens, and so on. Thus, the system of menus and submenus ties the set of user interfaces together into a set of capabilities that operate as a system.

Graphical User Interface (GUI)

In recent years, the standard proposed by many system professionals for the user interface has commonly been called the **graphical user interface (GUI)**. A GUI-driven system usually starts with a screen that displays various icons associated with different user applications. Each icon provides the user with access to the application it symbolizes. In this type of system, users normally use a mouse to select the icon and cause the application to execute. The execution of the application most often begins with the display of its menu (or another GUI), from which users select the option they wish the application to perform. This gives users a convenient and relatively simple way of gaining access to the capabilities provided by the system.

Frequently the selection of a GUI icon opens a section of the screen to display a menu of application options, thus opening a "window" for displaying application execution. The use of separate windows for application execution was originated by the Xerox Corporation and further refined by Apple Computer, Inc. and Microsoft Corporation. Many current systems that use icon-driven windowing methods are actually calling on systems developed by these companies to open and close windows for application execution. These applications include what is known as a *kernel* of code that causes the window to open, to be used, and to close.

The importance of obtaining a standard user interface cannot be overemphasized, and establishing any interface as the standard to be used for all systems, such as the graphical user interface, is the most significant and far-reaching standard yet proposed in information systems. The founding fathers of systems analysis and design have long proposed that users be shielded from the complexities of how a system works. **Information hiding** and **user transparency** have often been suggested as the strategy to follow while developing systems. What these terms mean is that users should not be forced to understand how a system works in order to use the system and gain access to the information that supports their job functions. To users, the information on how the system works should be *hidden* and *transparent*.

The most important part of adopting a specific user interface format as a standard is that each system developed will execute the same way. If all systems that interact directly with users are driven by the same GUI, special training on how to make the system execute is unnecessary. Each new application will have its own icon displayed on the users' screens, and they can select its execution the same way they select the execution of all existing applications. Furthermore, since selecting application execution remains the same, analysts can spend more time explaining the capabilities provided by applications and how to interpret and use application outputs. Users typically value this information more than gaining an understanding of how a system works. Documentation that helps explain how to interpret system output helps users employ system-supplied information in ways that help them perform their jobs better.

In recent years, most prototype applications have been created either with their own GUI or as part of an existing GUI-driven set of applications. When a GUI is used during prototyping, selection of an application icon causes a simulation of the execution of that application or a portion of that application. Behind the scenes, the same types of test data files are being used to accept and display data to users and simulate the way the system will respond to users when it exists.

For example, selecting an icon associated with a prototype application might cause a menu of the major execution options to be displayed horizontally or vertically across the screen (or window). If the user then moves the mouse to one of the options and selects it, a pop-down submenu or a new submenu of options is displayed for the user to select a particular option within the initially selected option. For example, the application selected could be the service orders application for National Golf & Tennis. Selecting this application would display a menu of options that correspond to the processes on the GTOP00 DFD of Figure 6-23 in Chapter 6. Selecting the menu option that corresponds to the VALIDATE ORDERS process on the GTOP00 DFD would display a submenu with three validating options that correspond to the three processes on the GTOP0005 DFD of Figure 6-26 in Chapter 6. Selecting the VALIDATE ORDER ENTRIES option on this submenu could then use a screen mask to display the data elements that make up the LOG-CUSTTRNS LDS used to enter or display a customer order.

If the option is selected, the screen mask created as part of the prototype screens will display this data. The data displayed on this screen will be data previously stored in the test data file used to simulate a customer's order. Figure 7-6 illustrates these actions and the subsequent screen displays. The screens are numbered to indicate the order of execution, as specified through mouse cursor arrow selection.

Overview Data Flow Diagrams (DFDs) Used During Prototyping

DFDs are frequently used to explain how data is to flow through a firm as a result of the development of a system. A valid interpretation of data flows, processing that must occur, and user involvement ensures that the design is progressing toward producing a system that correctly directs the flow and storage of data. Once users become accustomed to DFDs, an overview DFD allows them to see operations as interpreted by the analyst. For example, the GTOP00 level-1 DFD in Figure 6-23 of Chapter 6 can be shown to the user as part of the prototype, to verify, in general, that the analyst understands user requirements.

The analyst may use the processes on the DFD to create a top menu as a system-level menu. This menu would list the processes on this DFD as the major capabilities available to the user. The SERVICE ORDERS menu in Figure 7-6 illustrates a system-level menu that corresponds to the processes on the GTOP00 DFD. The top menu forms a system by combining the processes of the application and various submenus, data entry or reporting screen masks, function key and prompting interfaces, and forms. Later in this chapter, several examples for the NG&T case will illustrate creating menus and submenus to make DFD processes operational.

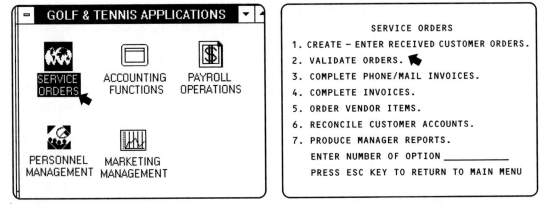

Figure 7-6. Screen displays for a GUI-driven prototype execution

Graphic Diagrams of Business Functions

Many graphics software packages allow the analyst to draw diagrams depicting the functioning of the business system and the users' part in it or the ways it affects them. The mechanics of data gathering, transmission, and processing can be visually portrayed for users to help ensure that the system is functionally sound relative to the physical interaction between the proposed system and user departments. When users are shown these diagrams, they usually look at themselves, their workplace, and their responsibilities from the perspective of a "third person." They are often able to identify areas of their own or others' responsibility not previously expressed to the analyst. This is a direct result of being forced to literally look at themselves in the third person through the use of graphic diagrams.

The example in Figure 7-7 simulates a graphic diagram drawn with one of these software systems. This diagram provides an overview of the operations included in

Customer Statement Diagram

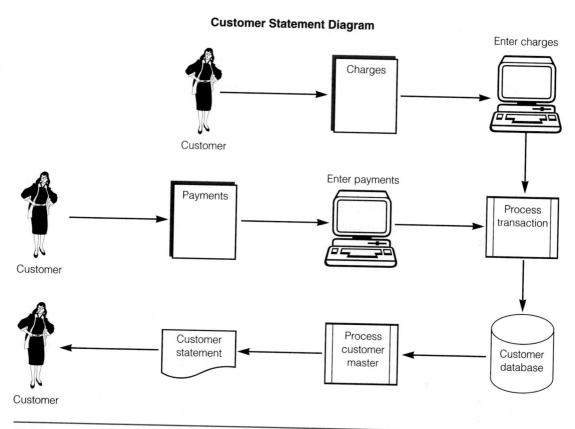

Figure 7-7. A graphic depiction of order processing activities

the proposed order processing system for NG&T. Note that people and system operations are also identified in this diagram.

Making a Prototype Operational

When driven by software, prototype screens for reports, data entry, inquiries, and updates provide a simulation of system execution. Users can run the prototype and use the on-line data entry screens to build small files of example data transactions, including inquiry, updating, and reporting activities, to see how the future system will operate.

Later in this chapter you will see how CASE systems facilitate prototype creation and execution. However, a prototype can be created with the help of most desktop database management systems or file processing systems. For example, the forms and reports capability in the dBASE software package, from Borland International, Inc., can be used to retrieve, display, update, and report values in database files. Users can use these screens to simulate the operations of the system before it exists.

Types of User Interfaces for Operational Prototypes

There are many ways to create a prototype that simulates the operations of an application and the types of user interfaces used. More particularly, the types of user interfaces used make the prototype appear to be operating as the system will function. There are eight major types of user interfaces:

- Commands entered or displayed on a fixed command line (usually at the bottom)
- User-prompting interface
- Menu-driven interface
- Function key–driven interface
- Screen mask interface with automatic cursor movement between entries
- Touch-sensitiven interface
- Pointer-driven or remote-driven interface
- Standardized GUI with windowing capabilities

COMMANDS DISPLAYED ON A FIXED COMMAND LINE Many systems use a fixed line at the bottom of the screen to relay a message to the user. Each time the system needs to say something to the user, it displays one of a fixed set of messages on that command line, and the user types responses on this line. Although this is one of the oldest types of user interfaces, it is still used by many systems.

USER-PROMPTING INTERFACE User-prompting interfaces display text on users' screens requesting that they do something, such as enter a data value on the keyboard. This data value is then used to perform some action. For example, users may be prompted for an employee ID number that is used by the system to select a particular employee's payroll data, which is then displayed on the screen. A prototype that uses this interface contains data corresponding to the prompt text that it displays in a specific location on the screen. When users enter an employee number, the prototype uses the data value to perform a search on the test data file used by the prototype. The data associated with that number is then displayed on the screen. When the system exists, it may perform calculations or logical comparisons to derive certain values that it returns to the user. The prototype test data file will have these values stored as part of simulated employee data.

MENU-DRIVEN INTERFACE Menu-driven interfaces were described in the earlier section "Menu Screens." The prototype contains the screen it uses to display the list of options the user can select. When a user selects one of the options, the prototype uses a particular test file already created to simulate the action that the user requests. For example, the option selected might be to calculate a particular value using data from one or more files. The prototype would be set up to select specific data from an existing test data file to simulate the calculation.

FUNCTION KEY–DRIVEN INTERFACE Many systems use specific function keys on a keyboard as a way for the user to request that certain actions be performed. A prototype that uses a function key–driven interface simulates the action associated with the function key by using the test data to simulate that action. Most businesses that use function key–driven interfaces set up standards regarding the use of function keys within and across computer applications. For example, depressing the F3 key might always be a save action whether it is done within a payroll, customer service, or manufacturing system for a particular company.

SCREEN MASK INTERFACE An application that uses a screen mask often displays the screen mask without data on it to the user. The user may then enter data in one of the data display positions (such as customer number) used by the system to retrieve related data. The remaining data element display positions on the screen mask (such as customer name, address, and phone number) are then automatically filled in by the system. A prototype that uses this type of interface would simulate the action by using one of its test data files to display data values on the screen mask.

TOUCH-SENSITIVE INTERFACE Many applications that need to be executed in hard-to-service areas of businesses use a touch-sensitive screen (often called a touch screen) for the user to enter requests for data. For example, it is often difficult to have a computer set up at different stations along an assembly line floor in a manufacturing company. Such firms often have touch-sensitive monitors hanging from the ceiling at key points along the assembly line to provide computer access without the need for an entire computer, which would clutter the work area.

These applications often have specific sections of the screen, or icons on the screen, that represent certain requests users might make while performing their job functions. For example, a touch screen might be used on the assembly line for an automobile manufacturer with icons representing specific sections of the assembly line. By touching a certain icon, a supervisor could request information on a section of the assembly line that appears to be slowing down. Touching this icon informs the supervisor that off-line assembly of a certain part has fallen behind, causing automobile assembly to falter. Once the problem is known, the supervisor might send utility personnel to that off-line position to help replenish the supply of this part and get the assembly line moving again. A prototype created for this purpose would use test data to display information to the supervisor and simulate this situation.

In recent years, voice-activated interfaces have begun to appear in places where computer keyboards and touch-screen monitors are difficult to use. For example, options displayed on a secured, enclosed monitor for location information are voice-activated in many major cities. Voice-activated and touch-screen interfaces function in very much the same way. The only real difference is in how the user responds or makes selections—by speaking or touching the screen, respectively.

POINTER-DRIVEN OR REMOTE-DRIVEN INTERFACE Pointer- or remote-driven applications use either a pointer device, such as a mouse, or a remote device, such as a television remote control, for the user to select actions that the application will perform. The pointer or remote may be used to move an arrow across a screen to select a particular action to be performed. These devices may be used to make selections from a list of actions, or they may be used in combination with a keyboard. Many applications developed for use by business executives use a remote device because many executives have an aversion to computer keyboards. By employing applications that use remote devices, these executives are able to satisfy many of their own information needs by using a device like those they use with their home television sets. A prototype that uses one of these devices displays the options available to the user on the screen; the device is used to position the cursor on the screen to select the option, and a test data file is used to display the data that simulates the action.

STANDARDIZED GUI   A prototype that uses a GUI often uses an existing system, such as Microsoft Windows, to display icons on the screen that correspond to different applications. When an icon is selected, a prototype menu screen may then be displayed for the user to select a particular action. When an action is selected, the prototype will likely use data from a test data file to simulate the selected action.

Many commercially available software systems already have an icon that represents the software system. Icons can also be created for computer applications created by the firm's programmers and analysts and for purchased applications that do not already have icons that can be used to represent them. When these commercially available and home-grown applications are installed, their icons are added to the existing GUI. To access an application, the user simply selects the application's icon from the GUI, which in turn activates the computer codes that cause the execution of the software application.

DESIGNING THE INPUT AND OUTPUT INTERFACES

During prototyping, the project team often either begins or continues work on the design of input and output interfaces. Some of this activity can precede or parallel the creation of detailed DFDs. However, the need for the design of additional screens is often identified as the DFDs are constructed.

The objectives of input/output interface design are:

- Minimize the number of each type of form, while adequately using the various types suitable for satisfying user requirements.
- Coordinate the design of input screen layouts.
- Use existing forms when possible.
- Consolidate similar forms.
- Design the user-friendly input/output screens.
- Construct interfaces that minimize possible user error.

Before discussing the actual design of input and output, it is appropriate to point out that analysts have two basic approaches to designing input/output forms. Depending on which approach they use, most analysts feel very strongly that one is superior to the other. The first approach works from the output backward: you define required system outputs first, and then you define the input necessary to produce these outputs.

The second approach starts with the inputs and works forward to the outputs. In this approach, the inputs are viewed as the stimuli that the system uses to form its outputs. Of the two strategies, working backward from the outputs is the method most widely accepted. You should be aware of both approaches and use the one that is better for the particular situation. The end result, regardless of the approach adopted, should be a comprehensive design of the input and output forms.

For both input and output forms and screens, the analyst should consider:

- Content
- Format
- Timeliness
- Volume
- Media

Content specifies what the form or screen should contain—that is, what data appears on it. Format specifies how the data is entered or displayed on the input or output form or screen. Timeliness refers to how often the data entry or display can be used or when it is appropriate for use. Volume specifies how much data is entered or displayed or how many times the screen or form can be used in a given period. Media indicates the way the forms and screens are presented to the user.

Designing Output

The output produced by a system is generally of two types: output produced for internal use and output produced to satisfy external reporting requirements. The internal reporting requirements satisfy the various information needs of users within the company. The external aspect usually includes reports to:

- Company clientele
- Suppliers of goods
- Creditors
- Owners of a business
- Subsidiary and parent companies
- Industry regulatory agencies
- Governmental regulatory agencies

These external reporting requirements are usually met by electronically transmitted reports or hard-copy reports.

Internal output requirements may also be met by reports and completed forms. Data types depicted as DFD data stores play an important role in identifying internal reporting. Recall that data stores usually represent data at rest. As a result, this data can be retrieved on command.

There are numerous questions that must be answered before adequate output can be designed. These questions include the following:

- What are all of the output requirements (the outputs necessary to satisfy user requirements) of the new system?
- What DFD processes are necessary to produce the needed output?
- What DFD inputs must be transformed to produce the desired outputs?
- What is the physical makeup of each form and how should each output be presented to the users?

Generally, output is either hard copy or soft copy. **Hard copy** consists of printed reports; **soft copy** is displayed on a terminal or desktop computer monitor. These reports may be either scheduled reports routinely produced by the system (often called periodic reports) or dynamically generated reports that may have a new format each time. The discussion here focuses on reports produced on a regular basis by the system, but many suggestions also serve the construction of dynamic reports.

Follow these guidelines when designing reports:

- Identify each report clearly with a heading.
- Design the report to be read from top to bottom and from left to right.
- Add descriptive characters ($, . + −, ...) to all numeric data items, and suppress leading zeros.
- Design the report with the reader in mind.
- Design reports for external users with special care.
- Use highlighting to direct attention to critical or exceptional data.

A report heading consists of:

- The title of the report
- The date the report was produced
- Column headings and line indicators where appropriate

Abbreviations should be kept to a minimum for the sake of clarity. In addition, descriptive words should be used for report, column headings, and line indicators.

Data items on the report should be in some logical order based on satisfying user requirements. For example, more important data items usually appear first, and totals appear either on the far right or at the bottom of the report.

The report should be reader-friendly. Appropriate line spacing can add greatly to the readability of a report. Segregate logical groupings of data with blank lines rather than with dashes. When possible, detail lines should be double-spaced.

Reports intended for external entities should be designed with even greater concern for detail and readability because generally no one from the firm will be available to explain any unclear portions of a report. Carefully planned reports also present a more professional appearance to the outside world. Furthermore, easily understood reports help create better relationships between the company and external personnel whose level of understanding regarding the firm's characteristics and service capabilities cannot be assumed.

Column headings and the order of information are even more important for external reports than for internal ones. Reports intended for external distribution are generally considered official documents. Therefore, understandability is even more critical. Figures 7-8 and 7-9 illustrate printed and screen report examples.

```
                        EMPLOYEE WAGE REPORT
    EMPLOYEE_ID   JOB_TITLE    WEEKLY_SALARY    YEAR_TO_DATE_SALARY
    XXXXXXXXXX    XXXXXXXXX      99,999.99          9,999,999.99
```

Figure 7-8. Printed report design format (hard copy)

```
                    CUSTOMER CHARGE HISTORY
    CUSTOMER_ID: _____    CUSTOMER_NAME: _____

    CHARGE_DATE: XX/XX/XX       CHARGE_AMOUNT: 9,999.99

    CHARGE_DATE: XX/XX/XX       CHARGE_AMOUNT: 9,999.99

    CHARGE_DATE: XX/XX/XX       CHARGE_AMOUNT: 9,999.99

    CHARGE_DATE: XX/XX/XX       CHARGE_AMOUNT: 9,999.99

    CHARGE_DATE: XX/XX/XX       CHARGE_AMOUNT: 9,999.99

    CHARGE_DATE: XX/XX/XX       CHARGE_AMOUNT: 9,999.99
```

Figure 7-9. Screen report example (soft copy)

Additional Guidelines for Screen Output Design

Many of the same rules apply for the design of screen output as for printed output. However, the following are some guidelines specifically for screen displays:

- Don't try to put too much information on one screen; design it carefully to fully utilize the space without crowding.
- Make error messages user-friendly; use simple everyday language that is meaningful to users *within* the application.
- Make error messages and prompting commands appear on the same part of all screens for different messages and applications.
- Use adequate spacing between columns and rows to make information easy to see.
- Do not have too much information highlighted or use too many colors; highlighting and color are most useful when they are not overdone.

In general, remember that the purpose of the output is to convey the needed information in the simplest form possible. Use the "KISS" (keep it simple, stupid) method at all times.

Designing Input

Data is input into a system in a variety of ways. For example, in the early days of information systems, nearly all input was in the form of punched cards. Punched cards are still used, but most data is now captured at its source in machine-readable form or is input through terminals or desktop computers by a variety of business personnel in shipping and receiving departments, sales departments, inventory departments, and so on. The input may be in a key-to-tape, key-to-disk, or on-line executable mode. In the first two cases, the operator is simply recording the data on tape or disk for processing in a batch mode at some later time. In the on-line mode, the operator is interacting directly with the system developed to process the data.

The following are guidelines to use in the design of input, regardless of the method of entry:

- Design the source document used to record the data to be read from top to bottom and from left to right.
- When possible, group numeric or alphanumeric data items together.
- Place any comments or system-generated instructions at the bottom of the form so they do not distract the user from the order in which the data is entered into the data entry screen.
- As with screen reports, keep the use of highlighting and color to an appropriate minimum; too much is just as bad as too little.

- Place filing or routing information in an obvious location on the form, usually at the bottom or on the left or right side.

Remember, keep the form simple; make it easy to understand and easy to insert the necessary information. Sample input forms are shown in Figures 7-10, 7-11, and 7-12.

```
                    CUSTOMER BILLING REPORT
CUSTOMER_ID: _____      CUSTOMER_NAME: _____
CURRENT_PERIOD_CHARGES:
    ORDER_NUMBER: _____    ORDER_DATE: XX/XX/XX   AMOUNT: 9,999.99
    ORDER_NUMBER: _____    ORDER_DATE: XX/XX/XX   AMOUNT: 9,999.99
    ORDER_NUMBER: _____    ORDER_DATE: XX/XX/XX   AMOUNT: 9,999.99
    ORDER_NUMBER: _____    ORDER_DATE: XX/XX/XX   AMOUNT: 9,999.99
CHARGE_BALANCES:
    PREVIOUS BALANCE: 99,999.99   CURRENT_BALANCE: 99,999.99
            PRESS ESC KEY TO SAVE AND EXIT DATA ENTRY
```

Figure 7-10. Example of a batch data entry screen

```
                    CUSTOMER CHARGE
CUSTOMER_ID: _____      CUSTOMER_NAME: _____
CUSTOMER_CHARGES:
ORDER_NUMBER: _____       ORDER_DATE: XX/XX/XX
    ORDER_ITEM: _____     QUANTITY: 999     PRICE: 9,999.99
    ORDER_ITEM: _____     QUANTITY: 999     PRICE: 9,999.99
    ORDER_ITEM: _____     QUANTITY: 999     PRICE: 9,999.99
                               TOTAL_ORDER_AMOUNT: 99,999.99
            PRESS ESC KEY TO SAVE AND EXIT DATA ENTRY
```

Figure 7-11. Example of an on-line data entry screen

```
                    CUSTOMER ORDER ENTRY
  ENTER CUSTOMER IDENTIFICATION NUMBER _____

  ENTER ORDER ITEM NUMBER _____

  ENTER ITEM QUANTITY _____
              PRESS ESC KEY TO SAVE AND EXIT DATA ENTRY
```

Figure 7-12. Example of a prompting data entry screen

Screen Design Considerations

Although many automated data entry methods exist, such as bar codes and optical character reading devices, data most often originates in the form of screen and hard-copy source documents, and both forms are equally important. As always, screen design should be as simple as possible, yet accomplish the purpose. Considerations in screen design include the following:

- Design the screen to match any original source documents so that the new data entry form capitalizes on previously learned data entry skills.

- Design the screen so that users can easily see what data items need to be entered, which data items are optional, how to edit previously entered data, and how to interpret messages generated by the system. Help keys, with accompanying menus of help options, are useful for these purposes.

- Use a flashing cursor to show the user the current location on the screen for data entry; reverse video (black on white or white on black) helps highlight the current input location.

- Design the screen so that a data item entry that *fills* the current data entry location causes the cursor to automatically move to the next data entry location.

- Use the Tab, Return, or arrow keys for movement from current to next data entry location when data entry *does not fill* a data item entry location.

- Tie multiple data entry screens together so that completing one data entry screen causes movement to the next screen.

- Design a touch-sensitive screen or a mouse to help when users' needs require rapid movement from one data entry location to another or from one screen to the next.

- Build editing features (such as tests for numeric data, blank data entry, validation of account numbers, and so on) into the screen design to reduce the number of possible input errors.

- Design the screen so that users can easily see how to exit the screen and save, transmit, or cancel the data entry.

On-line Data Entry

On-line data entry screens appear in three forms: menus (or lists), system prompts, and screen masks. The menu allows the user to select from a list of different displayed options. By selecting an option, the user automatically moves to a submenu screen, corresponding action, or data entry form. Menus may limit the flexibility of the user, but when used by inexperienced users, they virtually prevent many misunderstandings and aid in correct user action. On the other hand, for experienced users, going through several menus to get to a desired response point is often frustrating. Often these more experienced users can strike a sequence of keys to bypass some submenus and go directly to the user data entry or report screen. An example of a menu that could be used for data entry (as well as display of data) is shown in Figure 7-13.

The second form of on-line data entry, screen prompts, are messages displayed to the user by the system for a specific response. For example, the prompt "Please enter customer number" appears on the screen. The user responds appropriately through the keyboard, and the system accepts the response and displays the next prompt message. This method is very useful for certain types of questions such as "Would you like to continue?" It is not recommended for entering large amounts of data, because it slows data entry considerably. A data entry screen that uses a prompt is illustrated in Figure 7-14.

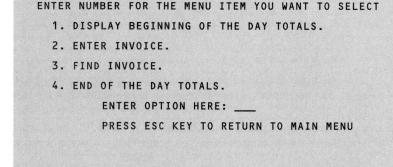

```
ENTER NUMBER FOR THE MENU ITEM YOU WANT TO SELECT
    1. DISPLAY BEGINNING OF THE DAY TOTALS.
    2. ENTER INVOICE.
    3. FIND INVOICE.
    4. END OF THE DAY TOTALS.
            ENTER OPTION HERE: ____
            PRESS ESC KEY TO RETURN TO MAIN MENU
```

Figure 7-13. Screen display menu example

```
                    CUSTOMER ORDER ENTRY
ENTER CUSTOMER_ID AT THE FLASHING CURSOR AND WAIT FOR
  NEXT PROMPT
ENTER DATA VALUE HERE:_____
          PRESS ESC KEY TO SAVE AND EXIT DATA ENTRY
```

Figure 7-14. Example of a data entry screen using prompts

```
                 EMPLOYEE WAGE CHANGE ENTRY
EMPLOYEE_ID:_____   EMPLOYEE NAME:_____
JOB_TITLE:_____   SUPERVISOR:_____
DATE_HIRED:_____    EDUCATION_LEVEL:_____
CURRENT_WAGE:_____    NEW_WAGE:_____
CURSOR AUTOMATICALLY MOVES TO THE NEXT ITEM AS VALUES
  ARE ENTERED
          PRESS ESC KEY TO SAVE AND EXIT DATA ENTRY
```

Figure 7-15. Example of a screen mask

The final form of on-line data entry, the screen mask, is an interface consisting of a screen display of a document stored on the computer in place of a hard-copy document. The user retrieves the screen mask and enters data on the screen from the keyboard instead of using a pencil or typewriter. The layout of the template should closely match the order of data entry and, if possible, the entire template should fit on a single screen. Automatic cursor movement usually occurs between data item entry locations. Figure 7-15 illustrates a screen mask.

In summary, the design of the input forms and screens is a very important part of the analysis and design phases. Two rules must always be kept in mind: Keep it simple and make it user-friendly.

PROTOTYPING FOR THE NATIONAL GOLF & TENNIS (NG&T) APPLICATION

When prototyping is combined with structured methods, the decision as to what data items to place on screens has already been documented. In the text methodology, the logical data structures (LDSs) created or referenced as relationship blocks in E/R expressions or data flows from or to entities and data stores on DFDs document the data items to paint on screens or use on forms. In this methodology, dictionary entries for LDSs shown as relationships on E/RDs document the data items to paint on screens. Thus, structured methods and prototyping are complementary methods within a comprehensive methodology, not alternative methods, as they are viewed by many systems professionals.

While analysts create the prototype, they should concern themselves primarily with *where* data items should be positioned, not *what* data items to place on the screen. Although any entity/relationship diagram (E/RD) or DFD level may be referenced while constructing prototype screens, the analyst should use mid-level and bottom-level E/RDs and DFDs as the best starting point for prototyping. Conversely, prototypes can also help the analyst to identify and describe the logical objects

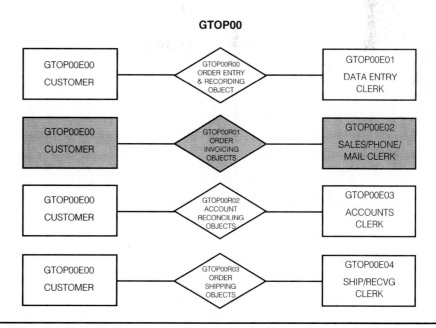

Figure 7-16. National Golf & Tennis GTOP00 level-1 E/RD

(LDSs) that need to appear on E/RDs and DFDs. In reference to the NG&T case, Figures 7-16, 7-17, 7-18, and 7-19 display the GTOP00 level-1 E/RD of Figure 5-37, the GTOP0002 Level-2 E/RD of Figure 5-38, the GTOP00 level-1 DFD of Figure 6-23, and GTOP0005 level-2 DFD of Figure 6-26, in Chapters 5 and 6. Prototype screens should be created for the LDSs portrayed as E/RD relationship symbols and the LDSs depicted as DFD data flows and data stores.

GTOP0002

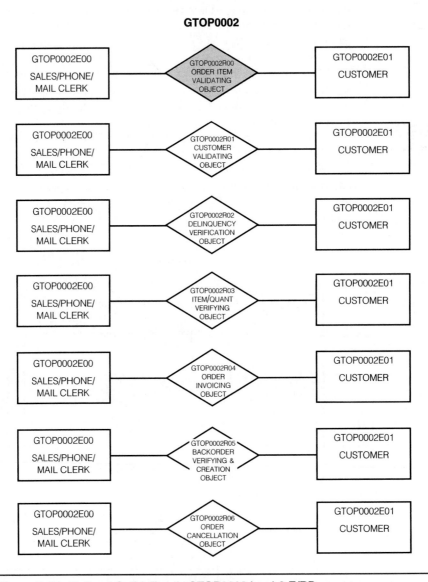

Figure 7-17. National Golf & Tennis GTOP0002 level-2 E/RD

GTOP00

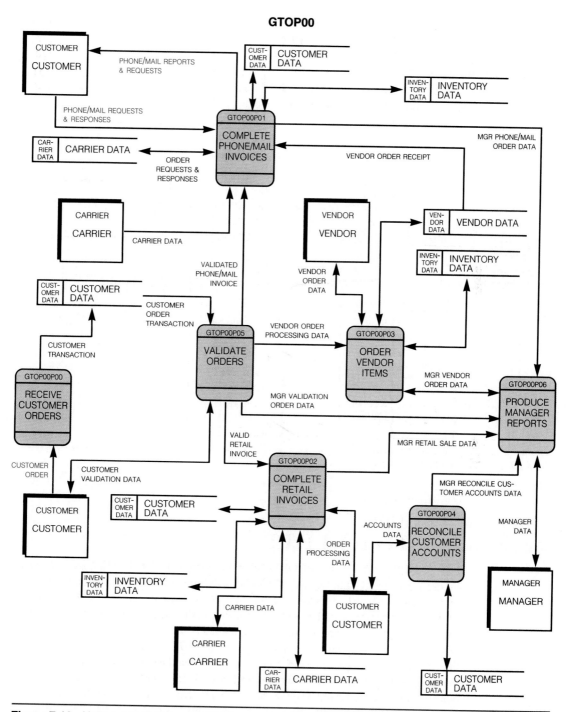

Figure 7-18. National Golf & Tennis GTOP00 level-1 DFD

GTOP0005

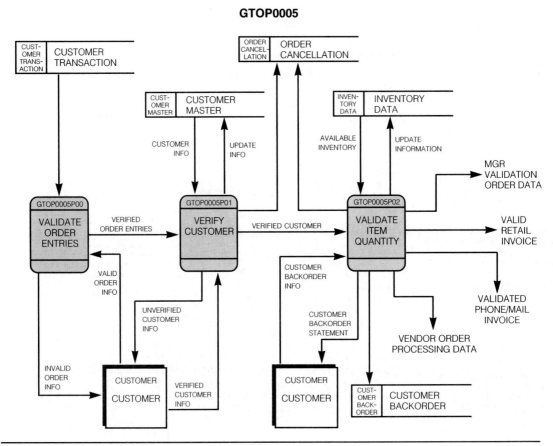

Figure 7-19. National Golf & Tennis GTOP0005 level-2 DFD

Prototype Creation
for the GTOP00 Level-1 E/RD

The ORDER ENTRY & RECORDING relationship in the first E/R expression in Figure 7-16 portrays the LOG-CUSTTRNS LDS illustrated in the dictionary entry in Figure 5-46 in Chapter 5. Project team members use the data elements composing this LDS to paint the on-line data entry screen mask shown in Figure 7-20 for the data entry clerk to use to record this data. Team members paint an additional screen to enter more data items for larger orders, as shown in Figure 7-21. The second screen is tied to the first screen so that clerks entering the last item on the screen in Figure 7-20 automatically go to the next screen, depicted in Figure 7-21, to enter additional order items. Note that this second screen can also be tied to the item ordering screen for suppliers.

In the GTOP0002 E/RD of Figure 7-17, order items are verified for filling the order. To assess filling item quantities, project team members create a screen mask to

```
                         CUSTOMER TRANSACTIONS
     CUSTOMER NUMBER: _____    ORDER NUMBER: _____

     CUSTOMER NAME: _____      CUSTOMER ADDRESS:

     DATE: _____       STREET: _____

                                           CITY: _____

                                           STATE: _____

                                           ZIP: _____

     TRANSACTION TYPE: _____   SHIPPING ADDRESS:

     EMPLOYEE NUMBER: _____        STREET: _____

     MAGAZINE: _____        CITY: _____

     REGION: _____        STATE: _____

     ORDER STATUS: _____         ZIP: _____

                           ITEMS ORDERED

       ITEM NUMBER: _____     ORDER QUANTITY: _____

       ITEM NUMBER: _____     ORDER QUANTITY: _____

       ITEM NUMBER: _____     ORDER QUANTITY: _____

       ITEM NUMBER: _____     ORDER QUANTITY: _____

          PRESS ESC KEY TO EXIT DATA ENTRY WITHOUT SAVING

          PRESS F3 KEY TO SAVE AND EXIT DATA ENTRY
```

Figure 7-20. Screen mask for the LOG-CUSTTRNS LDS

display the item quantity levels for all items appearing in LOG-CUSTTRNS. When insufficient item quantities occur, either a back order or an order cancellation is created. Team members create a screen mask to display items in the order for which there are insufficient quantities, as shown in Figure 7-22. They also include a function key selection for each item with insufficient quantities in the item quantity-level screen mask to register whether a back order is acceptable by the customer. The prompt appearing at the bottom of this screen directs the sales/phone/mail clerk to create either a back order/cancellation for a particular item or the cancellation of the entire order. The function key used by the clerk automatically causes a screen mask to be displayed that is either a back-order screen or an order cancellation screen.

Figure 7-23 illustrates how one team member creates a menu screen to display to the sales/phone/mail clerks the actions of entering an order, verifying item quantities, and creating an order invoice. The analyst builds this prototype menu screen to automatically switch to the screens shown in Figures 7-20 and 7-22 when the clerk selects options 1 and 2, respectively. When the clerk selects option 3, a screen mask is dis-

```
                    ADDITIONAL ORDER ITEMS
     ITEM NUMBER: _____     ORDER QUANTITY: _____
     ITEM NUMBER: _____     ORDER QUANTITY: _____
     ITEM NUMBER: _____     ORDER QUANTITY: _____
     ITEM NUMBER: _____     ORDER QUANTITY: _____
     ITEM NUMBER: _____     ORDER QUANTITY: _____
     ITEM NUMBER: _____     ORDER QUANTITY: _____
     ITEM NUMBER: _____     ORDER QUANTITY: _____
     ITEM NUMBER: _____     ORDER QUANTITY: _____
     ITEM NUMBER: _____     ORDER QUANTITY: _____
     ITEM NUMBER: _____     ORDER QUANTITY: _____
     ITEM NUMBER: _____     ORDER QUANTITY: _____
        PRESS ESC KEY TO EXIT DATA ENTRY WITHOUT SAVING
        PRESS F3 KEY TO SAVE AND EXIT DATA ENTRY
```

Figure 7-21. Screen mask for additional order items

```
                INSUFFICIENT ORDER ITEM QUANTITIES
  ITEM NO: _____   ORDER QTY: _____   QTY_ON_HAND: _____   ENTER{F1,F2,F3}
  ITEM NO: _____   ORDER QTY: _____   QTY_ON_HAND: _____   ENTER{F1,F2,F3}
  ITEM NO: _____   ORDER QTY: _____   QTY_ON_HAND: _____   ENTER{F1,F2,F3}
  ITEM NO: _____   ORDER QTY: _____   QTY_ON_HAND: _____   ENTER{F1,F2,F3}
  ENTER FUNCTION KEY FOR ACTION DESIRED FOR INSUFFICIENT ORDER ITEM
  QUANTITIES:
     ENTER F1 TO CREATE A BACK ORDER FOR AN ORDER ITEM
     ENTER F2 TO CANCEL THE ORDER FOR AN ORDER ITEM
     ENTER F3 TO CANCEL AN ENTIRE ORDER
             PRESS ESC KEY TO SAVE AND EXIT DATA ENTRY
```

Figure 7-22. Screen mask that uses function-key selection

```
                CUSTOMER ORDER PROCESSING ACTIONS
    1. RECORD A CUSTOMER ORDER.
    2. VERIFY ORDER ITEM QUANTITY LEVELS.
    3. CREATE ORDER INVOICE.
       ENTER SELECTION: ____
    SELECT OPTION BY KEYING THE NUMBER OF THE DESIRED OPTION
            PRESS ESC KEY TO RETURN TO MAIN MENU
```

Figure 7-23. Menu screen for SALES/PHONE/MAIL CLERK actions

played, which allows the clerk to enter order invoice data. The screen in Figure 7-23 becomes the first screen in the execution of this prototype.

Project team members create many prototype screens for many other relationship symbols on the NG&T E/RDs that depict LDSs. All of these prototype screens could be created during the creation of E/RDs or after their creation. User responses after execution of the prototype guide the analysts in refining E/RD documentation. For example, if a user recommends that the analyst add a data element to a screen, it might mean that a data element needs to be added to the LDS depicted on the screen. Thus, prototyping is used to refine user requirements, not as a replacement for the structured methods used to create them.

Prototype Creation for the GTOP00 and GTOP0005 DFDs

Each data flow emanating from or going to entities on the GTOP00 level-1 DFD in Figure 7-18 is a candidate for prototype screen creation. The LDSs depicted by these data flows comprise the data elements to paint on the screen. For the data flows depicting mass logical data structures (M-LDSs), the analyst may create separate screens for each LDS. For example, most of the data flows leading to the PRODUCE MANAGER REPORTS process depict M-LDSs, and multiple prototype screens need to be created for these. For data flows depicting a single LDS, a single screen usually suffices. For example, the CUSTOMER ORDER data flow leading from the CUSTOMER entity on the GTOP00 DFD of Figure 7-18 depicts the LOG-CUSTTRNS LDS, and the prototype screens shown in Figures 7-20 and 7-21 serve as the screens for this data flow.

The PHONE/MAIL REPORTS & REQUESTS and ORDER REQUESTS & RESPONSES data flows leading to and from the CUSTOMER entity in the top-left corner of the GTOP00 DFD depict M-LDSs that contain individual LDSs, which the

```
              CUSTOMER BILLING STATEMENT
  CUSTOMER NUMBER: _____
  CUSTOMER NAME: _____
  CUSTOMER ADDRESS:
    STREET: _____
    CITY: _____
    STATE: _____

                          BILL AMOUNT: _____
                          DATE: _____
       PRESS ESC KEY TO EXIT DATA ENTRY WITHOUT SAVING
       PRESS F3 KEY TO SAVE AND EXIT DATA ENTRY
```

Figure 7-24. PHONE/MAIL REPORTS & REQUESTS billing statement prototype form

```
                     CUSTOMER COMPLAINT
  CUSTOMER NUMBER: _____     CUSTOMER NAME: _____
  EMPLOYEE NUMBER: _____     DATE: _____
  COMPLAINT: _____
             _____
             _____
             _____
             _____
             _____

       PRESS ESC KEY TO EXIT DATA ENTRY WITHOUT SAVING
       PRESS F3 KEY TO SAVE AND EXIT DATA ENTRY
```

Figure 7-25. Customer complaints prototype screen

NG&T analyst uses to create prototype screens and forms. One of the LDSs for the PHONE/MAIL REPORTS & REQUESTS data flow depicts a billing statement mailed to the customer—a prototype form—and one of the LDSs of the ORDER REQUESTS & RESPONSES data flow depicts the recording of a complaint on a screen mask. Figures 7-24 and 7-25 show the prototype form and screen created for these LDSs.

The analyst creates prototype screens for all appropriate data flows and data stores throughout the NG&T DFDs. Prototyping is used to expand analysis and design documentation by including the design of the user interface. The analyst also uses prototyping to identify areas where the documentation that was produced while using structured methods needs to be changed.

Creating System-Level Menus for NG&T Applications

Earlier, we discussed how a set of menus can be created to combine a set of user interfaces that direct the execution of an application system. Figure 7-26 illustrates a system-level main menu for the service orders application depicted as the GTOP00 DFD in Figure 7-18.

Users can select one of the options from the menu in Figure 7-26 to have the system aid them in performing that business process. A selection of one of the options could cause a submenu to appear (as a replacement menu, as a pop-up menu, or as a menu in another window) that lists the processes of the next-level DFD. For example, Figure 7-27 illustrates a submenu for the VALIDATE ORDERS option from the menu in Figure 7-26.

The two menus in Figures 7-26 and 7-27 illustrate how a set of menu screens combined with other user interfaces being created for the NG&T application into an application system. Each option on the menu of Figure 7-26 corresponds to one of the processes on the GTOP00 DFD of Figure 7-18. Selection of one of these menu options produces a submenu of capabilities associated with that option or a data entry or display screen mask. Figure 7-27 illustrates the submenu for the VALIDATE ORDERS option that corresponds to the VALIDATE ORDERS process of the GTOP00 DFD of Figure 7-18. The selection of VALIDATE ORDERS from the menu

```
                    SERVICE ORDERS

        1. CREATE - ENTER RECEIVED CUSTOMER ORDERS.

        2. VALIDATE ORDERS.

        3. COMPLETE PHONE/MAIL INVOICES.

        4. COMPLETE RETAIL INVOICES.

        5. ORDER VENDOR ITEMS.

        6. RECONCILE CUSTOMER ACCOUNTS.

        7. PRODUCE MANAGER REPORTS.

                ENTER NUMBER OF OPTION _____

                PRESS ESC KEY TO RETURN TO MAIN MENU
```

Figure 7-26. SERVICE ORDERS main menu

```
                          VALIDATE ORDERS
      1. VALIDATE ORDER ENTRIES.

      2. VERIFY CUSTOMER.

      3. VALIDATE ITEM QUANTITY.

          ENTER NUMBER OF OPTION _____

          PRESS ESC KEY TO RETURN TO SERVICE ORDERS MENU
```

Figure 7-27. Submenu for the VALIDATE ORDERS option on the SERVICE ORDERS menu

in Figure 7-26 produces the submenu of options on Figure 7-27, which corresponds to the processes of the GTOP0005 DFD of Figure 7-19.

When system-level menus, such as the one in Figure 7-26, are combined with a GUI and windowing capabilities, a very powerful and easy-to-use system of interfaces is created for the user. For example, following logon, NG&T users could have an opening screen that displays icons corresponding to different systems they may use (the GUI in Figure 7-6 illustrates this). Selecting an icon with the mouse could then cause a window to open that displays the top menu for that application. Selecting one of the options from that menu would open either a submenu or another user interface for yet another level of interaction to support users' information needs.

Users who have desktop computers with larger memory capacities can be supported further through the combination of an opening GUI, system-level menus, submenus, and other user interfaces. These users may have multiple applications executing in different windows at the same time to perform different actions, either on the same data or on different data. In fact, they can easily transfer data being produced or changed in one application to a different application executing in a separate set of windows.

Not all menus and submenus will correspond directly to the processes on DFDs. However, keeping this possibility in mind helps the analyst to combine the many separate user interfaces into a harmonious set of interfaces that function more completely as a system.

CLOSING REMARKS ON PROTOTYPING PRACTICES

Project teams can also create prototype screens for the parts of other structured modeling methods, such as the Warnier/Orr (W/O) modeling method described briefly in Chapter 2. Data decomposed on W/O diagrams also documents the LDS to use in prototyping activities.

To clarify when and why a comprehensive methodology includes prototyping, remember: *Design is prototyped, not systems*. By using prototyping, analysts identify many changes to user requirements long before the more expensive activities of the development phase take place. The responses of users to prototypes help the analyst resolve many misunderstandings and create a more complete set of design specifications. The operation of the prototype helps the analyst get these user responses. You should view these responses as comments on design—that is, verification, needed changes, and so on. The prototype itself may not be retained after these responses are secured.

COMPUTER-AIDED PROTOTYPING

Overall, the use of CASE systems and other computer-aided tools makes prototyping a much more viable alternative in system development than it has been in the past. Many of these tools have the facilities to paint screens and the ability to let users interact with the prototype. Users can practice using on-line interfaces long before the system is actually developed. Data can be entered, modified, and used to generate either on-line or off-line reports so that users can quickly apprise the analyst of changes in user requirements relative to interaction with the prototype.

When CASE systems are used to build prototypes, previously entered documentation created while using structured methods is available to the analysts at the click of a mouse button. Analysts cause the CASE system to display this documentation while they build the prototype. Typically, analysts navigate through E/RDs and DFDs looking for places where prototype screens may facilitate the activities illustrated in the diagrams. LDS dictionary entries document the data elements to paint on the screen, and data element dictionary entries indicate the type, length, and format of the data elements to place on the screen. Data element dictionary entries also document the text entries that are placed beside or above data elements to use as prompts or column headings to classify them on the screen.

Middle CASE Prototyping

When middle CASE systems (analysis and design workbenches) are used to build the prototype, all the previously mentioned documentation is available to the analysts during prototyping activities. The documentation for the prototype is stored in the CASE dictionary (or repository) along with the documentation produced while using structured methods.

To perform prototyping activities, most middle CASE systems furnish a screen painting capability, and some systems permit temporary navigation through dictionary entries for diagrams, LDSs, and data elements to facilitate prototyping activities. Some middle CASE systems automatically position data item entry and display points on screens from dictionary length, type, and format entries for screen data items referenced by their dictionary IDs. Some middle CASE systems also automatically place text entries for data item prompts or column headings on the screen or report. Split-screen windowing capabilities that let the analyst see dictionary entries for pertinent diagrams, LDSs, and data items while they paint screens are provided by some middle CASE systems.

One of the better middle CASE systems, ProKit from McDonnell Douglas, expects the analyst to know that the requirements created while using structured methods influence prototype creation, and vice versa. With ProKit, an analyst indicates that a prototype screen "implements" a data flow on a DFD. The analyst selects the appropriate data flow from a list of all data flows on DFDs. The CASE system then builds a "scratch pad" that lists the data items composing the logical object depicted as the data flow, and displays it during the screen-painting function. The analyst selects individual data items from the scratch pad, and the CASE system enlarges the cursor to the dictionary-specified data item size. The analyst then uses a mouse to place the enlarged cursor on the specific position for that data item and anchors it to the appropriate place on the prototype screen. Using this CASE system, an analyst can paint a screen in a few seconds and integrate the requirements of structured methods with those of the prototype.

Middle CASE systems typically have two deficiencies with regard to prototyping: text entries often have to be keyed directly on the prototype screen, and the prototype is typically not a standalone executable. The first deficiency forces the analyst into needless clerical work while painting screens. Although screen headings should always be entered from the keyboard, the text in data item dictionary entries to classify the data items should be automatically placed beside, above, or below those data items painted on the screen. Many lower CASE systems can already do this, as you will see. The second deficiency stems from the fact that the prototype is executed within the CASE system; a separate programmed executable is not created by the CASE system. Therefore, the prototype execution does not completely simulate the way the system will operate when developed. In addition, users must be trained to log on and navigate through the CASE system to get to the prototype for execution.

Lower CASE Prototyping

Lower CASE systems contain screen-painting functions similar to those of middle CASE systems. When these systems are used by analysts for prototyping, the LDS displayed on the painted screen is constructed by indicating which physical data structures (PDSs) contain which data items. It also indicates which data items from these PDSs to paint on the screen. These systems usually display a list of these data items and allow the analyst to select from the list. They build something like the "scratch pad" described for the ProKit middle CASE system, and allow the analyst to position them, using a moving cursor, on the screen. While data items are positioned on the screen, classifying text labels for these elements are automatically positioned beside, above, or below the data item retrieval or display points. These text entries are retrieved from the lower CASE dictionary entries for these data items.

The best lower CASE systems also paint screens automatically in one of several formats. The analyst indicates that he or she wants to use the "auto-paint" feature, and the CASE system responds with a list of formats it uses to automatically paint the screen. The analyst then indicates the format, and the data elements of the constructed LDS are positioned appropriately on the screen. For example, one of the leading lower CASE systems, MAGEC, displays the following formats when the analyst selects the auto-paint facility:

OPTION 1 - LIST/2 - double space, one item per line
OPTION 2 - LIST/1 - single space, one item per line
OPTION 3 - COMPACT/2 - double space, multiple items per line
OPTION 4 - COMPACT/1 - single space, multiple items per line
OPTION 5 - SUPER-COMPACT - single space, multiple items per line,
                          NO TITLE
OPTION 6 - LIST/3 - one item per line, double space, left justified prompts
OPTION 7 - LIST/4 - one item per line, single space, left justified prompts

For example, if the analyst selects Option 2, each data element is positioned on a line by itself (including its text entry) in single-space line format.

Integrating Middle and Lower CASE Prototyping

To take full advantage of middle CASE and eliminate prototyping deficiencies, some analysts use another capability provided by these systems. Many middle CASE systems permit the analyst to download a file in ASCII format that is a facsimile of a painted screen (and LDS entries) as data structures in the format of many languages. These ASCII data structures can be imported into lower CASE systems and used to make the prototype a standalone executable that executes just like completed systems. Thus the prototype completely simulates the way the system will execute, and users do not require CASE-related training to access the prototype. Furthermore, text describing entries on the prototype screen need not be entered directly from the keyboard, thus saving clerical labor. When the analyst uses a middle CASE system to construct the prototype screens, he or she only marks data element display and retrieval points. After the prototype screen is dumped out in ASCII format and imported into a lower CASE system, it automatically places classifying text entries, such as prompts and column headings, associated with data elements on the prototype screen.

CASE and Graphical User Interface (GUI) Application Prototyping

In recent years, CASE software vendors have either developed their own proprietary utilities or used already available GUI development utilities for generating GUIs to accompany applications created using their CASE systems. When these CASE systems are used, the first screen created is usually the GUI for application selection. For the icons on the GUI, separate applications are generated by the CASE systems using the design specifications. The specific user interfaces associated with each application (menus, screen masks, and so on) are also created using the CASE system. The data item display positions on the user interface come from the logical data objects defined while creating E/RDs and DFDs. When this system is used to create a prototype, the data values displayed on or received via this user interface use the test data files to make the prototype simulate the way the system will operate. Thus, the CASE system helps the analyst to take advantage of already existing specifications while creating the prototype and having users operate it.

Rapid Application Development (RAD)

In the late 1980s and early 1990s, a new approach emerged for faster development of systems. This new approach is usually called **rapid application development (RAD)**. The basic premise of the RAD approach is to use rapid prototyping methods not just to simulate the system, but to actually develop it. The RAD approach gets the users together who have a vested interest in a new system, and analysts rapidly develop the specific user interfaces that provide access to the types of data and actions that will serve their information needs.

During RAD sessions, a lower CASE tool is often used to generate all user interfaces and programs that use them. As one analyst questions the users in the RAD session on their information needs, other analysts or programmer/analysts create the user interfaces and the programs that use those interfaces. The main specifications needed to create the prototype are:

- What data files or database objects to use to obtain the data
- What data items to use to combine files (ID numbers)
- What data items to extract from the combined files
- What data items to use for selection purposes
- What data items to use in special computations
- What data items to use in grouping data
- What data items to use for producing summaries
- What user interface to use in displaying the data

While one programmer/analyst uses the CASE system on one computer to create the specific user interfaces, another programmer/analyst may use it on another computer to enter the commands that will be used in generating specific actions to accept data from or display data on the user interface. The commands used to generate the program specifications may also be commands to perform various actions on data received via the interface or data displayed on it.

Using the RAD approach does not require that CASE be used; however, its use certainly increases the speed of developing the application. The main premise of RAD is that committed users should be brought together in a single room, ready to devote the time necessary to help develop an application more rapidly. While the user speaks in RAD sessions, the application is being built. As the system is built during these sessions, the user gets hands-on experience with it. Comments from users influence the modifications to user requirements and the changes to the application. Thus, the user watches the prototype progress toward the full-blown application in a relatively short period of time.

In between RAD sessions with the users, analysts and programmer/analysts usually continue to refine the specifications for development of the application. They do this so that the entire group of users is not burdened with modifications to some of the finer details of the application. Therefore, when the RAD sessions are reconvened, the users see an even closer fit to the capabilities and data access they want.

It is obvious that using the RAD approach leads to developing systems more quickly. However, it must be emphasized that the rapidly developed application specifications typically only pertain to what the computer system does, how it does it, how to make it execute, what its inputs are, what its outputs are, and how to interpret its results. The specifications created do not describe that area of the business, what it does, its functions and the job functions of those in that area, what those people do, what information they need to perform their jobs better, and how to use that information—in other words, the model of the business.

The RAD approach is useful when it is necessary to quickly produce systems, such as those needed to comply with newly passed governmental laws and regulations, to meet the changing demands of a volatile economy, and so on. To use it as the only approach in creating systems often keeps the most important documentation about a business in a very insecure form—in the minds of business and system personnel employed by the business. Keeping this important documentation in that form borders on disaster: these people could suddenly leave their positions for various reasons or, worse yet, be hired away by a direct competitor.

Exclusively using RAD approaches for system development can lead to even greater problems than those that already exist in information systems—namely, having even more systems out of alignment with what a business is and does. When RAD approaches are used, at some point in the future even more systems will become out of alignment with the business. To keep the business and its systems in alignment, it is best to create the model of the business using the data and process modeling methods described in this book, and to develop systems from the model. Furthermore, it is best if during maintenance actions, changes to the business model are made before making changes to the system, so that the business model is kept in synchronization with the system.

The RAD approach should be used only when systems *must* be created quickly. The remainder of the time, more complete analysis and design should be conducted to keep the model of the business in alignment with the systems created to support that model. In addition, after using RAD to quickly develop certain systems, it is best to create the business model on which the application should have been based. Thus, the analyst can take advantage of the benefits of using the RAD approach and help reduce the problem of systems that are out of alignment with business needs.

Prototyping in Joint Application Design (JAD) Sessions

Chapters 4, 5, and 6 described the purpose and practice of JAD sessions (JADs) and the way E/RDs and DFDs may be used during these sessions. In addition to using JADs to help gather and verify data and build E/RDs and DFDs, JADs can be used to create, review, verify, and modify prototypes.

During JADs, the use of CASE and visual-aid technologies, such as the overhead projector LCD panels described in Chapter 4, provide a way to quickly create portions of the prototype and obtain user feedback regarding it. A JAD may be set up with the class of users who will use the respective interfaces. As these users describe what data they want to access, how they want to access the data, and what they want to do with the data, project team members can create or modify portions of the prototype to reflect these user suggestions. Prototype screen masks and menus can be displayed on a large white screen and the LCD panels can be used to get immediate feedback from JAD participants.

A particularly helpful way to review prototypes and obtain feedback from users is to use networked desktop computers in hands-on sessions with the prototype during JADs. These hands-on sessions can be used to review prototypes completed since the last JAD or those created during the current JAD.

These same JADs can also be used to review and verify E/RDs and DFDs, as described at the ends of Chapters 5 and 6. As prototypes are created and reviewed, or just reviewed, E/RDs and DFDs can also be reviewed to verify that the prototype can make user requirements regarding data needs operational. Changes can be made to the prototype, the E/RDs, and the DFDs to keep them tightly integrated. As users suggest changes, scribes record those changes in real time. Thus, JADs can continue to contribute to the accuracy and completeness of the user requirements in a shorter period of time than more traditional approaches.

Distinguishing Between RADs and JADs

Many people confuse the RAD and JAD techniques, or assume that they are synonymous. Although these techniques may use some of the same data-gathering techniques, modeling methods, and technology, they are not the same. The main distinguishing characteristics of a RAD are more rapid creation of the system, and the use of prototyping as the main modeling method. Although E/RDs and DFDs may be used as part of a RAD approach, the data and process models created are not entirely comprehensive. The main purpose of the RAD is to quickly produce the computer system and put it into productive use. The prototyping modeling method is instrumental in supporting this purpose.

During JADs, project team members create, display for review, and make changes to detailed E/RDs, DFDs, and prototype specifications. They may be working on a faster schedule than they normally would; however, speeding up the process does not turn the JAD into a RAD approach. Their creation and use of a more complete set of specifications make the sessions a JAD and not a RAD.

REVIEW

Prototyping is the actual building of a model of the proposed system. The prototype created is not meant to be a fully functioning system that can go on-line when the prototype is finished. Its main purpose is to allow the analyst to detect and correct errors early in system development. System errors detected early in the design phase cost much less to correct than those detected later.

Prototyping is particularly useful in the design and modification of input and output screens and forms for the user interface. Overall, the goal of input/output interface design can be summarized as minimizing the number of each type of screens and forms, while adequately representing their various uses relative to user information needs.

The design of the input screen is just as important as the design of the input form. As much as possible, the input screen is designed to match the original source documents. User help functions are an important part of screen design. The user must always have a way out.

The menu, prompt, and screen mask are the most common forms of on-line data entry. The menu allows the user to select from a list of different screen options. The prompt asks the user for needed information. The screen mask, or template, is a document stored in the computer and displayed on the monitor. Data entry clerks enter data into the template from the keyboard instead of using a pencil or typewriter to fill out a preprinted form.

The set of user interfaces for an application can be tied together using a menu that contains options corresponding to DFD processes. These system-level menus can be combined with a GUI and windowing capabilities to create even more powerful prototypes for user review.

For the NG&T project, prototypes were created for screens that will provide user interfaces for various order servicing actions. The processes and data flows from the E/RDs and DFDs created in Chapters 5 and 6 were used as the basis for these prototypes, illustrating the integration of these modeling methods.

As with other modeling methods, CASE systems and joint application design sessions (JADs) are used in prototyping to automate some of the procedures and to coordinate user input to creation/review sessions. Another approach for faster development of systems, rapid application development (RAD), was described in this chapter. It differs from JAD in that its main purpose is to quickly produce the computer system using (primarily) the prototyping modeling method. Although E/RDs and DFDs may be used in RAD sessions, the data and process models created are typically very general.

QUESTIONS

1. What is prototyping? How is it used?
2. What is the main purpose of prototyping? Should it be used operationally? Why or why not?
3. List and discuss six characteristics of prototyping.
4. List and discuss the primary methods used in prototyping.
5. What is the importance of input/output design? How can prototyping help while this activity is performed?
6. List and discuss the objectives of input/output design.
7. What questions must be answered before adequate output forms can be designed?
8. Describe the guidelines to use in output design.
9. Why is output designed before input?
10. Discuss the additional guidelines for screen output design.
11. What is the "KISS" method? How does it apply to input/output design?
12. Discuss the general guidelines to use in input design.
13. What special considerations are used in input screen design?
14. Describe three useful methods to use in on-line data entry.
15. Describe how CASE software makes prototyping a much more viable alternative in system development than it has been in the past.
16. Define the RAD approach.
17. Distinguish between JAD and RAD.
18. List and explain the main specifications of a lower CASE system that may be used in a RAD or JAD to create a prototype.
19. Explain when a RAD is appropriate for system development and what should be done after the system is constructed using a RAD to make sure the business and the system remain in synchronization.
20. Explain what is the major problem when only a RAD approach is used for system development; e.g., having a RAD methodology.

EXERCISES

1. Create prototype screens and forms for LDSs represented on E/RDs for exercises completed at the end of Chapter 5. Create screens and forms of the following types (show E/RDs and the LDS for each screen or form type):

    a. Menu screen

    b. Batch data entry form

    c. On-line data entry screen

    d. Screen mask data entry

    e. Prompting screen data entry

    f. An output report form

    g. An on-line report screen

2. Create prototype screens and forms for LDSs represented on DFDs for exercises completed at the end of Chapter 6. Your completed exercise should be logically tied together using menus and submenus corresponding to the DFD processes on the DFDs created for Chapter 5 exercises. Use the examples shown in Figures 7-26 and 7-27 for the GTOP00 and GTOP0005 DFDs as the basis for creating your menus and submenus. Create screens and forms of the following types (show DFDs and the LDS for each screen or form type):

    a. Menu screen

    b. Batch data entry form

    c. On-line data entry screen

    d. Screen mask data entry

    e. Prompting screen data entry

    f. An output report form

    g. An on-line report screen

3. For your class project, conduct a JAD/RAD with participants from the company used, during which prototypes are reviewed, revised, created, and agreed upon. Prepare a report that describes all aspects of the JAD/RAD (remember to include preworkshop, workshop, and postworkshop activities).

SELECTED REFERENCES

Boar, B. H. 1984. *Application Prototyping*. New York: John Wiley and Sons, Inc.

Lantz, K. E. 1986. *The Prototype Methodology*. Englewood Cliffs, NJ: Prentice-Hall.

Naumann, J. D. and A. M. Jenkins. 1982. "Prototyping: The New Paradigm for Systems Development." *MIS Quarterly* 6, no. 3 (September).

CHAPTER 8

Logical Business and Information System Design

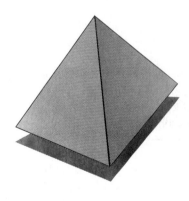

OVERVIEW

This chapter is the first part of a two-chapter sequence that focuses on the design phase of the system development life cycle. Here, the emphasis is on how to modify the diagrams and the accompanying dictionary entries created during the analysis phase to design a logical business solution for the identified problems. Chapter 9 describes how to implement the logical solutions by creating a physical design corresponding to the logical design.

This chapter takes you through the steps in the logical design by describing how to:

- Integrate IS with other corporate functions
- Identify categories of user requirements
- Develop the logical business design
- Modify diagrams and dictionary entries at National Golf & Tennis
- Conduct a logical design formal review
- Use CASE systems in logical design

KEY TERMS

Critical success factors (CSFs)
Generations of design
Logical business design
Logical DFD
Organizational chart
Physical DFD

B y using the National Golf & Tennis case, you will see how the principles and methods you have learned so far are used to develop a logical design that satisfies user requirements. Specifications have been gathered using methods such as interviews and questionnaires, as discussed in Chapter 4. With this information, systems analysts document the existing business system in the analysis phase, using the methods outlined in Chapters 5 and 6. The NG&T project has also been documented and analyzed in Chapters 5 and 6 using the E/RD and DFD modeling methods. Analysis helps the project team identify alternative solutions to the problem. The alternatives have been evaluated by participants during the review at the end of the analysis phase. Notwithstanding purchasing a new system, the result of evaluating these specifications leads the project team down one of two paths: either an existing business system is modified to meet user specifications, or an entirely new system is developed. Prototyping activities, as discussed in Chapter 7, have assisted in refining user requirements to use in either modifying an existing solution or designing a new system.

Figure 8-1 illustrates the part of the enterprise/methodology model on which this chapter focuses its attention: designing a logical business solution for identified problems. During this phase, E/RDs and DFDs are modified further according to user requirements, and a formal review is conducted before creating a procedure model that defines the logical procedures (covered in Chapter 9).

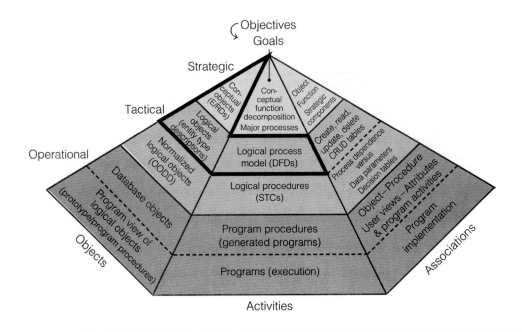

Figure 8-1. Enterprise/methodology model focus of Chapter 8

INTEGRATING INFORMATION SYSTEMS (IS) WITH OTHER CORPORATE FUNCTIONS

There are several aspects of the design phase that relate to a broader view of the project. Business systems under construction or modification need to blend with the rest of the systems in the firm, and at the same time to contribute to the overall goals and objectives of the firm. Taking a broader view, there are three main aspects to consider:

- How the project fits into the long-range plan of the organization
- How the system serves the formal and informal organization structures
- What critical success factors exist for the organization

In Chapter 1, you learned that the firm can be considered a system within an industry, and that this system consists of subsystems representing functional areas in the firm. Each of the functional areas usually has computer systems that supply information to the three levels of management and procedural personnel. Although functional area systems are designed to provide information for specific functional areas in

Functional Area

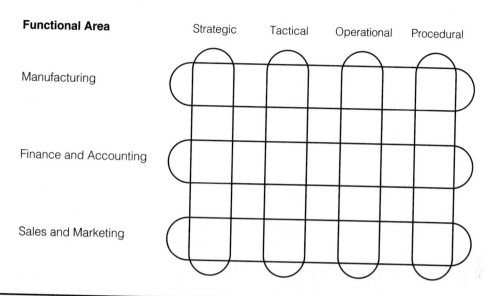

Figure 8-2. Integration of functional area systems

the firm, the information supplied must help each area's personnel perform their jobs satisfactorily in order to achieve the objectives of the entire organization. Since systems in functional areas are normally closely integrated and share many common data sources, any system developed or modified in support of one functional area has the potential of affecting systems in other functional areas.

Figure 8-2 illustrates the interweaving nature of the relationships between job functions and systems in different functional areas. From this diagram you can see that strategic planning, tactical policy setting, management of operations, and procedural task completion in a particular functional area depend on information supplied by systems designed for those areas and data contained in a companywide database.

Information typically travels through the organization along the managerial paths within the corporate organizational chart. An **organizational chart** is a diagram depicting the channels of command for a business. An example of a corporate organizational chart is shown in Figure 8-3. This figure illustrates that even though the channels of command are complete in each functional area, those channels all lead to a common ending point at the office of the chief executive officer (CEO). As a result, all functional area activities are the responsibility of the CEO. In addition, all information systems must provide information that is ultimately reported to the CEO.

The information supplied by various systems supporting functional areas is used by the CEO to determine whether the functional areas are operating in harmony relative to the overall objectives of the firm. To properly determine this, critical success factors must be identified for each functional area and evaluated with regard to the performance of personnel. **Critical success factors (CSFs)** are facets of the business

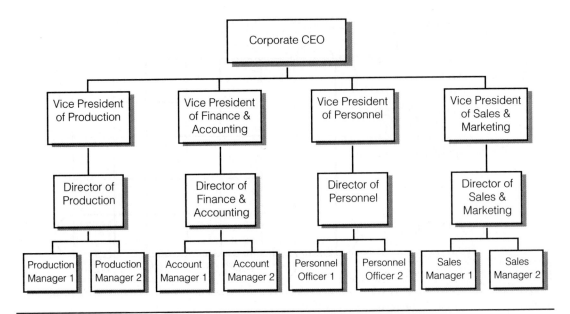

Figure 8-3. Organizational chart

that must be properly dealt with to ensure the success of the firm's activities. The identification and use of CSFs to aid organizational functioning was pioneered by John Rockart (1979, 1988). These factors may influence how successful the functional area or corporation is as a whole in reaching its objectives. For example, poor performance in one area of a production assembly line affects performance in later stages as well as the overall performance of the entire assembly line.

CSFs are usually defined at the corporate level of the firm and trickle down to individual functional areas. Executives typically identify corporationwide CSFs; managers identify CSFs for the functional areas that they govern.

Typically, six types of CSFs exist: factors that comprise facets of organizational functioning, factors that are used in the organization, factors that are created or offered by the firm, factors that affect or influence the organization, factors that are affected or influenced by the organization, and factors that simply need to be watched. Factors that constitute aspects of the organization are practices and procedures, types of personnel, revenues, and so on, that constitute what the business is and how it operates. Factors used by the firm consist of resources, capital equipment and land, legal agreements and patents, and so on, that the organization uses in seeking its objectives and solving its problems. Factors created or offered by the organization include various products and services, intermediate resources used for final creation, personnel expertise, and so on, used to achieve its objectives or solve its problems. Factors that affect or influence the firm include its direct competitors, governmental proclamations, consumer preferences, vendor actions, and so on, which cause the organization to modify its products, services, and actions. Factors that the organization affects or influences include competitor products, services, and actions, consumer satisfaction, vendor products, services, and actions, and so on. These factors are influenced by what the firm does or provides. Frequently, these factors are targeted by what the firm does or provides. Finally, factors that simply need to be watched are advances in technology, consumer preference changes, economic upturns and downturns, and so on, that may affect the firm in the future.

Information should be gathered about characteristics of these factors that affect the firm's operations and objectives. Information regarding CSFs is often embedded in components of systems that service the functional areas and characteristics of data objects. Consequently, the systems may contain automatic reporting functions to report deviations from expected characteristics of those CSFs.

In addition, the close integration of these systems, combined with data sharing between functional areas, usually causes disturbances in systems of one functional area to affect system performance in other functional areas. The strength of the entire corporate IS is determined by the strength of its weakest link (or system). Therefore, it is imperative that properly developed, maintained, and integrated systems exist for each functional area and that personnel in each area readily identify and evaluate CSFs, many of which provide the basis for user requirements.

IDENTIFYING AND REFINING USER REQUIREMENTS

The project team must document and present to users its interpretation of user requirements so that the users, in turn, may determine that the project team has correctly interpreted their needs. Figure 8-4 lists questions to consider in determining typical user requirements.

Responses to the questions in Figure 8-4 must be extensively reviewed to determine what capabilities the system project can provide within a reasonable time and budget. Users tend to ask for more than the project team can actually deliver, or more than is cost-effective relative to the benefits associated with certain features of the system.

A set of satisfactory user requirements is derived through long but critically important hours of presenting design documentation to users. User requirements are initially gathered during the analysis phase and the early portion of the logical design; they are refined as the logical design becomes more detailed.

User requirements usually continue to be refined throughout the development life cycle. For example, new requirements may surface during the system development phase as a result of showing the users additional capabilities provided by the system. Also, the traditional development life cycle is usually so long that user requirements may change before the completion of the project. However, the majority of user requirements are usually determined during the analysis phase and early in logical design.

1. What on/off-line reporting capabilities do users need?
2. What data values should be included in these reports?
3. How often do users need these reports, and when are they needed?
4. What on/off-line data entry capabilities do users need?
5. What data values do users need for their data entry capabilities?
6. What data inquiry capabilities do users want?
7. What data values should each user be able to view?
8. What updating capabilities do users want, and what updates can users correctly provide?
9. What data values can each user update?
10. What formats do users want for data entry, data access, and data reporting screens and documents?
11. What desktop and host computer capabilities do users need?
12. What desktop-to-host computer communication capabilities do users need?
13. What database data access is appropriate for users?
14. What desktop computer file formats are needed for data downloaded from the host computer?
15. What training do users need in new system requirements?
16. What is the desired level of security needed for each user?

Figure 8-4. Questions to help determine user requirements

Correctly and comprehensively determining user requirements early in the development life cycle is one of the best ways to increase the likelihood of developing or modifying an acceptable system on time and within budget. The graphs in Figure 8-5 illustrate that the largest percentage of errors occurs early in the development life cycle, and the largest error-correction effort centers around analysis and design, during which user requirements are determined. In fact, a large share of these errors concern the validity and comprehensiveness of the analyst's interpretation of user requirements.

In addition, the relative cost of correcting errors that occur early in a project rises as you progress through the life cycle phases. Correcting errors is relatively inexpensive as the analyst develops user requirements. However, correcting these errors after development begins or is completed can be extremely costly (an error that costs $1 in the analysis phase leads to $1000 in correction costs by the time the maintenance stage is reached). A valid and comprehensive determination of user requirements early in the project life cycle is extremely important to the remainder of the development life cycle. In fact, the recognition of this importance has in recent years led to a

Distribution of Bugs (%)		
Analysis and design		83
Requirements	56	
Design	27	
Code		7
Other		10

Distribution of Effort to Fix Bugs (%)		
Analysis and design		96
Requirements	83	
Design	13	
Code		1
Other		3

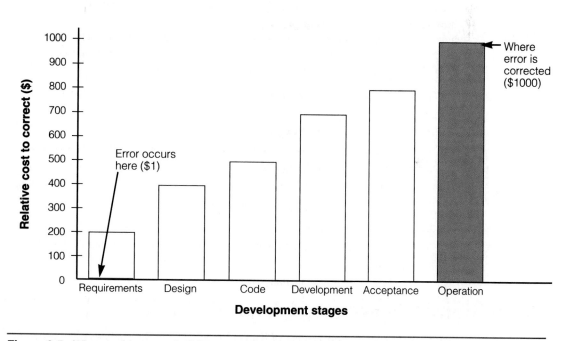

Figure 8-5. Where errors occur in A&D projects and their relative costs at different stages (adapted from J. Martin, 1984, and B. Boehm, 1981)

growing emphasis on analysis and design activities, prototyping, joint application design (JAD), and rapid application development (RAD).

Practicing analysts have learned to expect that in most systems, from ten to fifty defects typically occur per thousand lines of executable code in the system's programs. Furthermore, errors steadily decrease during maintenance activities in the first months following system implementation, and then begin to increase as a result of the aging of the system.

Once user requirements are tentatively determined and refined, the logical design begins in earnest. The **logical business design** involves modifying the diagrams produced during the analysis phase. This refinement provides details for the proposed system, business relationships or interactions that support operations, the inputs and outputs required, the LDSs needed to satisfy user requirements, and the processes required to produce results that satisfy user requirements. The remainder of this chapter explains and illustrates these activities, using the NG&T case as an example.

Developing the Logical Business Design

The logical design helps develop a logical model of the proposed system based on the analyst's interpretation of the problem and other related information gathered during the analysis phase. Analysts should develop the logical design with little regard for how the system will be physically implemented. Physical aspects of the proposed system are considered during the physical design. The logical design is developed from the analyst's understanding of how the various elements of the business system logically fit together. The major activities of the logical design are as follows:

1. Produce a composite evaluation of aggregated data gathered in the analysis phase.
2. Identify logical user requirements.
3. Modify analysis diagrams for easier evaluation of the analyst's proposed solution to identified problems.
4. Identify the major data structures necessary to support the proposed solution.
5. Identify the input and output forms to be used by the proposed system.
6. Create design dictionary specifications to accompany design specifications.
7. Review the results of the logical design by a committee of users and systems personnel.

Evaluation of Aggregated Analysis Data

To properly analyze the volume of data collected during the analysis phase, the data must be aggregated and categorized in a form that is easy to understand. This is normally done during the analysis phase while gathering data to evaluate the sources of problems. The data collected in entity/relationship diagrams (E/RDs), data flow diagrams (DFDs), and dictionary entries can be systematically evaluated by analysts and users to determine the best direction in which to proceed. By reviewing a logical solution, the project team and users determine whether the design is progressing in a direction acceptable to the users. Once users determine that the analyst correctly understands the problem, they usually decide to purchase a system, to modify the existing system, or to develop a new system that will satisfy user information needs and solve the problem.

Following a decision as to the type of solution, the analyst refines the design to reflect characteristics of this choice to more comprehensively satisfy user requirements. This usually involves refining the design diagrams (E/RDs, DFDs, and so on) and creating the remaining screen data entry and report formats, data structure descriptions, and dictionary entries associated with them.

User requirements continue to be refined during design iterations. Additional requirements are likely to surface as users continue to review design specifications. For example, additional query and updating capabilities desired by the users may emerge as the logical design is refined.

Design proceeds iteratively, with intermittent interaction between users and the project team. Design is a continuous activity wherein:

- Designers create or modify design specifications.
- Users review design specifications and respond to them.
- Designers modify or enhance the specifications in response to user responses.
- Designers move to the next phase of design or return to another round of user review and modifications.

Designers conduct these activities by using various modeling methods, such as E/RDs, DFDs, and prototyping.

Refined sets of specifications must be obtained for each of the user requirements identified in Figure 8-4. These refined requirements are generated as the analyst continues to present the progressively changing specifications to users and responds to their evaluation. The analyst continues to refine design diagrams, screen data entry and inquiry forms, on-line and off-line report forms, data structure specifications, and design dictionary entries for every design specification. User evaluations of these specifications and subsequent changes in them by the analyst eventually result in the creation of a detailed set of logical design specifications containing most, if not all, of the desirable requirements for the proposed system.

Modifying E/RDs and DFDs produced during the analysis phase provides a visual way for the analyst to present the proposed design. A top-down approach should be used regardless of the method. For example, E/RDs and DFDs are usually modified from the top-level diagram down through the detailed lower-level diagrams during the logical design.

Logical and Physical Data Flow Diagrams (DFDs)

Some modelers who use DFDs for process modeling distinguish between DFDs produced during analysis and those produced during design. The DFD produced during analysis reflects what already exists as the process model; these modelers often call this the **physical DFD,** meaning the business process model that already physically exists. Other modelers use physical DFDs to illustrate how to physically implement the logical DFD. These modelers view the **logical DFD** as what should exist and the physical DFD as a way to make what should exist actually exist. Still other modelers combine the two views, using the DFDs produced during analysis as physical DFDs to derive logical DFDs depicting what should exist, and then using physical DFDs to depict the way to make the logical DFDs a physical reality.

In each case, physical DFDs include graphical or text descriptions that depict physical realities of the business. In the text methodology, physical or time orientation in DFDs is avoided altogether. It takes a lot of work and expenditure of resources and time to complete DFDs (and other models of business aspects). When these models include current physical realities, they soon become dated with respect to time and/or technology. As a result, they have to be changed more frequently: each time physical circumstances change, the model must be updated. In the text methodology, an analysis DFD is produced to depict *what* is *currently* being done and *why*. During logical design, changes may be made to the DFD produced during the analysis phase; however, the changes still reflect *what* and *why*, not *how* a business process *should* be done.

The main reason that physical DFDs are avoided in the text methodology is to extend the life span of a DFD. The longer an existing DFD accurately and comprehensively portrays business processes, the more time the analyst can devote to modeling other areas of the business or the procedures that implement business processes and support data access. Thus, by avoiding references to current physical aspects of the business, greater reusability of DFDs is gained. The text methodology still distinguishes between current and more desirable business process models with analysis and logical design DFDs, but physical realities of the business are avoided so that DFDs can be used to depict business processes for a longer period of time.

Modifying Entity/Relationship Diagrams (E/RDs) at National Golf & Tennis

Designing a solution to problems often causes relationships between entities to change, causes new relationships to be identified, or causes additional data objects or properties of them to be identified. To keep design documentation current, members of the project team must revise E/RDs when they notice changes in existing relationships, identify new relationships, or identify new data objects (LDSs) or properties of them. Project team members may either change certain E/RD levels created during the analysis phase or create new E/RD levels. The NG&T project will illustrate how E/RDs may change as a result of changing relationships in business activities.

At the analysis review meeting, the committee decided that customers should be serviced by the same clerk for order entry and invoicing. Consequently, certain E/RD levels must be modified to reflect this change in customer order servicing. Figure 5-37 in Chapter 5 illustrated the relationship between the CUSTOMER entity and various clerical personnel on the GTOP00 level-1 E/RD. This E/RD showed the ORDER ENTRY & RECORDING OBJECT relationship between the CUSTOMER and DATA ENTRY CLERK entities. This E/RD then showed the relationship, ORDER INVOICING OBJECTS, between the CUSTOMER and SALES/PHONE/MAIL CLERK entity. The SALES/PHONE/MAIL CLERK in this E/R expression exploded to the GTOP0002 E/RD of Figure 5-38. Since the analysis review committee decided

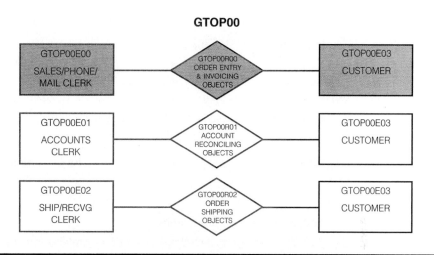

Figure 8-6. National Golf & Tennis GTOP00 level-1 E/RD

that the SALES/PHONE/MAIL CLERK should perform the ORDER ENTRY & RECORDING OBJECT relationship with the CUSTOMER entity, project analysts should modify the E/RDs in Figures 5-37 and 5-38 to reflect this change. Figure 8-6 shows the changed version of the E/RD in Figure 5-37.

The E/RD in Figure 8-6 reflects the fact that the SALES/PHONE/MAIL CLERK must now perform order recording and data entry as well as order invoicing and verification. This entity represents either a retail salesclerk or a phone/mail clerk. With the acquisition of on-line capabilities, these clerks can now satisfy all of these business relationships. Therefore, one E/R expression at the top of the original E/RD in Figure 5-37 has been eliminated: the CUSTOMER—ORDER ENTRY & RECORDING OBJECT—DATA ENTRY CLERK E/R expression. Figures 8-7, 8-8, and 8-9 contain the dictionary entries for the ORDER ENTRY & INVOICING OBJECTS relationship, the MLOG-CUSTORDR mass logical data structure (M-LDS), and the SALES/PHONE/MAIL CLERK entities, respectively.

The ORDER ENTRY & INVOICING OBJECTS relationship in Figures 8-6 and 8-7 represents all of the objects that support the interactions between customers and retail sales or phone/mail clerks. This relationship reflects the modification of sales and phone/mail clerk customer servicing responsibilities during order processing. The modification of responsibilities resulted from the decision made by the analysis review committee to make the clerks responsible for all of these business relationships. This relationship explodes to the MLOG-CUSTORDR M-LDS illustrated in Figure 8-8.

The MLOG-CUSTORDR M-LDS of Figure 8-8 is almost the same data structure to which the ORDER INVOICING OBJECTS relationship in Figure 5-37 exploded. There are several differences between these M-LDSs that reflect design modifications. This M-LDS now contains the LOG-CUSTTRNS, LOG-CUSTMAST, and LOG-CUST_ DELINQUENCY logical data structures (LDSs). These LDSs must be

Entry Type	Label		Dictionary ID
Relationship	ORDER ENTRY &		GTOP00R00
	INVOICING OBJECTS		

Explodes to:

   Data structure dictionary entry: <u>MLOG-CUSTORDR</u>

Relationship type: <u>Hierarchical multivalued</u>

Struct-Ele	E/O	Type	Key	Element Role

Text Description & Comments

This entry represents the relationship between retail sales or phone/mail clerks and customers during order processing. This process involves recording and entering customer orders, checking these orders for correctness, verifying customers relative to customer master records, checking inventory quantities for order filling, creating customer back orders for insufficient inventories, and/or canceling all or part of customer orders when they do not pass any one of the verification methods. This relationship is exhibited in the M-LDS called MLOG-CUSTORDR.

Figure 8-7. ORDER ENTRY & INVOICING OBJECTS relationship dictionary entry

available to the SALES/PHONE/MAIL CLERK entity to reflect the change in responsibilities. These clerks must now perform the following steps:

1. Record the customer order (LOG-CUSTTRNS).
2. Check the order for correctness.
3. Verify the customer (LOG-CUSTMAST).
4. Check the customer's delinquency record (LOG-CUST_DELINQUENCY).
5. Determine order item availability as well as what needs to be done for unavailable order items—that is, the remaining E/R expressions.

The dictionary entry in Figure 8-9 for the SALES/PHONE/MAIL CLERK entity also reflects the changed responsibilities for these clerical personnel. This entity explodes down to the GTOP0000 E/RD shown in Figure 8-10 (note that the ACCOUNTS CLERK entity in Figure 8-6 also explodes down to a separate E/RD).

The E/RD of Figure 8-10 represents a modified version of the GTOP0002 E/RD in Figure 5-38 of Chapter 5. Remember that the top E/R expression of Figure 5-37

Entry Type   **Dictionary ID**

Data Structure   MLOG-CUSTORDR

Alias: _CUSTOMER ORDER DATA_

Comment: _A M-LDS for customer order data._

Starting Volume: _____   Growth Potential: _____

No.	Ele/DS Name	DE/DS	SV/MV	Occurrences
01	LOG-CUSTTRNS	DS		
02	LOG-CUSTMAST	DS		
03	LOG-CUST_DELINQUENCY	DS		
04	LOG-ITEMMAST	DS		
05	LOG-CUSTORDR	DS		
06	LOG-CUST_BACKORDER	DS		
07	LOG-CUSTORDR_CANCELLATION	DS		

Figure 8-8. MLOG-CUSTORDR M-LDS dictionary entry

Entry Type   **Label**   **Dictionary ID**

Entity   SALES/PHONE/MAIL CLERK   GTOP00E00

Explodes to:

     E/RD: _GTOP0000_

     Data structure dictionary entry: _____

Text Description & Comments

This entity represents either retail sales or phone/mail clerks who process customer orders. These clerks record customer orders, check the orders for correctness, verify customers and their delinquency ratings, check inventory levels for order filling, create customer back orders for insufficient inventory, and/or cancel customer orders when they do not pass any one of the verification/validation methods. This clerk passes the customer order invoice (and/or back order) to the accounts clerk for order filling, customer billing, and/or vendor order creation.

Figure 8-9. SALES/PHONE/MAIL CLERK entity dictionary entry

GTOP0000

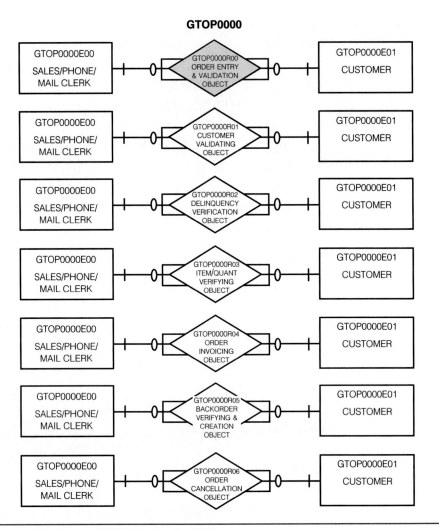

Figure 8-10. National Golf & Tennis GTOP0000 level-2 E/RD

was eliminated. Therefore, the SALES/PHONE/MAIL CLERK now has a dictionary ID of GTOP00E00. Thus, the explosion E/RD of Figure 8-10 has the dictionary ID GTOP0000, which conforms to the naming conventions for E/RDs explained in Chapter 5.

The main difference between the GTOP00 and GTOP0002 E/RDs of the analysis phase and the GTOP00 and GTOP0000 E/RDs of the design phase is the elimination of the E/R expression at the top of the analysis phase GTOP00 E/RD and the insertion of the top E/R expression on the GTOP0000 E/RD of the design phase. The GTOP0000 E/RD graphically portrays the changed responsibilities for SALES/PHONE/MAIL CLERK entities. Figure 8-11 illustrates the dictionary entry accompanying the

Entry Type	Label			Dictionary ID
Relationship	ORDER ENTRY & VALIDATION OBJECT			GTOP0000R00

Explodes to:

Data structure dictionary entry: LOG-CUSTTRNS

Relationship type: Complex multivalued

Struct-Ele	E/O	Type	Key	Element Role
CUSTNUM	E	SV	PRI	IDENTIFY CUSTOMER
CUSTNAME	E	SV	SEC	IDENTIFY CUSTOMER
STREET	E	SV		ADDRESS
CITY	E	SV		ADDRESS
STATE	E	SV		ADDRESS
ZIP	E	SV		ADDRESS
ORDER_NUMBER	E	SV		IDENTIFY ORDER
TRANTYPE	E	SV		RETAIL/PHONE/MAIL
SHIPSTREET	E	SV		SHIP ADDRESS
SHIPCITY	E	SV		SHIP ADDRESS
SHIPSTATE	E	SV		SHIP ADDRESS
SHIPZIP	E	SV		SHIP ADDRESS
ITEMNUM	E	MV		IDENTIFY ORD ITEM
QUANTITY	E	MV		ITEM ORD QUANT
DATE	E	SV		ORDER DATE
EMPNUM	E	SV		IDENTIFY ORD CLERK
MAGAZINE_SOURCE	E	SV		ADVERTISING SOURCE
REGION_SOURCE	E	SV		MAIL REGION

Text Description & Comments

This entry represents the relationship between retail sales or phone/mail clerks and customers during order processing. This relationship involves recording and validating customer orders for either retail sales or phone/mail orders. It is exhibited in the LDS called LOG-CUSTTRNS.

Figure 8-11. ORDER ENTRY & VALIDATION OBJECT relationship dictionary entry

ORDER ENTRY & VALIDATION OBJECT relationship at the top of Figure 8-10.

The dictionary entry in Figure 8-11 specifies that the ORDER ENTRY & VALIDATION OBJECT relationship explodes to a LDS named LOG-CUSTTRNS. This is the same LDS previously indicated as supporting the relationship between the CUSTOMER entity and the DATA ENTRY CLERK entity, now eliminated from the order

Entry Type   **Dictionary ID**

Data Structure   LOG-CUSTTRNS

Alias: _CUSTOMER ORDER TRANSACTIONS_

Comment: _A LDS for a customer order transaction._

Starting Volume: _____   Growth Potential: _____

No.	Ele/DS Name	DE/DS	SV/MV	Occurrences
01	CUSTNUM	DE	SV	
02	CUSTNAME	DE	SV	
03	STREET	DE	SV	
04	CITY	DE	SV	
05	STATE	DE	SV	
06	ZIP	DE	SV	
07	SHIPSTREET	DE	SV	
08	SHIPCITY	DE	SV	
09	SHIPSTATE	DE	SV	
10	SHIPZIP	DE	SV	
11	ORDER_NUMBER	DE	SV	
12	ITEMNUM	DE	MV	
13	QUANTITY	DE	MV	
14	DATE	DE	SV	
15	EMPNUM	DE	SV	
16	MAGAZINE_SOURCE	DE	SV	
17	REGION_SOURCE	DE	SV	
18	MPHY-CUSTORDR	DS		

Figure 8-12. LOG-CUSTTRNS data structure dictionary entry

processing subject area. Since LOG-CUSTTRNS is an individual LDS, the relationship dictionary entry in Figure 8-11 also includes entries that specify the roles for individual data elements. Figure 8-12 illustrates the dictionary entry for the LOG-CUSTTRNS LDS.

Figure 8-13 illustrates a dictionary entry accompanying the second relationship from the top of Figure 8-10.

The relationship illustrated in Figure 8-13 explodes to the LOG-CUSTMAST LDS that supports the CUSTOMER VALIDATING OBJECT relationship. The LOG-CUSTMAST LDS contains reference information concerning customers permitted to charge orders. The clerk uses this LDS to verify that those customers can charge orders. A similar connection exists between the DELINQUENCY VERIFICATION

Entry Type	Label			Dictionary ID
Relationship	CUSTOMER VALIDATING OBJECT			GTOP0000R01

Explodes to:

  Data structure dictionary entry: __LOG-CUSTMAST__

Relationship type: __Hierarchical single-valued__

Struct-Ele	E/O	Type	Key	Element Role
CUSTNUM	E	SV	PRI	IDENTIFY CUSTOMER
CUSTNAME	E	SV	SEC	IDENTIFY CUSTOMER
STREET	E	SV		ADDRESS
CITY	E	SV		ADDRESS
STATE	E	SV		ADDRESS
ZIP	E	SV		ADDRESS

Text Description & Comments

This entry represents the relationship between retail sales or phone/mail clerks and customers during order processing. This relationship involves verifying customers relative to customer master records and checking delinquency records to determine the credit rating for customers purchasing items on credit. It is exhibited in the M-LDS called MLOG-CUST_ VALIDATION.

Figure 8-13. CUSTOMER VALIDATING OBJECT relationship dictionary entry

OBJECT relationship and the LOG-CUST_DELINQUENCY LDS used by clerks to verify that customers do not have excessive delinquency records that prohibit them from charging orders.

The remaining relationships in Figure 8-10 depict inventory quantity verification, customer order invoice creation, back-order creation for insufficient inventory quantities, and order cancellation due to customer dissatisfaction. These relationships explode to the LOG-ITEMMAST, LOG-CUSTORDR, LOG-CUST_BACKORDER, and LOG-CUSTORDR_CANCELLATION LDSs, respectively. Since each relationship on the GTOP0000 E/RD explodes to a single LDS, this E/RD is the lowest-level E/RD for this path within the set of E/RDs.

The NG&T project team also revises the explosion E/RD for the ACCOUNTS CLERK entity appearing on the GTOP00 E/RD of Figure 8-6. The explosion E/RD is called GTOP0001 and reflects the revised CUSTOMER and ACCOUNTS CLERK interactions. The project team completes revised explosion E/RDs for the paths leading from the VENDOR, CARRIER, and MANAGER entities appearing on the GTOP E/RD in Figure 5-36 of Chapter 5 as well.

Modifying Data Flow Diagrams (DFDs) at National Golf & Tennis

The project team also revises DFDs to reflect changes in activities associated with the alternative selected by the analysis review committee. Remember that the M-LDSs and individual LDSs derived while creating E/RDs can be carried into data flow diagramming. DFDs revised during logical design reflect the changes in data flows and processes that occur as a result of selecting or revising a particular alternative to implement.

Figure 8-14 shows the top-level DFD for NG&T order processing. This is the same DFD that was completed during the analysis phase of the project. Notice that this DFD still has only one process, SERVICE ORDERS, and four entities: CUSTOMER, VENDOR, CARRIER, and MANAGER. This DFD still represents the context-level DFD, as previously stated. The SERVICE ORDERS process explodes down to the GTOP00 DFD in Figure 8-15.

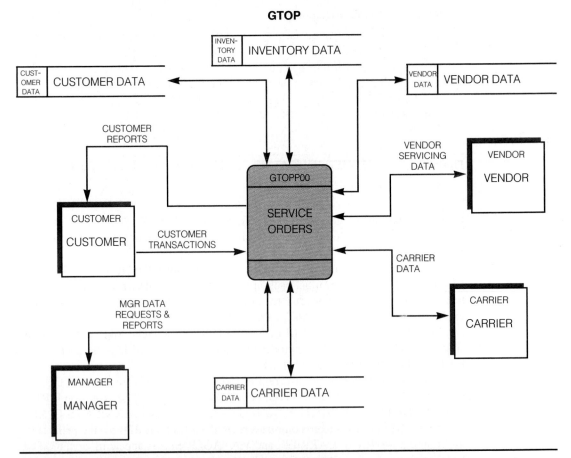

Figure 8-14. National Golf & Tennis GTOP context-level DFD

GTOP00

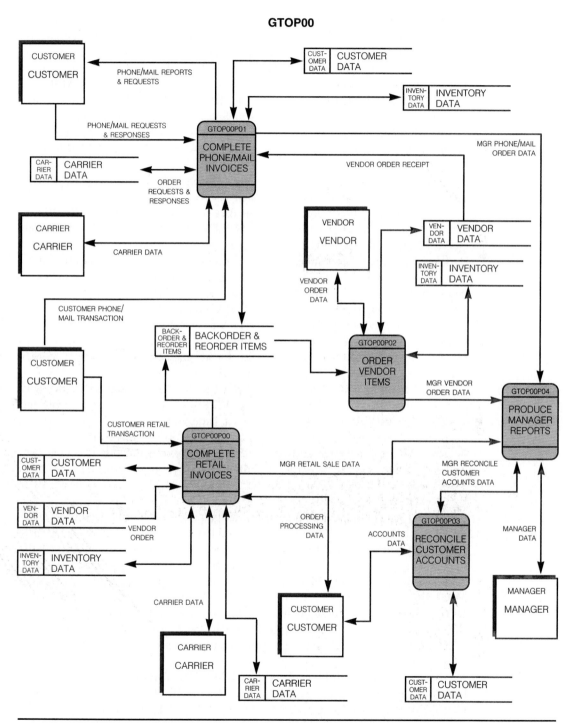

Figure 8-15. National Golf & Tennis GTOP00 level-1 DFD

The GTOP00 DFD in Figure 8-15 reflects the decision by the analysis review committee to install either microcomputers or terminals at points of sale. A comparison of the DFD in Figure 8-15 with the GTOP00 DFD of Figure 6-23 of Chapter 6 illustrates the changes motivated by this decision. Instead of separating sales creation and validating processes, these activities are included within the COMPLETE PHONE/MAIL INVOICES and COMPLETE RETAIL INVOICES activities. These activities are documented in the DFDs to which these two processes explode.

The two data flows from the CUSTOMER entity to the two invoice processes in Figure 8-15 are CUSTOMER PHONE/MAIL TRANSACTION and CUSTOMER RETAIL TRANSACTION, respectively. These data flows represent customer orders, and their dictionary entries both indicate an explosion to the LOG-CUSTTRNS LDS. This is the same LDS defined during the analysis phase.

An additional change to the DFD is the data store, BACKORDER & REORDER ITEMS, to which data flows from the COMPLETE PHONE/MAIL INVOICES and COMPLETE RETAIL INVOICES processes. This data store indicates how salesclerks create customer back orders and reorder items when inventory is insufficient to fill customer item order quantities. The dictionary entry for this data store indicates that it explodes to the MLOG-BACKORDER_REORDER_ITEMORDER M-LDS. This M-LDS comprises the LOG-CUST_BACKORDER and LOG-REORDER_ITEMORDER LDSs. A customer back order is created by retail or phone/mail clerks when they detect insufficient inventory quantities to fill item order quantities. A reorder item is created automatically when the system detects that an item reorder point has been reached.

The data in the BACKORDER & REORDER ITEMS data store was previously represented by the VENDOR ORDER PROCESSING DATA data flow from the VALIDATE ORDERS process in Figure 6-23. Order validation is now performed by the retail and phone/mail clerks. The BACKORDER & REORDER ITEMS data store depicts what happens when customer orders do not pass validation checking performed by these clerks on inventory quantities. Thus, both the COMPLETE PHONE/MAIL INVOICES and COMPLETE RETAIL INVOICES processes flow to the BACKORDER & REORDER ITEMS data stores.

Actual vendor item ordering occurs as part of the activities composing the ORDER VENDOR ITEMS process connected to the BACKORDER & REORDER ITEMS data store. These activities are performed by the accounts clerk, who identifies vendors that supply those items and places an order with the appropriate vendors.

Data flows from the VENDOR DATA data store to the COMPLETE PHONE/MAIL INVOICES and COMPLETE RETAIL INVOICES processes on the GTOP00 DFD to signify the receipt of goods resulting from vendor item ordering. These data flows are both labeled VENDOR ORDER RECEIPT. They explode to the LOG-VENDRCPT LDS, which triggers the processing that previously created customer back orders.

Notice that data still flows from the COMPLETE PHONE/MAIL INVOICES, COMPLETE RETAIL INVOICES, ORDER VENDOR ITEMS, and RECONCILE CUSTOMER ACCOUNTS processes to the PRODUCE MANAGER REPORTS process. These data flows still depict managerial monitoring and control data types that materialize during order processing. The only change is that a separate data flow to represent order validation monitoring and control does not exist. Since validation activities are part of retail and phone/mail order processing, monitoring these activities includes order validation monitoring and control.

Each of the processes on the GTOP00 DFD in Figure 8-15 involves a number of activities. Therefore, each of these processes explodes to a separate DFD. Figure 8-16 shows the dictionary entry accompanying the COMPLETE PHONE/MAIL INVOICES process. The other processes on the GTOP00 DFD have similar dictionary entries, with the explosion DFD and text description entries providing documentation appropriate for those processes.

The dictionary ID for the process in Figure 8-16 is GTOP00P01 (the GTOP00P00 dictionary ID is assigned to COMPLETE RETAIL INVOICES). This process symbol explodes to the GTOP0001 DFD in Figure 8-17. Notice that the dictionary ID for this process, and the DFD to which it explodes, conform to the naming conventions previously explained.

The DFD in Figure 8-17 contains five processes. The first process, CREATE ORDER, specifies the roles played by the phone/mail clerks during order creation. The CUSTOMER entity initiates order creation, aided by the phone/mail clerk's CREATE ORDER process. The output of this process is a customer order transaction illustrated by the CUSTOMER ORDER TRANSACTION data store. This data store explodes to the LOG-CUSTTRNS LDS.

Following order creation, the customer order transaction flows into the VALIDATE ORDERS process. This process explodes to a lower-level DFD in which all of the order validating activities are documented. Notice that this process has data flowing to and from the CUSTOMER entity. These data flows represent data used either to correct order entries and/or customer master data or to verify back-order acceptance by customers. This process has three main outflows of data. If insufficient inventory exists for order filling, then a customer back order is created or the order is canceled. This is documented by the flow to the CUSTOMER BACKORDER data store and the CUSTOMER DATA data store. The dictionary entry for the CUSTOMER BACKORDER data store indicates that it explodes to the LOG-CUST_BACKORDER LDS, while the CUSTOMER DATA data store includes the LOG-ORDER_CANCELLATION LDS. The LOG-CUST_BACKORDER LDS indicates the order and customer numbers as well as the items and quantities for which the back order is issued. If the order passes validation, the VALID ORDER data flows to the CREATE ORDER INVOICE process. The dictionary entry for this data flow indicates that it explodes to the LOG-CUSTTRNS LDS. This LDS now represents a validated customer order.

The CREATE ORDER INVOICE process represents creating a customer order invoice based on the customer order transaction. There are two possible outputs from this process: an order invoice and an item order. The order invoice is always produced and is represented by the ORDER INVOICE data store. The dictionary entry for this data store indicates that it explodes to the LOG-CUSTORDR LDS. The item order results when item reorder points are reached. The item order is represented by the

Entry Type	Label	Dictionary ID
Process	COMPLETE PHONE/ MAIL INVOICES	GTOP00P01

Explodes to:

   DFD: __GTOP0001__

   Structure chart: _____

   E/RD: _____

Location: __Phone/Mail Order Processing Department__

Type of process (Manual or Computerized): __Manual & computerized__

Process level (Managerial or Clerical): __Clerical__

Process triggered by: __Order receipt__

_____

Process triggers: __Order validation and filling__

_____

Text Description & Comments

This process represents all of the activities performed by clerical personnel during phone/mail order processing. The phone/mail clerk first validates the order. Order validation involves checking the order for valid data entries, verifying customers and checking their delinquency histories, and checking inventory availability relative to order item quantities. Orders not passing validation may result in either creation of a customer back order or cancellation of all or part of the order. If the order passes validation, these clerks will then create customer order invoices, update inventory quantities, and send the order invoice to the accounts clerk for order filling. Items reaching reorder point inventory levels cause an item order to be automatically initiated when order invoices are created. The accounts clerk then creates a shipping invoice, which will be sent to shipping/receiving, and processes customer accounts for billing and payment purposes. Shipping/receiving clerks create a carrier manifest record for the items being sent. This manifest is used to document goods that have actually been shipped. The goods are then delivered by the carrier based on the manifest entries.

Figure 8-16. COMPLETE PHONE/MAIL INVOICES process dictionary entry

GTOP0001

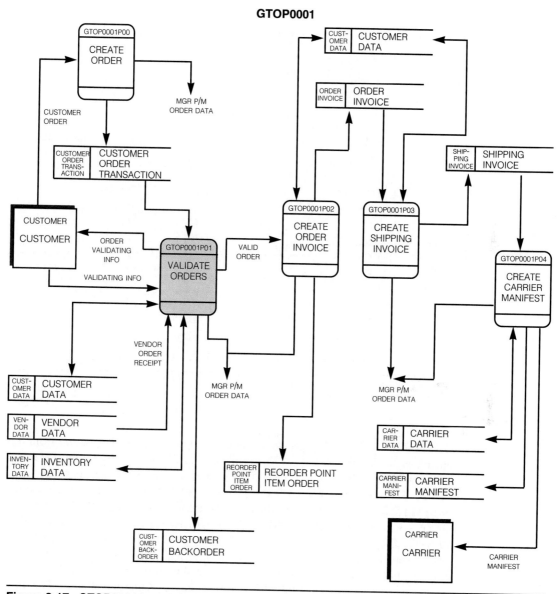

Figure 8-17. GTOP0001 level-2 DFD

REORDER POINT ITEM ORDER data store. The dictionary entry for this data store indicates that it explodes to the LOG-RECORD_ITEMORDER LDS.

Following order invoice creation, data flows from the ORDER INVOICE data store to the CREATE SHIPPING INVOICE process. This data flow indicates that the LOG-

Entry Type		Dictionary ID		
Data Structure		LOG-CUSTSHIP		

Alias: __CUSTOMER SHIPMENT__

Comment: __A LDS for customer shipments.__

Starting Volume: _____ Growth Potential: _____

No.	Ele/DS Name	DE/DS	SV/MV	Occurrences
01	ORDER_NUMBER	DE	SV	
02	CUSTNUM	DE	SV	
03	CUSTNAME	DE	SV	
04	SHIPSTREET	DE	SV	
05	SHIPCITY	DE	SV	
06	SHIPSTATE	DE	SV	
07	SHIPZIP	DE	SV	
08	ITEMNUM	DE	MV	
09	QUANTITY	DE	MV	
10	DATE	DE	SV	
11	EMPNUM	DE	SV	
12	MPHY-CUSTSHIP	DS		

Figure 8-18. LOG-CUSTSHIP LDS dictionary entry

CUSTORDR LDS will be used to create the shipping invoice. The output from this process is the SHIPPING INVOICE data store. The dictionary entry for this data store indicates that it explodes to the LOG-CUSTSHIP LDS. Figure 8-18 illustrates this LDS.

The last entry in Figure 8-18 is the MPHY-CUSTSHIP mass physical data structure (M-PDS). This M-PDS identifies the physical data structures (PDSs) where the data items in the LOG-CUSTSHIP LDS are actually stored. These PDSs are PHY-CUSTOMER_SHIPMENT, PHY-CUSTOMER_MASTER, and PHY-ITEM_QUANTITY. The first PDS supplies the shipping information for the shipping number, customer number, employee number, and date of shipment. The second PDS supplies reference information concerning the customer, such as name and address. The third PDS supplies the item numbers and quantities for items being shipped.

The MPHY-CUSTSHIP M-PDS establishes the link between logical and physical design and development, since PDSs often already exist. Even though the project team focuses on logical aspects during logical design, it often begins steps toward implementing the logical design early in the development project. Using a M-PDS provides one of the steps. More information on the subject of M-PDSs is presented in Chapter 10, which discusses the database environment. It is included here to explain the bottom entry that appears in many LDS dictionary entries.

The CREATE SHIPPING INVOICE process of Figure 8-17 specifies the activities performed to create a shipping invoice and update customer accounts. Customer account updates represent recording payment receipts for direct sales and updating customer balances for credit sales.

CREATE CARRIER MANIFEST is the last process logically performed on the GTOP0001 DFD of Figure 8-17. This process uses the LOG-CUSTSHIP LDS embodied in the SHIPPING INVOICE data store to create carrier manifest entries. The carrier manifest provides carriers with a list of items to deliver to indicated customer addresses. The data on shipping invoices provides data for these entries. The data flow and data store named CARRIER MANIFEST represent the entries created for order item distribution. The data flow with this label represents the manifest listing supplied to the carrier for customer order delivery. Figure 8-19 shows the dictionary entry for the CARRIER MANIFEST data store. A similar dictionary entry exists for the CARRIER MANIFEST data flow.

Your attention is directed to the five output interface data flows labeled MGR P/M ORDER DATA. These interfaces exist on the GTOP0001 DFD because the COMPLETE PHONE/MAIL INVOICES process on the GTOP00 DFD is connected directly to the PRODUCE MANAGER REPORTS process on the GTOP00 DFD. Again, we need to show the flow between these two processes. But when we explode on the COMPLETE PHONE/MAIL INVOICES process down to the GTOP0001 DFD, we do not carry the PRODUCE MANAGER REPORTS process down to this DFD.

It is also important to recognize that the MGR P/M ORDER DATA output interface leading away from the VALIDATE ORDERS process must also be shown on the DFD to which VALIDATE ORDERS explodes. For any process that explodes to a lower-level DFD that has an input or output interface leading to or from it, the lower-level DFD must also have an interface leading to or from one of its processes.

Entry Type	Label	Dictionary ID
Data Store	CARRIER MANIFEST	CARRIER_MANIFEST
Explodes to:		
E/RD: _____		
Data structure dictionary entry: __LOG-CARRIER MANIFEST__		

Text Description & Comments

This data store represents the carrier manifest entries created by shipping/receiving for customer shipping invoices. The carrier manifest entries provide records for goods actually shipped by carriers. The LOG-CARRIER_MANIFEST LDS contains entries for goods shipped regarding customer shipping invoices.

Figure 8-19. CARRIER MANIFEST data store dictionary entry

Therefore, the DFD that depicts the validation process must have an output interface leading away from one or more of its processes to correspond to the output interface leading away from the VALIDATE ORDERS process on the GTOP00 DFD.

Each process on the GTOP0001 DFD of Figure 8-17 has an accompanying dictionary entry. These dictionary entries provide descriptions for the activities associated with these processes. The VALIDATE ORDERS process is the only process on this DFD that explodes to a lower-level DFD. Figure 8-20 illustrates the dictionary entry for this process.

The dictionary entry of Figure 8-20 specifies that the dictionary ID for this process is GTOP0001P01 and that it explodes to the GTOP000101 DFD (conforming

Entry Type	Label	Dictionary ID
Process	VALIDATE ORDERS	GTOP0001P01

Explodes to:

DFD: GTOP000101

Structure chart: _____

E/RD: _____

Location: Order Processing Department

Type of process (Manual or Computerized): Manual & computerized

Process level (Managerial or Clerical): Clerical

Process triggered by: Customer order creation

Process triggers: Order invoicing

Text Description & Comments

This process represents all of the activities performed by clerical personnel during customer order validation. The order transaction must first be checked for correctness, followed by validation of the customer. Customer validation involves both comparing customer data on the order transaction with customer master data and checking delinquency records for the customer. The inventory level for order items is then checked to determine if order quantities can be filled. Transactions not passing any one of these validating tests may lead to back-order creation or order cancellation. This process explodes down to the GTOP000101 DFD, wherein the details of order validation are provided.

Figure 8-20. VALIDATE ORDERS process dictionary entry

to the naming conventions). The GTOP000101 DFD is essentially the same as the GTOP0005 DFD in Figure 6-26 of Chapter 6. The text description entry for the VAL- IDATE ORDERS process on the GTOP0001 DFD provides an overview of the processes performed on the GTOP000101 DFD. Figure 8-21 shows this DFD.

The DFD in Figure 8-21 contains three validation processes, VALIDATE ORDER ENTRIES, VERIFY CUSTOMER, and VALIDATE ITEM AVAILABILITY. The first process represents checking individual order entries for accuracy. The second process consists of comparing customer data on the order transaction with data retained by the company on its customers, as well as looking for excessive delinquencies in payments for previous orders by that customer. The third process consists of comparing order item quantities with the balance of inventory on hand for those items. Each of these processes has its own set of actions based on the results of validating customer orders.

The results of validation actions will be a customer back order, an order cancella-

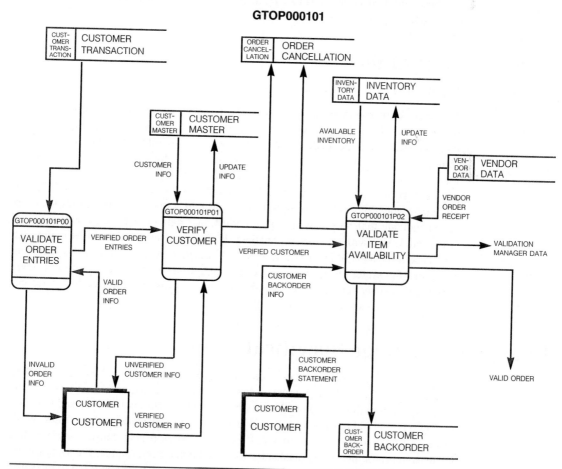

Figure 8-21. GTOP000101 level-3 DFD

tion, and/or a validated order transaction. A customer back order or cancellation is retained and documented by the CUSTOMER BACKORDER and ORDER CANCELLATION data stores, respectively. The validated order transaction is represented by the VALID ORDER output interface data flow. This output interface data flow represents the VALID ORDER data flow flowing out of the VALIDATE ORDERS process to the CREATE ORDER INVOICE process on the GTOP0001 DFD. The VALIDATION MANAGER DATA output interface data flow represents the output data flow interface from the VALIDATE ORDERS on the GTOP0001 DFD to the output interface, MGR P/M ORDER DATA.

Dictionary entries are created by the project team for each data entity, process, data store, and data flow on the GTOP000101 DFD. These dictionary entries provide descriptions for symbols more specific to order validation. These entries, combined with the dictionary entries for all symbols and connections on all of the DFDs, provide a comprehensive set of logical design specifications. These specifications will be reviewed and used as the basis for creating physical design specifications for the order processing system.

The Influence of the Prototype on Other Requirements

The purpose of prototyping, as stated in Chapter 7, is refining, not creating, user requirements. User interaction with the prototype can uncover many changes to be made to user requirements that were created while using other methods. The smallest change can be to LDSs. When users indicate other data items that need to be on a prototype form or screen, the typical response is to add a data item to the LDS that depicts this logical business object. The execution of screen data entry and display and menu selections can cause both E/RDs and DFDs to change. For example, users might indicate that they need to see an additional data object on a form or screen while interacting with a customer or client. In this case, an additional E/R expression may need to be added to an existing E/RD. As another example, if users indicate that they need the system to perform an additional action to be listed on a system-level menu, a DFD may need to have an additional process inserted on it with any accompanying data stores, entities, and data flows.

Changing Prototype Specifications

As discussed in Chapter 7, many of the LDSs identified and described while creating E/RDs and DFDs are used to create user screen masks and forms to receive data from or display data to the user. You also saw how menu screens could be created to reflect the actions specified as processes on DFDs. Any changes made to these LDSs while creating E/RDs or DFDs, or to DFD processes, should also cause corresponding changes to prototype screen masks, forms, and menus. For example, the system-level menu in Figure 7-26 of Chapter 7 contained seven options, corresponding to the seven

```
                          SERVICE ORDERS
          1. COMPLETE PHONE/MAIL INVOICES.
          2. COMPLETE RETAIL INVOICES.
          3. ORDER VENDOR ITEMS.
          4. RECONCILE CUSTOMER ACCOUNTS.
          5. PRODUCE MANAGER REPORTS.
                 ENTER NUMBER OF OPTION _____
                 PRESS ESC KEY TO RETURN TO MAIN MENU
```

Figure 8-22. Revised system-level menu for the GTOP00 DFD

processes on the GTOP00 DFD of Figure 6-23 from the analysis phase. Since the GTOP00 DFD changed during logical design, its system-level menu should also change to reflect only five options, corresponding to the five processes on the GTOP00 DFD of Figure 8-15 of the logical design. Figure 8-22 illustrates this new system-level menu that corresponds to the GTOP00 DFD of Figure 8-15.

REVIEW OF THE LOGICAL DESIGN

As you know, review should be a continuous activity as the design progresses through iterations of development, presentation, and evaluation. For the NG&T project, users involved in order processing are shown the results of project team efforts during and after completing logical design diagrams and dictionary entries. Responses of the users to logical design specifications allow the analyst to determine whether he or she has a clear understanding of user requirements. Users' responses to example forms guide the analyst in properly modifying the logical design as it progresses. By permitting users to review design specifications, the design continues to progress toward a set of specifications that more closely satisfies user requirements.

Formal Review

The purpose of conducting a formal review session at the conclusion of logical design is to confirm that the users and the project team agree that the results of project team efforts correctly embody desirable attributes for developing the system. See Figure

6-27 in Chapter 6 for a list of the elements of a formal review. The logical design review typically includes the same participants who were involved in the analysis review. Also, the project team prepares for the review using the same key considerations listed in the analysis review, which include site selection, preparation of presentation aids, round-table discussion, recording and summarizing evaluation responses, any additional investigation called for in the review, and follow-up. Finally, the activities of the logical design review are similar to those discussed in Chapter 6.

The main objective of the logical design review is to identify necessary changes in the design based on user responses. If the design needs further enhancements and modifications, the project team returns to logical design activities and changes the specifications to meet the new requirements. At the conclusion of these activities, another formal review should be held to present the changes to the users. This process continues until there are no new changes.

The logical design review should conclude with the signing of a document similar to the one shown in Figure 6-28 of Chapter 6. This document indicates that the review participants have reached agreement, and it is considered to be a contract committing the efforts of all participants to successful implementation of the logical design.

National Golf & Tennis
Logical Design Formal Review

The project team for NG&T presented the complete set of logical design specifications to the formal review committee. During the logical design presentation, a number of minor changes were made to dictionary entries associated with some of the diagram entries. Two major changes were also suggested during the design review. George Serve, the director of IS for NG&T, suggested the first major change. He noticed that manager data always appears as data flows or interfaces on the DFDs presented. He asked whether this data should be portrayed as a data store so that the DFDs would illustrate that this data would be routinely retained. As a result of this comment, the project team was commissioned to modify all the DFDs to reflect this action.

A second major change was suggested by Geraldine Gibson, the manager of phone/mail clerks. Geraldine noticed that an order cancellation did not result from the first validation action (CHECK ORDER ENTRIES) on the GTOP000101 DFD. She stated that phone/mail clerks frequently have trouble contacting customers regarding incorrect data. When this occurs, the clerk must issue an order cancellation. Mr. Serve also stated that this DFD did not appear to have enough detail to clearly explain all of the validating activities. He suggested that the project team develop a more detailed version of this DFD.

Figures 8-23 through 8-26 illustrate the changes made by the project team in response to these suggestions. These DFDs also represent the diagrams formally accepted by the review committee.

The project team inserted data stores for manager monitoring and control data to produce the DFDs in Figures 8-23 through 8-26. The dictionary entry for the MGR

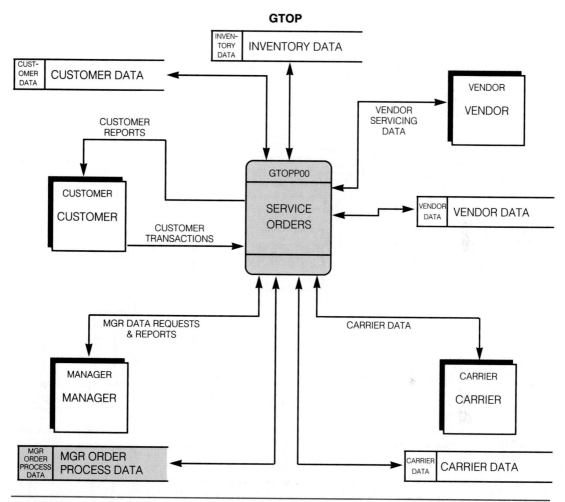

Figure 8-23. GTOP DFD following logical design review at NG&T

ORDER PROCESS DATA data store that appears in Figures 8-23 and 8-24 indicates that a M-LDS called MLOG-MGR_ORDER_DATA represents the retention of order processing data for managers. The dictionary entry for the MGR P/M ORDER PROCESS DATA data store in Figure 8-25 specifies that it explodes to a M-LDS called MLOG-MGR_P/M_ORDER_PROCESS_DATA. The dictionary entry for the VALIDATION MGR DATA data store in Figure 8-26 specifies that it explodes to a M-LDS called MLOG-MGR_ORDER_VALIDATION_DATA. The MLOG-MGR_ORDER_DATA M-LDS comprises the M-LDSs associated with the manager data stores on lower-level DFDs. The M-LDSs associated with data stores on lower-level DFDs comprise LDSs providing data for managerial monitoring and control.

GTOP00

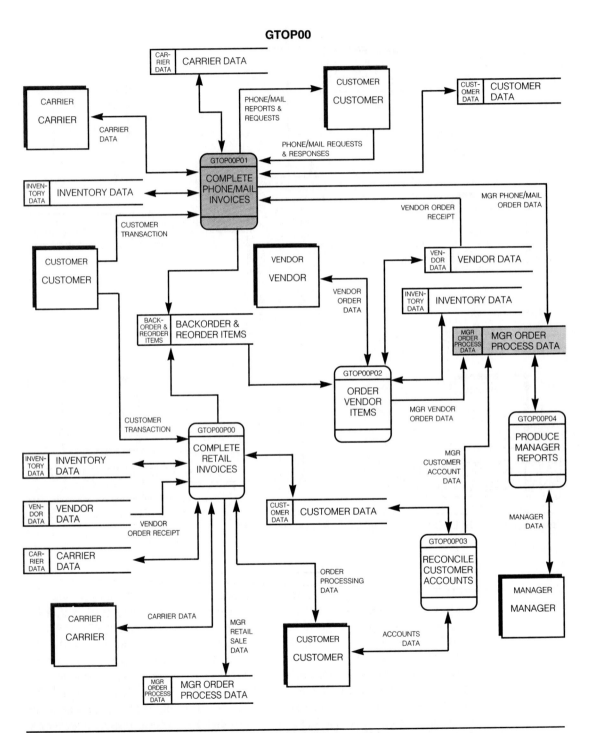

Figure 8-24. GTOP00 DFD following logical design review at NG&T

GTOP0001

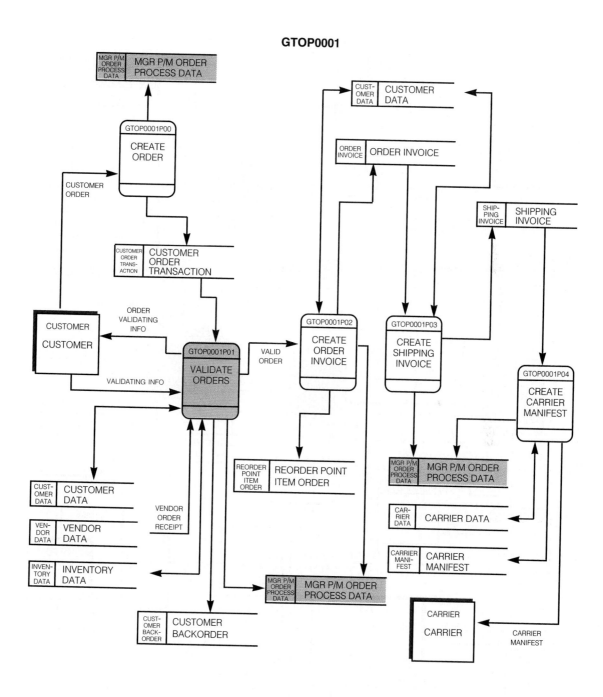

Figure 8-25. GTOP0001 DFD following logical design review at NG&T

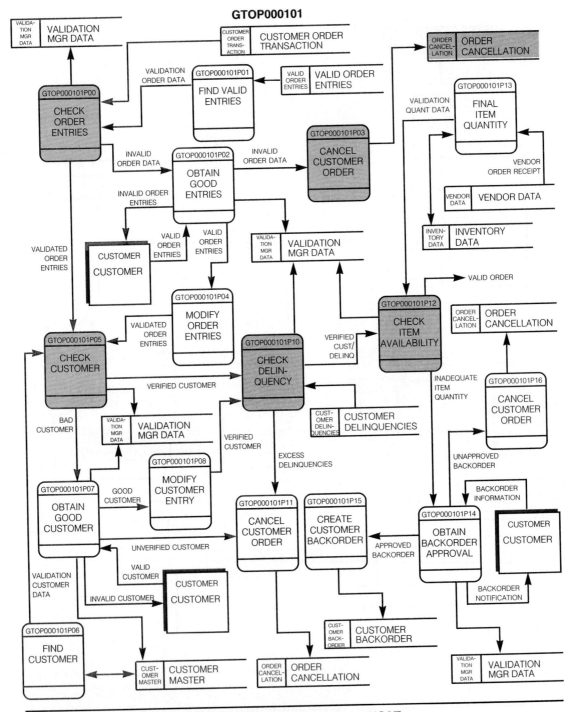

Figure 8-26. GTOP000101 DFD following logical design review at NG&T

The project team developed a more detailed version of the GTOP000101 DFD. Figure 8-26 illustrates this more detailed version of the DFD created for validation purposes. During this activity, the team copied the ORDER CANCELLATION data store into the GTOP000101 DFD of Figure 8-26 in a position to connect it to order entry validation. This change reflects the modification suggested by Geraldine Gibson during the analysis phase review.

The new GTOP000101 DFD reflects the order in which validation occurs. Starting from the upper left corner of Figure 8-26, the order entries are first checked for correctness. The entries are then compared with valid order entry values retrieved by the phone/mail clerk. Entries failing the comparison are communicated to customers, who are requested to supply correct order entry information. Failed attempts to contact customers result in order cancellations. When customers subsequently supply valid entries, the orders are modified by the MODIFY ORDER ENTRIES process and passed as the VALIDATED ORDER ENTRIES data flow to the CHECK CUSTOMER process. If the CHECK ORDER ENTRIES process finds valid order entries, the VALIDATED ORDER ENTRIES data flow is passed directly to the CHECK CUSTOMER process.

Customer checking involves comparing the customer on an order with those retained in the firm's customer master. The master is searched for the customer on this order. When customers are not found in the master, they are contacted to obtain valid customer information. If the customer on the order is valid but does not appear in the master, the customer is added to the master. If valid customer data cannot be obtained from the customer, the order is canceled. If valid data is obtained, the customer order is modified. If an order passes the CHECK CUSTOMER process or passes through the MODIFY CUSTOMER ENTRY process, a data flow labeled VERIFIED CUSTOMER flows to the CHECK DELINQUENCY process. The CHECK DELINQUENCY process retrieves the customer's delinquency records for excessive or outstanding delinquencies. If the customer has a bad delinquency record, the order is canceled. If a bad delinquency record is not found, then VERIFIED CUST/DELINQ data is passed to the CHECK ITEM AVAILABILITY process.

The CHECK ITEM AVAILABILITY process checks the item master for available inventory to fill the order; note the flow from the FIND ITEM QUANTITY process. When an inadequate quantity exists for order filling, the customer is notified concerning items for which a back order must be created. If the back order is refused, the order is canceled. If the back order is approved, a customer back order is created. If an order passes item quantity validation, a valid order is passed as an output interface labeled VALID ORDER. This interface represents the data flow between the VALIDATE ORDERS and CREATE ORDER INVOICE processes on the GTOP0001 DFD of Figure 8-25. Recall that the VALIDATE ORDERS process explodes to the GTOP000101 DFD.

The NG&T project team concludes the logical design formal review with an explanation of the activities to be performed during the physical portion of the design phase. They do this so that all participants in the review have an understanding of the next portion of the development life cycle. By doing this, they also ensure continued commitment to the development project.

COMPUTER-AIDED LOGICAL DESIGN

The iterations of logical design require that the analyst be able to navigate rapidly through the specifications for the proposed system in order to make changes and verify the validity and comprehensiveness of the design. The use of CASE systems greatly enhances this process. The sheer volume of work related to entering dictionary entries for design components can prove to be a formidable barrier to an analyst's work.

CASE software systems can be used to enter or modify all of the specifications for the logical design. Diagrams produced during the analysis phase can be modified easily to produce logical design specifications. Components of the diagrams can be documented using design dictionary entry capabilities embedded within CASE tools. CASE systems provide easier capabilities for modifying diagrams and dictionary entries as the logical design progresses. All of the graphical diagrams in this chapter are facsimiles of entries that could have been entered using many of the currently available CASE software systems, such as IEW from KnowledgeWare, Excelerator from InterSolv, IEF from Texas Instruments, or ProKit from McDonnell Douglas, to name a few. The design dictionary entry examples in this chapter are also facsimiles of dictionary entries for these systems.

CASE tools also permit more comprehensive integration of the design specifications. While an analyst is creating one set of design components, he or she can easily explode to another set of components that have a relationship with components on a currently displayed diagram. This explosion can occur from a DFD process to a separate DFD; from a DFD entity, process, data flow, or data store to the dictionary entry accompanying the respective DFD component; from a DFD data flow or data store to the dictionary entry for LDSs; or from a dictionary LDS entry to either another LDS entry or a dictionary entry for data elements within the LDS. As a result, the integration and comprehensiveness of design specifications are likely to be much better. The greatest benefit of CASE tools may prove to be the enhancement of the quality of design, rather than the increase in speed as many IS professionals suggest.

Text from a standard word processor can be imported into design specifications by many CASE dictionaries for a more detailed text presentation of design. Much of the design that requires user review involves long and detailed explanations. These explanations can be created or modified by the user on a standard word processor and imported into the design specifications.

Furthermore, detailed programming specifications written in pseudocode or structured English can also be created using text from a standard word processor. These specifications are usually incorporated into CASE-supported design specifications during conversion of logical design specifications into physical design specifications. The "Text Description & Comments" sections of procedure dictionary entries provide an excellent place for these entries. This action will be explained in Chapter 9. These specifications provide less complicated transitions between logical design, physical design, and system development.

An additional feature of many CASE tools is the built-in capacity for validating diagrams. Most modeling methods have rules to guide analysts in creating diagrams. For example, Chapter 6 identified rules governing DFD construction; many CASE systems can report on areas of diagrams that violate those rules, such as unbalanced inputs and outputs between DFD levels. In addition, these CASE systems report on portions of diagrams that do not have accompanying design dictionary entries—that is, incompleteness of specifications. As a result of using these validation capabilities, the analyst can identify diagram areas that need additional work. Consequently, the accuracy and comprehensiveness of the design specifications are likely to be greater.

Still another feature of the CASE environment is that several analysts can create design specifications off-line on desktop computers. These separately stored specifications can either be imported into composite specifications on a separate desktop computer or stored on host computer storage reserved for this purpose. Each specification, either entered or modified, is marked with the ID number of the person performing the activity. Thus, the set of specifications has built-in audit documentation for project management purposes.

Finally, a number of CASE tools provide a way to have multiple versions of A&D specifications. These multiple versions are frequently called **generations of design**. This useful feature allows analysts to compare specifications from different generations of design and determine how comprehensively design efforts are incorporating changes resulting from decisions based on analysis specifications. Chapter 16, on maintenance, will explain that this feature is also extremely important for retaining different generations of design specifications that result from maintenance activities.

Retracing all of the diagrams and dictionary entries in this chapter will help you understand the results of using CASE systems for design purposes. However, just looking at these specifications does not convey the ease of using these tools. To properly understand the benefits of using CASE tools, you need a hands-on demonstration: "Better felt than telt."

The CASE environment promises an exciting future for analysis and design. CASE tools have the potential to revolutionize the way system development projects are conducted. Chapters 5 through 9 provide a visual and explanatory demonstration of the capabilities of the CASE environment.

Joint Application Design (JAD) Sessions for the Logical Design

Chapters 4 through 7 described the purpose and practice of JAD sessions (JADs) and explained how E/RDs, DFDs, and prototypes may be used during these sessions. JADs can also be used to create, review, and change these specifications during logical design.

CASE tools and visual-aid technologies can once again be used to review E/RDs, DFDs, and prototypes. As users describe changes from analysis specifications to logical design specifications, project team members can create additional logical design specifications or modify analysis specifications. As users make suggestions, scribes either create new specifications or modify existing ones. Thus, JADs can continue to contribute to the accuracy and completeness of the user requirements as the project moves from the analysis phase to logical design.

REVIEW

This chapter discusses creating and refining the logical design to better satisfy user requirements. Attributes of user requirements are refined based on the results from the analysis phase and prototyping. A series of questions can be asked, the responses to which determine what capabilities the system project can provide within the time and budget allowed. The activities in logical design focus on developing a logical model of the system using E/RD and DFD modeling methods and dictionary entries. E/RDs and DFDs developed in the analysis phase are modified during this phase in order to conform to the proposed design.

Detailed examples from the NG&T case show how user responses influence changes in the design. A formal review of the logical design, similar to the review at the end of the analysis phase, is conducted. This review concludes with all participants signing an agreement committing them to the successful implementation of the logical design and to continuation of the system development life cycle.

Finally, using CASE systems and JADs during logical design is beneficial in reducing clerical tasks associated with modifying E/RDs, DFDs, and dictionary entries. They can also be used to validate diagrams, to allow several levels of diagrams to be opened at once, and to provide multiple versions of A&D specifications. With CASE systems, it is possible for several analysts to create design specifications off-line, and then to integrate various sets of specifications.

The combination of the activities described in this chapter prepares the way to developing the information system model that guides system development. The logical business model should now be complete and up-to-date. These specifications help to ensure that the design is solving the right problem with the best solution. Converting the business process model into a procedure model can now begin, with data modeling specifications reused as needed.

QUESTIONS

1. What are the three main aspects to consider relative to integrating system development/modification projects with the overall activities of the business? Explain why these factors are important.

2. For a company in your vicinity, describe how one of its systems projects affected the functional business.

3. Explain the relationship between the levels of management and systems designed to service functional areas of the business.

4. Define critical success factors and explain how they influence the success of activities.

5. For a company in your vicinity, identify and describe its CSFs.

6. Define user requirements and list five examples of them.

7. For a company in your vicinity, obtain a list of its user requirements for one of its systems projects.

8. When are the majority of user requirements ascertained?

9. What is one method of ensuring that systems will be developed on time and within budget, and will be acceptable to users?

10. Where do the largest percentages of errors occur in the development life cycle? Explain why recognition of the places where errors occur has increased the interest in analysis and design.

11. What types of errors lead to the largest expenditure of effort to correct?

12. What is constructed during the logical design and what is it based on?

13. List and describe the major activities of logical design.

14. When is data that is used during the logical design categorized and aggregated?

15. List and explain the steps in the iterative activities of design.

16. Why should the design be very close to completion at the point of the formal review?

17. What is the relationship between the diagrams produced during the analysis phase and those produced during logical design?

18. Thoroughly explain the relationship between prototyping and the diagrams produced during logical design.

19. Explain why there are differences between the E/RDs in Figures 5-37 and 8-6. List the main differences and explain them.

20. Explain why there are differences between the E/RDs in Figures 5-38 and 8-10. List the main differences and explain them.

21. What do the terms *single-valued* and *multivalued* mean relative to the type specifications for data element descriptions within relationship dictionary entries?

22. Explain why there is no VALIDATE ORDERS process on the GTOP00 DFD of Figure 8-15. Relate this to the decisions made by the analysis review committee.

23. Explain the purpose for the MPHY-CUSTORDR data entry and the accompanying dictionary entry for the LOG-CUSTTRNS LDS dictionary entry of Figure 8-12.

24. Explain the purpose for the CARRIER MANIFEST data store and data flows on the GTOP0001 DFD of Figure 8-17.

25. Thoroughly explain each process (purpose, results, and relationship to the other processes) on the GTOP000101 DFD of Figure 8-21.

26. Explain the purpose for the CUSTOMER BACKORDER data store on the GTOP000101 DFD of Figure 8-21.

27. Where is the processing of the data contained in the CUSTOMER BACK-ORDER data store documented in the set of order processing DFDs?

28. Explain how intermittent review by users, followed by design modifications, causes the logical design to more comprehensively conform to user requirements.

29. What is the purpose for the formal review at the conclusion of logical design?

30. Who should participate in the logical design formal review and why?

31. What is the main objective of the logical design formal review?

32. For a company in your vicinity, obtain a copy of the documentation for a logical design formal review for one of its systems projects.

33. Why should logical design conclude with a sign-off document, and what does this document represent to those who sign it?

34. For a company in your vicinity, obtain a copy of a sign-off document for one of its systems projects.

35. Explain the differences in the DFDs of Figures 8-14, 8-15, 8-17, and 8-21 and those in Figures 8-23 through 8-26 and explain why these changes were deemed necessary.

EXERCISES

Chapter 8 of the student workbook contains blank documentation forms to use in the following exercises.

1. Create a lower-level detail E/RD and accompanying design dictionary entries for an explosion on the ACCOUNTS CLERK entity of the GTOP00 E/RD of Figure 8-6.

2. Create a lower-level detail E/RD and accompanying design dictionary entries for an explosion on the SHIP/RECVG CLERK entity of the GTOP00 E/RD of Figure 8-6.

3. Create a lower-level detailed DFD diagram and accompanying design dictionary entries resulting from an explosion on the ORDER VENDOR ITEMS process of the GTOP00 DFD of Figure 8-24 (also include lower-level DFDs with accompanying dictionary entries).

4. Create a lower-level detailed DFD and accompanying design dictionary entries resulting from an explosion on the COMPLETE RETAIL INVOICES process of the GTOP00 DFD of Figure 8-24 (also include lower-level DFDs with accompanying dictionary entries).

5. Create a lower-level detailed DFD diagram and accompanying design dictionary entries resulting from an explosion on the RECONCILE CUSTOMER ACCOUNTS process of the GTOP00 DFD of Figure 8-24 (also include lower-level DFDs with accompanying dictionary entries).

6. Create a lower-level detailed DFD and accompanying design dictionary entries resulting from an explosion on the PRODUCE MANAGER REPORTS process of the GTOP00 DFD of Figure 8-24 (also include lower-level DFDs with accompanying dictionary entries).

SELECTED REFERENCES

Boehm, B. W. 1981. *Software Engineering Economics*. Englewood Cliffs, NJ: Prentice-Hall.

Martin, J. and C. McClure. 1988. *Maintenance: The Problem and Its Solutions*. Englewood Cliffs, NJ: Prentice-Hall.

Martin, J. and C. McClure. 1988. *Structured Techniques: The Basis for CASE*. Englewood Cliffs, NJ: Prentice-Hall.

Martin, J. 1984. *An Information Systems Manifesto*. Englewood Cliffs, NJ: Prentice-Hall.

Rockart, J. F. 1979. "Chief Executives Define Their Own Data Needs." *Harvard Business Review* 57, no. 2 (March–April 1979).

Rockart, J. F. and D. W. DeLong. 1988. *Executive Support Systems: The Emergence of Top Management Computer Use*. Homewood, IL: Dow Jones–Irwin.

CHAPTER 9

Physical Design Criteria Using Procedure Modeling Methods

OVERVIEW

During the physical design (or the information system design), the analyst adapts user requirements obtained during the logical design to information system requirements that will procedurally supply the user's information needs. The logical business design discussed in Chapter 8 represents what the user desires, and the physical design indicates how to meet and support these desires. This chapter discusses physical requirements of the system design and shows how to develop the physical design by describing:

- The principles of good physical design
- Modeling methods used in the physical design
- Physical design dictionary entries
- Identification of computer program boundaries and specifications
- Physical design formal review
- Computer-aided physical design

KEY TERMS

Application generators
Artificial boss
Boss module
Case structure analysis
Central area of transform
Cohesion
Control flag symbol
Control module
Coupling
Data flag symbol
First-cut STC
Information systems re-engineering

Labels
Local boss
Loop symbol
Or/selection symbol
Predefined procedure symbol
Procedure symbol
Refined STC
Size (of structure chart)
Span of control
Structure charts (STCs)
Transaction analysis
Transform analysis

The physical design provides guidance for development of the system. It results from mapping user requirements documented during logical business design into specifications for the physical aspects of the system, thus providing a blueprint for translating the logical design into the physical design. The physical design is then implemented in the development phase of the project life cycle, as you will see in Chapter 11.

The main physical requirement is the procedure model, which becomes the heart of the programs that compose the system. In Chapter 3 we discussed the alternatives for a system project: modify the existing system, replace the existing system with a purchased system, or replace the existing system with a system developed by the firm's systems analysts. This chapter focuses on creating a procedure model either as a replacement in th e existing system or as the main physical requirement for a system being developed within the business.

Analysts create a procedure model following the principles, activities, and diagramming methods of physical design described in this chapter. Computer program specifications are then identified from physical design specifications. Figure 9-1 illustrates the area of the enterprise/methodology model on which the actions of this chapter focus.

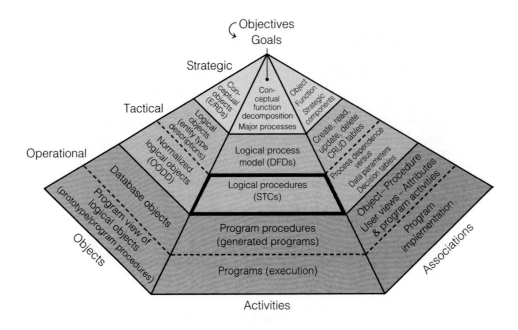

Figure 9-1. Enterprise/methodology model focus of Chapter 9

PRINCIPLES OF GOOD PHYSICAL DESIGN

During logical business design activities, the analyst produces user requirements for the business system with no regard for the physical information system. The analyst's only desire during this stage is to understand the needs of the user. The analyst defines the data and processing activities necessary to meet user information needs, constructing the logical solution without considering the physical information system or the constraints imposed by the physical environment of the firm. Once the logical business design is completed, the specifications provide the guidance necessary for physically implementing the needs of the user. *Mapping the logical business design into the physical design* represents adapting logical user requirements to physical specifications.

During the physical design, the analyst changes from the *what* and *why* orientation of logical business design to the *how* orientation of physical design. Logical design focuses on what processes are performed, what objects are served or used in those processes, and what data flows between processes. Physical design focuses on how processes are performed, how objects are served or used in those processes, and how data flows between processes. Physical design transforms processes identified during logical business design into procedures that indicate how to complete those processes.

During physical design, the analyst also specifies how to assemble the data elements that make up logical data structures (LDSs) to characterize objects served or used during those procedures. For example, procedures that create a payroll check must also specify the LDSs used as input to create the pay check amounts, such as gross wage, deduction amounts, and net wage.

PHYSICAL DESIGN MODELING METHODS

A number of modeling methods exist to aid the analyst in defining user requirements for the physical design. The physical design centers primarily on creating procedure models to implement the business process models. Some of the more popular methods used by practicing analysts are:

- Hierarchy plus input-process-output (HIPO) charts
- Nassi-Schneiderman charts
- Structure charts
- Warnier/Orr (W/O) diagrams
- Action diagrams

The text methodology uses the structure chart (STC) modeling method for procedure modeling. However, it would be a simple matter to replace the STC modeling method with any of the other procedure modeling methods without harming the completeness of the methodology. The main reason for using the STC procedure modeling method is that a method already exists to convert a business process model in data flow diagram (DFD) format into a procedure model in STC format. Since the text methodology uses the STC method, this chapter focuses on explaining this modeling method and using an enhanced version of the existing method to convert a DFD into a STC.

Structure Charts

Structure charts are probably the most widely accepted structured design modeling method used to create procedure models. **Structure charts (STCs)** are graphical models that provide an outline of physical program procedures; they are laid out in a style consistent with the principles of structured programming. STCs are blueprints for structured programs that contain the procedures necessary to facilitate processing and support the required data flows. STCs are models that typically decompose the procedures of a system on a single diagramming surface. That is, they have only one level, as opposed to the entity/relationship diagrams (E/RDs) and DFDs in Chapters 5, 6, and 8. Ed Yourdon and Larry Constantine pioneered the development of so-called optimal STCs for programs from a logical DFD, and Kathleen Dolan originated what is currently the most widely accepted method for converting DFDs into STCs.

Understanding Structure Charts

A STC can be an intermediate step between diagramming logical business requirements using DFDs and creating written specifications for structured programs to satisfy these logical user requirements. A STC is a physical design specification equivalent to the DFD that is used as an initial specification for a structured program. Once a STC is created, you have an outline of a structured program that is conceptually equivalent to the logical DFD. This outline contains the specifications for procedures to facilitate the input-process-output activities consistent with the way the firm's programmers create structured programs.

Programmers properly trained in structured programming methods view the procedures of a program from the top down, with separate program modules for separate procedures. A close look at a set of modules for a basic structured program will provide the basis for understanding the format of STCs and the purpose they serve in a structured methodology.

Since the early 1970s, structured programming has been recognized by personnel in IS departments as the desired approach for creating more easily maintained programs. The modules of a structured program represent separate sets of procedures to accomplish the purposes of the program. The first program module of a structured program is the basic **control module** for the program, sometimes called the driver routine or **boss module**. All other program modules are either called on for execution by the control module or subsequently called on by program modules already called on by the control module.

COBOL STRUCTURED PROGRAMMING EXAMPLE   In structured programs that use the COBOL programming language, the PERFORM statement is typically used to call for the execution of subsequent program modules. For example, the control module of a structured COBOL program usually only contains PERFORM statements that call for execution of the remaining program modules in the program. Commands similar to the COBOL PERFORM statement exist in other high-level languages used to create structured programs. Figure 9-2 illustrates the fundamental format for a structured COBOL program using the division of the COBOL language that describes the procedures of the program. Note that the CONTROL-ROUTINE procedure is the control module for this structured COBOL program. You should be able to envision a version of this example in other high-level languages.

The CONTROL-ROUTINE module represents the boss module for the structured program outline of Figure 9-2. Notice that this module contains no actual processing activities of its own. It only controls the way to call on each of the remaining program modules for execution. In addition, notice that the READ-ROUTINE module is called on for execution from within the LOOP-ROUTINE module. Structured programming permits the creation of short, easy-to-understand modules for the different activities required by the program, resulting in easy-to-understand and maintainable programs.

```
PROCEDURE DIVISION.
CONTROL-ROUTINE.
     PERFORM OPEN-FILES-ROUTINE.
     PERFORM READ-ROUTINE.
     PERFORM LOOPING-ROUTINE
          UNTIL EOF = 'Y'.
     PERFORM CLOSE-ROUTINE.
     STOP RUN.
OPEN-FILES-ROUTINE.
     OPEN INPUT ... OUTPUT ....
LOOPING-ROUTINE
     MOVE ....
     .
     .
     .
     WRITE ....
     PERFORM READ-ROUTINE.
READ-ROUTINE.
     READ ...
          AT END MOVE 'Y' TO EOF.
CLOSE-ROUTINE.
     CLOSE ....
```

Figure 9-2. Basic format of a structured COBOL program

Structure Chart Format and Basic Symbols

Structure charts are created using diagram symbols and a fundamental format. Figure 9-3 shows the symbols used to create a STC.

The **procedure symbol** in Figure 9-3 represents a procedure to execute a set of individual actions; it characterizes a portion of program logic to be created by programmers. Each procedure symbol usually signifies an intricate part of the procedures required to correctly process the data needed by that portion of a program. A procedure often becomes a program section with individual instructions in that section, such as the READ-ROUTINE of the COBOL program in Figure 9-2. A dictionary entry for a STC procedure symbol usually contains individual pseudocode statements for the instructions to execute for that procedure. Thus, calling on a procedure actually causes its set of instructions to execute, such as the "call" from the CONTROL-ROUTINE to the READ-ROUTINE in the COBOL example in Figure 9-2. The COBOL statement PERFORM READ-ROUTINE is functionally equivalent to a STC CALL statement.

The **predefined procedure symbol** in Figure 9-3 represents a procedure for which

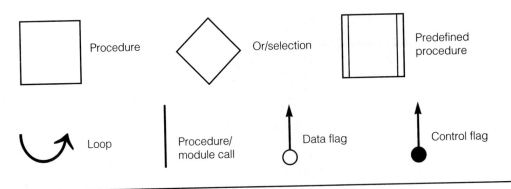

Figure 9-3. Basic structure chart symbols

a processing routine already exists to perform its actions. The appearance of a predefined procedure symbol on a STC indicates that this existing routine occurs at that point in the procedure. Thus, a call to a predefined routine executes all of the instructions contained in that predefined routine. These predefined instructions are usually expressed in reusable code that is available within the firm's IS department. Predefined routines may also specify manufacturer-supplied or home-grown utilities frequently needed by the firm's systems. For example, utility programs for sequencing data are usually acquired from the manufacturer of the computer. A predefined procedure may be called on before and during the execution of one of the firm's application programs. A STC created for these programs includes calls to predefined procedure symbols that symbolize these utilities at the appropriate points in the logic of the STC.

Labels inserted on the procedure and predefined procedure symbols identify the actions to perform at those points in the logic of the proposed program. These labels are functionally equivalent to the labels used for DFD process symbols, but they should imply *how* to proceed as well as *what* action to perform. Labels should concisely identify the purposes of the operations involved in the procedure. These labels sometimes become program section headings when the program is actually created, such as the READ-ROUTINE procedure name in the COBOL example in Figure 9-2.

The straight line (procedure/module call) in Figure 9-3 is used to connect STC procedures. The **procedure/module call symbol** is depicted as a connection between an upper procedure symbol and lower procedure symbols on a STC and actually specifies a call from the upper procedure to the lower ones. The STC format usually interprets procedure calls from the top of the diagram to the bottom and from left to right, following the top-down approach within structured programming principles.

The **loop symbol** in Figure 9-3 encircles calls to a sequence of procedures below the calling procedure to indicate that the calls occur in a repetitive fashion. The loop symbol is functionally equivalent to the iteration construct of good program design.

The **data flag symbol** in Figure 9-3 represents a logical data object and is inserted beside a call connection to indicate when calls from one procedure to another also pass a logical data object between the two procedures. The direction of the data flag arrow indicates the direction in which to pass data between the two procedures. For example, a call to a procedure that inputs data may have a data flag labeled "INPUT DATA" pointing up along the call to that procedure.

A **control flag symbol** inserted beside a call connection indicates when calls from one procedure cause a control condition to be passed between the procedures. For example, a call to a procedure to find a particular data object may return a control flag labeled "NOT FOUND" to signify that the data object was not found. This control flag can then be used to change the control of the STC to some other procedure. The direction of the arrow on the control flag indicates the direction in which to pass the control data value between procedures.

An **or/selection symbol** inserted at the bottom of a procedure with calls emanating from it indicates that the procedures below it are called on in an either/or fashion. Either the first procedure beneath the calling procedure containing the or/selection symbol is called on, or the next, or the next, and so on. A data flag or control flag passed from or to the calling procedure symbol often helps determine which procedure connected below it is called on.

SEQUENCE, ITERATION, AND SELECTION   Recall that a procedure model must conform to the three major constructs of good software engineering: sequence, iteration, and selection. The *sequence* of STC procedure calls normally occurs from the top down and from left to right, unless the sequence is interrupted by the detection of some control condition. This means that a STC normally issues calls from an upper procedure to all lower procedures connected to it from left to right. This also means that a call from a first-tier procedure to a second-tier procedure that calls on third-tier procedures causes execution of those third-tier procedures before continuing the execution of additional second-tier procedures connected to the first-tier procedure. To illustrate, consider the use of data flags and control flags, sequence, iteration, and selection of calls for the STC in Figure 9-4.

When the CONTROL-ROUTINE in Figure 9-4 calls on the READ-ROUTINE, it conceptually causes the DATA data flag to be passed from the READ-ROUTINE to the CONTROL-ROUTINE. The arrow points in the direction of the CONTROL-ROUTINE, indicating that the DATA logical data object passes from the READ-ROUTINE to the CONTROL-ROUTINE. This call causes the input of the first logical data object (equivalent to a record) in a set of serial data objects (equivalent to a file). This input action corresponds to the "prime-the-pump" input found in most structured programs that input and process *serial-access* data objects.

The prime-the-pump first input action occurs so that the routines that process data can be created such that they assume the input of the data. By making this assumption, they can be written without interrupting the flow of actions to perform on the data regarding what to do in processing it. At the end of the processing activities, an input action attempts to get the next data object. If a data object is input, the control module calls on the processing routine to process that data object and inputs the next data object. If the end of the data is reached (no data object is input), the control mod-

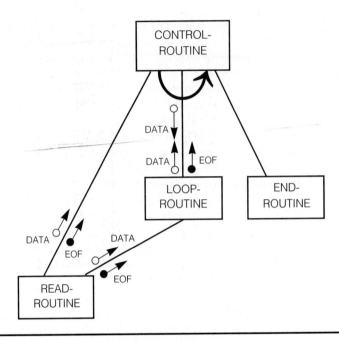

Figure 9-4. Example of a basic structure chart

ule does not call on the processing routine; it typically ends the program execution.

The call from the CONTROL-ROUTINE to the LOOP-ROUTINE in Figure 9-4, which is encircled by the loop symbol, causes the looping execution to commence, and it continues until no more DATA remains to be manipulated. The iterative calls continue until the LOOP-ROUTINE actually passes the EOF control flag up to the CONTROL-ROUTINE.

When the LOOP-ROUTINE in Figure 9-4 calls on the READ-ROUTINE, it conceptually causes the DATA data flag to be passed from the READ-ROUTINE to the LOOP-ROUTINE. The arrow points in the direction of the LOOP-ROUTINE, indicating that the DATA logical data object passes from the READ-ROUTINE to the LOOP-ROUTINE.

In Figure 9-4, the end-of-file (EOF) control flag pointing from the READ-ROUTINE is used to indicate when an end-of-data condition occurs. This control condition causes the end-of-data condition to be passed between the READ-ROUTINE and the LOOP-ROUTINE. The arrow for the EOF control flag points in the direction of the LOOP-ROUTINE from the READ-ROUTINE. Notice that the EOF control flag is then passed from the LOOP-ROUTINE to the CONTROL-ROUTINE. The control flag is a signal to the CONTROL-ROUTINE to call on the END-ROUTINE and stop the execution of the STC. Although the STC does not actually indicate this in the diagram, text entries in the dictionary entry of the CONTROL-ROUTINE procedure would specify what the EOF control flag indicates and causes in procedure control.

The STC in Figure 9-4 illustrates the basic procedures of a serial-execution routine that inputs a set of serially ordered logical data objects and processes them individually until the end of the logical data object set is reached. The STC calls in Figure 9-4 occur in the following order:

1. The CONTROL-ROUTINE boss module calls the READ-ROUTINE.
2. The CONTROL-ROUTINE boss module calls the LOOP-ROUTINE.
3. The LOOP-ROUTINE local boss calls the READ-ROUTINE.
4. The CONTROL-ROUTINE continues to call the LOOP-ROUTINE.
5. The CONTROL-ROUTINE boss module calls the END-ROUTINE.

In call number 1, the CONTROL-ROUTINE calls on the READ-ROUTINE to read the first logical data object—that is, the normal prime-the-pump data input for a structured program that acts on serially ordered data objects (as previously described). In call number 2, the CONTROL-ROUTINE calls on the LOOP-ROUTINE to process the first data object (notice the DATA data flag passed from the boss module to the LOOP-ROUTINE). In call number 3, the LOOP-ROUTINE calls on the READ-ROUTINE to get the next logical data object on which to act (note that this data object will be acted on in the next iteration of the call from the CONTROL-ROUTINE to the LOOP-ROUTINE). Call number 4 continues the calls from the CONTROL-ROUTINE to the LOOP-ROUTINE until the EOF control flag is passed from the READ-ROUTINE to the LOOP-ROUTINE and subsequently passed from the LOOP- ROUTINE to the CONTROL-ROUTINE. When the EOF control flag is passed up to the CONTROL-ROUTINE, call number 5 from the CONTROL-ROUTINE to the END-ROUTINE ends the STC execution.

CONVERTING LOGICAL BUSINESS DESIGN DATA FLOW DIAGRAMS (DFDS) INTO PHYSICAL DESIGN STRUCTURE CHARTS (STCS)

Remember that analysts create DFDs during analysis and logical business design activities without constraining their interpretations of business requirements with information system and physical environment considerations. Analysts consider only the actions users perform and their information needs, not how to physically perform those actions to satisfy those needs. After analysts create the DFDs representing the logical business design, they create specifications that show how to physically implement the logical business design. They may accomplish this by converting DFDs with a logical business orientation into STCs with a physical information system orientation. Figure 9-5 lists the steps involved in deriving STCs from DFDs.

Obtain a First-Cut STC

1. Identify the set of DFDs to convert to STCs.
2. Identify the boss (control*) module.
3. Perform transform and/or transaction analysis on DFDs.

Refine the First-Cut STC

4. Insert data flags and/or control flags as needed.
5. Determine cohesiveness of program modules.
6. Perform coupling/decoupling activities on program modules.
7. Evaluate the span of control for program modules.

*Hereafter, the terms *boss module* and *control module* should be considered synonymous.

Figure 9-5. Steps for deriving STCs from DFDs

Be aware that conversion of DFDs into STCs involves a certain amount of subjective judgment. Conversion normally follows a procedure that:

- Applies a systematic set of rules to obtain an initial or **first-cut STC**
- Applies a set of rules to obtain a **refined STC**

Thus, after applying systematic conversion rules, you must subjectively apply refining rules that require knowledge of the application and of how programs are normally structured.

Identifying Data Flow Diagrams to Convert to Structure Charts

It is important to realize that not all DFDs are converted into STCs. Selecting a DFD to convert into an equivalent STC requires subjective evaluation of the DFDs by the analyst. The upper-level DFDs only represent overviews of processes and data flows contained in the logical business design. The lower-level DFDs that represent process explosions on upper-level DFDs provide details that often require physical implementation. Usually, only lower-level DFDs are considered for conversion into STCs. However, more DFDs than just the very bottom-level DFD on an explosion path may be converted into STCs. Several DFD levels on a particular explosion path at lower levels may be selected to convert into STCs.

Designing the STC can entail a top-down approach similar to that used in designing DFDs, with each procedure symbol on a STC capable of exploding to a lower-level STC to depict even greater procedural details. The analyst might elect to create a

STC for one DFD level that contains separate process symbols that explode to even lower-level DFDs. The procedure symbols corresponding to these explosion processes on the converted upper-level STC would be described as exploding to the STCs converted from the lower-level DFDs to which those DFD processes explode.

Identifying the Boss Module

A DFD converted to a STC usually has a number of interrelated processes that share data. Kathleen Dolan furnished a formal method for converting DFDs to STCs that is currently the most popular conversion method. Dolan's conversion method represents a modification of an earlier Yourdon and Constantine approach.

The first conversion action identifies the control module—that is, the boss procedure. Dolan specifies that the boss should be selected from the area of the DFD where the most input/output (I/O) actions occur. Dolan assumes that by selecting a process from this area, you are isolating the area of the DFD that represents the main controlling section for the rest of the DFD. Using this basic premise, Dolan and others suggest the following two primary boss selection methods:

- Select the process on the DFD with the largest number of data flows going to and from it as the boss module.
- If no single process with the largest number of data flows exists, choose the DFD area containing two or more processes with the largest number of data flows. Then either select one of those processes as the boss, collapse those processes into a single process, or insert a new procedure symbol on the DFD (**artificial boss**) and connect it to the processes having the largest number of data flows.

Regardless of the boss selection criteria used, the area where the largest number of data flows occurs is called the **central area of transform**. Examples will help clarify these two boss selection criteria. Figure 9-6 shows a DFD for which a single process, RECORD TRANSACTION, has the most I/O connections. The process corresponding to using Dolan's boss selection method would be selected as the central area of transform and selected as the boss module. The dotted-line box around the RECORD TRANSACTION process symbol indicates that it is the boss module.

Figure 9-7 illustrates the next step in the conversion method. The process identified as the central transform is physically moved to the top of the diagram with all connections remaining intact between the remaining processes, stores, and entities. These retained connections move downward from the central transform process to the other processes. Notice that all connections still remain between the RECORD TRANSACTION process and other DFD symbols in Figure 9-7.

Figure 9-8 shows a DFD for which no single process contains the most I/Os. The two processes VERIFY CHARGE and RECORD CHARGE on this DFD both have the largest number of data flows (five). Notice that an area of the DFD encompassing both VERIFY CHARGE and RECORD CHARGE is boxed in as the central area of transform in Figure 9-8, with each process considered a candidate for the boss module.

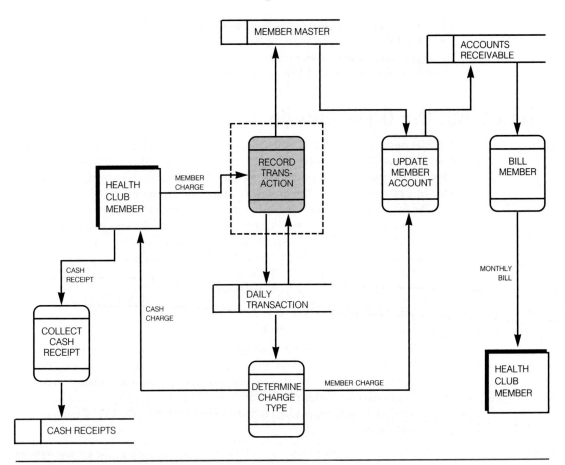

Figure 9-6. Boss selection DFD

Some analysts will simply select one of the processes as the central transform and use that process as the boss module. Other analysts will collapse these two processes into a single process and use this process as boss. When those processes are collapsed into a single process, that single process will retain all data flows leading into and out of all those original processes. A third option is to insert an artificial procedure symbol and connect it to all processes within the area of central transform. Regardless of the option selected, the boss module is then positioned at the top of the STC. Figure 9-9 illustrates the third option for boss selection for the DFD in Figure 9-8. You should be able to envision how to perform the first and second options from the example in Figure 9-8.

In Figure 9-9, COMPLETE UPDATE CHARGES is the artificially created central transform process. Notice that this process is connected to both VERIFY CHARGE

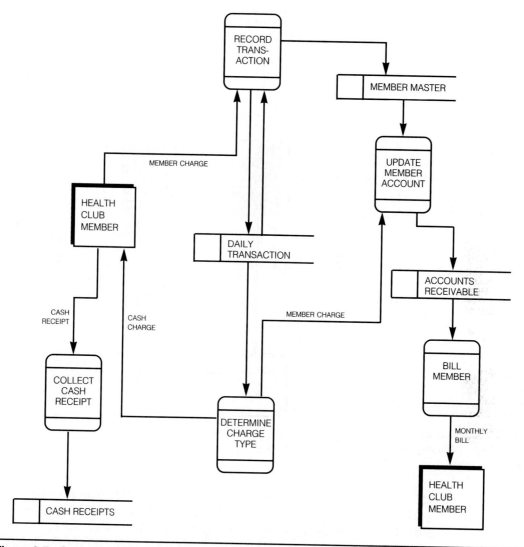

Figure 9-7. Central transform moved to the top as the boss module

and RECORD CHARGE and that all connections to these processes remain connected to the artificial boss.

For each example in Figures 9-7 and 9-9, applying the remaining steps of transform analysis would cause all the DFD process, entity, and data store symbols to become STC procedures. The data flows between these procedure symbols would then become calls between them, with data flags and control flags inserted as necessary.

Remember that design is always an iterative process involving the creation and modification of specifications for a system. The conversion of a DFD into the first-cut

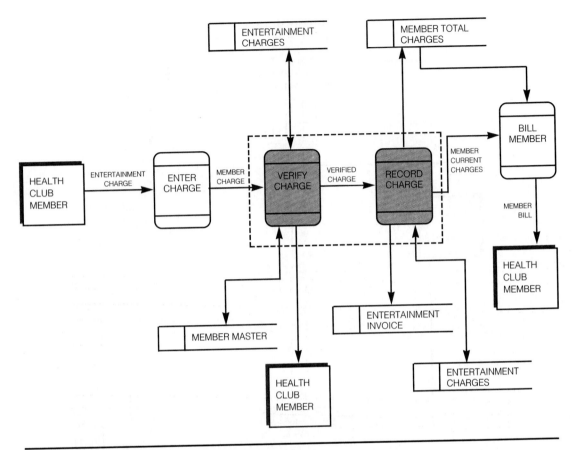

Figure 9-8. Artificially selected area of central transform

STC represents the first operation in converting logical DFDs into physical design specifications. Subsequent iterations of procedure modeling activities refine the STC derived as the first-cut equivalent of an original DFD. With this in mind, notice the call inserted between COMPLETE UPDATE CHARGES and the ENTER CHARGE process in Figure 9-9. Since entering charges occurs before verifying and processing charges, ENTER CHARGE should be the first procedure called on by the boss module. Hence, a connection is inserted between COMPLETE UPDATE CHARGES and the ENTER CHARGE process.

The artificial boss selection example illustrates how subjective judgment is used while adhering to a particular set of structured design rules. Design does not completely follow a "cookbook" method. You cannot closely follow some recipe for system design and expect a good design to result, even when carefully applying the rules of a structured methodology. There is a great deal of subjectivity within these rules. This requires that the analyst take off her business modeler's hat (or information engineer's hat) and put on her programmer's hat (or software engineer's hat).

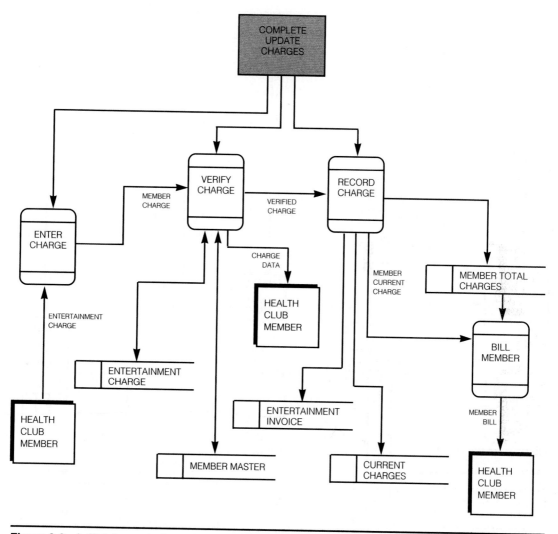

Figure 9-9. Artificially created central transform procedure

Recommended Boss Selection Method

There is a problem associated with using the first selection method of choosing the process with the most I/O data flows as the boss. As stated earlier, frequently several DFD levels along an explosion path require conversion to STCs. When this occurs, it often happens that the DFD process selected as boss on one DFD level, using Dolan's boss selection criteria, also explodes to a lower-level DFD. For example, the GTOP0001 DFD in Figure 8-25 of Chapter 8 would be a likely candidate for conversion to a STC. This DFD is reproduced in Figure 9-10.

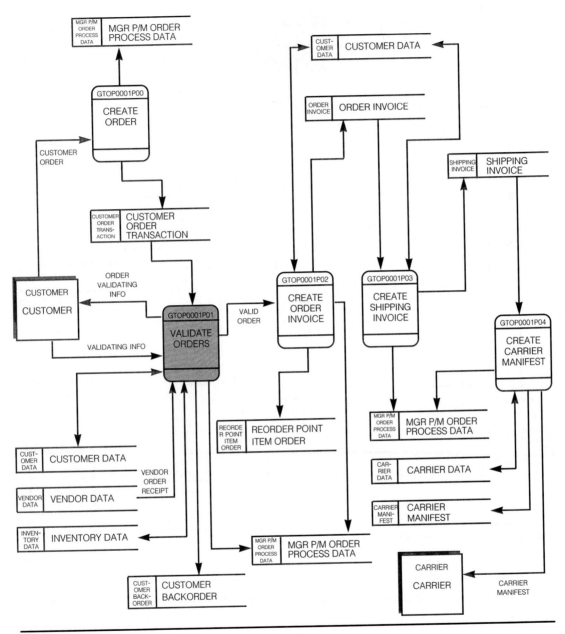

Figure 9-10. GTOP0001 DFD

Clearly, the process in Figure 9-10 to select as the boss, using Dolan's first selection method, is the VALIDATE ORDERS process, the process with the most data flows connected to it. Using this boss selection rule, the analyst would move this process to the top of the DFD and designate it as the control process for the entire STC converted from the GTOP0001 DFD. Recall from Chapter 8 that this process also explodes to a lower-level DFD (GTOP000101 in Figure 8-26), which contains the details of validating an order.

The boss module at the top of a STC is functionally equivalent to the control routine in a structured program. In a structured program, the only purpose of this routine is to control the calls to the remaining modules, where actual processing occurs. By selecting the VALIDATE ORDERS process and moving it to the top, you would now have a process as a boss that also explodes to a lower-level DFD. This lower-level DFD would also be converted into a STC equivalent. Thus, the boss on one STC would explode to a lower-level STC that would provide the details of the processing activities involved in validating an order. Since the only purpose of the STC boss is to control the remainder of the STC, having it also explode to a lower-level STC depicting the details of its processing makes absolutely no sense. Figure 9-11 depicts this senseless situation.

The top portion of Figure 9-11 illustrates the changes in GTOP0001 resulting from selecting the VALIDATE ORDERS process as the boss and moving it to the top of the DFD. The bottom of Figure 9-11 depicts the GTOP000101 DFD with an explosion path leading to it from the VALIDATE ORDERS process on the partially converted GTOP0001 DFD.

The situation depicted in Figure 9-11 frequently arises while converting multiple DFD levels into STCs. In fact, the process having the most I/O data flows is the process on any DFD that is most likely to explode to a more detailed lower-level DFD; it is the process that is doing the most. Thus, it appears that the first boss selection criterion is backwards. The process with the most connections is the *least likely* candidate for boss.

The first boss selection criterion would always work if only the lowest level DFDs were converted and if these DFDs were all functional primitives. However, it frequently happens that several DFD levels along an explosion path provide details requiring conversion to physical design procedures. Furthermore, it often happens that a DFD at the lowest level of explosion may have processes with more than two data flows attached to them. When this DFD is completely understood by the analysts and the users, an explosion on a DFD process with more than two data flows down to another level would only produce a trivial DFD and would therefore be needless. Remember that exploding down to functional primitives along each explosion path is only a *design goal*, not something that should always happen.

Every DFD level has a natural boss process. The natural boss for a level-2 DFD is the process from which explosion occurred on the level-1 DFD. For example, the natural boss for the GTOP0001 DFD in Figure 9-10 is the process from which explosion occurred on the GTOP00 DFD in Figure 8-24 of Chapter 8. This process is the COMPLETE PHONE/MAIL INVOICES process. Envision the GTOP00 and GTOP0001 DFDs in three-dimensional space. Also envision invisible connection lines between the COMPLETE PHONE/MAIL INVOICES process on the GTOP00 DFD and all of the processes on the GTOP0001 DFD. Flatten this picture out into two dimensions, and you have a DFD with a selected boss (COMPLETE PHONE/MAIL INVOICES) at the top of the DFD. Figures 9-12 and 9-13 symbolize these actions.

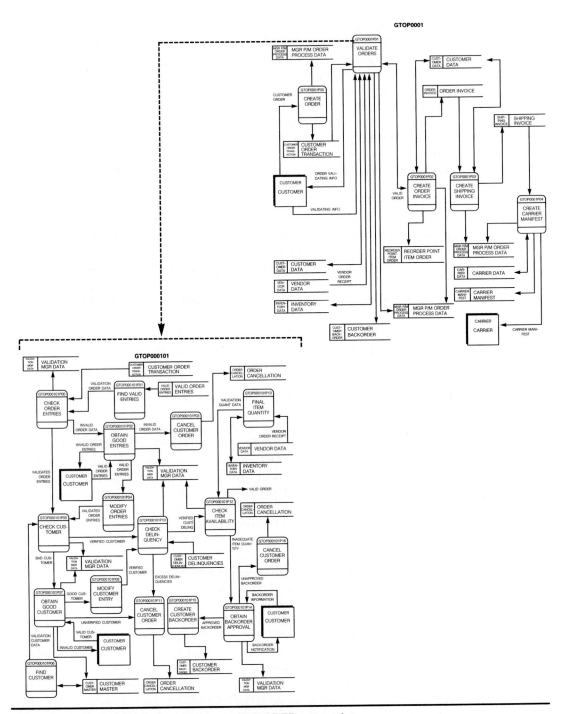

Figure 9-11. Boss selection problem for multilevel DFD conversion

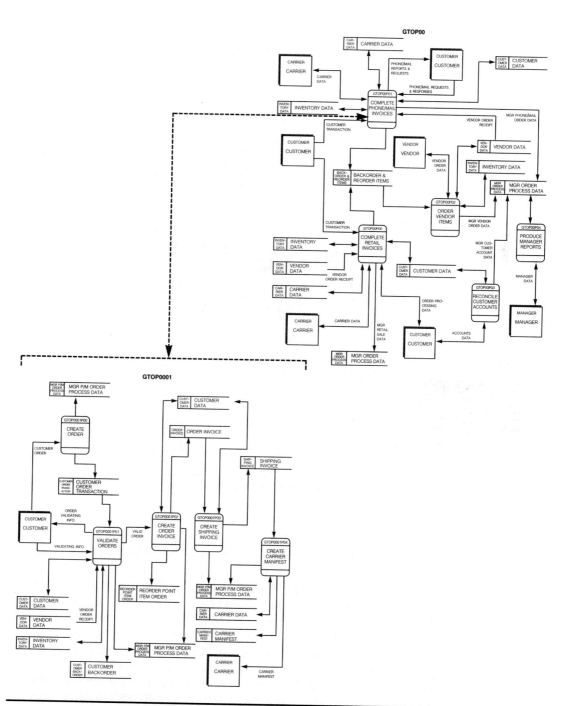

Figure 9-12. GTOP0001 with a boss from GTOP00

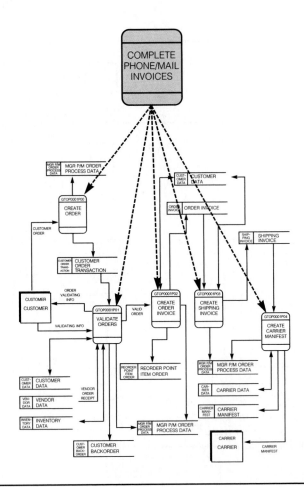

Figure 9-13. GTOP0001 with its selected boss

As Figures 9-12 and 9-13 show, the preferred method is to artificially insert the explosion process on the previous DFD level as a boss on a DFD being converted to a STC. Here, the boss for the GTOP0001 level-2 DFD in Figure 9-10 is the COM-PLETE PHONE/MAIL INVOICES process, the explosion process on the GTOP00 level-1 DFD above this level-2 DFD. Subsequently, the boss for the GTOP000101 level-3 DFD in Figure 8-26 is the VALIDATE ORDERS process, the explosion process on the GTOP0001 level-2 DFD. This boss selection criterion works under all circumstances and is also consistent with certain STC refining operations performed after completing the conversion to the first-cut STC. Figures 9-14 and 9-15 also sym-bolize three-dimensional to two-dimensional boss insertion for the GTOP000101 DFD of Figure 8-26. Notice that the VALIDATE ORDERS process from the GTOP0001 level-2 DFD becomes the boss for the GTOP000101 level-3 DFD during the conversion process.

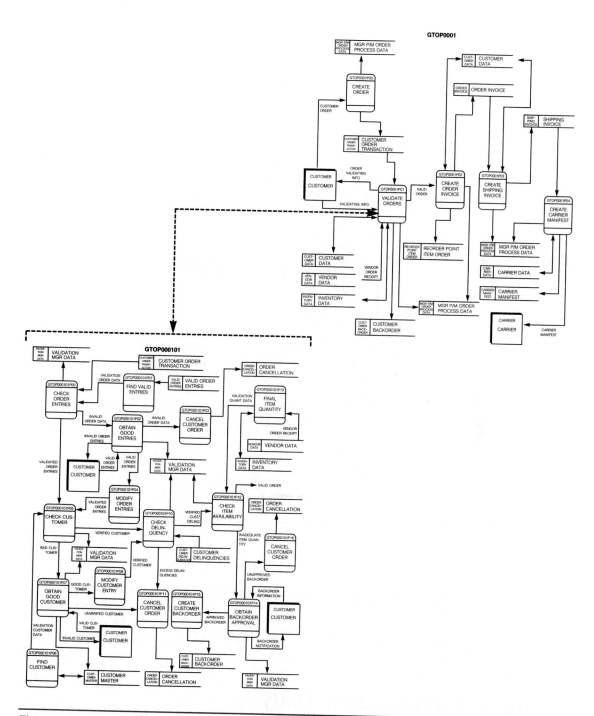

Figure 9-14. GTOP000101 with a boss from GTOP0001

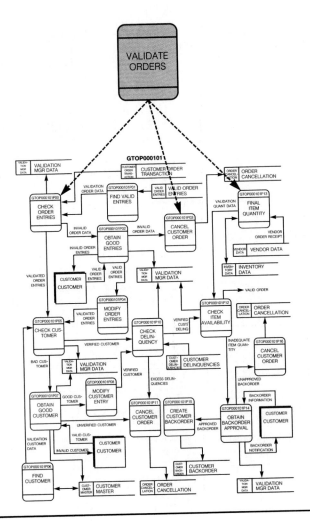

Figure 9-15. GTOP000101 with its selected boss

In summary, the boss for a STC converted from a DFD should be the process on the upper-level DFD on which explosion occurs down to the DFD being converted. For a level-3 DFD being converted to a STC, it is the process on the level-2 DFD that explodes to the level-3 DFD. For a level-4 DFD, it is the process on the level-3 DFD that explodes to the level-4 DFD, and so on.

Transform/Transaction Analysis

After identifying the boss module, the next step in converting DFDs into STCs is to perform transform and transaction analysis. **Transform analysis** represents the initial rules for DFD conversion. **Transaction analysis** represents additional rules necessary for detecting when a procedure needs to call on several lower procedure symbols in an or/selection attachment, where data or control flag values indicate which procedure to call. You will frequently perform both transform and transaction analysis while converting a DFD into a STC.

Transform analysis comprises a sequence of conversion steps for deriving a STC from a DFD that contains linear or sequential tasks. *Sequential tasks* means that the calls from one procedure symbol connected to procedure symbols below it *always* occur, and that they occur in a left-to-right sequence. As a result, the top procedure (the boss module) calls on the first procedure below it on the left. This symbol may have procedures below it that are also called on from left to right. After completion of all calls below the first procedure called on by the boss, the boss then calls on the second procedure from the left directly connected to it, and so on. Figure 9-16 shows a STC containing sequential tasks for validating student enrollment in a class.

The numbers in the upper-right corners of the procedure symbols in Figure 9-16 indicate the order in which the calls occur. The CONTROL MODULE calls on the INITIALIZE EXECUTION procedure first. This call is followed by a call to the GET STUDENT DATA procedure, followed by a call to the VALIDATE STUDENT MAS-

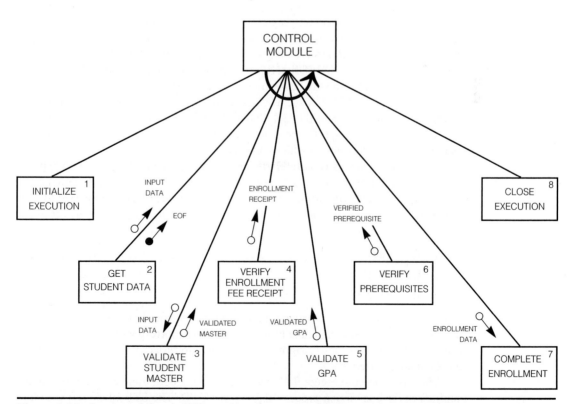

Figure 9-16. A sequential task STC resulting from only applying transform analysis conversion rules

TER, VERIFY ENROLLMENT FEE RECEIPT, VALIDATE GPA, VERIFY PRE-REQUISITES, and COMPLETE ENROLLMENT procedures. The CONTROL MODULE calls on these procedures (left to right) in a looping fashion (note the loop symbol) until the EOF (end-of-file) control flag is detected in a call to the GET STUDENT DATA procedure. The detection of an EOF flag causes the CONTROL MODULE to call on the CLOSE EXECUTION procedure, which is outside of the loop. Note that if the INITIALIZE EXECUTION procedure contained procedures below it, these procedures would be called on from left to right prior to the calls to looping procedures, as would also occur if any of these procedures also called on procedures below them.

The STC in Figure 9-16 illustrates the main difference between applying transform and transaction analysis: creating a STC with control calls from left to right versus or/selection calls.

Whereas only applying transform analysis is useful for system applications with linear or sequential tasks, such as program routines that involve serial processing of data (as previously described), transaction analysis is appropriate for case structure analysis. **Case structure analysis** means that a procedure with multiple procedures below it calls on only one of the procedures, depending on the circumstances of the case. The analyst performs transaction analysis by detecting places on the DFD where the data flows between a process and other symbols connected to it depend on a case structure situation. Situations occur in which different data flows leading away from or to a process do not all occur; they represent alternative flows. Therefore, converting these data flows into calls should designate them as alternative calls. For example, the INVALID ORDER DATA and VALIDATED ORDER ENTRIES data flows leading away from the CHECK ORDER ENTRIES process on the GTOP000101 DFD in Figures 8-26 and 9-14 represent alternative flows. If the order entries are correct, the flow to the CHECK CUSTOMER process occurs; if the order entries are incorrect, the flow to the OBTAIN GOOD ENTRIES process occurs. When these flows become calls on a STC, the case situation—whether the order entries are correct or incorrect—determines which call occurs.

Transaction analysis is particularly appropriate for menu-driven system applications in which different procedures need to be performed depending on which menu item the user selects. The menu selection represents an input data value used to indicate which processing routine to call. For example, a menu might have the following three options:

1. Copy files

2. Update data

3. Exit to higher menu

Each option would have a separate routine of program procedures. Selection of one of the three options would cause the program procedures corresponding to that option to execute. The STC for these program modules should reflect the or/selection calls to these optional procedures.

The STC shown in Figure 9-17 was created using both transform and transaction analysis in the conversion process applied to a DFD. The STC illustrates activities

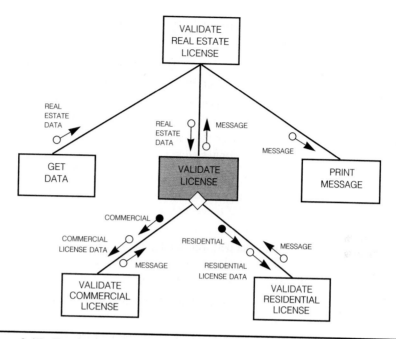

Figure 9-17. Transform and transaction analysis results

performed to validate either commercial or residential real estate licenses for an equivalent DFD that would have originally existed to reflect these actions. The top portion of this STC represents the portion resulting from applying only transform analysis rules to the DFD. The procedure symbols directly connected to the VALIDATE REAL ESTATE LICENSE procedure call on the three procedures connected to it sequentially from left to right.

The results of applying *transaction analysis* are illustrated by the calls from the VALIDATE LICENSE procedure to the two procedures below it. The VALIDATE LICENSE procedure calls on either the VALIDATE COMMERCIAL LICENSE or the VALIDATE RESIDENTIAL LICENSE procedure, depending on the type of data represented by REAL ESTATE DATA that the VALIDATE REAL ESTATE LICENSE procedure passes to the VALIDATE LICENSE procedure. This portion of the STC illustrates case structured execution. Only a particular validation procedure (COMMERCIAL or RESIDENTIAL) is called on, depending on the type of REAL ESTATE DATA being passed to the VALIDATE LICENSE procedure.

Steps in Transform Analysis

The two most notable methods to use in converting DFDs into STCs are the methods proposed by Yourdon and Constantine and by Dolan. The following list is a synopsis of the specific rules of transform analysis used as the prevalent conversion methods, as well as some additional rules supplied to make the conversion process more easily understandable.

1. Use the process on which explosion occurred on the upper-level DFD as the boss process for the lower-level DFD being converted.

2. Insert the boss process at the top of the DFD and connect it to the first process it would be most likely to call on.

3. Begin conversion with the first process connected to the boss and all DFD symbols connected to this process.

4. Convert DFD processing bubbles into STC procedure rectangles.

5. Make a process directly connected to a process that is already converted into a STC procedure subordinate to the process already converted.

6. Convert a data store and entity symbol into a STC input/output (I/O) procedure that performs the inputs the data depicted by the data store or data flows coming from or going to the entities.

7. Convert DFD data flow arrows into calls that perform data transmissions.

8. Make all I/O procedures subordinate to all other STC procedures connected to them.

9. Navigate through the entire set of processes on the DFD, converting the processes and the symbols connected to the processes to STC procedures, until all DFD symbols become STC symbols.

10. Rename STC procedure modules to imply *how* they occur.

11. Add data flag symbols to indicate data objects being passed along the call between the STC procedures.

12. Add control flags to indicate control, as needed.

Following boss selection, DFD symbols are converted into STC symbols. DFD processes become STC procedures. DFD entities and data stores become STC I/O procedures. New labels are assigned to these procedure rectangles that were data stores or entities that reflect a data I/O activity. The connections between procedure symbols that originally represented DFD data flows become STC calls. Figure 9-18 illustrates the conversion of DFD symbols into STC symbols.

To continue DFD-to-STC conversion, data flags are inserted on call connections for data flow contents. Recall that DFD data flows depict logical data objects, or LDSs. Finally, control flags are inserted on call connections where control data values need to be passed, to indicate that some condition occurred during the execution of that call. For example, a call to a data input procedure might need a control flag to signify the condition that the end of the file is reached, or that data is not found. To make the conversion process much simpler, you can insert data flags and control flags after performing the initial conversion activities. In fact, if you insert these symbols as you refine the STC, it is considerably easier to construct a STC that more closely resembles a structured program in outline form.

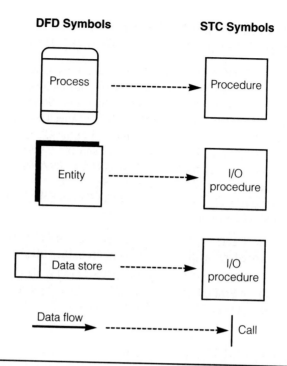

DFD Symbols   **STC Symbols**

Process ------------> Procedure

Entity ------------> I/O procedure

Data store ------------> I/O procedure

Data flow ------------> Call

Figure 9-18. DFD symbols converted to STC symbols

Converting the GTOP0001 Data Flow Diagram into a Structure Chart

For the GTOP0001 DFD, transform/transaction analysis begins by connecting the boss to the first DFD process it would call on, followed by changing this DFD process to a STC procedure. The next step is to change all the DFD symbols connected to this process to their STC equivalents. For example, the conversion of the GTOP0001 level-2 DFD into a STC begins by inserting the boss procedure, COMPLETE PHONE/MAIL INVOICES, at the top. This is the process from which explosion occurred on the GTOP00 level-1 DFD, and conforms to the recommended boss selection method. This boss procedure is then connected to the first DFD process it would call on, the CREATE ORDER process. The CREATE ORDER process is converted into a STC procedure symbol. Then all DFD symbols connected to this DFD process are converted to STC symbols.

Converting the CREATE ORDER
Process Area of the GTOP0001 DFD

Figures 9-19 and 9-20 illustrate conversion of the portion of the GTOP0001 DFD surrounding the CREATE ORDER process into its STC equivalent. In the conversion process, the boss procedure is connected to the CREATE ORDER DFD process, followed by converting it and DFD symbols connected to it to STC symbols. The CREATE ORDER DFD process is connected to the CUSTOMER entity, the MGR P/M ORDER PROCESS DATA data store, and the CUSTOMER ORDER TRANSACTION data store. The CUSTOMER ORDER TRANSACTION data store is in turn connected to the VALIDATE ORDERS process.

The following conversions to the DFD symbols in Figure 9-19 occur to produce the initial STC symbols in Figure 9-20:

- The CUSTOMER entity becomes the GET CUSTOMER ORDER DATA I/O procedure, with a call extending from the CREATE ORDER procedure.

- The MGR P/M ORDER PROCESS DATA data store becomes the CREATE MGR P/M ORDER PROCESS DATA I/O procedure, with a call extending from the CREATE ORDER procedure.

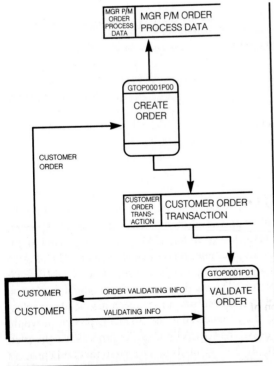

Figure 9-19. DFD-to-STC CREATE ORDER
DFD conversion area

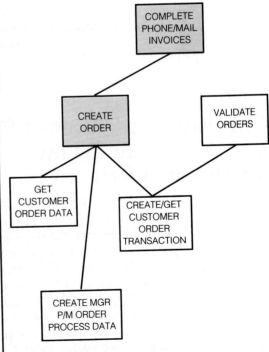

Figure 9-20. DFD-to-STC CREATE ORDER
initial conversion

- The CUSTOMER ORDER TRANSACTION data store becomes the CRE-ATE/GET CUSTOMER ORDER TRANSACTION I/O procedure, with a call extending from the CREATE ORDER procedure.
- The VALIDATE ORDERS DFD process becomes the VALIDATE ORDERS STC procedure, with a call extending to the CREATE/GET CUSTOMER ORDER TRANSACTION I/O procedure.

Notice that the VALIDATE ORDERS procedure was placed above the CRE-ATE/GET CUSTOMER ORDER TRANSACTION I/O procedure. This action reflects one of the structured programming rules of most IS departments: An I/O procedure should be subordinate to an actual processing procedure. Since the resultant program will be created with this rule in mind, it behooves the analyst to begin doing it while creating the STC procedure model. Therefore, the VALIDATE ORDERS procedure is placed above the CREATE/GET CUSTOMER ORDER TRANSAC-TION procedure with the call going from the VALIDATE ORDERS procedure to the CREATE/GET CUSTOMER ORDER TRANSACTION I/O procedure.

The label "CREATE/GET CUSTOMER ORDER TRANSACTION" reflects the fact that this procedure is both output (CREATE) and input (GET) for separate STC procedures. This occurs when you have either a data store or an entity connected to either the same or different DFD processes with *both* input and output data flows. An input data flow from an entity or data store becomes an I/O procedure with some word signifying input, such as GET or INPUT. Conversely, an output data flow to an entity or data store becomes an I/O procedure with some word signifying output, such as CREATE, SEND, or OUTPUT. When both input and output data flows occur to and from an entity or a data store, they become I/O procedures with words signifying both input and output, such as GET/CREATE, INPUT/SEND, or OUTPUT/GET. The word selected to signify input or output is not important; the important thing is that the I/O procedure is clearly recognized. Some IS departments specify a particular word to be used for I/O procedures, making their STC procedure models even more consistent between project team members.

Converting the VALIDATE ORDERS Process Area of the GTOP0001 DFD

For the GTOP0001 DFD, project team members now convert the symbols connected to the VALIDATE ORDERS process to their STC counterparts. Figure 9-21 shows the portion of the GTOP0001 DFD connected to the VALIDATE ORDERS process; Figure 9-22 illustrates the results of converting the DFD symbols in Figure 9-21 into their STC equivalents.

Notice that the STC conversion of VALIDATE ORDERS in Figure 9-22 includes the calls to procedures leading down to it from the boss module (COMPLETE PHONE/MAIL INVOICES through CREATE ORDER). The VALIDATE ORDERS DFD process in Figure 9-21 is connected to the CUSTOMER ORDER TRANSACTION data store, the CUSTOMER entity, the CUSTOMER DATA data store, the VENDOR DATA data store, the INVENTORY DATA data store, the CUSTOMER BACKO-

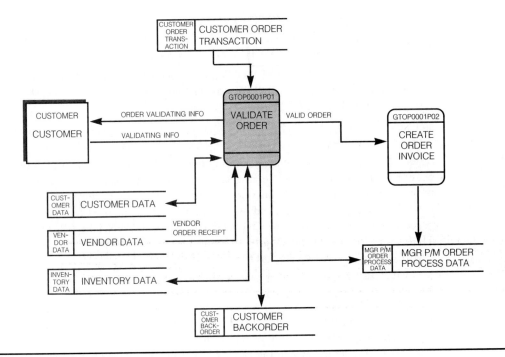

Figure 9-21. DFD symbols connected to the VALIDATE ORDERS process

RDER data store, the MGR P/M ORDER PROCESS DATA data store, and the CRE-ATE ORDER INVOICE DFD process. Each one of these DFD symbols becomes an STC procedure, with data flows between them becoming STC calls. All of these proce-dures become subordinate to the VALIDATE ORDERS procedure, as Figure 9-22 illus-trates. For example, the following conversions to the DFD symbols in Figure 9-21 occur to produce the STC symbols in Figure 9-22:

- The CUSTOMER ORDER TRANSACTION data store becomes the CREATE/ GET CUSTOMER ORDER TRANSACTION I/O procedure, with a call extend-ing from the VALIDATE ORDERS procedure. (This has already occurred while converting the CREATE ORDER process of the GTOP0001 DFD.)

- The CUSTOMER entity becomes the SEND/GET CUSTOMER INFORMA-TION STC I/O procedure, with a call extending from the VALIDATE ORDERS procedure.

- The CUSTOMER DATA data store becomes the GET/UPDATE CUS-TOMER DATA I/O procedure, with a call extending from the VALIDATE ORDERS procedure.

- The VENDOR DATA data store becomes the GET VENDOR ORDER RECEIPT STC I/O procedure, with a call extending from the VALIDATE ORDERS procedure.

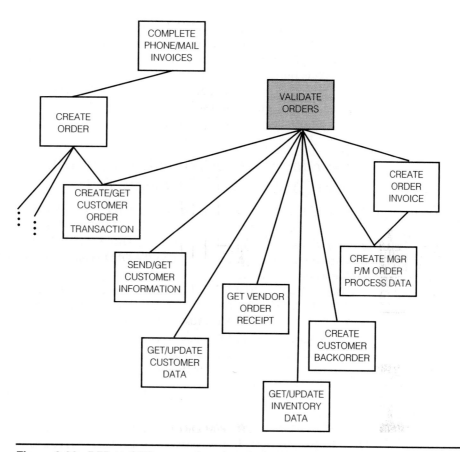

Figure 9-22. DFD-to-STC conversion of symbols connected to VALIDATE ORDERS

- The INVENTORY DATA data store becomes the GET/UPDATE INVENTO-RY DATA I/O procedure, with a call extending from the VALIDATE ORDERS procedure.

- The CUSTOMER BACKORDER data store becomes the CREATE CUS-TOMER BACKORDER I/O procedure, with a call extending from the VALI-DATE ORDERS procedure.

- The MGR P/M ORDER PROCESS DATA data store becomes the CREATE MGR P/M ORDER PROCESS DATA I/O procedure, with a call extending from the VALIDATE ORDERS procedure.

- The CREATE ORDER INVOICE DFD process becomes the CREATE ORDER INVOICE STC procedure, with a call extending from the VALI-DATE ORDERS procedure and to the CREATE MGR P/M ORDER PROCESS DATA procedure.

Notice that the CREATE ORDER INVOICE procedure is placed below the

VALIDATE ORDERS procedure in Figure 9-22. In the first-cut STC conversion rules, a DFD process connected to a DFD process that is already converted to a STC procedure typically becomes subordinate to the existing procedure. This may change as the STC is refined at a later stage, but it provides an easily understandable rule to apply for initially converting the DFD into a STC. At this point, analysts should be concerned only with conversion of the DFD symbols and proper subordination between different types of STC procedures.

Converting the CREATE ORDER INVOICE Process Area of the GTOP0001 DFD

Next, project team members convert the symbols connected to the CREATE ORDER INVOICE process to their STC counterparts. Figure 9-23 shows the portion of the GTOP0001 DFD connected to the CREATE ORDER INVOICE process, and Figure 9-24 illustrates the results of converting the DFD symbols in Figure 9-23 into their STC equivalents.

The CREATE ORDER INVOICE DFD process in Figure 9-23 is connected to the REORDER POINT ITEM ORDER data store, the MGR P/M ORDER PROCESS DATA data store, the CUSTOMER DATA data store, and the ORDER INVOICE data store. Each of these DFD symbols becomes a STC I/O procedure, with data flows

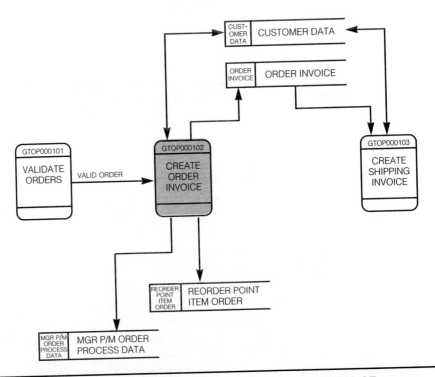

Figure 9-23. DFD symbols connected to the CREATE ORDER INVOICE process

between them and the CREATE ORDER INVOICE process becoming STC calls. All of these procedures become subordinate to the CREATE ORDER INVOICE procedure, as Figure 9-24 illustrates. For example, the following conversions to the DFD symbols in Figure 9-23 occur to produce the STC symbols in Figure 9-24:

- The MGR P/M ORDER PROCESS DATA date store becomes the CREATE MGR P/M ORDER PROCESS DATA STC I/O procedure (this already occurred while converting the VALIDATE ORDERS process on the GTOP0001 DFD), with a call extending from the CREATE ORDER INVOICE procedure.
- The REORDER POINT ITEM ORDER data store becomes the CREATE REORDER POINT ITEM ORDER STC I/O procedure, with a call extending from the CREATE ORDER INVOICE procedure.
- The CUSTOMER DATA data store becomes the GET/UPDATE CUSTOMER DATA I/O procedure, with a call also extending from it up to the CREATE ORDER INVOICE procedure.
- The ORDER INVOICE data store becomes the OUTPUT/GET ORDER INVOICE I/O procedure, with a call extending from it up to the CREATE ORDER INVOICE procedure.

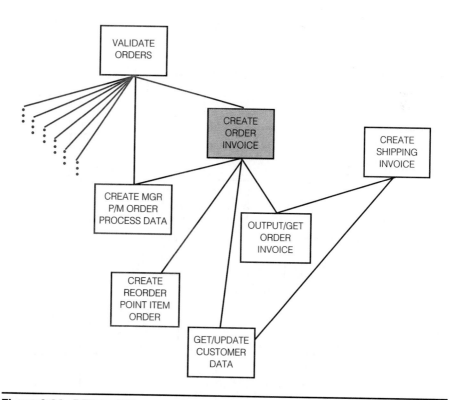

Figure 9-24. DFD-to-STC conversion of symbols connected to CREATE ORDER INVOICE

- The CREATE SHIPPING INVOICE process becomes the CREATE SHIP-PING INVOICE procedure, with a call extending down to the OUTPUT/GET ORDER INVOICE and GET/UPDATE CUSTOMER DATA procedures.

First-Cut GTOP0001 STC

Figure 9-25 shows the entire first-cut STC that results from following the guidelines for converting the remaining portion of the GTOP0001 DFD of Figure 9-10.

The first-cut STC of Figure 9-25 illustrates a number of actions required to create a STC from a DFD. Look at the DFD in Figure 9-10 and the STC in Figure 9-25 at the same time to gain a better understanding of the explanation that follows.

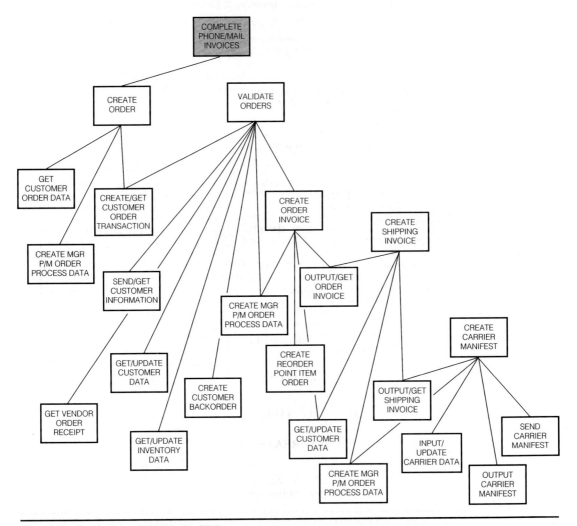

Figure 9-25. First-cut GTOP0001 STC

Notice that the CREATE ORDER procedure calls on the procedures below it in a sequential fashion, which conforms to the rules of transform analysis. This procedure represents a local boss module. A **local boss** is a procedure on a STC that has procedures below it over which it exerts control. A local boss procedure is the boss of the procedures below it, but is not the boss of the entire STC.

The second area of the DFD converted was the section that involves order validation, as illustrated in Figures 9-21 and 9-22. Notice that the CREATE/GET CUSTOMER ORDER TRANSACTION STC I/O procedure is called on by both the CREATE ORDER and the VALIDATE ORDERS procedures. Some analysts would anticipate refining activities and create separate CREATE/GET CUSTOMER ORDER TRANSACTION procedures rather than have two separate local bosses call on the same procedure (remember that a symbol on either a DFD or a STC that has the same label represents the same thing).

In the next area of conversion, since the CREATE ORDER INVOICE process was connected directly to the VALIDATE ORDERS process on the GTOP0001 DFD of Figure 9-10, the CREATE ORDER INVOICE procedure becomes subordinate to the VALIDATE ORDERS procedure on the STC in Figure 9-25. The CREATE ORDER INVOICE procedure is also a local boss for the procedures resulting from converting the DFD symbols connected to it. The conversion activities related to Figures 9-23 and 9-24 described how this section of the STC was created. Again, some analysts would anticipate refinement activities and create separate procedure symbols for the CREATE MGR P/M ORDER PROCESS DATA, OUTPUT/GET ORDER INVOICE, GET/UPDATE CUSTOMER DATA, and OUTPUT/GET SHIPPING INVOICE I/O procedures to prevent multiple local bosses connected to the same procedure.

The CREATE SHIPPING INVOICE DFD process with a flow from the ORDER INVOICE data store is converted into a STC procedure, with the connection from the ORDER INVOICE data store designated as a call from CREATE SHIPPING INVOICE to the OUTPUT/GET ORDER INVOICE STC I/O procedure. Notice that the CREATE SHIPPING INVOICE procedure is positioned above the OUTPUT/GET ORDER INVOICE STC I/O procedure. This conforms to the rule that DFD processes should never become subordinate to a procedure designated as an I/O procedure, as occurs when entities or data stores are converted into STC procedures.

CREATE SHIPPING INVOICE is a local boss controlling the procedures that result from converting the remaining DFD symbols in Figure 9-10 connected to it when it was a DFD process symbol. These activities resulted in the following conversions:

- Since the CUSTOMER DATA data store was already converted into the GET/UPDATE CUSTOMER DATA I/O procedure, the data flow from the CREATE SHIPPING INVOICE process was converted into a call extending from the CREATE SHIPPING INVOICE procedure (as well as the already existing call from the CREATE ORDER INVOICE procedure).

- The MGR P/M ORDER PROCESS DATA data store was converted into the CREATE MGR P/M ORDER PROCESS DATA I/O procedure, with a call from the CREATE SHIPPING INVOICE procedure.

- The SHIPPING INVOICE data store was converted into the OUTPUT/GET

SHIPPING INVOICE STC I/O procedure, with the data flow converted into a call to this procedure from the CREATE SHIPPING INVOICE procedure.

- Finally, the CREATE CARRIER MANIFEST DFD process with a flow from the SHIPPING INVOICE data store is converted into a STC procedure, with the data flow from the SHIPPING INVOICE data store converted to a call from the CREATE CARRIER MANIFEST procedure to the OUTPUT/GET SHIPPING INVOICE I/O procedure.

Again, many analysts would have anticipated refinement activities and created two separate procedure symbols for the SHIPPING INVOICE data store.

CREATE CARRIER MANIFEST is also a local boss that controls the procedures resulting from converting the remaining DFD symbols connected to it on Figure 9-10. These activities result in the following conversions:

- Since the MGR P/M ORDER PROCESS DATA data store has already been converted into the CREATE MGR P/M ORDER PROCESS DATA STC I/O procedure, the data flow from it to the CREATE CARRIER MANIFEST process becomes a call from the CREATE CARRIER MANIFEST procedure.
- The CARRIER DATA data store is converted into the INPUT/UPDATE CARRIER DATA STC I/O procedure, with the data flow converted into a call to this procedure from the CREATE CARRIER MANIFEST procedure.
- The CARRIER MANIFEST data store is converted into the CREATE CARRIER MANIFEST STC I/O procedure, with the data flow converted into a call to this procedure from the CREATE CARRIER MANIFEST procedure.
- The CARRIER entity is converted into the SEND CARRIER MANIFEST STC I/O procedure, with the data flow converted into a call to this procedure from the CREATE CARRIER MANIFEST procedure.

These activities complete the initial conversion of the GTOP0001 DFD. The STC of Figure 9-25 is refined in Figures 9-33 and 9-34, later in this chapter.

Notice that no data flags or control flags are inserted along the STC calls at this point in the conversion process. Although inserting these symbols is part of transform analysis rules, it is much easier to insert them after performing initial STC refinement actions. The initial refinement actions rearrange the STC procedures into a layout consistent with structured programs. It is best to perform initial refinement actions without data and control flags, which only encumber rearranging the STC into a more structured format. When these symbols are added to the STC, they provide data and control specifications that make the structured layout more understandable.

Converting the GTOP000101 Data Flow Diagram into a Structure Chart

The GTOP000101 DFD shown in Figures 8-26 and 9-15 is also converted to further demonstrate conversion activities. This DFD has three main areas of business processing: validating order entries, verifying the customer and checking for excess delinquencies, and verifying item availability for order filling. To more completely understand the conversion of this DFD into a STC, each of these main areas of processing is converted in separate actions with figures to illustrate the conversion of the areas of the GTOP000101 DFD.

Converting the CHECK ORDER ENTRIES Process Area of the GTOP000101 DFD

Figures 9-26 and 9-27 illustrate the check order entries area of the GTOP000101 DFD in Figures 8-26 and 9-15 and the portion of the STC created as a result of applying conversion rules to the DFD symbols in Figure 9-26.

To begin the STC conversion for the GTOP000101 DFD, the process on the GTOP0001 DFD that explodes to the GTOP000101 DFD—VALIDATE ORDERS—is converted into a procedure and inserted as the boss at the top of the STC. This procedure is connected to the CHECK ORDER ENTRIES process to represent a call from VALIDATE ORDERS to CHECK ORDER ENTRIES. The CHECK ORDER

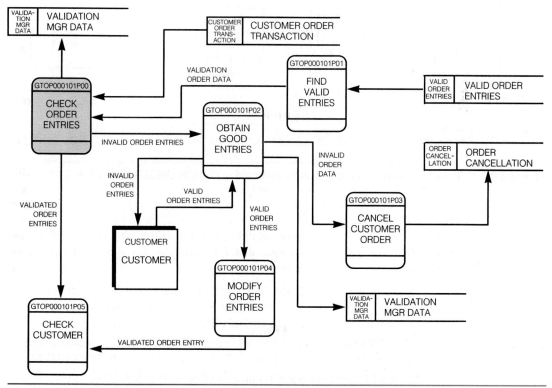

Figure 9-26. CHECK ORDER ENTRIES area of the GTOP000101 DFD

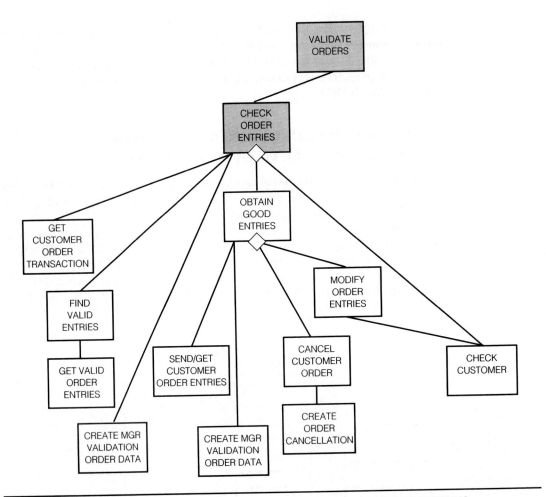

Figure 9-27. DFD-to-STC conversion of symbols connected to CHECK ORDER ENTRIES

ENTRIES DFD process is converted into a STC procedure, with DFD symbols connected to it also converted into equivalent STC symbols. The symbols are converted as follows:

- The CUSTOMER ORDER TRANSACTION data store becomes the GET CUSTOMER ORDER TRANSACTION STC I/O procedure, with a call extending from the CHECK ORDER ENTRIES procedure.
- The FIND VALID ENTRIES DFD process becomes a STC procedure with the same label, with a call to the GET VALID ORDER ENTRIES STC I/O procedure converted from the VALID ORDER ENTRIES data store.
- The VALIDATION MGR DATA data store becomes the CREATE MGR

VALIDATION ORDER DATA STC I/O procedure, with the data flow from CHECK ORDER ENTRIES becoming a STC call.

- The OBTAIN GOOD ENTRIES DFD process becomes a called procedure, with the same label and symbols connected to it changed as follows:
    - The CUSTOMER entity becomes the SEND/GET CUSTOMER ORDER ENTRIES STC I/O procedure called by OBTAIN GOOD ENTRIES.
    - The VALIDATION MGR DATA data store becomes the CREATE MGR VALIDATION ORDER DATA STC I/O procedure called by OBTAIN GOOD ENTRIES.
    - The CANCEL CUSTOMER ORDER DFD process becomes a called procedure with the same label that also calls on the CREATE ORDER CAN-CELLATION I/O procedure converted from the ORDER CANCELLATION data store.
    - The MODIFY ORDER ENTRIES DFD process becomes a called procedure with the same label that calls on the CHECK CUSTOMER procedure converted from the DFD process with the same label. Note that the CHECK CUSTOMER procedure also has a call extending down to it from the CHECK ORDER ENTRIES procedure that represented the data flow between them on the GTOP000101 DFD.

The final conversion action for this portion of the GTOP000101 DFD is an insertion of an or/selection symbol where the calls occur in an either/or orientation. Or/selection diamonds are inserted for calls from CHECK ORDER ENTRIES to OBTAIN GOOD ENTRIES and CHECK CUSTOMER, and for calls to the CANCEL ORDER and MODIFY ORDER ENTRIES procedures from the OBTAIN GOOD ENTRIES procedure. These procedures are in an either/or relationship because the order entries either are valid or need to be corrected, and either the customer provided order entry changes to modify the invalid entries or the order needs to be canceled. These areas of the GTOP000101 DFD represent case structured points in that portion of the DFD; therefore, transaction analysis is applied.

Converting the CHECK CUSTOMER and CHECK DELINQUENCY Processes Area of the GTOP000101 DFD

Figures 9-28 and 9-29 illustrate the check customer area of the GTOP000101 DFD in Figures 8-26 and 9-15 and the portion of the STC created as a result of applying conversion rules to the DFD symbols in Figure 9-28.

Notice that the conversion of the customer validation area of the GTOP000101 DFD in Figure 9-29 also includes calls leading down from the boss procedure (VALI-DATE ORDERS through CHECK ORDER ENTRIES). Since the CHECK CUS-TOMER DFD process is already converted into a STC procedure, the DFD-to-STC conversion continues with the DFD symbols connected to it on the portion of the

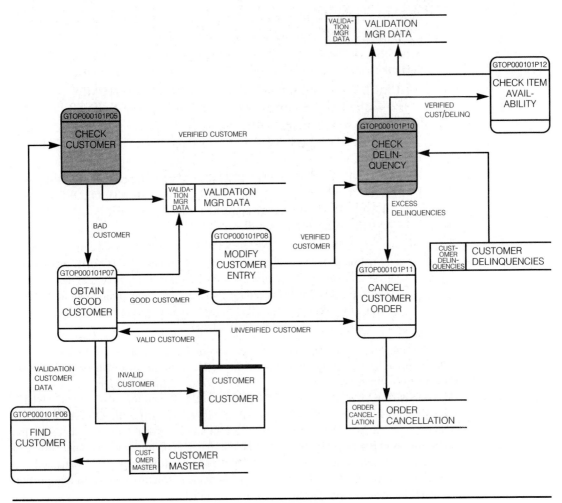

Figure 9-28. Check customer area of the GTOP000101 DFD

GTOP000101 DFD in Figure 9-28. The following conversions are applied to the portion of the GTOP000101 DFD in Figure 9-28 to produce the portion of the STC in Figure 9-29:

- The FIND CUSTOMER DFD process is converted into a called procedure with the same label, and the CUSTOMER MASTER data store is converted into the STC I/O procedure GET/UPDATE CUSTOMER MASTER, with a call extending from the OBTAIN GOOD CUSTOMER procedure.

- The OBTAIN GOOD CUSTOMER process becomes a procedure called on by the CHECK CUSTOMER procedure, with all remaining DFD symbols connected to it becoming STC symbols as follows:

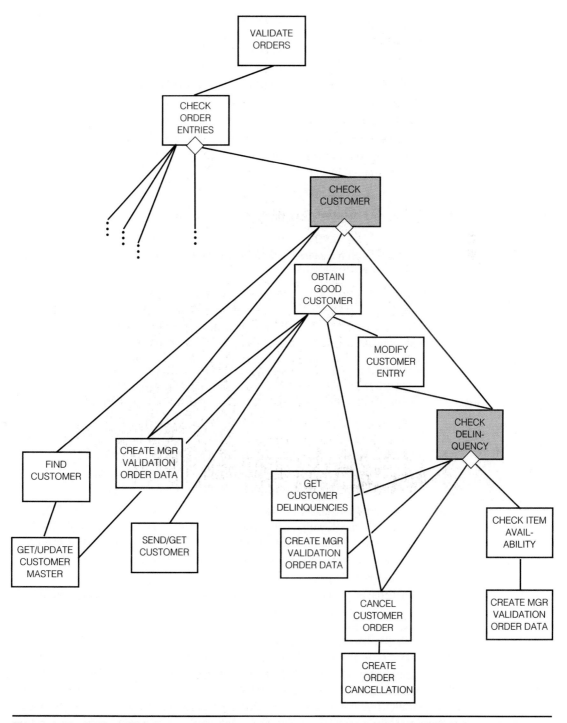

Figure 9-29. DFD-to-STC conversion of the symbols connected to CHECK CUSTOMER and CHECK DELINQUENCY processes

- Convert the CUSTOMER entity into the SEND/GET CUSTOMER I/O procedure, with the data flow converted into a call to this procedure from the OBTAIN GOOD CUSTOMER procedure.

- Convert the VALIDATION MGR DATA data store into the CREATE MGR VALIDATION ORDER DATA STC I/O procedure, with calls inserted to this procedure from the CHECK CUSTOMER and OBTAIN GOOD CUSTOMER procedures.

- Convert the CANCEL CUSTOMER ORDER DFD process to the CANCEL CUSTOMER ORDER STC procedure, with the data flow converted into a call to this procedure from the OBTAIN GOOD CUSTOMER procedure; also, convert the ORDER CANCELLATION data store to the CREATE ORDER CANCELLATION I/O procedure, with a call inserted to it from the CANCEL CUSTOMER ORDER procedure.

- Convert the MODIFY CUSTOMER ENTRY DFD process into a STC procedure with the same label and a call extending from the OBTAIN GOOD CUSTOMER procedure.

- Convert the CHECK DELINQUENCY DFD process into a STC procedure with the same label and a call extending from the CHECK CUSTOMER and MODIFY CUSTOMER ENTRY procedures, with the remaining DFD symbols connected to it also converted into STC symbols as follows:

  - Convert the CUSTOMER DELINQUENCIES data store to the GET CUSTOMER DELINQUENCIES I/O procedure, with the data flow converted into a call to this procedure from the CHECK DELINQUENCY procedure.

  - Convert the VALIDATION MGR DATA data store into the CREATE MGR VALIDATION ORDER DATA I/O procedure, with a call inserted to it from the CHECK DELINQUENCY procedure.

  - Insert a call to the CANCEL CUSTOMER ORDER procedure from the CHECK DELINQUENCY procedure.

  - Convert the CHECK ITEM AVAILABILITY DFD process into a STC procedure symbol, with a call made to it from the CHECK DELINQUENCY procedure, and copy the CREATE MGR VALIDATION ORDER DATA procedure into a procedure called on by the CHECK ITEM AVAILABILITY procedure.

The final conversion action for the portion of the GTOP000101 DFD in Figure 9-28 is the insertion of or/selection diamonds for case structured areas of the DFD. Two different sets of flows are in an either/or relationship on this portion of the GTOP000101 DFD: the flows leading from the CHECK CUSTOMER procedure to the OBTAIN GOOD CUSTOMER and CHECK DELINQUENCY procedures, the flows leading away from the OBTAIN GOOD CUSTOMER procedure to the CANCEL CUSTOMER ORDER and MODIFY CUSTOMER ENTRY procedures, and the flows leading from the CHECK DELINQUENCY procedure to the CANCEL CUSTOMER ORDER and CHECK ITEM AVAILABILITY procedures. An or/selection symbol is inserted for calls to the OBTAIN GOOD CUSTOMER and CHECK DELINQUENCY procedures from the CHECK CUSTOMER procedure because either the customer ID was correct or an attempt was made to obtain a good customer ID entry. An or/selection symbol is inserted for the calls to the CANCEL CUSTOMER ORDER and MODIFY CUSTOMER ENTRY procedures from the OBTAIN GOOD CUSTOMER procedure because either a valid customer ID was obtained or the order was canceled. An or/selection symbol is also inserted for the calls to the CANCEL CUSTOMER ORDER and CHECK ITEM AVAILABILITY procedures from the CHECK DELINQUENCY procedure because either excess delinquencies are present and the order is canceled or delinquencies are not present and a call is made to the CHECK ITEM AVAILABILITY procedure. These situations represent a case structured point in that portion of the GTOP000101 DFD; therefore, transaction analysis is applied.

Converting the CHECK ITEM AVAILABILITY Process

Figures 9-30 and 9-31 illustrate the check item availability area of the GTOP000101 DFD in Figures 8-26 and 9-15 and the portion of the STC created as a result of applying conversion rules to the DFD symbols in Figure 9-30.

Since the CHECK ITEM AVAILABILITY DFD process is already converted into a STC procedure, the DFD-to-STC conversion continues with the DFD symbols connected to it in Figure 9-30 when it was a DFD process. The following conversions are applied to the portion of the GTOP000101 DFD in Figure 9-30 to produce the portion of the STC in Figure 9-31:

- Convert the FIND ITEM QUANTITY DFD process into the FIND ITEM QUANTITY STC procedure, with the data flow converted into a call to this procedure from the CHECK ITEM AVAILABILITY procedure; also, convert the INVENTORY DATA data store to the GET ITEM INVENTORY STC I/O procedure called on by the FIND ITEM QUANTITY procedure; and convert the VENDOR DATA data store to the GET VENDOR ORDER RECEIPT STC I/O procedure that is also called on by the FIND ITEM QUANTITY procedure.

- Convert the OBTAIN BACKORDER APPROVAL DFD process into the OBTAIN BACKORDER APPROVAL procedure, with the data flow converted into a call to this procedure from the CHECK ITEM AVAILABILITY procedure and the remaining DFD symbols changed as follows:

  - Convert the VALIDATION MGR DATA data store into an I/O procedure labeled CREATE MGR VALIDATION ORDER DATA, with a call extending from the OBTAIN BACKORDER APPROVAL procedure.

  - Convert the CUSTOMER entity into the SEND/GET BACKORDER APPROVAL STC I/O procedure, with the data flow converted into a call to this procedure from the OBTAIN BACKORDER APPROVAL procedure.

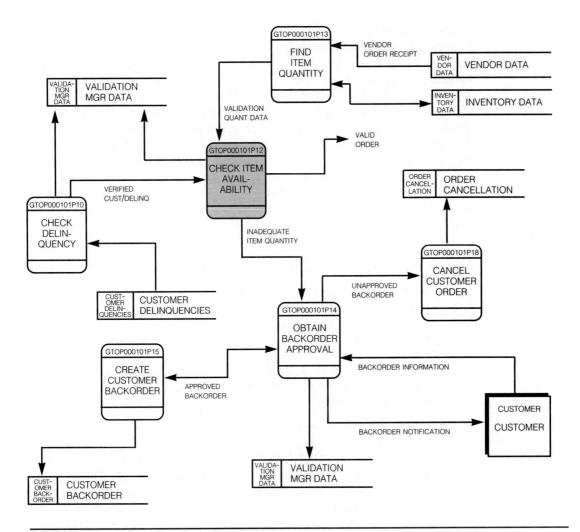

Figure 9-30. CHECK ITEM AVAILABILITY area of the GTOP000101 DFD

- Convert the CREATE CUSTOMER BACKORDER DFD process into the CREATE CUSTOMER BACKORDER STC procedure, with the data flow converted into a call to this procedure from the OBTAIN BACKORDER APPROVAL procedure; also, convert the CUSTOMER BACKORDER data store to the SEND CUSTOMER BACKORDER STC I/O procedure.

- Convert the CANCEL CUSTOMER ORDER DFD process into the CANCEL CUSTOMER ORDER STC procedure, with the data flow converted into a call to this procedure from the OBTAIN BACKORDER APPROVAL

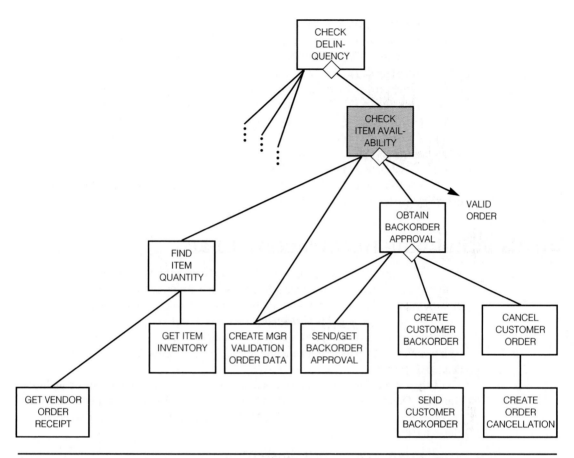

Figure 9-31. DFD-to-STC conversion of symbols connected to CHECK ITEM AVAILABILITY

procedure; also, convert the ORDER CANCELLATION data store to the CREATE ORDER CANCELLATION procedure, with a call inserted to it from the CANCEL CUSTOMER ORDER procedure.

- Insert an interface call from the CHECK ITEM AVAILABILITY procedure, with the VALID ORDER data flag inserted on the interface call. The interface call would become a STC I/O procedure labeled SEND VALID ORDER.

The final action in converting this portion of the GTOP000101 DFD is insertion of or/selection symbols for case structured areas of this portion of the GTOP000101 DFD. Two different sets of flows are in an either/or relationship in this portion of the GTOP000101 DFD: the flow leading from CHECK ITEM AVAILABILITY to OBTAIN BACKORDER APPROVAL and the interface flow labeled VALID ORDER, and the flows leading away from OBTAIN BACKORDER APPROVAL to

CREATE CUSTOMER BACKORDER and CANCEL CUSTOMER ORDER. An or/selection symbol is inserted for calls to the OBTAIN BACKORDER APPROVAL procedure and the VALID ORDER interface from the CHECK ITEM AVAILABILI-TY procedure because either inventory is available to fill the order or a back order needs to be approved by the customer. An or/selection symbol is also inserted for the calls to the CREATE CUSTOMER BACKORDER and CANCEL CUSTOMER ORDER procedures from the OBTAIN BACKORDER APPROVAL procedure because either the customer approves the back order or the order is canceled. These situations represent case structured points in that portion of the GTOP000101 DFD; therefore, transaction analysis is applied.

Figure 9-32 illustrates the entire first-cut STC created by using the conversion guidelines on the GTOP000101 DFD in Figure 9-15.

Goals in Refining the Structure Chart

When refining a STC, keep in mind that the final output will consist of physical design specifications for structured programs. In a structured program, each program module should be cohesive and loosely connected (coupled) to other program modules. Good structured programs have relatively self-contained program modules, with loose coupling between modules. For example, when a program module contains actions not related to its major function, these activities should be moved elsewhere or deleted altogether.

The main goal in creating STCs is to construct them with high cohesion and loose coupling. Other goals are to create STCs that are useful, have procedures with a limited span of control, are moderate in size, and have common storage areas. Four key characteristics of good STCs are:

- High cohesion
- Loose coupling
- Limited span of control
- Manageable size

High Cohesion

Cohesion is a measure of how tightly centered a STC procedure is regarding the other procedures with which it is connected. This means that procedures connected to an area of processing perform only one major action, with all of their procedures related to this action.

Since each program module should accomplish only one purpose, a cohesive local boss section contains all actions necessary to accomplish its central purpose. Thus, a highly cohesive STC local boss section does not rely on other sections of STC procedures for help. When looking at a STC section to check its cohesion, make sure that worker procedures under a boss help the boss. If any do not, they should be moved to areas of the STC where they do provide help. When checking for cohesion, study the

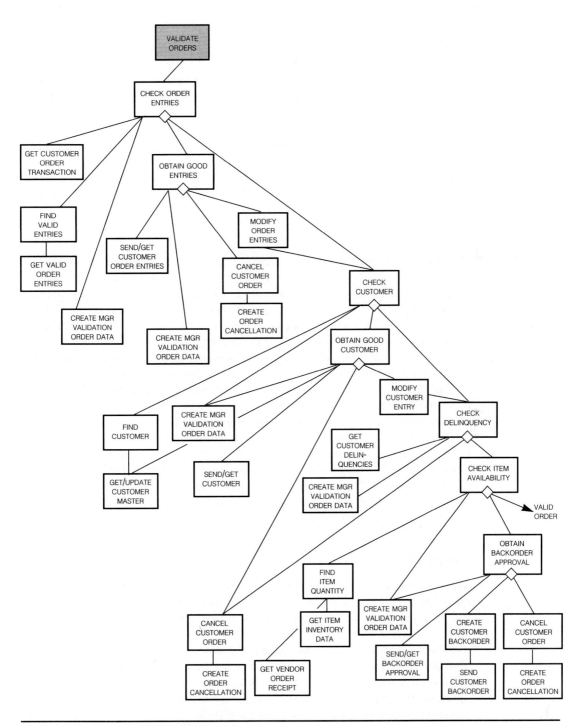

Figure 9-32. First-cut GTOP000101 STC

labels. In general, a label name should not contain a connective that strings together several tasks into an assembly-line task, or state an action to perform using terms that are general in nature.

For example, GET/UPDATE PAYROLL MASTER exhibits an assembly-line type of label that connects both the GET PAYROLL MASTER and UPDATE PAYROLL MASTER tasks. Furthermore, UPDATE PAYROLL MASTER includes many actions, such as GET UPDATES, VALIDATE UPDATES, FIND PAYROLL MASTER, and so on. UPDATE PAYROLL MASTER is a label with activities too general to represent the detailed actions that must be included in the procedure to perform the update actions. When selecting labels, use a direct active verb followed by a direct object—GET PAYROLL MASTER is a good name; PAYROLL UPDATING is not.

Loose Coupling

Coupling is a measure of the interdependence of the procedures connected together in one area of the STC. It refers to the integration and interaction between program modules. Since everything necessary for a local boss section to accomplish its function should be included in that section, the section should not be directly dependent on and connected to (coupled with) any other STC section. Connecting procedures together that exhibit dependencies is referred to as coupling. Since the independence of modules is a goal, local boss sections should be loosely coupled to each other. On examination, if it is determined that a local boss is connected to any nonessential procedure symbols below it, these nonessential procedure symbols are moved to places where they serve a purpose. This action often results in moving procedures (and sometimes sections of procedures) to other STC sections after initial conversion.

The number and types of data and control flags passed between local boss sections is a good indicator of the coupling within these sections. Check these STC sections to ensure that they do not get any data they do not need. On the other hand, check to make sure they receive enough data. If too many data and control flags are being passed, it is possible that the procedure symbol is trying to do too much. In that case, the procedure symbol can be decomposed into multiple procedure symbols.

Limited Span of Control

Span of control relates to the number of lower procedures connected to a specific procedure in a STC. The goal of good STC creation is to have a limited span of control. In general, a procedure should call on seven (give or take two) worker procedures. If it is obvious that a local boss does call on too many worker procedures, the local boss is probably trying to accomplish too much. On the other hand, if the calling procedure only calls on one worker procedure, the worker module is probably too trivial, and it should be considered as part of the actions of the calling procedure (remember that pseudocode statements in dictionary entries typically accompany the procedure and can be used to indicate these actions).

Moderate Size

There is no set length or module **size** for a STC. As a rule of thumb, many analysts feel that a STC should fit on one page or one screen. Remember, however, that the goal is to keep each local boss section achieving one purpose. If it takes a page and a half to accomplish this objective, there is nothing really wrong with that.

The Refined GTOP0001 Structure Chart

Figure 9-33 shows a partially refined version of the first-cut GTOP0001 STC in Figure 9-25, with procedures rearranged in a more structured layout. The STC in Figure 9-33 illustrates how cohesion checking, coupling, and size checking can be used to rearrange the STC procedures into a format consistent with the general layout of a structured program. Notice that many more procedures are directly connected (coupled) to the boss module and disconnected (decoupled) from each other. Also notice that the main boss and local bosses all have less than the recommended upper limit of the number of worker procedures coupled to them.

Rearranging Procedures

The rearranged first-cut GTOP0001 STC in Figure 9-33 illustrates how the assembly-line coupled procedures that often result from applying transform and transaction rules should be uncoupled and recoupled elsewhere whenever possible. The COMPLETE PHONE/MAIL INVOICES boss procedure is directly connected to the five major procedures of the converted STC. These major procedures are CREATE ORDER, VALIDATE ORDERS, CREATE ORDER INVOICE, CREATE SHIPPING INVOICE, and CREATE CARRIER MANIFEST. These procedures are called on by the boss procedure from left to right. These five local boss sections were decoupled from each other since they are not cohesive: they do not directly provide service to each other, nor are they part of each other's main purpose.

The five local boss procedures in Figure 9-33 perform five totally different sets of programming actions and should not be coupled together. They may share the same data flag or control flags. However, each of these sections has its own purpose and represents relatively independent sections of processing activity. For example, the VALIDATE ORDERS procedure was originally connected to (and calls on) the CREATE/GET CUSTOMER TRANSACTION procedure in Figure 9-25 to which the CREATE ORDER procedure was also connected (and which it calls on). The CREATE/GET CUSTOMER ORDER TRANSACTION procedure became two procedures, CREATE CUSTOMER ORDER TRANSACTION and GET CUSTOMER ORDER TRANSACTION, which are called on by the CREATE ORDER and VALIDATE ORDERS procedures, respectively.

A second refinement is the creation of separate procedure modules called on by

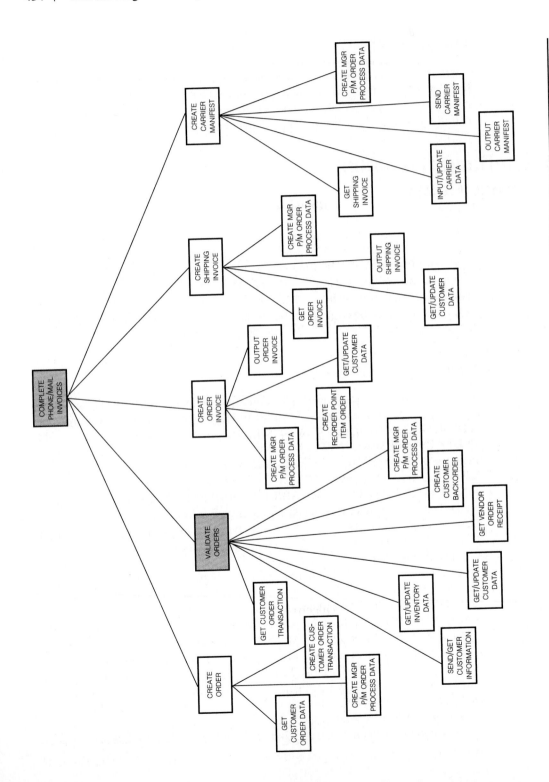

Figure 9-33. Rearranged first-cut GTOP0001 STC

multiple major sections of the STC. Notice that the CREATE MGR P/M ORDER PROCESS DATA procedure is now included as a separate procedure called on separately by the five local boss procedures. In the first-cut GTOP0001 STC in Figure 9-25, multiple calls to this procedure made many local boss procedures interconnected and coupled together.

Also notice that in the STC of Figure 9-33, no local boss procedure calls on more than seven procedures. In addition, the entire STC fits on a single page. Consequently, the refined STC conforms to the rules of thumb concerning span of control and size.

Inserting Data Flags and Control Flags

The next step in completing the STC in Figure 9-33 is to insert data flags and control flags along the calls between STC procedures. Figure 9-34 illustrates the completed refined GTOP0001 STC, with all data flags inserted along each call between procedures.

The COMPLETE PHONE/MAIL INVOICES boss procedure in Figure 9-34 first calls on the CREATE ORDER local boss procedure with accompanying data flags indicated along various calls. The CREATE ORDER procedure calls on the GET CUSTOMER ORDER DATA I/O procedure, with the CUSTOMER ORDER DATA data flag passed back to CREATE ORDER. The CREATE ORDER procedure then calls on the CREATE MGR P/M ORDER PROCESS DATA and CREATE CUSTOMER ORDER TRANSACTION procedures, with appropriate data flags sent to these I/O procedures.

After the CREATE ORDER local boss completes calling on the procedures below it on the refined GTOP0001 STC in Figure 9-34, the CUSTOMER ORDER data flag is returned to the COMPLETE PHONE/MAIL INVOICES boss procedure. This same data flag is sent from the COMPLETE PHONE/MAIL INVOICES procedure on the call to the VALIDATE ORDERS procedure. This data flag now represents the connection that initially occurred between the CREATE/GET CUSTOMER TRANSACTION and the VALIDATE ORDERS procedure on the first-cut STC conversion. Notice that VALIDATE ORDERS does not call on a procedure to get the customer order, as was the case in Figure 9-33; that procedure was eliminated because the CUSTOMER ORDER data flag is sent to VALIDATE ORDERS from the COMPLETE PHONE/MAIL INVOICES boss procedure.

The VALID ORDER data flag is inserted along the call from the VALIDATE ORDERS procedure back up to the COMPLETE PHONE/MAIL INVOICES boss procedure on the refined GTOP0001 STC in Figure 9-34. This same data flag is sent down along the call from COMPLETE PHONE/MAIL INVOICES to the CREATE ORDER INVOICE procedure. The VALID ORDER data flag takes the place of the call between the VALIDATE ORDERS and CREATE ORDER INVOICE procedures that appeared on the rearranged first-cut GTOP0001 STC of Figure 9-33. The boss procedure now passes this data flag between the two local boss procedures on which it calls to represent the way these two procedures share data.

The ORDER INVOICE data flag is inserted along the call from the CREATE ORDER INVOICE procedure to the COMPLETE PHONE/MAIL INVOICES boss procedure, and from this boss procedure to the CREATE SHIPPING INVOICE pro-

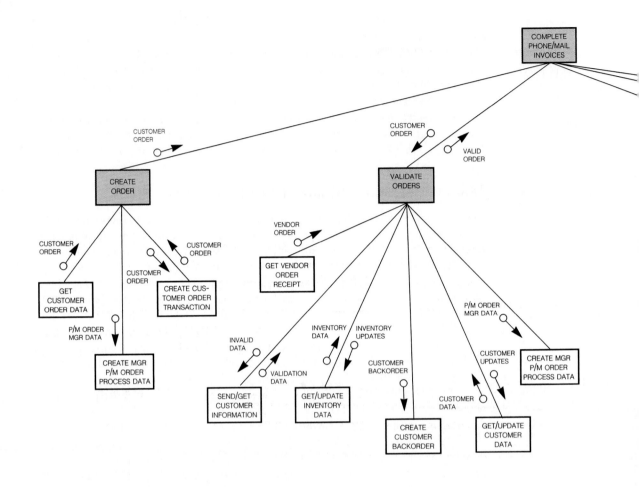

Figure 9-34. Refined GTOP0001 STC

cedure on the refined GTOP0001 STC in Figure 9-34. Passing the ORDER INVOICE data flag replaces having the OUTPUT/GET ORDER INVOICE procedure between the CREATE ORDER INVOICE and CREATE SHIPPING INVOICE procedures.

The SHIPPING INVOICE data flag is inserted from the CREATE SHIPPING INVOICE procedure to the COMPLETE PHONE/MAIL INVOICES boss procedure and from the boss procedure to the CREATE CARRIER MANIFEST procedure on the refined GTOP0001 STC in Figure 9-34. Passing the SHIPPING INVOICE data flag replaces having the OUTPUT/GET SHIPPING INVOICE procedure between the CREATE SHIPPING INVOICE and CREATE CARRIER MANIFEST procedures that appeared on the rearranged first-cut GTOP0001 STC in Figure 9-33.

As you can see, these sections of the STC have been easily decoupled, with data

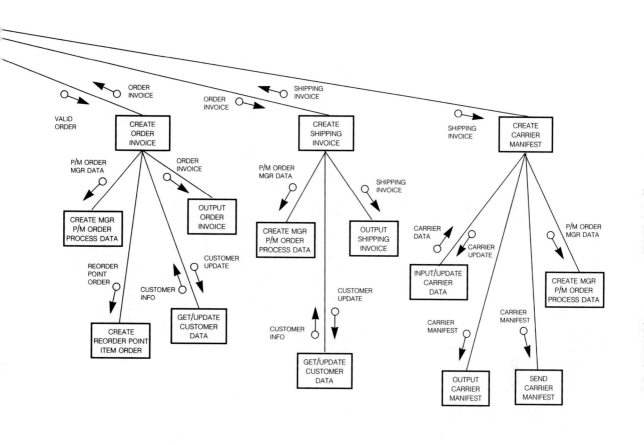

that passed between them passed to the boss procedure for appropriate distribution. The five local boss procedures also receive data from or pass data down to the procedures on which they call. All of these data flags represent many of the logical data objects depicted as either data flows or data stores in the original DFD. Dictionary entries for the calls and/or data flags indicate which logical data objects the data flags represent, as well as the specific pseudocode that the procedures use to accomplish their purpose.

As a final note, the VALIDATE ORDERS procedure on the refined GTOP0001 STC in Figure 9-34 is described in a dictionary entry as exploding to a refined version of the first-cut GTOP000101 STC that appears in Figure 9-32. This refined STC is shown after the steps in rearranging the first-cut STC and the insertion of data flags along various calls are illustrated.

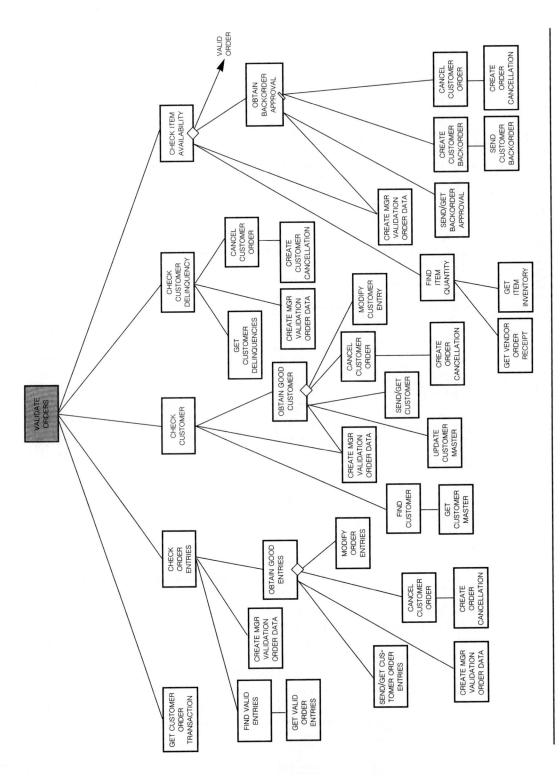

Figure 9-35. Rearranged first-cut GTOP000101 STC

The Refined GTOP000101 Structure Chart

Figure 9-35 illustrates rearranging the first-cut GTOP000101 STC in Figure 9-32 into a layout consistent with a structured program. This STC also illustrates how cohesion checking, coupling, and size checking can be used to rearrange the STC procedures into a format consistent with the general layout of a structured program. Notice that the four main procedures of the first-cut GTOP000101 STC in Figure 9-32 are disconnected (decoupled) from each other and directly connected (coupled) to the boss module. The GET CUSTOMER ORDER TRANSACTION procedure was also decoupled from the CHECK ORDER ENTRIES procedure and coupled to the boss procedure, as might occur in a structured program. Also notice that the main boss and local bosses all have no more than the recommended upper limit of the number of worker procedures coupled to them.

The next step in converting the STC in Figure 9-35 is to insert data and control flags where they need to appear along calls between procedures. Figure 9-36 illustrates the complete refined GTOP000101 STC after insertion of all data and control flags.

After the VALIDATE ORDERS procedure calls on the GET CUSTOMER ORDER TRANSACTION procedure and receives the CUSTOMER ORDER data flag, it calls on the four local boss procedures, with appropriate data flags passed between the boss procedure and the local boss procedures. Each local boss receives a data flag from the boss procedure and returns another data flag to the boss procedure that signifies the validation of that portion of the customer order. The data flags sent to the local boss procedures are the same data flags returned to the boss on the call to the previous procedure from the boss procedure. For example, the CUSTOMER ORDER data flag is returned to VALIDATE ORDERS from GET CUSTOMER ORDER TRANSACTION and then sent to the CHECK ORDER ENTRIES local boss procedure. When the CHECK ORDER ENTRIES procedure sends the VALIDATED ENTRIES data flag back to VALIDATE ORDERS, VALIDATE ORDERS sends the VALIDATED ENTRIES data flag down to the CHECK CUSTOMER local boss procedure for a check on the validity of the customer.

Each remaining local boss procedure receives a data flag from the boss and returns a data flag to pass to the next procedure on which the boss calls. These calls from the boss procedure determine the validity of the order and are used to indicate continuation of the entire set of procedures.

Since the VALIDATE ORDERS process exploded from the GTOP0001 DFD to the GTOP000101 DFD, the VALIDATE ORDERS STC procedure on the refined GTOP0001 STC in Figure 9-34 that corresponds to the GTOP0001 DFD process also explodes to the refined GTOP000101 STC in Figure 9-36 that corresponds to the GTOP000101 DFD. Thus, the relationship between the GTOP0001 and GTOP000101 DFDs is retained in the corresponding STCs. You should also notice that this retained relationship conforms to the recommended original boss selection criterion, namely that the boss of the refined GTOP000101 STC in Figure 9-36 is the procedure from which explosion occurred. In this case, it is the VALIDATE ORDERS procedure from which explosion occurred on the refined GTOP0001 STC in Figure 9-34.

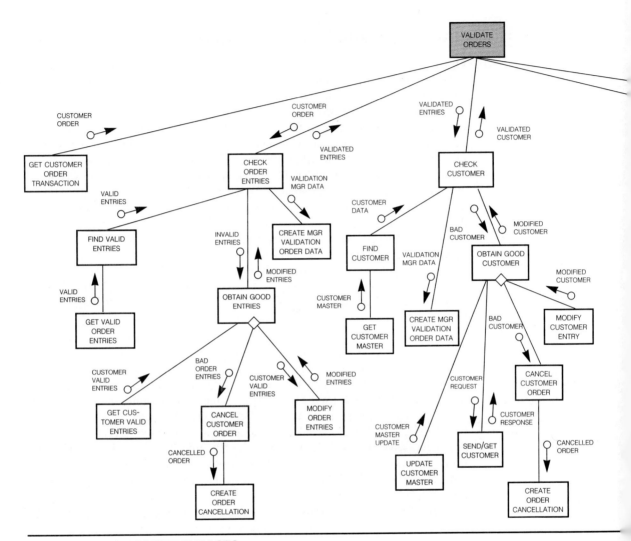

Figure 9-36. Refined GTOP000101 STC

Summary of Structure Chart Creation Guidelines

In summary, STC conversion rules should be viewed only as guidelines. They are not hard and fast rules to be applied exactly as described. The main point to keep in mind is that each module should be as self-contained as possible. Remember, the goal is to have loosely coupled, highly cohesive modules. By applying structured design methods, the analyst produces software having modules or programs with the characteristics listed in Figure 9-37. The STC is one popular method to produce software that has these characteristics.

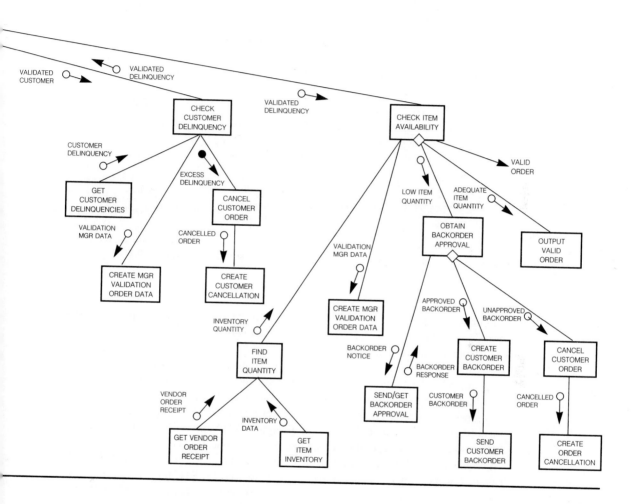

PHYSICAL DESIGN DICTIONARY ENTRIES

Diagrams that represent physical design specifications should be accompanied by design dictionary entries. Each component of each diagram should be sufficiently defined in the design dictionary. The more elaborate the dictionary specifications become (without redundant and trivial entries), the easier the physical design is to

**Characteristics of Software
Produced Through Structured Design**

- Each program or module conforms to rules for standardized structured programs.
- Each program or module solves only one specific problem or accomplishes only one program purpose.
- Each program or module contains a single overall control (boss) routine.
- Each program or module performs only one well-defined task.
- Each program or module uses utilities for reusable code to save coding.
- Each program or module only receives the data it needs to perform its function.
- Each program or module can only cause minor changes in design specifications.

Figure 9-37. Desirable program characteristics (adapted from Dolan, 1984)

explain to programmers who will be developing the programs for the proposed system. Consequently, the project team should seek to document all portions of the physical design in dictionary entries.

Each procedure, data flag, and control flag appearing in the refined STC should be thoroughly documented in design dictionary entries. It is recommended, with one exception, that the analyst only create dictionary entries for the refined STC since they more completely represent program specifications. For example, all of the components appearing in the refined STCs of Figures 9-34 and 9-36 should have design dictionary entries corresponding to the diagram components. The one exception is that a dictionary entry for the main boss procedure should accompany the first-cut STC. This dictionary entry can be used to explode to the refined STC for this first-cut STC. For example, Figures 9-38 and 9-39 show dictionary entries for the COMPLETE PHONE/MAIL INVOICES and VALIDATE ORDERS boss procedures for the first-cut GTOP0001 STC of Figure 9-25 and the first-cut GTOP000101 STC of Figure 9-32, respectively. Notice that each of these procedures explodes to the refined STC for the first-cut STC in which it appears.

The dictionary entries for the refined STCs include pseudocode that helps make each STC more easily understandable as a structured program specification. These specifications aid in understanding the basic programming logic under which the program will operate. Other dictionary specifications, such as "Triggered by," "Triggers," and so forth, also aid in understanding the operations to include in the program created for the refined STC. Figure 9-40 shows a design dictionary entry for the COMPLETE PHONE/MAIL INVOICES boss procedure from the refined GTOP0001 STC in Figure 9-34.

PROCEDURE   COMPLETE PHONE/MAIL INVOICES

Explodes to:

DFD: _____

Structure chart: _REFINED-GTOP0001STC_____

Program module: _____

Triggered by: _____

Triggers: _____

Location: _____

Text Description & Comments

This procedure represents the boss procedure for the first-cut GTOP0001 STC that explodes to the refined GTOP0001 STC.

Pseudocode

Figure 9-38. First-cut COMPLETE PHONE/MAIL INVOICES procedure

PROCEDURE   VALIDATE ORDERS

Explodes to:

DFD: _____

Structure chart: _REFINED-GTOP000101STC____

Program module: _____

Triggered by: _____

Triggers: _____

Location: _____

Text Description & Comments

This procedure represents the boss procedure for the first-cut GTOP000101 STC that explodes to the refined GTOP000101 STC.

Pseudocode

Figure 9-39. First-cut VALIDATE ORDERS procedure

PROCEDURE   COMPLETE PHONE/MAIL INVOICES

Explodes to:

DFD: _____

Structure chart: _____

Program module: _____

Triggered by: _Customer order._____

Triggers: _Creation of an order invoice, shipping invoice,_____

carrier manifest, customer back order, and order cancellation.

Location: _____

Text Description & Comments

This procedure represents the boss procedure for this refined STC.

Pseudocode

```
CALL CREATE ORDER
CALL VALIDATE ORDERS
IF ORDER IS VALID
    CALL CREATE ORDER INVOICE
    CALL CREATE SHIPPING INVOICE
    CALL CREATE CARRIER MANIFEST
```

Figure 9-40. COMPLETE PHONE/MAIL INVOICES dictionary entry

The pseudocode in the dictionary entry for the COMPLETE PHONE/MAIL INVOICES boss procedure contains only calls to the procedures below it, which is similar in operation to a control module in a structured program. All remaining procedures in the refined GTOP0001 STC in Figure 9-34 also include pseudocode in their dictionary entries. For example, Figure 9-41 illustrates the dictionary entry for the CREATE ORDER local boss procedure in Figure 9-34.

Three of the pseudocode statements in Figure 9-41 represent the calls to the procedures under the CREATE ORDER local boss procedure. Between the second and third calls, the CREATE CUSTOMER ORDER command executes, creating the order that is to be transmitted as output by the CREATE ORDER procedure and returned as the CUSTOMER ORDER data flag to the COMPLETE PHONE/MAIL INVOICES boss procedure. This pseudocode illustration shows how individual pseudocode commands are executed as part of a boss (local or main) procedure and between calls from it to other procedures on which it calls. The analyst and the programmer/analyst can be as detailed as they need to be in specifying pseudocode commands in order to provide a more complete set of program specifications.

PROCEDURE   **CREATE ORDER**

Explodes to:

    DFD: _____

    Structure chart: _____

    Program module: _____

Triggered by: _____

Triggers: _____

Location: _____

Text Description & Comments

This procedure represents a local boss for the refined GTOP0001 STC.

Pseudocode

```
CALL GET CUSTOMER ORDER DATA
CALL CREATE MGR P/M ORDER PROCESS DATA
CREATE CUSTOMER ORDER
CALL CREATE CUSTOMER ORDER TRANSACTION
```

Figure 9-41. CREATE ORDER STC procedure dictionary entry

Each procedure on which a local boss calls will also have a dictionary entry that includes pseudocode commands. For example, Figure 9-42 shows the dictionary entry for the GET CUSTOMER ORDER DATA STC I/O procedure.

All of the remaining procedures on the refined GTOP0001 STC in Figure 9-36 also have dictionary entries that include pseudocode and other specifications that make the program specification more understandable. Dictionary entries are also included for data flags and control flags to explain what they represent and what they mean to the STC. Some CASE systems, such as Intersolv's Excelerator, only permit dictionary entries for the call between procedures, not for individual flags that appear along the call. Regardless of how the dictionary entry appears or functions, it is important to indicate what data objects (LDSs) are depicted as data flags and what control flag values mean to the control of the STC.

For example, the EOF control flag that appeared on the example STC in Figure 9-4 would be explained in a dictionary entry as the internal switch that is turned on when the STC execution runs out of data. Figures 9-43 and 9-45 illustrate two types of dictionary entries for data flags appearing along a call. Figure 9-43 illustrates a dictionary entry that may be used to describe an individual data flag. This dictionary entry explains the CUSTOMER ORDER data flag that is returned to the COMPLETE PHONE/MAIL INVOICES procedure from the CREATE ORDER procedure.

PROCEDURE   GET CUSTOMER ORDER DATA

Explodes to:

    DFD: _____

    Structure chart: _____

    Program module: _____

Triggered by: _____

Triggers: _____

Location: _____

Text Description & Comments

This procedure represents an I/O procedure used to input a customer order.

Pseudocode

INPUT CUSTOMER ORDER

Figure 9-42. GET CUSTOMER ORDER DATA STC procedure dictionary entry

DATA FLAG   CUSTOMER ORDER

Explodes to:

    Data structure: _LOG-CUSTTRNS_____

    E/RD: _____

Triggered by: _Customer order entry._____

Triggers: _Completing and filling of the customer order._____

Text Description & Comments

This data flag depicts the unedited customer order that enters the service orders procedures through either a phone/mail or retail order.

Figure 9-43. CUSTOMER ORDER data flag dictionary entry

    The dictionary entry in Figure 9-44 illustrates the way the data flag depicts a LDS for a logical data object. This logical data object is the LOG-CUSTTRNS LDS that appeared as the ORDER ENTRY & VALIDATION object relationship in the GTOP0000 entity/relationship diagram (E/RD) in Figure 8-10 in Chapter 8, as the CUSTOMER ORDER data flow in the GTOP0001 DFD in Figure 9-10, and as the

CUSTOMER TRANSACTIONS screen masks in Figures 7-20 and 7-21 of Chapter 7. This set of entries illustrates the relationships among E/RDs, DFDs, STCs, and prototyping, as depicted in Figure 9-44. This figure illustrates how the data object identified as a logical object on an E/RD becomes a data flow or data store on a DFD, is passed as a data flag between procedures on a STC, and appears on a screen mask created while prototyping. Figure 9-44 also appeared as Figure 2-41 in Chapter 2 to explain how the modeling methods of the text methodology are related and how they share data, which brings full circle the application and integration of the modeling methods of the text methodology from analysis through design.

Figure 9-45 shows the dictionary entry that might be used for the call between the CREATE ORDER and CREATE CUSTOMER ORDER TRANSACTION procedures on the refined GTOP0001 STC of Figure 9-34. For this *call*, the logical data structures (LDSs) for each data flag need to be identified. Some CASE systems permit entering separate dictionary entries for each of these data flags, similar to the dictionary entry in Figure 9-43. Other CASE systems only permit dictionary entries for the call on which these data flags appear. Figure 9-45 shows a call dictionary entry of this type.

All remaining calls or data flags and procedures on the refined GTOP0001 STC of Figure 9-34 would have dictionary entries to make the program specifications easier to understand. Dictionary entries would also be created for the boss procedure on

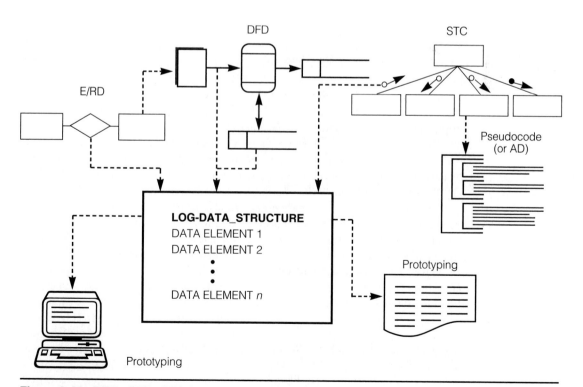

Figure 9-44. E/RD−DFD−STC−prototyping relationship

CALL   **CALL CREATE CUSTOMER ORDER TRANSACTION**

Explodes to:

    Data structure: <u>MLOG-CUSTOMER ORDER</u>

    E/RD: _____

Triggered by: _____

Triggers: _____

Text Description & Comments

This call depicts an unedited customer order passed to a procedure that creates a customer order, which in turn is used to service a customer through service orders procedures for either phone/mail or retail orders. The logical data objects (LDSs) that correspond to the two data flags are contained in the MLOG-CUSTOMER_ORDER M-LDS to which this call explodes.

Figure 9-45. Dictionary entry for the call from CREATE ORDER to CREATE CUSTOMER ORDER TRANSACTION

the first-cut GTOP000101 STC in Figure 9-32 and all remaining procedures, and calls or data flags on the refined GTOP000101 STC in Figure 9-36. Recall that Figure 9-39 illustrated the dictionary entry for the VALIDATE ORDERS boss procedure appearing on the first-cut GTOP000101 STC in Figure 9-32. This dictionary entry links the first-cut STC to the refined GTOP000101 STC for purposes of navigation through project specifications—note the explosion entry.

The design dictionary entry for the VALIDATE ORDERS procedure in Figure 9-39 illustrates how separate STCs created from separate DFDs can be related through the design dictionary. Notice that the procedure explodes to the refined GTOP000101 STC that appears in Figure 9-36.

The STC procedure dictionary entry can also illustrate how the explosion paths are retained for multiple DFD levels converted to corresponding STCs. In addition, the STC procedure dictionary entry can also show that the analyst should expect explosion procedures for many of the STCs created as a result of DFD conversion.

Figure 9-46 illustrates the dictionary entry for the VALIDATE ORDERS procedure on the refined GTOP000101 STC in Figure 9-36. The remaining procedures and all data flags or calls on the refined GTOP000101 STC in Figure 9-36 would have dictionary entries specifying logical data objects (LDSs) depicted as data flags along STC calls.

Notice that the design dictionary entry in Figure 9-46 includes text explanations to make it easier for a programmer to understand the operations necessary to create program code for the procedure. This documentation usually includes explanations and implications of codes, descriptions of data being accessed, explanations of indi-

PROCEDURE   VALIDATE ORDERS

Explodes to:

    DFD: _____

    Structure chart: _____

    Program module: _____

Triggered by: _Creation of an order._____

Triggers: _Creation of an order invoice, back order, or order cancellation._

Location: _____

Text Description & Comments

This procedure represents checking customer orders for the validity of data values. Data values in the order are checked for valid data types, valid range and code values, valid customer IDs, and the capacity to fill the order.

Pseudocode

```
CALL GET CUSTOMER ORDER TRANSACTION
CALL CHECK ORDER ENTRIES
CALL CHECK CUSTOMER
CALL CHECK CUSTOMER DELINQUENCIES
CALL CHECK ITEM AVAILABILITY
```

Figure 9-46. Design dictionary structure chart process entry

vidual operations using the accessed data, explanations of operations regarding repetitive procedures, relationships between procedures, explanations and implications of control flags directed toward the procedure, explanations and implications of transaction analysis–type specifications, and pseudocode for sets of instructions within that procedure. These specifications form the basis of explicit programming specifications that the project team must develop for programmers.

In a previous era, programming specifications were often written in longhand, from which programmers then used a procedure modeling method, such as a program flow chart, to determine the logic necessary to code the programs. The main problem with this method was that the procedure model was not directly tied to the business process model. When DFDs are created for business process modeling and STCs are created from these DFDs, the information system procedure model is directly integrated with the business process model.

The combination of the STC and accompanying dictionary entries provides specifications that programmers who fully understand structured programming principles can easily follow to create programs. The graphical picture of the STC and its accompanying dictionary entries are a better way of creating program specifications than those of previous eras because they show the logic necessary for the program.

PHYSICAL DESIGN PROGRAM SPECIFICATIONS AND BOUNDARIES

Typically, the activities of the physical design eventually leads to creating explicit specifications for the programs of the proposed system. Subsequently, these program specifications help guide programmers who are responsible for creating the programs.

Many IS departments train programmers to understand STCs, dictionary entries for components of the STCs, and the relationships between the STCs and the programs. These departments then use these specifications as program specifications themselves. The analyst in this setting simply indicates program boundaries within STCs. Programmers in this setting use bounded STCs and accompanying dictionary entries as guidelines to create the programs or parts of programs.

Personnel in many IS departments still find it necessary to create separate sets of program specifications to distribute to programmers. These program specifications are often created by the analyst using standard word processing software.

Identifying and Creating Program Requirements

Whether STCs, separate program specifications, or both are used, the majority of program requirements can be retrieved from design dictionary entries for components of physical design diagrams. Specifications are frequently retrieved, interfaced, and elaborated on to reflect physical design specifications for individual programs. These specifications should include all the processing requirements necessary for a programmer to completely understand the purpose of the program and how to write the program. Program requirements often include some combination of the following items:

- Narrative explanation of the purpose of the program, its major procedures, and its main processing operations
- Explicit text explanations for each main procedure
- List of the data structures to be accessed by each procedure
- Complete descriptions of all data structures accessed
- Complete descriptions of data items contained in the data structures accessed and meaning of data values associated with them
- Explicit explanations for all computations to be performed by the program, the

sequence in which they are to be performed, the data values to use in the computations, and what to do with the results of the computations

- Explicit explanations of all logical comparisons to be performed, what data values to compare, and what to do as a result of the comparisons
- Identification of batch and on-line procedures
- Explicit explanations for each batch and on-line procedure
- Explicit descriptions for each on-line data entry or report screen or forms used by the program
- Explicit descriptions of system programming procedures needed to support the execution of the program
- Explicit descriptions of communication system procedures needed to support the execution of the program
- Explicit descriptions of utility programs needed to support the execution of the program
- Explicit descriptions of calls to the database management system (DBMS) and accesses to the database needed by the program procedures
- Explicit description of data accessed by the DBMS

The level of program requirements that can be generated from dictionary entries depends on the amount of detail included in the dictionary entries and the ability to extract these details. These dictionary entries are usually those associated with the physical design procedure modeling method. For example, dictionary entries for STC procedures usually explain the procedure, its purpose, and how to cause it to accomplish its purpose. In addition, dictionary entries associated with data flags and control flags provide information for the data structures and data values associated with them. Furthermore, dictionary entries on prototype screen and form design specifications provide information regarding the structural form of data entry and reporting.

Word processing files are frequently created as program specifications. These files can contain retrievable dictionary specifications embedded within them, such as dictionary entries for STC components. For example, design dictionary entries can be created using standard word processing files for particular screen entry formats. The screen formats could be the same as those adopted by the installation as design dictionary screens. Also, the text explanations of the dictionary entries can be stored as a separate word processing file and rearranged in logical order. This file could then be enhanced with more detailed information about the requirements of the program and used as program specifications.

Dictionary software systems provide preformatted screens for this purpose. However, text entries within these screen formats can also be extracted and expanded for a clearer understanding. As a result, dictionary text specifications can be extracted, rearranged, elaborated on, and used as program specifications.

Regardless of the method used, program specifications can result from the use of dictionary entries. These specifications can then be used as explicit instructions for programmers to follow during program creation.

FORMAL REVIEW

The project team should conduct a formal presentation of the physical design specifications to users, managers, and information systems personnel. The purpose of this presentation is to review any deviations from the specifications formally reviewed at the end of the logical business design, identify and explain any hardware and software acquisitions, explain design specifications that have emerged during the activities of the physical design, and give management another opportunity for refusal of the system.

The formal review following the logical business design portion of the design phase concludes with the signing of a document representing agreement between the project team and the managers on logical design specifications. Any deviations from these agreed-upon design specifications must be approved by the managers. A review of the physical design should determine whether this has happened.

The project team often determines that additional software or hardware acquisitions are necessary for a proposed system. For example, the project team may decide that a smoother operation of the proposed system requires the use of a database management system or additional communications hardware and software. If required, these acquisitions must be approved prior to beginning any system development.

Additional user requirements may emerge as the analyst participates in physical design activities. These new user requirements may result from changes in business conditions, user responses to technological advances, or a host of other stimuli. The project team and users must formally agree that these new design criteria are necessary and represent valid modifications to original user requirements.

Finally, the physical design is the last activity before the firm begins to bear the tremendous cost of system development. The formal review represents the last opportunity for management to bail out of a development project prior to investing a great deal more money in hardware and software as part of the project development costs. By getting management to sign a physical design sign-off agreement document similar to the analysis phase sign-off document in Figure 6-28, the project team can rest assured that they have the support of management during the development and implementation phases of the development life cycle.

COMPUTER-AIDED PHYSICAL DESIGN

CASE systems permit the analyst to use the computer to create physical design diagrams and accompanying design dictionary entries. With these tools, the analyst can convert logical business design specifications into physical design specifications. In addition, many of these tools permit physical design prototyping activities.

The best versions of these tools provide ways to use desktop computers to enter elaborate dictionary specifications. These dictionary specifications can be printed, enhanced with standard word processing, and become explicit program specifications to be distributed to the programmers responsible for program creation.

Many of these tools can generate program code in various programming languages to represent I/O screens for user interfaces. These tools can also generate program code for data structures defined in the design dictionary and pro forma program code in the form of physical design diagrams. *Pro forma* program code represents program code of a particular type that is strung together to accomplish a specific purpose. A code layout in a particular style may be included in other program procedures. Including this code represents considerable savings in programming efforts relative to on-line system accesses. Programmers who can embed these entries in programs assigned to them will only be responsible for creating the additional program code for the procedures performed on accessed data.

Some CASE tools provide greater support than others for converting the logical business design into the physical design. For example, Computer Sciences Corporation has developed a CASE tool called Design Generator that can automatically produce a first-cut STC from a DFD. The analyst need only tell Design Generator which DFD to convert and what process should be the boss (one on the DFD or an artificially inserted boss).

Many of these tools also produce physical design specifications in a form that can be input to software systems capable of generating large portions of the physical system. These software systems are formally called **application generators** or lower CASE systems. In addition, a number of manufacturers of application generators have created utility routines that convert output specifications from the physical designs stored in CASE systems into specifications that can be input to the application generator. For example, utilities exist for converting specifications from various middle CASE systems into specifications for MAGEC from Al Lee and Associates, TRANSFORM from Transform Logic, and TELON from Computer Associates.

Prototyping the Physical
Design Using CASE Systems

The physical design represents the last portion of the project life cycle before actual creation or acquisition of the proposed system. It is important that users have the opportunity to respond to the relevant portions of the physical system prior to actual creation. This practice ensures that the physical design satisfies the users' information needs. Prototyping activities are frequently conducted for each physical data entry and reporting screen or form to ensure that they provide the desired level of functionality for users. In addition, the prototypes that correspond to physical design for other user interfaces should be created and reviewed.

A number of prototyping capabilities have become part of CASE systems to aid project teams in prototyping activities. These capabilities usually provide a way to operationally test all user interfaces so that users can appraise their suitability. They permit users to actually test the interfaces, including menu or prompting screens for operation selection, screen masks for data access and entry, screen report masks for data reporting activities, and preprogrammed files representing database accesses. Prototyping the physical design allows the project team to show the design specifications to users one last time before incurring the cost of developing the system—the greatest cost for the project.

Information Systems Re-engineering

Some CASE manufacturers also have utility programs that read existing programs and convert them into their equivalent procedure models, STCs, or action diagrams (ADs). For example, design recovery or reverse-engineering utilities are available that work with Texas Instruments' Information Engineering Facility (IEF), Knowledgeware's Information Engineering Workbench (IEW) and Application Development Workbench (ADW), and Intersolv's Excelerator. A whole area of recapturing program procedures at a higher level of abstraction, known as information systems re-engineering, has emerged regarding this capability. In fact, re-engineering has now moved up the ladder of abstraction to re-engineering the business model and the actual business. The implications of this are covered in Chapter 16 during discussions of post-implementation review and maintenance.

Information systems re-engineering typically involves executing a software system that restructures old program code into a more concise structured programming format and then re-engineering it in one of the procedure modeling formats such as STCs or ADs—that is, converting it into a procedure model at a higher level of abstraction. For example, Knowledgeware purchased a company that sold a restructuring software system used to restructure badly structured COBOL code. Knowledgeware now uses the output from this step as input to their re-engineering software system. This system takes the restructured COBOL code and creates an action diagram laid out in the same format as the restructured COBOL code. To provide detail, Knowledgeware's re-engineering software system substitues individual pseudocode statements for the COBOL instructions.

Intersolv also has a design recovery utility that recaptures the procedures of a COBOL program. This recovery utility converts the COBOL program procedures into a STC laid out in structured programming format in Excelerator. The program's detailed instructions appear as pseudocode in the Excelerator-based dictionary entries for the STC procedures. Programmers can then review and revise (re-engineer) the STC procedure model for better performance and clarity. The re-engineered STC can then be used as input into a lower CASE application generator to generate new code for the re-engineered code. For example, InterSolv uses these re-engineered STCs as input to APS, their lower CASE application generator. Thus, the recaptured COBOL code can be maintained as a STC procedure model, rather than just in the form of COBOL code.

REVIEW

This chapter explains how logical business design specifications are implemented in information systems and converted into physical design specifications that compose the information system procedure model.

You can use different procedure modeling methods during the physical design, but the text methodology uses structure charts (STCs) and their characteristics. Step-by-step methods for converting DFDs into STCs are given, and entries to the design dictionary for components of STCs are illustrated. These methods allow the analyst to identify program requirements and create detailed specifications for programmers.

Prototyping and reviewing physical design specifications are described. These processes represent the last major opportunities for the users and management to influence the system before system development actually begins.

Finally, CASE methods for developing physical design specifications are discussed. These methods assist analysts in physical design diagramming and in entering accompanying dictionary specifications.

The physical design represents the last major design effort of the project team. Additional physical design requirements may surface during the development phase of the project development life cycle. However, these requirements usually represent enhancements to existing requirements.

After completing the physical design and securing final approval for carrying the project forward, the project analysts assume the roles of coordinators and supervisors for the development phase. Programmers are selected, assigned responsibilities, and supervised during development activities. Users are trained in their new responsibilities and in the operations of the system. Finally, the project team coordinates the development activities of programmers, the training of users, and the acquisition of hardware and software required by the newly developed system. These activities represent the major activities performed by the project team during the development phase of the project life cycle. All of these activities will be discussed in Chapter 11, which covers the development phase.

QUESTIONS

1. Identify and explain the major activities of the physical design.
2. How do hardware and software influence the physical design?
3. What does the term *user interface* mean and what purpose does it serve for prototyping the physical design?
4. What does a STC represent relative to the design of a computer program as part of a system?
5. How are STCs related to structured programming?
6. What is the purpose of converting a DFD into a STC?

7. Distinguish between transform and transaction analysis by describing the relationship between them and the differences between them.

8. Identify and explain the steps involved in transform analysis.

9. Identify and explain the steps involved in transaction analysis.

10. Distinguish between data flags and control flags.

11. What is the purpose of the or/selection symbol, and what purpose does it serve relative to transaction analysis?

12. Why does the top-level DFD not represent a DFD that needs to be converted to a structure chart?

13. What does the central area of transform represent?

14. Distinguish between the methods used to identify the central transform relative to the traditional selection criteria.

15. Why is the central transform procedure moved to the top during the Dolan DFD-to-STC conversion method?

16. Why is a STC that is created using only transform analysis often called a sequential task STC?

17. What do data stores become during DFD-to-STC conversion?

18. How are data flows indicated on a STC?

19. Why is the or/selection symbol sometimes inserted below procedures on a STC?

20. Identify and distinguish among the four key characteristics of a STC.

21. What is the relationship between cohesion and coupling?

22. Explain the relationship between STC span of control and size.

23. Why must an additional procedure sometimes be inserted on a STC after a boss procedure has been selected when the Dolan method is used for boss selection?

24. What are the key criteria used to identify the boundaries of a program relative to STCs?

25. Identify and explain the requirements contained within program specifications.

26. For a company in your vicinity, obtain a copy of the instructions that analysts and programmers use in creating their program specifications. Explain these instructions.

27. Why is the physical design prototyped and what specifications represent those that are typically prototyped?

28. Why does the physical design contain a formal review at its conclusion?

29. What are application generators, and what purpose might they serve relative to the development of the system?

30. How is badly structured COBOL re-engineered into higher-level procedure models and carried forward into structured programs?

EXERCISES

Chapter 9 of the student workbook contains blank documentation forms to use in the following exercises.

1. Redraw the DFD in Figure 9-8 with one of the processes in the area of central transform selected as the boss and positioned at the top of the diagram.

2. Redraw the DFD in Figure 9-8 with the two processes in the area of central transform converted into a single process and positioned at the top of the diagram.

3. Convert the DFD created in exercise 3 of Chapter 8 into its first-cut STC equivalent, with an appropriate dictionary entry for the boss procedure.

4. Create a refined STC for the first-cut STC created in exercise 3. First create a rearranged version of the first-cut STC of exercise 3 without data flags, control flags, or dictionary entries. Create the final refined version of this rearranged STC that contains data and control flags and other STC symbols and all design dictionary entries for all procedures, data flags, control flags, or/selection symbols, and loop symbols appearing on the STC. Be sure to document any explosion to a lower-level STC.

5. Convert the DFD created in exercise 4 of Chapter 8 into its first-cut STC equivalent, with an appropriate dictionary entry for the boss procedure.

6. Create a refined STC for the first-cut STC created in exercise 5. First create a rearranged version of the first-cut STC of exercise 5 without data flags, control flags, or dictionary entries. Create the final refined version of this rearranged STC that contains data and control flags and other STC symbols and all design dictionary entries for all procedures, data flags, control flags, or/selection symbols, and loop symbols appearing on the STC. Be sure to document any explosion to a lower-level STC.

7. Convert the DFD created in exercise 5 of Chapter 8 into its first-cut STC equivalent, with an appropriate dictionary entry for the boss procedure.

8. Create a refined STC for the first-cut STC created in exercise 7. First create a rearranged version of the first-cut STC of exercise 7 without data flags, control flags, or dictionary entries. Create a final refined version of this rearranged STC that contains data and control flags and other STC symbols and all design dictionary entries for all procedures, data flags, control flags, or/selection symbols, and loop symbols appearing on the STC.
Be sure to document any explosion to a lower-level STC.

9. Convert the DFD created in exercise 6 of Chapter 8 into its first-cut STC equivalent, with an appropriate dictionary entry for the boss procedure.

10. Create a refined STC for the first-cut STC created in exercise 9. First create a rearranged version of the first-cut STC of exercise 9 without data flags, control

flags, or dictionary entries. Create a final refined version of this rearranged STC that contains data and control flags and other STC symbols and all design dictionary entries for all procedures, data flags, control flags, or/selection symbols, and loop symbols appearing on the STC.

Be sure to document any explosion to a lower-level STC.

SELECTED REFERENCES

Dolan, K. A. 1984. *Business Computer Systems Design.* Santa Cruz, CA: Mitchell Publishing, Inc.

Martin, J. 1988. *Information Engineering: Book I, Introduction.* Englewood Cliffs, NJ: Prentice-Hall.

Yourdon, E. and L. Constantine. 1989. *Structured Design,* 2nd Edition. Englewood Cliffs, NJ: Yourdon Press.

PART IV

Database Technologies and Developing and Implementing the Project Design

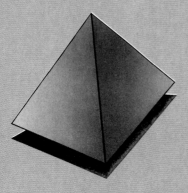

Once the physical design is complete, system development can begin in earnest. The primary concern of system development is the creation of a system that conforms to the physical design requirements. These physical design requirements and the development of the system can affect and be affected by database technologies. Proper database design and file organization methods ensure that users can obtain the information they need in a timely manner. Since many new systems require direct interaction with users, the design of data structures and the identification of the relationships among them take on special significance. Before the new system is actually turned over to users, they must be trained and the system must be thoroughly tested. The project life cycle should conclude with a formal review of the project by both IS personnel and users.

CHAPTER 10

Understanding Database Technologies That Influence the Design

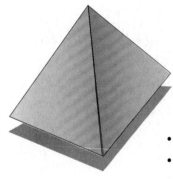

OVERVIEW

The use of a database enhances the comprehensiveness of the information supplied by a system. However, the use of a database also increases the complexities of the analysis and design process. This chapter explains database technology and discusses its influence on the analysis and design process by:

- Defining a database

- Explaining how to create the structure of a database

- Describing database management system models

- Explaining methods used to manipulate data in a database

- Describing usages and interfaces of the database

- Identifying methods to secure the database and ensure the integrity of its data

- Explaining normalization of database object type (file) formats

- Describing object-oriented database design

- Identifying hardware and software used in database environments

- Explaining system design criteria in the database environment

KEY TERMS

Active dictionary

Anomalies

Associative semantic object

Attribute

Client-server computer architecture

Complex network relationship

Composite semantic object

Compound semantic object

Data definition commands (DDCs)

Data dictionary

Data integration

Data integrity

Data manipulation commands (DMCs)

Database

Database administrator (DBA)

Database management system (DBMS)

Deletion anomaly

Determinant

Enciphering key

Encryption procedures

Foreign key property

Functional dependency

Generalized semantic object

Hierarchical database model

Host programs

Insertion anomaly

Intersection data structure

Journal files

Logical database structure

Logical view

Network database model

Normal forms

Normalization

Object-oriented database design
   (OODD)

Occurrence

Physical database structure

Physical view

Preprogrammed access procedures

Property

Relation

Relational database model

Schema

Semantic object

Simple network relationship

Simple semantic object

SQL

System tuning

Tree relationship

User view

The information explosion has fostered the rise of database technology, which attempts to provide the control necessary for obtaining appropriate and consistent information. Databases maintain large-scale accumulations of integrated data. This technology attempts to provide a source of data to be shared by persons with varying perspectives within the firm. Because the use of this technology is so common, analysts must understand how a database is defined, developed, and utilized. The technology of the database environment influences the activities of a development life cycle. With an understanding of this technology, the analyst can design systems in a more comprehensive manner.

461

This chapter provides definitions and explanations for understanding and using database technology in the design of computer systems; it explains the characteristics of this technology and identifies issues critical to analysis and design. No prior knowledge of database technologies is required.

The increased demand for information in business requires a large cache of data, and database technologies provide the vehicles by which this cache of data is managed. A system of software programs known as a **database management system (DBMS)**, under the direction of a system professional known as a **database administrator (DBA)**, creates and maintains the database. Designers of business systems either work closely with the DBA or perform some of the DBA's functions that are necessary to define or modify the database.

The same characteristics and skills described at the end of Chapter 1 for the analyst are also needed by the database administrator. The analyst uses investigative, organizational, technical, and interpersonal skills to mediate between the different information needs of functional area personnel, whereas the database administrator uses these skills to mediate between the different data requirements for different systems and users' on-demand inquiries.

The data contained in a database includes an accumulation of most of the facts about data types necessary for understanding the many different areas of the firm; it depicts the conditions facing the firm. Accessing the database provides a window through which users view the data that symbolizes the operations of the firm and the conditions facing it. For example, database files that describe customer complaints for NG&T may describe conditions that face its personnel in dealing with customers. Legitimate complaints may indicate changes in operations that NG&T could initiate to better serve its customers.

The same data types in a database may serve many different personnel in the firm. Individual data items for these data types often reside in a single storage location within auxiliary disk storage provided for the database. When needed, individual data items are made available to many different users in combination with other singly stored data items. These combinations of data items provide the information necessary to support the tasks performed by personnel within the firm.

Storing data items in single locations in the database that serve multiple users has two main advantages:

- Elimination of redundancy in data and effort
- Retention of the integrity of the stored data

Since individual data items reside in single storage locations within the database, two different employees in two different departments cannot enter conflicting information. **Data integrity** is the accuracy with which the data items and relationships portray their counterparts in the business environment. Integrity is maintained by preventing invalid (as opposed to unauthorized) modifications to the data. Therefore, users are more confident in using the data in support of their information needs. Storing individual data items in single locations also reduces the effort involved in keeping them current.

This chapter explains how to effectively create a nonredundant, accurate database.

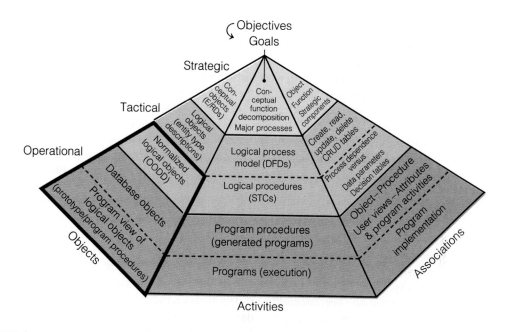

Figure 10-1. Enterprise/methodology model focus of Chapter 10

Figure 10-1 illustrates the part of the enterprise/methodology model on which this chapter focuses.

In this chapter, the logical objects of the business, as defined in logical data structures (LDSs), are used to create a database that is correctly formatted and relatively free of errors. Modified versions of each LDS are used in constructing the database for the system to use.

Many definitions of a database state that it is a collection of files that constitutes a base of related data. A database is not *just* a collection of separate files. A more complete definition is: A **database** is a collection of *integrated* data items that includes a *description* of the data therein, with names assigned and descriptions supplied to make those data items and collections of data items referable. A database differs from a design dictionary in that the description of the data is a part of the collection of data that composes the database.

STRUCTURE OF THE DATABASE

Combining relevant data items to describe a data type is made possible through the internal logical structure of the way the DBA directs the DBMS to build the database.

This internal structure provides for data integration, which makes it possible to readily combine separately stored but logically related data for specific purposes. **Data integration** is the ability to consolidate data items from different database files as either input or output to the IS or in response to an on-line user inquiry.

For example, a screen display of a customer's order may list characteristics of the customer, such as name, address, and telephone number, along with the characteristics of the order, such as order number, order date, order items, and order amount. The customer characteristics would be stored in a separate database file from the order characteristics. Commands to the DBMS would cause these data items to be combined for screen display so that a salesclerk could be better informed while talking to a customer about an order over the telephone. The analyst provides criteria concerning database design relevant to combining the logical relationships between appropriate data items for use as data sources for designed systems.

The DBMS establishes data integration by the way it "defines" the database in relation to the database's **logical database structure**, as perceived by users, and the **physical database structure**, which defines the way data is physically stored in the database. The analyst provides logical design criteria for integrating appropriate data in the database. The integration of data through the correlation of the logical and physical structures makes it possible for users with different information needs to share the data with little, if any, regard for where the data is physically stored in the database.

A database contains a description of itself that is used to store, retrieve, and integrate data items stored in different physical locations. This description allows separately stored data containing logical relationships to be collectively accessed. Since the DBMS defines the way data is logically viewed and physically stored, accesses to the database by programs or user inquiries do not require specification of where the data is stored. The DBMS is responsible for physical access. The embedded description (**physical view**) indicates physical storage locations of data items used to retrieve the integrated data items (**logical view**). This embedded description is known as the schema.

The Database Schema

The schema is the logical heart of the database and is the specification that separates a database from being just a collection of files. To be more precise, a **schema** is a description of the complete structure (logical and physical) of the database, including names and descriptions of all data items, sets of data, and collections of the data item sets. The names assigned in the schema are used to reference individual data items and collections of data items within the database. The schema relates the logical view (how the data is perceived to be stored) with the physical view (how and where the data is actually stored).

An example is the best way to understand the characteristics and uses of a database. Figure 10-2 shows a listing of six sets of data types (files) you might expect a hospital to maintain to support the information needs of some of its personnel.

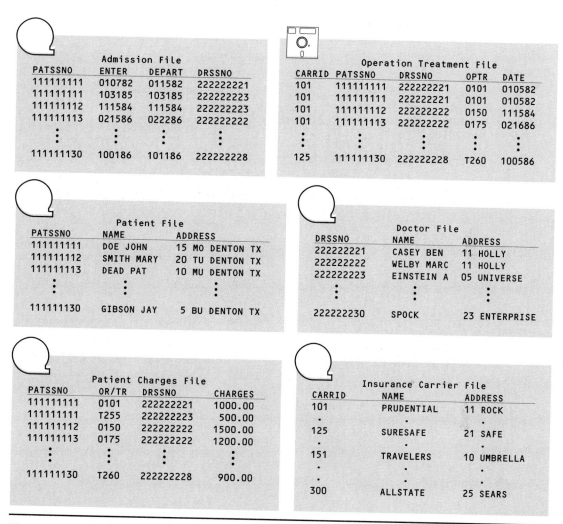

Figure 10-2. Hospital data file example

In Figure 10-2, if the hospital stored these sets of data types only as files, then each time an employee had a different information need from within a *new* combination of the six files, a complete application program would have to be created. This would be necessary because no general-purpose system like the DBMS exists that can be directed to access the data from these six files in a new form. Companies that use file processing have programs that access data in a specific format and perform specific procedures on the data. The company's personnel have to revise these programs to access different data, combine data differently, or perform additional actions on the data.

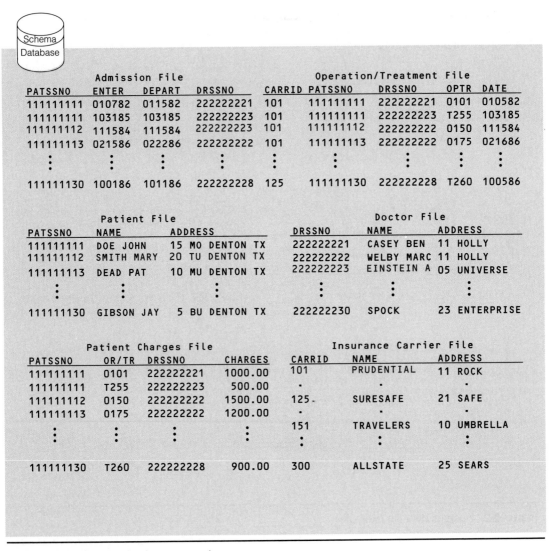

Figure 10-3. Hospital database example

If the hospital used a DBMS to maintain its data, names would be assigned in the schema to each separate database object type (or *file*—collection of data item sets) and each data item within the object type (or set of data items) of the database object type. The DBMS associates these names with the places where the data types and items are actually stored. As a result, these names can then be used in appropriate accessing commands to physically retrieve matched data. Figure 10-3 illustrates these files stored as a database in auxiliary disk storage.

Figure 10-3 illustrates how the database can be viewed as a large table with names assigned to sections that correspond to the data types in the database. Section names correspond to file names in file processing systems. Names are also assigned to data items (columns) within the sections that make up a database object type (table). These names correspond to field names in file processing systems. As a result of using these naming conventions for schema sections and data items, logically related data can be physically found by referring to its section name (file name) and specific data item names (field names). Hereafter, the terms *database object*, *database data type*, *database table*, and *database file* should all be considered synonymous.

For example, a hospital administrator may wish to access the name and address of Mary Smith along with her doctor's name and address, the day she was admitted, and the name of her insurance carrier from the database in Figure 10-3. This requires that data be accessed from the patient database file, the admissions file, the doctor file, and the insurance carrier file. More specifically, the access requires that the administrator:

1. Access the patient file, using "Mary Smith" to compare names until Mary Smith's patient file is retrieved.
2. Use the PATSSNO (111111112) from Mary Smith's patient file record to search the admissions file and find her admission record.
3. Use the DRSSNO (222222223) from Mary Smith's admission record to search the doctor file and find her doctor's record (A. Einstein).
4. Use the CARRID (101) from Mary Smith's admission record to search the insurance carrier file to find her insurance carrier record (Prudential).

The resulting display of the hospital administrator's access request would be:

Mary Smith 20 Tu Denton Tx. A. Einstein Prudential

A relatively simple access command could be used in a database environment to retrieve this information for the administrator, whereas in a file processing system, a programmer would have to create an entire computer program to perform this data retrieval. The program would contain the logical procedures to compare appropriate identification numbers from the separate files.

Figure 10-3 illustrates that the schema occupies part of the storage allocated to the database. The database is not actually stored as compactly as this illustration indicates (all on one disk pack). However, it can be conceptually viewed as if it were stored in this manner. For the sake of efficiency, the data sets are often stored on separate disk packs to prevent too many accesses to the same network channel or disk drive.

The DBMS uses the schema to correlate the logical view and the physical view of data in the database to support data integration. The logical integration of data provided for in the schema permits access of data items stored in completely different physical locations in such a way that the data appears to be physically stored together. The traditional concept of a record used in file processing environments completely changes as a result of the way the schema correlates the logical application of data and the physical storage of data in a database. Programs in systems and on-line user access commands can retrieve logically related data items for particular business applications without taking into account that the data comes from completely different physical locations. These programs and users treat each collection of data items as a physical record. A set of data items logically constituting a record for particular business purposes may in fact involve accessing data items in records from a number of different physical files in the database. As a result, there are, hypothetically, an infinite number of combinations of related data items that might constitute a logical record.

For instance, a billing program accessing data from the hospital database likely needs to access the charges from the patient charges file, the name and address of the patient from the patient file, and the patient's insurance company name and address from the insurance carrier file. After access, the programming application treats the combined access (patient charges, patient name, address, insurance company name, and insurance company address) as if it were a physical record. The access commands cause the DBMS to cross-reference the account numbers appropriate for each patient without requiring the access command to specify where the data items are physically stored.

DATABASE ADMINISTRATION

As previously stated, databases are created and maintained under the direction of an information systems professional known as the database administrator (DBA), using a system of software called a database management system (DBMS). The DBA and the DBMS function together to control the operations necessary to create or maintain the database.

The DBA performs the following functions relative to creating, maintaining, and using a database:

- Directs the DBMS to create or modify the schema and defines user views
- Manages all activities affecting the database
- Manages the DBMS
- Analyzes the environment of the database

The database administrator directs the DBMS to create or modify the schema either by issuing commands in command language or by keying the schema description in a dictionary system used by the DBMS. The DBA is responsible for setting up an environment in which he or she manages all activities that affect the database to ensure its integrity, security, completeness, and accessibility. Since the DBMS is just another software system, it must be monitored, managed, and maintained so that it provides appropriate and continuing access to the database.

Creation of the Schema

The database administrator directs the DBMS to define the database schema. The schema is defined in relation to the database design that best complies with the user requirements derived in the data modeling process described in Chapters 5 and 8. The DBA employs user requirements as the basis for defining a database that is comprehensive enough to meet the information needs of system users.

Names are assigned to database files and to individual data items. These names are usually selected to correspond to their functions within the firm; they usually represent standardized ways of referring to data within the business. Additional names, known as *aliases,* are assigned, which are synonymous with the "official" names. Aliases allow users to reference generally available data types and items by familiar names. For example, assembly line personnel may use the alias PART_NUMBER for the INVENTORY_NUMBER data item to refer to the ID number for an inventory item used in production. PART_NUMBER conveys an understanding more familiar to assembly line personnel for a part used in production. Aliases have appeared in some of the dictionary entries for data types and data items defined in earlier chapters.

Database Command Languages

The database administrator directs the DBMS to create the schema by issuing commands in a command language used to communicate with the DBMS. Each DBMS has a way for the DBA, the analyst, and the users to communicate with it. This communication language can be a rather cryptic language developed by the DBMS software developers or a macro version of the DBMS communication language. A macro database language is similar in concept to third generation programming languages listed in Chapter 1, such as COBOL and FORTRAN, that correspond to machine languages. These macro languages are generally called fourth generation languages, or just database languages.

The DBA uses certain commands within the command language, called **data definition commands (DDCs)**, to direct the DBMS to create or modify the schema. The CREATE command provided by the microcomputer DBMS packages dBASE III and IV is an example of a DDC. Although many DBMS manufacturers do create separate command languages, called *data definition languages (DDLs)*, to issue DDCs, most DDCs are simply those commands within the command language of the DBMS. These commands are used by the database administrator to cause the DBMS to assign names and descriptions to parts of the database. The assigned names make the respective data types and data items referable for data retrieval.

For instance, a schema used to define the medical database in Figure 10-3 might assign the names ADMISION, OPER/TRMT, PATIENT, DOCTOR, CHARGES, and INS/CARR to the six separate files, and the names PATSSNO, ENTER, DEPART, DRSSNO, OPTR, DATE, NAME, ADDRESS, CHARGES, and CARRID to the individual data items within those files. These names make those parts of the database referable for data retrieval purposes. In addition, a description of the individual data items is included in the schema. This description specifies the type of data (alphabetic,

R>LIST TABLES
Tables in the database HOSPITAL

Name	Columns	Rows	Name	Columns	Rows
ADMISION	4	14	PATIENT	3	7
DOCTOR	3	5	OPER/TRMT	5	20
CHARGES	4	20	INS/CARR	3	8

R>LIST ADMISION
Table: ADMISION
Read Password: NO
Modify Password: NO
Column definitions

#	Name	Type	Length	Key
1	PATSSNO	INTEGER	1 value(s)	
2	ENTER	INTEGER	1 value(s)	
3	DEPART	INTEGER	1 value(s)	
4	DRSSNO	INTEGER	1 value(s)	

R>LIST PATIENT
Table: PATIENT
Read Password: NO
Modify Password: NO
Column definitions

#	Name	Type	Length	Key
1	PATSSNO	INTEGER	1 value(s)	
2	NAME	30 characters		
3	ADDRESS	30 characters		

R>LIST DOCTOR
Table: DOCTOR
Read Password: NO
Modify Password: NO
Column definitions

#	Name	Type	Length	Key
1	DRSSNO	INTEGER	1 value(s)	
2	NAME	30 characters		
3	ADDRESS	30 characters		

Figure 10-4. R:BASE System V schema specification

numeric, and so on) and the amount of storage required for the data items. Figure 10-4 shows the schema that defines the medical database using a microcomputer DBMS, R:BASE System V. The LIST command in R:BASE System V is used to display the database schema consisting of the names of the database files (tables) and the names of the data items (columns) in each database table, including the descriptions of those data items. The CREATE command in the R:BASE System V language was used to create this database and to assign the table and data item names and descriptions.

Figure 10-4 begins by listing the names of the database tables, with information concerning the number of data items (Columns) and the number of records (Rows) for each table. The remainder of Figure 10-4 lists a portion of the database schema for three of its tables, including the names and descriptions of the data items in those tables.

High-level data definition software is often included as part of, or as a supplement to, the DBMS command language. This software prompts the database administrator for the names and descriptions of the parts of the database. The software package Application Express is an example of a high-level way to specify data definitions for R:BASE System V. Such programs often work by using preformatted screen displays with underscored sections that prompt the DBA to insert variable information regarding the database schema. With this variable information, the DBA provides the names and descriptions that define the database schema.

Modification of the Schema

The database administrator is also responsible for modifying the schema used to describe the database. The MODIFY command in dBASE III and IV is a DDC used to alter the schema for an existing database. The data contained in the database represents a conceptualization of conditions facing the firm. As the business changes, the information needs of the firm also change. Additional data may need to be collected and stored, and existing data may need to be modified or deleted. As a result of these changes in information needs, the analyst modifies the system, and the system modifications sometimes result in modifications to the database structure. Therefore, the schema may dynamically change as the business changes.

Modifying a database schema represents an investment in both overhead and operational expenses. While modifying a database structure, the current database may either be unavailable for access or be retained as a parallel database until the database is restructured. The use of a parallel database provides uninterrupted access by systems and users. While restructuring the database, the DBA attempts to redefine it in a manner that minimizes problems for existing systems.

Defining User Views for
Better Management of Activities

Defining the schema includes a set of specifications that provide a way to identify authorized users and the data they may access. Part of the management activities of the database administrator is to use these specifications, along with other DBMS functions, to secure the database from unauthorized access or modification. The database is a shared resource, and the DBA directs the DBMS to place restrictions on the portions of the database that are available for each user. In addition, restrictions are placed on the actions users can specify for those portions of the database. To do this, the DBA defines user views for each class of user.

The **user view** identifies the portions of the database a user can access and whether that user can perform modifications on the data items in that user view. Only qualified users are granted updating privileges for data values contained within their user views. User views provide better security for the data contained in the database. They make appropriate data items accessible across different files for different personnel in the firm. The analyst describes user views and modification privileges for the DBA to use.

To identify user views, the analyst or database designer must determine the logical objects that satisfy users' information needs and determine in which database objects the properties of these logical objects reside. The database designer then creates a table that lists the database objects users may access, the properties of those objects they may access, and the type of access they may have to those properties. These access specifications are related to the "Create-Read-Update-Delete (C-R-U-D)" activities that users are authorized to perform. It is not wise to permit all personnel to have access to all database object properties. Users should access only data types and data items for those data types that can help them complete their job responsibilities.

In addition to data definition commands (described earlier), the DBMS's communication language also has **data manipulation commands** (**DMCs**) that cause the DBMS to access appropriate data values within the database. Users either issue DMCs directly or call for the execution of IS programs that call on the database to gain access to the data in their user views. A more detailed description of DMCs appears in the section "Data Manipulation Commands (DMCs) and Command Languages," later in this chapter.

The DBA is responsible for managing all activities affecting the database, including user DMCs and calls to IS programs that access the database. The DBA usually does not actually perform the activities affecting the database, but must provide an environment conducive to successful and authorized completion of these activities.

Managing the Database Management System (DBMS) and Performing Configuration Analysis

Since the DBMS is a software system and the database is a collection of self-describing files residing on networked hardware, the efficient functioning of the entire environment can be monitored. The DBA analyzes the functioning of the DBMS, the performance of network hardware and software, the operations of the control software systems, access to data in the database, density of data in specific storage areas, and the functioning of utility and application software systems that use the database.

The DBA uses the DBMS to provide the most comprehensive and easily accessible database available for the information needs of the firm. To do this, the DBA periodically gathers statistical information related to database management actions. This information can be acquired by sampling the execution of DBMS directing functions, as well as by sampling actual system executions. The DBA also investigates user complaints about response time and validity of accessed information. He or she uses the information concerning the operations of the system to determine where changes should be made in order to alleviate problems.

As a result of analyzing statistical data and complaints from users, the DBA frequently performs a function known as **system tuning** to disperse data within a database among different auxiliary storage areas for increased efficiency. The DBA gathers data concerning how data has been accessed over a period of time. He or she then statistically analyzes data access performance and, based on the results of the analysis, reconstructs data storage in the database to more efficiently accommodate data accessing. One benefit of this is to speed up the response time when data is retrieved.

Problem sources may include the DBMS, the interface provided for application software, business systems that access the database, communication software that links users to the DBMS, the users themselves, or some combination of these.

If the source of the problem is the DBMS, the DBA may elect to acquire a more comprehensive version of the DBMS to service user accesses to the database. The DBMS is subject to the same problems evidenced in all vendor-supplied software. Most commercially acquired software is installed with varying degrees of comprehensiveness. During analysis of the firm's DBMS, it is sometimes determined that a pared-down version of the DBMS is more appropriate for the needs of the business. Alternatively, it is sometimes determined that additional options available from the DBMS manufacturer warrant acquisition. Consequently, the DBA may determine that an update of the DBMS itself is the solution to the observed problem. The remaining problem sources are addressed by changing application programs, modifying or replacing the current communication software, and/or training users in proper access methods.

Hardware/Software Configuration

In addition to reconfiguring the DBMS to better suit the firm's information needs, the DBA may help determine the specific configuration of hardware and software that makes up the firm's environment. This configuration includes:

- The computer hardware system
- A communication control system
- Application programs
- The DBMS
- The operating system for the computer
- The database stored on auxiliary disk storage

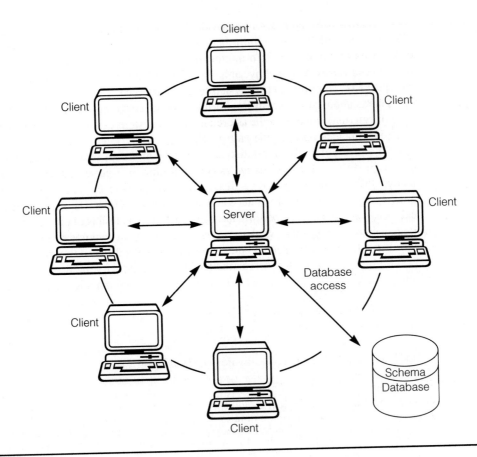

Figure 10-5. Client-server computer architecture

A preferred hardware configuration in today's environment is a configuration known as a **client-server computer architecture**, which uses host computers to access centrally stored databases that pass the database request to client computers, which in turn perform the actions on the retrieved data. Figure 10-5 graphically depicts the completeness of this configuration.

Each access to the database uses some combination of the elements of the hardware and software configuration. For example, a user may issue a command at his or her desktop client computer that causes an application program to execute and call on the host computer to retrieve the data from the database. This application program uses either embedded data manipulation commands (DMCs) or a call to a predefined data retrieval routine that directs the DBMS on the host computer to retrieve the data from the database. The application program on the client computer then continues executing to process the data retrieved from the host computer database. Alternatively, from the client computer, the user may issue an on-line communication control system command to send a DMC directly to the DBMS on the host computer for data retrieval. This DMC directs the DBMS to access the database stored on disk and display the results of executing the DMC on the user's screen.

The DBA determines a configuration of hardware and software for the client-server computer architecture that best meets the information needs of the users and the systems designed for processing data. The best configuration of hardware and software is decided on a cost/benefit basis, as are all decisions relative to expenditures of funds within the business. Acquiring and installing a DBMS entails expending additional funds for additional hardware and software used to support database technologies. Typically, additional acquisitions consist of increased internal computer memory, disk drives and disk packs, channels for communication, and ports of entry into the computer system. Increased acquisitions are also made in system software, communication software, and application software. Furthermore, the hardware and software configuration is periodically reviewed by the DBA to determine whether it warrants modification. The DBA determines which acquisitions are warranted on a cost/benefit basis to provide an environment conducive to effective and efficient use of the database.

The Analyst's Role in Database Administration

A deeper discussion of the DBA's activities is beyond the scope of this text. However, practicing analysts should be familiar enough with these activities to recognize their dependence on the DBA for better functioning of their systems. By understanding each other's responsibilities, the analyst and the DBA help establish an air of cooperation that spreads throughout the business and the systems that serve it. The analyst should also understand that the majority of the DBA's functions are performed by enlisting the help of the DBMS, which also performs activities related to creating, maintaining, and using the database.

DATABASE MANAGEMENT SYSTEMS

A DBMS was defined earlier as a software system used to create and maintain a database. DBMS software has evolved over the years and has produced an array of different types of systems to act on databases. These software systems are generally based on a particular database model that emerged as DBMSs evolved.

Database Management System Models

Commercially available DBMSs have been developed based on a specific type of database model to define relationships among the different data contained in databases. The available DBMSs use three major ways of structuring relationships among data:

- Tree (or hierarchical) relationship
- Simple network relationship
- Complex network relationship

Each of the different types of relationships represents a particular type of relationship among different data types.

The **tree relationship** (also known as a hierarchical relationship) specifies a *one-to-many (1:M)* relationship. It is a structuring of the data relationships based on individual data items in one set of data (a data type) that have relationships with a number of data items in the other set (data types). The data type on the "one" side of the relationship is known as the *parent* data type; the data type on the "many" side is known as *child* data. The main characteristic of a tree relationship is that parent data types can be associated with many child data types, but a child data type can be related to only one parent data type.

For instance, two files that NG&T might maintain are a vendor (supplier) file and a file of current invoices for items ordered from the vendor. An individual vendor record may have many current invoices, but each invoice can only be associated with only one vendor. Another example is a dormitory-to-student relationship. A dormitory may have many students, but it makes no sense for a student to live in more than one dormitory.

A **simple network relationship** is a data relationship in which the parent data types have one-to-many relationships with corresponding child data types, but child data types may have relationships with multiple parent data types. The characteristic that makes this a "simple" network relationship is that the multiple parents for a particular child *must* be from different data types (different files). For example, a customer order for NG&T has a simple network relationship with employees and customers. An employee may record and file many customer orders, and a customer may issue many orders, resulting in one-to-many relationships for customer-to-order and employee-to-order. The child records in this situation are capable of having multiple parents (two), but the different parent records are of different types of records (employees and customers). Thus it matches the main distinguishing characteristic of simple network relationships: one-to-many relationships between parent and child data, with child data type capable of having multiple parents as long as the parents come from different data types. Another example is the relationship between trucks and order shipments, and customers and order shipments. The shipment data type may have parents from the truck and the customer data types, while both of these parent data types may have multiple shipments.

A **complex network relationship** is a data relationship in which a parent data object may have a relationship with many child data objects, and a child data object may have a relationship with many parent data objects (even parents of the same data type). Another term for this type of relationship is a *many-to-many (M:N)* relationship. For example, the records in a vendor file and in the firm's inventory file usually have a many-to-many relationship. Each vendor supplies many goods retained in inventory, and each good retained in inventory may be supplied by many different vendors. Another example is the class enrollment-to-student relationship. A class may have many students enrolled in it, and a student may enroll in many classes.

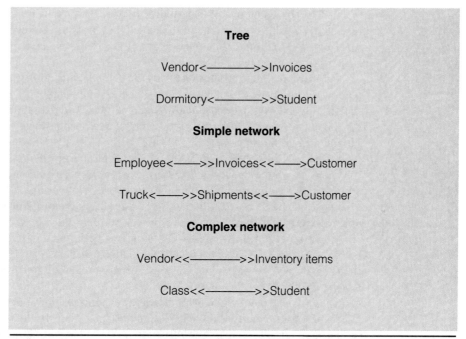

Figure 10-6. Three ways of structuring relationships among data

The diagrams in Figure 10-6 illustrate the three different types of relationships. The single and double arrows indicate the one-to-many (<———>>) and many-to-many (<<———>>) relationships between data items.

To identify the type of relationship between the objects of the different data types, the analyst and the database designer should review the cardinality relationship between the entities that represent the data types on an entity/relationship diagram (E/RD). Recall from Chapter 5 that the three different cardinality relationships are 1:1, 1:M, and M:N.

Commercially available DBMSs have been developed with the capacity for easily modeling one main type of relationship. These DBMSs are based on one of the following:

- Hierarchical (tree) model
- Network model
- Relational (complex network) model

An example of a hierarchical DBMS is Information Management System/Data Language/I (IMS/DLI). The most prevalent simple network-based DBMS is IDMS/R. Examples of relational DBMSs are ADABAS, Interaction Graphics and Retrieval System (INGRES), DB2, Oracle, Paradox, and R:BASE System V.

A DBMS based on one of these particular types of models is capable of structuring data relationships in any one of the three types of data relationships when necessary. However, the internal characteristics of each DBMS make it more capable of using one of the three types of relationships over the others.

A **hierarchical database model** is a DBMS model that defines data relationships by primarily using trees. It may also model data that has simple and complex network relationships. DBMSs based on the hierarchical database model decompose simple and complex network relationships into multiple tree relationships, while representing tree relationships directly.

A **network database model** defines data relationships using simple networks. DBMSs based on the network database model are also capable of modeling related data normally having tree and complex network relationships. Network DBMSs decompose complex network relationships into multiple simple network relationships, while representing tree and simple network relationships directly.

A **relational database model** can more easily define data relationships using complex networks. DBMSs based on the relational database model can also model related data types that have tree and simple network relationships. Relational DBMSs are capable of representing all three different types of relationships directly, without decomposing the type of relationship into a lower-form relationship.

The three different types of database models may also use link-list and inverted-list database data structures. (See Appendix A for a detailed discussion of link lists and inverted lists.) These database data structures may be used to allow more efficient access to data that has either tree, simple network, or complex network relationships.

Figure 10-7 illustrates the characteristics of the three different types of models and the type of database data structures that they may use. The arrows leading from simple and/or complex networks down to the left imply the decomposition of the higher-level relationship into multiple occurrences of lower-level relationships for the particular lower-level database models. This means that a DBMS based on the tree model can model simple network and complex network relationships. To do so, it decomposes these higher-level relationships into multiple trees that effectively represent the higher-level relationships. Figure 10-7 also indicates that a simple network-based DBMS can model complex network relationships. It models complex network relationships by decomposing them into multiple simple networks. The complex-network-based DBMS (relational) can model all three types of relationships directly without having to decompose them into a relationship in a lower-level form.

The Relational Model

As you can see from the examples in Figure 10-7, most of the modern commercially available DBMSs are based on the more powerful relational model. This model depicts higher-level relationships more conveniently and efficiently than the other models. Consequently, it is appropriate to study the characteristics of this type of DBMS model more carefully.

The relational model conceptually portrays the data contained in the database as a large table. For instance, the hospital database in Figures 10-3 and 10-4 can be con-

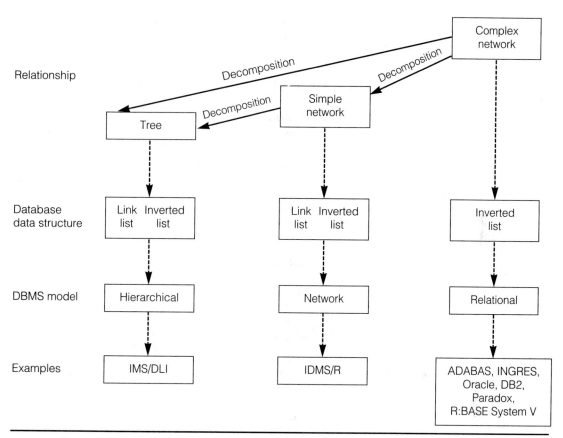

Figure 10-7. Relationship/database data structure schematic for the three different types of database models

ceptually viewed as a large two-dimensional table, with subsections of the table referenced by the names ADMISIONS, OPER/TRMT, PATIENT, DOCTOR, CHARGES, and INS/CARR. Individual data items in the table subsections are referenced by the names assigned to them in the schema. The relational model refers to the subsections (files) of the database (table) by the name **relation**; to individual data items (fields) in these subsections by the name **attribute**; and to a collection of individual data items that depict a real-world object by the name **occurrence** (record). *Relation* implies that the collection of data items represented maintain some relationship with each other. The collection of data items (occurrences) represents the recording and storing of data (records) concerning a transaction or other data object *occurring* within the business. Each data item in the recorded transaction represents an *attribute,* or characteristic, of that transaction. Accessing data items in a relational database requires only that the attribute and relation names be specified, or only the attribute name if it is unique. This is the same as specifying the coordinates of the data item by their positions in the table of data items. These names are assigned when the schema is defined.

The terms *instance* and *tuple* are sometimes used in place of the term *occurrence*. *Instance* refers to a specific data object in a list of "instances" of data objects in that relation. *Tuple* refers to the fact that each data object is defined by the specific data items that define the relation. A data object type with three data items for the relation would be a *three-ple*, one with five data items a *five-ple*, and so on. *Tuple* is a general reference to the fact that each data object type defined as a relation is composed of a number of data items.

Because of its greater capabilities and conveniences, the relational model for DBMSs is emphasized in this text. In the relational model, database files are normally termed *tables*, and data items are normally termed *attributes*. This text uses the terms *file*, *table*, and *relation* synonymously to refer to database files, and the terms *attribute*, *property*, and *data item* to refer to fields of database files.

Data Dictionaries

It is important to understand the relationship between the DBMS and a software system known as a data dictionary. Data-defining specifications in the schema are also included as part of the data dictionary that accompanies many DBMSs. The **data dictionary** contains a list of table and data item names and descriptions that define the database schema. The data dictionary also includes references to users, how they identify themselves, what data items they may access, and what operations they are allowed to perform on those data items. As previously stated, user view entries regarding the users and their database accesses are also part of the database schema. A data dictionary is often used to enter these specifications into the schema. The design dictionary often provides the basis for the entries in the database data dictionary.

In Chapter 3, the *design dictionary* was defined as a comprehensive collection of the design specifications used to define and describe all of the components of a system. A data dictionary defines and describes all the components of the database. A data type is referred to by the name assigned to it in the data dictionary; its data items are also referred to by the names assigned to them in the data dictionary.

The data dictionary provides stored documentation of ways to reference any portion of the database. DBMS command languages include commands used to display portions of the data dictionary. These commands help obtain a listing of the names assigned in the schema specifications. The command appearing before the listing of the portions of the schema in Figure 10-4 (LIST */tablename*) is a type of data dictionary command for R:BASE System V.

Data dictionary software packages may also be purchased separately from software vendors and interfaced with the DBMS command language. These data dictionary packages are used to create and display data dictionary entries for appropriate portions of the defined schema. A particular DBMS may or may not have a data dictionary package associated with it.

Current research is attempting to develop interfaces between existing design dictionaries and the data dictionary packages of DBMSs. The purpose of this interface is to convert the design dictionary entries into a form that can be used as input to the

DBMS data dictionary package, and vice versa. The data dictionary system then imports the converted design dictionary entries and uses them as the basis for the design of the database.

This research is beginning to show the greatest promise in areas where an **active dictionary** is used. Active dictionaries are dictionaries that do more than just serve as a reference library for database structures and user access definitions; they permit the database administrator to enter specifications for the schema in a higher-level dictionary format. Subsequently, these specifications are used by the dictionary to generate corresponding data definition commands. As a result, an active dictionary acts as a reference library for the database environment, as well as a generator and maintainer of the database structures.

Database Management System Functions

The following are some of the more important functions that the DBMS provides:

- Creation of the database, including the schema describing the database
- Storage, retrieval, and updating of data contained in the database
- Provision for the integrity of the data contained in the database
- Security of the database from unauthorized entry and unauthorized or invalid modification
- Synchronization of user accesses
- Crash protection and recovery from failure

Creation and Use of the Database

Earlier, we discussed how the database administrator directs the DBMS to create and modify the database schema. The DBA issues the schema-defining commands, but the DBMS actually creates the schema. The data definition commands (DDCs) and/or dictionary entries specify the structure that the DBMS is to use in creating or modifying the schema. Many of the statements that described the responsibility of the DBA in the earlier sections, "Creation of the Schema" and "Modification of the Schema," also pertain to the responsibility of the DBMS in defining or modifying the database schema.

The DBMS performs all data access to the database regardless of the type of access (update or input/output), and whether a user issues a data manipulation command (DMC) or a program issues a call to the DBMS. These types of access are described later in this chapter in the section "Usage of the Database."

Database Integrity

As defined earlier in this chapter, *data integrity* is related to the validity of the data values being accessed. Database users must be confident that the data values being accessed consistently represent values pertaining to real-world data objects in the business. In addition, they must have confidence in the consistency of data value reporting. Databases are defined that specify that each data item, if at all possible, must be stored in a single storage area in the database. Database designers accomplish this by eliminating redundancy when they find it.

The DBMS allows different users to access the same data value from this single location. Consequently, the same data value is reported for the different user accesses. Any updating of this value alters the data value stored in the single location for all accesses. Therefore, the data has integrity as a shared resource. For example, the STREET data items for NG&T customers should be stored only in the CUSTOMER database file. If a data value for STREET appears on a screen or report for some other data type, such as CUSTOMER ORDER, users can be confident that the street address actually came from the CUSTOMER database file, not the CUSTOMER_ ORDER database file. If STREET were also stored as part of the CUSTOMER_ ORDER file, it would be redundant. If STREET were redundantly stored in two or more database files, the specific street address for a particular customer could get out of synchronization in the different files. A database update for a customer with a change of street address may only modify the street address in one of the files in which it appears. Thus, the street address for that customer could be incorrect in one of the files in which it appears; its data integrity would be in question.

Database Security Methods

User views defined by the database administrator are usually included as part of the data dictionary for the database. Recall that the data dictionary contains a list of data items each user can access and a way of identifying each user. Users are commonly identified by comparing the identification numbers and passwords that they enter when accessing the database with those specified for them in the data dictionary. Using checks for user IDs and passwords helps determine whether the user is authorized to access those portions of the database. It also provides a way to determine whether the user is authorized to perform the action on data items referred to in his or her inquiry.

The analyst usually conveys information to the DBA concerning user views. The DBA may elect to periodically change IDs and passwords assigned to users, further securing the database from unauthorized access. The DBA also bestows on appropriate employees in the personnel department the responsibility for deleting user access when users leave the firm.

Databases distributed among computers at different locations and accessed in a dial-up mode over public communication facilities (telephone lines) offer additional problems in securing the database. This is especially problematic now, with the advent of dial-back systems that may include program code that randomly generates logon IDs and passwords for repeated attempts to gain access to the firm's system from a remote location. Securing database access in these circumstances often involves executing software procedures at the location of origin to code user IDs, passwords, and transmitted data. Subsequently, these values are decoded by software at the distributed destination to help identify users and prevent accidental or purposeful disclosure of information from the firm's database. These coding procedures are called encryption (or enciphering) procedures.

Encryption procedures consist of a series of manipulations that use an **enciphering key** used to produce a coded version of the IDs, passwords, and data values to transmit. Securing the database from unauthorized access through encryption methods is further supported by periodic changes in the enciphering key and modifications in the encryption procedures. Such modifications prevent access to the database by individuals who might procure user IDs and passwords but are not familiar with the encryption procedure or the precise key used in coding the values to transmit.

Using encryption methods represents an overhead investment in operations to secure the database from unauthorized access. Each transmission must go through the enciphering and deciphering procedures and devices, and costs more for that reason. Therefore, these procedures should be used only for access to sensitive data that could cause the firm to be embroiled in legal battles or lose its competitive advantage. For example, the transmission of formulas used in making products, such as the KFC "secret recipe," might require encryption prior to transmission. The analyst provides information concerning sensitive materials needing protection through encryption methods.

The fact that a company uses encryption methods can make its services more attractive to the general public. The perception of increased security is sometimes conveyed by the marketing efforts of a firm that uses encryption methods to protect data transmission. The general public perceives this as increased privacy for themselves and for their property.

Access Synchronization

Frequently the same data items are accessed simultaneously by different users. For example, different airline ticketing agents at different locations often attempt to simultaneously access the same data representing a seat on a departing airplane for passenger assignment. The DBMS ensures that the concurrent access of the same data item by different users is *synchronized*.

One way of synchronizing access, as well as providing additional integrity for the data values accessed, is to reserve (*lock*) portions of the database from access by other users while updating actions are performed. The analyst designates the portion of the database that requires locking during updating procedures. In the airline example, when a ticketing agent is considering a seat assignment for a customer calling in on the telephone, he or she may issue a command to lock a particular seat to prevent it from being assigned to someone else while the customer decides.

Locking portions of the database involves considerable overhead and slows down response time for all users accessing the database during the locked period. Concurrent accesses are often permitted when gains in response time far outweigh the loss of benefits that would be gained by locking accessed data items. The analyst often performs a cost/benefit analysis to determine whether users should be locked out of certain data values while updating operations occur. As a result, database locking is employed only when it is imperative that data values be reserved while someone is updating a portion of the database.

Database Crash Protection and Recovery

The DBMS also provides for crash protection and recovery from failure. In a "crash," the database is destroyed or rendered unusable by hardware, software, or human error. Considering the propensity of people, hardware, and software for making mistakes, becoming overburdened, or wearing out, the DBA can usually expect a database crash to occur and should formulate plans for recovery. The DBMS can detect circumstances that might lead to a crash; for example, too many users attempting to access the same data at the same time, or telephone lines going down between locations. Upon detecting an impending crash, the DBMS can then perform actions to help make the database environment more secure and recoverable.

Formal crash protection typically involves collecting database update actions in temporary storage and backing out of those actions when the DBMS detects a condition leading to a crash. An access occurring at the point of detecting crash conditions is reapplied after the conditions are rectified. Any accesses during the time when the database is shut down are either temporarily stored and then applied to the database or reissued by the inquiring user after access is restored.

All hardware and software systems are subject to failure; therefore, database recovery procedures are an important part of maintaining the database. The most frequently used method of preventing database loss or ensuring recovery after failure consists of a periodical backup of the database and reapplication of update accesses to the database. These accesses represent all updates occurring since the creation of the last backup copy of the database.

Normal updating practices usually involve creating separate files known as **journal files**, which are used to store all updating accesses that occur during the period between backup executions. After a database is destroyed or rendered invalid, journal file update entries are reapplied to the previous backup copy of the database during database reconstruction. Backup and/or recovery operations constitute an overhead cost in the maintenance and use of the database. Any accesses that occur during backup and/or recovery procedures are temporarily stored. The temporarily stored accesses are applied once the procedure ends and a current version of the database is released for use. The backup of a database requires a considerable expenditure of time. Therefore, the frequency of database backup is analyzed to determine the most cost-effective frequency.

USAGE OF THE DATABASE

The database serves as both on-line access for personnel within the firm and input/output (I/O) for execution of the firm's information systems. Business personnel access the database in on-line mode to gain immediate access to information that aids them in performing their job responsibilities. These accesses consist of immediate displays of current data values, formatted reports of current data values, or immediate updates of current data values stored within the database. To use the database as I/O, programs typically "call" the DBMS to retrieve data from the database rather than issue specific I/O commands to access data for use in executing their procedures. Except for data retrieval, programs execute the same as if they executed I/O commands for data access. Data manipulation commands provide the basis for on-line data access.

Data Manipulation Commands (DMCs) and Command Languages

The DMCs of the DBMS provide a way for users to access data from the database directly. Users issue DMCs to cause data items to be stored, retrieved, or modified in the database.

Database inquiries require a syntactically (grammatically) correct DMC to retrieve the data values referenced by designated names for database files and attributes within the DMC. DMCs that express ways to cause the retrieval of the appropriate data values are known as *procedural* commands. Most commercially available DBMSs, however, provide a more user-friendly means of accessing data values. These methods for expressing DMCs are usually macro-language versions of DBMS accessing commands or separate macro command languages purchased from software vendors, called *query languages*. Many fourth generation languages serve the database environment in this capacity. These DMC languages are known as *nonprocedural* DMC languages, since they only require specifying what to access, not how to cause the data values to be accessed. Specifying what to access requires referencing the names assigned to data types and data items in the database—that is, the names for files and fields in the database schema.

For example, the following DMC causes data from the ORDER and CUSTOMER database files to be displayed on a computer screen:

```
FIND CUSTOMER HAVING ORDER WITH DATE > 1/1/94
```

This DMC causes the CUSTOMER and ORDER database files to be combined with an order date greater than 1/1/94 used to determine which combination to display on the user's screen. The user does not need to know where the relevant database files are stored or how to cause them to be combined to issue this retrieval command.

Preprogrammed Database Accesses and Screen Templates

IS personnel frequently create preprogrammed accesses as a more convenient way for users to express inquiries. These **preprogrammed access procedures** complete the inquiry in the appropriate syntax of the DMC. The user is only required to issue a simple command and identify data items to be accessed. The user-specified command causes the preprogrammed procedure to execute, which in turn causes the DBMS to access the specified portions of the database.

Though these methods restrict access to the database, they do provide a simple way for users to access the database, which prevents many erroneous inquiry operations. Costs associated with the "misinformed" user often warrant constraining access to the database for some users. The analyst creates the preprogrammed procedures based on information from users.

Using DMC languages often generates preformatted screen displays (screen masks). *Screen masks* (or templates) were defined in Chapter 7 as pictorial screen displays of business forms or reports, such as an inventory invoice voucher or a vendor receipt report. Input screen masks typically include underscored sections in which variable information is inserted to reference data items that are to be displayed or modified. Screen mask access methods represent a special form of preprogrammed access. These masks cause the screen to be "painted" with a visual display that prompts the user for the variable information used in the access. The analyst either generates these screens to access data or provides the criteria used as the basis for them. Once entered, the variable information is used by the preprogrammed access to retrieve and process data in the database.

Standardization of DBMS Command Language

Over the years, database users have sought a standard language for issuing queries, such as the third generation languages that emerged in the 1960s and 1970s. In 1981, the American National Standard Institute (ANSI) proposed the query language SQL as the standard query language for DBMSs. SQL is a DBMS language developed at the IBM San Jose research facility. **SQL**, which stands for *S*tructured *Q*uery *L*anguage, is a DBMS language developed in the 1970s under the name SEQUEL, a descendant of an earlier language known as SQUARE. Many vendor-supplied DBMSs, such as DB2 and Oracle, have adopted SQL as their command language for desktop computers, minicomputers, and mainframe computers. The software vendors incorporate software used to interpret SQL into the specific language of their DBMS product. This activity is synonymous with the creation of compiler programs for translating programs written in macro languages, such as COBOL and FORTRAN, into the specific machine languages of particular computers. The advantage of this is that database users need not be familiar with multiple DBMS languages.

The use of preprogrammed procedures (such as procedures for downloading or uploading of data between computers), screen masks, and standard DBMS command languages provides transparency for database activities. *Transparency* means that the person accessing the database facilities need not be concerned with the different operations required to accomplish data access. Transparency of data accessing allows analysts to focus on more critical design issues, since they can assume that the DBMS will accomplish the data access. Therefore, A&D projects can focus on the procedures that act on the retrieved data to meet the information needs of the firm.

On-line Access to the Database

Regardless of how comprehensive and versatile the firm's information systems are, they cannot satisfy all of the information needs of the user, especially as business conditions change. Users frequently need immediate access to data that conceptually represents current conditions facing them. They often need information more current than what is normally supplied to them by the information systems of the firm. In addition, they might need to gain quicker access to information the IS does supply.

Users also need to directly receive reports on data values within the database or perform direct updates when unusual sets of events occur within the firm's operations—activities that are not part of the normal functions of the firm's computer systems. Before the arrival of database technologies, reports that were not part of normal system functions could be produced only through the creation of additional programs. On-line accesses fill the gap between normal execution of the systems of the firm and additional information required by the firm's personnel.

Users can issue DMCs from client computers to a DBMS residing on a server computer. These DMCs direct the server DBMS to retrieve the data from the database and return these data values to users on their desktop client computers. Technically proficient users, sometimes called *power users*, can issue their own DMCs to meet their information needs.

Interfacing Computer Systems to the Database

A database, as previously defined, represents an accumulation of related data to be used in support of business functions. Computer systems are designed to meet these information needs. Much of the data used by computer systems is retrieved from the database. These systems use the database as input and/or output.

The link between the client computer application programs and the database is provided by using DMCs embedded within the application programs. These programs are sometimes called **host programs** because they "host" the DMCs. The DMCs direct the DBMS to access data from the database for data manipulation operations in the host program. Instead of normal input or output commands in these programs, DMCs are inserted to direct the DBMS to retrieve and/or replace data values within the database. The requirements for actually retrieving the appropriate data are the responsibility of the DBMS. Therefore, in the creation, maintenance, and use of computer systems, the analyst can focus on the actions to perform on logical data objects, with little regard for where the data is stored or how to retrieve it for manipulation in the application program. After the embedded DMCs cause the data to be accessed, the program on the client computer performs normal program actions using the data passed to it by the DBMS.

The DBMS can be viewed as a system of supporting software (not replacement software) for performing the data-accessing functions included in computer systems. Consequently, a DBMS is just another tool and a database is just another data storage method that analysts use in their continuing effort to design and develop systems that meet the information needs of the firm.

Program Execution in a Client-Server Architecture

The applications that execute on client computers but rely on the server computer for data retrieval require design specifications for both the server and the client computer applications. Earlier, you saw how user requirements often consist of retrieving and/or manipulating logical data objects, objects that must be reconstructed from database objects. Commands to the server execute to retrieve database objects and reconstruct these logical data objects (LDSs). These LDSs are then manipulated by the procedures of the application that execute on the client computer. Figure 10-8 illustrates the operations that are performed for applications that execute in a client-server computer architecture.

The client application software is based on the procedure model of the physical design, which is either a structure chart (STC) with accompanying pseudocode or an action diagram (assume a STC procedure model). Included within this procedure are either DMCs or a call to a DBMS data accessing routine that contains DMCs, to be sent to the server to retrieve database objects. These DMCs may include JOIN and PROJECTION commands that execute in the server to reconstruct the logical data objects of interest to the user. The JOIN command retrieves and combines the data-

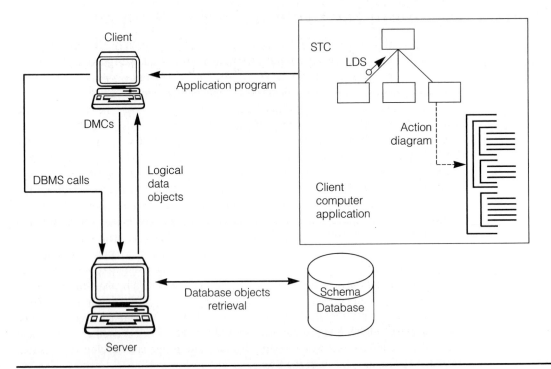

Figure 10-8. Client-server architecture application execution

base objects that contain the data items of the logical data object. The PROJECTION command causes the specific data items of the logical data object to be transmitted to the client computer application. The logical data objects (LDSs) are then returned to the client computer to be acted on by the client application software. The procedures embedded in the client application software are the actions to be performed on logical data objects. These actions are derived by creating a STC procedure model from a data flow diagram (DFD) business process model. These client computer application procedures manipulate the logical data objects as originally stipulated in the STC.

Relating Logical and Physical Data Structures

At the beginning of this chapter, we stated that user accesses to a database to satisfy logical needs for data are likely to cause data items stored in completely separate physical areas of the database to be accessed. The analyst should have documented these accesses to logical data structures (LDSs) with design dictionary entries while creating entity/relationship diagrams (E/RDs) and data flow diagrams (DFDs). The dictionary entries for these LDSs were illustrated in Chapters 5, 6, and 8.

A good way to distinguish between the LDSs and the physical data structures (PDSs) is to view LDSs as strings of data that users want to access together and PDSs as strings of data physically stored together for the sake of efficiency and error-free access.

The design of the database must be based on design criteria outlined earlier in this chapter, and these two views (logical and physical) of the database should be reconciled. A good technique for integrating these two views and capitalizing on previously entered specifications is to have design dictionary entries for both LDSs and PDSs and an entry that integrates these two sets of data structures.

Figure 10-9 is a reproduction of Figure 8-12 in Chapter 8, which contains a LDS for a customer order transaction. This LDS contains the following data items that make up the LDS depicting a customer order: CUSTNUM, CUSTNAME, STREET, CITY, STATE, ZIP, SHIPSTREET, SHIPCITY, SHIPSTATE, SHIPZIP, ORDER_NUMBER, ITEMNUM, QUANTITY, DATE, EMPNUM, MAGAZINE_SOURCE, and REGION_SOURCE.

The data items in Figure 10-9 would usually be stored in several PDSs. Based on good database design principles, data items for the customer would be stored in a customer master file, data items on customer orders would be stored in an order file, and data items on items ordered would be stored in an order-items file. In the following section, on applying normalization principles, you will see why LOG-CUSTTRNS contains data items from three database files. Let's assume that these physical files are called PHY_CUSTOMER_ORDER, PHY_CUSTOMER_MASTER, and PHY_ITEM_QUANTITY, respectively.

A simple way to integrate LDS descriptions and the PDSs contained in the database is to include a final entry on the LDS representing a mass physical data structure (M-PDS) to indicate the PDSs that contain the data items within the LDS. Note that

Entry Type   **Dictionary ID**

Data Structure   LOG-CUSTTRNS

Alias: _CUSTOMER ORDER TRANSACTIONS_

Comment: _A LDS for a customer order transaction._

Starting Volume: _____   Growth Potential: _____

No.	Ele/DS Name	DE/DS	SV/MV	Occurrences
01	CUSTNUM	DE	SV	
02	CUSTNAME	DE	SV	
03	STREET	DE	SV	
04	CITY	DE	SV	
05	STATE	DE	SV	
06	ZIP	DE	SV	
07	SHIPSTREET	DE	SV	
08	SHIPCITY	DE	SV	
09	SHIPSTATE	DE	SV	
10	SHIPZIP	DE	SV	
11	ORDER_NUMBER	DE	SV	
12	ITEMNUM	DE	MV	
13	QUANTITY	DE	MV	
14	DATE	DE	SV	
15	EMPNUM	DE	SV	
16	MAGAZINE_SOURCE	DE	SV	
17	REGION_SOURCE	DE	SV	
18	MPHY-CUSTTRNS	DS		

Figure 10-9. LOG-CUSTTRNS LDS dictionary entry

Figure 10-9 contains an entry called MPHY-CUSTTRNS to represent such an entry.

Figure 10-10 shows a dictionary entry for this M-PDS called MPHY-CUST-TRNS, which contains PHY-CUSTOMER_MASTER, PHY-CUSTOMER_ORDER, and PHY-ITEM_QUANTITY. The entry of MPHY-CUSTTRNS as the last entry in the customer order LDS of Figure 10-9 integrates the logical LOG-CUSTTRNS with the physical database files containing the data items within LOG-CUSTTRNS. Although this technique is not formally a part of the text methodology, using it may help keep track of where data comes from for LDSs. This technique is not recommended as a hard and fast rule; it is only a recordkeeping suggestion to aid in integrating the physical and logical views of data.

Figures 10-11, 10-12, and 10-13 contain the dictionary entries for PHY-CUS-

Entry Type   **Dictionary ID**

Data Structure   MPHY-CUSTTRNS

Alias: _CUSTOMER_ORDER_TRANSACTIONS_

Comment: _A M-PDS for a customer order transaction._

Starting Volume: _____ Growth Potential:_____

No.	Ele/DS Name	DE/DS	SV/MV	Occurrences
01	PHY-CUSTOMER_MASTER	DS		
02	PHY-CUSTOMER_ORDER	DS		
03	PHY-ITEM_QUANTITY	DS		

Figure 10-10. Dictionary entry for MPHY-CUSTTRNS PDS

Entry Type   **Dictionary ID**

Data Structure   PHY-CUSTOMER_MASTER

Alias: _CUSTOMER_MASTER_

Comment: _A PDS for a customer master record._

Starting Volume: _____ Growth Potential: _____

No.	Ele/DS Name	DE/DS	SV/MV	Occurrences
01	CUSTNUM	DE	SV	
02	CUSTNAME	DE	SV	
03	STREET	DE	SV	
04	CITY	DE	SV	
05	STATE	DE	SV	
06	ZIP	DE	SV	
07	SHIPSTREET	DE	SV	
08	SHIPCITY	DE	SV	
09	SHIPSTATE	DE	SV	
10	SHIPZIP	DE	SV	
11	DATE	DE	SV	

Figure 10-11. Dictionary entry for PHY-CUSTOMER_MASTER PDS

Entry Type   **Dictionary ID**

Data Structure   PHY-CUSTOMER_ORDER

Alias: _CUSTOMER ORDER TRANSACTIONS_

Comment: _A PDS for a customer order transaction._

Starting Volume: _____ Growth Potential: _____

No.	Ele/DS Name	DE/DS	SV/MV	Occurrences
01	ORDER_NUMBER	DE	SV	
02	CUSTNUM	DE	SV	
03	EMPNUM	DE	SV	
04	DATE	DE	SV	
05	MAGAZINE_SOURCE	DE	SV	
06	REGION_SOURCE	DE	SV	

Figure 10-12. Dictionary entry for PHY-CUSTOMER_ORDER PDS

Entry Type   **Dictionary ID**

Data Structure   PHY-ITEM_QUANTITY

Alias: _ITEM QUANTITIES_

Comment: _A PDS for order item quantities._

Starting Volume: _____ Growth Potential: _____

No.	Ele/DS Name	DE/DS	SV/MV	Occurrences
01	ORDER_NUMBER	DE	SV	
02	ITEM_NUMBER	DE	SV	
03	ITEM_QUANTITY	DE	SV	

Figure 10-13. Dictionary entry for PHY-ITEM_QUANTITY PDS

TOMER_MASTER, PHY-CUSTOMER_ORDER, and PHY-ITEM_QUANTITY.

A final note on the use of logical and physical design dictionary entries: The physical design entries can capitalize on the thoroughness of logical design data structure dictionary entries. All of the data item descriptions entered during the logical design of data structures can be incorporated into PDS dictionary entries. Thus, much of the database designer's clerical work has already been accomplished with the logi-cal design dictionary entries. The use of the same dictionary descriptions for data items further integrates the logical and physical designs. The same dictionary entries for data items are referenced in both.

Reconstructing Logical Data Objects from Database Objects

The bottom portion of the objects side of the pyramid in Figure 10-1 is labeled "Program view of logical objects." This view of data represents the logical data objects originally defined in entity type descriptions (LDSs) in the logical (functional) portion of creating the data model on this pyramid. These logical data objects were identified while creating E/RDs and are used to create normalized database objects (as defined later in this chapter). Earlier in this chapter, you learned that logical data types (LDSs) often consist of data items from a number of physical data types (PDSs) in the database. In the next section, you will learn how database designers use a process known as normalization to complete the physical design of the database from the logi-cal data types identified and described during logical design.

Chapters 2 and 5 described how a large portion of user requirements consists of simply viewing the properties of these original logical objects. These user require-ments are made operational through user views (discussed earlier) that specify what data users can access and what they can do with that data. To view these logical object properties that compose a person's user view, physical database objects that contain these properties are accessed and joined together with only the properties of the logical object extracted. These "joins" of database objects and "projections" of appropriate properties onto user screens and reports reconstruct the logical objects of the business from its database objects. These join and projection actions are usually transparent to (hidden from) the user. The user views the set of logical object proper-ties as if they were stored together in the database and, in fact, often believes this to be the case.

Figures 7-20 and 7-21 in Chapter 7 illustrated two screen mask user interfaces that might be used to enter or display the data items for the LOG-CUSTTRNS LDS. These user interfaces may either be a part of DMCs issued directly by the user, part of a preprogrammed DMC access, or part of an IS program for user interaction with the system and the database. These screen mask user interfaces are reproduced in Figures 10-14 and 10-15.

When commands execute that use the user interfaces in Figures 10-14 and 10-15, database access commands execute on the three PDSs that make up the LOG-CUST-TRNS LDS. Figure 10-16 illustrates the actions that are performed to employ the user interfaces in Figures 10-14 and 10-15.

Users may issue JOIN and PROJECTION commands directly from their client computer stations to the DBMS that resides on the server in order to retrieve the data-base objects and reconstruct desirable logical data objects. The client-server connec-tions make these direct actions possible.

```
                        CUSTOMER TRANSACTIONS
     CUSTOMER NUMBER: _____        ORDER NUMBER: _____

     CUSTOMER NAME: _____          CUSTOMER ADDRESS:

     DATE: _____         STREET: _____

                                            CITY: _____

                                            STATE: _____

                                            ZIP: _____

     TRANSACTION TYPE: _____       SHIPPING ADDRESS:

     EMPLOYEE NUMBER: _____          STREET: _____

     MAGAZINE: _____                 CITY: _____

     REGION: _____                   STATE: _____

     ORDER STATUS: _____           ZIP: _____
                            ITEMS ORDERED
          ITEM NUMBER: _____      ORDER QUANTITY: _____

          ITEM NUMBER: _____      ORDER QUANTITY: _____

          ITEM NUMBER: _____      ORDER QUANTITY: _____

          ITEM NUMBER: _____      ORDER QUANTITY: _____

          PRESS ESC KEY TO EXIT DATA ENTRY WITHOUT SAVING

          PRESS F3 KEY TO SAVE AND EXIT DATA ENTRY
```

Figure 10-14. A screen mask for the LOG-CUSTTRNS LDS

Accessing Data from Multiple Database Management Systems

Firms often maintain databases on mainframe computers, minicomputers, and desktop computers. Hereafter, the term host computer will be used to signify either mini- or mainframe computers used for central database control and storage. To transfer data between host computers and desktop computers, someone must be familiar with both host computer and desktop DBMS languages. Preprogrammed procedures to transfer appropriate portions of databases between computers are often created by information systems professionals. Communication software systems are also used for this purpose. Preprogrammed procedures provide relatively simple ways for users to gain access to the data appropriate for their job functions. These users are frequently unaware that a transfer of data between computer systems is occurring. The analyst

```
                    ADDITIONAL ORDER ITEMS
    ITEM NUMBER: _____      ORDER QUANTITY: _____
    ITEM NUMBER: _____      ORDER QUANTITY: _____
    ITEM NUMBER: _____      ORDER QUANTITY: _____
    ITEM NUMBER: _____      ORDER QUANTITY: _____
    ITEM NUMBER: _____      ORDER QUANTITY: _____
    ITEM NUMBER: _____      ORDER QUANTITY: _____
    ITEM NUMBER: _____      ORDER QUANTITY: _____
    ITEM NUMBER: _____      ORDER QUANTITY: _____
    ITEM NUMBER: _____      ORDER QUANTITY: _____
    ITEM NUMBER: _____      ORDER QUANTITY: _____
    ITEM NUMBER: _____      ORDER QUANTITY: _____

      PRESS ESC KEY TO EXIT DATA ENTRY WITHOUT SAVING
      PRESS F3 KEY TO SAVE AND EXIT DATA ENTRY
```

Figure 10-15. A screen mask for additional order items

usually provides the specifications for the access needs that are met by preprogrammed procedures.

DATABASE DESIGN AND NORMALIZATION OF DATABASE FILE FORMATS

The logical data types (LDSs) form the basis for creating the physical data types (PDSs) that compose database files. As discussed earlier, multiple PDSs are often created from LDSs. These PDSs are created by eliminating redundant LDSs, creating a database file for each data type in the LDS, eliminating repeating data items in the LDS, and properly inserting keys for different data types that aid in linking the PDSs that make up the LDSs.

The logical data types typically contain irregularities, called **anomalies**, that cause redundancy and other problems associated with proper storage of data in the database. Database anomalies often result in giving users incorrect information, caus-

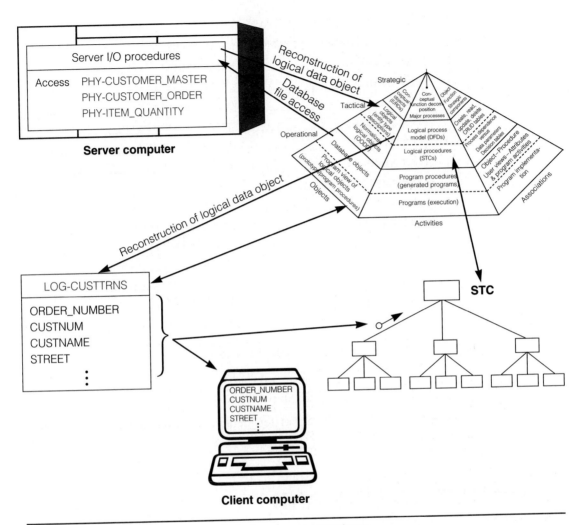

Figure 10-16. Physical access for LDS displays on user interfaces

ing them to be misinformed concerning business conditions. Anomaly conditions usually occur as a result of the way database files are physically formatted.

Anomalies create the greatest problems during normal database updating activities. The two most prevalent anomalies occur while data items are added or deleted within the database. Certain physical file formats can create a situation called a **deletion anomaly**, in which deleting data items from the database that need to be deleted also causes the loss of data not intended for deletion. In addition, certain physical file formats can create a situation, called an **insertion anomaly**, in which adding data items to these files requires adding data items not necessary for the firm's normal business operations. Figures 10-17 and 10-18 illustrate deletion and insertion anom-

Major/Club/Fee File				Major/Club File			Club/Fee File	
ST-ID	MAJOR	CLUB	FEE	ST-ID	MAJOR	CLUB	CLUB	FEE
11011	MIS	Theater	150.00	11011	MIS	Theater	Concerts	250.00
11011	ACCTG	Films	200.00	11011	ACCTG	Films	Films	200.00
11150	MRKTG	Sports	100.00	11150	MRKTG	Sports	Sports	100.00
11200	FIN	Theater	150.00	11200	FIN	Theater	Theater	150.00
11225	ECO	Concerts	250.00	11225	ECO	Concerts		
11275	OM	Films	200.00	11275	OM	Films		
11425	FIN	Concerts	250.00	11425	FIN	Concerts		

Figure 10-17. Deletion anomaly example

alies, using files that a college might have in its student records database for student majors and extracurricular clubs.

Figure 10-17 shows three separate files: Major/Club/Fee, Major/Club, and Club/Fee. Major/Club/Fee has a file format that promotes a deletion condition. Let's assume that the club fees are stored only in this data structure for this database and that student 11150 is the only student signed up for the Sports club. If student 11150's data object were deleted from the database (for example, the student dropped out of the club or dropped out of school), we would also lose the fact that the fee for the Sports club is $100. (Remember that this is the only place where club fees are stored.)

The typical remedy for the anomaly condition is to decompose the file that has an anomaly condition into separate files that do not have that particular anomaly condition. To correct the deletion anomaly present in the Major/Club/Fee file, you could decompose it into the Major/Club and Club/Fee files. When this is done, student 11150 can be deleted from the Major/Club file without losing the amount of the fee for the Sports club, since club fees are now stored in the Club/Fee file.

Correcting one anomaly condition can lead to database files with still other anomaly conditions. For example, although the deletion anomaly condition present in the Major/Club/Fee file in Figure 10-17 is corrected by decomposing it into the two other files, the Major/Club file has an insertion anomaly condition. In the Major/Club file, a student can have multiple majors and can sign up for multiple clubs.

An insertion anomaly exists in the Major/Club file in Figure 10-17 because no relationship exists between what majors students have and what clubs they join. For example, student 11011 has two majors, MIS and ACCTG, and has joined two clubs, Theater and Films. Just having these two occurrences (records) of student 11011 in the Major/Club file makes it appear that as an MIS major the student joined the Theater club, while as an ACCTG major he joined the Films club. To be more correct, the following two additional occurrences for student 11011 would be added to the Major/Club file:

```
11011      MIS         Films
11011      ACCTG       Theater
```

Adding these occurrences does not add any additional knowledge to the database; it only corrects misunderstandings that may occur. As a result, you are forced to add data you do not actually need while adding data that you do need, creating an insertion anomaly.

To correct this insertion anomaly, a database administrator would decompose the Major/Club file into two separate files that separate the multiple occurrences of student/major and student/club. Figure 10-18 illustrates decomposing the Major/Club file into files free of the insertion anomaly.

In Figure 10-18, the Major/Club file is decomposed into the Student/Major and Student/Club files to correct the insertion anomaly condition. This example actually demonstrates the anomaly condition addressed by the fourth normal form rules (which will be discussed in the next section) and illustrates its remedy.

The normalization of data types effectively secures the database against four main conditions:

- It eliminates redundancy resulting from having the properties of one data type included with the list of properties of another data type.
- It makes sure that each data type has its own database file.
- It does not allow repeating data items in a database file.
- It facilitates the insertion of keys to link the data from logically related data types that are stored in different physical storage places.

The properties of each data type should not be stored in multiple places, or you will have redundancy and the possibility of getting the data items out of synchronization, which were discussed earlier in this chapter. Each data type should have its own database file. If you embed all the properties of one data type inside another data type,

Major/Club File			Student/Major File		Student/Club File	
ST-ID	MAJOR	CLUB	ST-ID	MAJOR	ST-ID	CLUB
11011	MIS	Theater	11011	MIS	11011	Theater
11011	ACCTG	Films	11011	ACCTG	11011	Films
11150	MRKTG	Sports	11150	MRKTG	11150	Sports
11200	FIN	Theater	11200	FIN	11200	Theater
11225	ECO	Concerts	11225	ECO	11225	Concerts
11275	OM	Films	11275	OM	11275	Films
11425	FIN	Concerts	11425	FIN	11425	Concerts

Figure 10-18. Insertion anomaly correction example

you will create a deletion anomaly condition like the one in Figure 10-17. Repeating data items should not be permitted in a database file because of the problems caused by variable-length records. Data that has a logical relationship within the information needs of users is frequently stored in separate database files. It is important to include keys in these database files that aid in retrieving them together to satisfy these information needs. The normalization process can be performed by using the normal forms, which provide increasingly better database design criteria as you apply them.

Normal Forms

Improved database design criteria have been developed in the past ten years or more to eliminate anomalies. Called **normal forms**, these database design criteria prevent identified anomalies from occurring as a result of the way database files are defined. Table 10-1 shows a list of the normal forms proposed by researchers involved in studying database design methods. Although you may not understand all of the terminology in

Table 10-1	Classification of normal forms

Normal Form	Normalization Rules
First normal form (1st/NF)	No repeating data items are allowed.
Second normal form (2nd/NF)	All nonkey attributes are dependent on *all* of the key, and also follows the first normal form rule.
Third normal form (3rd/NF)	No transitive dependencies are allowed, and also follows the second normal form rules.
Boyce-Codd normal form (B-C/NF)	Every determinant is a candidate key, and also follows the third normal form rules.
Fourth normal form (4th/NF)	Multiple independent multivalued dependencies are not allowed, and also follows the B-C/NF rules.
Fifth normal form (5th/NF)	All join constraints are implied by keys, and the size of the domain of primary attributes (attributes that are part of the key of the relation) must be $\geq C(n,[n/2])$—the combination of n things taken $n/2$ at a time (fraction is dropped if n is odd), and also follows the fourth normal form rules.
Domain key normal form (DK/NF)	This is a subjective attempt to express every constraint on a relation (user requirement) as a logical consequence of the definition of domains and keys. It involves enforcing domain definitions contained in the data dictionary via editing and requiring key attributes to be unique.

this figure, you can see that each new normal form, as you go down the list, requires increasingly strict criteria for eliminating the occurrence of possible anomalies.

The process of applying the normal form database design criteria is known as **normalization**. When a particular file format violates one of the normal forms, normalization typically causes this file to be decomposed into multiple physical file formats that do not violate that particular normal form. Normalization involves checking all physical file formats in the database to see that they conform to all of the criteria for that normal form. For example, to obtain a database normalized through the third normal form, each file format is checked to see whether it has repeating data items (1st/NF), and to make sure that all nonkey data items are dependent on all of the key (2nd/NF) and that no transitive dependencies exist (3rd/NF).

A key to understanding anomalies and normalization is to realize that data items that may inherently be logically strung together may not be physically stored together because of the possibilities for anomalies. For example, suppose that a physical file in a college database contains the name of a student, the name of the physical education (PE) activity in which he is enrolled, and the registration fee for the PE activity. Assume that the PE activity registration fee is stored only in this physical file in the database. If only one student is registered for a particular PE activity, deleting that student's record will also cause a loss of information concerning the registration fee for the PE activity. In this case, the conditions for a deletion anomaly exist.

The normalization process in this example would decompose the student/PE activity file into two files: one containing student name and PE activity name in which she is enrolled and the other containing PE activity name and registration fee. As a result, deleting a student would not cause additional data loss regarding the registration fee for PE activities.

Since normalization typically breaks database files into multiple files, it slows down user inquiry response time. Because of this, many IS personnel only normalize through the third normal form, since the first three normal forms take care of the most frequently occurring anomalies.

First Normal Form (1st/NF)

The 1st/NF states that a database file should not have a data item that repeats itself. For example, a customer order may have multiple items on it as a logical object (LDS). Since it complicates matters when a data item name represents more than one data item for a particular data type—especially when the number of occurrences varies—it is best to restructure the file into multiple files to prevent this condition. To eliminate repeating order items in the database file structure for the customer order file, a separate file is created that contains separate records for each order item and the key of the order to be able to link them. Figure 10-19 illustrates the unnormalized LDS for the customer order and the two data structures that result from applying the 1st/NF rule (do not permit repeating order item/quantity data items). The unnormalized order data structure is the LOG-CUSTTRNS LDS for customer phone/mail and retail orders from the NG&T case. Note that the MV (multivalued) entries for the ITEMNUM and QUANTITY data items designate them as repeating data items.

Unnormalized LDS		First Normal Form		Normalized Data Structures	
ORDER	**SV/MV**	**ORDER**	**SV/MV**	**ORDER_ITEMS**	**SV/MV**
CUSTNUM	SV	CUSTNUM	SV	ORDER_NUMBER	SV
CUSTNAME	SV	CUSTNAME	SV	ITEMNUM	SV
STREET	SV	STREET	SV	QUANTITY	SV
CITY	SV	CITY	SV		
STATE	SV	STATE	SV		
ZIP	SV	ZIP	SV		
SHIPSTREET	SV	SHIPSTREET	SV		
SHIPCITY	SV	SHIPCITY	SV		
SHIPSTATE	SV	SHIPSTATE	SV		
SHIPZIP	SV	SHIPZIP	SV		
ORDER_NUMBER	SV	ORDER_NUMBER	SV		
ITEMNUM	MV	DATE	SV		
QUANTITY	MV	EMPNUM	SV		
DATE	SV	MAGAZINE_SOURCE	SV		
EMPNUM	SV	REGION_SOURCE	SV		
MAGAZINE_SOURCE	SV				
REGION_SOURCE	SV				

Figure 10-19. Normalizing using 1st/NF conversion

In Figure 10-19, the ORDER and ORDER_ITEMS data structures resulting from applying the 1st/NF rule are normalized only through the 1st/NF; other anomalies may exist that have not yet been addressed. The ORDER data structure that is derived contains all of the data items of the LOG-CUSTTRNS LDS except ITEMNUM and QUANTITY. Since these data items are MV, they are moved to a separate data structure designated as ORDER_ITEMS. The ORDER_ITEMS data structure also includes the ORDER_NUMBER data item so that it can be easily linked back to its specific order object in the ORDER data structure.

Second Normal Form (2nd/NF)

The 2nd/NF states, in addition to prohibiting repeating data items, that all nonkey attributes are dependent on *all* of the key. To understand the condition specifically being addressed by the 2nd/NF, you must understand the concept of functional dependencies. A **functional dependency** is a relationship that exists between data items wherein data values for one data item are used to identify data values for another data item. Stated another way, if you know the value for data item X, you can functionally determine the value(s) for data item Y. For a functional dependency, one of the data items will be designated as the **determinant**. For this example, data item X is the determinant for the functional dependency between data items X and Y.

The condition addressed by the 2nd/NF is one in which you have a key for a data structure that comprises several data items, and one of those data items is a determinant for other properties of the LDS. The real problem is that you may have properties of one data type embedded in another data type. When this occurs, you may have redundancy for those embedded properties or the possibility of a deletion anomaly.

Redundancy should always be avoided because (as we have discussed previously) the values for redundantly placed data items may get out of synchronization when they are changed in one place but not in another. When different users access the same data item redundantly stored in different locations in the database, they may not be able to communicate properly, because one of them may have the true value for this data item while the other has an old and incorrect value. For example, assume that a customer credit rating is a data item in two separate files in the database for NG&T. Different salesclerks may access the customer credit rating from these two different files and draw different conclusions regarding the advisability of permitting a particular customer to purchase additional items on credit. This situation would be especially problematic if the true credit rating in one of the files indicated that the customer is a bad credit risk.

The deletion anomaly condition that the 2nd/NF addresses involves having one data type totally included in another data type. When this happens, you may accidentally delete properties of an object of the embedded data type while correctly deleting an object of the original data type.

The ORDER data structure in Figure 10-19 that results from applying the first normal form rule exhibits the condition addressed by the second normal form. Assume that the key for the ORDER data structure is composed of the CUSTOMER_NUMBER and ORDER_NUMBER data items. A functional dependency exists between the CUSTOMER_NUMBER and the CUSTNAME, STREET, CITY, STATE, and ZIP data items. By knowing the customer number, you can functionally determine the customer's name and address data values. If a CUSTOMER data structure exists that also has these properties, you have redundantly embedded the CUSTOMER properties in the ORDER data structure. Alternately, if this is the only place where these customer properties are stored, you may lose important data about a customer when you delete data about a particular order. As an example, if a particular customer has mailed only a single order, which ends up being canceled, you may also delete the only reference to this customer if you delete his or her order. Figure 10-20 illustrates the unnormalized and normalized data structures for the customer order.

The normalized ORDER data structure in Figure 10-20 now contains properties that refer only to characteristics of the customer's order. All properties pertaining to the customer have been removed except the CUSTNUM data item. This property remains so that the order can be linked to the specific customer placing the order. All remaining properties of the customer and the CUSTNUM data item have been placed in the normalized CUSTOMER data structure. The ellipsis below the ZIP property

Unnormalized LDS		Second Normal Form		Normalized Data Structures	
ORDER	SV/MV	ORDER	SV/MV	ORDER_ITEMS	SV/MV
CUSTNUM	SV	ORDER_NUMBER	SV	CUSTNUM	SV
CUSTNAME	SV	DATE	SV	CUSTNAME	SV
STREET	SV	EMPNUM	SV	STREET	SV
CITY	SV	CUSTNUM	SV	CITY	SV
STATE	SV	SHIPSTREET	SV	STATE	SV
ZIP	SV	SHIPCITY	SV	ZIP	SV
SHIPSTREET	SV	SHIPSTATE	SV	.	
SHIPCITY	SV	SHIPZIP	SV	.	
SHIPSTATE	SV	MAGAZINE_SOURCE	SV	.	
SHIPZIP	SV	REGION_SOURCE	SV		
ORDER_NUMBER	SV				
DATE	SV				
EMPNUM	SV				
MAGAZINE_SOURCE	SV				
REGION_SOURCE	SV				

Figure 10-20. Second normal form example

indicates that the CUSTOMER data structure may have additional properties that pertain to a customer.

When the properties of one data type are removed from another data type and you need to leave the key of one of the data types as a foreign key property in the other data type, you need to know the cardinality relationship between the data types to decide which data type retains the key. A **foreign key property** is a data item in one data structure that may be used to reference a data object of another data type. For example, when the CUSTOMER properties are removed from the ORDER data structure, the CUSTNUM data item remains in the ORDER data structure as a foreign key property. Remember that the cardinality relationship could be one-to-one (1:1), one-to-many (1:M), or many-to-many (M:N). This example contains a 1:M cardinality relationship from CUSTOMER (1) to ORDER (M), as indicated by the cardinality relationship depicted in the GTOP0000 entity/relationship diagram (E/RD) of Figure 8-10 in Chapter 8. By indicating the cardinality relationship between the CUSTOMER entity and LOG-CUSTTRNS data type depicted as the ORDER ENTRY & VALIDATION OBJECT relationship symbol on the GTOP0000 E/RD, specifications have been entered that are appropriate to use to properly normalize the data. The other two types of cardinality relationships will be addressed in the section "Object-Oriented Database Design," later in this chapter.

Third Normal Form (3rd/NF)

The 3rd/NF also pertains to anomaly conditions that may exist because of functional dependencies. The third normal form prevents functional dependencies among three data items, wherein knowing the value for property X, you can functionally determine the value(s) for Y; and knowing the value for Y, you can functionally determine the value(s) for Z. Again, the real problem is that you may have redundancy or properties of one data type totally embedded in another data type.

To illustrate, assume that a customer's credit rating functionally determines his or her purchase amount limit. If the CREDIT_RATING and PURCHASE_LIMIT properties are both included as part of the CUSTOMER data structure, you have the conditions that the third normal form addresses. A transitive dependency exists among CUSTNUM, CREDIT_RATING, and PURCHASE_LIMIT. By knowing the customer's ID number, you can determine the CREDIT_RATING for that customer, and by knowing the CREDIT_RATING for that customer, you can functionally determine his or her PURCHASE_LIMIT. If the CREDIT_RATING and PURCHASE_LIMIT data items are stored only as part of the CUSTOMER data structure, either you may not know the purchase amount limitation for some credit ratings, or some credit rating and purchase amount limit combinations may be accidentally deleted if you delete the only customer who has a particular credit rating from the CUSTOMER data structure. Figure 10-21 illustrates the CUSTOMER data structure that includes the CREDIT_RATING and PURCHASE_LIMIT data items and the normalized data structures that would exist after applying the main rule of the third normal form.

In Figure 10-21, the CREDIT_RATING and PURCHASE_LIMIT data items have been moved to their own data structure. Now you do not have to wait for a particular customer to have a specific credit rating to know his or her corresponding purchase limit amount. Also, you do not have to worry about a possible deletion anomaly for some CREDIT_RATING and PURCHASE_LIMIT combinations that only a single customer may currently have.

Unnormalized LDS		Third Normal Form		Normalized Data Structures	
CUSTOMER	SV/MV	CUSTOMER	SV/MV	LIMIT_PURCHASE	SV/MV
CUSTNUM	SV	CUSTNUM	SV	CREDIT_RATING	SV
CUSTNAME	SV	CUSTNAME	SV	PURCHASE_LIMIT	SV
STREET	SV	STREET	SV		
CITY	SV	CITY	SV		
STATE	SV	STATE	SV		
ZIP	SV	ZIP	SV		
CREDIT_RATING	SV				
PURCHASE_LIMIT	SV				

Figure 10-21. Third normal form example

Boyce-Codd Normal Form (B-C/NF)

The B-C/NF also addresses the anomaly condition in which the properties of two data types have been combined into a single database file. This normal form identifies the condition under which you have a functional dependency whose determinant is not a part of the key for the file, as addressed by the second normal form rules. The functional dependency here is also not a part of a transitive dependency, as addressed by the third normal form rules. To illustrate, assume that JOB is a data item that identifies personnel job classifications in the LOG-EMPLOYEE_MASTER LDS used to describe the employee data type for the NG&T case. (Note that the different entities associated with personnel on NG&T E/RDs could explode to this LDS.) Also assume that an additional data item in LOG-EMPLOYEE_MASTER called PAY_GRADE has data values that are functionally dependent on data values in the JOB data item. Figure 10-22 illustrates the LOG-EMPLOYEE_MASTER LDS retained as a database file called EMPLOYEE_MASTER, with some of its data objects displayed.

If the PAY_GRADE is stored only in the EMPLOYEE_MASTER file, as depicted in Figure 10-22, you have a deletion anomaly condition that must be addressed. To understand this anomaly condition, assume that Terry Byrd is the only employee with job classification 151 and that he decides to retire. When you delete Terry Byrd from the EMPLOYEE_MASTER file, you also lose the fact that JOB 151 has a PAY_GRADE of 60,000.00. The problem is that there is a functional dependency between JOB and PAY_GRADE; however, JOB is not a possible key for the CUSTOMER_MASTER file.

The B-C/NF states that the determinant for a functional dependency must be a candidate for the key of the database data type. For this to be true, a new data type must be created for JOB/PAY_GRADE that stores data values for these functional dependencies. Figure 10-23 illustrates the normalized files that would result from applying B-C/NF rules to the EMPLOYEE_MASTER file in Figure 10-22.

B-C/NF asserts that a determinant that could not be the key for an existing file identifies the key of a completely separate data type contained in that file that should

EMPLOYEE_MASTER File

EMP_ID	NAME	JOB	PAY_GRADE	STREET	CITY	STATE	ZIP
101111	Tom Marshall	125	55,000.00	115 Cary	Auburn	AL	33445
101120	Terry Byrd	151	60,000.00	125 Moores	Auburn	AL	33445
101170	Mike Whitman	100	10,000.00	130 Kentucky	Auburn	AL	33445
101200	Marc Miller	100	10,000.00	150 Atlanta	Auburn	AL	33445
101250	Tom Roberts	125	55,000.00	175 Murfree	Auburn	AL	33445
101325	Mark Wright	175	70,000.00	160 Louisvil	Auburn	AL	33445
101375	Kent Fields	175	70,000.00	145 Hwy 280	Opelika	AL	33450

Figure 10-22. EMPLOYEE_MASTER unnormalized example

EMPLOYEE_MASTER File								JOB/PAY File	
EMP_ID	NAME	JOB	STREET	CITY	STATE	ZIP	JOB	PAY_GRADE	
101111	Tom Marshall	125	115 Cary	Auburn	AL	33445	100	10,000.00	
101120	Terry Byrd	151	125 Moores	Auburn	AL	33445	125	55,000.00	
101170	Mike Whitman	100	130 Kentucky	Auburn	AL	33445	151	60,000.00	
101200	Marc Miller	100	150 Atlanta	Auburn	AL	33445	175	70,000.00	
101250	Tom Roberts	125	175 Murfree	Auburn	AL	33445			
101325	Mark Wright	175	160 Louisvil	Auburn	AL	33445			
101375	Kent Fields	175	145 Hwy 280	Opelika	AL	33450			

Figure 10-23. Boyce-Codd normalization example

have its own file. In this example, the JOB/PAY file separates this data type from the EMPLOYEE_MASTER file. Doing this allows access to every job/pay grade combination in the database regardless of whether anyone currently has a particular combination.

Fourth Normal Form (4th/NF)

The 4th/NF addresses anomalies that may occur as a result of having more than one functional dependency in the same file. The anomaly condition occurs when these separate functional dependencies can produce multiple values in that file for a given determinant and the functional dependencies are not related to each other; they are independent functional dependencies. Figure 10-18, which illustrated the traits of an insertion anomaly, also illustrated having multiple, independent, multivalued functional dependencies in the same file. This example began with the Major/Club file, which contained two independent, multivalued functional dependencies:

```
ST_ID ---> MAJOR
ST_ID ---> CLUB
```

If the ST_ID is known, you can separately determine multiple values for MAJOR and CLUB; in other words, both MAJOR and CLUB can have multiple values for the same ST_ID. Determining multivalues for the determinant of a functional dependency is not the problem; the problem is having more than one multivalued functional dependency in the same file that are also not related. To remedy this condition, you should separate the functional dependencies into their own separate files, as was done in Figure 10-18 for the Student/Major and Student/Club files and for the EMPLOYEE_MASTER and JOB/PAY files in Figure 10-23.

Fifth Normal Form (5th/NF)

The 5th/NF is the most difficult to understand and apply, even though it addresses a problem that frequently occurs. Many database accesses combine the data items of multiple database files and display them on a computer screen. Users sometimes combine these "joins" of database files with joins of other database files, and then join these data items with data items from other database files. After issuing several JOIN commands to the DBMS, the user may forget which database files are the original source of the data items he or she is viewing. The fifth normal form addresses this problem by specifying rules to aid in returning to the original database files from a screen that displays combined data items from multiple database files that resulted from issuing several JOIN commands.

Explaining the fifth normal form and its remedy in greater depth is beyond the scope of this text. It is sufficient that you understand it in principle, especially since it is the normal form that is least applied in actual practice.

Domain/Key Normal Form (DK/NF)

The DK/NF emerged when a researcher named Fagin (1981) discovered that regardless of the anomaly condition, the remedy is always the same. Fagin noticed that correcting the anomaly condition involves either decomposing the anomaly-ridden file into multiple files and assigning them their own "keys," or specifying "domains" that constrain the data values for data items. In the examples for the other normal forms, you will notice that the remedy always decomposes the anomaly-ridden file into separate files with their own keys assigned. Explaining how to apply correction factors using domain specifications is beyond the scope of this text. Suffice it to say that you can prevent some anomaly conditions by placing limitations on data values for data items within and between database files. Thus, the DK/NF gets its name from the way the anomaly condition is corrected.

The DK/NF can address any anomaly condition that may be detected, not just a specific anomaly condition, as expressed by the major rule for the other normal forms. It offers the same remedy for any new anomaly condition that some research may find: correct the condition by the way you decompose files and assign keys or by the way you constrain data values for data items using a domain specification. To apply the DK/NF, you must be able to detect the anomaly condition. Therefore, an analyst/DBA who applies the DK/NF during database normalization should be familiar with the other normal forms and the conditions they address.

Understanding the DK/NF in greater depth and using it for normalization are beyond the scope of this text. It is sufficient to understand that the DK/NF put to rest the identification of any additional normal forms. Rather than have any new rules to address any new anomaly condition that someone discovers, the DK/NF suggests that database designers simply determine how to correct the problem by the way they decompose the file and assign keys or the way they express domain specifications.

Normalization in Practice and the Technology That Supports It

In practice, databases are usually normalized only through the 3rd/NF or the B-C/NF, when normal form rules are applied. Software has emerged to aid the analyst and the DBA in normalizing the schema through these levels. This software generally uses an algorithm that progressively decomposes current physical file formats in a database into multiple file formats until a desired level of normalization occurs. This software supplements CASE software used during the analysis and design of application systems.

Identifying and correcting anomalies through improved design methods based on application of normal form rules is very complicated and somewhat subjective. Only experience provides the analyst with the skills necessary for eliminating or reducing the possible occurrence of anomalies by using these rules. A full understanding of the discovery and remedy of anomaly conditions using the normal forms can be pursued through further reading. The "Selected References" section at the end of this chapter lists a number of books on database concepts that provide more detailed descriptions of this and other database principles and practices.

A more easily understood method for identifying anomaly conditions, and part of the text methodology, is the application of object-oriented database design principles. Using this method also integrates very well with conceptual and logical data modeling, as described in Chapter 5. Where conceptual and logical data modeling ends, object-oriented database design begins.

OBJECT-ORIENTED DATABASE DESIGN

In recent years, a new concept has emerged regarding how to apply the normalization process. Called **object-oriented database design (OODD)**, it uses the concept of proper semantic object identification and description to apply anomaly correction rules and establish normalized physical database objects. A semantic object is synonymous with a logical data type, as identified in data-gathering efforts, modeled as entities and relationships on E/RDs, and described in entity type descriptions. The basic premise of this approach is that data structures are retained in the business for semantic objects inside and outside of the business. These data structures describe these semantic objects so that information concerning them will be retained in the firm's database.

A **semantic object** is a data type for objects inside or outside of the firm, such as people, places, things, events, or concepts, that influence or are influenced by the firm's business activities. Examples of semantic objects are departments in the business, governmental agencies, competitors, clients, and client transactions. Appropriate characteristics must be used to describe these semantic objects sufficiently, to understand the influence of the firm's activities on them or their influence on the firm's activities. A characteristic of a semantic object is called a **property**. An example of properties for a customer semantic object would be name, address, when the customer began doing business with the firm, and other information sufficient for the firm's information needs regarding customers.

All properties of the semantic object important to the business must be identified, but not all information is useful; for example, in most situations, the way customers dress is not a property retained in the customer database file in order to sufficiently describe a firm's customers. The way they dress is certainly a characteristic of customers, but it does not provide the type of information the firm is likely to retain.

Most requirements for applying OODD principles have already been documented in the E/RDs and entity type descriptions created during project analysis and design phases. The entities and relationships appearing throughout the E/RD explosion paths represent semantic objects important to the business. The dictionary entries for the individual logical data structures (LDSs) that depict these semantic objects provide most of the data needed to apply OODD principles.

Semantic Object Categories

The principles of OODD identify five different types of semantic object categories. All semantic objects inside and outside the business fit within one or a combination of these categories:

- Simple semantic objects
- Composite semantic objects
- Compound semantic objects
- Associative semantic objects
- Generalized semantic objects

Which category a semantic object belongs to depends on a combination of the properties and relationships required to describe that semantic object. A close look at the LDS used to describe the semantic object provides the information necessary to determine the category.

A **simple semantic object** has only single-valued (nonrepeating) non-object properties. *Single-valued* in this context means that each property of the semantic object requires only an individual data value to provide that characteristic of the semantic object. An example of a multivalued property is the repeating item number/quantity data items appearing in a LDS for a customer order, which list multiple items as part of the same order. *Non-object property* means that this semantic object does not contain properties of another semantic object within the properties listed for it. An example of an object property is a collection of data items used to identify a customer within the LDS representing a customer shipment. A LDS used to identify the customer master is an example of a simple semantic object. Figure 10-24 illustrates this data structure. Notice that this LDS has only single-valued data items (properties) and no references to properties of another semantic object.

Entry Type		Dictionary ID		
Data Structure		LOG-CUSTMAST		
Alias: _CUSTOMER MASTER_				
Comment: _A LDS for customer master data objects._				
Starting Volume: _____		Growth Potential: _____		

No.	Ele/DS Name	DE/DS	SV/MV	Occurrences
01	CUSTNUM	DE	SV	
02	CUSTNAME	DE	SV	
03	STREET	DE	SV	
04	CITY	DE	SV	
05	STATE	DE	SV	
06	ZIP	DE	SV	

Figure 10-24. LOG-CUSTMAST data structure dictionary entry

A **composite semantic object** is a semantic object having at least one multivalued property. A **compound semantic object** is a semantic object having at least one object property; therefore, it contains the properties of another semantic object embedded within its properties. In a compound semantic object, one semantic object receives some of its properties from the list of properties of another semantic object. The LOG-CUSTTRNS LDS in Figure 10-25 illustrates both the composite and compound semantic object concepts.

In Figure 10-25, notice that the ITEMNUM and QUANTITY data items are multivalued. Therefore, the semantic object portrayed by this data structure has the traits of a composite semantic object. Also, notice that many of the data items actually pertain to the customer semantic object (CUSTNAME, STREET, CITY, STATE, ZIP). This collection of data items represents an object property (one semantic object receiving some of its properties from the list of properties of another semantic object). Therefore, the semantic object portrayed by this LDS also has the traits of a compound semantic object. This example shows how a semantic object may also be a cross between categories, called a *hybrid* semantic object.

An **associative semantic object** is a semantic object that exists as the result of a relationship between two or more other semantic objects. Associative semantic objects document the relationships between the other semantic objects by having properties that reference the other semantic objects. Associative semantic objects may also have properties supplementary to the properties that reference the other semantic objects. For example, in the NG&T order processing application, there is a LDS called LOG-VENDITEM that documents the relationship between vendors and the items supplied by them to NG&T. Figure 10-26 illustrates this data structure.

Entry Type   **Dictionary ID**

Data Structure   LOG-CUSTTRNS

Alias: _CUSTOMER ORDER TRANSACTIONS_

Comment: _A LDS for a customer order transaction._

Starting Volume: _____   Growth Potential:_____

No.	Ele/DS Name	DE/DS	SV/MV	Occurrences
01	CUSTNUM	DE	SV	
02	CUSTNAME	DE	SV	
03	STREET	DE	SV	
04	CITY	DE	SV	
05	STATE	DE	SV	
06	ZIP	DE	SV	
07	SHIPSTREET	DE	SV	
08	SHIPCITY	DE	SV	
09	SHIPSTATE	DE	SV	
10	SHIPZIP	DE	SV	
11	ORDER_NUMBER	DE	SV	
12	ITEMNUM	DE	MV	
13	QUANTITY	DE	MV	
14	DATE	DE	SV	
15	EMPNUM	DE	SV	
16	MAGAZINE_SOURCE	DE	SV	
17	REGION_SOURCE	DE	SV	
18	MPHY-CUSTTRNS	DS		

Figure 10-25. LOG-CUSTTRNS LDS dictionary entry

In Figure 10-26, notice that LOG-VENDITEM contains two combinations of data items pertaining to vendors and items, respectively. The VENDNUM, VENDNAME, STREET, CITY, STATE, and ZIP data items all pertain to the vendor semantic object; the ITEMNUM and ITEMDESC data items pertain to the item semantic object. Also notice that the data items VENDOR_ITEM_DISCOUNT and DATE are data items that pertain only to the associative semantic object (supplementary to the properties establishing the relationship).

A **generalized semantic object** is a semantic object representing a class of semantic objects. For example, a union personnel semantic object is an aggregation of people who belong to the union. Thus, *union personnel* is a generalized semantic object. A generalized semantic object may also have traits normally used to identify simple, composite, compound, and associative semantic objects.

Entry Type   **Dictionary ID**

Data Structure   LOG-VENDITEM

Alias: __VENDOR ORDER ITEMS__

Comment: __A LDS linking vendors to the items they supply.__

Starting Volume: _____   Growth Potential: _____

No.	Ele/DS Name	DE/DS	SV/MV	Occurrences
01	VENDNUM	DE	SV	
02	VENDNAME	DE	SV	
03	STREET	DE	SV	
04	CITY	DE	SV	
05	STATE	DE	SV	
06	ZIP	DE	SV	
07	ITEMNUM	DE	SV	
08	ITEMDESC	DE	SV	
09	VENDOR_ITEM_DISCOUNT	DE	SV	
10	DATE	DE	SV	

Figure 10-26. LOG-VENDITEM LDS dictionary entry

Normalized Database Design Using Object-Oriented Database Design

There is a set of rules for constructing normalized PDSs for each semantic object category. These rules are listed in Table 10-2. Identifying the semantic object types and applying the appropriate set of rules accomplishes database normalization without requiring the arduous task of applying the rules of the normal forms. In applying the OODD rules, the key that identifies a particular object of one data type may be placed in another data type as a foreign key property to establish a relationship between those two data types. In effect, normal form rules are applied within the application of OODD rules.

Simple Semantic Object PDS Creation

Table 10-2 states that the PDS used to represent a simple semantic object will have all of the same data items as the LDS for the semantic object. Since the LDS for the customer master is a simple object, all of the same data items of LOG-CUSTMAST will be included in a PDS created to represent this semantic object. The convention is to

Table 10-2	OODD rules for semantic object categories

Object Category	Normalized PDS Construction Rules
Simple object	Create a single PDS consisting of all of the data items in the LDS.
Composite object	Create a PDS for the original object and a PDS for each separate multivalued property (or set of related multivalued properties), with the key of the PDS for the original object used as part of the key for the PDSs created for the multivalued properties.
Compound object	Create a PDS for the original object and remove the properties of each object embedded in the original object, with foreign keys assigned appropriate to the way the objects are related (1:1, 1:M, or M:N).
Associative object	Remove the properties of the objects having the association from the associative object. Create a separate PDS for the associative object itself, with keys to the related objects appearing as foreign key attributes in the PDS created for the original associative object, along with data items pertaining to the associative object.
Generalized object	Create a PDS relative to what traits of other object types the generalized object exhibits.

name PDSs with a prefix of PHY-, similar to the use of LOG- as a prefix to all LDS names. Thus, you would define a PDS named PHY-CUSTOMER_MASTER with all of the same data items appearing in LOG-CUSTMAST.

Composite Semantic Object PDS Creation

PDSs are created for composite semantic objects relative to the way repeating data items are treated. The LDS in Figure 10-27 illustrates how to apply composite semantic object conversion rules. The two multivalued (MV) data items, ITEMNUM and QUANTITY, should be treated as a single set of related multivalued data items. To correct the anomaly condition of this composite object, a PDS would be created for the original semantic object representing the customer order, with a separate PDS for the order items and quantities.

Identifying a composite item and applying its rules for creating PDSs corresponds to applying the rule of the first normal form: no repeating data items. A similar application of normal form rules occurs as a result of identifying other types of semantic objects and applying their rules for creating PDSs. Figures 10-28 and 10-29 illustrate the two normalized PDSs created for the LOG-CUSTORDER data structure.

Entry Type   **Dictionary ID**

Data Structure   LOG-CUSTORDER

Alias: _CUSTOMER ORDER_

Comment: _A LDS for a customer order._

Starting Volume: _____   Growth Potential: _____

No.	Ele/DS Name	DE/DS	SV/MV	Occurrences
01	ORDER_NUMBER	DE	SV	
02	CUSTNUM	DE	SV	
03	ITEMNUM	DE	MV	
04	QUANTITY	DE	MV	
05	DATE	DE	SV	
06	EMPNUM	DE	SV	

Figure 10-27. LOG-CUSTORDER data structure dictionary entry

Entry Type   **Dictionary ID**

Data Structure   PHY-CUSTORDER

Alias: _CUSTOMER ORDER_

Comment: _A PDS for a customer order._

Starting Volume: _____   Growth Potential:_____

No.	Ele/DS Name	DE/DS	SV/MV	Occurrences
01	ORDER_NUMBER	DE	SV	
02	CUSTNUM	DE	SV	
03	DATE	DE	SV	
04	EMPNUM	DE	SV	

Figure 10-28. PHY-CUSTORDER PDS dictionary entry

Notice that the prefix PHY- has been assigned to both data structures in Figures 10-28 and 10-29. Also notice that the PHY-CUSTORDER PDS contains all of the data items that pertain only to the order. Finally, you should note that PHY-ITEM_QUANTITY contains the key of the original order semantic object (ORDER_NUMBER), along with its ITEMNUM and QUANTITY properties.

Entry Type	Dictionary ID			
Data Structure	PHY-ITEM_QUANTITY			

Alias: _CUSTOMER ORDER ITEMS_

Comment: _A PDS for order items._

Starting Volume: _____ Growth Potential: _____

No.	Ele/DS Name	DE/DS	SV/MV	Occurrences
01	ORDER_NUMBER	DE	SV	
02	ITEMNUM	DE	SV	
03	QUANTITY	DE	SV	

Figure 10-29. PHY-ITEM_QUANTITY PDS dictionary entry

Separating the ITEMNUM and QUANTITY properties into their own PDS eliminates having a repeating data item in the database file. It causes the items that are ordered to be stored as multiple occurrences in a separate file. As a result, creating a customer order causes records to be created in the two database files. For a customer order for five items, one PHY-CUSTORDER occurrence and five PHY-ITEM_ QUANTITY occurrences would be created.

Compound Semantic Object PDS Creation

Constructing PDSs for compound semantic objects depends on how a given object and the object embedded in it are related. These objects can be related on a one-to-one (1:1) basis or according to one of the three types of binary relationships explained earlier: tree (1:M), simple network (1:M with multiple parents of different types), and complex network (M:N). Table 10-3 illustrates the PDS construction for the different ways the semantic objects in a compound semantic object may be related.

Regardless of the type of relationship between data types, correcting the anomaly for the compound object involves removing the data items of the data type embedded in the compound object and placing them in their own PDSs. Retaining the relationship between these different data types involves placing keys of the different normalized PDSs where they aid in linking those data types together.

NORMALIZING A 1:1 RELATIONSHIP   For compound objects with a one-to-one (1:1) relationship type, the properties of the data type embedded in the compound object are removed and placed in their own PDSs, and the key of one of the data types is inserted as a foreign key attribute in the PDS for the other data type. Which PDS receives the

Table 10-3	Compound semantic object PDS construction

Relationship Type	Normalized PDS Construction Rules
One-to-one	Create a separate PDS for each object, with the key of one of the objects included as a foreign key data item in the PDS of the other object.
Tree	Create a PDS for each separate object, with the key of the parent object included as a foreign key data item in the PDS of the child.
Simple network	Create a PDS for each separate object, with the key of each parent object included as a foreign key data item in the PDS of the child.
Complex network	Create a PDS for each separate object, with a third PDS created that contains only keys for the related objects as data items.

key of the other data type does not matter in a functional sense; it only matters that one of the PDSs has the key of the other PDS so that they may be readily linked together. Although it does not matter which PDS receives the key, just as long as one does, a semantic interpretation often leads to choosing one PDS as the more practical choice.

As an example, assume that employees at NG&T can register a car for parking in the NG&T parking lot, but that a car registration must be associated with only a single employee, a 1:1 relationship. Also assume that car registration data items appear as part of the LOG-EMPLOYEE_MASTER LDS. Figure 10-30 illustrates this LDS.

The last four data items listed in Figure 10-30 pertain to the automobile registration data type. Applying normalization rules to this compound object causes the automobile registration data items to be removed and placed in their own PDSs. One of these PDSs would then have the key of the other PDS as a foreign key attribute. It does not really matter which one of these data types receives the key of the other data type. However, it makes more sense to place the EMP_ID key of the PHY-EMPLOYEE_ MASTER PDS in the PHY-AUTO_REGISTRATION PDS because not all employees register cars, but a registered car must have an employee assigned to it.

The cardinality relationship between the two data types provides some insight into which data type should receive the key. For a 1:1 relationship with a mandatory and an optional specification for the two data types, place the key of the mandatory data type in the optional data type. For example, PHY-AUTO_REGISTRATION would have an optional cardinality relationship designation because an employee does not have to register an automobile. Conversely, PHY-EMPLOYEE_MASTER would have a mandatory cardinality relationship designation because an employee must exist for a registered automobile. For cardinality relationships with both data types designated as either optional or mandatory, which PDS receives the foreign key attribute is a judgment call in which it largely does not matter which data type receives the foreign key attribute.

Entry Type

Dictionary ID

Data Structure   LOG-EMPLOYEE_MASTER

Alias: __EMPLOYEE_MASTER__

Comment: _A LDS for an employee master._

Starting Volume: _____   Growth Potential: _____

No.	Ele/DS Name	DE/DS	SV/MV	Occurrences
01	EMP_ID	DE	SV	
02	NAME	DE	SV	
03	JOB	DE	SV	
04	PAY_GRADE	DE	SV	
05	STREET	DE	SV	
06	CITY	DE	SV	
07	STATE	DE	SV	
08	ZIP	DE	SV	
09	AUTO_REG_NUM	DE	SV	
10	LICENSE_NUMBER	DE	SV	
11	AUTO_MAKE	DE	SV	
12	REG_DATE	DE	SV	

Figure 10-30. Employee master with embedded car registration data

Figures 10-31 and 10-32 illustrate the two PDSs for the PHY-EMPLOYEE_ MASTER and PHY-AUTO_REGISTRATION data types following application of compound object normalization. Notice that all automobile registration data items have been removed from the PHY-EMPLOYEE_MASTER PDS, and the key of the PHY-EMPLOYEE_MASTER PDS (EMP_ID) is placed in the PHY-AUTO_REGISTRA-TION PDS as a foreign key attribute to retain the link between the two data types.

NORMALIZING A 1:M TREE RELATIONSHIP   For compound objects with a one-to-many (1:M) tree relationship type, the properties of the data type embedded in the compound object are also removed and placed in their own PDSs. To retain the link between the data types, the key of the data type on the "one" side of the relationship is placed in the data type on the "many" side of the relationship as a foreign key attribute. The "many" side (child data type) receives the key, since to do the reverse, you would cause the parent data type to have a repeating data item for the keys of the many child data types. Placing the keys of the child data types in the parent data type would transform the parent into a composite object; you do not want to create a new anomaly condition while correcting an already existing anomaly condition.

Entry Type   **Dictionary ID**

Data Structure   PHY-EMPLOYEE_MASTER

Alias: _EMPLOYEE MASTER_

Comment: _A PDS for an employee master._

Starting Volume: _____   Growth Potential: _____

No.	Ele/DS Name	DE/DS	SV/MV	Occurrences
01	EMP_ID	DE	SV	
02	NAME	DE	SV	
03	JOB	DE	SV	
04	PAY_GRADE	DE	SV	
05	STREET	DE	SV	
06	CITY	DE	SV	
07	STATE	DE	SV	
08	ZIP	DE	SV	

Figure 10-31. Normalized employee master with car registration removed

Entry Type   **Dictionary ID**

Data Structure   PHY-AUTO_REGISTRATION

Alias: _AUTOMOBILE REGISTRATION_

Comment: _A PDS for an automobile registration._

Starting Volume: _____   Growth Potential: _____

No.	Ele/DS Name	DE/DS	SV/MV	Occurrences
01	AUTO_REG_NUM	DE	SV	
02	EMP_ID	DE	SV	
03	LICENSE_NUMBER	DE	SV	
04	AUTO_MAKE	DE	SV	
05	REG_DATE	DE	SV	

Figure 10-32. Normalized automobile registration PDS

Even though the automobile registration data items are removed, the PHY-EMPLOYEE_MASTER PDS in Figure 10-31 is still a compound object because of the JOB/PAY data type embedded in it. This example illustrates once again that correcting one anomaly condition does not necessarily correct other anomaly conditions that may exist. For the PDS in Figure 10-31, a 1:M relationship exists between the JOB/PAY and EMPLOYEE_MASTER data types contained in the compound object; that is, an employee can have only one job classification, but a specific job classification can be assigned to multiple employees. The PHY-EMPLOYEE_MASTER and PHY-JOB_PAYGRADE PDSs in Figures 10-33 and 10-34 illustrate the anomaly-correcting remedy for a compound object with a 1:M relationship. For this normalization action, the data items for the JOB/PAY data type are removed and placed in their own PDS in Figure 10-34, and the key of this parent data type is placed in the PHY-EMPLOYEE_MASTER PDS in Figure 10-33 as a foreign key attribute.

Figures 10-33 and 10-34 effectively duplicate Figure 10-23, which were used to illustrate the B-C/NF. The PHY-EMPLOYEE_MASTER PDS in Figure 10-33, which resulted from the removal of the JOB/PAY data items, effectively duplicates the EMPLOYEE_MASTER file in Figure 10-23; the PHY-JOB_PAYGRADE PDS in Figure 10-34 duplicates the JOB/PAY file in Figure 10-23. This example illustrates how applying the normalization rules for a compound object can be the same as applying the normalization rules for the B-C/NF, showing once again how these two different normalization methods are related.

Entry Type		Dictionary ID		
Data Structure		PHY-EMPLOYEE_MASTER		
Alias: _EMPLOYEE_MASTER_				
Comment: _A PDS for an employee master._				
Starting Volume: _____ Growth Potential: _____				

No.	Ele/DS Name	DE/DS	SV/MV	Occurrences
01	EMP_ID	DE	SV	
02	NAME	DE	SV	
03	JOB	DE	SV	
04	STREET	DE	SV	
05	CITY	DE	SV	
06	STATE	DE	SV	
07	ZIP	DE	SV	

Figure 10-33. Normalized EMPLOYEE_MASTER PDS with JOB/PAY removed

Entry Type		Dictionary ID		
Data Structure		PHY-JOB_PAYGRADE		

Alias: __JOB_PAYGRADE__

Comment: _A PDS for a job paygrade._

Starting Volume: _____   Growth Potential: _____

No.	Ele/DS Name	DE/DS	SV/MV	Occurrences
01	JOB	DE	SV	
02	PAY_GRADE	DE	SV	

Figure 10-34. Normalized PHY-JOB_PAYGRADE PDS

NORMALIZING A SIMPLE NETWORK RELATIONSHIP   The simple network relationship is essentially a tree relationship, except that child objects can have multiple parents that come from different data types. The LDS in Figure 10-35, containing objects in a simple network relationship, is used for a carrier invoice for products that NG&T ships to customers and items it receives from vendors. Figure 10-36 illustrates the PDS created from it.

The LDS in Figure 10-35 contains two different data types that have a relationship with a carrier invoice. These data types are the sender and receiver of the carrier delivery. These objects would be individually defined in PDSs created to describe them. To identify them, the carrier invoice needs only their identification keys. Assuming that SENDER_NUMBER and RECEIVER_NUMBER are these keys, notice that the PHY-CARRIER_INVOICE PDS in Figure 10-36 contains these keys as foreign key attributes. Thus, the PHY-CARRIER_INVOICE child object includes keys of the two different types of parents as foreign key attributes.

NORMALIZING A M:N COMPLEX NETWORK RELATIONSHIP   The complex network relationship causes an extra PDS to be created as an index file to document the many-to-many (M:N) relationship between the semantic objects. This data structure is sometimes called an **intersection data structure**. The only data items in an intersection data structure are the keys of the PDSs for the data types that have the M:N relationship.

Assume that NG&T has stores in different cities and multiple stores in many cities. As a result, the same carrier may serve multiple stores and an individual store may have multiple carriers, a M:N relationship. Figures 10-37 and 10-38 illustrate the data structures for these two semantic objects. Figure 10-39 illustrates the PDS for the intersection data structure.

Entry Type   **Dictionary ID**

Data Structure   LOG-CARRIER_INVOICE

Alias: _CARRIER_INVOICE_

Comment: _A LDS for a carrier invoice._

Starting Volume: _____   Growth Potential: _____

No.	Ele/DS Name	DE/DS	SV/MV	Occurrences
01	MANIFEST_NUMBER	DE	SV	
02	SENDER_NUMBER	DE	SV	
03	SENDER_NAME	DE	SV	
04	SENDER_ADDRESS	DE	SV	
05	RECEIVER_NUMBER	DE	SV	
06	RECEIVER_NAME	DE	SV	
07	RECEIVER_ADDRESS	DE	SV	
08	DELIVERY_AMOUNT	DE	SV	
09	DATE	DE	SV	

Figure 10-35. LOG-CARRIER_INVOICE LDS dictionary entry

Entry Type   **Dictionary ID**

Data Structure   PHY-CARRIER_INVOICE

Alias: _CARRIER_INVOICE_

Comment: _A PDS for a carrier invoice._

Starting Volume: _____   Growth Potential: _____

No.	Ele/DS Name	DE/DS	SV/MV	Occurrences
01	MANIFEST_NUMBER	DE	SV	
02	SENDER_NUMBER	DE	SV	
03	RECEIVER_NUMBER	DE	SV	
04	DELIVERY_AMOUNT	DE	SV	
05	DATE	DE	SV	

Figure 10-36. PHY-CARRIER_INVOICE PDS dictionary entry

Entry Type		Dictionary ID		
Data Structure		LOG-STORE		
Alias: ___STORE DATA___				
Comment: _A LDS for a NG&T store._				
Starting Volume: _____ Growth Potential: _____				

No.	Ele/DS Name	DE/DS	SV/MV	Occurrences
01	STORE_NUMBER	DE	SV	
02	MANAGER_NUMBER	DE	SV	
03	STREET	DE	SV	
04	CITY	DE	SV	
05	STATE	DE	SV	
06	ZIP	DE	SV	
07	DATE	DE	SV	
08	STORE_TELEPHONE	DE	SV	
09	CARRIER_NUMBER	DE	MV	
10	CARRIER_NAME	DE	MV	
11	CARRIER_TELEPHONE	DE	MV	

Figure 10-37. LOG-STORE LDS dictionary entry

The LDSs in Figures 10-37 and 10-38 contain properties of each as part of their respective semantic objects. The LDS in Figure 10-37 contains the CARRIER_NUMBER, CARRIER_NAME, and CARRIER_TELEPHONE from the LOG-CARRIER LDS. The LDS in Figure 10-38 contains the STORE_NUMBER, STORE_NAME, and STORE_TELEPHONE from the LOG-STORE LDS. The CARRIER_NUMBER, CARRIER_NAME, and CARRIER_TELEPHONE in the LOG-STORE LDS in Figure 10-37 that refer to the carrier semantic object are all designated as multivalued (MV). The STORE_NUMBER, STORE_NAME, and STORE_TELEPHONE data items in the LOG-CARRIER LDS in Figure 10-38 that refer to the store object are all designated as multivalued (MV). When two semantic objects have a M:N relationship, the LDS of one or both of the semantic objects often contains data items from the other semantic object. When the original semantic objects are defined in PDSs, the data items in them that refer to the other semantic objects will be removed, in keeping with the main action to perform to normalize a compound object. For this example, the carrier properties are removed from the store data object, while the store properties are removed from the carrier data object. Subsequently, an intersection PDS will be created to support the M:N relationship. Figure 10-39 illustrates the PDS for the intersection between the carrier and store semantic objects.

Entry Type   **Dictionary ID**

Data Structure   LOG-CARRIER

Alias: _CARRIER DATA_

Comment: _A LDS for a carrier._

Starting Volume: _____   Growth Potential: _____

No.	Ele/DS Name	DE/DS	SV/MV	Occurrences
01	CARRIER_NUMBER	DE	SV	
02	CARRIER_NAME	DE	SV	
03	CONTACT_PERSON	DE	SV	
04	STREET	DE	SV	
05	CITY	DE	SV	
06	STATE	DE	SV	
07	ZIP	DE	SV	
08	DATE	DE	SV	
09	CARRIER_TELEPHONE	DE	SV	
10	STORE_NUMBER	DE	MV	
11	STORE_NAME	DE	MV	
12	STORE_TELEPHONE	DE	MV	

Figure 10-38. LOG-CARRIER LDS dictionary entry

Entry Type   **Dictionary ID**

Data Structure   PHY-STORE_CARRIER

Alias: _STORE CARRIER_

Comment: _A PDS for a store carrier._

Starting Volume: _____   Growth Potential: _____

No.	Ele/DS Name	DE/DS	SV/MV	Occurrences
01	STORE_NUMBER	DE	SV	
02	CARRIER_NUMBER	DE	SV	

Figure 10-39. PHY-STORE_CARRIER PDS dictionary entry

Associative Semantic Object PDS Creation

An associative semantic object differs from an intersection data structure in that it has properties of its own as well as the keys for the semantic objects that it associates. Intersection data structures have only key data items that refer to the semantic objects that have the M:N relationship; they do not have any nonkey data items. Normalizing an associative semantic object causes PDSs to be created for each semantic object having an association, and a separate PDS to be created for the original associative semantic object. Figure 10-40 illustrates an associative semantic object for vendor-supplied items in the NG&T order processing application. Figure 10-41 illustrates the PDS created to represent the original associative semantic object.

In Figure 10-40, the data items that are part of the vendor and item semantic objects will be removed as part of the normalization process similar to the action performed for compound objects. The only data items from the vendor and item retained in the PHY-VENDITEM PDS in Figure 10-41 are their key data items, VENDNUM and ITEMNUM. In addition to these data items, the normalized associative semantic object in Figure 10-41 contains the VENDOR_ITEM_DISCOUNT and DATE properties. Since these nonkey data items also pertain to the associative semantic object, the data structure in Figure 10-41 is not an intersection data structure.

Entry Type   **Dictionary ID**

Data Structure   LOG-VENDITEM

Alias: _VENDOR ITEMS_

Comment: _A LDS for vendor items._

Starting Volume: _____ Growth Potential: _____

No.	Ele/DS Name	DE/DS	SV/MV	Occurrences
01	VENDNUM	DE	SV	
02	VENDNAME	DE	SV	
03	STREET	DE	SV	
04	CITY	DE	SV	
05	STATE	DE	SV	
06	ZIP	DE	SV	
07	ITEMNUM	DE	SV	
09	ITEMDESC	DE	SV	
10	VENDOR_ITEM_DISCOUNT	DE	SV	
11	DATE	DE	SV	

Figure 10-40. LOG-VENDITEM LDS dictionary entry

Entry Type		Dictionary ID			
Data Structure		PHY-VENDITEM			

Alias: __VENDOR ITEMS__

Comment: __A PDS for vendor items.__

Starting Volume: _____   Growth Potential: _____

No.	Ele/DS Name	DE/DS	SV/MV	Occurrences
01	VENDNUM	DE	SV	
02	ITEMNUM	DE	SV	
03	VENDOR_ITEM_DISCOUNT	DE	SV	
04	DATE	DE	SV	

Figure 10-41. PHY-VENDITEM PDS dictionary entry

Generalized Semantic Object PDS Creation

Creating PDSs to represent generalized semantic objects does not require any special rules beyond those rules already explained. Generalized semantic objects simply refer to a class of individual semantic objects. A generalized semantic object may be a simple, composite, compound, or associative semantic object. The appropriate set of normalization rules should be applied depending on the type of generalized semantic object. For example, the NG&T project might have a LOG-DEPARTMENT LDS to identify and describe important properties of central office and store departments. Figure 10-42 illustrates the LOG-DEPARTMENT LDS dictionary entry.

The LOG-DEPARTMENT LDS in Figure 10-42 has characteristics similar to those of a simple semantic object; it has only single-valued, non-object properties. Therefore, its LDS is already in a normalized form, and its LDS and PDS will have the same formats. If the LOG-DEPARTMENT LDS contained additional properties that pertained to the department head semantic object, such as NAME, JOB, and DATE_APPOINTED, this LDS would be a compound semantic object. If the LOG-DEPARTMENT LDS were a compound semantic object, the department head properties would be removed, and the key of the department head semantic object, DEPARTMENT_HEAD, would be retained as a foreign key attribute.

This DEPARTMENT/DEPARTMENT_HEAD compound semantic object is an example of a compound semantic object with a 1:1 relationship and a mandatory-mandatory cardinality relationship specification.

Entry Type   **Dictionary ID**

Data Structure   LOG-DEPARTMENT

Alias: DEPARTMENT

Comment: A LDS for a department.

Starting Volume: _____   Growth Potential: _____

No.	Ele/DS Name	DE/DS	SV/MV	Occurrences
01	DEPARTMENT_NAME	DE	SV	
02	DEPARTMENT_HEAD	DE	SV	
03	DEPARTMENT_TELEPHONE	DE	SV	
04	OFFICE_STORE	DE	SV	
05	STREET	DE	SV	
06	CITY	DE	SV	
07	STATE	DE	SV	
08	ZIP	DE	SV	

Figure 10-42. LOG-DEPARTMENT LDS dictionary entry

The Relationship Between OODD and A&D

Figure 10-43 illustrates the relationships between creating the logical design data model, the normalized data types, and the program procedures that retrieve and act on database data. The figure shows how logical data types are identified and described by using entity/relationship diagrams (E/RDs) and entity type descriptions (LDSs) for the logical data types depicted on E/RDs. These LDSs are the semantic objects on which OODD starts its normalization process. These LDSs are used to create normalized physical database PDSs through the application of normalization rules by OODD. Applying these rules results in creating normalized PDSs to use for database object definition in the schema. When programs or data manipulation commands execute, the DBMS on the server computer accesses the normalized PDSs to reconstruct the logical data types (LDSs). After the call to the DBMS, IS program procedures based on structure chart procedures execute on the client computer. They act on those LDSs that the DBMS on the server reconstructs from the normalized PDSs for data types in the database. The programs then employ user interface screen masks, produced during prototyping activities, to display the reconstructed LDS on the user's client computer.

Identifying anomalies and applying normal-form or OODD normalization rules requires a great deal more study than this text can provide. The discussion here is only an overview, which includes the influence of analysis and logical design specifications. An excellent book that covers these subjects in greater detail is *Database Processing: Fundamentals, Design, Implementation*, by David Kroenke.

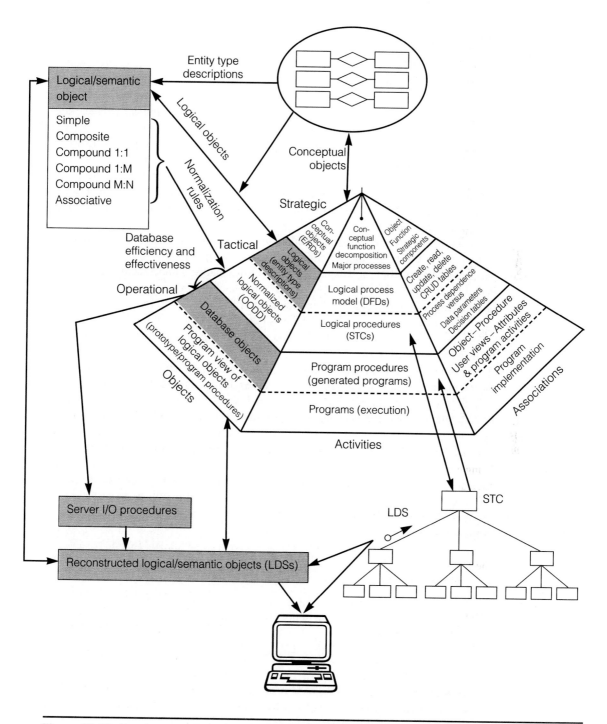

Figure 10-43. Database design relationship to A&D specifications

NORMALIZATION AS A DESIGN ISSUE

Normalization is a design issue. By physically storing strings of logically related data items together, the time required to complete the access is reduced. Consequently, a trade-off often exists between eliminating conditions for anomalies and making access faster. When a string of data items is frequently accessed as a group, the need for more efficient access may override eliminating conditions for anomalies. In these situations, the type of access permitted to users will be constrained so that the anomaly does not occur. These are the design specifications that must be transmitted from the analyst to the DBA.

Additional database design normalization criteria are subjective; they rely on the analyst's full understanding of proper database design criteria to aid the DBA in designing an anomaly-free database. The better the analyst's understanding, the easier it will be for the DBA to meet the goal of completely eliminating the possibility of *any* anomalies in the database, while providing efficient access to the database.

Given the subjective nature of database design criteria, you must be able to recognize possible anomaly conditions. You are encouraged to obtain a more detailed understanding of all of the normal forms and of the anomaly conditions each normal form proposes to eliminate. A thorough understanding of object-oriented database design principles and how applying them causes database normalization will be very helpful to you as an analyst. The list of normal forms and the presentation of object-oriented database design principles are provided to help you identify areas in which you may need more detailed study. If you can identify these areas as an analyst, you are halfway to solving the problem of designing a database without anomaly conditions.

Summary of Database Design Criteria

The elements of design criteria relative to systems and users operating in a database environment are as follows:

- Identify the data items that require link lists and inverted lists for more efficient access of related data items. (See Appendix A for a discussion of link lists and inverted lists.)
- Know when not to normalize database files in the interest of providing more efficient access.
- Know when constrained access is necessary so that anomalies do not occur.
- Identify tree, simple network, and complex network relationships.
- Specify screen mask database access commands.

- Specify preprogrammed data access and access between computer architectures.
- Define user views.
- Identify sensitive data and necessary security measures.
- Identify data and files for which enciphering of access and transmission is necessary.
- Specify where it is necessary to lock sections of the database.
- Specify on-line access capabilities.

REVIEW

The characteristics of database technologies have an ever-increasing influence on the analysis and design of computer systems. Understanding the definition, structure, and maintenance of databases permits the analyst to design systems in a more comprehensive manner. Critical design issues related to the design of a database shared by all systems must be considered while creating and maintaining the database. More detailed knowledge of database technology, of particular database management systems (DBMSs), and of the database administrators' responsibilities is required to fully understand how the database influences or is influenced by an A&D project. This knowledge can be acquired through in-house training courses, manufacturers' training courses, professional seminars, college database courses, journal articles, textbooks, and reference manuals.

Understanding what constitutes a database and how it is used involves understanding a database schema and languages used to create and use the database. A data dictionary aids in defining the database schema and establishing user views that constrain user access to the database. The schema definition and use of a database depend on the type of model on which the specific DBMS is based. Currently, the most popular model is the relational model.

To create a database that best suits the firm, anomalies should be eliminated and one or more methods for normalization applied. The three normalization methods most often cited are successive application of normal form rules, the domain/key method, and object-oriented database design (OODD). The application of the normal forms is the oldest method for normalization, with normalization typically proceeding through the third normal form. OODD is a normalization method that is more closely integrated with conceptual and logical data modeling. The OODD normalization method uses entity/relationship diagrams (E/RDs) and entity type descriptions to identify and depict semantic objects used in the method.

Finally, database use and protection require establishing information systems and on-line access to the database, and preventive, protective, and corrective measures to ensure continued productive use of the database. The firm's information systems use the database as input and output for the procedures they perform. The DBMS and the database normally reside on the server computer and are directed to access the physical data structures (PDSs) whose data items compose the logical data structures (LDSs) that help satisfy user needs. The user's client desktop computer typically performs its operations on the data returned to the desktop computer by the DBMS operating on the host server computer. For more immediate access, users can use data manipulation commands (DMCs) to direct the DBMS to retrieve the data they need. By understanding how database technology influences analysis and design and vice versa, the analyst better prepares the way for actual development of the system, the topic of Chapter 11.

QUESTIONS

1. What distinguishes a database from a mere collection of files?

2. How does a database come into existence? Who participates in its creation, and what factors are involved?

3. What does *data integrity* mean and what problems can it cause?

4. What advantages does a database have over a collection of files?

5. Explain what *integration* means regarding the data in a database. Explain how data from separate database files becomes integrated and how the schema and the DBMS facilitate data integration.

6. Distinguish between logical and physical database structures.

7. Define *schema* and explain what it means.

8. Distinguish among the major functions performed by the DBA.

9. Distinguish between data definition and data manipulation commands.

10. What is a user view and of what does it consist?

11. Explain how statistics helps the DBA maintain a better environment for systems and on-line accesses of data in a database.

12. Explain the concept of client-server architecture, its components, the purpose of each component, the interaction between components, and the sharing of data between client and server components.

13. What is a host program and how is it used for database accessing and data processing?

14. Distinguish among the three types of data relationships and identify the type of DBMS model associated with each relationship.

15. Distinguish among the three different types of DBMS models. Identify a DBMS based on each of the three models not specified in this chapter.

16. Distinguish among the terms *relation, attribute, tuple,* and *occurrence* in relational DBMS environments.

17. Explain what *table* refers to in the relational model vocabulary (vernacular). What is the underlying interpretation of the way a relational database is viewed?
18. Explain what *tuple* means.
19. Explain what a data dictionary is, how it supports creating a database schema, and the difference between it and a design dictionary.
20. Distinguish among the major functions performed by the DBMS.
21. Explain how data integrity is facilitated by decreasing redundancy in the database.
22. Explain how database data is enciphered for distributed transmission.
23. Why is synchronization of database accessing important?
24. Explain how a database recovers from failure.
25. Distinguish between procedural and nonprocedural DBMS query commands and languages.
26. How is standardizing DBMS query languages related to the standardization of programming languages that occurred in the third generation?
27. What advantages does on-line access provide over IS program execution?
28. Explain the execution of host programs in a client-server environment.
29. Explain how logical data types and database data types are related and how the logical data types are reconstructed from database data types, and why.
30. Explain the relationship between the logical data types displayed on user interfaces and the physical data types in a database.
31. Define *anomaly* and explain the two types of anomalies that may exist in logical data types.
32. Provide an example of a LDS not illustrated in this text that contains a deletion anomaly, and explain where the deletion anomaly condition is for this LDS.
33. Provide an example of a LDS not illustrated in this text that contains an insertion anomaly, and explain where the insertion anomaly condition is for this LDS.
34. Explain the purpose of the normalization process and the typical remedy associated with applying the normalization process.
35. Distinguish among the different types of normal forms.
36. Provide an illustration of separate LDSs not depicted in this text that violate the 1st/NF, the 2nd/NF, the 3rd/NF, and the B-C/NF.
37. Provide an illustration of a LDS not depicted in this text that violates the 4th/NF. Is this an actual object or just the relationship between other data types in a M:N relationship? Explain why or why not.
38. Explain *functional dependency* and what purpose the determinant serves for the functional dependency.

39. Illustrate and explain a functional dependency that is contained in a LDS not depicted in this text.

40. What normal forms correct anomalies that exist because of the incorrect file formats for LDSs with functional dependencies?

41. Explain what a foreign key attribute is and what purpose it serves.

42. Distinguish between applying normalization through successive application of the normal forms and applying the DK/NF.

43. What must you know about the other normal forms to apply the DK/NF?

44. Distinguish between the different types of semantic objects in OODD.

45. Provide an illustration of a LDS not depicted in this text that is a simple semantic object. Explain this object and what makes it a simple semantic object.

46. Provide an illustration of a LDS not depicted in this text that is a composite semantic object. Explain this object and what makes it a composite semantic object.

47. Provide an illustration of a LDS not depicted in this text that is a compound semantic object with a 1:1 relationship. Explain this object and what makes it a compound semantic object.

48. Provide an illustration of a LDS not depicted in this text that is a compound semantic object with a 1:M relationship. Explain this object and what makes it a compound semantic object.

49. Provide an illustration of a LDS not depicted in this text that is a compound semantic object with a M:N relationship. Explain this object and what makes it a compound semantic object.

50 Provide an illustration of a LDS not depicted in this text that is an associative semantic object. Explain this object and what makes it an associative semantic object.

51. Provide an illustration of a LDS not depicted in this text that is a generalized semantic object. Explain this object and what makes it a generalized semantic object. What characteristics of one or more other semantic objects does this semantic object exhibit?

52. For the semantic object in question 45, illustrate its normalized PDS.

53. For the semantic object in question 46, illustrate its normalized PDS.

54. For the semantic object in question 47, illustrate its normalized PDS.

55. For the semantic object in question 48, illustrate its normalized PDS.

56. For the semantic object in question 49, illustrate its normalized PDSs. Make sure to include the intersection record.

57. For the semantic object in question 50, illustrate its normalized PDS.

58. For the semantic object in question 51, illustrate its normalized PDS.

59. Explain what *hybrid semantic object* means.

60. Provide an illustration of a LDS not depicted in this text that is a hybrid semantic object. Explain this object and what makes it a hybrid semantic object.

61. For the semantic object in question 60, illustrate its normalized PDS.

62. Explain how normalization using the normal forms is related to the normalization performed in OODD.

63. For the LDS that violates the 1st/NF in question 36, what semantic object does it represent? For the LDS that violates the 2nd/NF, what semantic object does it represent? For the LDS that violates the 3rd/NF, what semantic object does it represent? For the LDS that violates the B-C/NF, what semantic object does it represent?

64. For the LDS that violates the 4th/NF in question 37, what semantic object does it represent?

65. Explain what an intersection data structure is, its purpose, and what normal form and semantic object to which it relates in the normalization process. Distinguish between an intersection data structure and an associative semantic object.

66. Thoroughly explain the design criteria to consider in a database environment.

67. Clearly distinguish between link lists and inverted lists. (See Appendix A.)

68. What is the difference between a two-way and a ring link list? (See Appendix A.)

69. Explain the design characteristics that influence the number of link lists or inverted lists created for a database. (See Appendix A.)

EXERCISES

Chapter 10 of the student workbook contains blank documentation forms to use in the following exercises.

1. Provide the same sequence of descriptions as in Figures 10-9 through 10-13 for a vendor order LDS called LOG-VENDORD, the LDS that supports one of the relationships between a VENDOR entity and one of the types of clerks in Chapter 8. Your exercise should combine and integrate the LDS for the vendor order and the physical database data structures where the data items of that LDS are likely to reside. You should include the following entries: a LOG-VENDORD LDS that includes a reference to a mass PDS, a dictionary entry for the mass PDS, and all PDSs contained in this mass PDS for the logical vendor order LDS.

2. Provide the same sequence of descriptions as in Figures 10-9 through 10-13 for a customer shipment LDS called LOG-CUSTSHIP, the LDS that supports the relationship between the CUSTOMER and SHIP/RECVG CLERK entities in Chapter 8. Your exercise should combine and integrate the LDS for the customer shipment and the physical database data structures where the data items

of that LDS are likely to reside. You should include the following entries: a LOG-CUSTSHIP LDS that includes a reference to a mass PDS, a dictionary entry for the mass PDS, and all PDSs contained in this mass PDS for the logical customer shipment LDS.

3. Provide the same sequence of descriptions as in Figures 10-9 through 10-13 for a vendor order receipt LDS called LOG-VENDRCPT, the LDS that supports the relationship between the VENDOR and ACCOUNTS CLERK entities in Chapter 8. Your exercise should combine and integrate the LDS for the customer shipment and the physical database data structures where the data items of that LDS are likely to reside. You should include the following entries: a LOG-VENDRCPT LDS that includes a reference to a mass PDS, a dictionary entry for the mass PDS, and all PDSs contained in this mass PDS for the logical vendor receipt.

4. Provide the same sequence of descriptions as in Figures 10-9 through 10-13 for an item back-order LDS called LOG-ITEMBACKORDER, the LDS that supports the relationship between the VENDOR and ACCOUNTS CLERK entities in Chapter 8. Your exercise completion should combine and integrate the LDS for the customer shipment and the physical database data structures where the data items of that LDS are likely to reside. You should include the following entries: a LOG-ITEMBACKORDER LDS that includes a reference to a mass PDS, a dictionary entry for the mass PDS, and all PDSs contained in this mass PDS for the logical item back order.

SELECTED REFERENCES

Alagic, S. 1986. *Relational Database Technology*. New York: Springer-Verlag.

American National Standards Institute. 1981. *Proposed American National Standard for a Data Definition Language for Networked Structured Databases*. ANSI X3H2.

Atre, S. 1980. *Data Base: Structured Techniques for Design, Performance, and Management*. Chichester, NY: John Wiley and Sons.

Chen, P. 1976. "The Entity-Relationship Model—Toward a Unified View of Data." *ACM Transactions on Database Systems* 1, no. 1 (March).

Codd, E. F. 1970. "A Relational Model of Data for Large Shared Databanks." *Communications of the ACM* 13, no. 6 (June).

Courtney, J. F. and D. B. Paradice. 1992. *Database Systems for Management*, 2nd edition. Homewood, IL: Irwin.

Date, C. J. 1981. *An Introduction to Database Systems*, 3rd edition. Reading, MA: Addison-Wesley.

Fagin, R. 1981. "Multivalued Dependencies and a New Normal Form for Relational Databases." *Transaction on Database Systems* 6, no. 3 (September).

IBM Corporation. 1981. *SQL/Data System General Information*. GH24-5012-0. White Plains, New York.

Inmon, W. H. and T. J. Bird. 1986. *The Dynamics of Database*. Englewood Cliffs, NJ: Prentice-Hall.

Kroenke, D. M. 1992. *Database Processing: Fundamentals, Design, Implementation*, 4th edition. New York: Macmillan.

Pratt, P. J. and J. J. Adamski. 1991. *Database Systems: Management and Design*. Boston: Boyd and Fraser.

Tsichritzis, D. C. and F. H. Lochovsky. 1982. *Data Models*. Englewood Cliffs, NJ: Prentice-Hall.

Vetter, M. 1987. *Strategy for Data Modeling*. Chichester, NY: John Wiley and Sons.

CHAPTER 11

System Development: Implementing the Physical Design

OVERVIEW

Using the various methods presented in this chapter, the project leader, programmers, and operational personnel move a system from logical design to a concrete set of programs that can be installed into production. These programs supply the information that users need to support their responsibilities in the firm. The major tasks in implementing the physical design include:

- Supervising the project
- Creating application programs
- Using structured programming in programming activities
- Creating program and user documentation
- Categorizing systems and files
- Preparing for system implementation
- Creating error and crash recovery routines
- Using new technologies for faster systems development
- Using computer-aided system development principles

KEY TERMS

Active dictionary

Application generators

Batch processing systems

Check digit routines

Checkpoint

Chief programmer team

Client-server environment

Code generators

Computer program

Cross system architecture (CSA)

Data editing routines

Distributed systems

Downsizing

Edit programs

Expert system

Fifth generation development

Fourth generation languages (4GLs)

Generation data groups

Help files

Interactive system

Job Control Language (JCL)

Job stream

Keys

Knowledge base

Knowledge-based systems

Natural language programming (NLP)

Object-oriented programming (OOP)

Open system architecture

Operations documentation

Parameter data

Procedural languages

Procedure library

Programmer workbenches

Programming standards

Random access files

Real-time systems

Rehosting computer systems

Remote job entry system (RJES)

Sensitivity analysis

Sequential access files

Structured programming

System architecture

Time-sharing systems

Traditional programming languages

User documentation

Once the analyst completes the physical design, system development can begin in earnest. System development includes system creation, environment modifications, and user support. The primary concern is to create a system conforming to the physical design requirements.

The main goal in program development is to build reliable, usable, understandable, and maintainable programs. A *reliable* program provides failure-free system execution and correct output. A *usable* program serves business personnel in their job functions: it is easy to use, convenient, and tolerant of user errors, and it provides the information needed. If you build an *understandable* program, users will know how to

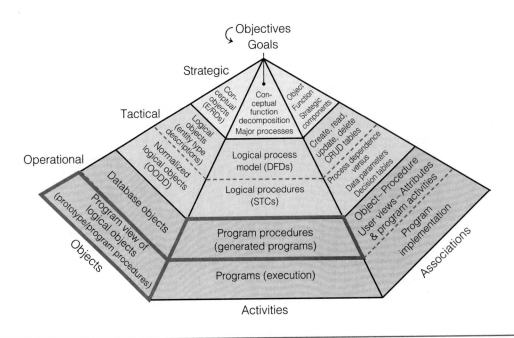

Figure 11-1. Enterprise/methodology model focus of Chapter 11

use the system properly; they will know what inputs are required and how to interpret system outputs. A *maintainable* program makes it easy to correct errors, enhance system performance, and adapt the system to changes in the business environment. All of these attributes should be built into the system during system development.

The enterprise/methodology model focus of this chapter, as shown in Figure 11-1, centers around taking the procedure model and the operational data model and developing a system that performs those procedures on operational data. Chapter 10 discussed how the logical data types defined as LDSs during creation of entity type descriptions are normalized and used to build database files. Chapter 9 discussed how the business process model is converted into a procedure model to help implement business processes. The procedure models perform actions on the logical data types (LDSs) defined in the entity type descriptions. When these procedures are made operational in computer programs, they need to include the calls to the database management system (DBMS) to reconstruct the logical data type (LDS) from the database data types. These programs also need to base their operations on the procedures included in the procedure models. These programs combine the operations to call on the DBMS to reconstruct the logical data type and the operations to be performed on those logical data types.

Programmers and operational personnel usually perform the activities in system development, but the leader of the project team must assign personnel to specific tasks and properly coordinate activities to ensure timely completion. As an emerging analyst, you should understand your dual responsibility as supervisor and manager of the project.

PROJECT SUPERVISION

Chapter 1 presented a list of roles taken by the analyst. One of these roles was that of supervisor. The analyst assumes the role of a supervisor during the development phase of the project life cycle. Any managerial activity must begin with a plan; managing the development phase also conforms to this rule. Creating the development plan involves identifying the tasks to perform, scheduling those tasks, allocating available resources to them, and monitoring and supervising the progress of the plan. The primary tasks of a project development plan are as follows:

- Assign responsibility for individual programs
- Create application programs
- Create procedures to direct system and communication software
- Create documentation
- Convert existing software and data storage formats to support the system
- Acquire supporting hardware and software
- Create or modify the database and procedures to direct the DBMS to access the database
- Create error recovery routines
- Create crash recovery procedures

The topics in this list are discussed in the remainder of this chapter either as major topics, in combination with other topics, or as sections within a major topic. The list is intended for use as a reference point while completing system development, not as an ordering of topics in this section or in the remainder of this chapter.

Assigning and Scheduling Program Creation

Traditionally, the creation of application programs by the firm's programmers is a separately defined and controlled development task. The project leader assigns individual programmers to create particular programs based on a combination of program complexity, programmer experience, and programmer qualifications. Superior programmers are assigned to more complex programs or combinations of programs, for example. Some companies use the chief programmer team concept to counterbalance problems associated with the more complex programs and portions of programs. A **chief programmer team** is managed by a more experienced and highly skilled programmer who assumes general control for the design and construction of assigned programs. The chief programmer governs all creation and testing of programs, as well as personally constructing some of the more complex programs and portions of programs.

The assigned programmers are given the specifications created during the latter stages of physical design—for example, the program design specifications explained at the end of Chapter 9. The programmers are also given a time estimate for creating programs and a schedule for the creation of combinations of programs by the project leader or chief programmer. The project leader monitors the progress of each task assigned to these programmers and tracks the progress of program completion. In case of any deviation from anticipated completion of programming tasks, the supervising analyst should become more actively involved in overseeing them, encouraging programmers to get back on schedule.

Assigning Multiple Programmers to Programs

Sometimes the supervising analyst assigns more than one programmer to a program, or part of a program, that requires greater thought and effort. Such a program may benefit from the contributions of more than one person's ideas and experiences. Joint program assignments have advantages and disadvantages, of which the analyst should be aware. Organizations that typically do this claim the following advantages:

- Faster creation of programs as a result of joint effort
- Greater adherence to programming standards
- Programs with more efficient computer code
- Reduction of individual programming idiosyncrasies
- Fewer program errors in the delivered program

Assigning multiple persons to program creation encourages adherence to the firm's programming standards because each programmer reminds the others when they move outside of those standards. Multiple programmers are also likely to take the time to create more effective computer code because they can share efficient program routines from prior projects that may be used on the current project. Stylistic differences between multiple programmers tend to negate each other as portions of the programs are revised. Finally, having two persons involved in tracking program logic helps identify more errors that might otherwise remain in delivered programs.

Some disadvantages of joint programming assignments are:

- Difficulty identifying responsibility for delivered programs
- Tendency for personality problems to occur
- Difficulty integrating program modules when programmers use different programming styles
- Additional time and expense of communication between programmers

On multiprogrammer assignments, it is difficult to tell who is responsible for good and bad code in the programs—especially when programmers of different skill levels are paired. Also, when programmers share the review and modification of all portions of the program, it is difficult to assign individual responsibility. This problem can be remedied to some extent by assigning different programmers to work on different portions of the same program.

Joint efforts undertaken by humans are subject to personality conflicts, which may disturb the flow of work. Individual behavioral eccentricities often clash, making it difficult to work cooperatively and produce better programs. Stylistic differences, although they can be an advantage, can also be a hindrance to completing joint program assignments. The programming styles of different programmers may be so different that it may be difficult to integrate their code. Furthermore, to integrate and complete programs assigned to multiple persons, the programmers must take time to discuss various aspects of the program. Discussing the characteristics of a joint program assignment typically contributes to better quality; however, some discussions between programmers digress from the topic, causing program completion to take longer.

CREATING MAINTAINABLE SYSTEMS AND DOCUMENTATION

A computer system consists of individual computer programs executed in a particular sequence or recalled individually for execution. A **computer program** is a sequence of instructions that causes a computer to process data in the pattern prescribed by the program's specifications. Programs operate on the principles of sequence, selection, and iteration: they execute a set of instructions in a particular sequence, make selections of actions based on specific conditions, and repeat certain actions in a looping fashion. These principles form the basis for the operations of a computer program, which consist of:

1. Instructions causing storage areas for data to be set aside and made referable
2. Instructions causing data to be stored in the storage areas that have been set aside
3. Instructions causing data manipulation by referencing data storage areas
4. Instructions causing a change of execution control
5. Instructions causing the transmission of generated output data to external storage mediums, to user interfaces, and to devices being controlled by computer systems in real time.

The first type of instruction (1) assigns variable names to storage areas reserved for data. An example of this type of instruction is the data names and accompanying descriptions specified in Data Division entries in COBOL programs (other languages have equivalents to this example). These entries specify the type and amount of storage to set aside and the variable name assigned to reference these storage areas.

The second type of instruction (2) is either an input-type instruction (READ statement) or an instruction specifying that data values be placed in specified storage areas. Data input instructions cause data to be retrieved from external storage media and placed in the reserved storage areas. These instructions may be record retrieval instructions within file processing systems or calls to a DBMS to retrieve data when the program acts as a host program (see Chapter 10). Other data value insertion instructions can be used with one of a number of other instructions—for example, VALUE clauses, MOVE statements, and COMPUTE statements in a COBOL program.

The third type of instruction (3) represents all instructions used to manipulate data. The major classes include instructions to:

- Copy data from one storage area into another storage area
- Use data in computations
- Use data in comparison operations

Examples of these classes of instructions are the MOVE, COMPUTE, and IF instructions in COBOL programs. Again, other languages have equivalents to these instructions.

The fourth type of instruction (4) causes a branch of control from one point in a program to another point in the program. These instructions cause control to:

- Branch indefinitely to some other point in a program
- Branch to some other point in the program and return after the execution of a series of instructions
- Branch to a set of instructions a specified number of times
- Branch to a set of instructions until a certain condition is detected

Examples of this type of instruction are the GO TO, PERFORM, PERFORM with a TIMES option, and PERFORM with an UNTIL option instructions in COBOL programs. Again, other languages have equivalents to these instructions.

The fifth type of instruction (5) causes data contained in data storage areas to be transmitted to external storage mediums, back to the user interface, or to devices being controlled by the computer application. These instructions may be record transmission instructions within file processing systems or calls to a DBMS for data transmission when the developed program acts as a host program (see Chapter 10). An example of this type of instruction is the WRITE instruction in a COBOL program for file processing applications or a CALL to an output routine to a DBMS. For interactive encounters between users and the system, the stored data is transmitted to the users' display monitors. For systems called *real-time systems*, which often help operate other devices in the business, the output is often transmitted to these devices to activate or control them. For example, a real-time system that facilitates manufacturing of steel products could operate a steel mill with a computer system that uses the temperature gauge as input and fuel intensity to the firing points as output. This computer system transmits output in the form of fuel delivered to the firing points to ensure that the temperature inside the vat remains consistent.

Program creation involves specifying the correct sequence of instructions and proper references to data. The analyst creates program specifications that generate this sequence of instructions, which indicate what data items to access, what data manipulation operations to perform on the accessed data, what to do to cause the output data to be transmitted, and how to present the output. The programmer follows these guidelines and creates a program with control branching actions that cause the data to be processed as indicated in the specifications. All of the instructions are based on the logical routines of the STC procedures, as described in Chapter 9.

Developing Maintainable Programs

Considering the amount of time and effort devoted to maintaining existing programs, programmers must make every effort to build easily maintainable programs from the beginning. Most companies spend roughly 70 to 80 percent of their time and resources on maintaining systems rather than developing them. Remember that a good system is maintainable, usable, reliable, and understandable. Some of these attributes are considered during the physical design phase; some are considered during the development phase. All of these attributes are manifested in the development phase.

Developing usable software starts with determining what constitutes usability from a user's standpoint. Properly conducted prototyping activities, as described in Chapter 7, go a long way toward ensuring that software is usable. During prototyping activities, users verify the functioning of the prototype. They review the types of actions they can perform, data they can access, actions they can perform on the data, user interface formats, and the ease of using the prototype. These specifications become part of the user requirements for developing the programs. Thus, prototyping verifies that the use of the system matches the desires of the user. JAD and RAD techniques, as described in Chapters 4 through 8, help the analyst determine how usable the software is from the perspective of users.

By developing efficient software, programmers ensure that users remain satisfied with program performance. When users are satisfied with program performance, it usually follows that maintenance requests decrease, extending the usability of the program. Efficiency often means using faster processing methods, faster human-machine communication, and possibly faster hardware.

Reliable software performs correctly, consistently, and completely with no (or infrequent) breakdowns. Programmers must understand the meaning behind program instructions and test developed software thoroughly to ensure the accuracy of processing methods and of the output generated. The result of each routine in the program should be checked for correctness. JAD and RAD sessions may provide the opportunity for users to review the correctness of software execution. Reliability also involves how consistently the software executes and how consistently outputs are generated from execution to execution. When software stops in midexecution, or produces questionable results, users become very dissatisfied with a program and typically stop using the software. A final trait of reliability is the completeness of the processing and of the resulting output. Again, RAD and JAD sessions provide a way for users to assess the completeness of software execution. When users perceive that complete processing occurs in developed software, their requests for changes decrease. When the results of software execution generate additional questions from users that can be answered by providing additional information, the software cannot be considered complete.

Finally, a maintainable program should be easy to modify or adapt to changes in the business environment. Programmers should be able to change programs without losing the basic structure and function of the programs. Keeping the logic of programs simple usually makes them more easily understood and modifiable. The more generic a program is, the more easily understood and modifiable it will be. Establishing rules regarding stylistic conventions makes programs more easily understood. One such set of rules is called structured programming.

Structured Programming

Most IS departments have adopted conventions to guide programmers in developing programs. By adopting a set of conventions, the department ensures that programs developed by different programmers have the same appearance and basic program logic. Thus, the programs should be easier to understand and maintain.

Business programming conventions are called **programming standards. Structured programming**, the recognized programming standard since the early 1970s, represents a modular, top-down programming method that uses hierarchical execution control. Structured programming standards for an organization may also establish rules regarding how to code programs, for example:

- Naming conventions for files, data structures, records, fields, and program modules
- Structural format of the overall program
- Stylistic presentation of the program, such as indentation rules
- Coding methods for instructions used to set aside storage
- Modular program logic structure
- Hierarchical execution of program modules within the program
- Entrance, execution, and exit methods used in program modules
- Stylistic framework for individual instructions within the programming language
- Usage of particular instructions
- Usage of options for particular instructions
- Documentation embedded within programs

The purpose of adopting a set of rules to govern all programming activities is to make sure that programs developed by one programmer are easily understood by other staff programmers, and therefore can easily be modified later by other programmers. Generally speaking, the more detailed the structured programming rules and the greater the controls exercised over programmer compliance with these rules, the more easily understood and maintainable the program becomes. A complete list of structured programming rules for companies using the COBOL programming language is provided in Appendix B. Similar structured programming rules may be established for other computer languages. COBOL is used as an example simply because it is still the language preferred by most businesses.

Structured programming rules prescribe an explicit programming style. Properly enforced, this programming style causes programs to be stylistic clones of each other. Adopting structured programming conventions for all program creation ultimately reduces maintenance costs.

Programming Logic

Regardless of the programming style, all programs in business contain either a single logical routine or a combination of logical routines from within a set of fourteen basic logical routines. Five of these logical routines are typically used in batch processing programs; nine of them are typically used in on-line processing programs. All of these routines involve either information reporting or data updating functions. Data is being processed to generate a report, processed relative to a query by the user, processed to update the firm's retained data, or stored for future updating activities. Figure 11-2 lists the fourteen different types of logical routines that make up the basic logic for batch and on-line programs.

Batch Processing Logical Routines

1. Simple read-write routines, including various calculations
2. Read-write routines, including a summary of processed data
3. Control group processing routines
4. Multiple record type processing routines
5. Matching files processing routines

On-line Processing Logical Routines

6. Add data to a database or file processing routine
7. Change data in a database or file processing routine
8. Delete data from a database or file processing routine
9. Display data in a database or file processing routine
10. Duplicate data with changes in a database or file processing routine
11. Retrieve next data item in a database or file processing routine
12. Locate (or browse) data items in a database or file processing routine
13. Scan (or query-by-example) data in a database or file processing routine
14. Find (nonkey search) data in a database or file processing routine

Figure 11-2. Fourteen basic logical routines for programs

The list of actions in Figure 11-2 involves the basic logic of a typical program, not additional logic that may be a part of some programs. For both batch and on-line processing, sort and merge routines are typically completed external to the program as actions to perform on data prior to using it as input, or as actions to perform on the output data. Although these routines can be included as part of an executable program, they are not considered to be part of the main processing routines that make up the program.

In batch processing, a number of transactions are accumulated and then processed at the same time. Every batch processing program in business systems contains either one of the logical routines listed in Figure 11-2 or a combination of several of them. The logical routines selected depend on the type of processing prescribed by the system design.

On-line programs are programs that directly interact with end-users and use the computer screen and keyboard to facilitate the interaction. On-line programs may include one or a combination of the last nine logical routines listed in Figure 11-2. Although these routines are also used in more sophisticated file processing systems, they are primarily used to either update or retrieve data contained in the firm's database.

Developing System Program Procedures

Program execution requires the assistance of programs contained in the organization's system library (collection of system software). Control commands to the firm's operating system, called **Job Control Language (JCL)** commands, may be needed to guide system execution. Sequences of JCL commands cause an operating system program to find and retrieve the application program for execution; find and retrieve utility programs for execution; set execution limits for time and resource usage; identify, find, and retrieve data required for program execution; and communicate with operations staff. Combinations of application programs and utility programs frequently execute in a predefined sequence, with data passing between the application and utility programs during execution. A set of JCL commands called a **job stream** is developed to cause the retrieval and execution of application programs (and utility programs) in a desired sequence. This job stream also includes JCL commands that identify the places where data is stored for access purposes. Figure 11-3 illustrates a partial job stream for JCL used to sort input time-card data (STEP1 EXEC command), execute a program to check input time-card data (STEP2 EXEC command), and update the payroll master file (STEP3 EXEC command). Note that the first program executed is a sort program to sequence the time-card data prior to using it for error-checking routines in the program execution in STEP 2. The operating system commands in Figure 11-3 are those that might execute in an IBM host computer environment. Equivalent operating system commands exist for program/system execution in other computing environments.

JCL job streams are typically stored in a portion of auxiliary storage known as the **procedure library**, which may be retrieved to direct the execution of a program or a system of programs. When it is desirable to cause the execution of a particular program or system of programs, users merely reference the name that was assigned to

```
//UPDTJOB JOB ...
//STEP1 EXEC PROGRAM=SORTD, ...
//INPUT DD FILE=INTIME, ...
//OUTPUT DD FILE=TIMESORT, ...
//STEP2 EXEC PROGRAM=TIMECARD_EDIT, ...
//INTIME DD FILE=TIMESORT, ...
//OUTTIME DD FILE=TIMEEDIT, ...
//STEP3 EXEC PROGRAM=PYRLUPDT, ...
//INDATA1 DD FILE=TIMEEDIT, ...
//INDATA2 DD FILE=PYRLMAST, ...
//OUTDATA DD FILE=PYRLMAST, ...
```

Figure 11-3. An example of a JCL job stream

the JCL procedure at the time it was stored in the procedure library. This way, users can cause the program or system to execute without having to include the specific JCL required for the execution.

Although *JCL*, *job streams*, and *procedure libraries* are often equated with the IBM-based computing environment, the use of these terms in this textbook is intended to be more general in nature. All computing platforms have equivalent forms of these instructions to the control system (or operating system), equivalent ways to sequence operating system commands, and equivalent ways to refer to storage locations for use by the control system commands in periodic application system execution.

Programmers are usually responsible for developing the set of JCL commands to cause the proper execution of programs. They are also responsible for developing JCL job streams to cause a set of programs to be executed in a predefined sequence. After developing programs and JCL commands, programmers conduct test executions to determine if the program and the control commands harmoniously and correctly perform the processing required. Program and system testing will be explained in detail in Chapter 12.

Developing Communication Program Procedures

Programs operating in an on-line environment, or in one where data is distributed between different locations, must be supported by communication systems. Consequently, sequences of control commands must be developed that direct programs in the communication system to execute. These sequences of commands often cause the transmission of screen formats to users' computer screens and the transmission of data keyed by users on these screens to the program for processing. In addition, sequences of control commands are necessary to direct the communication system to transmit data back to users in some data reporting format. This format frequently involves the use of preformatted report screens such as those discussed in Chapter 7, on prototyping. Programmers are usually responsible for developing these sets of communication control commands and for testing the programs and sets of commands to ensure that they perform operations to access data and process it properly.

Programs containing screen mask user interfaces for data entry, program execution direction, and reporting functions must include instructions to:

- Define the screen used as the user interface
- Cause the screen display to be transmitted and displayed on users' screens
- Accept users' data entry or insert data retrieved for output purposes

A combination of these three types of program commands is necessary to access a user screen interface.

User Interfaces

The screen displayed as the interface between the user and the computer program is defined and stored as part of the program's computer storage. This storage area contains text that is displayed on the screen telling users how to direct program execution, where and how to enter data values, or what values are being displayed as program output. In some computing environments, these screen masks become a part of the command-level portion of the operating system, as in IBM's CICS operating system.

The three most popular interfaces to aid users in making selections among various options and entering data on the screen are:

- Menus (lists) that offer users a choice of actions
- Prompts that direct users to perform actions or enter data values
- Screen masks that have specific locations for data entry or display

Menus display a list of optional actions from which users select the one that they need the application system to perform. (Another way to list options—a graphical user interface, or GUI—was described in Chapter 7 and is discussed in more detail later in this chapter.) For menu-driven systems, the specific menu is typically stored as a list of constant values and transmitted to users as a block of text displayed on their monitors. Each of the menus illustrated in Chapter 7 could be created as a text block and transmitted to a user's screen as a single output.

Following the display of the menu on the user's screen, a data retrieval command in the program is executed to receive the menu selection keyed in by the user. The COBOL ACCEPT command is an example of this type of data retrieval command.

Menus almost always contain text that explains each menu selection and how to provide additional data values, if necessary. Screen-level help, which can be initiated by pressing a particular key, such as F1, is often provided on-line to guide the user in menu selection. By pressing the help function key (F1 for example), text description regarding the purpose of the screen, data entries on the screen, how to enter and save data entered, and how to back out of a screen entry are displayed on the user's monitor. Sometimes, the same key or a separate Help key is used to display help text for a particular data entry. As the user moves to data entry points on the user interface, pressing the Help key at a particular data entry point causes help text for that entry to appear on the monitor.

Programs with user interfaces that include messages that prompt the user for directions and data values contain instructions to display the prompt, followed by a data retrieval command that accepts the value entered by the user in response to the prompt. Screen prompts are data constants stored as part of the program's computer storage and transmitted to the user. Each response by the user is transmitted to the program via the data retrieval command following the prompt. The response value is used either to direct program execution or as a data value during execution. For example, a user at National Golf & Tennis (NG&T) could be prompted for a date range to use in selecting customer orders that occurred during a particular period of time.

Screen masks contain positions on the screen for data entry, with the data entry points defined as part of the program storage for the screen mask. This storage contains intermittent, constant, and variable storage areas. The screen mask is transmitted to users as a block. The display has text-type values to guide users in entering data in blank areas, which can be either underscored or highlighted for the user's convenience. After the screen mask is displayed and data is entered by the user, data retrieval commands cause the values entered by the user to be retrieved for processing purposes.

A number of other methods also exist to provide the user interface for on-line program execution, but they are based on the same principles as the menus, prompts, and screen masks described here. The important thing to remember is that storage is used by the program to define the displayed values and data entry positions, and commands are executed to display portions (if not all) of the interface display values. Subsequently, commands are executed to accept the data values entered by the user.

SCREEN MASK REUSABILITY   To prevent "reinventing the wheel," screen user interfaces (menu and data entry) are sometimes independently defined and stored for use in a number of programs. In addition, a computer installation may maintain a library of screen masks. The screen mask is usually developed in the same language as the application program and retrieved and compiled with the application program. Thus the same screen mask may be used by different programs for different purposes. In addition, an existing screen mask may be retrieved and modified for use in a particular program. The modification of the screen mask affects only the program for which it was modified.

TECHNICAL CHARACTERISTICS AND CATEGORIES OF SYSTEMS

Systems used by businesses can be categorized by their technical characteristics; for example, a batch processing system has different characteristics from those of an on-line system. However, a system may fit into one or more of these categories, and the entire system may be made up of one or more of the types of systems discussed here. By understanding the basic premises of system categories, the analyst is better prepared to design systems that fit the general categories or share characteristics with them, but is not limited to a strict set of design rules.

Batch and Random Access Processing Systems

The earliest and most longstanding systems are **batch processing systems**, which are characterized by the accumulation of a collection or "batch" of transaction data objects to be processed together. These types of systems execute on a cyclical basis, with the processing performed on a daily, weekly, monthly, or longer basis. The interval of time between processing sessions is largely governed by the circumstances of the business and the volume of transactions that accumulate during a business interval. A payroll system is an example of a system that typically operates in a batch processing mode to produce weekly, biweekly, and monthly payroll checks.

Batch processing systems typically use **sequential access files** as input to the system. The records in sequential access files must be read serially, beginning with the first record in the file and continuing through succeeding records. In other words, the fifth record in the file cannot be accessed without accessing the first four records in the file. Even though the input of a batch processing system is usually a sequential access file, the system may also access data from a random access file or data in a another format in the database. When used with a database, batch processing systems typically use the data values from the sequential access files to retrieve or store data in the database. Many programs that update databases use batch processing routines to input sequential access data.

Batch processing systems may also use **random access files**, which allow immediate access to any record in the file without accessing preceding records first. Batch processing systems often accumulate a batch of transaction records and process them in combination with records that are randomly retrieved from one of the types of random access files. For example, many data updating programs process updates that are accumulated as a batch, such as time-card data, with a random access master file, such as the payroll master.

In on-line processing routines, random access files provide quicker access for users: a request for specific data will cause retrieval of the specific data object that contains the data. For example, a random access file might use ID numbers as keys for random record retrieval. Users enter the ID number and cause direct access of the record matching that number, such as an employee ID number for a file containing payroll records. Sequential and random access files will be discussed further in Chapter 12.

Systems that execute largely in a batch processing mode consist of various programs that execute consecutively while passing outputs from one program execution to become inputs to the next program execution. As a result of this and other characteristics of these types of systems, certain problems occur. The main problem is that the information produced is only current on a periodic basis—whenever the system executes. For example, a payroll system update program that executes once a month only has updated data once a month. After an update execution and prior to the execution for the next month, the files and database objects being updated may not reflect current data values for particular business objects that are part of those data types.

An additional problem associated with batch processing systems is the inability to generate ad hoc reports and routines. To obtain more timely information than that provided by the periodic execution of the batch program, a complete execution of the entire system or of components of the system is required. Since this is impractical, users who depend on batch processing systems for information must obtain the output from the last execution of the system and wait until the next scheduled execution for more current information.

The fact that batch processing systems are executed in a serial fashion also contributes to problems. A failure in one of the portions (commonly called an *execution step*) of the system often affects subsequent steps of the system. The serial nature of batch processing also contributes to the failure of a complete component when a single record in the file fails to process.

These are just a few of a number of problems that can result from using batch processing systems. Batch processing system problems may occur whether current systems are being modified or new ones are being developed or purchased and modified to better support a particular business. In spite of these problems, batch processing continues to be a viable form of program processing for data that does not have to be processed at the point of creation, because it conserves computing time during business hours. During the day, the data objects are accumulated in a holding file that is used as initial input to the batch program execution runs that take place after regular working hours.

Batch Processing at NG&T

The project team at NG&T decides to use batch processing for customer account processing. Customer bills are to be compiled and mailed once a month for charge customers. During the month, customers can charge up to their charge limits; their accounts receivable data accumulate the charge amounts. Individual bills are computed as part of the batch processing of the accounts receivable data. The NG&T analyst derives program specifications for the batch processing–oriented program.

Interactive Systems

In an **interactive system**, users issue commands and requests through a terminal or desktop computer keyboard to the computer system and receive responses on their screens. Users supply parameters to guide the system in properly responding to their requests; in return, the computer system uses the screen to display information to the user that requires a response. An interactive system is sometimes called a conversational system, because it appears to support conversations between the user and the system. An example of an interactive system is one that provides ways for business personnel to customize the production of a particular product. The customized product may be based on the stated desires of the customer and the available combination of resources interactively displayed on the terminal screen. For instance, a screen mask might display a business form with data entry points that are used to enter the specific requirements (make, model, engine size, color, and so on) for an automobile. During the course of the day's production, an automobile with these characteristics would then be produced.

Some of the key characteristics of interactive systems are on-line data entry and retrieval, interactive user responses to screen displays from the system, interactive guidance of the system by the user during processing, and interactive responses from both the user and the system during execution. Another important trait is a convenient and easy-to-use human-machine interface. This interface may be provided in many forms, but the most prominent form involves users interactively selecting from menu options and prompts that direct them as to how to respond to the system, as described in Chapter 7.

This type of system often allows users to perform **sensitivity analysis**, a method of determining the effect on system outputs relative to changes in the values of key input parameters. Users interactively alter the values of certain key inputs to see what effect they have on the outputs generated by the system. For example, a user could enter different price data values for a product into a system that predicts demand for that product based on pricing data from market research surveys. Each different price entry and output would allow the user to assess profitability based on the sensitivity of demand to changes in the price of the product.

Like batch processing systems, interactive systems also suffer from certain problems. The most common one is a poorly designed and implemented user interface. The interface is intended to provide flexibility for the user to respond and guide the system during its execution, while providing a convenient and easy way to direct it. These objectives for the interface often conflict. To provide a convenient and easy-to-use interface, it is often necessary to restrict what the user can ask the system to do.

Interactive systems also suffer from an inadequate knowledge base. In order for the system to respond to the many types of user responses, it is necessary that a large **knowledge base**, in the form of a large collection of data, be made available to the system. However, restrictions on the amount of storage reserved for this data collection often prevent the amount of knowledge available to the system from being very large. Consequently, the system may not have enough data, or the right type of data, to respond properly to requests.

A third problem that occurs frequently in interactive systems is slow response time due to overextended hardware and software capacity. Interactive systems use a large amount of available resources in both hardware and software. As more users are added to the system, the response time becomes slower for all users. To help combat slow response time, some companies reserve interactive systems for critical applications under the direction of key personnel in the firm. However, adopting this policy also conflicts with a basic premise of computing: to make as much computing power available to as many users as possible. Therefore, managers must find a compromise in the use of interactive systems, one that places the power of computing in the hands of more personnel without increasing response time for all users beyond an acceptable amount.

A final problem associated with interactive systems is insufficient user control during processing. Behind all systems are programs written to respond in a preordained fashion to input stimuli. The system cannot do anything that is not already programmed as a fixed procedure. As a result, it does not allow flexible guidance on the part of users who may be inclined to direct the system in a way that is not a part of the program. For example, some of these systems are used for data retrieval only. If users at some point during system execution want to update the data for a particular data object by using values retrieved from another data object, they will typically have to manually record these changes and use some other method to update those data values.

NG&T's Interactive Order Processing System

At NG&T, the project team decides to use an interactive system for POS (point-of-sale) phone/mail or retail order processing. An interface with windows is to be used to display the top menu for servicing orders. Figure 11-4 illustrates the NG&T top menu for servicing orders. This is the same menu that was illustrated as the system-level menu for the GTOP00 DFD in Figure 8-22 in Chapter 8.

To complete a phone/mail customer order, the sales/phone/mail clerk selects option number 1 from the system-level menu in Figure 11-4. For this selection, a win-

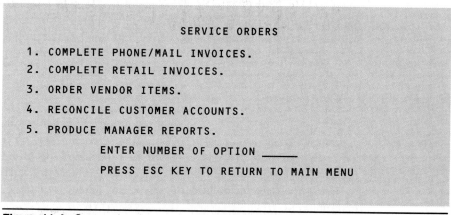

Figure 11-4. System-level menu for the GTOP00 DFD

```
                    COMPLETE PHONE/MAIL INVOICES
    1. CREATE ORDER.

    2. VALIDATE ORDERS.

    3. CREATE ORDER INVOICE.

    4. CREATE SHIPPING INVOICE.

    5. CREATE CARRIER MANIFEST.

            ENTER NUMBER OF OPTION _____

            PRESS ESC KEY TO RETURN TO MAIN MENU
```

Figure 11-5. Complete phone/mail invoice submenu

dow opens that displays a submenu for completing the order. This submenu displays options for the processes listed on the GTOP0001 DFD illustrated in Figure 8-25 in Chapter 8. Figure 11-5 shows this menu.

When the sales/phone/mail clerk selects option number 1 on the submenu, a third window opens for entry of the customer's order. The screen masks in Figures 7-20 and 7-21 in Chapter 7 are the screen masks used for customer order entry. Remember that these screen masks were used to enter the data values for the LOG-CUSTTRNS LDS. Figures 11-6 and 11-7 illustrate these screen masks for entry of all of the data values that are part of the LOG-CUSTTRNS LDS.

As the clerk discusses the order on the phone with the customer, he or she uses the interfaces in Figure 11-6 and 11-7 to enter the order. For current NG&T charge customers, the system automatically displays the customer data when the customer ID is entered. The sales/phone/mail clerk completes the order entry while talking to the customer on the phone. Then he or she completes the order by selecting the remaining options from the submenu in Figure 11-5. The system communicates interactively with the clerk while he or she selects and completes the remaining options on the submenu in Figure 11-5.

Real-Time Systems

Real-time systems provide data recording, processing, and response in actual time periods that affect user decisions or operation of machinery. As a transaction occurs, it is recorded, transmitted, and processed. As something happens in the business environment, the conditions are recorded, transmitted, processed, and acted on. There is no time lag between the occurrence of the event and the response of the system to the occurrence.

Examples of real-time systems can be found in manufacturing systems, airplane

```
                        CUSTOMER  TRANSACTIONS
      CUSTOMER  NUMBER: _____      ORDER  NUMBER: _____

      CUSTOMER  NAME: _____       CUSTOMER  ADDRESS:

      DATE: _____             STREET: _____

                                             CITY: _____

                                             STATE: _____

                                             ZIP: _____

      TRANSACTION  TYPE: _____      SHIPPING  ADDRESS:

      EMPLOYEE  NUMBER: _____        STREET: _____

      MAGAZINE: _____         CITY: _____

      REGION: _____         STATE: _____

      ORDER  STATUS: _____          ZIP: _____
                            ITEMS  ORDERED
        ITEM  NUMBER: _____      ORDER  QUANTITY: _____

        ITEM  NUMBER: _____      ORDER  QUANTITY: _____

        ITEM  NUMBER: _____      ORDER  QUANTITY: _____

        ITEM  NUMBER: _____      ORDER  QUANTITY: _____
          PRESS  ESC  KEY  TO  EXIT  DATA  ENTRY  WITHOUT  SAVING
          PRESS  F3  KEY  TO  SAVE  AND  EXIT  DATA  ENTRY
```

Figure 11-6. Screen mask for entering customer orders

on-board systems, airline reservation systems, stock market transaction recording and processing systems, and financial institution systems. These systems all have a single most important characteristic: the necessity of recording and processing externally originated input stimuli in real time. Manufacturing systems are often real-time systems that control product assembly. These systems must continually respond to environmental conditions to consistently produce the same products. An airplane headed toward the ground must be adjusted in real time by its on-board system. Financial transactions of the stock exchange and of financial brokerage firms depend on real-time processing for successful operation. Banking institution systems must respond in real time in large-scale transactions involving millions of dollars.

The three most common problems associated with real-time systems are reliability of the system, validity of information, and response time. System reliability refers to how often the system fails in the performance of its assigned duties, is harmfully affected by external sources such as disk failures, or is not available for use in real time. The desired—albeit elusive—goal is to have a real-time system that never fails

```
                        ADDITIONAL ORDER ITEMS
        ITEM NUMBER: _____      ORDER QUANTITY: _____
        ITEM NUMBER: _____      ORDER QUANTITY: _____
        ITEM NUMBER: _____      ORDER QUANTITY: _____
        ITEM NUMBER: _____      ORDER QUANTITY: _____
        ITEM NUMBER: _____      ORDER QUANTITY: _____
        ITEM NUMBER: _____      ORDER QUANTITY: _____
        ITEM NUMBER: _____      ORDER QUANTITY: _____
        ITEM NUMBER: _____      ORDER QUANTITY: _____
        ITEM NUMBER: _____      ORDER QUANTITY: _____
        ITEM NUMBER: _____      ORDER QUANTITY: _____
        ITEM NUMBER: _____      ORDER QUANTITY: _____
           PRESS ESC KEY TO EXIT DATA ENTRY WITHOUT SAVING
           PRESS F3 KEY TO SAVE AND EXIT DATA ENTRY
```

Figure 11-7. Screen mask for additional order items

to perform satisfactorily, never is harmed by external sources, never suffers downtime, always provides valid information, and always provides rapid response.

Real-Time Processing at NG&T

The customer ordering system illustrated in the previous section also executes in real-time mode. To keep accurate data on the relationship between customer accounts receivable and customer charge limits, each customer order is processed in real time. Each time a customer orders NG&T products, either on a phone/mail or a retail sale basis, the accounts receivable data is updated and compared to the customer's limit for charge amounts. When a current order makes a customer's accounts receivable exceed the charge limit, a screen automatically opens that displays the customer's previous accounts receivable, current charge, credit limit, the amount by which the current charge would exceed the credit limit, and a rating of the customer's charge record. Figure 11-8 illustrates this output screen mask.

When salesclerks see the user interface in Figure 11-8, they make the decision either to permit the sale and warn customers about reaching their charge limit, or to disallow the sale and refer customers to the store manager if they wish to place the order. Salesclerks can make this decision based on a set of standards regarding the customer's credit rating and the amount by which the credit limit is exceeded. These

```
                    CREDIT LIMIT EXCEEDED REPORT
     CUSTOMER NUMBER: _____        ORDER NUMBER: _____
     CUSTOMER NAME: _____          CUSTOMER ADDRESS:
     DATE: _____                     STREET: _____
                                            CITY: _____
                                            STATE: _____
                                            ZIP: _____
     CURRENT ACCOUNTS RECEIVABLE: _____
     CURRENT CHARGE: _____         CREDIT LIMIT: _____
     AMOUNT BY WHICH CHARGE EXCEEDS LIMIT: _____
     CUSTOMER CREDIT RATING: _____        1 - EXCELLENT
                                             2 - GOOD
                                             3 - POOR
```

Figure 11-8. Customer credit limit exceeded screen mask

standards are based on business rules within NG&T policies. Regardless of whether the order is completed or not, a manager exception data object is created. This will be used to produce manager reports that may cause a letter to be sent to the customer. These letters result from weekly batch processing execution of manager reporting.

Remote Job Entry Systems

A **remote job entry system (RJES)** is (as its name suggests) a system located in a central computer facility, that receives data from and transmits outputs to locations separate from the central facility. These systems provide centralization of remotely triggered processing. A RJES provides on-site information needs from a centrally located computer system to all of the remote locations where computing capability is required. An example of a RJES is a weather processing system. It receives remotely recorded data on weather conditions and processes the data to inform inhabitants of current conditions. Another example is the remote entry of product orders to a company's warehouse from stores located away from the warehouse.

A RJES can operate in batch or interactive mode. Data can be entered on remote input devices and either transmitted individually and accumulated in a batch of data objects, or accumulated as a batch on the remote data entry device and transmitted all at once to the computer system for processing.

The two most prevalent problems with RJES are the difficulty of securing the system and the vulnerability of the system to external disturbances. Since the transmission of the data and output often occur over public access communication networks such as the Internet, safeguarding these systems from inadvertent or purposeful security breaches is difficult. In addition, the failure of public access networks also causes the failure of the RJES.

NG&T and Remote Job Entry

NG&T does not have a RJES, but the interaction between a local server and the host computer at NG&T headquarters exhibits RJES characteristics. When the local server needs additional data from the host computer at NG&T headquarters, systems on the host may execute to complete the request from the local server. These requests occur at a remote location and cause local execution by the NG&T headquarter's host computer. These are the same characteristics as those of an execution of a RJES.

Distributed Systems

It is often necessary to decentralize processing of data. For example, a company with headquarters in New York might have marketing offices distributed throughout the United States and the world. Remote responsibility for actual processing provides the flexibility desired for many business applications. **Distributed systems** have decentralized computing power that allows the distribution of processing to a number of different locations. Computer hardware and software systems are strategically located to serve a distinct population of persons in the business community. These distributed systems are connected over a wide area network (WAN) to allow conversations between the computer systems while allowing the systems to function independently. An example of a distributed system is the system that a major corporation has distributed over different marketing locations. For example, computer manufacturers such as IBM typically have a distributed system for placing or tracing orders created for products.

A prevalent example of distributed processing is the proliferation of desktop computers in the business community in the past ten years. These devices bring the power of computer systems to the work site and a certain amount of self-sufficiency to the independent worker. Networking desktop computers to share large caches of data and major computing power also has the advantages of providing significant computing power while still permitting independence of control.

The most common problems associated with distributed systems are the loss of central control of the information systems' function, difficulty in securing the system from accidental or purposeful fraudulent entry, inability to ensure the validity of shared resources, and lack of communication among the decentralized computer systems.

NG&T's Distributed Systems

The connections between the local servers at NG&T stores and the host computer at NG&T headquarters illustrate the use of a distributed system. Each time a user request cannot be completed by accessing data on the local server, a transmission between the local server and the host computer may occur. Furthermore, the data on customers in the NG&T database is distributed between the local servers and the host computer at NG&T headquarters. NG&T provides this connection via a WAN and includes appropriate security measures to prevent the confidentiality of customer data from being violated.

Expert Systems

Although expert systems are not frequently cited as a type of system used in developing organizational applications, some characteristics of expert systems can be incorporated into a firm's application systems. As a result, the aspiring analyst should understand this type of system. An **expert system** draws on a knowledge base to actually perform decision making normally performed by an expert in that business area. An expert system mimics the way human experts might respond to certain situations based on their knowledge, experience, learned reasoning capabilities, and insight. Expert systems contain a set of programmable rules governing what to do and how to respond to various conditions detected in the business environment. These rules consist of a large set of IF-THEN instructions, which, when applied to known facts and stored knowledge of the business situation, attempt to emulate the way a person in the same position would perform necessary functions in response to the situation. An expert system is nothing more than a program attempting to model human behavior for a particular class of people in particular situations.

Expert systems have a noble origin in research in the information sciences. Developers of expert systems believe that it is possible to program a set of rules and provide a base of stored knowledge to emulate the way an expert in a particular area would perform if consulted about certain conditions. Early in the history of expert systems it was recognized that programming a computer to perform simple IF-THEN operations while using a database as a source of data, and picking the brain of an actual expert in an area for the particulars of the IF-THEN operations, was not a trivial task. Problems rapidly surfaced when it was determined that too many rules, too much knowledge, and infinite combinations of both were necessary to effectively emulate an expert in a programming form.

A true expert system is something that is grown, not developed in the same way and time frame as application systems. As a result, the only expert systems that have been effectively completed by businesses are those that address simple tasks.

The most prevalent problems with expert systems are as follows:

- The set of rules is often too large for the current era of computing, which uses small, independent modules.
- The knowledge base requires too many database resources.
- The combination of possibilities required to truly emulate an expert is too extensive to realistically be serviceable.

The use of expert systems in business will increase, or their traits will be included in typical business systems, as computer speeds and storage capacities increase, and

I/O access times decrease. Consequently, aspiring analysts should be prepared to take advantage of these systems as part of their project completion activities.

Expert Systems at NG&T

Though NG&T does not actually use an expert system, the example used for real-time systems can illustrate how an expert system functions. Remember that a customer order that causes the customer's credit limit to be exceeded displays the output report shown in Figure 11-8. As previously stated, when salesclerks see the user interface in Figure 11-8 appear on their screens, they can decide whether or not to permit the sale based on a customer's credit rating and on criteria for excess credit limit amounts. Instead, this decision could be automatically made by the system, with the result displayed on the bottom line of the screen in Figure 11-8. The combination of the credit rating and the amount by which the order exceeds the customer credit limit is the "expert knowledge" that the system would use to make the decision, eliminating the need for subjective judgment on the part of clerks.

Time-Sharing Systems

Time-sharing systems share the available computer resources across a range of users and application programs, or even between firms. Although time sharing is more of an operating system function than a true category of systems, its technicalities need to be considered while creating systems. In the types of systems presented in this chapter, developers share the resources of the computer systems with functional area personnel and the application programs that serve them. Both groups access the shared resources through some form of command entry terminal or desktop computer and suffer the consequences of sharing resources for two explicitly different purposes. These consequences include the possible unavailability of a particular resource and slower response times. The two groups typically share hardware, software, and data stored in files and databases.

Since computer facilities can be concurrently used by a number of users, a user requesting a resource that is already in the possession of another user must wait for that resource to become available. In addition, concurrent access to the same data items may lead to problems with the integrity of the data. If you have ever found someone already sitting in your "assigned" seat on an airplane, you have experienced the consequences of an inadequate time-sharing system. In this case, your travel agent may have simultaneously accessed the seat record and assigned the seat to you while another travel agent was doing the same for his or her customer.

The other problem associated with time-sharing systems, slow response time, arises when the capacity of the system for sharing resources reaches its limit. Situations in which a large number of users concurrently access the system and its resources will cause a bottleneck for the firm's information channels. The more users accessing the computer system and the more they cause the system to do, the slower the response time for all users.

All businesses experience increased access to computer facilities at strategic points during the day and the month. Peak computing times occur at the beginning, middle, and end of a month for many businesses. During the work day, peak computing use occurs at the beginning of the day, immediately before and after lunchtime, and just before the end of the day. Since greater demands are made on shared resources at these times, users experience greater problems with the immediacy of responses.

Time-Sharing at NG&T

NG&T uses a time-sharing system for the POS processing of customer orders. All personnel in a particular store use the same system and share the resources as customer orders are processed. Additionally, computing resources at NG&T headquarters are shared by systems that operate on computers at different stores. Salesclerks enter the order on their individual POS terminals or desktop computers. Retail sales are supported by POS terminals, while phone/mail ordering is supported by desktop computers. The server to which the clerks' systems are connected performs the database accesses necessary to support the customer ordering process. The NG&T host computer may periodically download data to a local server for data not retained at the local server. Thus, time-sharing occurs throughout the NG&T computer systems.

DEVELOPING DOCUMENTATION

Maintainable and usable systems must have documentation for the inner workings, use, and operations of the systems. To provide this, information systems personnel work with four main categories of documentation:

- Design/development documentation
- User documentation
- Operations documentation
- Training documentation

Design/development documentation serves as a reference for the system throughout its life span. Some of this documentation resides internally within program logic; other design/development documentation is external, or separate from programs. User documentation provides guidelines for users on how to use a system, how to respond to system prompts, and how to interpret outputs generated by the system. Operations documentation provides guidelines for operations personnel regarding activities involved in system execution. Training documentation, for both users and IS personnel, is used in conjunction with courses that teach specific technology and job responsibilities.

Design/Development Documentation

System design specifications that have been illustrated throughout the chapters on analysis and design represent the major form of external system documentation. Analysis and design specifications such as entity/relationship diagrams (E/RDs), data flow diagrams (DFDs), structure charts (STCs), prototype interfaces, and accompanying dictionary entries represent the major forms of design/development documentation. Discussion of this documentation here does not imply that it is created at this point in the system development life cycle; it is too late in the life cycle to develop it now. It should be continuously developed during each phase of the life cycle, when the analyst is more knowledgeable about design/development criteria associated with the activities of that phase.

Program specifications developed during physical design represent the main external documentation for programs. These specifications guide programmers in developing programs. Additional external documentation may be generated by the programmer to document the way the program was developed, what each module includes, and what users need to know in order to initiate program execution and interpret results.

Programmers frequently include additional documentation explaining how the developed program implements program design specifications. This documentation may either be written separately and included with physical design program specifications, embedded within program code, or both.

Separate documentation concerning program development is normally included when the program design specifications are insufficient to explain how the program was developed. This is needed when the logic of the program is more complicated than the program design specifications indicate.

Internal program documentation usually consists of comments embedded by programmers at the beginnings of major sections of the program being developed. These embedded comments explain the portion of the program that follows, in order to make it easier to modify the program in the future. Comments may be found at the beginnings of file and record descriptions and of work-area storage definitions, and at the beginning of each program module.

At NG&T, design/development documentation exists in the form of data, process, and procedure models, as well as program specifications for individual programs. This documentation is to be maintained so that it remains an accurate picture of NG&T and its systems. Chapter 16 will discuss maintaining this documentation.

The design/development documentation serves a very important function for NG&T: it provides a baseline understanding of NG&T data, operations, and systems. For decisions that might affect NG&T operations or systems, this documentation is reviewed in joint application design (JAD) sessions that involve NG&T managers, staff, and IS personnel. During these JADs, important decisions can be reached while reviewing their possible effect on NG&T and its systems. These decisions may cause NG&T operations to change, existing A&D projects to change, or new A&D projects to commence. This documentation can also serve to educate new employees regarding NG&T data, operations, and systems.

User Documentation

System development entails more than just creating application programs. It involves establishing an environment to support system execution that includes user documentation. Programs requiring input from users, such as data values that set ranges on a particular data item the user wants processed, must provide documentation for the user to follow when furnishing the data. In addition, program execution frequently results in generation of different outputs. When different output is produced by the same program, users must be provided with documentation so that they can properly interpret the results generated for a particular program execution. This type of documentation is often provided by the programmer as separate documentation for the developed program.

The name **user documentation** implies documentation that the user needs for all facets of the system execution. Users require detailed instructions to initiate the execution of the programs of a system, to correctly enter requested data values, and to interpret the outputs generated by system executions. User documentation guides users in the use of the system and in the interpretation of system responses and outputs. Good user documentation ensures the understandability of the system, which results in reduced system maintenance activities. To ensure proper completion, these activities must be properly planned, scheduled, monitored, and supervised by the project team leader.

User documentation to initiate system execution and interpret output includes:

* Instructions for scheduling system execution
* Instructions detailing how system execution is initiated
* Explanations of input parameters required of users
* Explanations of user responsibilities during execution
* Explanations of how the user is to interpret outputs generated by the system relative to a particular execution

Systems frequently prescribe that programs are to be executed in a particular order so that output from one program can be used as input to another program. Different systems initiate system execution differently. For example, some systems operating on the desktop computer may execute within Microsoft Windows, whereas others may need to execute at the DOS operating system level. As a result, user documentation must include different methods for initiating execution. When system execution requires that users enter data values—commonly called **parameter data**—either to guide processing or to be used during processing, the user must correctly supply these data values to ensure proper program execution.

Systems also provide a host of possible types of outputs, and users must be capable of properly interpreting the different outputs. Some of the most important documentation that users need in regard to output answer these questions:

* What do the different output values mean relative to their job responsibilities?
* What data values were used to develop the output values?
* What actions (from the perspective of the user) were performed on the data values to create the output data values?

User documentation is normally provided in two forms: printed and on-line. The traditional form of printed user documentation manuals is usually developed through the joint efforts of analysts and programmers. As the system is being developed or modified, user documentation is being developed or modified. This documentation is then printed and distributed to appropriate users as a guide to initiating system execution and interpreting output.

User documentation can also be stored on auxiliary storage media and made available in various on-line forms called **help files**. Users can retrieve these files on-line either prior to, during, or following system execution. The ease of use of this type of documentation and its tendency to be more up-to-date are its greatest advantages. Frequently, help files are either page-, line-, or data entry point–specific regarding responses to user requests. This is a form of documentation known as *context-sensitive documentation*.

User Documentation at NG&T

At NG&T, the project team decides to produce screen and data entry help for all of its on-line users. Help can be accessed for each menu or screen mask by pressing the F1 function key. This screen-level help explains the purpose of the screen, how to enter responses, various decisions users may need to make regarding entries, how to transmit the entries, and how to back out of a current or previous entry. Data entry–level help is accessed by pressing the F2 function key when the data entry cursor is located at a particular data entry point, and is context-sensitive to the purpose of that particular entry. For example, as users enter specific values on screen mask data entry interfaces, they can press the F2 function key to open a window on their screen. The window displays text explaining the purpose of that specific entry and any other information relevant to entering data.

NG&T also decides on context-sensitive documentation to support all of its systems that function as decision support systems (DSSs), such as systems that support managerial decision making regarding customer complaints and delinquencies.

For its batch processing systems, NG&T managers decide on printed user documentation manuals. Even though NG&T managers are aware of the possible integrity problems with printed documentation, they believe that it will provide users with documentation in a form that best suits the situation. This documentation includes a volume table of contents and index that support easy access to data regarding any information on NG&T batch processing transaction systems.

Operations Documentation

System execution requires coordinating a number of resources and enlisting the cooperation of a number of people—those responsible for scheduling and assisting system execution. These personnel need explicit instructions regarding their responsibilities prior to, during, and following system execution. Operations documentation serves this purpose.

Operations documentation covers instructions for the actions people perform to assist system execution. For example, different generations of files and data storage must be properly maintained; program execution must be properly matched with data to use during execution; backup procedures must be properly documented in order to assure successful backup of important data; and run-time logs must be properly implemented to dynamically document system execution activities. Operations documentation serves a variety of these types of activities.

NG&T operations documentation covers operations on desktop computers, server computers, and the host computer at NG&T headquarters. For individual desktop computers, regular maintenance operations are performed daily when the user performs logon or logoff operations. These daily maintenance operations include backup of current data on the desktop computer and transmission to the network server of data accumulated as a batch on the desktop computer. The user is prompted by the system for information it needs to complete these operations. For example, the control system prompts the user to insert a specific disk for data backup operations for current data on the desktop computer.

The network server and host computer operations documentation provides guidance regarding daily service operations such as data backup, transmission supporting actions, error prevention actions, and error recovery actions. This documentation facilitates smooth operations between these systems and the many purposes for which NG&T personnel use them.

Training Documentation

Training documentation is created to support training courses for users and systems professionals. This documentation is provided in courses that:

- Teach users the purposes and values of using a particular system
- Teach users how to interpret output and use it in supporting their job responsibilities
- Train users and systems professionals in the use of a particular technology in an application system
- Train IS personnel in methodologies, principles, practices, and technologies used in system development, as well as the technologies that support an application system

PREPARATION FOR SYSTEM IMPLEMENTATION

Once the programs and documentation are created, the project leader must manage the conversion and modification of existing systems and the acquisition of new hardware or software. A number of activities must be performed prior to implementing the system to prepare the environment in which the system will operate. Chapter 13 covers these topics in greater detail; however, they are discussed briefly here since they can affect system development.

Converting Existing Software and Data Formats

Existing software maintained by the IS department may require modification to effectively support the functioning of the developed system. Company data currently stored in files and databases may require reformatting in a style conducive to the execution of the developed system. In addition, data stored in formats used by the previous system or in formats previously used by a system being modified may require conversion to the format needed for the new or modified system. These conversion activities are also performed during the development phase by the programmers under the supervision of the project team.

When converting existing software and data formats, remember that software and data used by the system under development are probably being used by programs in other systems. As a result, changes can affect those systems as well as the system under development. The analyst must compare the benefit of changing the software and data formats for the system being developed to the costs associated with modifying those other systems before undertaking conversion activities.

Converting Software and Data Formats at NG&T

For the NG&T project, all point-of-sale (POS) data needs to be converted to formats consistent with batch and interactive processing of order data. Most of this data currently resides in filing cabinets in printed form. George Serve predicts that to convert these data objects into an electronic form will take several months of concentrated work by data entry clerks. To save time and avoid hiring additional data entry clerks, George decides to out-source this activity to Mark Wright's Customer Data Entry Service, a local San Diego firm.

Hardware and Software Acquisitions

Many programs within the system being developed or modified may require special hardware and software acquisitions prior to testing. For example, if the system being developed uses a new database management system (DBMS), the DBMS must be acquired and installed during the development phase. These types of acquisitions should occur during and following the development of programs and accompanying control commands. They must be made well in advance of their intended use to allow time for installation, testing, and any modifications necessary to ensure consistency with the existing environment and the overall project system. Training may also be required.

Evaluation of these acquisitions would have taken place during review of the logical and physical design, with alternatives assessed, appropriate ones selected, and acquisition approval obtained. Since additional funds will be spent on these acquisitions, personnel responsible for these expenditures would take part in deliberations regarding the alternatives. Small purchases can be approved and made by personnel with the skills to evaluate alternative purchases. Larger purchases need to be approved by managers in the departments that will be supported by the technology. For these purchases, it is a good idea to have personnel skilled in the use of the technology make recommendations.

Hardware and Software Acquisitions at NG&T

The decision by NG&T to use POS processing of customer orders means that the company needs to acquire POS terminals, desktop computers, and communication software to connect with the local server and central host computer. These acquisitions are made through contacts with vendor representatives, purchases at retail outlets, purchases from wholesalers or distributors, and/or purchases from used technology outlets. George Serve decides to use IBM's DB2 database management system at NG&T; however, the purchase needs to be approved by Tim Richardson because of the purchase amount and the far-reaching nature of installing a particular DBMS.

The purchase of new hardware and software by NG&T is reviewed and analyzed by the director of MIS, George Serve, and the owners, Tim and Jason Richardson. As previously stated, they have decided to purchase and use POS terminals for retail sales and desktop computers for phone/mail sales. Alternative choices for this hardware are evaluated and a selection is made. They decide on 3270 IBM-style terminals and 486/66, Pentium-based desktop computers for greater power, expandability, and future use. The desktop computers are purchased from a distributor of clone computers, a San Diego company called EverGreen Clone Computers.

With the acquisition of POS terminals and desktop computers, NG&T must acquire additional software as well. For the POS terminals, control and communication system software is purchased for execution on local server computers and on the headquarter's host computer. For the desktop computers, the desktop version of the Windows/NT operating system is purchased from Microsoft, along with the current version of DOS. Additional communication software is purchased, as well as various end-user computing software, including a spreadsheet, a word processor, and an electronic mail system.

Database Modification and Creation

Systems that require database accessing may cause the structure of the firm's existing database to be modified or a new database structure to be developed. Chapter 10 defined a database as a shared resource for the firm's different systems. This database may not currently contain certain data items required by the project system. Or it may not exist if the firm is just converting to systems that require databases. Consequently, database modification or creation activities must be performed during the development phase, prior to system testing.

Database Modification and Creation for NG&T

The normalized data types described in Chapter 10 for NG&T business objects should be used to develop a database to support order processing. IS personnel at NG&T decide to acquire and install IBM's DB2 and build a database for all of the normalized data types resulting from applying object-oriented database design principles (as described in Chapter 10). Developing this database results in developing systems that interact with DB2 for data input and output. As a result, some of the on-line, interactive portions of the order processing system are created in SQL, the DBMS query language made standard by IBM. You can see that the choice of a DBMS influences not only the way the data is stored, but also the form the system uses to act on the data.

ERROR PREVENTION AND CRASH RECOVERY PROVISIONS

The creation and use of computer systems that depend on people and electromechanical and electronic hardware and software provide many avenues for error, and errors have potentially devastating effects on the operations of the firm. Employees depend on the firm's computer systems to provide the information they need to support their job functions. When these systems produce erroneous results or become inoperable, work cannot get done. The project team must develop systems that provide for prevention of errors, strategic error recovery routines, and methods for recovery when complete system crashes occur.

Error Prevention Methods

The development team should expect that users will sometimes provide the system with erroneous data or direct the system erroneously. For example, a user may enter text data for a data item that should consist of numbers for computational purposes. In other cases, users may direct the system to the wrong version of data to be used in generating a report for a previous quarter of business activities. Programs should be designed to detect and correct errors, and to prevent many of them altogether. The two main error prevention methods included as part of developed systems are data editing routines and routines that identify and assist users.

Data editing routines (or data validating routines) are usually in separate programs that execute at the front end of a system to check the validity of data being supplied as input. If initial input data is not correct, subsequent program executions will produce erroneous results. These erroneous results will then cause users to incorrectly interpret the conditions facing them in performing their job responsibilities—a serious consequence of having bad data. The main sources of error prevention regarding gathered and stored raw data are the creation and use of programs to check the data's validity and appropriateness, and the verification of permission to perform the action directed by a particular user. Programs used to check the validity of raw data are called edit programs.

Edit Programs

Edit programs contain routines that compare actual data with expected values for the data. Edit program routines involve the creation of:

- Procedures for checking the existence of a condition or data object
- Check digit routines for checking key data items
- Data value type checking routines
- Zero insertion routines for numeric data
- Range checking routines for numeric data
- Discrete data value checking routines
- Response checking routines for on-line system execution
- System response routines to verify on-line actions specified by users

This list seeks only to illustrate some of the traits of edit programs, not to be a complete list of edit program routines.

CONDITION OR DATA EXISTENCE CHECKS   Sometimes data to be acted on may not exist yet because of transmission problems, transcription problems, lost data, and a host of other errors that may occur regarding the data. An edit program should first check for the existence of the data before proceeding to further checks. If the data does not exist, executing the remaining checks is pointless.

Some programs process specialty conditions detected within data. For these programs, data editing (validation) should include checks for these conditions, with remaining checks performed on data that passes the condition-checking edit. For example, edit routines should be performed only on inventory data that the company currently holds and uses in its operations. Inventory items of a previous era may be retained in inventory files, but an inactive code value in one of the data items should be used to specify their current status. Edit routines for inventory data in this example should be performed only on the inventory data objects that pass the check for current inventory, not on those that have an inactive inventory status.

CHECK DIGIT ROUTINES   **Check digit routines** are used to test the validity of data items used as keys for input data. **Keys** are data items assigned to particular real-world objects for identification purposes, such as account numbers, employee identification numbers, inventory item numbers, and so on. Since keys often control the places where succeeding data items are to be applied in the business, the first step in a check digit routine is to verify the key (or identification number). For example, checks and deposits must be applied to the correct account in a banking system. To ensure that this occurs, the bank account number must be verified. The check digit procedure is a method used to verify identification numbers with close to 100 percent accuracy.

The check digit routine prescribes that an additional digit, known as the check digit, be added to identification numbers. This is normally the rightmost digit of the identification number. The check digit is computed and inserted into an identification number when the number is initially assigned. Computing the check digit involves dividing the assigned identification number by a particular value known as the *modulus number*. Dividing the identification number by the modulus number produces a remainder. The remainder becomes the check digit. This digit is assigned as the rightmost digit of the identification number. Figure 11-9 gives an example of the calculation of a check digit for a seven-digit bank account number using a value of 11 for the modulus number.

The computed check digit (9) is added to the initial bank account number (596484), to give the full bank account number assigned to the customer (5964849). Subsequently, any banking transaction involving that account number may be checked to make sure the transaction is applied to the correct account. If the verification routine computes an incorrect check digit, the validity of the account number would be in question, and applying the transaction to an account of the bank would be delayed until it is determined why the transaction account number did not pass the check digit edit checking routine.

DATA TYPE CHECKING ROUTINES   Many program operations expect certain classes of data, such as numeric or text, for correct processing to occur. Edit programs usually contain routines to determine if the data values used as input actually contain the correct type of data. For example, calculation operations in programs require numeric data. An edit program would check the input data values to determine if the data value represents a numeric value. Most programming languages have a data type checking command.

LEADING ZEROS IN NUMERIC DATA ITEMS   Users seldom enter the leading zeros for all of the digit positions in a numeric data item entry with a fixed number of digits.

Assume:
    Initial bank account number = 596484
    Modulus number = 11

Check digit computation:
    596484 / 11 = 54225 with remainder of **9**
    Check digit = **9**

Bank account number (including check digit) = 596484**9**

Figure 11-9. Example of the computation of a check digit

When leading spaces are not replaced with zeros, programs typically treat expected numeric data values as having nonnumeric characters, and may interrupt execution of that operation. Edit programs contain instructions that cause leading spaces to be replaced by leading zeros for data in fixed-length data item entries.

DATA RANGE CHECK EDITING   Many data items used as input data have a prescribed range (upper, lower, or between certain data values) for their values. Edit programs contain instructions to compare the values of certain data items with an expected data value range. For example, it may be known that the hours-worked data item is not to exceed 40 hours (no overtime hours). The edit program would contain an instruction to compare the value of the hours worked data with the value of 40.

DISCRETE DATA VALUE EDITING   Many data items used as input may contain a specific data value taken from a specific list of data values. Some of these discrete data values act as a code to identify the type of data item being used as input. The edit program contains routines to compare these data items against the list of discrete data values to check for possible correctness. For example, assume that a banking transaction contains a data item identifying the type of transaction. The code values might be C for check, D for deposit, and W for cash withdrawal. An edit program could check the transaction code of each transaction to determine whether it equals C, D, or W. Any transaction with an erroneous or missing transaction code would be included in an error report generated by the edit program.

USER RESPONSE CHECKING ROUTINES AND VERIFICATION   In on-line system execution, users enter parameter values (menu selections, data prompting responses, and so on) either to guide processing or to be used as data during processing. The data values supplied by users frequently pass through checks to test their validity. If the data value does not pass the edit check, the user is notified of the incorrectness of the parameter value and prompted for a new parameter value.

There are also cases in which users employing an on-line system should be able to confirm the actions that they direct the system to perform. An edit routine may respond by echoing the action entered back to the user's computer monitor and asking whether or not to proceed. This gives the user the opportunity to cancel the action before it is applied. For example, a user may direct that an on-line system for updating data to delete a certain record in the system. The edit routine echoes the action and the identification number of the data to be deleted back to the user and asks whether to proceed or not: "Y or N." This gives the user an opportunity to confirm that the identification number is correct and deletion should proceed.

Another function of edit routines is to determine if users are authorized to initiate the actions that they direct the system to perform. An edit routine could be included that compares users' account numbers and passwords with the user views described in the firm's dictionary or database management system. User views, as explained in Chapter 10, describe the data items users may access and the actions they may perform on the data items. When users direct the system to retrieve data from the firm's data storage, the system should determine whether the data specified is within the user view. In addition, the actions specified by users could be checked against the list of authorized actions within the user view. Any deviation from authorized access would result in users' being informed that they are not authorized for the access specified.

ERROR PREVENTION AT NG&T   For error prevention, NG&T decides to use edit routines that execute on the server for POS terminals and on the desktop computer for POS client computers. These edit routines check all data entries for order processing as orders are processed by clerks. Additional error prevention is provided by assignment of appropriate user views, logon/logoff daily maintenance operations, and periodic user action tracking using a "WHERE-USED" function in the control system for NG&T. Restricting users' access to data and operations within their job capabilities helps prevent unknowledgeable users from making errors that affect NG&T. The automatic execution of daily maintenance during user logon/logoff helps ensure that users back up appropriate data on the server and host computers based on daily user actions. Periodic tracking of actions by users will help to identify areas where they may need additional training, and to assess their effectiveness in serving NG&T customers.

Error Recovery Routines

Valid execution of the firm's computer systems requires that people, software, and hardware function properly. If there is one fact of life, it is that people, software, and hardware will sometimes be in error or completely break down. Consequently, systems must be developed that anticipate errors or breakdowns and prescribe ways to recover from them.

Many programs in systems require correct completion on a regularly scheduled basis. In addition, many programs apply changes to data being retained by the firm as the program executes. It is common for these programs to experience difficulties during execution. To simply reexecute the program from the beginning creates a situation wherein data-modifying actions already performed are being performed again. As a result, the integrity of the data being retained by the firm may be in question. It is desirable in many instances to restart a program execution at a point at which valid execution was occurring. This is usually accomplished through the use of checkpoint routines embedded within the logic of programs.

Checkpoint Routines

A **checkpoint** is a place in the execution of a program in which valid processing actions were being performed. It is a point between the beginning of program execution and its termination at which all previous actions performed by the program are valid actions.

Many program languages have commands that can be used to insert a checkpoint code value in a reserved storage area in the computer periodically during the execution of the program. These checkpoints help determine which data item was the last data item correctly processed before program execution was interrupted.

Consequently, when program execution resumes, it can begin at a point at which execution validity is assured.

Checkpoints are implemented by periodically storing appropriate values to identify processing points. When program interruption occurs, the last set of checkpoint values identifies the point where execution must resume when the program is restarted. Companies that use checkpoint routines usually have utility programs that restart program execution using the set of checkpoint values. The execution of the restart program uses the checkpoint values and permits program execution to resume at its last safe execution point.

CHECKPOINT ROUTINES FOR NG&T   George Serve decides that all batch executions should occur in the evening, when fewer demands are placed on network servers and on the host computer at NG&T headquarters. He also decides that these batch processing programs should all have checkpoint routines. By including checkpoint routines, the batch processing programs can continue execution at some strategic point prior to the point where their execution was interrupted by an exceptional situation. This will permit quicker completion of these batch program executions and will control their use of resources on the server and host computers.

Recovery of Data and Software

All systems eventually break down. Disk drive heads fall onto the surfaces of disks, destroying programs and data files stored on the disks. Software routines break down when given an instruction to which they are unprepared to respond. People enter incorrect data or specify actions from which the system cannot recover. A good system is one that people expect to eventually replace, along with the data it uses.

The main form of crash protection is periodic creation of backup versions for data files, databases, and software files. During the period following the creation of a new version of a data file or database, all data used to modify the data file or database is retained. The discussions of database technologies in Chapter 10 explained that data-modifying actions were retained as journal files. In a file processing environment, backup generations for data files and modifying actions are retained in storage and are known as generation data groups.

Generation data groups are families of data files and software used during certain periods of processing. Each time a new version is created, the previous version becomes the previous generation. In addition, older backup versions become one more generation removed from the new current version. Most companies retain generation data groups for data files, files used for modification actions, and application software.

To recover destroyed data files and databases, the backup (previous generation) version of the data file or database is designated as the current version of the data file or database objects. Subsequently, the data-modifying actions retained since the previous backup are reapplied to the data file or database in the same order in which they were originally applied. Thus, the current version of the data file or database is recovered, and it includes all database updates that have occurred since the last backup was created. As a result, the data file or database is brought up to date to the point at which its destruction occurred.

An advantage of generation data groups is that they permit the firm to retain data expressing the conditions facing it at some particular point in time. Any desired data reporting concerning an earlier period may be re-created simply by indicating in a system command that a particular generation of data files is to be used during program execution. In this way, the processing results will reflect the condition of the firm during the previous period. For example, it is common to produce quarterly reports during a subsequent quarter of the business year. These reports can be generated by forcing the system to use the generation of data files that were current during that quarter.

The recovery of software destroyed because of human, software, or hardware errors proceeds in much the same manner as the recovery of data files and databases. A backup version of the software is installed as the current version, and an additional backup copy of the software is created.

A final note on the recovery of destroyed data and software: Typically, business transactions continue during the time in which recovery activities occur. For example, bank transactions are not discontinued because the system or files are down. The computer system of the firm retains these ongoing transactions in a separate file (frequently a journal file), to be applied upon recovery. During recovery, it is a good idea to inform users that there may be unusual delays in processing.

DATA AND SOFTWARE RECOVERY AT NG&T   George Serve decides that generation data groups should be used for all updates to the NG&T database. The update files used as input to batch processing update programs are to be retained as different generations of updates, accumulated on a daily and weekly basis. In addition, journal files are retained that chronicle all update accesses to the database as they occur. A backup of the entire NG&T database is to be created on a monthly basis so that twelve generations of it are maintained for the current year, and four quarterly generations for the current and prior years. Generations of backup versions of the NG&T database are created during weekend processing activities on a monthly or quarterly basis.

If NG&T should experience any problems that render the current version of the database unusable, they can reapply all update accesses recorded in journal file entries to the previous generation of the database to reconstruct a current generation of it. In addition, they could reapply updates accumulated in the current generation of batch and on-line updates that occurred at the time of the database failure.

TECHNOLOGIES SUPPORTING FASTER SYSTEMS DEVELOPMENT

Several technologies facilitate system development beyond the capabilities in the third generation of computing. Some of the technologies that improve system development practices are fourth generation languages (4GLs), natural language programming, object-oriented programming (OOP), standard system architecture, open system architecture, client-server application development, and rehosting computer architectures. Additional advances in programming languages and user interfaces are helping to avoid some of the common pitfalls in developing systems. Standardized interfaces, object-oriented and natural language programming, and friendlier languages, such as fourth generation languages, are making it possible to develop less error-prone systems in a more efficient way. Companies that adopt either their own proprietary standard system architecture or an **open system architecture** ensure greater compatibility between different computer systems within the company and/or between it and many external computer installations. Many companies are switching to a client-server architecture; others are replacing existing host computers with new ones (rehosting computer architectures).

Fourth Generation Languages (4GLs)

Most fourth generation languages came into existence in the 1970s and 1980s to support database environments. They emerged as a result of the need for greater use of database technologies and greater speed in developing a system to satisfy user requirements. **Fourth generation languages (4GLs)** are normally used to direct a DBMS regarding what data retrieval is desired, not how to perform the set manipulation operations required for physical data retrieval. The most widely known 4GL is SQL (Structured Query Language), which was described in Chapter 10 as the proposed standard query language to direct a database management system (DBMS). DBMS vendors either produce their own proprietary query language to use with their DBMS, such as the language called Natural for Software AG's ADABAS DBMS, or they use SQL.

The DBMS is actually responsible for data retrieval. A DBMS treats database files as if they were mathematical "sets" and performs various set manipulation operations, such as set union, intersection, difference, join, and so on, to properly combine data for retrieval or transmission purposes. These set manipulation operations represent the procedural methods required for performing data retrieval. Therefore, languages in which data manipulation commands specify set manipulation operations are called **procedural languages**. Fourth generation languages do not require the inclusion of these types of commands.

Fourth generation languages are commonly used for on-line data manipulation. They are easy to learn and require much less time for program development. They are able to make intelligent assumptions regarding what the user wants. As a result, less is required of the user. It is also assumed that the DBMS will be capable of properly manipulating the sets of data in a database to accomplish the desired data retrieval specified by 4GLs.

The adoption of 4GLs is hampered by the fact that most systems are acquired as complete packages from software vendors who have historically produced packaged systems in one of the third generation languages—usually COBOL. As a result, firms that wish to adopt 4GLs must deal with incompatibility between third and fourth generation languages.

Although 4GLs provide a powerful data manipulation option for users and are becoming much easier to use, they require a great deal of the computing resources of the firm. Until now, the development of hardware storage media and communication software has largely encouraged products in support of third generation languages. As a result, 4GL application development has suffered and enthusiasm has waned in the past few years. However, many computer installations consider the convenience provided by 4GLs worth the additional expenditure in resources.

Fourth Generation Use at NG&T

George Serve decides to not use 4GLs for actual system development for NG&T systems; instead, the firm will use COBOL as the language for programs in the order processing system. Therefore, most of the menu-driven application for order processing at NG&T is created in the form of COBOL programs. George decides to use SQL for more immediate access to the NG&T database. NG&T programmers create some preprogrammed queries that would likely be needed on a periodic basis. However, only a few of these preprogrammed SQL queries are created, and any remaining database queries using SQL procedures are to be created by individual users at NG&T. This means that some users will take part in training programs on SQL and its use with the NG&T database.

Natural Language Programming (NLP)

The field of artificial intelligence in recent years has seen the rise of a form of human-machine communication known as **natural language programming (NLP)**, in which people create programs using human languages ("natural" languages) to direct the computer. These languages fall under the classification of knowledge-based systems, as does an expert system.

Knowledge-based systems use a storehouse of knowledge composed of facts and rules to apply against some input data, and act as the controlling factor in communication with the computer. The facts used in the knowledge base are of a general nature; they are not about specific conditions that the company faces. The rules for the knowledge base consist of business rules that guide business actions and systems. The system uses these rules and facts in processing input data that describes the variable characteristics of the problem being addressed, and produces output to guide company decisions and operations.

Knowledge-based characteristics aid in equating natural language statements with statements in one of the traditional programming languages, such as COBOL or SQL. When users enter an NLP command, the knowledge-based system uses the rules to interpret the command. Remember that the computer is an electronic device capable of performing a fixed number of operations (commands). A program is simply a set of commands created to direct the computer to perform some of these operations in a desired order. **Traditional programming languages** provide a vocabulary and syntax of a higher-level language that causes the computer to perform a desired sequence of operations.

In a natural language programming environment, a vocabulary and syntax are gradually constructed in which communication terminology natural to humans becomes associated with the vocabulary and syntax of another computer language. A processor interprets the NLP commands and converts them into equivalent software code vocabulary and syntax. For example, an item number is frequently used as the data value for retrieval of an inventory record. In the traditional programming environment, a properly constructed (vocabulary and syntax) command in a programming language must be issued to read the inventory item, using the item number value as a key to select the desired inventory record. In a NLP environment, a knowledge base could be constructed such that the value-driven READ command could be initiated in a variety of forms familiar to humans. For example, "Get item using part number 1111235" or "Retrieve item number 1111235" may be interpreted by the natural language processor as fundamentally equivalent to the vocabulary and syntax of a traditional programming language command to input a particular data object. In constructing the knowledge base used by the natural language processor, the developer seeks to increase the vocabulary and syntactical forms in which commands may be issued to the computer.

Fully compatible natural language programming does not currently exist. However, as the vocabulary and syntactical forms of the knowledge base increase, more natural human-machine communication will become a reality.

George Serve decides to use natural language programming with an interpreter that converts its NLP commands to SQL. He decides to use NLP in place of native SQL commands for all on-line access outside the normal on-line access provided by the order processing application. His thinking is that using NLP will help people feel more comfortable with the vocabulary and syntactical rules, and that therefore they will be able to retrieve the most up-to-date information from the system.

Object-Oriented Programming (OOP)

Object-oriented programming (OOP) constructs programs using some of the same principles of object-oriented analysis and design that were discussed in Chapter 2. Object-oriented programming extends these principles by encapsulating in an object the attributes of the object and the procedures (called services) to perform while using those attributes. By pointing to an icon or referencing an object, a programmer causes the procedures encapsulated in the object to execute using the attributes of the object. Two examples of OOP languages are C++ and SmallTalk.

One of the main benefits of using an OOP language is the increased productivity gains from programming efforts. A single instruction in an OOP language is equivalent to approximately twenty-five instructions in a third generation language such as COBOL. Therefore, programmers produce much more code in shorter periods of time.

An additional advantage of OOP is the reusability of routines created while using the technology. Each OOP routine can be assigned its own icon and can be reused as part of another routine or copied in and modified as a completely separate routine.

The main drawback of OOP is the completely different perspective on constructing programs that programmers must have. Rather than creating a set of instructions to construct a specific procedure, OOP programmers create a set of references to specific objects that cause their procedures to execute. This is a completely different orientation to programming from those of typical third and fourth generation languages.

Object-Oriented Programming at NG&T

George Serve decides to not use an OOP language in current operations because of the training required. He also decides that the current investment in third generation language technology, and in operations based on it, makes OOP too expensive for consideration at this time. However, George believes that object-oriented methods are the methods of the future, and should be reconsidered on a periodic basis—once a year for now.

Standard System Architecture

In Chapter 2, we stated that *architecture* defines and interrelates data, hardware, software, and communications resources to support the organization's conceptual, logical, and physical structures. A **system architecture** defines and interrelates data, hardware, software, and communications resources to support the organization's systems. For many years, manufacturers of computers have proposed standards for various aspects of the system architecture. Three main areas in need of standardization are:

- The user interface
- The programmer interface
- Communication control program protocols

These three areas are often collectively called a computer installation's *system architecture*. In fact, IBM, Digital Research Corporation, Unisys, and others have proposed a standard architecture comprising these three areas. IBM's standard architecture is called System Application Architecture (SAA); Digital's is called Cohesion.

System Architecture at NG&T

With some reservations, George Serve decides to use IBM's SAA to support the already substantial investment in IBM-related products: an IBM 3890 mainframe computer used as the host at NG&T headquarters; IBM AS 400 minicomputers used as servers at each store; IBM 3270 terminals used for retail sales; desktop computer clones of the IBM PS/2 486/66 desktop computers; and DB2 as the DBMS used on desktop computers, server minicomputers, and the NG&T headquarters host computer.

George realizes that he may need to move to another architecture in the future, should SAA not continue to become more open, as it now appears to be doing.

Standardized User Interface

The standardized user interface proposed by most computer experts is a graphical user interface (GUI), previously described in Chapter 7. Acceptance of a GUI as the standard user interface diminishes the need for specialized training when new applications are constructed. Since in a completely standardized world, each application has a GUI, users need not be trained in order to make the application execute. All applications execute the same way—by having the user point to and select an icon on the GUI for the application desired.

When a GUI is the chosen standard for user interfaces, all applications requiring conversational interaction with the user should be constructed with a GUI. This requires additional construction during system development to create the GUI and make it the means of conversing with the user. Most, if not all, of the additional effort required to create a GUI-driven application can be recovered by reusing many existing GUIs as new applications are constructed. Many installations construct a library of GUIs for reuse with newly developed or modified applications.

Statements made here about the GUI are only intended to indicate why it is important to have a standard user interface, not to make a GUI a sacred object. The use of menu-driven applications has similar advantages to those of using GUIs. The emphasis is on using a standard interface, not on which standard interface is actually chosen. GUIs force standardization on the human-machine interaction, because the presentation and selection of available application systems have a standard format. Figure 7-6 in Chapter 7 illustrates a GUI that could be used for NG&T application selection and execution.

Standardized Programmer Interface

The second major aspect of a computer architecture involves a standard way for programmers to link applications with the computer. Having a standard programmer interface decreases the need for additional links to help the application fit into the computing environment. In a standard computer architecture, programs either are coded in a form that is consistent for each computer used by the company, or undergo transformation into a common format between computer types.

CROSS SYSTEM ARCHITECTURE   In recent years, system professionals have attempted to devise ways of using the same system development specifications across different computer platforms: mainframes, minis, and desktop computers. Dubbed **cross system architecture (CSA)**, these systems facilitate creating a single set of code that can be readily carried to the different computer architectures (platforms) and used for information system applications to execute on those platforms. A prominent example is the Cross System Product software offered by IBM; equivalent software is offered by other major computer companies.

With the advent of downsizing and switching to client-server computing, interest has shifted from having the same executable code on different computer platforms to having more specialized use of the platforms. The main premise of this movement is to make different portions of the computing environment responsible for only those operations they do best and most cost-effectively. The intention is to have powerful host computers operate the larger storage devices where the databases reside, while inexpensive client desktop computers perform all of the internal processing of data sent to them by the server.

Until information technology advances one way or the other, in cross system or client-server architecture, the system architecture of many companies will be a cross between host and desktop computers. Many systems professionals predict that most, if not all, companies will fully operate in a client-server architecture soon. They also predict that systems that can be used on different computer platforms will continue to be used for many years while the transition is made from the practice of using the same programs on different computer platforms to using each platform for special purposes.

PROGRAMMING ARCHITECTURE AT NG&T   NG&T adopted the client-server architecture in the early stages of development. All of the software purchased or developed by NG&T is completely restricted to this architecture. As a result, no cross system architecture technology is considered by George Serve and others at NG&T.

Standardizing the Communication Program Interface

For many years, companies have complained about the incompatibility between different computer platforms, especially those at different companies, that makes it difficult to share data and programs. The problem arises because of the different communication control program protocols and rules governing the ways to communicate with the computer.

Many companies take advantage of particular computer platforms because they are especially well suited for different areas of their business. However, some of the advantages of using these different platforms are lost when they try to share data and programs with other computer platforms in the company, and between the company and affiliate companies (companies they share and do business with).

In today's highly competitive business environment, many companies take advantage of each other's strengths by entering into joint ventures and other formal agreements that permit them to share resources. Here, too, they find that sharing resources is more complicated when they have different computer platforms. Incompatibilities between ways of communicating with these different computer platforms make it difficult to transport data between two companies—data needed to fulfill their agreement.

Another aspect of this problem appears when external information available for all companies resides on a particular computer platform that has its own communication control program protocol. These external sources include various governmental or industry reports, consumer interest group reports, stock market data, and so forth. To take advantage of this available data, some companies must translate signals in one protocol into signals in their computer installation's protocol. This incompatibility makes it more costly for businesses to take advantage of the externally available data.

Open Systems Architecture

The goal of **open systems architecture** is to foster the sharing of computer resources between software and computer platforms by eliminating incompatibilities between different software and computer protocols. The term *protocols* refers to the rules and principles that support the software and computer system, such as the format expected for input data, conversion rules for communicating between systems, and so on. In an open systems architecture, data flows freely between software and computer platforms without elaborate conversion that sometimes causes incompatibilities.

An open systems architecture includes a standard user interface, program interface, and communication program interface. By using these standard formats and practices, data and communication flow more freely within an open systems architecture and between separate architectures that are open. To participate freely but securely, companies that subscribe to the open systems philosophy must make it easy for authorized users to function in the environment while still protecting themselves against unauthorized use of their facilities. Since the control systems of an open systems architecture are responsible for this, analysts who create systems for it need only concern themselves with the specifications of the system.

Client-Server Application Development

In recent years, many computer installations have moved away from a computer architecture with almost complete dependence on a central host mainframe computer to smaller computer platforms distributed throughout the company. This process is called **downsizing**. When companies choose to downsize their computer platforms, application development specifications must reflect the characteristics of the new computer platform; they must be changed to fit the new environment.

A close relative of downsizing is creating applications to run in a client-server environment. In a **client-server environment**, the server computer platform is used to manage and retrieve the collections of data files and databases, while the client computer platform is where the data is actually processed. Developing applications to execute in this type of environment requires developing the portion of the application that directs the server as well as the portion of the application that directs the client to process the retrieved data. Thus, additional system development requirements are necessary for the application.

Figure 10-8 in Chapter 10 illustrates program execution in a client-server computer architecture. Programmers who work in this environment must create both the calls for data (and sometimes the specific instructions to accomplish the calls) from the server, and the client computer actions to perform on the logical objects returned by the server. The client computer procedures embody the program procedures depicted in the STC procedures, as illustrated in Chapter 9. The server procedures access data in the database and reconstruct the logical objects used by the business. Figure 11-10 illustrates a modified version of Figure 10-8 in Chapter 10 that also depicts how program specifications include server and client requirements. Notice that these program specifications include the user interfaces developed while prototyping, the call routines to the DBMS on the server to reconstruct the logical objects, and the program procedures that originated as STC procedures to act on the logical data objects.

Rehosting Computer Architectures

A relatively recent development in computer architectures, called **rehosting computer systems**, is the practice of retaining a host computer platform, but replacing the existing host computer with another computer. Moving to the new host may be a form of downsizing, moving to an equivalent host, or moving to a more powerful host. The major reasons for installing a new host computer are to:

- Take advantage of increased capacity
- Take advantage of decreased costs
- Take advantage of special hardware and software available in the new host computer environment

Programmer/analysts must be prepared ahead of time for system development activities in the new host computer environment. Rehosting affects system development in the modifications required to make system commands (including operating system, communication system, and database management system commands) compatible with the new host computer. Thus, training must be completed before and during the transition to the new host computer environment.

COMPUTER-AIDED SYSTEM DEVELOPMENT

Actual development of the computer systems can benefit from the move toward using computer technology to complete development activities. Many of the technologies discussed here are incorporated in a suite of tools provided by computer-aided software engineering (CASE) vendors. Still other CASE tools help integrate many of the system development practices discussed here. For example, many CASE tools either produce client-server computer applications now, or will do so in the near future.

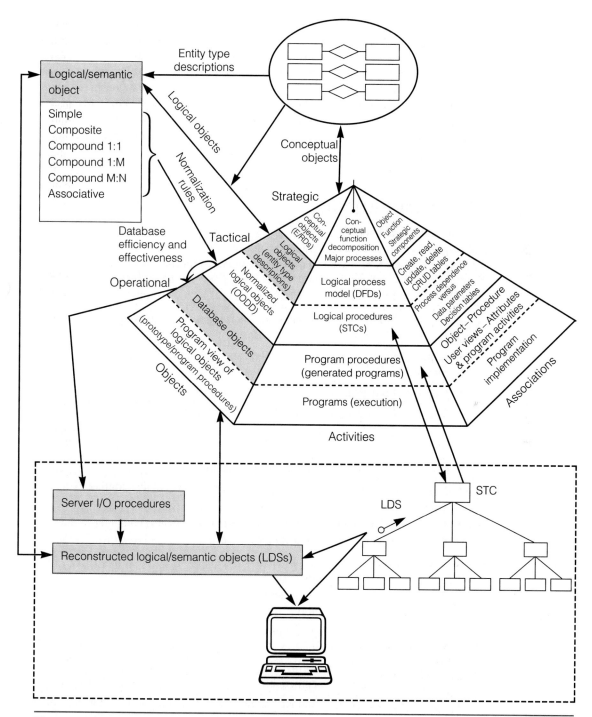

Figure 11-10. Program specifications for the client-server environment

Previous chapters introduced you to CASE tools that support different aspects of the entire process of system development. This new era of system development also includes software that supports programmers in developing programs and systems of programs, and is capable of generating computer code either for individual programs or for complete applications. CASE systems use either procedure models combined with data structure descriptions and user interface formats or prototype-oriented specifications to generate programs. All of these software systems, known as programmer workbenches, code generators, application generators, and lower CASE application development systems, are useful in the physical design stage.

Programmer Workbenches

Programmer workbenches are software systems with a number of software tools to aid the programmer in developing and testing newly developed or modified programs. Two prominent examples are MicroFocus' COBOL Workbench and the Telon programmer workbench from Computer Associates. There are many such systems available that aid in every aspect of physical design. Tools include software:

- Capable of easily retrieving physical file formats with names assigned to the files and the data items within the files
- Capable of retrieving previously stored and preformatted program modules for often-used routines
- Capable of retrieving screen mask data entry program specifications
- Capable of retrieving screen mask printed report program specifications
- To retrieve program modules of database access commands to be embedded in host programs
- To establish a subset of live data for testing purposes
- Capable of establishing a desktop computer environment that emulates a host computer environment
- Capable of downloading subsets of live data from the host computer to the desktop computer for initial testing purposes
- Capable of uploading the programs developed on the desktop computer into a host computer environment
- To retrieve previously established system and communication job streams needed for program execution
- Capable of integrating separate program executions for proper sequencing of execution and data sharing
- Capable of retrieving preformatted documentation screens for generating development and user documentation to accompany the developed programs
- To assist in special programmer functions such as program flow charting, cre-

ation of on-line system software manuals, and pro forma (already formatted) computer code commands

Programmers often use their desks as workstations and retrieve the necessary software to support the type of program development activity in which they are currently involved. The workstation may include a comprehensive configuration of hardware and software to support the programmer during programming activities. Operating in a workstation environment, programmers can retrieve previously stored file formats and select portions of the files to use in their current programming assignments. These file formats are usually stored in places known as *copy libraries*. Programmers may also retrieve previously stored program modules and modify them to fit the physical design specifications of the current application. Programs in various source languages are also stored in libraries that are managed by a librarian software system. The concept of reusable code assumes a dynamic nature when programmers use either entire programs or modules of programs from such a library. In addition to code, screen mask and report program entries can be retrieved and either used as is, or modified to suit screen or report forms in the current programming assignments.

Database access commands are often embedded in the programs of application systems. The same database access specifications may be used in a number of application programs. Programmers can retrieve previously created and stored sets of database access commands and insert them into the programs of the current application. These commands may then be modified to more appropriately direct the DBMS relative to data access.

Programmers can also force the creation of a subset of existing live data based on their file selection and formatting specifications. They can use existing desktop computer software that permits the desktop computer environment to emulate a host computer environment for program development and testing purposes. This permits the programmer to use an off-line environment for program development and initial testing purposes. Still other software available to programmers is capable of downloading data from the host computer environment and reformatting the data to permit the desktop computer to emulate retrieving and storing data in the same manner as the host computer environment. Programmers can then use software that uploads the programs developed and tested on the desktop computer onto the host computer for final testing in a live environment.

Programmers may use software that retrieves previously created system and communication software procedures to use them as a basis for creating operation and communication commands for a current programming assignment. They may use software that integrates the newly developed or modified program into the system environment being maintained by the firm. Finally, they may use software containing screen masks for entering development and user documentation. The comprehensiveness of this programmer workstation environment provides computer-aided methods for each of the different tasks performed by programmers during program development or modification.

Many special-purpose software systems have a reference ID number in the catalog of programmer workbench software systems. One such system is software that the programmer/analyst may use to draw program flow charts on terminal or desktop computer screens. This software system provides the graphics for drawing a program flow chart to be stored on auxiliary storage. On-line help manuals for system software are also available as a component of the programmer workbench. Many of the instructions used in structured programs have particular requirements for the format of the instruction. These formats may be stored as pro forma versions of the instruction and made available for retrieval by the programmer within the workbench. Many more special-purpose software components of programmer workbenches exist; the ones selected for a particular workbench depend on the needs of the particular programming staff.

Code Generators

Code generators are software systems capable of generating computer code. Programmers key in specifications for individual computer programs, and the code generator generates computer programs based on those specifications. Code generators produce computer code in a particular computer language using a particular framework for logical routines embedded in the code generator. The programmers specify particular characteristics for the desired program, and the code generator produces a program with those characteristics.

Some code generators use a main logical routine composed of several different logical routines. The programmer specifies which of the routines to include as part of the main logic of the generated code. As a result, programs are generated with the same basic logic, with different programs distinguished by which portions of the main program logic have been included. RPG is one of the earliest code generators of this type; it is used to generate programs that produce the types of data reports normally used by business. Another early code generator is APS from InterSolv, whose code-generating functions are now incorporated in the APS lower CASE system provided by InterSolv and integrated with Excelerator, InterSolv's analysis and design CASE tool.

A code generator may be one of the tools included in a programmer's workstation. Instead of directly coding programs, the programmer enters specifications into the code generator. Programmers operating in this environment are called on to develop programs that would be difficult to generate using the code generator. They develop these programs either by traditional methods or by a method that uses programmer workbench capabilities, followed by entering the specifications into the code generator.

In recent years, interest has grown in developing code generators that generate computer code from physical program design models or pseudocode specifications. In this environment, programmers create design procedure models (such as structure charts, pseudocode specifications, action diagrams, and so on) used as input to the code generator. The code generator then generates computer code corresponding to the actions specified in the procedure mode. Thus, the code is generated using the type of specifications that programmers normally use as a prelude to traditional program creation.

Application Generators

Software systems that can generate almost complete computer application systems are known as **application generators**. These software systems generate large portions of the system, whose remaining portions are produced by creating program modules to supplement the generated portion. The generated portion is assembled from physical development specifications used as input to the application generator.

Application generators are different from programmer workbenches in that programs within the applications are completely generated by the application generator rather than constructed by a programmer using tools within the workbench. The application generator may be included among the tools available to the programmer operating at a workstation; however, it will largely replace many of the programmer workstation tools. Use of application generators usually requires substantial training.

The following list of specifications must be included as input to application generators to properly generate the application system:

- Identify specific data files and items to access
- Indicate the type of data access (read-only, read-write) needed to access those files
- Specify how to combine (JOIN) data types from different data files or database objects
- Specify what data items to retain from the joined data files or database objects
- Indicate summary data to produce for data items retained from the joined data files or database objects
- Indicate special grouping of data within and between data objects included in the joined data files or database objects
- Indicate the format of the user interface to be used for screen data entry (screen mask, menu-driven, data entry prompting, and so forth)
- Identify and specify sequence, selection, and iteration of the procedures used to process the application's data
- Identify the data to be generated as the application's output
- Identify the type and format of output to be generated by the application (report form, screen display, file updating, and so on)
- Indicate system and communication software commands to be retrieved from procedure libraries to support program execution
- Identify or create DBMS calls to use in combination with the programs
- Identify users who can initiate program execution
- Identify on-line and batch specifications to support execution
- Indicate program execution sequencing and scheduling

Application generators provide a variety of stylistic methods for entering these specifications, including menu-driven, input prompting, and many others. The effort expended to develop the application largely consists of development methods provided by the application generator and instructions issued to the application generator by the programmer/analyst.

Application generators are seldom capable of producing the entire application. Certain portions of the application system are so intricate that they require individual development activity by programmers because of weaknesses in the application generator. However, the fact that large portions of the application have been generated by the application generator provides great savings in development time and effort.

Lower CASE (Fifth Generation Application Development Systems)

Lower CASE systems (operational CASE) provide a way for programmers to enter program generation specifications and additional program actions to be inserted within the generated code. Operational CASE systems either perform operations in combination with front-end CASE (A&D CASE) systems, or function as standalone systems into which the programmer enters system generation specifications directly.

When lower CASE is used in combination with front-end CASE, the design specifications for the programs are used as input to the lower CASE system. These design specifications usually consist of the logical procedures in the form of one of the procedure modeling methods, user interface formats, file and record (data structure) layouts, and computer environment specifications. For example, these specifications may include structure charts derived from data flow diagrams, screen and report formats to use with the program procedures, data structures defined as data objects to display on the screens and/or use in the program procedures, and operating system and communication system commands to cause and support program execution.

The **fifth generation development** of computing is characterized by creating programs using specifications for the desired program actions, not the explicit commands needed to accomplish them. Consequently, the main characteristic of the fifth generation is specification-driven command syntax for program and system creation. The component of the development system that makes the fifth generation possible is an active development dictionary.

The Active Dictionary

An **active dictionary** is a dictionary capable of generating specifications or software from descriptions entered into it. It is more than just a dictionary used to enter and reference the specifications it contains. An active dictionary has three major components:

1. A database of empty storage where characteristics of the environment in which the application system is to exist and explicit characteristics of the application system are stored

2. A framework for the types of procedural commands desired within typical application systems

3. An "activator" capable of combining the characteristics of the environment and the application being developed with selected procedural command frameworks to be embedded within the programs generated for the application system

The comprehensiveness of the interactions among these three components provides the necessary ingredients for the success of the fifth generation development system.

First, characteristics of the firm's computing environment are stored in the active dictionary's database. This makes it unnecessary for application developers to describe the computing environment for each application they develop. The characteristics needed are the identification of operating system and communication software systems, database management systems, descriptions of various additional software, and descriptions of hardware availability. These characteristics are stored in the database of the active dictionary when the fifth generation development system is first installed, or come already installed in the computer storage occupied by the active dictionary. Subsequently, specifications for individual application systems are entered in some of the remaining available storage areas set aside for the active dictionary. These specifications describe the characteristics of the system to be developed.

Second, a framework for the typical types of logical routines used by business systems is embedded within the active dictionary of the fifth generation development system. This framework is made up of the fourteen different logical routines identified at the beginning of this chapter, in Figure 11-2. Additional frameworks for logical command specifications, such as types of comparisons to perform and data to compare, are also embedded in the fifth generation development system. These specifications are dynamically entered within the overall logic of programs during application development activities.

Following the insertion of characteristics of the environment and the application, the activator combines them with procedural framework specifications to generate programs in the application system being developed. The lower CASE active dictionary can generate these programs in whatever language is consistently used by the computer installation.

Support for Documentation, Reusable Code, and Complete System Development

Another attribute of the fifth generation system development tool is the ability to generate development and user documentation and make the documentation available in various formats. Embedded in the design of systems is a large cache of valuable documentation for both developers and users. Fifth generation development systems can make this documentation available on demand. Thus, the often-neglected portion of the development life cycle (creating documentation) is automated, making the developed system more easily understandable and maintainable.

Many systems that are developed using a fifth generation development system will have similar characteristics used as input to the application generator, making many physical design specifications reusable during development or maintenance projects. With fifth generation development systems, reusable physical design specifications will assume a place of importance alongside reusable code.

The operational fifth generation development system is not difficult to understand. An active dictionary has been used for years within the database environment to generate schemas and user access specifications. It has only recently been recognized that this same methodology can be used in the development of application systems. A number of development tools have emerged with many of the characteristics of a fifth generation development system. However, to actually be designated as a fifth generation development system, the development system must be an *extremely active* dictionary, and *100 percent of the application* must be generated by the development tool.

System developers operating within the fifth generation development environment initiate system development by calling on the active dictionary. They enter characteristics of the system being developed (for example, files to access, data items to manipulate, type of processing to perform, comparison and computational command characteristics, and so forth). They then request that programs be generated and that accompanying design and user documentation be made available, and the system is developed completely in a computer-aided mode.

Active dictionary-based application generators complete the support provided by CASE systems for system development and maintenance. The CASE analyst workbench provides support for analysts during system development and maintenance projects. Subsequently, programmer/analysts use the active dictionary-based application generator to generate programs, operating system commands, DBMS calls, user documentation, and so on. In this way, CASE systems provide support for the analysis, design, and development phases of the system development life cycle, as well as support for maintaining systems developed in a CASE environment.

Computer-Aided Software Engineering and Fourth Generation Languages

CASE systems and application/code generators now exist for most of the third and many of the fourth generation languages. These systems use one of the methods previously described to generate programs in a specific third or fourth generation language. For example, certain of these systems generate COBOL and SQL language programs.

Some of these systems can also generate programs in different third or fourth generation languages. Part of the input to these systems indicates the language in which to generate the program, as well as the other application generation specifications. To generate programs in a particular language, these systems must understand the format, syntax, and vocabulary of that language.

Some of these systems only generate programs to work within particular computer environments. Often, these systems can generate the operating system, communication system, and DBMS commands to support program execution.

Computer-Aided Software Engineering and Object-Oriented Programming Languages

Although object-oriented programming (OOP) languages have not been around for long, CASE systems are now emerging that can generate programs in OOP languages. Using specifications similar to those used to generate a prototype, these systems generate the OOP commands needed to access, combine, process, store, change, and delete instances of object classes and types (object classes and object types were defined in Chapter 2). An object class is similar in concept to a generalized data type; an object type corresponds to an individual data type.

Specifications here indicate which object classes and types to access, which ones to combine with other object classes and types, and what services (procedures) to cause to execute. These specifications may be in either a graphical or a text format.

Computer-Aided Software Engineering and Graphical User Interface Application Generation

Most of the more advanced CASE systems now generate a graphical user interface (GUI) for conversational (interactive) applications. When programs generated by these systems execute, they display the GUI to get instructions from the user regarding program execution. Therefore, part of the input to these systems must consist of specifications that describe the GUI, the menus used, the options available, and the program procedures attached to the options displayed.

It deserves to be repeated that adopting a standard user interface (GUI or other form) is one of the most important advances in system development. If a GUI is used, the point is not that a GUI is so wonderful, but that each application executed with a GUI uses the same user interface. Since all GUI-driven applications execute in a similar fashion, user training and support are reduced regarding the way to select an application to execute. This makes the transition from application to application much easier for users. Users often feel that they know how to make all applications execute with little or no specific training when the system first comes into existence. Again, a consistent, well-developed standard format for menus supporting menu-driven application systems can accomplish the same thing in regard to user interface standardization.

Computer-Aided Software Engineering and Cross System Architecture Development

Ever since computing began, systems professionals have dreamed of the day when the same set of application specifications could be used to generate applications for all computing environments. In Chapter 1, we discussed these *spanned system architectures*. Earlier in this chapter, we introduced another name for these systems: *cross system architecture (CSA)*.

The premise behind CSA is that the programmer/analyst creates a single set of system development specifications, used by the CASE system or repository to generate an application that will work in all of a company's computer architectures. In practice, this works because the CASE system or repository is capable of generating applications to work in a number of computer architectures. Thus, the current version of CASE-supported CSA software is coded to accept input from the programmer/analyst to indicate the computer architecture in which the programs are to execute. Indicating the computer architecture causes the operating system and other architecture commands that must accompany the generated programs to be generated as well.

Computer-Aided Software Engineering and Client-Server Application Generation

The interest in downsizing and client-server applications has also caused CASE systems to change. Many CASE systems now work on smaller computer platforms. Also, the drive to produce system development specifications for client-server applications in recent years has ushered in an era in which CASE systems use input specifications from IS personnel that is essential to direct both client and server computers.

In the CASE environment, the specifications for the client and server computers are combined as a single set of system development specifications. Portions of these specifications direct the server computer regarding data access and reconstruction of logical business objects; other portions provide programs based on logical procedure models to direct the client computer regarding data processing actions.

Application Generation in Downsized Computer Architectures

Downsizing causes a change in the CASE input specifications that indicates the appropriate computer architecture in which to generate the program, a switch to a new version of the existing CASE system, or the replacement of existing CASE systems with a system that works in the new computer architecture. If the CASE system uses CSA that includes the downsized computer, it will only be necessary to change the indicator for the architecture of the program. If the existing CASE system is not a CSA system, but a different version of the CASE system exists for the new architecture, then a simple switch to this version will likely occur. It should be remembered that switching to a new version of an existing system does not preclude the need for additional training in the intricacies of the new version. If the CASE system is not a CSA system, or if a new version of it exists for the downsized computer architecture, a completely new CASE system will need to be installed—an installation loaded with all of the complexities of changing a fundamental software system.

Client-Server-Supporting CASE Systems

Several prominent CASE systems generate applications for the client-server environment. These systems have either separate or combined specifications for the client and server computers. When separate specifications are the norm, the portion of the application that directs each of these computer architectures is created separately and used to generate that portion of the application. The separately generated portions are then combined to produce the completed application, a task that usually requires some direct coding of commands to combine the client and server commands into a single application.

Some CASE systems used in a client-server architecture permit programmer/analysts to create a single set of program development specifications that direct the server for data retrieval and the client for logical object processing. These CASE systems assume the responsibility for separating server and client code to produce a fully functional application.

Combined client-server specifications are used when the CASE system or the repository is capable of distinguishing between specifications directed toward the client and toward the server. These CASE systems then generate the server and client commands from the specifications and automatically combine them into a single application, a much more effective method of generating client-server applications.

REVIEW

During the activities of the system development phase, the analyst assumes the role of supervisor. Proper project supervision includes assigning and scheduling programmers for program creation and assigning multiple programmers when it is desirable. The analyst and the project team strive to create maintainable, usable, understandable, and reliable programs in the application system. Creating maintainable programs includes creating structured programs, as well as taking the time to create system program procedures, communication program procedures, and DBMS access procedures to support program execution.

The analyst should be familiar with the different technical categories of systems in order to include aspects of them in the system development project. Characteristics of batch processing systems, interactive systems, remote job entry systems, and distributed systems are useful in the development of new or modified systems. The analyst should also oversee the creation of design/development, user, operations, and training documentation to accompany system development specifications.

The project team prepares the environment for system implementation by converting existing software and data formats, acquiring appropriate hardware and software to support the project application system, creating or modifying the database, and providing for error prevention and crash recovery. The project team should be familiar with technologies supporting faster system development, such as fourth generation languages (4GLs), natural language programming (NLP), object-oriented programming (OOP), standard system architecture, standardized user and programmer interfaces, cross system architecture (CSA), open system architecture, client-server application development, and rehosting computer architectures. These technologies, or aspects of them, can be used in the various implementations of system design.

Finally, project team members should continue to take advantage of computer-aided support during actual system development. They should clearly understand the differences between programmer workbenches, computer code generators, application generators, and fifth generation CASE active dictionaries. They should also be familiar with how CASE systems support other system development concepts, such as developing GUI-driven applications and generating applications for the client-server architecture.

QUESTIONS

1. What is the main role assumed by the project team during the development phase of the system development life cycle? What is the importance of this role during the development phase?

2. Identify the tasks to be accomplished during the system development phase of the development life cycle.

3. What is the criterion used to determine program assignment responsibilities?

4. Why is creation of one program sometimes assigned to multiple programmers? Explain the advantages and disadvantages of this practice.

5. List and explain the general operations performed by computer programs.

6. Identify and explain the five characteristics of a maintainable program.

7. What is meant by *programming standards*, and why is it important that an installation have programming standards?

8. For a company in your vicinity, obtain a list of its programming standards. Explain these standards.

9. Explain what structured programming is and explain its importance.

10. How does the design of a database influence the physical design?

11. List the major categories of structured programming rules.

12. Explain the concept of top-down (hierarchical) program module development.

13. Identify and explain the five main logical programming routines normally used in batch processing.

14. Identify and explain the nine main logical programming routines normally used in on-line processing.

15. Distinguish between design/development, user, training, and operations documentation.

16. For a company in your vicinity, obtain a copy of each of the four different types of documentation listed in question 15. Explain the examples.

17. What is program documentation and what is its purpose, who is responsible for creating it, and how is it created and used?

18. What is the purpose of user documentation, who is responsible for creating it, and how is it made available to the user?

19. What are the major specifications for user documentation?

20. What is the purpose of operating system commands to accompany application programs and who is responsible for creating them?

21. Explain the concept of a job stream and how it is used in the execution of a sequence of programs.

22. For a company in your vicinity, obtain a copy of one of its job streams and explain it.

23. Explain what a procedure library is, its purpose, and the advantages it provides to the user relative to program execution.

24. When is it necessary for a programmer to create sets of communication system commands to accompany the execution of newly developed programs?

25. Why is it often necessary to convert existing software and data formats when a program is initially created?

26. Why is it sometimes necessary to acquire additional hardware and software during or following development activities?

27. Why might it be necessary for a database to be modified during and following development activities?

28. What are the two main error-prevention methods included in the development of a system?

29. Identify and explain the seven main routines included in an edit program.

30. What is a check digit, what is its purpose, and how is it computed?

31. How are user views used during error-prevention activities within system execution?

32. What is the main error recovery routine used to recover program execution at an error-free point of its execution?

33. Explain the concept of checkpoints, their purpose, what they consist of, and the advantage of using them.

34. What is the main method by which crash recovery is performed, how is it accomplished, and what is used for restoration?

35. Explain the concept of generation data groups, their purpose, and the advantages they provide.

36. Explain how generation data groups may be used to provide reports relative to data values that were current during prior periods of the firm's business year.

37. Explain what fourth generation languages are. Distinguish between them and

third generation languages and fifth generation development systems. List some of each.

38. What are programmer workbenches, what is their purpose, and what advantages do they provide during system development?

39. List and explain the software tools available within a programmer workbench.

40. What is a code generator, what is its purpose, how is it directed to generate computer code, and where does the procedural logic of the program come from?

41. What is an application generator, how is it different from a code generator, and what forms the basis for the specifications used by an application generator?

42. Identify and explain the specifications required as input to an application generator.

43. What are the main characteristics of a true fifth generation development system?

44. Define and explain the concept of an *active dictionary*, its components, and what each component consists of.

45. Explain how a fifth generation development system using an active dictionary can be used for system development, how specifications for different systems are made available for the active dictionary, and what causes the system and the documentation to be generated.

EXERCISES

1. a. Create a complete set of physical design program specifications for the structure chart created in exercise 4 of Chapter 9. Be sure to include specifications for user interfaces and I/O forms and reports, and DBMS access on the server computer, as well as specifications for the STC procedures to execute on the client computer.

   b. Use the program specifications created in exercise 1a to create a structured program using the rules of structured programming specified in Appendix B of this textbook.

2. a. Create a complete set of physical design program specifications for the structure chart created in exercise 6 of Chapter 9. Be sure to include specifications for user interfaces and I/O forms and reports, and DBMS access on the server computer, as well as specifications for the STC procedures to execute on the client computer.

   b. Use the program specifications in exercise 2a to create a structured program using the rules of structured programming specified in Appendix B of this textbook.

3. a. Create a complete set of physical design program specifications for the structure chart created in exercise 8 of Chapter 9. Be sure to include specifications for user interfaces and I/O forms and reports, and DBMS access on the server computer, as well as specifications for the STC procedures to execute on the client computer.

   b. Use the program specifications created in exercise 3a to create a structured program using the rules of structured programming specified in Appendix B of this textbook.

4. a. Create a complete set of physical design program specifications for the structure chart created in exercise 10 of Chapter 9. Be sure to include specifications for user interfaces and I/O forms and reports, and DBMS access on the server computer, as well as specifications for the STC procedures to execute on the client computer.

   b. Use the program specifications created in exercise 4a to create a structured program using the rules of structured programming specified in Appendix B of this book.

SELECTED REFERENCES

Baker, F. T. 1972. "Chief Programmer Team Management of Production Programming." *IBM Systems Journal* 11, no. 1.

Baker, F. T. and H. D. Mills. 1973. "Chief Programmer Teams." *Datamation* 19, no. 12 (December).

Dijketra, E. 1972. "The Humble Programmer." *Communications of the ACM* 15, no. 10 (October).

Miller, E. F. and G. E. Lindamood. 1973. "Structured Programming: Top-Down Approach." *Datamation* 19, no. 12 (December).

Parnas, D. L. 1972. "A Technique for Software Module Specification with Examples." *Communications of the ACM* 15, no. 5 (May).

Wirth, N. 1971. "Program Development by Stepwise Refinement." *Communications of the AMC* 14, no. 4 (April).

CHAPTER 12

File Organization and System Testing

OVERVIEW

User requirements collected in the analysis phase provide the background information for the analyst's decision as to what type of file organization and access to recommend for the system. Files and the data contained within the files are also determined from user requirements. It is very common in today's business world to manage all data through a database management system, as described in Chapter 10. Although managing the data is complex, it is all transparent to the users. In other words, users need not have any technical expertise to access the data. This makes it even more important that the file organization and access be set up properly and that the system be thoroughly tested before being turned over to users. The type of testing needed is in large part determined by the system's file organization and access method.

To determine the type of file organization and testing required for successful system development, you need to understand:

- File organization and access methods
- Multiple levels of testing
- Testing procedures
- Types of tests
- Importance of carefully designed test data
- Automated methods of testing

KEY TERMS

Acceptance testing

Automated testing tool

Black-box approach

Direct access

Direct file organization

Direct random access method

Dynamic testing tool

EXHIBIT statement

File access

File organization

Functional tests

Hashing algorithm

Hashing random access method

Indexed sequential file organization

Integration test plan

Integration testing

Limit tests

Live test data

Modified live test data

Peak load testing

Performance testing

Procedure testing

Program testing

Random access

Recovery testing

Sequential access

Sequential file organization

Simulated test data

Static testing tool

Storage testing

Stress tests

Structure tests

Synonym

System testing

TRACE statement

Unit testing

User procedure testing

User testing

Volume tests

White-box approach

File organization schemes are a fundamental ingredient in understanding system development and subsequent testing of the system. Testing must be performed on the integration of the input access procedures, on formats used by users to interact with the system, on all procedures that are part of the programs, on integration of programs in the system, and, finally, on integration of the system with the firm's other systems. Figure 12-1 illustrates this chapter's focus on the enterprise/methodology model.

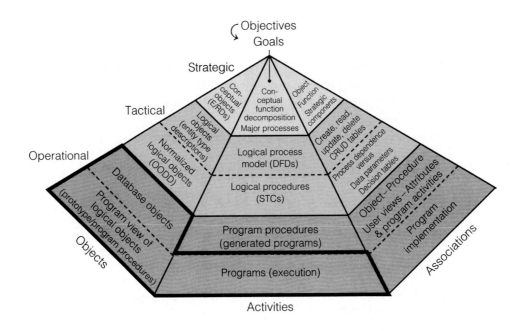

Figure 12-1. Enterprise/methodology model focus of Chapter 12

FILE ORGANIZATION AND ACCESS METHODS

Many system professionals use the terms *file organization* and *file access* interchangeably, but there is a difference. **File organization** is the way data is physically stored on tape or disk and the way the records relate to one another. **File access** is the way the data is retrieved and processed. File organization is a physical reality for the file, whereas file access represents the type of data access for a particular record.

File Organization Methods

Of the numerous file organization methods used in industry, three common ones are:

- Sequential
- Indexed
- Direct

These organization methods may be used in an environment that is oriented strictly toward batch file processing, or in an environment that uses an interactive database approach. For both environments, the term *physical data object* refers to a physical record in a file.

Sequential File Organization

Sequential file organization stores physical data objects one after another in a particular order, usually based on the sequence of one of the data items in the data objects, such as social security numbers for employee records. Normally, the physical data objects are stored in some logical order, such as by customer number or by employee Social Security number. In this case, the customer number or employee Social Security number is the key field or primary key, also called a *sort* or *control* key, within the physical data objects. Figure 12-2 shows how a customer file is organized sequentially. The records are physically organized in the sequence of the values of the primary key—in this example, in ascending order of CUSTOMER_NUMBER.

The user's view, or logical view, is the same as the physical view in sequential file organization. Thus, a change in the physical view requires a change in the logical view, and vice versa. This makes it time-consuming and costly to make changes in files stored under the sequential method. Under this method, physical data objects may be stored either on tape or on a direct access storage device (DASD), such as a disk.

Sequential file organization is appropriate when a large percentage of the physical data objects is processed each time the file is accessed—for example, when batch processing is used. This method is not appropriate when only a single record or a small percentage of physical data objects is processed each time the file is accessed—for example, in on-line real-time processing.

Indexed Sequential File Organization

The second type of file organization method uses a technique similar to sequential organization to structure the file. However, under **indexed sequential file organization**, in addition to the physical data object being stored sequentially by the primary or key field, the system also maintains a separate index file. Basically, the index file contains two data items: the value of the key field and the address or location of the physical data object associated with this key field. With this method, a user can enter a key data item, such as a customer number, for the system to use in searching the

CUSTOMER_NUMBER	CUSTOMER_NAME	BALANCE
111	Bill	400.00
222	Joan	300.00
333	John	700.00

Figure 12-2. Sequential customer file

index of customer numbers until it finds the requested one. It is then able to access the correct physical data object based on the address found in the index. This example is a common form of an indexed sequential file organization known as the *indexed sequential access method (ISAM)*.

Figure 12-3 illustrates the indexed sequential file organization on a DASD. Here, the master index would indicate which disk cylinder contained the record. On each cylinder, another index would indicate on what track the record was stored. For example, the record for customer 111 would be stored on cylinder 1, track 2.

Under the indexed sequential file organization method, the information must be stored on disk, not on tape. Tape supports only sequential organization because a physical object in the middle of the tape must wait until all data objects in front of it are read before that middle point in the file is reached. Making an update such as an insertion, deletion, or modification in a sequential file involves rewriting the entire file. In indexed sequential organization, changes can be made without rewriting the entire file.

Direct File Organization

Direct file organization stores the physical data objects based on a particular address on the disk. The actual storage address is usually either the key field in the physical data object or a result of its manipulation. Figure 12-4 illustrates direct file organization.

In the first case shown in the figure, the key field in the data record determines the actual storage disk address, so the record for customer number 111 would be stored at record address 111 on the disk. In the second case, in which the disk address

Master Index for Cylinders

Cylinder	Highest Primary Key
1	200
2	300
3	400

Track Index for Cylinder 1 Data Records Range 101–200		Track Index for Cylinder 2 Data Records Range 201–300		Track Index for Cylinder 3 Data Records Range 301–400	
Track	Highest Key	Track	Highest Key	Track	Highest Key
1	110	1	210	1	310
2	120	2	220	2	320
.	.	.	.	.	.
.	.	.	.	.	.
.	.	.	.	.	.
10	200	10	300	10	400

Figure 12-3. Indexed sequential file organization

Storage Address = Key Field

Data Records		Actual Disk Address
111	————————————>	111
222	————————————>	222
333	————————————>	333

Storage Address = Manipulation of Key Field

111	————Algorithm————>	Disk Address
222	————Algorithm————>	Disk Address
333	————Algorithm————>	Disk Address

Figure 12-4. Direct file organization example

is calculated from the key field, the customer number is manipulated to yield a disk address. This concept is explored further in the next section, on types of access.

In direct file organization, the physical view is separate from the logical view. In other words, the way the user logically views the data is not the way it is physically stored. In contrast to the sequential method, in which the physical and logical views are the same, direct file organization is more flexible. The users can change their logical view of the system without affecting the physical view.

The response time to access any one physical data object is much faster in direct file organization than in the other two methods because no indexes are needed, as in indexed sequential organization, and the system does not need to read all records in front of the requested record to access it, as in sequential organization. Direct file organization is particularly appropriate for query requests, which often occur in a database environment. Low-activity applications—those in which a small percentage of the physical data objects is processed on each access—are prime candidates for direct file organization. The key to determining whether direct organization is warranted and possible is whether immediate access of data objects is desirable and whether a key item can be used directly or manipulated to obtain record addresses. Records with large differences in ID numbers and instances in which the algorithm is too difficult to identify make it difficult to use direct file organization.

File Access Methods

File access is the way data is retrieved and processed. In other words, it indicates how to access a physical data object or data item for particular access instances. There are two main file access methods:

- Sequential
- Random

Sequential Access

As its name implies, **sequential access** retrieves physical data objects one after another. To locate a particular physical data object within the file, you start at the beginning and read each physical data object until you get to the one you want. For example, if information is needed about the eighth physical data object in a sequential file, the first seven physical data objects must be accessed first. The system does not go directly to the required physical data object. Another way of saying this is that physical data objects are accessed in the order in which they appear in the file. In Figure 12-2, in order to read the record for customer number 333, records 111 and 222 must be read first when the file is being accessed in sequential access mode.

Sequential access allows rapid access only to the next physical data object in the sequence. Relatively little space is wasted between files. A file in sequential organization can only be accessed sequentially. Sequential file organization and access are particularly appropriate for large files in which physical data objects are processed one after the other. Weekly payroll processing, in which all employee physical data objects are processed one after another on a weekly basis, is a good example of an application particularly suited to sequential access. Files with a random file organization can also be accessed sequentially. Their organization makes it possible to access them randomly, but they may also be sequentially accessed.

Random Access

The second file access method avoids the need to start at the beginning of the file when a specific physical data object must be accessed. Using **random access**, the system is able to go directly to the required physical data object. Thus, if the eighth physical data object is needed, the system is able to go directly to that physical data object and retrieve it. This type of access is also called **direct access**.

Random access is possible because the system initially calculates an actual storage address from some key within the physical data object. When the particular physical data object is needed again, the system performs the same operation on the same key and gets the same address. It is then able to go directly to the calculated address and retrieve the requested item. Quick access and retrieval are possible for low-activity files. If only a small percentage of physical data objects is processed each time the file is accessed, random access is appropriate. Only files with random organization— indexed sequentially or direct—can be accessed in a random access mode.

Two basic methods of assigning and accessing data under the random access method exist: direct and hashing.

DIRECT RANDOM ACCESS METHOD   The **direct random access method** of data access uses an actual field value within the physical data object as the storage address, or a facsimile of the address. For example, if the customer number is the key field within a physical data object, the value within this field may also be the actual storage address. For example, as illustrated in Figure 12-4, a customer number of 111 could correspond to a storage address of 111, which corresponds to the position of the data object relative to the start of the file. This is a simple and quick method. However, it is also quite inflexible, because the values of the key fields must be structured around available storage addresses. In addition, the fields must all be numeric.

HASHING RANDOM ACCESS METHOD   The **hashing random access method** derives the storage address by applying a hashing algorithm to the key field and using the result of the calculation as the actual storage address. A **hashing algorithm** is really nothing more than a mathematical formula. The number of possible algorithms is limitless, but the most common is the prime number division/remainder algorithm. In this method, the key field is divided by a predetermined prime number; the remainder becomes the actual storage address.

The following example helps to illustrate this process: Assume a storage location is being calculated for a customer physical data object with a customer number of 111. A predetermined prime number, such as 23, is divided into 111, giving a remainder of 19. Here is the computation:

$$\text{Prime number} \ \rightarrow \ 23 \ \overline{\smash{\big)}\ 111} \atop \begin{array}{r} 4 \\ \hline 92 \\ \hline 19 \end{array} \ \leftarrow \ \text{Remainder and disk address}$$

Since the remainder gives the actual storage address, the customer physical data object would be stored or accessed at address 19.

Unfortunately, there are some potential problems associated with hashing algorithms if they are not set up correctly. First, they should provide an even distribution throughout the storage area. Second, synonyms should be minimized. A **synonym** means that the same address is calculated from different key values using the same hashing algorithm. The system has several ways of handling synonyms, but these are beyond the scope of this text. All you need to know is that synonyms are possible and that good hashing algorithms both minimize and accommodate them.

File Organization and Access Methods as a Basis for Testing

The needs of the user determine the type of file organization and access required. (Batch processing systems require different organization and different access methods from on-line systems.) These file organizations, in turn, provide the basis for creating test data used to test the programs developed for the application.

Once the system is designed and the code written, A&D project team members test the system to ensure that it meets user requirements. A carefully designed testing process helps avoid the surprises that often occur during system development. This can be compared to buying a new car: few buyers are willing to purchase a new car without first taking it for a test drive to determine whether it meets their specifications. System testing checks the proposed system to make sure it meets user specifications. The objective is to turn a system over to users that does not produce costly errors when used in regular production.

A common misconception is that testing applies only to application programs. Testing program code determines whether the program performs as desired; however, this is only one part of overall system testing. The testing philosophy extends to all phases of the system development life cycle. Testing only the code is like checking only the engine in a new car. Though the engine is a major part of the car, there are many other parts, such as the cooling system and the braking system, that must work in unison for the car to operate properly.

To carry the car-buying analogy a bit further, purchasers often request unnecessary but desirable options for their new car. Testing only the code of an information system does not ensure that the system works properly, nor does it guarantee compliance with other functional and cosmetic desires of the user. The remainder of this chapter discusses testing in detail, from both a program and a system viewpoint. An overview of the testing philosophy is presented first. Then, since program testing is the more traditional view of testing, it is presented next; a discussion of system testing follows.

LEVELS OF TESTING

Testing is a multilevel process, as shown here:

SYSTEM TESTING
Testing the interaction among programs
PROGRAM TESTING
Testing the interaction between modules
UNIT TESTING
Testing the individual program module

Notice that unit testing is at the lowest level of testing and system testing is at the highest level. Figure 12-5 presents a view of testing known as a top-down approach. This approach to testing corresponds to the concept of structured programming and structured analysis and design. The underlying premise behind these concepts is that the best way to solve a large complex problem is to break it down into smaller, less complex parts, called *modules*.

Top-down testing views a program as a series of interrelated modules, with testing conducted from the most general to the most detailed levels. In other words, top-down testing is implemented in stages, starting at the top and proceeding to the bottom. This systematic approach ensures that the overall logic works before the detailed modules are written. In Figure 12-5, module 1.0 would be tested first; then 1.1, 1.2, and 1.3; then 1.11, 1.12, and so on.

The other standard approach to testing is the bottom-up approach. In this

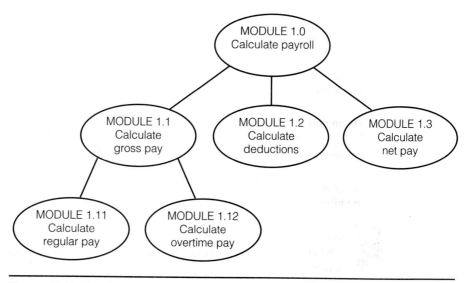

Figure 12-5. Top-down approach to testing

approach, interest centers on the detailed levels first and proceeds to the more general levels. If the bottom-up approach were applied to Figure 12-5, testing would begin at modules 1.11 and 1.12 and work upward. The main problem with the bottom-up approach is the difficulty of overall planning and program integration. For this reason, top-down program design and testing is usually preferred.

Influence of Structure Charts on Testing

In Chapter 9, we showed how project team members use transform and transaction analysis to create a structure chart (STC) from a data flow diagram (DFD). The STC then serves as the basis for writing programs, as described in Chapter 11. Because of the hierarchical nature of STCs, the top-down approach to program design and testing follows naturally. However, it is sometimes best to use a combination of top-down and bottom-up testing. Testing programs that have been derived from STCs are becoming more widely accepted because many firms use a structured methodology in their design process with STCs used for IS procedure modeling.

TESTING PROCEDURES

Testing various levels and procedures ensures that the code is complete, reliable, correct, and maintainable. As shown in the previous section, these procedures and levels include:

- Unit testing
- Program testing
- System or integration testing

Unit testing is used to remove errors, both syntactical and logical, from a single module or unit of a program. For instance, a sales program might be designed to produce subtotals and totals using a routine that is often called a *control break subroutine*. For that program, a unit test could be used to test only the control break subroutine. Unit testing can take two main approaches to different types of tests, sometimes classified as the black-box and white-box approaches. These approaches are illustrated in Figure 12-6.

The Black-Box Approach

The **black-box approach** to testing is output-oriented. The analyst knows what the output should look like from the input submitted to the programs. If the output produced by the programs is what is expected, the system is considered functionally correct. In other words, the black-box approach checks the inputs and outputs in detail without analyzing the way the processing that converts them actually performs. The processing is considered a "black box." You do not concern yourself with what goes on inside the box; for correct outputs, you do not care. The key to properly using this

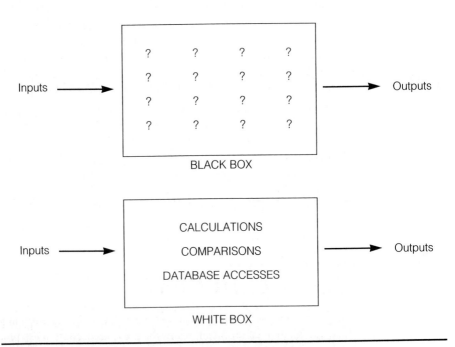

Figure 12-6. Black-box and white-box approaches to testing

approach is to use each different combination of input data the system was designed to process and to make sure the output produced is the expected output.

The black-box approach is used mainly for functional tests. **Functional tests** are used for known results. From a unit testing standpoint, this involves more than just output from a module. It also includes testing to see how the module handles exceptions. For example, if a program runs out of data to process, does it end normally? Another example might be checking the way a file-handling module handles an empty file.

The White-Box Approach

Under the **white-box approach**, the inner workings of the module are explicitly tested. The analyst is interested not only in what the inputs and outputs look like, but in what goes on inside the box as well. This approach to testing checks the programming logic included in the box. The white-box approach is used mainly for structure tests. **Structure tests** emphasize what goes on inside the box (the program). One aspect of structure testing—path testing—tests the various logical paths through a program module. For simple modules, it is possible to test every logical path through a module. However, as the program modules grow in complexity, the number of paths grows geometrically, as shown by the following formula:

$$P = 2^{n + 1}$$

where:

P = possible paths through a module, a program, or a system

n = number of different loops

As the number of loops increases in a module, the number of paths geometrically increases. For example, if there are two possible loops in a module, there are $P = 2^{2 + 1}$ or 8 paths through it. If the number of loops increases to 15, there are 32,768 possible paths. Obviously, the number of paths becomes very large very quickly.

For this reason, it is often impossible to actually test all paths through a module. Care must be taken in deciding which paths to test, followed by designing appropriate test data to accomplish the task. Unfortunately, path testing does not guarantee the correctness of the module, as would testing for arithmetic errors. For example, the computation $A = B/D + C$ produces different results from the computation $A = B/(D + C)$. Only test data carefully designed to produce known results reveals this type of error.

Program Testing

After completing unit testing, project members combine the different modules and perform program testing. **Program testing** ensures that all of the various modules within the program function properly while executing the whole program. The same methods used for unit testing are also used in program testing. The main difference is that the program is treated as a unit. The tests become more complex, but the testing principles remain the same.

For example, functional tests may involve using the black-box approach. Again, the concern is with the outputs and not with the processing that takes place to produce them. The analyst must know what outputs to expect and make sure that the program produces those outputs. Thus, for a payroll program whose ultimate objective is to produce a payroll check and a payroll register, the analyst must determine that the individual checks and records on the register are properly produced.

The white-box approach to program testing uses structure tests in a manner similar to unit testing. Path testing must still be done. However, the number of possible paths through a program becomes much greater than the number of paths through a program module. In addition, passing data from one module to another requires checking to ensure that there is no loss of data integrity. As in unit testing, carefully designed test data for known results helps reveal possible errors.

Debugging Aids

Specific debugging statements in particular languages will not be discussed here, but a brief example will illustrate them. The most common business programming language is COBOL (Common Business Oriented Language). Two particularly useful statements available for testing COBOL programs are the TRACE and EXHIBIT statements. Other computer languages have debugging statements of equally important usefulness for testing purposes.

The **TRACE statement**, combined with path testing, helps check the order in which program sections and paragraphs (units or modules) are executed. The READY TRACE instruction causes the name of each section and paragraph of the program to be listed, in the order of their execution. As the program executes, each branch to another paragraph or section of the program causes that paragraph or section name to be listed. The names of all paragraphs or sections that execute are listed until the RESET TRACE command executes. By following the order of execution of different paths through the program, potential trouble spots can be identified. Here are some sample statements using a TRACE statement:

```
000-CONTROL PROCEDURE.
    READY TRACE.
        COBOL Statement
        COBOL Statement
        COBOL Statement
    RESET TRACE.
```

This TRACE statement would list each program paragraph name, in the order of their execution. For a program with loops, you could follow the list of paragraph names to review the order of program module execution. The READY TRACE and RESET TRACE commands could be strategically positioned within a program to test specific areas of a program or the entire execution of the program.

The **EXHIBIT statement** allows the programmer or analyst to see the names and data values for selected data items each time they are encountered in the program. If a particular data item does not have the value it should have during any point of program execution, an EXHIBIT statement can indicate where the value changed to an incorrect value. The following example shows sample statements using an EXHIBIT statement:

```
GROSS_PAY.
    COMPUTE GROSS_PAY = HOURS * RATE
NET_PAY.
        .
        .
        .
    COMPUTE DEDUCTIONS = ...
    COMPUTE NET_PAY = GROSS_PAY - DEDUCTS.
DEBUG_NET_PAY.
    ON 5 AND EVERY 5 EXHIBIT NAMED GROSS_PAY,
        HOURS, RATE, NET_PAY, DEDUCTIONS.
```

This EXHIBIT statement causes the values of GROSS_PAY, HOURS, RATE, NET_PAY, and DEDUCTIONS to be listed for every fifth physical data object processed. Here is an example of the output:

```
GROSS_PAY = 120.00 HOURS = 40.0 RATE = 3.00 NET_PAY = 95.00 DEDUCTS = 25.00
```

Debugging aids such as the TRACE and EXHIBIT statements are particularly useful in testing program execution in combination with different types of input data contained in files with sequential and random organization that are accessed sequentially and randomly. The execution of program statements such as the READY TRACE and EXHIBIT statements can be the action to perform when an IF statement determines that a record with a particular data value in a data item is encountered, such as a particular data value for an employee SSNUMBER. For example, when a particular SSNUMBER data value is encountered, an IF (condition) statement would determine that it has been encountered and cause a READY TRACE to execute. As that record and subsequent records are input into the program, each paragraph or section name for the program would be listed as they are branched to for execution. During the execution, EXHIBIT statements might also execute to display the data values for particular data items. Program execution could continue to be traced until a particular data value for SSNUMBER is reached, at which time another IF statement could cause the RESET TRACE statement to execute to cause the trace of program execution to stop.

The previous example could be used to test program execution that uses a particular sequential or random file in either sequential or random access modes. The execution of the program's debugging statement could be controlled by the use of specific records in the files. For this example, strategically positioned records in the files could help determine that these files are being processed properly in the appropriate sequential and random access modes.

SYSTEM TESTING

System testing, often called **integration testing**, is used to determine whether all the different programs interface correctly and operate as a complete system. The object of system testing is to ensure that the system performs as promised in the user requirements phase. System testing actually consists of two major parts: integration testing and acceptance testing.

Objectives and Scope of Integration Testing

Specifications in the design phase determine the scope of the testing process. The testing process is typically designed around these specifications. The object of integration testing is to prove the workability of the overall system and to ensure its readiness for release to the user.

The analyst often develops a plan called the **integration test plan** to identify the tests to perform, the order in which to apply them, the hardware and software to use, the files to use during execution, and the documentation required. This plan then serves as a guide throughout the system testing process. The integration test plan is reviewed by the users, the design team, the steering committee, and the acceptance team. Only when they agree on the completeness of the plan and its feasibility should system testing proceed.

Testing the File Organization and Access Methods

The test plan is influenced by the file organization and type of access required to meet user needs. If the application developed is basically a batch-oriented system, then the testing must include a variety of tests. The ability of the system to process a given number of transactions within a given time frame and to produce required reports on a timely basis is particularly important. Of equal importance are tests to ensure that the processing logic is correct and that sufficient backup and recovery procedures are built into the system. These tests are typically used to test the execution of sequential access routines for either sequential or random files.

The test plan for on-line systems will include some of the same testing logic as that for batch systems, but will also need to test response times, number of users that can access the system at any given time, appropriate security measures, and user-friendliness. These tests typically test the execution of random access routines for processing random files. The system tests described in the next section can apply to both batch and on-line systems, but the emphasis differs depending on the type of system tested.

Special Types of System Tests

The purpose of system testing is to ensure that the system meets the specifications identified in earlier phases of the system life cycle. Special tests used for this purpose are:

- Peak load testing
- Performance testing
- Recovery testing
- Storage testing
- Procedure testing
- User testing

Peak load testing helps determine whether the system performs properly when operating at the upper limit of its capacity during periods of high demand for computer execution. For example, a university may install a student information system to help students register for classes without long waits and to provide up-to-date information about a student's physical data objects during peak periods of class registration. The system may function properly during the semester, when only a moderate number of requests occur. Peak load testing determines how the system would perform in periods of high demand, during actual registration for classes. It would help determine whether response time gets much longer during class registration, or whether the system goes down altogether. Designers and users want to know how the system reacts during these busy periods.

Several types of peak load testing actually exist: volume tests, stress tests, and limit tests. Though all three of these tests are closely related, there are subtle differences among them, such as:

- **Volume tests** inspect a system while it is executing a particularly large job.
- **Stress tests** help determine how the system reacts to loads within specified limits.
- **Limit tests** submit the system to conditions outside of its designed limits to determine whether an adequate safety margin has been included in the design.

An example will help to clarify the differences among these three tests. Using the student registration system as a reference, a volume test might include listing all the students attending the university, along with their calculated GPAs. A stress test for the system might be an attempt to access student physical data objects during peak registration. If the system is designed properly, any degradation in response time will be within acceptable ranges. Finally, a limit test might determine how well the system performs when 1200 daily requests are made to a student information system designed to handle 1000 requests per day. Tolerance for overload is a particularly useful test for a rapidly growing application, such as one that processes a growing number of students at a university, or a rapidly expanding customer base.

Performance testing determines the length of time required for certain system operations. This test often involves examining transaction data processing. Examples of performance testing range from testing the amount of time required to execute a batch payroll program that includes sequential access of sequential and random files to testing the response times of a real-time, on-line airline reservation system for various types of transactions performed during random access of random files. The analyst conducts performance tests on the system when it is operating in a normal mode and when it is operating near capacity.

Recovery testing examines the ability of the system to recover from a failure. This failure can take many forms: data loss because of a disk head crash, equipment destruction because of fire, sabotage that changes important data values, processing of the wrong transaction data against a master file, and so on. Regardless of the failure, the goal of the system should be to recover the data and restart the system from a particular point in time.

Situations are simulated to determine how the system will perform under adverse circumstances. The system must fail and then recover. Though not all possible adverse conditions can be tested, the ones deemed the most important must be tested. The particular application determines the particular types of tests to run. The recovery should include the recovery of both sequentially and randomly organized files.

Storage testing determines the ability of the system to store a maximum amount of data. For example, for a system designed to store 100,000 transactions on a particular day, a storage test helps determine whether the system can actually store that number of transactions on disk. When determining the amount of storage needed, it is always a good idea to have a large margin for error, particularly for a fast-growing application whose storage requirements are expected to increase rapidly. Storage testing should be performed for all sequentially and randomly organized files in system execution in both sequential and random access modes.

Procedure testing provides a basic test of both system and user documentation. System documentation provides directions in a procedures manual for both operations personnel and user personnel to follow when they encounter certain problems. Examples of procedure testing for operations personnel include the procedure to perform when there are system malfunctions or equipment breakdowns.

User procedure testing mainly involves testing the user manual, which guides users in initiating system execution or accessing on-line help facilities. To test the procedure manual, users should be asked to perform a procedure exactly as shown in the manual. If they have difficulty with the procedure, the manual probably needs revising.

User testing, often called *human factors testing*, determines how the system is actually used. Factors to consider are clarity of documentation, ease of use, how well the system satisfies user information needs, and the opinions of the users about the system. This form of testing often leads directly into acceptance testing.

Acceptance Testing

The toughest test of all is meeting the requirements set by the users. If the system passes **acceptance testing**, the users are ready to sign off on the system; they verify that it meets the original goals and specifications determined during the analysis and design phases.

The components of the acceptance test include: a report that shows the results of the various testing procedures to users, verifying that proper and timely training has occurred, and comprising a detailed plan for system conversion and changeover. The purpose is to assure users that everything possible has been done to guarantee that the system will function properly when it is put into operation.

When users sign off on a system, the responsibility for the system is transferred to them. This does not mean that the systems department will no longer be involved with the system. Usually, they will still be responsible for its maintenance. It means that the system team is not responsible for meeting additional user requirements for the original project.

User sign-off should not be taken lightly, either by the users or by the systems department. Sign-off from the user's point of view only relieves the IS department from the development phase of the life cycle. If users sign off on a system that does not meet their requirements, additional changes are typically considered another project and will cost more money, even if these requirements could have been part of the original design.

From the point of view of the systems department, a major goal is to satisfy user requirements. If this is not accomplished, even though users may sign off on the system, hard feelings result—feelings that come back to haunt the team on future projects. It is not beneficial to anyone to have dissatisfied users. Thoroughly testing the system helps ensure that it meets user information needs. An integrated test plan and properly designed test data (discussed in the next section) provide the best way to thoroughly test the system.

DESIGNING TEST DATA

Test data is either live or constructed data used during test execution of a newly developed or modified system for an A&D project. Properly designed test data is derived from the type of file organization and the access methods used in the system. For example, to test a sequentially organized file may require using a large number of transaction records as input to the system in order to determine whether program logic executes correctly and whether the system is producing the correct output. The format of the output is already known, along with data values for correctly computed output data items such as subtotals and totals. In this case, test data is processed and compared against known results to ensure that the system is working properly.

On the other hand, test data for on-line systems is designed to simulate the types of queries users may issue. The results of each query should already be known. The actual results are compared to predetermined results to determine whether the system is accessing the data and executing properly.

Regardless of the file organization or access method being tested, the test data comes from two sources: live data and artificially designed or simulated data. In some systems, both types of test data can be useful.

Sometimes the best way to convince users that the system is functioning as promised is to use their own data in the test. **Live test data** is actual data currently used in the business. It is used in either original or modified form. Used in its original form, live test data is common for volume testing and user acceptance testing.

Live data that has been changed to test certain modules of a program, called **modified live test data**, can also be used. For example, actual data may be modified to test for error conditions that may occur. These modifications may include modifications to the file structure (data items in file records), the file organization (random to sequential and vice versa), or the actual data records in the files. Testing must also ensure proper handling of exceptions. Live data can be modified to include exception data to check how the program handles such situations.

Simulated test data is data produced specifically to test a particular module or program. It does not come from the company's files or database. An independent team may design test data to ensure proper execution for all conditions and paths through a program. Live test data may not test all conditions and paths—a weakness of this type of test data, since some conditions that may occur in the business may not be currently present and reflected in data values in live data files. Simulated data can overcome this problem.

In theory, all paths and conditions should be tested in a program; however, it is not always practical to do so. As explained earlier in the chapter, it may only be feasible to execute a certain number of tests. Therefore, the project team must determine what needs to be tested the most. Generally, tests need to be performed on data designed to expose errors in normal processing and system execution that occur under extreme conditions. The most complex parts of the system need to be tested the most, but this does not mean that the simpler parts should be overlooked. Many IS personnel have regretted a decision to put a system into action when only the more complex portions of the system have been tested.

AUTOMATING THE TESTING PROCESS

System testing is a long and tedious process. Large amounts of programmer time are required for setting up the tests, creating test data, collecting test results, and interpreting the results. Fortunately, the entire process does not have to be performed manually. Computer systems can help perform these actions.

There are hundreds of automated testing tools available. An **automated testing tool** is a software system that relieves the programmer of much of the clerical work associated with testing. These tools are designed to test programs written in virtually all of the popular, and some of the not so popular, programming languages.

Though there are many possible ways to classify testing tools, perhaps the most useful classification divides them into *static* testing tools and *dynamic* testing tools. This classification distinguishes between the structural aspect of the program and its actual execution. For example, static analysis is concerned with program documentation and the actual appearance of the program. Most companies using COBOL now require that COBOL programs be written in a structured form. The advantages of using the structured format are many, and have been explained at various points throughout this text.

A **static testing tool** checks a program to determine whether it is written in structured format. In addition to errors in coding, static testing tools can check for consistent usage of variable names throughout the program and correct interfaces between modules. They can also make sure that data items are given values before being used in the program.

The components of a static testing tool include:

- Front-end language processor for the particular language used
- Database for creating necessary tables
- Error analyzer for determining error type and scope
- Report generator for generating a list of errors found

These tools vary widely; the main difference is the number of command-level statements the programmer can add. In other words, how flexible is the tool for different applications? Since the program is not actually executed by a static analysis tool, these tools are particularly deficient for analyzing programs dealing with data items that vary during program execution, such as the subscripts for table elements. Table 12-1 lists some of the more popular static testing software systems.

A **dynamic testing tool** actually tests the program during execution. Debugging statements such as the EXHIBIT and TRACE statements illustrated earlier are often part of a dynamic testing tool. Some of these tools also track the CPU time associated with a certain program or a particular module of a program.

Automatic test data generators also fall into the category of dynamic testing software systems. Test data generated automatically by the system helps test a greater variety of conditions and paths, in much less time, than test data prepared manually by the programmer.

Since it is often impossible to test all paths in a system, it is important that these types of test generators permit programmers to specify how paths through the program should be tested. A programmer can specify that certain paths, a random sample of paths, or the maximum length of a path should be analyzed. The software then gen-

Table 12-1 Examples of static testing tools

Software	Language Supported	Major Functions
AUTOMATED TEST DATA GENERATOR	FORTRAN	Unit testing, program testing
COBOL/DV	COBOL	Generates test data from COBOL code
SADAT	PL/1	Path testing, data flows, auditing
DOCUTOOL	PASCAL	Documents FORTRAN from source code

Table 12-2   Examples of dynamic testing tools

Software	Language Supported	Major Functions
ATTEST	FORTRAN	Test data generator; produces a data flow report
DISSECT	FORTRAN	Divides complex programs into segments and generates test cases
EFFIGY	PL/1	Proofs of correctness, TRACEs
SMOTL	COBOL	Text data generator; regression testing

erates test data based on the characteristics of the particular program. Table 12-2 categorizes some of the major dynamic testing software systems.

In summary, automating the testing process takes much of the tedious clerical work out of the hands of the programmer. When combined, static and dynamic testing tools greatly simplify the testing process, freeing programmers to do more creative work. In addition, many dynamic testing software systems automatically generate test data. When used in conjunction with live data, tests that use generated data help ensure that the system meets all user requirements.

TESTING AT NATIONAL GOLF & TENNIS (NG&T)

To give you an example of appropriate testing for a specific system, various types of system tests applicable to the NG&T case are provided in Figure 12-7. This example employs a question-and-answer format to help the analyst determine whether they are sufficiently testing the system to assess whether the requirements for the system are being met. (This is not meant to be a complete list of all tests required.)

Figure 12-8 illustrates how test data could be designed in the NG&T case. Keep in mind that this is only a sample, not a complete set of test data. Testing sales and accounts receivable programs helps ensure that the system meets user requirements for accurate and reliable data. Simulating a live environment, sample transactions are entered from each POS terminal, accompanied by the testing of Administration processing. The samples are specifically designed to test all phases of data validation and process control. In addition, these samples are manually calculated, and the resulting totals and updates are compared to system-generated output.

PEAK LOAD TESTING

Question: Can the new system handle the volume of transactions that may occur at peak levels of processing activity? If all business sections enter sales and customer updates at the same time, can the system support them effectively?

Response: The new system capacity is designed to handle eighteen remote terminals simultaneously. The new system will be implemented with only four POS terminals and two dumb terminals, leaving considerable excess capacity for future expansion. The need for only four terminals per store was determined from the project team's analysis of current needs.

STORAGE TESTING

Question: Does the POS terminal hard disk have adequate storage capacity to record all daily transactions and that particular area's sales program?

Response: If each POS terminal handles 1000 customer transactions per day, with a maximum of 419 bytes per transaction, the required space will be a total of 419,000 bytes. The POS terminal hard disk can store up to 100 megabytes of data. If every customer completed a transaction during one day, the total of 4000 transactions would require less than 2 megabytes of storage space. Since the data on the hard disk is uploaded and purged at the end of each day, the hard disk capacity of 100 megabytes will never be reached. This also permits the storage of programs, such as the sales program, on the hard disk.

Question: Does the new system have adequate storage capacity to record daily transactions on the Administration hard disk?

Response: The hard disk on the Administration host computer has a storage capacity of 800 megabytes plus off-line storage in the form of unlimited tapes and disks. If each of the four POS terminals uploads 4000 transactions daily, a maximum of 8 megabytes will be used for daily storage. After these transactions are sorted and processed, they will be transferred to tape and removable disks, releasing the hard disk storage used. Thus, the host computer will have an excess of storage on a daily basis to store programs and handle processing.

PERFORMANCE TIME TESTING

Question: Will the response time for each POS terminal request meet user expectations of less than three seconds each for inquiry and transaction processing?

Figure 12-7. System testing at NG&T

Response: These POS terminals will operate with a one-second response time for transactions and inquiries.

Question: How long does the system take to implement backup procedures for processing if the POS hard disk fails?

Response: If the host computer or local network computer detects failure in its interface with a POS terminal, it will automatically restart and reload that area's sales program and interface to its POS terminal. This process will require 15 seconds to complete.

Question: How long will it take to sort transaction types and update the sales and accounts receivable files?

Response: The host computer or local network computer can sort a maximum of 16,000 transactions (4000 from each POS terminal), using a sort utility, in less than one minute. Updating existing accounts receivable files will take five minutes to retrieve old member balances, sort, update, and reload new balances.

RECOVERY TESTING

Question: Is the system able to recover data and restart after failure?

Response: Since all on-line transactions are uploaded simultaneously to the Administration host computer hard disk, the POS terminals are fully backed up. In the event of an electrical failure, manual sales tickets and procedures are available. When the on-line system is reestablished, these manual sales tickets can be entered, to be included with previous data entered on regarding POS terminal sales.

PROCEDURE TESTING

Question: Are the programs user-friendly and is the documentation easy to follow?

Response: Procedures for operating the POS terminals, networks, and host computers are documented for each module. Training is provided for all users to meet their particular training needs. Programs designed to prompt the users for required information are validated on-line.

HUMAN FACTORS TESTING

Question: Is the system designed to prompt the user for required data and keep the user informed as to the state of transaction processing?

Response: The user can exit menus at will for reporting and sorting data. If invalid data is keyed for a transaction, the program will return an error message asking the salesperson to rekey the previous data element. While a program is executing, a message will be displayed on the terminal, indicating what its processing is doing and the expected length of time for completion.

Figure 12-7. System testing at NG&T *(continued)*

DATA ELEMENT ASSURANCE

Question: Is the data keyed for each field of a transaction valid?

Reason: The on-line system validation must reject the entry of alphabetic data in a numeric field (and vice versa) and notify the salesperson of the error. Blanks and special characters are not permitted in critical fields. Each customer number entered must be verified against the Administration master file for credit sale limits.

Test: A test of 100 transactions created with bad data is keyed into each POS terminal to test whether the program will detect the error and display an error message for the user to correct the input data.

VERIFICATION AGAINST MASTER FILE

Question: Is the customer number valid? Are credit files up to date?

Reason: If the customer number is not valid, credit sales cannot be billed. Proper approval of credit is effective only when credit information is current. Inadequate information indicates problems with collecting receivables.

Test: Enter 100 credit sales transactions that require verification of customer numbers against the master file. For numbers not in the file, sales cannot be completed without authorization from Administration. The transactions test is designed to include seventy-five active customer numbers and twenty-five not on the master file. In addition, these credit sales test the credit limit verification against the master file and reject those sales exceeding the credit limit. Also, credit sales for forty active accounts will exceed their account credit limits.

PROCESSING VERIFICATION

Question: Determine whether all data is completely and correctly processed by the system.

Reason: Lost, double-counted, or incorrect data indicates unreliable output.

Test: Manually trace 300 transactions from daily batch totals for sales files forward through posting to customer accounts receivable files and billing. Compare manually computed totals for certain data with those totals that result from system execution.

TRANSACTION SEQUENCE CHECK

Question: Determine whether all transactions are recorded properly and represent actual sales.

Reason: Failure to record sales transactions results in an understatement of sales and accounts receivable. Fictitious sales overstate revenue and accounts receivable and cause misleading financial statements.

Figure 12-8. Design of test data for NG&T

Test: Check the numerical sequence of 300 transactions from the daily sales file for missing numbers. Voided sales receipts must be retained by the sales area, and lost tickets must be reported and logged. For the system test execution, compare total cash sales recorded by sales registers to total cash receipts for the day as recorded by the system, and signatures on credit sales slips to customer signatures on file.

PRICE TABLE VERIFICATION

Question: Determine whether prices in price tables within the system's programs agree with the posted price list on purchase items.

Reason: Clerical errors in inserting price data on system tables may cause a loss of revenue or incorrectly recorded price tags on purchase items. Overstated prices on the table antagonize customers and create collectible account problems.

Test: Using the sample of 300 sales transactions, verify the prices of each item against the manual price list.

Figure 12-8. Design of test data for NG&T *(continued)*

REVIEW

User requirements determine the particular types of file organization and access methods used in the system. The three main types of file organization methods are sequential, indexed, and direct. Sequential organization is used for only batch processing; indexed files can be used for both batch and on-line processing; direct files are typically used for on-line real-time processing.

File access refers to the way data is actually retrieved and processed. The two main file access methods are sequential and random. Sequential access reads physical data objects one at a time, in the order in which they appear in the file, and must search through all preceding physical data objects to get to a specific one needed for processing. Random access may use a hashing algorithm or a specific data value to obtain the address of a physical data object to be directly retrieved. One problem associated with random access is the possible creation of synonyms. A synonym results when a hashing algorithm assigns the same address to two different data objects.

System testing before turning a system over to the user is a significant part of the system life cycle. It is estimated that over 50 percent of the cost of a software project is directly related to testing. Basically, testing involves identifying and correcting errors in a system before releasing it to operations.

The type of file organization and the access methods used help determine how a system must be tested. Different testing procedures apply to batch systems and on-line systems. There are several approaches to testing, the most common one being the top-down approach. Top-down testing proceeds from the most general level to the more specific levels, and ensures that the overall logic works before writing detailed code.

Another view of testing looks at the system as a black box and/or a white box. In the black-box approach, the analyst is not concerned with the processing, but only with ensuring that the output is correct. The white-box approach tests the actual process routines that convert inputs into outputs. A combination of the two approaches is usually preferred.

System testing is a multilayered approach to unit testing, program testing, and overall system testing, which proceeds from the simplest modules to integration of the entire system. The ultimate test is the acceptance test, in which responsibility for the system actually passes from the systems department to the user. Acceptance testing checks to make sure that the system meets user requirements.

Testing systems usually requires designing test data, which can be a combination of live data from the actual business operations and simulated data that has been produced specifically to test a particular program. The tedious clerical tasks involved in designing test data and performing actual system testing can be eliminated by using the testing software. Programs available for automating the testing process fall into two major categories: static and dynamic testing tools. Dynamic testing tools also generate test data.

QUESTIONS

1. What is a file organization method? How does it differ from a file access method?

2. List and discuss the three most common forms of file organization.

3. For a company in your vicinity, identify at least one file it retains in each type of file organization. Explain why these files are retained in this orientation.

4. Define *file access*. Describe the difference between the two main types of file access methods.

5. For the files in your response to question 3, indicate where they are used in both sequential and random access modes (random access mode is only appropriate for random files). Explain why these files are used in these type access modes.

6. What is meant by *hashing algorithm*? Under which file access method is it used?

7. For the company used in question 3, identify and explain where it uses a hashing algorithm for one of its direct files.

8. Describe what is meant by a synonym and how it may occur.

9. For the example used in question 7, identify and explain where synonyms are present.

10. Why is it necessary to match file organization and access methods to the needs of the user?

11. For the responses to question 5, explain how these examples match the needs of the user, and why.

12. What is testing? Why is it important in the overall system development process?

13. Distinguish between the top-down and bottom-up approaches to testing. Which do you prefer? Why?

14. What is the purpose of program testing? List and discuss the various testing levels.

15. What is the black-box approach to testing? Do you like this approach? Why or why not?

16. For a company in your vicinity, explain where it used the black-box approach to testing for either a newly developed system or a modified system. Explain why this test was determined to be sufficient.

17. What is the white-box approach to testing? How does it differ from the black-box approach?

18. For a company in your vicinity, explain where it used the white-box approach to testing for either a newly developed system or a modified system. Explain why the IS personnel decided to use this approach.

19. Describe path testing. Why is it sometimes impossible to test all paths through a program? Is this a problem?

20. What is system testing? How does it differ from unit and program testing?

21. What is the integration test plan? What are its components?

22. For a company in your vicinity, explain how it used integration within and between systems for a newly developed or modified system.

23. Describe the various types of special system tests.

24. For a company in your vicinity, explain how it used special system tests for a newly developed or modified system.

25. Name and discuss the three aspects of peak load testing.

26. For a company in your vicinity, explain how it set up and performed peak load testing for a newly developed or modified system.

27. How important is user testing to the overall testing process?

28. For a company in your vicinity, explain how it used user testing to test a newly developed or modified system.

29. How is test data used to help determine the accuracy of the system?

30. For a company in your vicinity, explain how and why it used certain types of test data for a newly developed or modified system.

31. Name the two sources of test data. What are the two types of live test data? When would each be used?

32. For a company in your vicinity, explain where and why it used different types of test data to test a newly developed or modified system.

33. Why is the testing process a likely candidate for automation?

34. Name and describe one classification scheme for automatic testing tools.

35. For a company in your vicinity, identify automated testing software systems it uses, how it uses them, and why.

EXERCISES

1. Create a complete set of testing specifications, including creating test data, for the program specifications created in exercise 1 of Chapter 11, using the following guidelines:

    a. Unit testing   b. Program testing   c. System testing

2. Create a complete set of testing specifications, including creating test data, for the program specifications created in exercise 2 of Chapter 11, using the following guidelines:

    a. Unit testing   b. Program testing   c. System testing

3. Create a complete set of testing specifications, including creating test data, for the program specifications created in exercise 3 of Chapter 11, using the following guidelines:

    a. Unit testing   b. Program testing   c. System testing

4. Create a complete set of testing specifications, including test data creation, for the program specifications created in exercise 4 of Chapter 11, using the following guidelines:

    a. Unit testing   b. Program testing   c. System testing

5. For a program in your semester project, create a complete set of testing specifications, including test data creation, using the following guidelines:

    a. Unit testing   b. Program testing   c. System testing

SELECTED REFERENCES

Beizer, B. 1990. *Software Testing Techniques*. New York: Van Nostrand Reinhold.

DeMillo, R. A., W. M. McCracken, R. J. Martin, and J. F. Passafiume. 1987. *Software Testing and Evaluation*. Menlo Park, CA: Benjamin/Cummings Publishing Company.

Hansen, O. 1982. *Design of Computer Data Files*. Rockville, MD: Computer Science Press.

Ould, M. A. and C. Unwin. 1986. *Testing in Software Development*. Cambridge, England: Cambridge University Press.

CHAPTER 13

Training, Implementation, and Formal Review

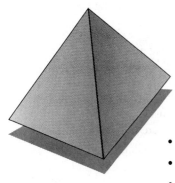

OVERVIEW

The final phase of system development consists of training, implementation, and formal review. After the formal review, the system is turned over to the user. There should be no surprises when this happens; users must feel comfortable with the system from the start. This chapter covers the elements of successful implementation of the new system:

- The purpose and importance of training
- Methods for effective training
- Elements of a training plan
- Procedures for conversion of data, programs, and business practices to the new system
- Methods for changeover to the new system
- Aspects of formal review and user acceptance
- CASE usage in training, implementation, and formal review

KEY TERMS

Acceptance testing

Changeover

Conversion

Crash changeover

Financial accumulations

Formal review

Hash totals

Librarian system

Library

Parallel changeover

Phased changeover

Pilot changeover

Record counts

System balances

Training

Training plan

Utility programs

The main aspects of system implementation—training, conversion, changeover, formal review, and user acceptance—deserve equal emphasis with the early stages of development if you are to implement a system that operates as planned. Unfortunately, many IS departments tend to neglect one or more of these aspects. They are often under considerable pressure to get the system operational. Experience shows that overlooking or minimizing the significance of these factors often leads to serious trouble later. By including the methods discussed here in the final stage of development, the IS department will make the transition from developer to maintainer. (Maintenance is discussed in Chapter 16.)

The implementation of technology, such as an IS, should always be considered a business decision. In recent years, some firms have moved away from centralized technological groups; these firms now employ technology workers within various work groups. Technology specialists work alongside personnel involved with the firm's regular functions. In these firms, conversion, training, and implementation may be occurring throughout the organization. Regardless of whether the organization is centralized or decentralized, training, conversion, and implementation are conducted in similar ways.

TRAINING

Training is a recognized component of the corporate environment. Employees who aspire to higher organizational positions generally perceive training as a prerequisite to advancing in the corporate hierarchy. Training is also a vital element in the success of an information system.

The way in which users operate a system can lead to its success or failure. Poorly trained users are hesitant about using the new system. Managers will not get the information they need to make a timely decision, not because it is not available, but because they have not received proper training. They may feel intimidated by the system or reluctant to show co-workers that they do not know how to use it. Without training, many of the objectives of the new system will never be met. Proper training can be conducted either by system developers or by outside consultants or vendors. Advantages and disadvantages of various types of trainers are discussed later in this chapter.

Although training is normally associated with the latter phases of the system development life cycle, it should take place throughout the life cycle. Figure 13-1 illustrates the position of training in the overall life cycle.

It is incorrect to think that training is conducted only for the use of the hardware and software. Training begins in the problem definition phase, when a user first thinks about what is wrong with the old system and what the new system should do, or when the analyst explains that what the users perceived as a problem was not an actual problem. In the analysis and logical design phases, users get training on the system during prototyping activities or while they evaluate E/RDs or DFDs. In the physical design and implementation phases of the system development life cycle, users learn specifically how the system works and what to do when various situations arise, such as an incorrect attempt to log on to the system or a crash of the system.

Training consists of a sequence of experiences designed to modify behavior.

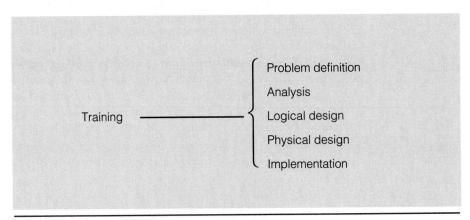

Figure 13-1. Training in the development process

People are trained for one reason: to change their behavior. For example, a shipping/receiving clerk may be accustomed to manually entering a receipt or shipment invoice on a printed form while another clerk stocks the receipt or loads the shipment. With computerization of the receipt or shipment invoice, much less time is required for invoice entry, and a single clerk may be able to enter the invoice as well as stock the receipt or load the shipment. For the new system, users are trained to change from one way of performing a task to another. They need to be trained in the purpose of the system, how the system affects them, how to use it, and how to interpret the results of system execution. Furnishing users with the best possible training on system use makes them comfortable with the new system in the best possible way.

If users thoroughly understand how to use the system, their time will be spent solving problems rather than trying to figure out what command to enter next or what button to push to get the information they need. Adequately trained users should experience no surprises when implementing the new system.

In addition to users, support personnel, such as computer operators, are also trained in system use. These people need training in how to handle errors and emergencies. For example, support personnel need to know how to restart the system if it goes down. They also need to be trained in how to handle routine as well as nonroutine system operations.

Output from the system gives users certain facts that they need to perform their jobs and make decisions that aid the mission of the firm. Well-trained users know how to interpret the output of the IS. They also know what to do regarding what the output means, who needs to be included in their decisions or actions, and what areas of the business may be affected by these decisions or actions.

Training Effectiveness

Many different methods of conducting training exist, but some basic criteria are common to most of them. First, effective training appeals to the senses of hearing, sight, and touch. Within the context of the firm, the training program should meet the following criteria:

- Senior management commitment
- Job relatedness
- Small group size
- Qualified trainers
- Isolation of the training program

If employees know that senior management believes in the system and expects them to operate it properly, they are more likely to apply themselves to the training program. The training program must also show trainees exactly how the task for which they receive training relates to their new job. If they feel that the training relates to someone else and not to them, they tend not to be as receptive to the training program.

A large training room filled with trainees is not a good training environment. Employees like to feel they are receiving individual attention. A class size of ten to fifteen is ideal. The trainer should spend time with each employee on an individual basis. Trainers should understand the material and know how to present it; departmental supervisors or systems analysts from the development project do not make good trainers. Professional trainers should be used. Software and hardware vendors often have people specially trained as instructors. Many companies have separate training departments.

Whenever possible, training should be held off site. If this is not possible, employees should be told to expect to spend the entire time in training, and not to leave early or come late—especially important for managerial training. Day-to-day activities of trainees must not interrupt the training process. This is why top management support is important. Manager trainees are much less likely to leave if they know that their boss supports the program.

Sensory Approach to Training

As previously stated, effective training programs appeal to three senses: hearing, sight, and touch. Figure 13-2 illustrates the sensory approach to training. Trainees need to hear a friendly, unintimidating voice, and need to feel free to ask questions and express concerns without fear of ridicule.

Visual aids reinforce what trainees hear. Some of the more common visual aids are overhead transparencies, computer screen LCD panels (the same as those suggested for interactive JADs), computer screen displays, CD-ROM presentation files, slide presentations, movies, and flip charts or blackboards.

To appeal to the sense of touch, trainees should receive hands-on experience with the system they will be using. Including actual work on the system in an environment similar to the one in the trainee's work environment reinforces training. The execution of the prototype by users (as discussed in Chapter 7) goes a long way toward orienting the user regarding the need for training.

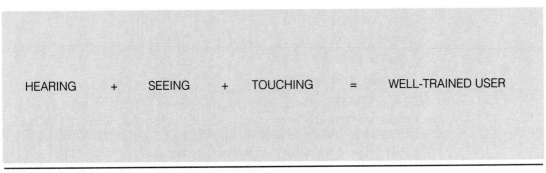

HEARING   +   SEEING   +   TOUCHING   =   WELL-TRAINED USER

Figure 13-2. Sensory approach to training

Training Plan

You train people because you want them to be able to perform required tasks. Who needs training for a new system? The people who have to use the new system, but do not yet know how. The goal is to design appropriate training programs for the people who need them. To design a plan that will train employees to use the system effectively in their job environment, ask yourself these questions:

- What type of training is best suited for training different groups of employees?
- What is the length of the training program?
- How long before implementation should training be performed?
- Do managers at different levels require different types of training? For instance, should the trainer assume that top-level managers already know how to use a desktop computer?

Training becomes a reality via the **training plan**, which is an outline of specific objectives, materials required, methods to be used, schedules, and staffing required.

Specific Objectives of Training

The first step in a training plan is a clear statement of the training objectives. These should be specific objectives that can be measured, not general objectives. Specific objectives must be measurable. Training objectives that are difficult to quantify are probably too general. For example, objectives like "understanding the system" or "learning to use the system" are far too vague. Specific objectives, such as successfully retrieving ten records in five minutes or entering fifteen invoices in thirty minutes, are much better.

A performance test should be applied to determine when training objectives are met. For instance, training should continue until the clerk can handle error-free deletes, adds, and updates.

Training Materials

The training plan specifies in detail the requirements for training materials, documented for each training group and for each major function of the system. The key training material components are the materials used during training sessions, user manuals, and manuals for operations and data control (operator manuals). The training materials are prepared by the trainer or by the consultant conducting the training. The manuals for users and operators are generally prepared by the project team.

After training sessions have been conducted, manuals for users and operations and data control are updated to make them clearer. Though employees may not need to use training manuals extensively right after training, they often forget as time goes by how to use all of the system functions. In addition, new employees often need to learn to use the system without the benefit of a training program.

Part IV: Database Technologies and Developing and Implementing the Project Design

Training Methods

The training plan also identifies specific methods to use in conducting training sessions. These methods include seminars, workshops, computer-aided instruction, and, most important, hands-on usage. The project team selects the most appropriate methods for both the type of user and the system task to perform. Seminars and workshops are used to give the future users, usually managers, an overview of the new system and how it interfaces with other related systems. Computer-aided instruction is used to guide users through the system at their own pace. Finally, hands-on usage is needed for all users.

When deciding on the method of training, the project team should be sensitive to the different needs of different types of employees. It is wise to separate the training of managers and clerical personnel, for example. Workers may feel uneasy and hesitant to ask questions if their boss is in the same session with them. Also, many managers feel awkward with hands-on usage simply because of poor typing skills. As a result, manager training may require keyboard instruction, whereas training for data entry clerks may not.

Staffing

The training plan includes specific staff assignments for conducting training. The schedules for outside trainers must be considered if they are being used. Scheduling for inside trainers is less complicated, but still must be planned, as well as approved by their supervisors.

Different types of training call for different trainers. For example, it is unlikely that the same trainer who conducts the overview seminar or the workshop will also conduct the hands-on session. The types of material being presented are entirely different, and different training skills are needed. The trainer conducting the overall seminar needs a much broader view of the system and how it interfaces with other systems, whereas the hands-on trainer must be technically superior. If outside trainers are used, the project team must be certain that they are adequately briefed on particular aspects of the system, as well as aspects of the business.

Training Schedule

After determining material requirements and methods, the project team member(s) responsible for training makes up a schedule for specific training sessions. A sample schedule of training dates and activities for the mail-order department at National Golf & Tennis (NG&T) is shown in Figure 13-3. Assuming that two five-hour training sessions are appropriate, the sessions are conducted on the two nonworking days, and four one-hour training sessions are conducted each day prior to the week of implementation. For example, on January 23, from 8:00 AM until 1:30 PM, a training session will be conducted for full-time employees on a system overview and an order entry overview. On January 25, part-time employees will undergo the same training. Notice that on January 27, 28, and 29 and February 1, no training is scheduled.

MAIL-ORDER DEPARTMENT

Date	Workday Shift	Training Shift	Training Session
JANUARY			
23	Part-time	Full-time	#1
24	Part-time	Full-time	#2
25	Full-time	Part-time	#1
26	Full-time	Part-time	#2
27	Full-time		
28	Full-time		
29	Full-time		
30	Part-time	Part-time	#3
31	Part-time	Part-time	#4
FEBRUARY			
01	Full-time		
02	Full-time	Full-time	#3
03	Full-time	Full-time	#4
04	Full-time	Full-time	#5
05	Full-time	Full-time	#6
06	Part-time	Part-time	#5
07	Part-time	Part-time	#6
08	IMPLEMENTATION DAY		

****** LEGENDS ******

	Date	Time	Training Topic
Session #1	Jan 23	8:00 AM - 10:00 AM	System Overview
	Jan 25	10:00 AM - 10:30 AM	Recess
		10:30 AM - 1:30 PM	Order Entry
Session #2	Jan 24	8:00 AM - 10:00 AM	Inventory Control
	Jan 26	10:00 AM - 11:00 AM	Shipping
		11:00 AM - 11:30 AM	Recess
		11:30 AM - 1:30 AM	Management Functions
Session #3	Jan 30	7:00 AM - 8:00 AM	Order Entry
	Feb 02	11:00 AM - 12:30 PM	Order Entry
Session #4	Jan 31	7:00 AM - 8:00 AM	Order Entry
	Feb 03	11:00 AM - noon	Order Entry
Session #5	Feb 04	11:00 AM - noon	Inventory Control
	Feb 06	7:00 AM - 8:00 AM	Inventory Control
Session #6	Feb 05	11:00 AM - noon	Inventory Control and Shipping
	Feb 07	7:00 AM - 8:00 AM	

Figure 13-3. National Golf & Tennis training schedule

TRAINING AT NATIONAL GOLF & TENNIS (NG&T)

This section describes the training at NG&T. Decisions on whom to train, what topics to cover, and who is to conduct the training are made in the training plan developed by the project team in consultation with the users. They decide that a description of general training topics, standard for all users, should be covered first. Then more specific training, designed especially for different types of users, is covered. Since this is a small company and revenues are not large, members of the project team will actually conduct the training. Furthermore, John Matsumoto, one of the project members, is placed in charge of training because of his experience as a professional trainer with a large consulting company.

General Topics

General training will give everyone in the organization the same introduction to the system. The information covered ranges from how to operate the hardware to an overview of how data is collected, how it flows through the system, and how it is finally made available to those who need to know. Routine training for all users includes:

- How to operate the hardware
- How to enter, store, and retrieve data
- How the system gathers and distributes information
- How information on error messages is received from the system
- Whom to contact in the event of system malfunctions
- What user and operations documentation manuals are needed

Training for Point-of-Sale (POS) Terminal Users

Training on POS terminals is designed specifically for retail sales clerks who directly use the system to enter customer orders. The main purpose of this training is to get these employees ready to take orders from the customer and to answer questions about the status of a particular order. They are trained in how to enter orders, what data items to enter for the system to accept an order, and what information about customer orders the order-taker can access. Sales personnel also need training in operating the new POS terminals, such as:

- How to enter their user IDs and passwords
- What transactions they may record via their particular sales area menus

- What data is required to record a transaction
- How to use special keyboard keys

In addition to learning how to use the terminals, sales personnel are trained in their security responsibilities and in new policies and procedures for their department.

Administrative Users

The accounting and IS personnel receive more extensive training to prepare them to monitor system control functions, interact with data being processed, and provide reports to management. Administrative personnel need to know overall systems operations; their training includes:

- How to enter their user IDs and passwords
- How to use the master menu and understand each option and its corresponding programs and associated file contents
- How to retrieve information from POS terminals for daily processing
- How to input accounting adjustments and generate accounting reports and financial statements
- How to monitor internal controls such as batch balances
- How to update the item price list table
- How to use the printer
- How to understand and maintain system documentation
- How to perform backup of files
- How to locate and retain data on hard disk, tape, floppy disk, and paper

Practical training is supplemented with a general understanding of common equipment, software malfunctions, resources available to resolve problems, security responsibilities of administrative personnel, and new policies and procedures for system operations and internal controls.

One person has additional training requirements: understanding the security access process and how to retrieve and monitor the weekly security history file. This person assigns and deletes user IDs as personnel change, and limits access to particular data types for personnel assigned these user IDs, data items within those data types, and type of access for that data. These specifications make up the user view for a particular user, as discussed in Chapter 10.

CONVERSION

At the same time as training is taking place, the project team prepares the new system for use by performing conversion activities involving certain aspects of the business and system environment. **Conversion** denotes transferring all data, programs, and procedures from the old system to the new system. Though many IS professionals also use *conversion* to mean the actual operational change from the old system to the new system, this text uses the term *changeover* for that action. The next section of this chapter deals with various types of changeover strategies.

Two common situations exist when converting from an old system to a new system: New computerized methods are replacing manual operations, and new computerized methods are replacing old computerized methods. Table 13-1 depicts the various types of conversion from the standpoints of data, programs, and business practices.

Table 13-1 Types of conversion

NEW COMPUTERIZED METHODS REPLACING MANUAL METHODS

Type of Conversion	Changes Required
Data	Keyboard entry or use of scanners; extensive conversion control required
Programs	Special input and editing routines
Business practices	Extensive employee training; complete replacement of forms and reports

NEW COMPUTERIZED METHODS REPLACING OLD COMPUTERIZED METHODS

Type of Conversion	Changes Required
Data	Some manual conversion required; automated conversion tools are useful; control not as extensive; conversion of file processing data to database data; conversion of old database data to new database data
Programs	Some old programs or modules used (reusable code); documentation of old programs to determine usefulness; language conversion for some code
Business practices	Less extensive training of employees; some old reports and forms may be used

Data Conversion

For the purposes of this discussion, data conversion and file conversion are synonymous. New files should be ready for use before the new system is installed. For instance, if you are changing a payroll system to make it more accurate and up-to-date, payroll data should be converted prior to the first run of the new system.

Data conversion problems are usually not severe when an existing computerized system is replaced with a new computerized system. Programs often exist or can be written to perform this type of conversion automatically.

When you are computerizing a new system to replace an old manual system, the file conversion problems multiply. For example, persons who convert data should take special care to ensure against overlooking or improperly recording data records. Several control methods are available to guarantee proper conversion. These methods include record counts, hash totals, financial accumulations, and comparison of system balances.

Record Counts

Record counts guarantee the entry of all records from the existing system into the new system. A record count might proceed as follows: All of the records are grouped into batches containing 100 records per batch, with each batch numbered. During data entry, the new system counts the number of records entered and compares them with the number in the batch to verify that the totals match. A final check verifies that the total number of records in the new system matches the total number of records that were converted from the old system.

Hash Totals

Hash totals are the sums of various nonmonetary data elements within records. All data values in records are added together and compared with a total accumulated by the old system; discrepancies are noted and corrected. The procedure begins by measuring nonfinancial data to verify its correct entry into the new system. To accomplish this, sums of part numbers, customer telephone numbers, customer credit card numbers, and so on are calculated for each batch of records entered into the system. These hash totals are then compared to the totals calculated by the new system, with no further transfer of data until the two match.

Financial Accumulations

Every data element that has a monetary value associated with it is counted in **financial accumulations**. As you can guess, it is extremely important to ensure correct transfer of these data items. The procedure begins by calculating a financial total for things such as inventory totals, account balances, or order quantities for each batch of records to be converted from the existing system. While records are entered into the new system, financial totals are recalculated by the new system and compared with the manually calculated totals. If the values do not match, the manually calculated totals are recalculated and, if necessary, records are reentered. In addition, a preconversion financial total for all records are compared to the overall total from the new system. If the two totals do not match, conversion terminates until the discrepancy is found and corrected.

System Balances

System balances compare the totals of the two systems at a given point in time. The two systems are often executed concurrently (as discussed in the "Changeover" section of this chapter, below) until analysts and users are satisfied regarding the accuracy of the new system. For example, the total of accounts receivable on the old system is compared to the total of accounts receivable on the new system to verify that the two balances are equal. This procedure begins by manually calculating system balances at the end of a month of operation of the old system and comparing them to the totals generated by the new system in the same period. If discrepancies are found, revisions are made either to the new system or to procedures used by it, to ensure agreement between the balances of the two systems.

Conversion Strategy

In summary, the project team must use appropriate measures to ensure correct transference of all data and files. Verifying the accuracy of both financial and nonfinancial data is an essential step in the conversion process. Table 13-2 gives an example of a file conversion strategy. When this is carried out correctly, the problems associated with the implementation of the new system are minimized.

Table 13-2 File conversion strategy	
Files Used by Existing System to Be Converted	**Files Used by New System to Be Created**
House account file	Retail house account file
UPS file	Mail-order status file
Customer mailing list	Retail and mail-order files
Inventory file	Inventory file, retail transaction file, mail-order transactions, and mail-order reports

Program Conversion

Converting from a manual system to a computerized system requires little program conversion; however, most conversions move from one computerized system to another, such as switching from a host computer environment to desktop computers. When the new system requires few new programs, conversion typically takes the form of converting certain modules within programs rather than converting an entire program.

For example, assume that NG&T replaces its batch-oriented inventory system with a new on-line system. Many of the formulas used to calculate the value of ending inventory, cost of goods sold, work in process, raw material inventories, and so forth, remain the same. These portions of old programs can be converted to the new system.

Two alternatives exist for converting programs from the old system into the required format for the new system: let programmers do it, or buy software that performs the conversion. When a large number of virtually identical programs exist in the new and old systems, software may be available that can automate conversion of programs in other languages, such as converting COBOL into visual basic or object-oriented COBOL. These conversion software systems are particularly useful for converting a system to work with different hardware components. Because of the expense of these conversion systems, it is a good idea to perform a cost/benefit analysis to determine the most economical alternative. The cost of having the programs converted by programmers must be weighed against the purchase price of the conversion software. Two factors to consider are any training that might be required on the conversion system and the availability of the programmers.

There are also a number of software systems for converting older "spaghetti" code into a structured program form. These systems operate on programs in different languages; however, most convert unstructured COBOL programs into structured versions. Many vendors of computer-aided software engineering packages have structured programming conversion routines as part of the utility programs that support their CASE tools.

A final consideration in program conversion is the quality of existing program documentation. For programs not written in structured code, or those that do not have accompanying documentation, a complete reprogramming is often less costly and less time-consuming than trying to salvage existing poorly created programs. This often happens while working with older systems not designed or maintained using a structured methodology.

Business Practices Conversion

Two main aspects of business practices conversion are (1) getting employees used to the new system and (2) converting old forms and reports into new ones. Though neither of these conversions is particularly complex individually, together they embody a sizable project.

People Conversion (Overcoming Resistance to Change)

People have a natural resistance to change; they often surround themselves with familiar objects, practices, and habits to combat the stresses associated with change. By understanding that change fosters anxiety, and the loss of productive time associated with it, trainers can incorporate techniques into the conversion process that diminish problems associated with change.

Employees' acceptance of and familiarity with the system are the measures of its success. When an old system is replaced with a new one, tasks usually change, co-workers may change, and employees must use new procedures and follow new guidelines. Careful handling of these conversions can prevent resistance to implementing and using the new system.

Providing an adequate training program constitutes the most effective way to ensure employee cooperation. There should be no surprises when implementation time arrives. Employees should know exactly what to expect from the system as it relates to their job functions. Management bears an equal responsibility with the project team in getting employees acquainted with the new system. Management must emphasize the importance of the new system's working properly and the obligation of each employee to see that it does. The proper working of the system is accomplished by adequate training and user involvement throughout the various phases of the system life cycle.

People conversion (like training) is not just one project, but multiple ongoing projects during the course of the analysis and design process, as illustrated in Figure 13-1. Training and user involvement throughout the analysis and design process removes most surprises when the system is implemented.

Form and Report Conversion

Form conversion entails making sure the new forms are available when the new system is installed. IS personnel and managers must make sure that all required forms are sent to the print shop or ordered in time to be ready for the new system installation. Nothing frustrates users more than to have a new system ready to go, but not really usable because of delays in printing new forms. Typically, the project team does not directly order the new forms but must oversee the ordering process and occasionally check on their status.

Since most report formats should already have been designed, conversion is a relatively simple matter of checking that new reports are distributed to the proper personnel on time. Report routing usually changes from the routing used in the old system, and everyone should be notified of new timetables and reports to be distributed. For properly trained personnel, report routing is not a major problem.

All new forms and reports are presented and discussed in training sessions before the system is implemented. Clerical and managerial personnel are given practice in filling out the new forms. Reports are generated, distributed, and discussed by all personnel who will receive them. In this, as in other implementation procedures, the goal is to have as few surprises as possible when the system becomes operational.

Reusable Code

The conversion process is greatly accelerated if existing code is used in new systems for either the same or similar sets of actions. The term *reusable code* refers to the practice of incorporating existing code into either a new application or a modification of an application. In Chapter 6, we stated that reusable code is computer code that does not change over time or in use from application to application. The same reusable code typically appears in many application systems that need to perform those same program actions.

Reusable Code Within Programs

Reusable code comes either in the form of a program module to insert into an application or as a completely separate and executable module to execute between different programs of an application. For example, many IS departments have used the same program module to convert Julian dates to calendar dates for programs needing to perform that action. Either reusable code is physically inserted in the correct position and becomes part of the application program, or it is a standalone module called by the executing program.

For a standalone module, the programmer enters a call statement in the application's language that calls on the reusable module to execute at the appropriate point. Figure 13-4 illustrates a COBOL program using an internal call to an external executable module.

Reusable Code as a Standalone Utility Between Programs

Many IS departments create or purchase programming routines, called **utility programs** (or modules), that execute between different programs within an application. Hardware and software vendors sell these utility programs for common processing routines. External sort programs are one type of utility program. They execute as part of a system prior to executing application programs that process the sorted data. The sort routines rearrange the data into a sequential order that is expected by the application programs. For example, transaction files, which are created as business transactions occur, often need to be sorted before they are used to update a master file.

Figure 13-5 illustrates how operating system commands developed for an IBM mainframe computer environment call on a sort program between application programs. The first program called on in STEP1 of this stream of JCL (Job Control Language) is an on-line program used by a shipping clerk to fill a customer order. The transaction records created as a result of filling orders are then passed to a sort program (STEP2 in the job stream), which sequences those records in the correct order to pass them to the third program called on in STEP3: the master file update program.

In Figure 13-5, the first step in the job stream executes the order-filling program using unsorted customer order records (/F1) as input and creating unsorted order-fill-

```
PROCEDURE DIVISION.
CONTROL-ROUTINE.
        PERFORM . . . .
        PERFORM PROCESSING-ROUTINE.
          .
          .
          .
        PERFORM . . . .
        EXIT.


PROCESSING-ROUTINE.

    MOVE . . . .
      .
      .
      .
    CALL JUL-CAL-CONVERSION . . . .
      .
      .
      .

    **********  END OF INTERNAL CALLING PROGRAM   **********
```

Figure 13-4. Calling on a reusable module within a program

ing records as output (/F2). In STEP2, the sort program utility executes, using the unsorted order-filling records as input (/F2), and creates a sorted order file (/F3). In STEP3, the master file update program executes, using the sorted order file (/F3) and the old master file (/F4) as input, and creates an updated version of the master file (/F5) as output. This job stream illustrates a batch program execution that updates a sequential access master file.

BENEFITS OF REUSABLE CODE   One of the benefits of reusable code is an increase in programmer productivity. When reusable code exists, programmers can focus on the more specialized code of the application. Also, existing code reused within a program need not be tested as rigorously as new code developed for the application. The reusable code should have already undergone rigorous testing procedures when it was first created and placed in the program library.

```
//...          JOB ...
/STEP1         EXEC PGM=FILORDR ...        Order filling program
/F1            FILE ...                    Unsorted customer orders
/F2            FILE ...                    Filled order file
/STEP2         EXEC PROC=SORTD             Sort program
/F2            FILE ...                    Filled order file
/F3            FILE ...                    Sorted filled order file
/STEP3         EXEC PGM=UPDTMAST ...       Master file update program
/F3            FILE ...                    Sorted filled order file
/F4            FILE ...                    Old master file
/F5            FILE ...                    New master file
```

Figure 13-5. Reusable code between application programs

Employing reusable code also cuts down on creating the same routine over and over. Novice programmers might rewrite the same routines many times in different programs before they realize they can reuse the code.

Reusable code contributes to creating programs in a standard format. When a routine is appropriate in many different circumstances, creating that routine once, and then reusing it, encourages program standardization.

A final benefit of reusable code is a reduction in the amount of storage required for the company's programs. When the same code is used in several applications, the source and/or executable code for that routine need only be stored once in the company's library.

Program Libraries

Utility programs are usually stored in an executable form in a central location called a **library**. The library is also used to store the company's application programs. IS departments almost always have a complete system, called a **librarian system**, to manage application programs and utility libraries. A librarian system manages libraries of both source and executable programs.

CHANGEOVER

After the conversions required for the new system are completed, the changeover process begins. **Changeover** consists of replacing the existing system with the new system. It may be gradual or all at once; users make the final decision as to which changeover process to use. However, the project team must make the users aware of their options and the strengths and weaknesses of each. Changeover strategies include crash, pilot, phased, and parallel.

Crash Changeover

Crash changeover is the "out with the old, in with the new" philosophy. Employees may leave on Friday afternoon after working on the old system and return Monday morning to an entirely new system. At no time are both the old system and the new system working together.

This method of changeover forces users and IS professionals to make the system work immediately because the old system is not available to fall back on. In effect, applications cannot be run until the new system works. The IS department must do a thorough job of planning and testing before turning the system over to the user—the main advantage of this type of changeover.

Many companies and analysts minimize the use of crash changeover because of its risks. However, in some situations, this method of changeover is appropriate. Small applications and applications being computerized for the first time are good examples. Also, applications not critical to a firm's overall success are likely candidates. For example, a firm that has traditionally processed its own health insurance claims manually for its employees might consider a crash changeover to computerized claim processing.

Pilot Changeover

A **pilot changeover** produces a working version of the system that is installed in only part of the organization. This changeover method is often used for applications that are new to the firm. For instance, an IS department may not have previous experience with this type of system. Since it is new, they may not know what to expect or whether it will work correctly from the start. In this case, they install the system, evaluate it for errors, and then redesign it before implementing it in the remainder of the firm.

Installing automatic teller machines (ATMs) is a good example of an appropriate application for pilot conversion. A bank that plans to install fifty ATMs around the city may install one or two initially, evaluate problems that occur, and make needed changes in the design before installing the rest of the ATMs.

After completing the pilot study, the changeover proceeds with one of the other three changeover methods discussed here. One important point to note is that the pilot method deals with an entire system, not just one part of a system. The entire system is installed in a pilot area of the firm; it is not a trial (pilot) system installed throughout the firm. An advantage of starting with a pilot area of the business is that personnel who participate in the pilot changeover can aid personnel in other areas when the system is implemented.

Phased Changeover

Whereas the pilot method involves evaluating an entire system, **phased changeover** means changing over to parts of the system at various times. This particular method is appropriate for very large applications that are simply too big and complex to install all at once. A phased changeover is a good choice when a company designs an entirely new system, such as an accounting system that includes various subsystems such as payroll, accounts receivable, accounts payable, and inventory control. Instead of installing all these subsystems at one time, the company might elect to bring them on line one at a time. Payroll might be the first, followed by accounts receivable, accounts payable, and inventory.

There is nothing magical about the phased order. The actual order is determined by the needs of the business. If management views accounts receivable as the highest-priority application, it is implemented first. The important point is that phased changeover involves the gradual implementation of parts of a much larger system over an extended period of time.

The main advantage of the phased changeover strategy is that users do not have to wait until the entire system is finished to use a portion of it. Thus, a key application such as accounts receivable can be implemented before completing the payroll application. In addition, the system is checked in phases for the correctness and suitability of its use.

Implementing only a portion of a system is dangerous unless adequate precautions are taken. Interfaces that must exist between one subsystem and others can be overlooked when a subsystem such as accounts receivable is designed by itself. Accounts receivable must interface with sales, billing, purchasing, collections, and many more applications. Analysts must consider these interfaces, or the accounts receivable subsystem will not function properly. How, then, can a subsystem be implemented without the entire system being completely designed? The answer lies in the structured design methodology described earlier in this text.

Using a structured methodology to thoroughly design user requirements in the early stages of the process helps pinpoint important interfaces. Furthermore, describing the entire system from a top-down vantage point, using graphic modeling methods such as data flow diagrams or process dependency diagrams and structure charts, provides a comprehensive, systematic view of the system. A top-down approach identifies interfaces early in analysis and design and initiates the work needed to integrate them into subsystem design.

Parallel Changeover

The safest changeover method, **parallel changeover**, runs both the existing system and the new system side by side. Since two systems are available, one acts as a backup to the other and as a benchmark for comparison of how well they function. If the new system fails, the existing system remains in place to take over processing.

Parallel changeover is typically the choice for applications considered critical to the firm's success. Applications involving cash flow, such as accounts receivable and accounts payable, are often candidates for parallel changeover. The firm cannot allow applications like these to be down for any period of time. Since the existing system and the new system both execute, this method provides the highest form of system validation. Results of complete system executions can be compared before completing the changeover.

Parallel changeover has its disadvantages. First, it is the most expensive changeover method. It may require additional personnel. Executing systems side by side is time-consuming and costly, and IS departments do not always have the staff and facilities to concurrently execute both systems. Finally, users often resist running two systems concurrently. This is understandable when you consider that employees expect the new system to make their jobs easier. Imagine their surprise when they have to operate not only the new system, but the old one as well. Fortunately, the analyst may overcome this resistance by keeping employees involved in the design process, keeping them informed about the new system, and assuring them that parallel execution will only last a short time.

Deciding on a Changeover Strategy

In summary, one of the four changeover methods is used in most system development projects. However, more than one of the changeover methods may be used in a very large project. Part of the project may use parallel conversion, another part a pilot test, and still another a crash changeover. None of the changeover strategies is necessarily superior to the others. It all depends on the particular situation and the needs of users. Figure 13-6 illustrates the four types of changeovers.

FORMAL ACCEPTANCE

During **formal review**—often called **acceptance testing**—users perform the final tests on the system before agreeing that it meets their requirements and can be turned over to them. Two points of view exist in formal review and acceptance: the user's point of view and the IS department's point of view.

User Point of View

Formal acceptance is the time to make sure the system runs as expected and is free of errors. Users may wish to run some of their own data through the system to ensure that it produces expected results. Before formal acceptance, users will want to:

- Confirm that they understand the purpose of the system

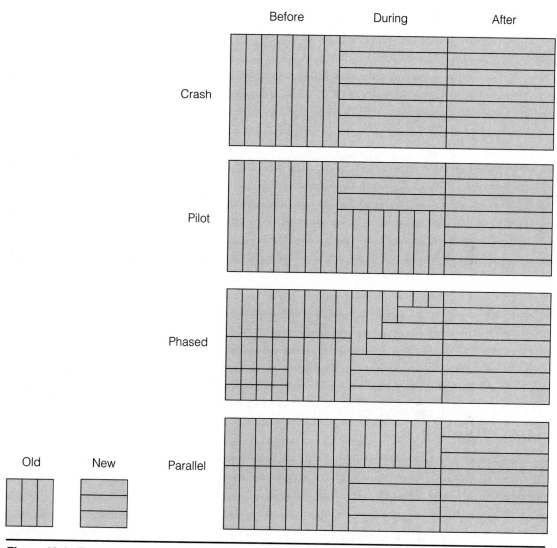

Figure 13-6. Types of changeovers

- Confirm that the system runs correctly
- Confirm the usability of the documentation
- Confirm that they understand how to direct system execution and provide input to the system
- Confirm that they understand the system output—what it is and what it means

- Identify those responsible for system maintenance
- Understand that changes not accounted for in the original requirements constitute additional costs that the company may bear

Confirming the usability of documentation means determining that instructions are clear and detailed enough. Has the documentation been updated to represent any late changes made in the system? Is the documentation understandable? Finally, are appropriate procedures for backup, requests for change, and report distribution clearly defined?

Personnel who will perform future maintenance on this system should be identified at this time. Users often prefer someone from the development project—someone they already know and trust. Chapter 16 discusses this topic more fully.

Finally, users need to know that following system sign-off, additional changes or training may be considered as extra costs for the project. Therefore, they should determine that all necessary training has been completed and that they feel comfortable with the new system. Upon resolving these concerns, users are ready to accept the system. Figure 13-7 is a sample checklist that could be used to perform a final test of the system.

Administrative Data

Application/module: _____

Date/time of test: _____

User in charge: _____

Staff in charge: _____

Technical Data

Resource Needed	Location	Availability
1. Test transaction	_____	_____
2. Master files/database	_____	_____
3. Operator instruction	_____	_____
4. Special media/forms	_____	_____
5. Acceptance criteria	_____	_____
6. Input support personnel	_____	_____
7. Output support personnel	_____	_____
8. Backup/recovery plan	_____	_____
9. Security plan	_____	_____
10. Error message actions	_____	_____

Figure 13-7. User acceptance test checklist

Information Systems
Department Point of View

The users' formal acceptance relieves the IS department of certain responsibilities. It marks the end of many months, sometimes years, of work on the part of the IS department. They generally feel relief, but expect to see the system again. Ensuring that the system performs according to user expectations benefits the IS department immensely. Figure 13-8 provides an example of an IS department's installation checklist; not all items are appropriate for all companies. Each company should have its own checklist that more appropriately lists the hardware and software it might use. Even after completing a checklist as extensive as the one in Figure 13-8, users should expect system changes to be needed in a dynamic business environment—changes that require system maintenance.

COMPUTER-AIDED SUPPORT FOR SYSTEM IMPLEMENTATION

CASE has already become important in providing support for system implementation. It allows for better management of the system through the repository. The formal review of the system is aided by having documentation for both the business model and the system model stored on-line.

Repository Support

The main portion of the CASE environment that supports system implementation is the repository. Recall from Chapter 2 that the repository stores the different CASE-created specifications for the system. By centrally storing specifications for various systems, the repository helps integrate those applications with other applications. The repository is also a central storehouse for reusable code, existing job streams, user access to data, and different data needed by all the various systems.

Repositories also manage the different versions of project specifications and executable applications. Version control, wherein IS departments maintain different generations of both data and programs, has been practiced for over twenty years. The repository helps manage the different versions of programs by maintaining the specifications for them. This also helps to keep different versions of the business model in synchronization with the correct version of the system.

The repository also facilitates creating a single set of specifications for systems that may need to execute in different computing environments. Some CASE reposito-

INSTALLATION CHECKLIST

I. Hardware

  A. Electrical Outlets

    1. Desktop Computers

      a. Sales Manager's Office   ____

      b. Data Entry Area (five outlets)   ____

      c. Stockroom   ____

      d. Dock   ____

      e. Retail Store Manager's Office   ____

      f. Executive Conference Room (nine outlets)   ____

    2. Point-of-Sale (POS) Terminals

      a. Retail Store Sales Desk   ____

      b. Executive Conference Room   ____

    3. Printers

      a. Sales Manager's Office   ____

      b. Stockroom   ____

      c. Dock   ____

      d. Retail Store Manager's Office   ____

      e. Retail Store Sales Desk   ____

      f. Executive Conference Room (five outlets)   ____

  B. Cabling and Connectors for LAN

    1. Sales Manager's Office   ____

    2. Data Entry Area (five connections)   ____

    3. Stockroom   ____

    4. Dock   ____

    5. Retail Store Manager's Office   ____

    6. Retail Store Sales Desk   ____

    7. Executive Conference Room (ten connections)   ____

  C. Supplies

    1. Backup Diskettes (two) — Mail-Order System   ____

Figure 13-8. Installation checklist

2. Backup Diskettes (two) — Retail System   ____

3. Folios to Hold Diskettes (four)   ____

4. Printer Ribbons

    a. Four High-Speed Printers   ____

    b. One Receipt Printer   ____

5. Printer Paper

    a. Computer Paper   ____

    b. Receipt Paper   ____

    c. Multipart Carbonless Paper   ____

6. Binders

    a. Manuals   ____

    b. Reports   ____

D. Planning Forms

    1. CORE System Installation Planning Chart   ____

    2. Local Area Network Diagram   ____

E. Workstation Device Installation

    1. Mail-Order System

        a. Desktop Computers

            1. Sales Manager's Office   ____

            2. Data Entry Desk 1   ____

            3. Data Entry Desk 2   ____

            4. Data Entry Desk 3   ____

            5. Stockroom   ____

            6. Dock   ____

F. Systems Software

    1. MS-DOS   ____

    2. Windows   ____

    3. XENIX   ____

    4. Windows/NT   ____

    5. OS/2   ____

    6. Novell Network   ____

Figure 13-8. Installation checklist *(continued)*

G. Systems Security

    1. Passwords _____

    2. Menu Security _____

    3. List Security File _____

    4. Backup Security File _____

II. Software

A. Mail-Order System

    1. Signed Copy of Contract _____

    2. Create System Subdirectories _____

    3. Load Mail-Order System _____

    4. Load Test Files _____

    5. Build Master Files

        a. Mail-Order Status File _____

        b. Mail-Order Customer File _____

        c. Mail-Order Inventory File _____

        d. Mail-Order Transaction File _____

        e. Mail-Order Inquiry File _____

        f. Mail-Order Report Detail File _____

        g. Box Dimensions File _____

        h. System File _____

    6. Convert Existing Files

        a. House Account File _____

        b. UPS File _____

        c. Customer Mailing List File _____

        d. Inventory File _____

        e. Other: _____ _____

    7. Reconcile Converted File Information

        a. Check Error Report _____

        b. Correct Identified Errors _____

        c. Signed File Conversion Acceptance Form _____

Figure 13-8. Installation checklist *(continued)*

8. Train Personnel

    a. Full-Time Employees

        1. Manager   ____

        2. Supervisors   ____

        3. Bookkeeper   ____

        4. Accounting Clerks   ____

        5. Data Entry Operators   ____

        6. Inventory Clerks   ____

        7. Shipping Clerks   ____

    b. Part-Time Employees

        1. Accounting Clerks   ____

        2. Data Entry Operators   ____

        3. Inventory Clerks   ____

        4. Shipping Clerks   ____

9. Begin Normal Operations

    a. Update Files   ____

    b. Generate Invoices   ____

    c. Generate Pull Sheets   ____

    d. Generate Bills of Lading   ____

    e. Process Inquiries   ____

    f. Prepare Reports   ____

B. Retail System

    1. Signed Copy of Contract   ____

    2. Create System Subdirectories   ____

    3. Load Retail System   ____

    4. Load Test Files   ____

    5. Build Master Files

        a. Retail House Account File   ____

        b. Retail Store Customer File   ____

        c. Retail Store Inventory File   ____

        d. Retail Transaction File   ____

Figure 13-8. Installation checklist *(continued)*

6. Convert Existing Files
   a. House Account File   ____
   b. Customer Mailing List File   ____
   c. Other: _____   ____
7. Reconcile Converted File Information
   a. Check Error Report   ____
   b. Correct Identified Errors   ____
   c. Signed File Conversion Acceptance Form   ____
8. Train Personnel
   a. Full-Time Employees
      1. Manager   ____
      2. Bookkeeper   ____
      3. Accounting Clerks   ____
      4. Salesclerks   ____
   b. Part-Time Employees
      1. Accounting Clerks   ____
      2. Salesclerks   ____
9. Begin Normal Operations
   a. Update Files   ____
   b. Generate Customer Receipts   ____
   c. Prepare Reports   ____

Figure 13-8. Installation checklist *(continued)*

ries can take a set of system specifications on how to process data and generate different versions of the application to execute on different computing platforms. These repositories generate different sets of operating system commands, communication system commands, and database management system commands, and then modify the system specifications to generate an application to use those commands.

Conversion and Changeover Support Through the Repository

CASE systems can be used to convert documentation, data files, and programs. Businesses maintain a great deal of documentation, stored in many locations and in many forms, about how they operate and how systems support their operations. Utility routines in CASE systems help centralize existing documentation and convert it into a more standardized format.

CASE systems also help convert existing programs into a form consistent with the one the system uses to document project specifications. They help convert programs into different languages used by different computing environments, and they can be used to convert existing batch programs into a format consistent with on-line program execution. For example, many companies use CASE systems to generate a graphical user interface (GUI) that accepts responses and data from users and uses those responses and data within calls to existing executable batch programs. The program generated along with the GUI will typically include a call routine to call on the programs from the existing system. In this way, CASE helps extend the usable life span of some existing systems.

Since users have seen many of the capabilities of the system and how they can interact with it during project prototyping activities, their knowledge and acceptance of the system are strengthened. By using CASE systems during prototyping, both simulated applications and standalone prototypes can be created that simulate actual execution. During these sessions, users work with prototype screens and reports, which give them an opportunity to make sure that system design is progressing toward satisfying their information needs.

Although CASE systems do not help with the selection of a changeover method or the actual changeover, their contribution to well-designed systems and documentation helps increase confidence in new systems. As confidence in a new system rises, personnel may feel more confident about using the crash changeover method or shortening a parallel changeover. This saves resources used in the changeover process, since the firm changes to the new system more quickly. Furthermore, by completely switching to the new system sooner, users can experience the benefits of a new system's greater capabilities more rapidly.

Computer-Aided Software Engineering and Formal Review

The formal review is one of the areas in which CASE shines. By having the design and development documentation for both the business model and the information system stored on-line, CASE systems make it easier to direct system development, check system completeness, and see how the system operates. Users who participate in the formal review can evaluate more than just the IS to determine a project's success. For example, they can review data objects identified in E/RDs, business processes in DFDs that use those same objects, and prototype user interfaces to display those objects. A thorough review is likely to provide additional design specifications needed to verify that the system satisfactorily supports business operations.

Joint application development (JAD) or JAD-like sessions may be used in the formal review to show a set of related design specifications and the portion of an executing system supporting them. Using enlarged computer displays, users may simultaneously view design specifications while viewing system execution on another portion of the same display.

Furthermore, the CASE repository management system can be directed in the JAD-like sessions to display specifications from the new system in combination with specifications from existing systems already familiar to the user. Thus, users learn the details of the new system while judging it on the basis of benchmarks from existing systems. This capability gives the user a more comprehensive view of the organization and of the systems serving it.

CASE systems also help eliminate redundancy and inconsistencies in application specifications. By eliminating these problems prior to review, they allow users to concentrate on those areas of the new system that need more of their attention. CASE systems help locate inconsistencies in the functional business model and in the information system, thus helping to make sure that they remain in synchronization.

A major problem in information systems has always been that existing systems eventually become inconsistent with current operations of the business. Most systems are created over a long period of time. What is hard-coded in many systems serves a business of a previous era, not the business that exists today. By using CASE systems, users and project team members can more readily verify that the functional business model, the information systems model, and the system execution are aligned. Therefore, users can feel confident that the newly completed system does in fact serve the needs of the current business.

REVIEW

The importance of training to the acceptance of a new system cannot be overemphasized. At this stage of the system life cycle, even though some training has been conducted during development, the project team must develop a specific plan for training different types of employees. Users must feel comfortable with the new system in order to use it effectively.

Successful training programs incorporate senior management commitment, job relatedness, small group size, qualified trainers, and isolation of the training program. In addition, they emphasize the three senses of hearing, sight, and touch. Hands-on experience is a particularly useful training method in computer-based systems.

A training plan outlines the objectives of training, which should be specific and measurable. The plan specifies the materials required, the appropriate method to use (seminars, hands-on usage, and so forth), the training schedule, and the staffing required.

Training prepares users for system conversion and changeover. Conversion transforms data, programs, and procedures from the old system to the new system. In data conversion, record counts, hash totals, financial accumulations, and system balances are methods that help ensure proper data conversion.

Changeover is the actual replacement of the old system with the new one. One or a combination of the crash, pilot, phased, and parallel changeover methods may be used for any system changeover.

Finally, formal acceptance involves signing over the new system to the users. Users need to make sure that the system performs as promised and includes proper documentation. After formal acceptance, an IS department is usually happy to be finished with the project. However, they should expect to see the system again in the maintenance phase of the system life cycle.

QUESTIONS

1. Why is training necessary? What is the purpose of training?
2. Explain the most important aspects of effective training programs.
3. For a company in your vicinity, obtain a copy of its training program for some of its applications. Explain aspects of this training program.
4. What senses are most important in training? Explain how each relates to an effective training program.
5. Why is a training plan important? List and discuss the components of an effective training plan.
6. Define *conversion*. What importance does conversion play in the overall system life cycle?
7. For a company in your vicinity, explain the conversion it performed for one of its system projects, including data and program conversion.
8. Describe the process of data conversion.
9. List and discuss four methods used to ensure the accuracy of the data conversion process. Give an example of each for the company in question 7.
10. What is program conversion? Describe the options available in designing programs for the new system. Explain one of the program conversions for the company in question 7.
11. Describe the two aspects of procedure conversion. In your opinion, which is the more important? Why?
12. What is changeover? How does it differ from conversion?
13. Describe the four strategies available for system changeover. When would you use each?
14. For a company in your vicinity, describe how it used each changeover method for one or more of its projects.
15. What is meant by formal acceptance?
16. For a company in your vicinity, obtain a copy of formal acceptance documentation for one of its projects.

17. Describe similarities and differences between the user's and the IS department's views of formal acceptance.

18. Why is the user point of view so different from the information system view? Can the differences be reconciled?

19. Explain how CASE could be used to facilitate training, conversion, and formal review at NG&T.

EXERCISES

1. Expand the NG&T training plan in Figure 13-3 to include training in any additional I/O created for exercises completed in Chapters 6, 8, 9, and 10. (Remember that end-users need to understand the purposes of procedures and what they do for them, not their inner workings.)

2. Create a conversion plan for NG&T that uses and expands on the conversion guidelines indicated in Table 13-1.

3. Create separate changeover plans for NG&T for the types of changeover listed below and thoroughly explain how appropriate each plan would be for the NG&T case. (You may choose to create different changeover plans for different portions of the NG&T project.)

    a. Direct or crash

    b. Pilot

    c. Phased

    d. Parallel

4. Create a plan and script for the formal review session for NG&T that indicates the format of the session, who should attend, how the session should be conducted, what should be included, the order of review, what results should be expected, and what should be done as follow-up.

5. For your class project, create and conduct a JAD-like review session that uses overhead and computer displays to review various aspects of your business model, system model, and system execution. Conduct the session with the users from your project. Prepare and use a formal sign-off document to obtain confirmation of your project's completion. Your presentation should display a portion of your E/RDs, DFDs, STCs, and system execution. It should also illustrate LDSs depicted on E/RDs, DFDs, and STCs, and LDSs displayed on user interface screens. Finally, it should illustrate the way the executing system implements procedure models and supports the business data and process models.

PART V

Justifying and Managing Analysis and Design Projects

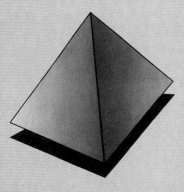

The activities covered in Part V, justifying and managing the project, are performed throughout the project life cycle. A project must be justified before it is started as well as at various points in its development. Proper management of the project is necessary throughout its life cycle. These topics are placed at this point of the textbook to keep from interrupting the natural flow of project design. They are also placed here in the belief that only after understanding the analysis and design activities that lead to developing a system can a new analyst understand the importance of justifying and managing the project.

These chapters could be read at the beginning of project analysis and design and referred to many times throughout the system development life cycle, as it is described in the first thirteen chapters of this text.

CHAPTER 14

Justifying the Project

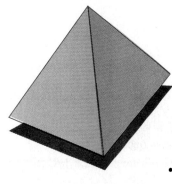

OVERVIEW

After collecting and analyzing data, the analyst defines user requirements and proposes various solutions to meet them. Before a project begins, the analyst must justify the project; that is, he or she must show that the benefits to be derived from the new system outweigh the costs of completing it. The analyst then evaluates each alternative to determine its feasibility and selects the best one to implement. This chapter provides the groundwork for justifying the project by describing:

- Areas of feasibility
- Classifications of costs and benefits
- Categories of costs and benefits within the classifications
- Various methods for performing cost/benefit analysis
- Influence of the real value of money
- Criteria for cost/benefit analysis
- Computer-aided cost estimation procedures
- An example of cost justification at NG&T

KEY TERMS

Break-even analysis
Cost/benefit analysis
Economic criteria
Efficiency criteria
Financial criteria
Direct cost or benefit
Fixed cost or benefit
Function point
Future value
Indirect cost or benefit
Intangible cost or benefit

Interest
Legal feasibility
Net present value
Pay-back analysis
Performance criteria
Present value
Tangible cost or benefit
Technical feasibility
Timing feasibility
Variable cost or benefit

Project feasibility should be considered from the beginning to the end of an analysis and design project. In Chapter 3 we discussed the preliminary feasibility study, which is conducted before the analysis and design project begins. Although feasibility (covered here) and project management (the subject of Chapter 15) should both be considered early in a project, they are discussed at this point in the text because of the need for continuity in the coverage of material in Chapters 1 through 13. With a thorough knowledge of project activities, you will better understand the importance of these subjects.

This chapter identifies and discusses the types of costs and benefits associated with system solutions; special attention is given to economic justification of the project. Methods are presented that allow you to evaluate alternatives and recommend optimal solutions to user requirements.

MAJOR AREAS OF FEASIBILITY

The feasibility of a project is determined in order to decide whether or not an organization should undertake that particular project. There are some obvious, and some not so obvious, factors to consider when determining feasibility. Six major areas that should be addressed before a project is approved are:

- Operational feasibility
- Timing feasibility
- Technical feasibility
- Legal feasibility
- Organizational feasibility
- Economic feasibility

Operational Feasibility

Operational feasibility is affected by organizational practices, employee skills, technology used, or any combination of these influences on operations. As defined in Chapter 3, it mainly concerns whether the current organizational operating environment is capable of supporting the new system. Particular operational practices may be inconsistent with the activities needed by the information system to be produced by the A&D project; they may, therefore, cause problems during the project. For example, developing an on-line application to support shipping and receiving may be unnecessary and unwanted because knowledge of up-to-date inventory does not change functional decisions.

Employee skills may influence operations and system development. For example, a preponderance of employees without computer skills may render a project infeasible that depends on having computer-capable personnel.

The use of particular technologies may influence the feasibility of an A&D project. For example, proposing an on-line, real-time system to a company that still runs mostly batch jobs may not be realistic without a major investment in equipment, software, and personnel training.

Timing Feasibility

Timing feasibility encompasses two main elements: the correct time to do what the project requires and the ability to complete the project in a timely manner. The analyst must determine whether the current time period is appropriate to introduce a new system in the firm. For example, will this new system help contribute to the firm's overall goals in a timely manner? Second, is it possible to implement the system in the time frame desired by the user?

The user may feel that if the system cannot be made operational within six months, other alternatives should be considered. If examination reveals that system implementation requires a minimum of twelve months, the proposed system is not feasible from the standpoint of timing.

Technical Feasibility

Existing project team expertise and available technology should be assessed to determine **technical feasibility**. Is the proposed system practical in relation to acquiring the necessary staff and technology? If technical expertise and capability are not available within the company, the analyst determines whether the firm can acquire the expertise and technology, and whether it is cost-efficient to do so, in order to complete an important project.

Legal Feasibility

A great many laws govern business, and a variety of reports must be produced to satisfy various governmental agencies. Examples of laws affecting business are those concerning privacy rights of employees and income tax rates; reports range from environmental impact statements to employment of disabled people. The **legal feasibility** of a project is determined by evaluating current and proposed legislation at the local, state, and national levels and deciding whether the proposed system is flexible enough to handle current and anticipated legal requirements.

Organizational Feasibility

Organizational factors [handwritten margin note]

As we explained in Chapter 3, the way the new system fits within the firm's existing environment determines organizational feasibility. Does the system have management support at all levels, or will some level of management try to undermine the new system? Implementing a new information system always requires change. Not all parties necessarily support these changes. Social and political factors are also important in assessing organizational feasibility. Employees' job descriptions, their work hours, or even the departments in which they work may change. All these factors must be considered when a particular type of system is recommended. Keeping employees informed about the changes that will take place is the best way to minimize disruption within the organization.

Organizational feasibility is assessed in five areas that can affect the success of the introduction of any change in the organization, whether it is a change in technology, in business practices, or in some other aspect of the business. These areas of feasibility are organizational structure, social orientation, company politics, managerial capabilities, and personnel capabilities.

Influence of Organizational Structure

For many years, companies were largely built around a hierarchical, authoritarian organizational structure. In the past, best-selling management books preached that an employee needs a fixed structure, including one supervisor who has responsibility for that employee. In recent years, more forward-looking management principles suggest that rather than a fixed structure, a team-based structure is needed in which multidisciplinary teams form to complete a project and then disband upon project completion. These principles also suggest that project assignments should always be based on employee skills and experience, not on some rigid hierarchy of organizational responsibility.

For companies that still adhere to rigid organizational structures, it is difficult to assign personnel to projects outside of their existing lines of authoritarian responsibility. As a result, the best person for completing the project may not be available. In addition, budgets and other resources assigned to specific areas within a rigidly structured organization may not be available for use in a particular project. For example, excess resources from manufacturing operations may not be available for a marketing IS project. As a result, the marketing project may lack what it needs to make it feasible, while the resources needed for project completion languish in the production budget.

Influence of Company Politics

Because of the human nature of business, internal politics influence all of its activities. The formal organizational structure does not always reflect the hierarchies of power that actually control the firm's activities. Many times, personnel establish a political base of power outside of the normal chains of command depicted in the organizational chart. Changes in the organization brought about by IS projects may threaten the political base of some of these informal hierarchical power bases. As a result, the project team must be astute regarding informal organizational politics in order to increase the feasibility of project completion and the use of the IS that results.

Influence of Social Orientation

Business organizations are composed of people and, therefore, are influenced by the social nature of their personnel. An organization that is composed of bright, energetic, forward-thinking personnel carries an uplifting air of achievement. Personnel in this type of organization are always looking for better ways of performing their jobs and completing projects. You rarely hear the statement, "That's the way we always do this"—and that statement, of course, is not the deciding factor when changes are being made. Personnel in an organization of this type treat change as a normal state of events. They embrace change because they view it as better for the organization and for them individually.

On the other hand, many organizations are composed of personnel who want things to remain the same. They feel more secure in what they do because changes of any real consequence are avoided. They typically embrace consistency in what is being done, why it is being done, and how it is being done, even at the expense of the organization's success.

An IS project by its very nature introduces change into the organization and into the lives of its personnel. Organizational personnel can receive more and better information, make more and better decisions as a result, assume greater responsibility, and become more independent regarding their job responsibilities. However, for the IS project to be successful, the social nature of the organization must be considered. A very closed-spirited social climate makes it more difficult to introduce beneficial change into the organization. On the other hand, making changes just for the sake of change leads to inconsistencies in organizational practices and hinders the ultimate success of the project.

The project team must correctly discern the social nature of those affected by the project and prepare for completing and implementing the project within that social climate. Regardless of the preparation and the success of the project in making positive changes in organizational practices, the true nature of personnel in the organization may make a project infeasible. This true nature needs to be understood and the feasibility of completing the project must be analyzed relative to this understanding. If those responsible for the success of the project have extremely negative attitudes toward change of any kind, a project that initiates many changes may be doomed from the start.

Influence of Managerial and Personnel Capabilities

Good management practices have been studied, verified, and reported on for many years. Nevertheless, organizations hire and retain managers who refuse to learn and apply these principles. In addition, movement up the corporate ladder often causes people to be promoted to management positions beyond their level of competency; this is called the "Peter Principle," from a book of the same name in which it first appeared. Where poor managers exist, the introduction of any change, let alone the major changes involved in implementing a new or dramatically modified IS, are doomed to failure. Without competent, committed managers, an IS project will not receive the support it needs in the way of resources and personnel. Thus, the capabilities of managers in areas affected by an IS project influence the feasibility of the project.

When an information system causes changes in job responsibilities and actions that personnel perform, the current capabilities of employees also influence the success of the project. For example, many people are averse to technology of any type. They often prefer manual methods to any method that causes them to become familiar with and use technology. These persons may resent having to learn how to use computer terminals or desktop computers to retrieve data that they can retrieve from metal filing cabinets. Some personnel who already use technology may resent having to learn new ways of performing the same activity. Still other personnel may be incapable of acquiring the skills that added responsibilities force on them.

An information system introduces change toward the use of technology, replacement of existing technology, and the need for personnel to acquire new skills or for the firm to acquire personnel who have those skills. When project feasibility is being determined, current capabilities of personnel must be analyzed in relation to the additional skills that an IS requires.

Economic Feasibility

In Chapter 3 we introduced *economic feasibility*, which is determined by appraising the monetary costs and benefits associated with a project. Analysts use economic analysis to evaluate viable alternative solutions to the information system problem. Identifying project costs and benefits and viable alternatives is not a simple task. The visible costs of a system can turn out to be just the tip of the iceberg. As with an iceberg, the unseen part often causes the most serious problems, such as cost overruns. (A cost overrun occurs when actual costs exceed estimated costs.)

It can be difficult to assign specific monetary values to the benefits of a system. For example, there is no straightforward means of measuring the dollar value of improved employee morale or more timely information for managerial decision making. A possible method of assessing this value is to estimate the retention rate of employees after implementation of the new system and compare it with the current retention rate, then use the cost of recruitment and training to make the comparison.

Analysts should identify all the various costs and benefits and weigh them against each other. In addition, they usually consider several alternative solutions to the problem. Each alternative has its benefits and costs. For instance, one alternative might significantly reduce the total dollar value of inventory at the cost of longer lead times for filling customer orders. Another alternative might increase customer satisfaction, but significantly increase the total dollar amount of inventory. By identifying and quantifying the costs and benefits associated with each alternative, analysts can recommend several alternatives from which managers may choose the best.

The three major costs to consider in economic feasibility analysis are:

- Developmental costs
- Utilization costs
- Maintenance costs

Developmental costs are those associated with developing a new system or modifying an existing system. These costs include all costs from the time of problem identification through system implementation. Hardware, software, and the development team's time are also examples of developmental costs.

Utilization costs are the costs of using the system after it is developed. These include the cost of supplies, such as computer paper and printer ribbons, and overhead costs, such as electricity to run the system. Some companies charge users for the actual amount of time they use the computer. In such a case, time usage on the CPU and I/O devices is also a utilization cost.

Maintenance costs are incurred as changes are required in the system after it is implemented. Conditions within the firm constantly change. As a result, users' needs also constantly change. Maintenance costs are often the most expensive part of the system life cycle, making up 70 percent or more of the total cost of a system.

Economic feasibility is the main area of feasibility considered by management. The decision to go forward with the project is made by management. The project team helps management identify the costs and benefits and make a decision regarding project feasibility.

The remainder of this chapter focuses on economic feasibility, starting with the identification of different types of costs and benefits associated with completing and using an IS.

CLASSIFICATIONS OF COSTS AND BENEFITS

Costs and benefits must be measured and quantified to justify a project or a new system. Identifying the costs associated with developing the system and the benefits to be derived from the operational system requires a great deal of thought, hard work, and ingenuity. The task is made somewhat easier if the analyst has a way to identify and classify both the costs and the benefits associated with the new system. Typically, costs and benefits fall into three classifications:

- Fixed versus variable
- Tangible versus intangible
- Direct versus indirect

The analyst has a demanding task in assigning dollar amounts to many types of costs and benefits, and this task should be undertaken with a great deal of care.

Fixed Versus Variable Costs or Benefits

The term *fixed* implies constant or unchanging. A **fixed cost or benefit** exists across different time periods, but may increase in amount from period to period. On the other hand, *variable* means changing. Examples of fixed costs include one-time hardware charges or exempt employee salaries (*exempt* means there is no increase in salary with overtime). An example of a fixed benefit is the reduction of total employee salaries because the new system requires fewer people to operate it.

A **variable cost or benefit** changes both in its existence and in its amount, depending on circumstances. CPU time charged is an example of a variable cost; the cost depends on the amount of CPU time used. A variable benefit would be the time saved in processing a sales invoice. The total amount of time saved would depend on the number of invoices processed.

Tangible Versus Intangible Costs or Benefits

The term *tangible* means something touchable and nonabstract. Thus, a **tangible cost or benefit** is concrete and easily identified and measured. The cost of new hardware or equipment is a tangible cost determined by the invoice price. Employee time savings expected from using this new equipment is an example of a tangible benefit.

The term *intangible* means something abstract or vague. An **intangible cost or benefit** is generally easy to identify, but difficult to measure. In spite of this, the analyst must consider intangible costs and benefits during economic feasibility determination. Examples of intangible costs are lost confidence in information systems or dissatisfaction caused by changes in the way end-users must use the system. Intangible benefits might include elevated user self-esteem resulting from being able to function with a more elaborate human/machine interface and an improved corporate image.

Direct Versus Indirect Project Costs or Benefits

A **direct cost or benefit** relates directly to a particular action. The salaries of three programmers assigned 100 percent to a particular project are an example of a direct cost. A direct benefit might be the ability to ship orders two days sooner because of a new order entry system.

An **indirect cost or benefit** is difficult to associate with any particular project. For example, the electricity used by a firm would be an indirect cost for a project. It is difficult, if not impossible, to allocate a fair amount of the total cost to any single user of electricity. Improved decision making as a result of installing a new system is an indirect and intangible benefit of installing a new system. Improved decision making is difficult to measure quantitatively.

Classifying Cost and Benefit Categories

You can list the cost and benefit categories within the business according to the three classifications, to help you judge their relative values. Once the costs and benefits are classified, they are used to perform the actual cost/benefit analysis, as explained in the next section of this chapter.

In addition to understanding the three types of cost and benefit classifications, the analyst should be familiar with individual categories within the classifications as they relate to developing new or modified systems. Tables 14-1 and 14-2 list possible cost and benefit categories, respectively. The costs and benefits listed in these tables can be further classified according to whether they are fixed versus variable, tangible versus intangible, or direct versus indirect.

Table 14-1	Classifying examples of cost categories

Category	Cost	Classification
Personnel	Salaries	Fixed - Tangible - Direct
	Fringe benefits	Variable - Tangible - Direct
	Hourly wages	Variable - Tangible - Direct
	Worker behavior	Variable - Intangible - Indirect
Hardware	CPU	Fixed - Tangible - Direct
	Monitors	Fixed - Tangible - Direct
	Printers	Fixed - Tangible - Direct
	Disk drives	Fixed - Tangible - Direct
	Tape drives	Fixed - Tangible - Direct
	Communication	Fixed - Tangible - Direct
Software	Operating system	Fixed - Tangible - Direct
	Compilers	Variable - Tangible - Direct
	Utilities	Variable - Tangible - Direct
	Vendor-supplied systems	Fixed - Tangible - Direct
Operations	CPU time	Variable - Tangible - Direct
	Communications	Variable - Tangible - Direct
	Quality	Variable - Intangible - Indirect
	Quantity	Variable - Tangible - Direct
Supplies	Computer paper	Variable - Tangible - Direct
	Printer ribbons	Variable - Tangible - Direct
	Tapes	Variable - Tangible - Direct
	Disks	Variable - Tangible - Direct
Facilities	Rent/purchase	Fixed - Tangible - Indirect
	Utilities	Variable - Tangible - Indirect
	Air conditioning	Variable - Tangible - Indirect

COST/BENEFIT ANALYSIS

After the costs and benefits have been identified and quantified, the next step is a
cost/benefit analysis, in which each cost or benefit is evaluated in relation to each
alternative. Numerous methods are used to accomplish this task. The following are
some cost/benefit analysis methods:

- Pay-back analysis

Table 14-2	Classifying examples of benefit categories	
Category	**Benefit**	**Classification**
Performance	Increased processing speed	Fixed - Tangible - Direct
	Fewer errors	Variable - Tangible - Indirect
	Easier maintenance	Variable - Tangible - Direct
Developmental	Tax advantages	Fixed - Tangible - Direct
	Equipment resale	Fixed - Tangible - Direct
	Developer satisfaction	Variable - Intangible - Direct
Operational	Reduced operating expenses	Variable - Tangible - Direct
	Improved cash flow	Variable - Tangible - Direct
	Improved decision making	Variable - Intangible - Indirect

- Break-even analysis
- Present value analysis
- Net present value analysis
- Cash flow analysis
- Depreciation modelst
- Return on investmen

Though the analyst may use all of these methods, the four most common are pay-back, break-even, present value analysis, and net present value analysis. These four methods are illustrated in this chapter. Most advanced accounting or finance texts explain the final three methods and provide more information on all of the methods described here.

Pay-Back Analysis

Pay-back analysis determines the time it takes for the benefits to equal the initial investment. With this method the analyst calculates how long it takes for the benefits to pay back the costs incurred during development and usage. The simplest form of this determination is:

$$\text{Pay-back} = \frac{\text{Investment}}{\text{After-tax yearly savings}}$$

For example, assume that a project requires an initial investment of $1,000,000 with a yearly after-tax savings of $250,000 resulting from completion of the project. The formula now becomes

$$\text{Pay-back} = \frac{1,000,000}{250,000}$$

$$= 4 \text{ years}$$

This proposed system pays for itself in four years. Is this acceptable? That depends on the pay-back guidelines established by the company. Many companies have a pay-back guideline that a project must meet before it can be considered. If the guideline is six years, then the project stays well within the guideline. However, if the pay-back guideline is three years, this project is not acceptable on the basis of its pay-back.

Several considerations guide the analyst in using pay-back analysis. First, pay-back analysis does not allow for the time value of money. (You will learn more about this in the section "Real Value Monetary Costs," below.) Second, it indicates only the acceptability of projects, not how "good" or "bad" they are. Therefore, analysts consider it dangerous to use pay-back analysis alone to compare alternatives. For example, one project could have a longer pay-back period, but could be more beneficial to the organization in the long run. Analysts often use pay-back analysis in conjunction with more comprehensive cost/benefit analysis procedures.

Break-Even Analysis

Break-even analysis determines the point at which the cost of the proposed system equals the cost of the current system, or the cost of a new system equals its benefits. After determining the break-even point, the analyst subjectively evaluates conditions evidenced in the project to assess its acceptability. Notice that whereas pay-back analysis determines when the total benefits of candidate systems outweigh their total costs, break-even analysis uses expected conditions to compare costs of current and proposed systems. The present value method uses cost/benefit analysis to compare projects, including the time value of money.

Figure 14-1 shows a generalized break-even diagram for a proposed system and the current system. This figure shows the typical situation in which, initially, the costs of the new system investment outweigh the costs of the current system. In Figure 14-1, 1000 units constitute the break-even point, or the point at which both systems cost the same ($20,000). After reaching the break-even point, the company experiences a profit (the costs of the old system are higher than the costs of the new system). As you can see in Figure 14-1, up to 1000 units, the old system is more economical than the new system. After 1000 units, the proposed system becomes more economical. Notice that if the company's future needs indicate that its processing will not exceed 1000 units, the company should remain with the old system.

Break-Even Analysis Example— Financial Analysis Package

A software vendor produces a financial analysis package. To copy-protect the package, the firm considers two alternatives:

- A parallel-port ROM chip security device manufactured by another firm
- A key diskette to mount in the A drive while executing the package

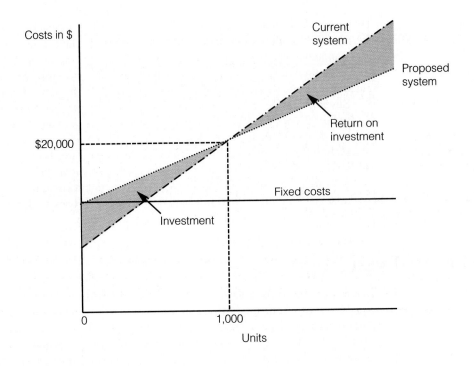

Figure 14-1. Break-even analysis

An outside firm has offered to produce the ROM chips at a cost of $8 per unit if a minimum of 500 units are purchased. The company can create key diskettes at a cost of $4 per unit with an overhead cost of an additional $4000, to be included in the cost of this alternative. To decide between the alternatives, the break-even point for each is computed and compared.

Solution:

Total cost for producing in-house: $TC_1 = \$4000 + \$4X$

Total cost for outside production: $TC_2 = \$8X$

Calculation of break-even sales level:

$TC_1 = TC_2$ (set two alternatives equal to each other)

$4000 + 4X = 8X$

$4X = 4000, X = 1000$ (solve for X)

The break-even point is 1000 units, meaning that for 1000 units, each alternative would cost the same ($8000). At fewer than 1000 units, the firm should choose external production of the ROM chips, the less costly alternative. However, for sales of more than 1000 units, the firm should choose creating the key diskettes in-house as the best alternative.

Real Value Monetary Costs

The first two cost/benefit analysis methods, pay-back and break-even, do not allow for the time value of money, whereas the present value and net present value methods do. To understand present value and net present value analysis, you need to understand the effects of the time value of money on project cost analysis.

In evaluating project costs and benefits, the value of money over the period required to develop and/or install the system must be taken into account. Analysts should consider the real value of money relative to the prevailing interest rate when analyzing alternatives. This real value of money reflects using money for investment purposes rather than for financing development projects. In addition, firms often find it necessary to borrow money to finance development costs. As a result, the firm must bear the costs associated with the interest rates being charged.

Interest is the cost of using borrowed money (or the income that may be received from loaning money). Interest rates are usually computed on an annual basis. The interest *rate* can be defined as the ratio of the amount paid or received for the use of the money to the amount of the money. The following example illustrates a simple interest rate calculation:

Length of loan = 1 year

Amount borrowed = $500

Interest paid = $50

Interest rate = Interest paid ÷ Amount borrowed = 50 ÷ 500 = 10%

Table 14-3 identifies formulas that can be used to analyze alternatives that consider project costs and benefits based on the present and future values of money.

Table 14-3	Cost/benefit formulas that consider present and future values of money

Formula Type	Formula
Future value formula	$F = P(1 + i)^n$
Present value formula	$P = F \div (1 + i)^n$
Equal payment series future value	$F = A \times ((1 + i)^n - 1) \div i$
Equal payment series sinking fund	$A = F \times i \div ((1 + i)^n - 1)$
Equal payment series capital recovery	$A = P \times (1 + i)^n \times (i \div ((1 + i)^n - 1))$
Equal payment series present worth	$P = A \times ((1 + i)^n - 1) \div (i \times (1 + i)^n)$

where P = principal sum or present value
F = future value, compounded amount of the principal sum
i = nominal rate of interest
n = number of interest periods
A = single payment

Present and Future Value of Money

To assess costs or benefits, analysts often need to calculate the future value of money currently in hand and/or the present value of money to be obtained in the future or throughout a future period. **Future value** is the final accumulated value of a sum of money currently invested at a specified interest rate (rate of return). The analyst uses the following formula to compute the future value with the proper notation as defined in Table 14-3:

$$F = P(1 + i)^n$$

The **present value** of money reduces a future amount of money to what it is worth now (its present value). An alternative definition might be the amount that one must invest now to produce a known future amount. Actually, future value and present value are two ways of looking at the same process. Note that mathematically manipulating the future value formula leads to a formula for present value:

$$P = F \div (1 + i)^n$$

Business people expect that the amount of money invested today will increase as time passes due to the profit they earn on that investment. Thus, the amount of money available for investment today is more valuable than an equal amount not available until some future date. Therefore, the value of a certain sum of money today exceeds its value at some future date. An example should clarify the present value/future value concept.

EXAMPLE: Assume your company invests $100 today at an annual interest rate of 8 percent. You should expect $100 invested today to have a future value of $108 one year from today. Conversely, $108 expected a year from today has a present value of $100 if you expect to earn 8 percent on the investment.

Additional examples in the following sections illustrate the present and future value concepts.

Future Value Analysis

Future value analysis considers the time value of money in determining project costs and benefits. It has two major applications in the analysis and design area. Two examples will help clarify the concept. The first is a cost example; the second involves revenues. Both examples use the same future value formula:

$$F = P(1 + i)^n$$

For the first example, assume that your company considers purchasing new hardware upgrades that cost $15,000. To make the purchase, the firm needs to borrow the $15,000 for three years at an annual compound interest rate of 10 percent to finance the project. How much will the new equipment actually cost the firm? To determine the cost, you simply insert the attribute values into the future value formula:

$$P = \$15{,}000$$

$$i = .10$$

$$n = 3$$

$$F = \$15{,}000 \times (1 + .10)^3$$

$$F = \$19{,}965$$

The firm must pay an actual cost of $19,965 for the computer equipment.

The second example of future value analysis involves an income example. Assume that the company has $15,000 to invest. The company would like to know the future value of the $15,000, invested at 10 percent annual compound interest, in three years. The same calculation can be used to show that the future value of the present $15,000 is $19,965.

Present Value Analysis

Assume now that your company will need $25,000 at the end of three years to make a hardware purchase. How much money do you need to invest now at an annual compound interest rate of 10 percent to produce the $25,000 in three years? This amount can be determined by using the present value formula. This formula represents an algebraic reformulation of the future value formula:

$$P = \frac{F}{(1 + i)^n}$$

Inserting numbers in the example produces

$$P = \frac{25{,}000}{(1 + 10)^3}$$

$$P = \$18{,}782.87$$

The company needs to invest $18,782.87 today to have $25,000.00 in three years at 10 percent interest compounded annually.

Present Value Analysis
Example for Evaluating Alternatives

Unlike the pay-back method, the present value cost/benefit method considers the time value of money. To illustrate, assume an analyst considers two alternatives that provide identical services for a project. Each system is expected to have a useful life of five years. Costs vary from year to year and between projects. Also assume an annual interest rate of 10 percent. Figure 14-2 compares these two alternatives (A and B) using present value analysis to compare the costs throughout the lifetime of the project. Note that alternative B would have a lower present cost if the analyst considered only present costs. However, using present value analysis shows that initial impressions can be misleading. The analyst would prefer the alternative with the lowest present value cost estimate over the full lifetime of the project. The accumulated present value cost for A is $39,295, and that for B is $39,758. Therefore A is the lower-cost alternative.

Year	Direct/Indirect Project Costs A	B	Present Value Multiplier*	Calculated Yearly Present Value Costs A	B
1	10,000	16,000	.909	9,090	14,544
2	10,000	10,000	.826	8,260	8,260
3	15,000	11,000	.751	11,265	8,261
4	12,000	10,000	.683	8,196	6,830
5	4,000	3,000	.621	2,484	1,863
	$51,000	$50,000		$39,295	$39,758

* This multiplier is calculated from the formula:

$$P = \frac{F}{(1 + i)^n} = F \times \frac{1}{(1 + i)^n} \text{ and}$$

$$\frac{1}{(1 + i)^n} = \text{the respective multiplier with .10 and year number inserted}$$

For example:

$$\frac{1}{(1 + 10)^1} = .909 \text{ for year 1}$$

$$\frac{1}{(1 + 10)^2} = .826 \text{ for year 2}$$

$$\frac{1}{(1 + 10)^3} = .751 \text{ for year 3}$$

$$\frac{1}{(1 + 10)^4} = .683 \text{ for year 4}$$

$$\frac{1}{(1 + 10)^5} = .621 \text{ for year 5}$$

Figure 14-2. Present value analysis of two projects

Net Present Value Analysis

To truly evaluate alternatives, the analyst must also determine the present value of benefits derived from the alternatives. This analysis calculates a **net present value**, or benefits less costs for each alternative (again, A and B) for each year of the life cycle. To illustrate this analysis method, benefits and expenses derived for each year during the useful life span of the system are included. Assume an active and useful life span of ten years for this particular system. The time frame of ten years is used only for purposes of the example. In today's fast-paced world, with technology changing so rapidly, a useful life span may be more in the neighborhood of three to five years. Figure 14-3 compares the two alternatives using net present value.

The accumulated net present value for A is $16,078, and that for B is $11,780. Since A has the higher net present value, it should be the selected alternative.

Additional Financial Consideration Examples

A number of additional quantitative financial analysis formulas exist. A project's specific characteristics help determine which formula to use. The following sections describe four methods, with an example of the circumstances and the formula used for each.

	Alternative A		Alternative B			Net Present Value	
Year	Cost	Benefit	Cost	Benefit	Multiplier	A	B
1	10,000	1,000	16,000	0	.909	−8,181	−14,544
2	10,000	4,000	10,000	3,000	.826	−4,956	−5,782
3	15,000	6,000	11,000	5,000	.751	−6,759	−4,506
4	12,000	7,000	10,000	6,000	.683	−3,415	−2,714
5	4,000	7,000	3,000	8,000	.621	1,863	3,005
6	5,000	20,000	3,000	18,000	.565	8,475	8,475
7	6,000	24,000	5,000	22,000	.514	9,252	8,738
8	6,000	24,000	6,000	25,000	.467	8,406	8,873
9	7,000	22,000	7,000	22,000	.425	6,375	6,375
10	8,000	21,000	9,000	19,000	.386	5,018	3,860
						$16,078	$11,780

Figure 14-3. Net present value analysis of two projects yearly

Equal Payment Series Future Value

This analysis determines a future value for a series of equal payments over a particular number of periods at a specific interest rate. An example helps illustrate how to use this method and its accompanying formula.

EXAMPLE: A local firm wants to enter into a contractual maintenance agreement with an electronics shop that will provide maintenance services. The agreement calls for the firm to hold $2000 in an interest-bearing account at 12 percent until the end of the year. This is to pay for the service for a four-year estimated life of the agreement. What actual sum (F) does the firm pay over the life of the agreement?

$$F = A \times ((1 + i)^n - 1) \div i$$
$$F = 2000 \times ((1 + .12)^4 - 1) \div .12$$
$$F = \$9,558.66$$

Equal Payment Series Sinking Fund

This analysis determines the series of payments necessary to accumulate a desired future amount over a particular number of periods at a specific interest rate. An example illustrates the use of this method, including the appropriate formula.

EXAMPLE: Suppose the maintenance agreement in the previous example called for $20,000 to be paid at the end of four years. What payment amount (A) does the firm need to invest to ensure accumulating the requested amount?

$$A = F \times i \div ((1 + i)^n - 1)$$
$$A = 20,000 \,(.12 \div ((1 + .12)^4 - 1)$$
$$A = \$4,184.69$$

Equal Payment Series Capital Recovery

This analysis determines the series of payments necessary to amortize (pay off) an amount borrowed over a particular number of periods at a specific interest rate. An example illustrates the use of this method, including the appropriate formula.

EXAMPLE: A computer manufacturing company must borrow $1 million to finance new product development. A bank agrees to lend this firm the capital, to be recovered over a five-year period in equal year-end payments at an interest rate of 14 percent. What will be the year-end payments (A)?

$$A = P \times (1 + i)^n \times (i \div ((1 + i)^n - 1))$$
$$A = 1,000,000 \times (1 + .14)^5 \times ((.14) \div ((1 + .14)^5 - 1))$$
$$A = \$294,270$$

Equal Payment Series Present Worth

This analysis determines the combined present value for a series of dollar amounts received in equal amounts over a particular number of periods at a specific interest rate. An example illustrates the use of this method, including the appropriate formula.

EXAMPLE: A firm estimates that it will save $5000 a year in operating expenses for the next five years by subscribing to a commercially available wide area network. What is the present value (*P*) of these savings at an interest rate of 10 percent?

$$P = A \times ((1 + i)^n - 1) \div (i \times (1 + i)^n)$$
$$P = 5000 \times ((1 + .10)^5 - 1) \div (.10 \times (1 + .10)^5)$$
$$P = \$18,953.93$$

As you can see, determining the most cost-beneficial alternative involves elaborate financial analysis. Using the financial analysis methods presented in this chapter should not be taken lightly. Proper use of appropriate financial analysis methods helps the analyst ensure that system costs and benefits will be acceptable to management.

ESTABLISHING CRITERIA FOR PERFORMING COST/ BENEFIT ANALYSIS

A systematic approach to evaluating information system proposals is the best way to assure optimal project selection decisions. As an analyst, you need to establish a set of criteria to evaluate each project and use the same set each time for projects of the same type. Evaluation could be based on one or more of the following criteria:

- Performance criteria
- Economic criteria
- Efficiency criteria
- Financial criteria

Performance criteria include accuracy, growth potential, integration, responsiveness, and usability. Accuracy is the ability to provide consistently correct information. Growth potential is the ability to expand system capacity to meet changing needs. Integration is the ability to interface with other business systems, such as accounts payable and general ledger. Responsiveness is the ability to produce timely information. Usability relates to a new system's ease of use.

Economic criteria are the decreased costs and/or increased revenues that the new system brings to the firm. These criteria center around the main purposes of the system.

Efficiency criteria are related to the ratio of output to input. An example is the ability to accomplish more work while holding the number of workers steady. In the NG&T case, for example, the firm is able to ship more orders without increasing the number of shipping department employees.

Financial criteria help determine the advisability of pursuing a project from a monetary point of view. Possible methods to use include net present value, internal rate of return, and pay-back period, as previously described.

The next step in evaluating IS proposals is to derive a scale that rates the importance of each set of criteria in the overall process of selecting the best system. The scale is typically specified by managers involved in the areas affected by the A&D project. An **importance scale**, as shown here, can be used to assign relative weights to the important criteria identified:

Description	Weight
Very important	3
Somewhat important	2
Less important	1

Now each set of criteria is assigned a weight to rate its importance, such as:

Criteria	Weight
Performance	2
Economic	3
Efficiency	1
Financial	2

In this case the project team has determined, based on talks with users, that economic criteria are very important and efficiency criteria are relatively unimportant. The weight of each set of criteria is based on its value as viewed by the user.

The last step in the process is to rate each alternative, using the weight that has been assigned to the set of criteria, and then rate various attributes within each set of criteria. The criteria are rated on the following scale:

Rating Description	Rating Score
Excellent	4
Good	3
Fair	2
Poor	1

At this point, the various attributes of performance, economic, efficiency, and financial criteria are rated for alternative A based on the preceding scale. Figure 14-4 illustrates this process.

Each additional system alternative identified in the analysis phase is rated the same way, based on its importance as viewed by the user. The total number of points

Criteria Rating	Importance Rating	Attribute Rating	Total
Performance	2		
Growth potential	2	4	8
Accuracy	2	3	6
Responsiveness	2	2	4
Usability	2	2	4
Economic	3		
Decrease costs	3	3	9
Increase revenue	3	4	12
Efficiency	1		
Increase work load	1	4	4
Hold work force steady	1	1	1
Ship more orders	1	4	4
Financial	2		
NPV	2	4	8
IRR	2	3	6
Pay-back	2	1	2
Alternative A total points			68

Figure 14-4. Ratings for alternative A

for each alternative are compared, and the alternative with the most points is a strong candidate for implementation.

This model can be modified to meet the needs of a particular firm. For example, some firms might place a significantly higher value on financial criteria.

COMPUTER-AIDED COST ESTIMATION

A number of estimating software systems aid the analyst in determining economic feasibility for proposed systems. These software systems operate on the principle of entering attributes of the system development environment to determine cost estimates relative to developing, using, and maintaining system solutions. Analysts enter attribute values such as experience level of participants, percentage of existing and reusable code, programming language employed, amount of computer-aided technology employed, and a number of other attributes that describe environmental characteristics. These estimates are used by the software to approximate the cost of developing, using, and maintaining the new system.

Cost estimating software systems frequently employ an estimating method known as *function point analysis*, which analysts can use to determine the magnitude (size) of a system project. A **function point** is a point in the logic of a program where a certain activity occurs. These function points are operations such as input/output activities, full-screen interactive activities, and so forth. Researchers have discovered that knowing the number of function points leads to accurate estimates of the number of instructions (code lines) in programs—that is, the magnitude of system development.

Separate research projects at IBM laboratories, under the direction of A. J. Albrecht and T. Capers Jones, led to the development of function point analysis. The IBM research teams tracked the number of function points in several thousand programs and developed an algorithm to estimate the number of code lines for programs. The researchers compared the results of using this algorithm against programs each of which had a known number of code lines and function points. The results indicated that function point analysis did indeed help determine the magnitudes of programming tasks. Conversely, the researchers found that knowing the number of lines of code could lead to accurately estimating the number of function points in the programs.

As a result of this research, analysts can use either an estimated number of code lines or the number of function points to determine the magnitude of effort involved in system projects. The analyst either enters the number of function points explicitly into the cost estimation software or enters the expected number of code lines for a proposed system, and the software automatically computes the number of function points.

The number of lines of code can also affect the complexity of the system development task; however, it is not the only influence on the complexity of the system development task. The experience of project team participants and other internal and external environmental characteristics also contribute to the complexity of the development process. For example, a team of highly experienced project members should be able to complete a reasonably complex development system much faster, with fewer delivered errors, than a team of new systems professionals.

A few estimating systems combine function points and other contributing factors to produce estimates for a system development project with various characteristics. To produce these estimates, the analyst enters parameter values for factors that contribute to project complexity that the software uses to compute estimates, such as cost to develop the system, time to complete the project, number of delivered errors in the system, and cost to maintain the system after installation. The accuracy of the estimates depends on the confidence that one has in the underlying algorithm.

Not many experienced analysts are likely to stake their careers on a single estimate coming from out of these systems, even if they trust the underlying algorithms. However, repeated use of the estimating system with different parameter values entered for a single project provides an estimating range that an analyst can use confidently. In addition, repeated use of the estimating system should permit experienced analysts to obtain benchmark estimates for use as important project development indicators. As analysts continue to use the estimating system, they should learn how to properly enter parameter values to produce more accurate estimation ranges.

COST JUSTIFICATION AT NATIONAL GOLF & TENNIS (NG&T)

This section illustrates some typical cost/benefit analysis procedures for the National Golf & Tennis (NG&T) case. It is not intended to be complete; additional documentation, such as analysis of other areas of feasibility, would normally be required. Figures 14-5 through 14-8 illustrate the procedure. Figure 14-5 contains a brief executive summary. Next, Figure 14-6 details the disadvantages of alternative 1 and estimates the cost of the first alternative recommended in the executive summary. Similar cost estimates could be done for alternatives 2 and 3. Figure 14-7 outlines the advantages of the first alternative. Similar analysis might be done for the other two alternatives. Finally, Figure 14-8 provides a net present value analysis of the three proposals. Assumptions are made about alternatives 2 and 3 for illustrative purposes. Note that because the third alternative has the highest net present value, it is the preferred system.

Figure 14-5 provides a brief executive summary of the project team's recommendations for the retail and mail-order sales handling procedures at NG&T. It offers three alternatives and a summary of the cost/benefit analysis.

Figures 14-6 and 14-7 provide details of cost and benefit estimations for alternative 1. These figures include both advantages and disadvantages of this alternative.

The purpose of this proposed study is to review the current system at NG&T for handling retail and mail-order sales and determine how to improve it. We need this study because the current system does not appear to adequately support the company's rapid growth. Problems experienced by management include inadequate control over inventory, inability to follow up on customer mail orders, large volumes of paperwork, and limited management reporting. A preliminary investigation was conducted prior to actually designing the new system. The project team studied information about the current system, policies and procedures, problems experienced, and key concerns of management. This information was documented using data flow diagrams, system flow charts, and a data dictionary.

After analyzing the situation at NG&T and deciding against doing nothing, the project team identified several alternatives:

- An IBM personal computer token ring network with specially developed software
- An IBM personal computer token ring network with purchased software
- An NCR Tower 32 minicomputer system

Figure 14-5. Executive summary of recommendations for NG&T

In conclusion, it appears that NG&T's needs will be best served by an on-line order entry and inventory control system. It also appears that this system would be best supported by the NCR Tower 32 minicomputer system.

In determining the economic feasibility of the proposed system, the project team found it necessary to compare economic costs and benefits over time. Because of the concern for cash flows at NG&T, the project leader chose the discounted cash flow method to evaluate alternative solutions. This method computes a net benefit for each year based on the projected costs and benefits given elsewhere in this proposal. The net benefit for each year is discounted to the present to take into account the time value of money. In the simplest terms, this method recognizes that a dollar today is worth more than a dollar in the future. For our analysis, the project leader chose a discount value of 18 percent. The results for each of the three proposed system alternatives appear on the following pages.

Figure 14-5. Executive summary of recommendations for NG&T *(continued)*

Adopting a PC Token Ring Network—Specially Developed Software
Disadvantages

1. NG&T personnel have little understanding of an operating system featuring magnetic disk storage and a local area network. Therefore, training is required. However, this is a one-time cost, included in consultant costs.
2. New computer programs have to be written and tested before implementing them; this is also included in consultant costs.
3. The use of personal computers as terminals does not take full advantage of their capabilities of performing standalone tasks such as spreadsheet operations or word processing. Consequently, using them requires purchasing computer power that may not be used.
4. The industry has not yet accepted this configuration as adequate for remote access. Costs of individual workstations increase more than those of unintelligent terminal counterparts. Further, analysts expect degradation of processing capability with the addition of more terminals when needed as the result of new retail store openings.

Figure 14-6. Cost estimation for alternative 1

Costs

Equipment

IBM Model 95	$ 5,945
Monitor (15)	2,625
DOS 6.0 (15)	1,500
IBM MAU	525
IBM Model 70 (15)	18,225
Token ring adapter/A	575
Token ring adapter (15)	8,625
IBM LAN program v. 1.3	130
IBM LAN support program (16)	640
Tripp-lite surge protector (16)	1,463
IBM Quietwriter III (3)	6,045
Subtotal	46,298
Consultant costs	40,000
Total costs	$86,298
Annual costs:	
Maintenance	$4,000

Figure 14-6. Cost estimation for alternative 1 *(continued)*

Adopting an IBM Token Ring Network—Specially Developed Software

Advantages

1. Use of a vendor that specializes in POS terminals
2. Increased efficiency and accuracy in handling mail orders
3. Increased control of inventory by automatically indicating reorder items using an on-line facility to update inventory records
4. Ability to respond immediately and accurately to customer inquiries concerning the status of an order, resulting in improved customer satisfaction
5. On-line editing of information to correct errors at terminals
6. More accurate invoices that reduce customer complaints and possible losses due to incorrect charges
7. Ease in maintaining customer mailing informatio
8. Improved management reporting in areas such as sales performance, advertising effectiveness, and inventory turnover
9. Ability to develop software to specifically meet NG&T needs

Figure 14-7. Benefit estimation for alternative 1

Tangible Benefits
No tangible savings are expected, since the new system will require additional personnel.

Estimated Intangible Benefits
It is expected that the new system will increase both customer satisfaction and management control of the business, resulting in additional sales. We estimate that there is a 50 percent chance that a customer might purchase 5 percent more goods, a 20 percent chance that a customer might purchase 25 percent more goods, and so on. Given these assumptions, an estimated percentage increase in sales (using mail-order sales as the base figure) can be calculated as follows:

Increase =
.50 × .05 increase
.20 × .25 increase
.10 × .45 increase
.05 × 1.00 increase
= .17 increase in sales

Applying this increase to the anticipated $5,000,000 in sales yields .17 x $5,000,000 = $850,000.

Figure 14-7. Benefit estimation for alternative 1 *(continued)*

Analysis for PC Token Ring with Specially Developed Software

Year	Benefit	Cost	Net Benefit	P.V. Multiplier	Present Value
0	0	86,298	(86,298)	—	(86,298)
1	850,000	86,298	763,702	.833	636,163
2	850,000	86,298	763,702	.694	530,009
3	850,000	86,298	763,702	.579	412,183
4	850,000	86,298	763,702	.482	368,104
5	850,000	86,298	763,702	.402	307,008
Present value					$2,283,467

Figure 14-8. Net present value analysis for project

Analysis for IBM Token Ring Network with Purchased Software

Year	Benefit	Cost	Net Benefit	P.V. Multiplier	Present Value
0	0	77,050	(77,050)	–	(77,050)
1	971,296	150,300	820,996	.833	683,890
2	971,296	150,300	820,996	.694	569,771
3	971,296	150,300	820,996	.579	475,357
4	971,296	150,300	820,996	.482	395,720
5	971,296	150,300	820,996	.402	330,040
Present value					$2,377,728

Analysis for NCR Minicomputer

Year	Benefit	Cost	Net Benefit	P.V. Multiplier	Present Value
0	0	111,869	(111,869)	–	(111,869)
1	971,296	23,928	947,368	.833	789,158
2	971,296	23,928	947,368	.694	657,473
3	971,296	23,928	947,368	.579	548,526
4	971,296	23,928	947,368	.482	456,631
5	971,296	23,928	947,368	.402	380,842
Present value					$2,720,761

Figure 14-8. Net present value analysis for project *(continued)*

If the decision as to which system to implement were based purely on net present value analysis, alternative 3 would be chosen, since it has the highest net present value. However, as discussed earlier in this chapter, other criteria may also be important, and a weighted procedure, similar to the one presented in the section titled "Establishing Criteria for Performing Cost/Benefit Analysis," above, may be needed.

REVIEW

Determining project feasibility is an ongoing process throughout the analysis and design of a system. Analysts determine project costs and benefits for the company by identifying areas of feasibility, such as economic, operational, and technical; also by classifying costs and benefits into fixed versus variable, tangible versus intangible, and direct versus indirect. By classifying costs and benefits in different categories, such as personnel, operations, hardware, software, and so on, analysts can get an overall view of the relative values of the categories. Though it might be difficult to assign monetary values to certain types of costs and benefits, analysts must attempt to do so in order to justify a project.

After costs and benefits have been identified and quantified, the analyst applies various methods of cost/benefit analysis to evaluate the alternatives in relation to one another. The four most common methods are pay-back, break-even, present value, and net present value. Analysts should include the time value of money in evaluating alternatives; they should realize that the value of money today exceeds its value at some future time.Establishing criteria for evaluating system proposals and applying these same criteria to every proposal encourages optimal selection among alternatives. The analyst is aided in determining economic feasibility for proposed systems by the use of cost estimating software systems, many of which use function point analysis to determine the magnitude of a system project.

Finally, an example of cost justification at NG&T shows typical documentation used to recommend a new system for handling retail and mail-order sales.

QUESTIONS

1. What are the three major costs involved in the lifetime of a system?
2. Clearly distinguish between fixed and variable costs, tangible and intangible costs, and direct and indirect costs.
3. For a company in your vicinity, list fixed and variable costs, tangible and intangible costs, and direct and indirect costs.
4. List five cost categories, with examples; identify the cost types.
5. List three benefit categories, with examples; identify the types of benefits.
6. Explain what a pay-back calculation involves.
7. If $500,000 is used to purchase a new computer system that produces $125,000 savings in computing usage in a year, how long will it take to pay back the initial investment?
8. What purpose does break-even analysis serve?
9. If alternative A has a fixed cost of $200,000 associated with it and an incremental cost of $500 per use of the system, and alternative B has an incremental cost of $1000 per use of the system without any fixed cost, what is the break-even point between the two alternatives?
10. Why should the real value of money be considered in A&D projects?
11. What is the present value of $15,000 to be paid in four years, if the nominal interest rate is 12 percent?
12. Distinguish between present value and net present value.
13. Define function points; explain what function point analysis involves and what it actually measures.

14. Identify the attributes of a development project that contribute to the complexity of system development.

EXERCISES

1. Create a set of analysis criteria to use in assessing the costs and benefits of the alternatives for the NG&T case.

2. Create a cost analysis for alternative two (IBM personal computer network with purchased software) of the NG&T case, using Figure 14-6 as a guide.

3. Create a cost analysis for alternative three (NCR minicomputer system) of the NG&T case, using Figure 14-6 as a guide.

4. Create a benefit analysis for alternative two (IBM personal computer network with purchased software) of the NG&T case, using Figure 14-7 as a guide.

5. Create a benefit analysis for alternative three (NCR minicomputer system) of the NG&T case, using Figure 14-7 as a guide.

6. Create a summary of the three alternatives that selects the best alternative. Include a complete explanation of why the particular alternative is the best.

7. Create a cost/benefit analysis for each alternative using the pay-back analysis method, using Figure 14-8 as a guide.

8. Create a cost/benefit analysis for each alternative using the break-even analysis method, using Figure 14-8 as a guide.

9. Create a cost/benefit analysis for each alternative using the present value analysis method, using Figure 14-8 as a guide.

10. For your semester project, create a cost/benefit analysis using net present value for two system development alternatives. Which is the best and why?

SELECTED REFERENCES

Couger, J. D., M. A. Colter, and R. W. Knapp. 1982. *Advanced Systems Development/Feasibility Techniques*. New York: John Wiley and Sons.

Moyer, R. C., J. R. McGuigan, and W. J. Kretlow. 1984. *Contemporary Financial Management*. St. Paul, MN: West Publishing Co.

Putnam, L. H. and A. Fitzsimmons. 1979. "Estimating Software Costs." *Datamation* 25, no. 9 (September).

Weston, J. F. and E. F. Brigham. 1982. *Managerial Finance*, 6th Edition. Hinsdale, IL: The Dryden Press.

CHAPTER 15

Project Management

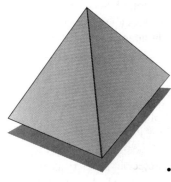

OVERVIEW

As a project leader, you must adequately plan, monitor, and control projects to produce the desired results. Using project management techniques and tools helps project leaders finish projects on time and within budget. This chapter introduces aspiring analysts to time-proven project management techniques. In addition, methods for estimating overall time and costs to complete projects are discussed. Essential elements of project management include:

- Project planning and control
- Project charting methods
- Factors in time and cost estimation
- Computer-aided project management
- Project management at NG&T

KEY TERMS

Crashing the system

Critical path

Critical path method (CPM)

Duration time

Earliest start time

Gantt chart

Latest start time

Milestone chart

Program evaluation and review
    technique (PERT)

Project management software

Project network

Project schedule

Slack time

Stochastic determination

Proper management methods help analysts complete projects on time and within budget. Because of the complexity of many system development projects, it is critical that analysts define and schedule the activities required to complete the project, including time estimates, resource usage, costs, and methods to monitor the progress of projects. Project management is one strategy to conduct large, complex projects. However, all projects need proper management, regardless of their size and complexity. Project management methods include the critical path method (CPM), program evaluation and review technique (PERT) charts, Gantt charts, and milestone charts. There are specific time and cost estimating methods, as well as ways to monitor the progress of projects, that help the analyst maintain control and be prepared for changes that inevitably take place during the system life cycle.

As with project feasibility, covered in Chapter 14, analysts should administer project management from the start of an analysis and design project. Coverage of the topic is positioned in this chapter in order to give you a thorough understanding of systems analysis and design practices before you study project management practices.

PROJECT PLANNING AND CONTROL

A *project* can be defined as a series of tasks having a beginning, an end, and a set of deliverable end products. It is an organized effort to reach a predefined goal. Project planning helps minimize the number of "crises" that can occur in the analysis and design process. These crises often take the form of incomplete or delayed tasks, missed deadlines, cost overruns, and even project abandonment. With proper management, a project can provide the expected benefits within the cost and time estimates determined during feasibility analysis. The goal of achieving system benefits within cost estimates is better accomplished by identifying and avoiding detrimental crises during the system project. In general, planning and managing a system project involve:

- Defining tasks
- Creating a network
- Estimating duration of tasks
- Deriving a schedule
- Monitoring resource availability
- Estimating unit costs of resources
- Estimating resource usage per task
- Estimating the total cost and duration of the project
- Monitoring and controlling the project

Defining Tasks

Defining tasks begins with a clear definition of the project scope. In Chapter 3 we discussed problem domains and the relationships among problem scope, subjects, objects, and objectives. Problem domains also help to establish project domains. The goal is to determine boundaries for the proposed system; in other words, to determine what functional areas of the business will be affected by the proposed system.

As an example of defining boundaries early in the development process, consider an on-line order entry system that could encompass sales, accounts receivable, shipping, purchasing, and inventory. Perhaps the company is not yet ready to implement a new system in all of these areas, so management defines the scope of the project to omit purchasing and inventory. These functions may be developed at a later time.

Once project leaders define project boundaries, they can create an exhaustive task list within those boundaries. What the system must do to meet the needs of the users is detailed by making a list of all the tasks necessary to accomplish the project within the desired time frame. For example, a task list to complete the portion of the on-line application dealing with sales might include the following tasks:

- Identify all interactive screen user interfaces
- Eliminate redundant access by combining similar user interfaces
- Create user interfaces to use with the on-line application
- Identify user views within the application to identify interfaces, data access using an interface, and actions permitted
- Revise interface screens to facilitate actions users are permitted to perform on the data they can access

- Test the prototype user interfaces with users
- Revise interface screens
- Create programs that implement the interfaces
- Test program/interface with live data and user execution

While composing the task list, project leaders spend time detailing the system requirements and tasks necessary to accomplish each task. As a result, time spent in preparing to manage the project contributes to meeting user requirements in a comprehensive way.

Creating the Network

Once project leaders have defined the tasks, they create a graphical representation of the task sequence. This graphical representation indicates which task completions precede the start of the next task. Determining what is to be done and in what sequence is a result of careful analysis of the project by the project leader.

A complete diagram should indicate tasks to be completed on a parallel basis and those that precede and succeed each other. Diagrams showing task relationships are known as a **project network**, as illustrated in the discussion of the CPM (critical path method) technique later in this chapter.

Estimating Duration of Time for Tasks

Upon completing the network, project leaders must estimate the duration of each task. Task duration time estimates, called **duration time**, are estimates of the time it will take for each task in hours, weeks, months, or even years. These time estimates are then used to derive the duration of the entire project. Detailed descriptions of various methods used in estimating duration time are provided later in this chapter, in the section titled "Time Estimation."

Deriving a Project Schedule

After project leaders identify tasks, create a network, and obtain time estimates, they can devise a project schedule relatively easily. A **project schedule** is a timetable in which to complete project tasks.

The goal is to create a schedule that is optimal in terms of time and cost. The schedule must also take into consideration any restrictions placed on the project in terms of cash flow, resource availability, events that may affect the project, and any outside approvals needed. For example, if the money needed to order the hardware is not available until a certain date, or if approval from someone at another location is needed before the project can begin, it is reflected in the project schedule. Deriving the project schedule will become more clear as you progress through this chapter.

Monitoring Resource Availability

When the network is created, project leaders estimate the amounts of resources needed and their availability. Now that a project timetable has been established, project leaders must continually monitor the availability of resources needed to meet that timetable. These resources include both physical equipment, such as computers and storage devices, and personnel, such as analysts, programmers, and data entry clerks. If sufficient resources are not available, project leaders must modify the project timetable.

Estimating Unit Cost of Resources

The unit cost of each resource must be determined once availability is confirmed. For example, project leaders determine the cost of CPU time per second, or the hourly rate of pay for programmers and analysts. Resource unit costs help the project leader determine the costs of the entire project. Unit costs are typically available within the company for most of the resources used in A&D projects.

Estimating Resource Usage for Task Completion

Project leaders obtain an initial estimate of the amount of resource usage for each task. For instance, they may estimate how much time the analyst will spend in the problem definition phase. Methods to estimate the required time and resource usage are discussed later in this chapter in the section "Time Estimation." After project leaders define tasks, derive resource usage for each task, and establish the resource unit cost, they can easily estimate the cost of each activity.

Knowing the people involved in a typical system analysis and design project makes estimating resource usage easier. It also helps in assigning personnel to specific tasks and estimating the costs of completing those tasks. Given the variety of people involved, proper resource management requires that project leaders have extensive managerial skills. The following is a list of the key participants in a major A&D project:

- Information systems managers and project managers
- Project team members, such as programmers and analysts
- Other information systems personnel, such as database administrators, computer operators, and data control personnel
- Functional area managers
- Functional area personnel involved with or affected by the project
- A steering committee of participants, such as the functional manager for the project area, the director of IS, and so on
- A committee of IS and functional area personnel created to review A&D results

Estimating Duration and Cost of the Entire Project

Once project leaders obtain estimates for completing each task, they can derive estimates of the duration time and costs for the entire project. They periodically compare these estimates with actual time and costs during the project to make adjustments to help keep the project within a reasonable range of its expected time and costs.

Project task monitoring is an ongoing process. To keep up with changes and to determine whether the project is on schedule, project leaders continually compare actual duration times with estimated duration times for tasks.

Monitoring and Controlling the Project

Once the project begins, the project leader compares initial time, resource usage, and cost estimates with actual time, resource usage, and costs. If estimates differ greatly from the actual amounts, project leaders adjust tasks to keep them from overextending the available use of resources, or they reassign excess resources. The project leader may reassign excess resources (personnel, computing facilities, supplies, and so on) to other tasks to make sure that the project continues within a reasonable range of the estimates. For example, when programmers finish their own programming tasks, they can be reassigned to help complete other programming assignments.

PROJECT MANAGEMENT METHODS

There are several well-established methods for precisely planning a project's content, timing, and costs. The critical path method (CPM) and the program evaluation and review technique (PERT) are especially helpful in charting the timing of tasks; Gantt and milestone charts help define tasks and milestone events that should occur. A *milestone event* is an event that marks some level of completion or achievement for a project. For example, completing one of the phases of an A&D project may be considered a milestone event.

Critical Path Method (CPM)

The **critical path method (CPM)** uses tasks or activities (called *events*) and completion dates to design a network model of the proposed system that identifies tasks that must be completed on time or else the entire project will be delayed. Project leaders often use CPM for projects that require coordinating large amounts of resources over a lengthy time period. Circles on a CPM diagram represent the beginning or completion of a task (event), and arrows represent the task itself. Together, these CPM ingredients make up a diagram defined earlier as the project *network*.

In general, CPM demonstrates the interdependence of tasks by showing which task must be completed before the next one begins. It also shows all the possible paths through the diagram from the start to the end of the project. By determining which path takes the longest, project leaders identify the critical path. The **critical path** defines the longest path from the start to the end of a project, and thus the earliest time to complete the project. Figure 15-1 shows a CPM chart.

The CPM diagram in Figure 15-1 is a simple project having only four events, shown in the four circles, and five activities, labeled t_{12}, t_{13}, t_{23}, t_{24}, and t_{34}. Notice that the CPM chart also shows the time for each activity. For example, t_{12} takes 1 time unit, and activity t_{34} takes 3 time units. The CPM chart in Figure 15-1 illustrates:

- A project with four events and five activities (tasks)
- The time for each activity
- Event 2 cannot start until activity t_{12} is completed
- Event 3 cannot start until activities t_{12}, t_{13}, and t_{23} are completed
- Event 4 is not reached until all five activities are completed

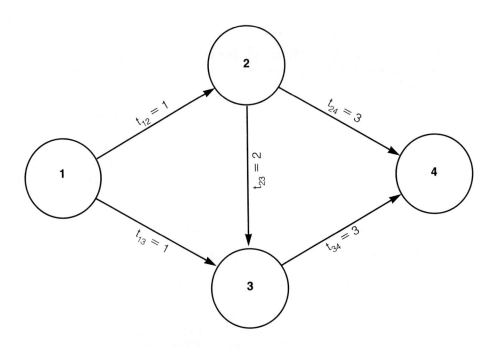

Figure 15-1. CPM chart example

Critical Path

The critical path has been defined as the path with the most time required from the start to the finish of the project. The critical path can be derived by tracing the total duration time for all tasks for every path from the start to the end of the project. The path with the longest duration time is the critical path.

Looking at Figure 15-1, you can identify the following paths through the diagram along with their associated times:

$$\text{Path 1: } t_{12} + t_{24} = 1 + 3 = 4$$
$$\text{*** Path 2: } t_{12} + t_{23} + t_{24} = 1 + 2 + 3 = 6 \text{ ***}$$
$$\text{Path 3: } t_{13} + t_{34} = 1 + 3 = 4$$

Since path 2 has the longest total time, 6 units of time, it is the critical path. Thus, the earliest time to complete the project is 6 time units. Time units can be minutes, hours, days, weeks, months, or years.

Earliest and Latest Start Times

Two other computations in analyzing a CPM diagram are the earliest start time and the latest start time to begin an event, shown as:

$$ES_i = \text{Earliest start time for event } i$$
$$LS_i = \text{Latest start time to reach event } i \text{ without delaying the project}$$

The **earliest start time** for each event is the *highest sum* of task times immediately preceding an event plus the ES_i of all events from which those tasks emanate. The following shows the calculations of the earliest start times for various events in Figure 15-1:

$$ES_1 = \underline{\mathbf{0}}$$

$$ES_2 = t_{12} + ES_1 = 1 + 0 = \underline{\mathbf{1}}$$

$$ES_3 = t_{23} + ES_2 = 2 + 1 = 3$$
$$\text{or} \qquad\qquad = \underline{\mathbf{3}}$$
$$t_{13} + ES_1 = 1 + 0 = 1$$

$$ES_4 = t_{24} + ES_2 = 3 + 1 = 4$$
$$\text{or} \qquad\qquad = \underline{\mathbf{6}}$$
$$t_{34} + ES_3 = 3 + 3 = 6$$

Thus the earliest start of each event is as follows:

Event 1 = time 0
Event 2 = time 1
Event 3 = time 3
Event 4 = time 6

From a planning standpoint, this means that event 3, for example, cannot begin before time unit 3, the time to complete both activities t_{23} and t_{13}, as well as activity t_{12}.

The **latest start time** (LS_i) constitutes the time the event *must* begin before delaying the overall project. To calculate LS_i, the analyst needs to work backward from the terminating event—that is, event 4 in Figure 15-1. LS_i is the *smallest difference* between the latest start time of an event minus the duration time for tasks on paths leading away from that event, starting with the earliest start time of the terminal event. The following illustrates the calculation of the LS_i for each of the four events in Figure 15-1:

$$LS_4 = LS_4 - 0 = \underline{\mathbf{6}} \quad \text{[The earliest start time of the terminal event]}$$

$$LS_3 = LS_4 - t_{34} = 6 - 3 = \underline{\mathbf{3}}$$

$$LS_2 = LS_4 - t_{24} = 6 - 3 = 3$$
$$\text{or} \qquad\qquad = \underline{\mathbf{1}} \quad \text{[Smallest difference]}$$
$$LS_2 = LS_3 - t_{23} = 3 - 2 = 1$$

$$LS_1 = LS_2 - t_{12} = 1 - 1 = 0$$
$$\text{or} \qquad\qquad = \underline{\mathbf{0}} \quad \text{[Smallest difference]}$$
$$LS_1 = LS_3 - t_{13} = 3 - 1 = 2$$

Thus, the latest start time for each event is as follows:

Event 4 = 6 time units

Event 3 = 3 time units

Event 2 = 1 time unit

Event 1 = 0 time units

In other words, reaching any event later than its latest start time will delay the project by that amount of time. For example, if event 2 is reached any later than 1 time unit, the project will be delayed. Figure 15-1 can be redrawn to incorporate the features of critical path, earliest event start time, and latest event start time. Figure 15-2 shows this revised CPM chart.

Slack Time

One final concept to understand relating to CPM charts is called slack time. **Slack time** constitutes the time to spare for completing tasks on a project network. A task's slack time is the amount of time a task can be delayed from its earliest start without affecting the earliest starts of succeeding tasks. Slack times for tasks are calculated by subtracting the duration time of the task, plus the earliest start time of the preceding node, from the latest start time of the succeeding node. The following illustrates the calculation of slack time for the CPM diagram in Figure 15-2:

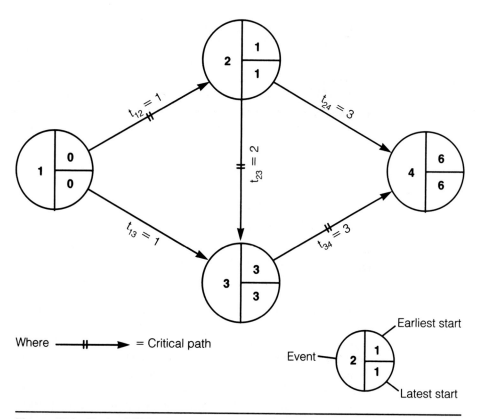

Where ————⊩———▶ = Critical path

Figure 15-2. Revised CPM chart

$$\text{Slack time for } t_{24} = LS_4 - ES_2 - t_{24}$$
$$= 6 - 1 - 3$$
$$= 2$$
$$\text{Slack time for } t_{23} = LS_3 - ES_2 - t_{23}$$
$$= 3 - 1 - 2$$
$$= 0$$

Thus, the slack time for t_{24} is 2 time units. This means that t_{24} can start any time between time unit 1 and time unit 3 and still be completed by time unit 6, when the entire project is scheduled for completion. From the standpoint of allocation of resources, slack time is extremely useful. Resources may be assigned to task t_{23} as early as time unit 1 or as late as time unit 3. This knowledge gives the project leader flexibility in allocating resources. One final note on slack time: All tasks on the critical path have a slack time of zero, meaning that they must begin and end on time or a delay will occur in the entire project.

Time Estimation

Up to this point, it has been assumed that the project leader knew the time required to complete each task. Actually, the project leader must derive these times using a time estimating method. The most widely used methods for estimating activity duration times include:

- Informed guessing
- Historical analysis
- Weighted averages
- Statistical methods

Informed Guessing

Experienced analysts can make an informed guess as to the duration times for tasks, based on their years of experience. Though not very analytical, this is the simplest method and often proves to be fairly reliable for experienced analysts. Problems occur with this method when the bias of an analyst enters into the estimation process and his or her assumption that the proposed project resembles a past project proves to be incorrect. If either of these problems occur, the estimate becomes nothing more than a wild guess. In addition, the informed-guessing method is useless for a project having a high degree of uncertainty.

Historical Analysis

In the historical analysis method, the analyst uses data about tasks on previous projects for estimating duration times on the current project. Many project leaders combine this method with their own experience to provide more valid estimates.

There are two major problems with the historical analysis method: Many companies do not keep adequate records, making data unavailable for task duration estimates, and the assumption that tasks on a current project will be similar to tasks on previous projects may be incorrect. Actually, the second problem occurs less often, since many projects do have many similarities. Like informed guessing, this method proves to be less useful for projects that involve a great deal of uncertainty.

Weighted Time Estimation

In many cases a single time estimate for task duration, as used in CPM, is not sufficient. A more realistic time estimate can be obtained by computing a weighted average for tasks. When an expected time for each task is derived from several different estimates, the CPM network diagram becomes a **program evaluation and review**

technique (PERT) diagram. The main difference between CPM and PERT is the use of weighted time estimates for task duration times. The remainder of the previous discussion on CPM also applies to PERT. In a PERT diagram, project leaders use the following three different times to estimate project tasks:

1. The optimistic time (T_o) is the least time required by the project if everything goes right and the project experiences no problems.

2. The most likely time (T_1) is the time the activity requires if normal problems and delays occur.

3. The pessimistic time (T_p) is the time required according to Murphy's Law: If anything that can go wrong, it will.

To compute the weighted average, project leaders calculate a weighted average of the three times: T_o, T_1, and T_p. The project leader may use the following formula to calculate the weighted average, the expected time (T_e) for task T:

$$T_e = \frac{T_o + 4T_1 + T_p}{6}$$

This formula indicates that the optimistic and pessimistic times are equally likely to occur, and the most likely time is four times more likely to occur than either T_o or T_p. The following example illustrates the use of this formula.

Assume a project leader needs to estimate the time to complete the task of installing computer hardware. If nothing goes wrong, the project leader estimates that two weeks will be required; with a normal amount of problems, three weeks; and if Murphy is correct, eight weeks. What is the estimated time for installation?

$$T_e = \frac{T_o + 4T_1 + T_p}{6}$$

$$= \frac{2 + 4(3) + 8}{6}$$

$$= \frac{22}{6}$$

$$= 3\frac{2}{3} \textbf{ weeks}$$

The estimated time (T_e) from the formula is 3⅔ weeks for installation. Most project leaders use weighted averages to derive task duration times for use in tracking projects because they furnish a more realistic estimate of the time needed for project completion.

Statistical Methods

Statistical methods are another way of estimating task duration time; this is often called a **stochastic determination** of time estimates. This method involves calculating the statistical variance for each task on the critical path and the statistical standard deviation of the project as a whole. From the activity variances, the project leader can calculate the standard deviation along the critical path. With this information, several important questions about the project can be answered. For example, by using a measure known as *Z-scores*, project leaders can calculate the probability of completing the project within a certain number of days. Thus, they can assess the risk of completing tasks by certain dates.

If you wish to pursue the use of statistical methods, consult any good textbook on the principles of management science. Many of these books now come packaged with software that makes the statistical methods operational.

Gantt Charts

A **Gantt chart** is a diagramming method used to chart and define project tasks, identify when they start and end, and indicate their duration time. Figure 15-3 shows a simple Gantt chart. This figure shows that the analysis phase of the project is scheduled for weeks 1 through 5, the design phase for weeks 3 through 11, the development phase for weeks 9 through 18, the implementation phase for weeks 15 through 21, and the project evaluation for weeks 21 through 22. The chart indicates that the project leader expects to complete the project in 22 weeks.

A Gantt chart also permits the project leader to start with an overview of general activities and decompose each activity into more detailed tasks on a separate Gantt chart. For example, the design phase could be shown as an activity on an overview Gantt chart, as in Figure 15-3, and then decomposed on a separate Gantt chart into all the design subtasks.

The main benefit of using Gantt charts is that they force the analyst to define the

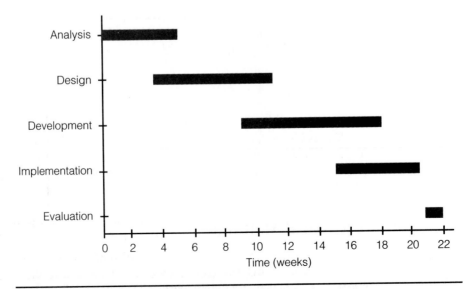

Figure 15-3. Gantt chart example

activities that must be accomplished to finish a project and to define the time needed for each task. They also facilitate assigning responsibilities to each task and subtask and show parallel completion of tasks. The major disadvantage of these charts is that they do not show dependencies. For example, Gantt charts do not show which tasks must be completed before other tasks are started. Project leaders typically use Gantt charts for smaller projects.

Milestone Charts

A *milestone* marks a significant point in a project, such as a task completion. The project leader determines the most important milestones for the project—for example, ordering hardware or completing software development—and incorporates them into a milestone chart. Like a Gantt chart, a **milestone chart** is a bar-type chart. However, a milestone chart only defines critical tasks that must be completed on time or the entire project becomes delayed. Thus, a milestone chart specifies completion dates for critical tasks; for example, the date when hardware must be received, or user training completed, in order to remain on schedule. Any event deemed critical by the analyst is a candidate for a milestone chart.

Figure 15-4 shows an example of a milestone chart indicating the tasks on the critical path during the analysis phase. Notice that the analysis phase is broken into

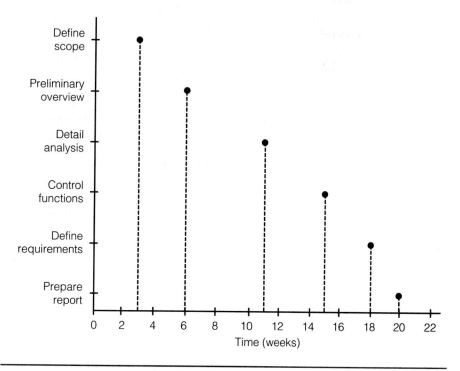

Figure 15-4. Milestone chart for the analysis phase

six critical tasks to complete, each having an expected time of completion. You can see, for example, that defining the scope is to be completed at the end of week 3, the detailed analysis is due at the end of week 11, and the prepared report is due in week 20. The chart helps project leaders monitor the progress of the project and adjust time and resource requirements as needed.

Time and Cost Trade-offs

Notice that up to this point, only time estimates have been considered. However, project leaders must also control project costs. Analysts frequently estimate project costs ahead of time. For example, the analyst may determine that a project expected to take thirty weeks will cost $400,000 to complete.

Consider what happens when a project leader needs to shorten project completion time. For example, suppose that your business is growing rapidly and the president determines that a new sales system needs to be installed sooner than anticipated. The obvious solution to the dilemma is to speed up the project to complete the system faster than originally expected—a process often called **crashing the system**. Project leaders use two important variables, time and cost, to derive estimates for crashing a system.

Before a system can be crashed, project leaders must determine whether the entire project can be shortened. Describing the crash procedure helps project leaders determine the amount of time they might save by crashing a system. They calculate this possible time savings by determining where they can shorten tasks on the critical path with a minimum expenditure of additional resources. Examples of possible ways to shorten a task include assigning more personnel to the task, assigning personnel who are more experienced to the task, making more or better equipment available, and purchasing some of the required software rather than coding it in-house. The goal is the greatest reduction in project completion time for the least increase in cost.

You must spend more money to reduce the time for a task on the critical path. Determining the least-cost crash involves analyzing the relationship between time and cost. Figure 15-5 shows a simple time/cost graph for a task along the critical path of a project.

According to Figure 15-5, the normal time for the task is 3 units at a cost of 10 units. The crash time is 1 unit at a cost of 30 units. Assuming a linear curve, the project leader can compute the cost slope by using the following formula:

$$\text{Cost slope} = \frac{\text{crash cost} - \text{normal cost}}{\text{normal time} - \text{crash time}}$$

$$= \frac{30 - 10}{3 - 1}$$

$$= \frac{20}{2}$$

$$= 10$$

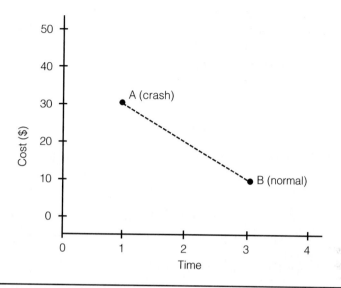

Figure 15-5. Time/cost graph

This slope indicates that for every decrease of 1 unit in time, cost increases by 10 units.

It should be noted here that a limit exists for reducing time. At some point, task time cannot be reduced any further, regardless of the amount of money spent. Also remember that resources and time (that is, people and months) are not totally interchangeable. For instance, if ten programmers can do the job in one year, twenty programmers cannot necessarily do the job in six months. The decision remains as to whether a project leader willingly spends the money necessary to shorten task completion time and, subsequently, the entire project.

Finally, remember that when you are crashing a system, crashing only those tasks on the critical path helps shorten the overall project. A company may spend much money and devote huge quantities of resources to reducing tasks not on the critical path and not gain anything. Look back at Figure 15-1 to see that the project leader could shorten the project only by devoting extra resources to tasks on the critical path—that is, path 2. Devoting additional resources to noncritical task along path 1 or path 3 would not reduce the project completion time at all.

FACTORS IN TIME AND COST ESTIMATION

In the earlier discussion of project management methods, you learned how important it is to calculate the time required for each task. This section provides some guidelines for determining the times to use in those calculations. The two main factors to consider when determining the time required for a task are:

- Complexity of the task
- Capability of the person assigned to the task

Complexity of the Task

Since it is easier to estimate time and cost for a simple project than for a complex project, as a project leader you should try to break down a project into manageable units. Not only does this make estimation easier, but assigning duties will be much smoother.

The project leader determines the components that make up the system, and then breaks up the programming effort into various tasks and assigns a person or a group of people to each task. There are numerous standard components in most software. Some of these components are:

- Report generation to produce needed information for users
- Update modules that update given files, such as the master file in a batch processing environment
- Edit modules that allow input to be checked for validity and accuracy before it actually enters the system
- Processing modules in which the actual calculations are carried out, such as calculating gross pay or a customer's total bill
- Utilities that perform standard functions, such as sorting the transaction file before processing
- Database extract routines that allow users to get needed information, such as querying the status of a particular order

The project leader might want to assign one group of programmers to report design, another group to writing database extract routines, and yet another group to working on update and edit modules. This separation of tasks clearly defines the responsibilities of each group and makes it easier for the project leader to determine the overall completion status of the programming phase. Also, if one group is behind schedule, the project leader can take whatever action is necessary to get it back on schedule.

Time Needed for Each Phase

From a computer project viewpoint, it helps to know (estimate) the amount of time needed in each project phase. For example, Figure 15-6 identifies possible guidelines to be used by the project leader. Whether the project breakdown in Figure 15-6

Activity	% Time
Analysis	15%
Design (logical)	20%
Development (physical)	55%
Implementation	5%
Documentation	5%
	100%

Figure 15-6. Guidelines for time estimates of each phase (including documentation)

represents a reasonable breakdown or not depends on the organization and the methods and tools used.

For example, if the analyst uses a computer-aided software engineering tool (such as an analyst workbench), you should shift more of the percentage of time into the analysis and logical design phases and less into the physical development phase. Each firm needs to develop a set of guidelines like the one in Figure 15-6 to more accurately estimate cost and resource usage in each project phase.

Capability of Personnel

The knowledge and experience of the person(s) assigned to the tasks determines to a large extent the time required to complete the activity. As a project leader, you can evaluate the capability of programmers by their:

- Experience with the computer system within which the programs will execute
- Knowledge of the programming language used
- Years and type of programming experience
- Creativity and imagination
- Willingness and drive in completing tasks

One important point to keep in mind is that programmers are not additive—that is, two programmers cannot create a program twice as fast as one programmer. The same attributes and concerns apply to all members of the design team. The knowledge and experience of all members of the team must be considered in estimating the time for project completion. Increasing the number of analysts working on the project does not necessarily mean that the project will be completed any sooner.

COMPUTER-AIDED PROJECT MANAGEMENT

Applying project management principles while developing information systems was one of the first project activities to be computerized. Project management got its start in the late 1950s and early 1960s, when defense contractors needed ways to manage large projects. Since by definition a project has a beginning, a middle, and an end, the building of 50 jet airplanes or 500 tanks was ideal for the project management concept. Needless to say, drawing PERT diagrams with 10,000 activities became a very time-consuming and tedious task, not to mention redrawing the diagrams countless times as conditions changed.

When computers became more readily available, much of the tedious work associated with project management could be shifted to the computer. Unfortunately, early project management software systems were generally mainframe-based and, even worse, used batch processing.

The increased interest in project management on the part of IS professionals has been due partly to the emergence of new technology. Desktop computer–based **project management software** systems enable IS managers and project leaders to track and control projects in an interactive mode, and many of these systems cost under $1000. Examples of desktop computer-based project management packages include Microsoft Project from Microsoft Corporation, Harvard Project Manager from Software Publishing Company, Project Management Workbench from Applied Business Technology, and SuperProject from Computer Associates.

Reasons for Using Project Management Software

There are many reasons for using project management software in the development of an information system, but perhaps the best reason is that it permits early planning by the project team. By using computer-based project management systems, project leaders experience reduced clerical workload, greater accuracy of project estimates, and the ability to track data values of interest. As a result, project leaders spend more time in planning and controlling projects and less time in directly applying project management principles.

Another advantage of using project management systems is the ability of the system to quickly respond to project changes. For example, schedules, budgets, and reports can be changed as user needs change. An indirect advantage of using computer-aided project management is improved decision making because of the availability of more accurate information derived from the project management system. Typical project management software systems allow you to do the following on the computer:

- CPM, PERT, Gantt, and milestone charting

- On-line editing
- Allocating of resources to each activity
- Comparing actual with expected times and report variances
- Analyzing time/cost trade-offs for crashing systems
- Using adaptive calendar features
- Scheduling, including user-defined priorities

PROJECT MANAGEMENT AT NATIONAL GOLF & TENNIS (NG&T)

The National Golf & Tennis (NG&T) project leader prepares Gantt charts, estimates activity duration times and costs, and institutes procedures to monitor the project. Figures 15-7, 15-8, and 15-9 illustrate the project management Gantt charts for the NG&T project. They depict Gantt charts for the analysis phase, the design phase, and the entire project, respectively. Notice that these figures show both scheduled and completed work.

Figures 15-10 through 15-13 supply detailed cost and manpower estimates for the analysis, design, and development phases, as well as for the entire project. The project leader vitally needs these estimates to prepare the schedule used to develop the project Gantt chart.

REVIEW

Methods for planning and managing projects include CPM (critical path method), PERT (program evaluation and review technique) charts, Gantt charts, and milestone charts. All of these methods serve as useful ways to monitor system projects, accompanied by estimating task and project completion times. Various ways of calculating time estimates, and considering earliest and latest start times and slack time, can be incorporated in the charts.

In addition to time concerns, the project leader must be concerned with costs. Crashing a project involves determining how to shorten project completion by spending more money to decrease the duration time for critical path activities.

Some factors to consider when estimating the time and costs of a project include the complexity of the task and the skill of the analyst or programmer assigned to the tasks. Application systems can be broken down into functional components to make estimating time and assigning duties easier for the analyst.

Finally, computer-aided project management is a way to reduce the time spent on

CURRENT DAY MARKER

ACTIVITIES		1	2	3	4	5	6	7	8	9	10	11	12	13	14	15
WEEK		MTWTF	MTWTF	MTWTF	MTWTF	MTWTF	MTWTF	MTWTF	MTWTF	MTWTF	MTWTF	MTWTF	MTWTF	MTWTF	MTWTF	MTWTF
MONTH		SEP	SEP	SEP	SEP	OCT	OCT	OCT	OCT	NOV	NOV	NOV	NOV	DEC	DEC	DEC
DATES		05-09	12-16	19-23	26-30	03-07	10-14	17-21	24-28	31-04	07-11	14-18	21-25	28-02	05-09	12-16
						V										
TOTAL PROJECT																
(Projected)	(35%)	***	*****	*****	*****	*****	*****	*****	*****	*****	*****	*****	*****	*****	*****	***
(Completed)		XXX	XXXXX	XXXXX	XXXXX	XXX										
ANALYSIS REPORT																
(Projected)		***	*****	*****	*****	***										
(Completed)	(100%)	XXX	XXXXX	XXXXX	XXXXX	XXX										
PRELIMINARY STUDY																
(Projected)		***														
(Completed)	(100%)	XXX														
SYSTEM SCOPE																
(Projected)			*													
(Completed)	(100%)	X	XXX													
CONCLUSION & RECOMMENDATION																
(Projected)			***													
(Completed)	(100%)		XXX													
STUDY OF PRESENT SYSTEM																
(Projected)			*****	*****												
(Completed)	(100%)		XXXXX	XXXXX												
PERFORMANCE SPECIFICATION																
(Projected)				***	*****											
(Completed)	(100%)			XXX	XXXXX	XXX										

LEGEND
% = Percent Completed
* = Scheduled Time
X = Work Completed
V = Present Date Pointer

Figure 15-7. Analysis phase Gantt chart

CURRENT DAY MARKER

ACTIVITIES		WEEK	1	2	3	4	5	6	7	8	9	10	11	12	13	14	15
		MONTH	SEP	SEP	SEP	SEP	OCT	OCT	OCT	OCT	NOV	NOV	NOV	NOV	DEC	DEC	DEC
		DATES	05-09	12-16	19-23	26-30	03-07	10-14	17-21	24-28	31-04	07-11	14-18	21-25	28-02	05-09	12-16
			MTWTF	MTWTF	MTWTF	MTWTF	MTWTF	MTWTF	MTWTF	MTWTF	MTWTF	MTWTF	MTWTF	MTWTF	MTWTF	MTWTF	MTWTF
TOTAL PROJECT																	
(Projected)	(35%)		***	*****	*****	*****	*****	*****	*****	*****	*****	*****	*****	*****	*****	*****	***
(Completed)			XXX	XXXXX	XXXXX	XXXXX	XXXX										
DESIGN REPORT																	
(Projected)			***	*****	*****	*****	*										
(Completed)	(100%)		XXX	XXXXX	XXXXX	XXXXX	X										
SYSTEM SCOPE																	
(Projected)			***														
(Completed)	(100%)		XXX														
SYSTEM FLOW CHARTS																	
(Projected)				*****	*****	*											
(Completed)	(100%)			XXXX	XXXXX	XXXXX	X										
SYSTEM INPUT/OUTPUT																	
(Projected)				*****	*****	*											
(Completed)	(100%)			XXXX	XXXXX	XXXX											
PERSONNEL & TRAINING																	
(Projected)				**	*****	*											
(Completed)	(100%)			XX	XXXXX	XXXXX	X										
DESIGN FILES																	
(Projected)					*****	*											
(Completed)	(100%)				XXXX	XXXXX											
SYSTEM CONTROLS																	
(Projected)				**	*****	*											
(Completed)	(100%)			XX	XXXXX	XXXXX	X										
PROGRAM SPECIFICATIONS																	
(Projected)					**	*****	*										
(Completed)	(100%)				XX	XXXXX	X										
PLANS & COST SCHEDULE																	
(Projected)					*	****											
(Completed)	(100%)				X	XXXX											

Figure 15-8. Design phase Gantt chart

CURRENT DAY MARKER — marker (V) shown at Week 14

ACTIVITIES	WEEK	1	2	3	4	5	6	7	8	9	10	11	12	13	14	15
	MONTH	SEP	SEP	SEP	SEP	OCT	OCT	OCT	OCT	NOV	NOV	NOV	NOV	DEC	DEC	DEC
	DATES	05-09	12-16	19-23	26-30	03-07	10-14	17-21	24-28	31-04	07-11	14-18	21-25	28-02	05-09	12-16
		MTWTF	MTWTF	MTWTF	MTWTF	MTWTF	MTWTF	MTWTF	MTWTF	MTWTF	MTWTF	MTWTF	MTWTF	MTWTF	MTWTF	MTWTF
TOTAL PROJECT (Projected)		***	*****	*****	*****	*****	*****	*****	*****	*****	*****	*****	*****	*****	*****	***
(Completed) (100%)		XXX	XXXXX	XXXXX	XXXXX	XXXXX	XXXXX	XXXXX	XXXXX	XXXXX	XXXXX	XXXXX	XXXXX	XXXXX	XXXXX	XXX
ANALYSIS REPORT (Projected)		***	*****	*****	*****	***										
(Completed) (100%)		XXX	XXXXX	XXXXX	XXXXX	XXX										
PRELIMINARY STUDY (Projected)		***														
(Completed) (100%)		XXX														
SYSTEM SCOPE (Projected)		*	***													
(Completed) (100%)		X	XXX													
CONCLUSION & RECOMMENDATION (Projected)			***													
(Completed) (100%)			XXX													
STUDY OF PRESENT SYSTEM (Projected)			*****	*****												
(Completed) (100%)			XXXXX	XXXXX												
PERFORMANCE SPECIFICATION (Projected)			***	*****	***											
(Completed) (100%)			XXX	XXXXX	XXX											
PLANS & COST SCHEDULE (Projected)			*****	**												
(Completed) (100%)			XXXX	XX												
DESIGN REPORT (Projected)		***	*****	*****	*****	*										
(Completed) (100%)		XXX	XXXXX	XXXXX	XXXXX	X										
SYSTEM SCOPE (Projected)		***														
(Completed) (100%)		XXX														
SYSTEM FLOW CHARTS (Projected)			****	*****	*****	*										
(Completed) (100%)			XXXX	XXXXX	XXXXX	X										
SYSTEM INPUT/OUTPUT (Projected)			****	*****	****											
(Completed) (100%)			XXXX	XXXXX	XXXX											
PERSONNEL & TRAINING (Projected)			**	*****	*											
(Completed) (100%)			XX	XXXXX	X											

Figure 15-9. Project Gantt chart

CURRENT DAY MARKER														V	
ACTIVITIES	MTWTF	MTWTF	MTWTF	MTWTF	MTWTF	MTWTF	MTWTF	MTWTF	MTWTF	MTWTF	MTWTF	MTWTF	MTWTF	MTWTF	MTWTF
WEEK	1	2	3	4	5	6	7	8	9	10	11	12	13	14	15
MONTH	SEP	SEP	SEP	SEP	OCT	OCT	OCT	OCT	NOV	NOV	NOV	NOV	DEC	DEC	DEC
DATES	05-09	12-16	19-23	26-30	03-07	10-14	17-21	24-28	31-04	07-11	14-18	21-25	28-02	05-09	12-16
DESIGN FILES (100%)															
(Projected)			*****	*****											
(Completed)			XXXX	XXXXX											
SYSTEM CONTROLS (100%)															
(Projected)		**	*****	*****	*										
(Completed)		XX	XXXXX	XXXXX	X										
PROGRAM SPECIFICATIONS (100%)			**	*****	*										
(Projected)			XX	XXXXX	X										
(Completed)															
PLANS & COST SCHEDULE (100%)		*	*****												
(Projected)		X	XXXX												
(Completed)															
DEVELOPMENT PHASE (100%)															
(Projected)					***	******	*****	*****	*****	*****	*****	*****	*****	**	
(Completed)					XXX	XXXXX	XXXXX	XXXXX	XXXXX	XXXXX	XXXXX	XXXXX	XXXXX	XX	
APPROVAL OF VENDORS (100%)						*****	*								
(Projected)						XXXXX	X								
(Completed)															
PLANS COST ESTIMATES (100%)						****									
(Projected)						XXXX									
(Completed)															
SYSTEM MANUAL (100%)						**	*****	*****	*****	*****	*****				
(Projected)						XX	XXXXX	XXXXX	XXXXX	XXXXX	XXXXX				
(Completed)															
PROGRAMMERS MANUAL (100%)							**	*****	*****	*****	*****	**			
(Projected)							XX	XXXXX	XXXXX	XXXXX	XXXXX	XX			
(Completed)															
OPERATORS MANUAL (100%)							**	*****	*****	*****	*****	***			
(Projected)							XX	XXXXX	XXXXX	XXXXX	XXXXX	XXX			
(Completed)															
USERS MANUAL (100%)									****	*****	*****	*****	*****		
(Projected)									XXXX	XXXXX	XXXXX	XXXXX	XXXXX		
(Completed)															

LEGEND
% = Percent Completed
* = Scheduled Time
X = Work Completed
V = Present Date Pointer

Figure 15-9. Project Gantt chart (*continued*)

	Lead Analyst	Analyst	Analyst	Analyst
Hours	40	40	40	40
Pay Rate	$60	$40	$40	$40
Total Pay	$2,400	$1,600	$1,600	$1,600
Total Payment				$7,200
Total Hours				160

Figure 15-10. Analysis phase cost and manpower estimates

	Lead Analyst	Analyst	Analyst	Analyst
Hours	60	60	60	60
Pay Rate	$60	$40	$40	$40
Total Pay	$3,600	$2,400	$2,400	$2,400
Total Payment				$10,800
Total Hours				240

Figure 15-11. Design phase cost and manpower estimates

	Lead Analyst	Analyst	Analyst	Analyst
Hours	100	100	100	100
Pay Rate	$60	$40	$40	$40
Total Pay	$6,000	$4,000	$4,000	$4,000
Total Payment				$18.000
Total Hours				400

Figure 15-12. Development phase cost and manpower estimates

	Lead Analyst	Analyst	Analyst	Analyst
Hours	200	200	200	200
Pay Rate	$60	$40	$40	$40
Total Pay	$12,000	$8,000	$8,000	$8,000
Total Payment				$36.000
Total Hours				800

	Total Hours	Total Costs
Analysis Phase	160	$7,200
Design Phase	240	$10,800
Development Phase	400	$18.000
	800	$36,000
Miscellaneous		$ 4.000
Estimated Total		$40,000

Figure 15-13. Project cost and manpower estimates

routine, tedious tasks. Computer-based project management systems provide automated charting capabilities, on-line editing, easy analysis of time/cost trade-offs for crashing systems, and many more functions that help managers spend more time on project planning and control and less time applying detailed project management principles.

QUESTIONS

1. Define *project management*.
2. What are the steps in project planning? How does planning help avoid the crises that often occur in system projects?
3. What does CPM stand for and what does it mean?
4. Describe how CPM can be useful in planning and controlling a systems project.
5. What is meant by earliest start time and latest start time for an event? What is the significance of each?
6. What does *slack time* mean, and what is its significance?
7. What is the critical path on a CPM diagram? Why is it important?
8. Distinguish between the PERT and CPM methods.
9. What is a Gantt chart? List its benefits and disadvantages.

10. How does a milestone chart differ from a Gantt chart?

11. What are three methods used for time estimation? Compare and contrast the three methods.

12. Why is the weighted time estimation method useful?

13. Define the phrase *crashing the system*. Explain its significance.

14. What are the two main factors to consider when estimating task duration times?

15. Why is project management a prime candidate for introducing a computer-aided method to apply its principles?

16. Discuss the reasons for using project management in developing a system project.

EXERCISES

1. Expand the analysis phase Gantt chart in Figure 15-7 to include specific tasks to complete the E/RDs created at the end of Chapter 5 in exercises 4 through 6 and the DFDs created in exercises 3 through 7 of Chapter 6.

2. Expand the portion of the Gantt chart in Figure 15-8 that addresses logical design, to include specific tasks for completing the prototype actions indicated in exercises 1 and 2 of Chapter 7, the logical design E/RDs of exercises 1 and 2 of Chapter 8, and the DFDs of exercises 3 through 6 of Chapter 8.

3. Expand the portion of the Gantt chart in Figure 15-8 that addresses physical design to include specific tasks for completing the structure charts created in exercises 3 through 10 of Chapter 9 and exercises 1 through 4 of Chapter 11.

4. For your class project, create a Gantt chart for the individual tasks within the analysis phase of the project. Create a project network and compute the critical path through your project.

5. Repeat question 4 for the logical design, physical design, and development and testing phases of your project.

SELECTED REFERENCES

Anderson, D. R., D. J. Sweeney, and T. A. Williams. 1978. *Quantitative Methods for Business*, 2nd Edition. St. Paul, MN: West Publishing Co.

Moder, J. J. and C. R. Phillips. 1983. *Project Management with CPM, PERT and Precedence Diagramming*, 3rd Edition. New York: Van Nostrand Reinhold.

PART VI

Maintaining and Securing the System

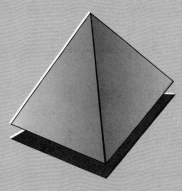

After the system is turned over to the user, an evaluation is conducted to determine whether it accomplishes the intended objectives, as described in user requirements established during the analysis, design, and development phases of the project. In addition, since the system must operate in a dynamic environment, changes may need to be made at the conclusion of the project. These changes may consist of enhancements to the system, or they may herald the start of the maintenance phase of the system life cycle.

The abundance and widespread use of computerized systems contribute to the growing concern for security and ethical use of systems and their associated data. Security measures need to be established by using preventive and corrective measures to secure the system and data from unauthorized access. Computer ethics involves analyzing the infringements of data representation and privacy.

CHAPTER 16

Post-Implementation Review and Maintenance

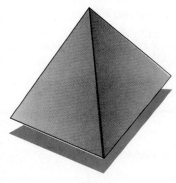

OVERVIEW

The analyst conducts a post-implementation review of the system several months after it has been put in place. This is a formal review to evaluate whether the project met expectations and was completed on time and within proposed guidelines. Most important, it reveals successes and failures that can be copied or avoided in the next project. At this stage, the system moves into the period in the system development life cycle that represents up to 70 percent of the information dollar: maintenance. To complete the cycle of system development, this chapter covers:

- The need for evaluation and post-implementation review
- The need for maintenance
- Major types of maintenance
- Proper management of the maintenance function
- Maintenance activities
- Maintenance tools and methods
- Methods to maintain business and system models
- Computer-aided maintenance

KEY TERMS

Adaptive maintenance

Benchmark testing

Charge-back scheme

Corrective maintenance

Legacy systems

Maintenance

Modifiable system

Ongoing maintenance

Parameter data values

Perfective maintenance

Periodic audit checking

Portable system

Program structuring system

Ripple effect

System consistency

System dependence

System maintainability

System re-engineering

Total quality management (TQM)

Understandable systems

A common misconception assumes that after implementation of the system, the work is almost completed. Actually, it has just started. Post-implementation activities consume the largest portion of the total resources devoted to the system. Estimates of this portion range from 60 to 90 percent, with variation between firms. Suffice it to say that a major portion of the cost associated with a system is incurred *after* implementation. The two major activities performed after implementation are post-implementation review and maintenance.

POST-IMPLEMENTATION REVIEW

After turning the system over to the user for initial use, the analyst conducts a post-implementation review to determine how well the system performs. This formal review determines whether or not the system has been successfully implemented. The project team leader should allot enough time between implementation and review for users to thoroughly examine the system, usually several months. Formal review should not be conducted immediately after implementation because some problems may not have surfaced, and users are not yet familiar with enough aspects of the system to provide adequate feedback.

Since typically the original development team has been disbanded, the responsibility for the post-implementation review must be assigned elsewhere. If one exists, a steering committee may be responsible for authorizing the review, assigning members to a review committee, and supervising the review. The review committee is usually independent of the original project team and user organization. However, some project team members and users involved in the project may be part of the committee; other members should have skills and organizational status similar to those of persons involved in the original A&D project.

The post-implementation review team reviews the project, prepares a post-implementation review work plan, conducts fact-finding activities, and prepares and presents reports to the steering committee. Key questions the review process attempts to answer include these:

- Were the expected benefits actually realized?
- Do problems exist with the system that need further investigation, which may lead to further enhancement and modification of the system?
- Was the project completed on time and within estimated guidelines?
- What was learned from this project that can be transferred to other projects?
- Was the system completed in a way that exhibits quality in the development process, and did it result in a high-quality system?

Exploring each of these questions in depth provides a greater understanding of their importance.

Assessing the Benefits

During the project's feasibility study, the analyst identified the system's expected benefits in measurable terms. These benefits were derived after intensive interviews with users to determine their requirements. The steering committee should now be able to actually measure what the system does versus the users' expectations of the system. For example, management at National Golf & Tennis (NG&T) can determine whether the expected number of orders can be processed in a day, or whether the elapsed time from receiving the order to shipment falls within the stated guidelines, as specified during the analysis and design phases.

Other evaluations might include operational guidelines, such as actual versus desired response time and actual versus expected throughput time. Good systems analysts consider operating efficiency as an important part of proper system design.

Investigating Problems Requiring Enhancement and Modification

During the time devoted to system development or modification, changes may occur in technology and business conditions that affect how well the system meets current information needs for company personnel. Furthermore, it is naive to expect that system development or maintenance can be completed without errors or neglected aspects of how the system may serve the company. Some of these errors and areas of neglect surface as users put the newly developed or modified system to use.

When projects are completed in traditional ways, the system delivered as final output often does not match some of the current information needs and capabilities of the business. Changes in the system may be warranted by a new or modified technology. Many types of technological advances may be foreseen while completing an A&D project, with changes in the system made during various project completion phases. However, some advances are difficult to forecast, and may emerge as the system is delivered for review. Users often expect that the newly delivered systems will permit them to use the latest advances in technology, where appropriate. When they recognize that a system does not use a technology that would enhance the capabilities provided, they are less satisfied with the system at delivery.

The analyst is the judge of whether the inclusion of a newly developed technology will actually enhance system capabilities or whether altered business conditions warrant changes in the delivered system. A user, dazzled by some new technology, may suggest that it be included, but it may not actually be necessary to satisfy user requirements. Analysts should determine the feasibility of including the technology and making changes to the system in the same way as they determine feasibility throughout the project. If the technology is a better way to meet user requirements, every attempt should be made to include it.

If analysts determine that the technology and changes to the system do not warrant a delay in system delivery, they should make every attempt to explain to users why the changes are not being made. Keeping users informed about the system and its characteristics at delivery promotes acceptance of the system and a feeling of mutual respect.

Changes in business conditions can often be forecast during completion of project phases. Many of these changes can affect the criteria on which an A&D project is based and, as a result, immediate changes may be warranted in the system delivered by a newly completed A&D project. Other changes in business conditions have little or no effect on a project; still others may need to be addressed when the system enters the continuous cycle of maintenance. Analysts must continually assess business conditions and make changes that they deem necessary, ignore those that do not affect the project, and delay those that may need to be addressed during maintenance of the system.

Errors identified in the system during final review are corrected as part of the original A&D project. Many of these errors may require a substantial investment of time, effort, and money. Typically, users are "good consumers" in their judgment of the end product of an A&D project, the system. They tend to judge the entire system based on specific characteristics they either like or dislike. If the system is delivered with known errors, however small, users may largely discount the many benefits of the system because of these errors. To prevent systems from being judged poor by users, all errors or problems with system operations detected during initial execution of the system should be corrected or resolved before the project is considered completed.

Just as problematic is a newly completed project that has areas of support that were neglected during the project. When users notice ways in which the system does not support their information needs, they become dissatisfied with the system.

Neglected areas of support often signify incomplete user requirements. When these areas are identified at the final review, the analyst should make every effort to include them and change the system so it supports them.

Assessing Timely Completion

In the planning stages of a project, the analyst lists all of the activities required to complete the project, along with the resource usage and costs required for each task. Chapter 15, on project management, explained how to accomplish this chore. The leader of the post-implementation review should compare estimated and actual figures on benefits, development costs, operation costs, and return on investment. The overall post-implementation report should contain tables with these comparisons to be presented to the steering committee at the end of the review. The steering committee can then compare these figures with the actual time and cost for completion.

Determining Transferable Lessons

Regardless of a project's uniqueness, post-implementation review follows the same basic process for all projects. The objective is to learn the best ways to complete project tasks and to learn from previous mistakes, so that you will function better during future projects. Analysts often perform tasks in ways that they learned were better during previous projects. Be careful to examine all aspects thoroughly, to avoid a false sense of success or failure, and to take with you what you have learned from a current project. Analysis and design is a continuous learning experience. The more you strive to learn, the better you will be as a systems analyst.

Review what went right and what went wrong during the project and look for changes that can be made to the development process to improve it. Some examples will help clarify this concept.

Suppose that project completion time was estimated at eighteen months, but the project was actually completed in twenty-four months. First impressions might suggest that the project team was poorly managed. However, initial estimates may have been unrealistic. An enthusiastic project manager may have had unrealistic expectations and assigned unattainable time estimates for certain tasks. A more realistic approach on future projects might be to use three different time estimates—optimistic, realistic, and pessimistic—to get an expected time. This procedure was outlined in the discussion of PERT in Chapter 15. A comparison of the actual time to pessimistic time may reveal that the project was completed well within worst-case estimates. The actual project completion time might be within normal standards for that company.

Another example of how a firm might learn from past mistakes involves the user interface designed for the system. Assume, for example, that the system was designed for inexperienced users, with system response slowed down in order to display instructions for each entry on a computer screen. Later this firm finds that its users are much more knowledgeable than had been assumed, and that instructions for each entry need not be displayed. Eliminating these screens helps decrease data entry time and improve the overall efficiency of the system.

Post-implementation review is a necessary process that can help determine the overall effectiveness and efficiency of a newly implemented system. It also helps provide information on what went wrong on a project and how to use this information to improve the system development process for future projects. The post-implementation review team submits a final report on the system to the steering committee for evaluation.

The results of the review can be used as a source of suggestions for modifications or enhancements of the operational system. Many of these identified changes are implemented in the maintenance phase of the system development life cycle.

Assessing the Quality of a Project and the Resultant System

The interest in quality in recent years affects the review and acceptance of the system delivered from an A&D project. The term **total quality management (TQM)** refers to building quality into business processes rather than merely attempting to inspect quality in outputs that result from business processes. For many companies, quality is addressed only after something is constructed; that is, they inspect the product for quality, rather than create a process that has quality. TQM typically involves continuous assessment of business and system processes, with changes made that further the cause of *continuous improvement* for those processes. TQM activities should also be performed to assess how well the system performs and how well system outputs support business activities.

Improving the processes used in A&D projects involves correcting erroneous processes, enhancing existing processes, deleting unnecessary processes, or adding new processes to those already performed. The intent is to make A&D project activities perform better, which will result in higher-quality systems.

One way to improve the quality of delivered systems is to make changes in system design and development specifications that will cause the system to more completely and correctly meet the timely information needs of users. To do this, additional quality checks need to be performed as portions of the system are completed. These quality checks may take the form of more test executions for the system, more prototyping-supported interactions between analysts and users, and more managerial review by IS and functional managers of design specifications.

FACTORS IN MAINTENANCE

Once implemented, a system enters the period of its life known as **maintenance**, which represents the greatest expenditure of effort and resources for computer systems. As mentioned earlier, most businesses spend at least 70 percent of the information system dollar on maintenance activities; some spend over 90 percent of the IS dollar on maintenance.

The information needs of businesses constantly change in response to external and internal factors. External factors that may require system changes include the general business climate, a competitor's introduction of new products and services, and imposition of new rules and regulations by governments. Internal factors include changes in user requirements and responses to methodological and technological changes. In addition, all systems contain inadequacies and errors overlooked during system development. Existing systems—whether they are newly developed and installed systems or older systems that are still in service—require the following modifications:

- Improving and enhancing the system
- Correcting errors
- Interfacing systems with other applications, systems, and technologies

The implementation of these changes is the reason why maintenance consumes more time, effort, and money than do new system development activities for the business.

Maintaining Legacy Systems

For most businesses, the importance of maintaining existing, longstanding systems, called **legacy systems**, far exceeds that of developing new systems. In fact, many important new systems development projects become part of a backlog of projects or a business that can extend seven years or longer.

Many characteristics of legacy systems need to either be completely eliminated or modified so that the system functions better, become more easily understandable, or becomes more easily modifiable. To make these systems easier to maintain, some portions need to be recoded altogether, while other portions need restructuring or refurbishing. Entirely replacing legacy systems is a very arduous task; therefore, most of them are only modified.

Some portions of these systems perform so poorly or are so difficult to understand that they need to be completely replaced. When analysts identify a portion of a legacy system that exhibits these characteristics, they may decide to completely replace that portion.

Many legacy systems were created prior to the adoption of structured programming as a standard by IS departments. The programs in these systems are sometimes restructured to make them easier to understand and maintain. The company's programmers may perform restructuring directly on simple programs or on programs that can be greatly helped by a little restructuring. Software now exists that will take existing unstructured code in many languages and produce a structured version of the program. Some CASE companies use this software to convert existing unstructured code into a format they can use to translate the program code back to a procedure model in either a structure chart or an action diagram format. The process of converting existing code back to a more abstract procedure model is often called *reverse engineering.*

Refurbishing legacy systems involves giving them a newer look and feel so that they appear to function and provide user access in a way that is consistent with more recently developed systems. Refurbishing tasks include recoding some of the routines, creating additional routines, replacing user interfaces, and creating utility routines that call on portions of the legacy system or are called at some point in the legacy system.

Some legacy systems only need changes to existing code or additions to that code. In these situations, programmers in the IS department code the changes or additions directly and add them to the existing code for the legacy system.

When user interfaces do not exist or are old and outdated, a more contemporary user interface can be created and installed, and the code updated to provide for more direct action between users and the system. These modifications are typically made to the existing code in specific programs in the legacy system.

Routines that perform additional processing or use better input or output formats, such as an on-line user interface, can also be created and added to legacy systems. To combine these additional routines with a legacy system, CALL routines are either added to the new routine or inserted into the legacy system. When the call is part of the additional routine, it causes this routine to be "wrapped around" the legacy system, with many external interactions with the legacy system actually made through the additional routine. When the additional routine is called by the legacy system, a CALL statement is placed at the appropriate point in the legacy system and control is passed to the additional routine. Regardless of how the additional routine and the legacy system are combined, using them together hides the archaic traits of the legacy system from the user and makes it appear more useful.

External and Internal Influences on Maintenance

The firm does not exist in isolation. Therefore, analysts must consider external factors, such as the general business climate, in systems maintenance. For example, boom-and-bust climates require the firm to change modes of action, or international expansion might require the development of interactive networks, among a host of other challenges. In addition, governmental regulations and demands affect the business's activities, creating accompanying changes in information demands. For example, numerous governmental reports on the hiring of minorities and handicapped individuals are required. The firm responds to these demands by modifying its activities and its computer systems.

Regulatory agencies within various industries also force changes in business. In addition, competition forces the firm to change as the industry changes. Better customer service often requires updated information systems. If your competitors are providing improved service, then you must do the same. For example, independent mail and package carriers such as UPS and Federal Express now provide immediate information regarding the delivery status of all packages. Once one of them provides this service, all mail and package carriers feel compelled to provide it.

Technological advances also put pressure on the firm to change in order to maintain a competitive edge. Advances in hardware and software require firms to update their technology to meet changing information needs. These advances frequently require modifying the firm's computer systems. For example, as the internal clock speed of desktop computers increases, more systems begin to have problems with hardware and software that were created to perform at slower clock speeds.

Internally, changes in business needs and changes in the character of users are two main influences on maintenance. Businesses frequently change their modes of action, lines of business, and levels of business activity. Likewise, users change their information needs, expect more of the system, and change jobs frequently. Also, there is an increasing level of computer literacy among managers and users that leads to more people using computer systems. These changes cause a continuing need for maintenance actions. For example, businesses that change from indirect to direct interaction with customers by converting from a mail-order business to a retail outlet must have systems that function on demand in a more interactive mode.

Evolution of Software

The development of a computer system follows a development life cycle like the one presented in this text. However, once developed, computer software must often be changed to prevent obsolescence. Modifying software can make the system more complex and more difficult to maintain. Eventually, the system may become so complex that it is more cost-effective to develop a new system. Figure 16-1 depicts the circular life span of systems.

A system is more than software. It consists of personnel activities, prescribed procedures, support activities, and resource utilization. However, the term *system maintenance* commonly refers to modifying programs within the firm's computer systems. During maintenance, systems personnel usually:

- Modify actions within a module of a program
- Modify actions within and between program modules
- Restructure a program and modify module activities
- Rewrite a program and replace it with a better program

Which action they perform depends on a number of factors, with each situation requiring subjective determination. The details of these factors are discussed in the remainder of this chapter.

Maintenance of Design and Systems

Systems personnel expend a great deal of energy gathering user requirements and designing a system to meet those requirements. However, after implementation, these same personnel often modify a system with little regard to updating the meticulously created business models and design specifications. As a result, modifications throughout the remainder of a system's life span eventually cause a loss of design, resembling the patchwork system. This situation occurs needlessly, especially when design speci-

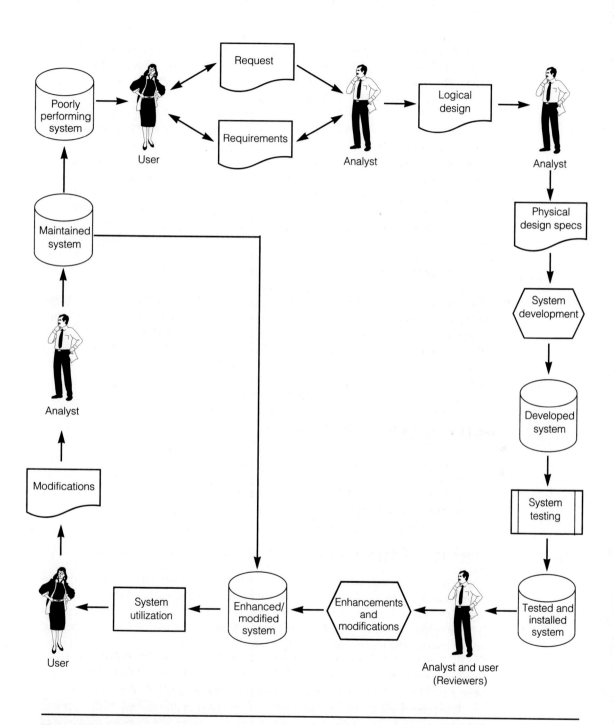

Figure 16-1. System life cycle

fications reside in an on-line dictionary or repository. Any change to a system should first be reflected in design specifications. In fact, modifying design specifications before modifying the system should guide system changes. In this way, the analyst assures a software life cycle of continuing development.

Any problem that leads to a system maintenance activity is actually a *business problem*. It is not a system problem that can be corrected by merely changing the computer system. The problem must be examined in the context of how it affects the entire organization or a portion of the organization. This business problem should be examined in its proper setting within the existing business model. By analyzing the problem with respect to the current business model, the analyst can better understand what the problem is, why it is important that it be resolved, and how best to resolve it.

Unfortunately, the demands of rapid change and the staffing levels of IS departments may dictate that system modifications are not preceded by modifications to the business model and system design specifications. Thus, the eventual outmoding of the business model and the demise of the system are assured. For example, the economic downturn in the early 1990s that caused companies to seek better ways to provide their products and services while cutting staff was disguised as business downsizing. The completion of more A&D projects can help make a company more competitive, which stimulates a greater demand for company products and services. However, completing these projects requires more personnel—a need that conflicted with various approaches to downsizing taken by many companies.

TYPES OF MAINTENANCE

Systems professionals provide the support necessary to keep systems current. As the information needs of the business change, systems professionals modify the firm's system to meet these needs. Consequently, each type of maintenance represents an organizational system-support activity.

Ongoing Maintenance

The firm has **ongoing maintenance** needs, which are usually taken care of by programs that perform some type of maintenance on a regular basis. They update files, update records and data items within files, update business accounts, reset totals, modify table entries, and perform a host of other activities. Files and databases are backed up and copied. The number of files within a firm is reduced as a result of purging inactive files and records. Storage space for data is reduced by reorganizing files, indexes, and directories. Files undergo conversions involving formats, media, and physical locations. New versions of vendor software and hardware may replace older versions.

This type of maintenance is normally not included in discussions of the types of maintenance, and it is not the main concern here. However, it influences the types of maintenance we will discuss next.

Maintenance Categories

Maintenance can be classified as:

- Corrective maintenance
- Perfective maintenance
- Adaptive maintenance

Corrective maintenance entails actions to eliminate errors and failures. Perfective maintenance represents actions to improve or maintain system performance. Adaptive maintenance embodies actions to adapt systems to new methodologies, functions, or technologies.

Corrective Maintenance

Corrective maintenance eliminates errors through changes in procedures, techniques, computer code, and documentation. These corrections involve operations personnel, users, programs within the system, and all forms of documentation.

The principal type of corrective maintenance is correcting problems associated with the integrity and/or reliability of a system's programs. Integrity problems result from inadequate data validation, invalid data usage, improper or invalid processing, or inadequate or invalid reporting. Reliability refers to error-free execution with minimal downtime. If a system is down too much, users typically consider it unreliable, even if it is relatively error-free. Such problems result from inadequate testing of systems following development and maintenance activities. Software that periodically performs auditing activities or benchmark software can be used to identify integrity and reliability problems.

Operations personnel are the data entry personnel, computer operators, and data librarians who are responsible for scheduling and assisting system execution. These personnel must be properly trained and have clear, up-to-date operations procedures available to them. Procedures and techniques followed by operations personnel and users are parts of any system. The proper performance of these procedures influences the correctness of system execution. Corrective maintenance often involves changing the procedures that operations personnel or users follow. These procedures may have been developed incorrectly from the start or may need to be changed because of business changes.

Additional training in new or changed procedures is also part of corrective maintenance. Chapter 13 covered training as it relates to implementing a new system, but training is just as important to maintenance activities. Errors may occur simply because operations personnel or users lack proper training. Firms that leave training to area personnel, or avoid retraining, encourage carrying misunderstandings forward to subsequent generations of employees.

Proper maintenance of documentation complements procedural and training maintenance activities that keep up with changes in personnel and operations. This is an often overlooked corrective maintenance activity. Documentation serves as a guide to operations personnel and also guides users in operating the system and interpreting the results of system execution.

Two other forms of corrective maintenance are periodic audit checking and benchmark testing. **Periodic audit checking** tracks the processing of data following maintenance activities to compare processing results with values known to be correct. **Benchmark testing** involves testing a system to determine whether it performs according to expectations. Periodically executing benchmark tests is one way to detect when software deteriorates following continued maintenance.

Early in the life of a system, corrective maintenance is the dominant type of maintenance activity. As a system matures, proper maintenance generally decreases the number of bugs, and maintenance shifts to enhancement activities for perfective or adaptive system modification.

Perfective Maintenance

Perfective maintenance seeks to enhance system performance, improve system cost-effectiveness, and improve system maintainability. Performance enhancements increase the efficiency of the system and maintain speedy response times. Many elements of the system can contribute to its efficiency: well-written algorithms or processing techniques in programs, well-designed forms for input and output, updated computer languages and language translation optimizers, improved storage formats, faster communications software and hardware, and faster computer processors.

Perfective maintenance represents the re-engineering of an existing operational system based on functional premises. The term **system re-engineering** refers to redesigning and/or developing an existing system. In its simplest form it involves restructuring or enhancing the performance of archaic code in system programs. In its more complex form, it involves the redesign and implementation of an existing business system, which may include changing the ways in which the business and the information system function. A perfective maintenance project may involve either simple or complex system re-engineering.

SYSTEM PERFORMANCE   An example of a more efficient processing technique is the use of a *binary table search* for tables containing data values in ascending or descending order. For example, a sequential search of a thousand-element table for a value not in the table would normally execute the search routine a thousand times before determining that the value does not appear in the table. In contrast, a binary search would execute the search routine only nine times before determining that the table does not contain the search argument value.

In a table search, the data value being searched for is often called the *search argument*. A binary search routine performs a more efficient table search by iteratively halving the table and testing to see whether a middle data value is greater than or less than the search argument data value. For example, if the data values in the table are stored in ascending order and the middle data value is greater than the search argument data value, then the match for the search argument can only be in the first half of the table. This eliminates a search of all the data values in the last half of the table. The first half of the table would then be halved and the middle data value compared to the search argument, with an appropriate half of the table selected to continue the search. The binary search would continue halving and comparing the middle data value with the search argument until either the data item is found or the end of the table is reached (the search argument data value is not found).

Another example of using perfective maintenance to improve system performance is in an early system that may have been coded in an inefficient language. Many small manufacturing companies used (and still use) the 30-series computers from IBM. The applications created to execute in these systems are in a language called RPG (report program generator). When these companies migrated to more advanced minicomputers in the 1990s, they were able to replace programs in their existing systems with programs written in a more efficient language than RPG.

Frequently, programmers who have been maintaining systems written in inefficient languages ignore the benefits of using efficient subroutines in other languages. In addition, systems in these older languages seldom have optimizing language translators. Converting an often-used program into a more efficient language, such as assembly language, geometrically increases system efficiency. The same thing occurs when efficient subroutines are called within programs.

Optimizing language translators are a recent development affecting program efficiency. These translators create machine code in a more efficient manner than conventional translator software. As a result, complete systems may become more efficient in terms of execution.

Changing record blocking factors illustrates a perfective maintenance project involving storage formats. As enhancement of storage devices provides denser data storage, the blocking factor for records should be changed to accommodate this greater density. When blocking factors remain the same over a number of years, space is wasted at the ends of disk tracks.

COST-EFFECTIVENESS   Perfective maintenance can also be used to improve the cost-effectiveness of systems. For instance, if a system generated a full complement of reports upon program execution, a perfective maintenance project might insert a routine calling for the user to enter a data value to indicate only those reports actually needed for the current execution. This modification would result in cost savings each time a user requested only certain reports rather than the full complement normally generated by the system.

MAINTAINABILITY   Once a system becomes difficult to maintain, it becomes a candidate for the system scrap pile. As a result, the company loses the tremendous investment it has in the system. Keeping programs maintainable is a vital part of perfective maintenance. One way to increase maintainability is to perform maintenance in a more careful and deliberate fashion. Changed programs often lose their structure or already exist in a less maintainable form. A perfective maintenance project may redevelop a program in a more maintainable format. For example, software now exists that converts unstructured source language code into a structured equivalent. Applying this software to older, unstructured programs may render them more maintainable.

Adaptive Maintenance

Adaptive maintenance responds to changes in the internal or external environment and may involve enhancements to the related systems. External factors such as those we have discussed previously—the general business climate, competition from other firms, or regulations from various governmental agencies—may require changes within the firm and its IS. Internally, the firm's systems and communication hardware and software undergo constant change, and changes in the level and type of business activity may also create the need to adapt systems.

As the general business climate moves between boom and bust times, the firm must conduct business differently; or the federal government may require new information that the current system cannot produce; or the firm's industry may institute new customer services that require a new customer information system for the firm. These changes may also cause information requirements for the firm's personnel to change. An adaptive maintenance project responds to such changes.

An example of changes in hardware and software is the emergence of enhanced storage media, implemented by company personnel. Such a change frequently causes adaptive maintenance projects to be undertaken. In addition, changes in users and in their computer awareness normally result in changes in data and processing requirements, which create pressure to modify systems.

During an adaptive maintenance project, the analyst should determine whether parameter data values entered at execution time may make a system adaptable on a continuing basis. **Parameter data values** are used as input to a system, either for direct use by the program or as a guide for the program in processing other data. For example, some reports may use data from a previous time period and therefore need to reflect the fact that the output pertains to that time period. In this case, the execution of the system's programs would require that the user enter the date that should appear on the report.

As an example of how parameter data values are used to guide programs in processing other data, consider an output report that displays data grouped on a certain data item in the report, such as a state code. The data item used for grouping the output data is called a *control group*. The report displays the output data grouped on different data items for the control group data item. For instance, if the control group is a state code, the output data will be displayed in groups based on the state code in the individual output records. When a program can be grouped on different types of data items, such as state codes or regions, each system execution may require that the user submit an appropriate parameter data value to indicate how to group the output data.

The use of parameter data builds adaptability into a system. When types of adaptability are known, the system can be developed or modified to make it more flexible in satisfying user information needs. When types of adaptability are not known, but are subsequently identified, adaptive maintenance projects occur.

The following examples illustrate requests for the three types of maintenance requests that occur in business.

Perfective Maintenance Example

A small company in the southwestern United States manufactures products for one of the large door-to-door sales firms. Raw materials are weighed at shipping and receiving and recorded on a terminal connected to the firm's minicomputer. Shipping and receiving clerks have been complaining to their supervisors about the length of time required for each data entry. The minicomputer capacity is much greater than the needs of the company. Thus, the problem resides in the shipping and receiving transaction processing system, not in the capacity of the computer.

Shipping and receiving clerks write a request for maintenance service and submit it to their supervisor. After reviewing the request, the supervisor formalizes it and sends it to the supervisor of IS maintenance. Figure 16-2 shows the formalized request.

After reviewing the request, the maintenance supervisor gives the request to

---

Novelty Manufacturing Maintenance Request Form

Requestor: <u>Mark Wright, Supervisor of Shipping/Receiving</u>

Telephone Number: <u>555-4148</u>

System(s) Involved: <u>Shipping/Receiving Transaction Processing</u>

Problem Explanation: <u>Recording shipping/receiving transactions takes two minutes per transaction regardless of the number of items included in the transaction. This causes clerks to spend a great deal of time waiting for the transaction to be processed.</u>

Date of Request: <u>8-03-93</u>

Estimated Implementation Date: <u>2-01-94</u>

Request Justification: <u>Shipping/receiving clerks are paid $10.00 an hour with an average number of 20 transactions processed per hour. As a result, the daily loss to the company in idle work time is approximately $53.00 indirect wage loss. Indirect cost such as lost opportunities for worker utilization contribute even more to the loss to the company.</u>

Request Priority:	1	2	3
(Circle one)	Immediate attention	Very soon	When convenient

Figure 16-2. Perfective maintenance request

Riggs Williams, a maintenance staff member already experienced in the shipping/receiving system. Riggs contacts Mark Wright, the shipping/receiving supervisor, to set up the first meeting and secure permission to question shipping/receiving clerks. He then interviews shipping/receiving clerks and has each one record a transaction while he looks on. Riggs discovers that the time reported for processing a transaction is indeed correct. He then decides to review design and development documentation to determine the cause of the slow response time.

The design/development documentation indicates that a complete execution of the inventory update system occurs while each transaction is entered. Riggs interviews all area supervisors in the manufacturing section to determine whether it is necessary that inventory records be continuously updated. During these interviews, it is determined that an on-demand execution of the inventory system would suffice for any immediate needs. Otherwise, an update execution at the end of the day would be sufficient for all concerned. As a result, Riggs determines that shipping/receiving transactions may be accumulated during the course of the day and processed during the normal execution of the update system at the end of the workday.

Riggs modifies the design/development documentation to indicate accumulating shipping/receiving transactions in a sequential access file as goods arrive or leave the section. He then writes a small program to act on requests for transaction processing by the shipping/receiving clerk. He changes the connection to the menu item of the shipping/receiving clerk so that the transaction processing option causes this new front-end program to execute. Riggs also adds a new option to the shipping/receiving menu that causes the update program to be invoked on demand. After eliminating initial bugs, testing the modified transaction processing system reveals that it is bug-free. In addition, Riggs notes that normal transaction processing now takes less than three seconds. Everyone is pleased. At the conclusion of the maintenance project, the users who requested the change certify that the modified system meets their needs.

Adaptive Maintenance Example

The Phillips/Matsumoto Advertising Agency, owned and operated by Stew Phillips and Marcy Matsumoto, supplies advertising to a cross section of clientele. The agency uses a medium-sized mainframe to retain various records needed by the firm. One of the files maintained in support of the firm is the advertising clientele file. This file contains information about the amount of business activity generated by the firm's clientele. Until recently, the largest yearly advertising total was $5 million. However, the Phillips/Matsumoto Agency just acquired the advertising rights to the Leonard Mauer Fish franchise. Phillips/Matsumoto's management expects that this franchise will generate $12 million of advertising business. This makes it necessary to extend the significant digits of the advertising total data item from seven to eight digits to the left of the decimal. Thus, a maintenance project must adapt the firm's systems to the modified data format. Figure 16-3 shows the request for this modification.

The request is reviewed by Michael Brawner, systems manager, and passed on to programmer/analyst Jack Berry. Jack knows that changing a data field in a file may

Phillips/Matsumoto Advertising Maintenance Request Form

Requestor: <u>Larry Leseur, Supervisor of Accounts</u>

Telephone Number: <u>555-2264</u>

System(s) and/or Files Involved: <u>Clientele File</u>

Problem Explanation: <u>The acquisition of a large advertising account makes it necessary to extend the length of the advertising total data item from seven to eight significant digits to the left of the decimal position.</u>

Date of Request: <u>2-04-94</u>

Estimated Implementation Date: <u>3-01-94</u>

Request Justification: <u>Self-explanatory</u>

Request Priority: 1   2   3

(Circle one)   Immediate   Very soon   When
                attention   convenient

Figure 16-3. Adaptive maintenance request

affect all programs that access the file. As a result, accesses to the file during the past few months must be scrutinized. Jack decides to use a program to monitor the computer log of actions performed on this file for this purpose. This program reads a tape of the log file for a specified activity. Thus, accesses to the clientele file may be determined. Subsequently, programs may be identified as candidates for modification as a result of converting to the new file format. These programs may all need to be changed before switching to the new file format.

Jack Berry directs the system to print out a current source code listing of the identified programs, including a cross-reference list for variable names assigned to data items. Jack uses these listings to determine where changes need to occur and whether there is a need for additional modification. A close look at the computer code identified in the cross-reference listing indicates that all references, except one, to the advertising total field would be unaffected by the change to the new file format.

The single reference affected by the field length change consists of a computation in which the advertising total is used. This computation results in a data value used as output to another file. Extending the length of the advertising total by one digit also causes the length of the computed data value to be increased by a single digit. Thus, the log tape needs to be searched once again for the second file affected by the change in the advertising total field. Fortunately, a review of the programs that access this file reveals that no other files or programs are affected further. Jack Berry then makes the changes to the programs affected, changes the file formats, and updates the documentation to reflect these changes.

This example reflects how changes in one file and/or program can cause changes to be made in other files and/or programs. Using the log tape pointed to possible problems in making the desired change. It was the perseverance and thoroughness of the programmer/analyst that assured that the change would be instituted in a trouble-free manner. This example also makes a strong case in favor of using relational database management systems that use standard names and descriptions for data items in logical database objects.

Corrective Maintenance Example

Following the field length change, Jack Berry tests and installs a modified program that uses the file as input. Two weeks after the updated program was implemented, it fails in an execution. Initially, it appears that modifying the program had created the problem. However, during a preliminary investigation, it is determined that a program module unaffected by the recent change actually caused the failure. This module was designed to process a special type of data. The special data had not been processed until the time when the failure occurred. A close look at the program module created for this data reveals that the module contains errors in its logic. Thus, a corrective maintenance project needs to be performed for errors that should have been caught in testing when the system was first developed. Corrective maintenance projects often occur because of insufficient testing following system development or a previous maintenance action performed on the system.

Jack consults with the systems manager, Michael Brawner, concerning the need for further modification of the program. Michael states that the additional maintenance activity actually represents a new project. However, since Jack had not completely signed off on the project, the additional modification could be included with the original request. Michael also states that the requesting user should be told why the failure occurred and that he must consent to being responsible for the additional maintenance. Michael then calls Larry Leseur, the supervisor requesting the original change. Larry consents to the additional maintenance actions that result in a continuation of the project.

Jack Berry decides to review the documentation concerning the special data and to interview personnel regarding its purpose and how it should be processed. He thinks that the original programmer must have misunderstood the purpose of the data and coded the program module incorrectly. After careful review of documentation and questioning of users, Jack corrects the module and tests it. To test the modification, he uses the same version of the file that was used as input when the failure occurred. The test execution is completed without errors and Jack conducts a formal review of the project. This review includes signing a separate corrective maintenance sign-off form.

This example illustrates how a need for additional maintenance often surfaces while another maintenance project request is serviced. When this happens, the analyst must first decide whether the additional problem represents a completely new maintenance project or can be corrected as part of the existing project. Second, the user must be told of the need for additional work and must consent to being responsible for any additional maintenance actions.

Maintenance Tools and Methods

Project team members use the same tools, methods, sequences, and formats no matter what type of maintenance they are performing: corrective, perfective, or adaptive. Many of the tools and methods that are used in development projects also serve maintenance personnel in their activities. For example, software systems that restructure programs help in the process of maintaining a system. Furthermore, the practice of having programmers who develop systems become the persons who maintain the programs during future maintenance projects helps the maintenance process. A number of other tools provide ways to improve maintenance. The use of these tools and methods does not ensure good maintenance. Systems are maintained by people, not by methods or tools. However, using them provides valuable assistance to those who maintain systems.

The three main types of tools and methods used in supporting maintenance include design and development tools and methods, monitoring methods, and documenting tools and methods. Design and development tools and methods support maintenance activities directly. CASE tools provide the most comprehensive set of tools to support developing and maintaining systems. Monitoring tools and methods provide ways to determine when maintenance is required. Many companies have software systems that monitor system executions to determine when certain types of conditions exist. Documenting tools and methods are used to upgrade documentation during maintenance activities.

Tools that support maintenance design and development activities are:

- Prototyping
- Modeling methods and tools supporting them
- Structured methods and tools supporting them
- Design/development dictionaries
- Designer/developer CASE workbenches
- Computer-aided tools and methods such as CASE utility software

As you can see, these are the same tools, described in earlier chapters, that are used in the development of a project. The difference is that maintenance personnel use them to *modify* a system instead of to create one.

Prototypes help to determine desirable changes in user interfaces and options available to users. Various design diagrams may clearly identify changes required for the system. A structured, top-down approach simplifies system modifications. Maintenance personnel sometime use a program structuring system as an additional tool before redevelopment. A **program structuring system** is a software system capable of converting unstructured or poorly structured code into structured code. The maintenance staff may also use a design/development dictionary or repository to update design/development specifications.

We discussed prototyping in Chapter 7. During maintenance, prototyping helps determine desirable changes. The design dictionaries that were created in the logical design stage, discussed in Chapter 8, can now be used to update design/development specifications.

Design/development CASE workbenches provide a wealth of tools to aid maintenance personnel during modification activities. Computer-aided tools, from cost estimators through application generators, provide efficient and thorough assistance to maintenance personnel. Computer-aided maintenance principles will be discussed in a separate section later in this chapter.

Maintenance personnel use a number of tools to provide information regarding the efficiency and validity of system execution. These tools and methods are created by software manufacturers and by personnel within the firm. Some of these tools perform continuous monitoring and some can be used on demand. For example, there are software systems that continuously monitor the average response time for user queries. When these systems detect an average response time outside of an acceptable range, a message is sent to the appropriate person in the IS department. An example of an on-demand tool is the use of a querying system to search the log file for the company computing center to determine whether recorded values are substantially different from those expected. These queries cause exception data values to be displayed for log entries, such as the number of repeat queries per user, the number of errors in entering queries for particular users, and so forth. With these tools, analysts can sometimes identify problems in systems before users notice them and before they become too costly.

MANAGING MAINTENANCE

Understanding the types of maintenance and the influences on it, regardless of the type, provides the basis for managing maintenance. Managing maintenance also involves preparing systems for easier maintenance, training personnel about maintenance, providing proper control for maintenance, and making functional personnel aware of their responsibilities regarding maintenance.

Building in Maintenance

As you know by now, the initial preparation for maintenance activities occurs while a system is developed. A well-structured, top-down approach to system development goes a long way toward building in system maintainability. The more structured and consistent the design of the system, the more maintainable the system is likely to be. Structured methods break complex systems down into smaller, less complex components that are easier to maintain. Building in maintainability also includes creating (and maintaining) thorough development documentation. The more thorough and up-to-date documentation is, the easier it is to understand where and how to change systems.

System maintainability refers to whether a system is easily understood, easily modified without loss of functionality, and easily transported to a new environment without the need for major changes.

Certain characteristics must be built into a system for it to be easily understood. **System consistency**, which is achieved through consistency of technique and style, is one of these characteristics. Consistent technique and style should be present within programs, between programs, and between systems. Structured methods encourage these types of consistencies. Easily understood programs contain deliberate and simple program logic. The problem should be faced head-on in the simplest manner; creating business software is not a time to demonstrate eccentric programming capability.

Understandable systems are characterized by how completely the programs perform their actions and how easy it is to follow a program's logic while analyzing it. A **modifiable system** is an understandable system that employs common (or general) problem-solving logic. A structured, top-down approach to design supports creating understandable, modifiable systems.

A **portable system** exhibits flexibility and machine independence. Systems that have these characteristics accommodate varying environments; they have built-in flexibility and execute in a multitude of hardware and software environments. As a result, when changes are made in their existing environments, or when they are used in a new environment, these systems usually execute without major modifications. An example of a portable system is an inventory system designed for use in one factory that can be used at other locations, even though different software running on different hardware is in place at the various locations.

Staffing and Training for Maintenance

When a system is designed to be consistent, understandable, modifiable, and portable, maintenance projects should be conducted in a manner that promotes the continuation of these attributes. Proper staffing and training of personnel help the system manager retain these characteristics within the firm's systems. Two primary approaches to staffing exist, each with its advantages and disadvantages:

- Systems personnel assigned to represent a particular group of users in both development and maintenance
- Systems personnel divided into two separate groups, one responsible for development and one responsible for maintenance

The user representative approach provides users in a particular functional area with dedicated IS personnel assigned directly to them. These IS professionals develop and maintain systems for just that group of users. As a result, they often become more familiar with users' needs in a particular functional area of the business and with the existing systems that service them. Managed properly, this approach can be successful in servicing those users. However, this approach may encourage pockets of system biases that become difficult to integrate across the firm.

IS personnel who spend all of their time on systems for a particular functional area frequently know very little about other functional areas and the systems they use. When systems that support different functional areas lack integration, many of the same actions may be performed on the data being retained by the company. Furthermore, since many systems that support different functional areas share the same data, changes made to this data by a system in one functional area may create problems for the execution of systems that support other functional areas. In addition, rapid turnover in systems professionals frequently decreases the likelihood that these personnel will become truly knowledgeable about a particular functional area and its systems.

The second approach to staffing creates an environment in which personnel specialize in either development or maintenance. However, good development and maintenance practices are very similar in nature for companies having a history of effective maintenance activity. In this approach, a development team member is often reassigned to maintain the system after it is developed. As a result, some maintenance staff members are thoroughly familiar with all aspects of the system's design and understand why certain parts of the system work as they do.

The main disadvantage of separating staff into development and maintenance personnel is that some maintenance staff personnel may not initially understand the basis and functioning of newly developed systems. They will have to learn how the system is structured and how it works through maintenance actions performed on these systems—a task that may be difficult for large, complex systems.

Both types of staffing arrangements have proven to be workable. How to arrange the staff is often less important than how the staff is managed. Regardless of the type of arrangement, both expertise regarding the functioning of the business and technical specialization should be encouraged. IS personnel should attempt to learn as much as possible about all functional areas of the business so that they understand how aspects of a particular system may affect the business. Furthermore, the more they know about all the areas of the business, the better prepared they will be to work on A&D projects that support those areas. It is impossible for every system professional to be an expert on every facet of a computer system. Therefore, permitting a person to become the resident expert in certain technical areas of a system provides a way to focus that person's attention and make him or her a more valuable resource. At the same time, a system manager should not depend on a single person for a particular type of maintenance. This is especially true in the volatile world of the systems professional, where job changes occur often.

Once the staff is properly assigned, they must be trained in maintenance practices. This is an area that is frequently neglected but is critically important to the success of the IS department. Training should begin when a person first joins the IS department, and systems managers must make sure that learned maintenance practices are used by all maintenance personnel. This requires extensive review of the staff's maintenance activities.

Maintenance Planning

Maintenance usually follows an underlying pattern or cycle. IS managers must recognize this pattern and anticipate maintenance activity associated with the pattern. In addition, IS managers must anticipate technological changes that result in modifying systems. Finally, they must recognize that all systems eventually become dysfunctional or obsolete, and plan for system replacement.

Many companies approach maintenance planning by establishing a regular maintenance schedule. The IS staff accumulates requests to modify systems during the period between maintenance cycles. At the scheduled time of maintenance, these requests are acted on by the maintenance staff. Of course, IS managers must distinguish between requests that need immediate attention and those to accumulate for scheduled maintenance. This can be a difficult decision, since users tend to think that each of their requests deserves immediate attention. To merit immediate attention, a request should involve:

- Major integrity problems
- Compliance with governmental regulations
- Preventive measures regarding subsequent legal involvement of the firm

Any request not meeting these criteria is a candidate for the scheduled maintenance cycle.

A maintenance project follows a life cycle similar to that of a development project (see Chapter 3 on the system development life cycle). In general, the maintenance staff defines the problem, identifies alternative solutions, selects a solution, and modifies system design to conform to updated user requirements.

Through closely following the life cycle and properly updating design and development documentation, a system is likely to remain maintainable. Quick fixes without accompanying documentation updates are leading causes behind the demise of systems. A company that does not allocate enough time and resources to properly update development documentation wastes its investment in system documentation. Treating maintenance projects in the same way as development projects and closely supervising these projects helps to prolong the life of a system.

Retesting and Validation

Just as throwing a small stone into a lake causes ripples on the surface of the lake, a small change in a system may cause ripples of disturbance throughout all of its elements. This is especially likely when systems are tightly integrated. As a result, maintenance activities in one area of a system may affect other areas of the system. This is commonly called the **ripple effect**.

To diminish the ripple effect, maintenance personnel should evaluate a request for change relative to its total effect. In addition, the request should undergo a cost/benefit analysis prior to modification of the system. After the request is satisfied, the system should be thoroughly tested to determine its validity and reliability following modification. Finally, the system should undergo thorough validation to determine whether it still does what it is supposed to do.

MAINTENANCE ACTIVITIES

A number of different factors influence maintenance activities. Understanding these influences provides a way to determine how to control or adjust for them. The major influences on maintenance include:

- Type of application
- Age of the system
- Size of the system and programs
- Complexity of the system and programs
- Dependence within and between systems
- Quality and completeness of development documentation
- Level of user understanding of the system
- Level of user involvement in the project

These influences vary from project to project, but individually or collectively, they affect the maintenance of projects. The system manager anticipates these influences and makes adjustments in the schedule to allow for their proper handling.

Application Types

It is generally simple to modify a straightforward transaction processing application, but it becomes complicated when you must modify MIS applications involving many different users and many different options that the system provides to the users. In addition, some applications tend to change more often than other applications. For example, the information needs of users of on-line systems are much more dynamic than those of users of batch-oriented systems. More volatile applications require greater maintenance resources and care during maintenance projects. The different influences exerted by different applications should be anticipated, and supervision of the project should be adjusted accordingly.

Age, Size, and Complexity of the System

As previously stated, programs in older, legacy systems often need to be restructured as well as modified. They may have been created in an unstructured era, or they may have lost their structure during years of maintenance activities.

Larger systems and programs generally involve more difficult maintenance activities. They tend to have more integrated factors, with greater potential for ripple effects during changes. Similarly, the more complex a system is, the more difficult it is to maintain. Complexity may be due to overall system characteristics or to individual program characteristics. In either case, care must be taken, since small changes tend to have a greater effect on the validity and reliability of the system.

System Dependence

The reliance of one program on actions performed in another program, within or between systems, is referred to as **system dependence**. The dependence often takes the form of one program depending on actions performed on data that is used by another program. Systems that have greater dependence within their programs tend to be more difficult to maintain, since a change in one program may affect what is shared between it and other programs. For the same reason, systems with greater dependence on other systems tend to be more difficult to maintain. An order-entry system that interfaces with inventory control, purchasing, and accounting will be much more difficult to maintain than a personnel system that has minimal integration with other systems in the company.

An extensive evaluation and cost/benefit analysis at the start of maintenance projects for these types of systems helps prevent disruptive ripple effects.

Documentation and Maintenance

Three equally important forms of documentation are:

- Design/development documentation
- User documentation
- Operations documentation

Design/development documentation provides a detailed understanding of a system. The greater the quality and completeness of this form of documentation, the easier it is to understand the framework and inner workings of the system. The easier it is to understand a system, the easier it is to maintain the system. It is the responsibility of IS managers to make sure that this form of documentation retains its quality and completeness.

User confidence in a system directly affects system maintenance. A system without well-written, complete documentation appears faulty to users; they question its validity and reliability. Therefore, it is important to the maintenance effort that user documentation retain its quality and completeness throughout the life of a system.

Finally, IS managers must make sure that the documentation created for the operations staff retains its quality and completeness. This documentation represents instructions for execution setup, output distribution, scheduling, and other forms of operational instructions accompanying a system. Poor-quality operations documentation may lead to improper system execution. This may result in more maintenance activity than is actually necessary and a loss of user confidence.

Managing User Requests

Just as enhancement requests at the conclusion of a development project often get out of hand, maintenance requests by users may become unruly. Users tend to think that systems are easily modified. One of the greatest fears of the systems professional is a user requesting a "small change" requiring little time and effort. A small change, such as extending the length of a data field, can have hidden ramifications that greatly influence a maintenance project. Proper management of user requests can prevent maintenance efforts from becoming difficult to manage.

There are several major control actions for maintenance that systems managers use. When applied selectively or collectively, these actions can lead to fewer and more knowledgeable requests for maintenance service. Systems managers might take the following steps to control maintenance requests:

1. Ensure that the user is properly educated concerning the system.
2. Ensure that user documentation is readily available and easily understandable.
3. Require that users justify maintenance requests.
4. Establish a procedure to service requests by users.
5. Establish a charge-back scheme for maintenance request charges (an antiquated practice that many people feel inhibits the use of information systems).

The more completely users understand the system, the more likely they will be to understand the complexity of their requests. Detailed training of users ensures that their requests become more realistic and better thought out. In addition, systems managers build in better control of user requests when they enforce retention of good user documentation.

IS managers find that they can achieve better control over user requests by establishing a formal method for submitting requests. This method may require the user to thoroughly justify the request and submit it on a form specifically designed for service requests. Requests may also follow a prescribed channel from users to the IS department. Requiring users to justify requests forces them to more judiciously consider the importance of the request and the activities involved in the request. The more information contained on the request form, the more serviceable the request becomes. Analysts should provide a request form for users to fill out that includes the following information:

- Description of the service requested
- Reason for the request
- Who is making the request
- What system is involved
- Documentation justifying the request

- Estimate of when the modification needs to be implemented
- Specification of the priority of the request

Establishing a formal channel for maintenance requests can decrease user requests considerably and help desensitize users to refusals. Without a formal channel, users may treat IS personnel as personal consultants and tend to bombard them with requests that are not well thought out. The following scheme illustrates a sequence of steps to better manage maintenance "shops."

1. Individual users formalize their own requests.
2. Individual user requests are viewed by the user's manager.
3. Approved requests are rewritten by the user's manager.
4. Rewritten requests are transmitted to IS managers.
5. IS managers review formal user requests.
6. Approved user requests are distributed to maintenance personnel by the IS manager.
7. Maintenance personnel notify the requesting user manager concerning the start of the project.
8. The first meeting of concerned parties involves the requesting user (and supervisor), maintenance personnel, and the systems manager.

A **charge-back scheme** is a framework to charge the costs of servicing a request to those responsible for submitting maintenance requests and those benefiting from its completion. A charge-back scheme usually includes personnel costs, computer costs, training costs, resource usage costs, and purchase costs for items required to service the maintenance request. Once users become familiar with maintenance costs, they tend to treat requests for service more seriously and frivolous requests decrease. As previously stated, many people believe that a charge-back scheme inhibits the use of information systems and is not in the best interests of the company.

MAINTAINING THE BUSINESS AND SYSTEM MODELS

The analyst's attitude and maintenance goal must always be to keep both the business and information system models up to date and in complete alignment. Achieving this goal is difficult; however, striving for it assures more efficient functioning of the system. In previous eras, maintenance often meant merely changing the programs of the system; these changes may not have taken into account the complete interests of the business. Figure 16-4 illustrates what took place regarding maintenance actions in previous eras and what takes place in the current era.

In previous eras, requests for changes led to changes in the code only, often without corresponding changes to business models and system specifications (which often

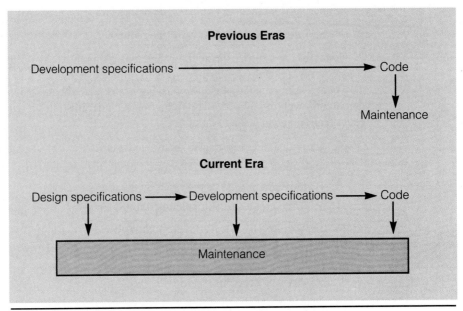

Figure 16-4. System specification maintenance then and now

did not exist at all). As a result, system specifications and code often became out of alignment, rendering the specifications virtually useless for continuing maintenance actions. Furthermore, when maintenance actions only change the code, the essence of the design is lost and is never regained. This corresponds to having a mechanic fix parts of a car without knowing how a car is designed to work.

Business decisions and problems that surface may lead to maintenance actions. When analysts address the effect of a decision or problem at the business level, rather than at the code level, they find a more appropriate solution to the problem. Code makes a business decision or problem solution operational. To anticipate the effects of a major decision or to solve a business problem, you must understand it; to understand it, you should model it. To make the solution operational, business model changes are translated into code used in the operational environment. The illustration of the current maintenance era in Figure 16-4 illustrates this process.

Approaching maintenance from a business system specification ensures the maintenance of the more important documentation. This documentation includes both the business model and the system model. The business model should always be viewed as data about the business, data that provides knowledge about the way the business operates, and data needed to operate the business. The business model provides a far-reaching picture that can be used to view and study the business and its environment. Each portion of the business model should be viewed as important to those working in that area of the business.

When analysts engineer system changes by making changes to the business model, they address the problem at its source and carry the solution forward into the operations of the firm's information systems. Those who use this approach understand the real problem and make more perceptive and purposeful changes. Analysts more easily and skillfully apply the system solution, because they forward-engineer the solution to the business problem into the information system.

In Chapter 8 we described how to make changes to the analysis specification (entity/ relationship diagrams and data flow diagrams) to derive the logical design specifications. These modifications changed the business data object and process models from the analysis phase depiction of what the business is to the design phase depiction of what these models and the business should be. Maintenance activities should also result in changes to these models. Thus, maintenance activities should continue to approach problems from their business perspective by making modifications to conceptual and logical entity/relationship diagrams and data flow diagrams. Business model changes should then be carried forward into the information systems model.

COMPUTER-AIDED MAINTENANCE

Many developers of CASE tools state that the main advantages of these tools are speed and consistency of system development. However, it could be said that maintaining systems is the real advantage of using computer-aided approaches. Once analysts store design and development specifications on-line, they can review and reuse a wealth of documentation. In addition, on-line storage of design makes it easier to maintain the *design* of the system. Thus, the design is always known and may be used to direct system modifications from design modifications.

The thorough maintenance of design and systems in the CASE environment requires that more solid interfaces be created between design and development tools. As these interfaces continue to become more powerful, maintenance becomes an enhanced design function. A request for a change will then result in modifying design documentation. The modified design specifications will in turn guide system modification. As the interface becomes more comprehensive, modifying design specifications will automatically cause appropriate system modifications.

Currently, CASE-supported maintenance requires that the program modules of the system document the design specifications leading to them. This requires that developers update design specifications to reflect the program modules and accompanying documentation. Once they do this, future changes to design specifications become a guide to changing programs and documentation. These changes become automatic as the analyst uses application generators. However, some companies still make system changes manually, using programmer/analysts to manually change programs and user documentation.

In some CASE tools, such as Texas Instruments' Information Engineering Facility (IEF) and Knowledgeware's Information Engineering Workbench (IEW) or Application Development Workbench (ADW), system code comes directly from design documentation. For systems produced while using these CASE tools, the best (and sometimes the only) way to make changes to system code is to make changes in design documentation.

The important point is that storing design specifications on-line provides a way to maintain these specifications and permit systems to be maintained in alignment with the business model. This should lead to an increase in the life expectancy of systems and a decrease in the amount of resources dedicated to maintaining systems.

MAINTAINING THE BUSINESS AND SYSTEM MODELS AT NATIONAL GOLF & TENNIS (NG&T)

Management at NG&T decided that having their own sales delivery service could give them a competitive advantage over competing retail and mail-order companies that furnish golf and tennis supplies and equipment. By making this decision, they ensured that both the business and information systems models would require modifications to reflect the results of the decision. Figures 16-5 and 16-6 reflect the changes to the business model. Changes to the information systems model would be reflected in changes to the structure chart (STC) created for the data flow diagram (DFD) in Figure 16-6.

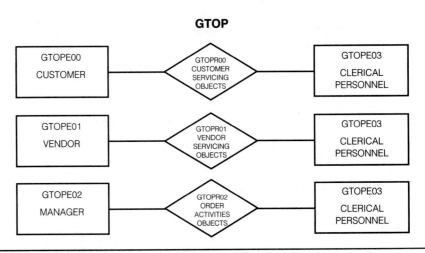

Figure 16-5. Changes to the top-level E/RD reflecting NG&T's change to in-house sales delivery

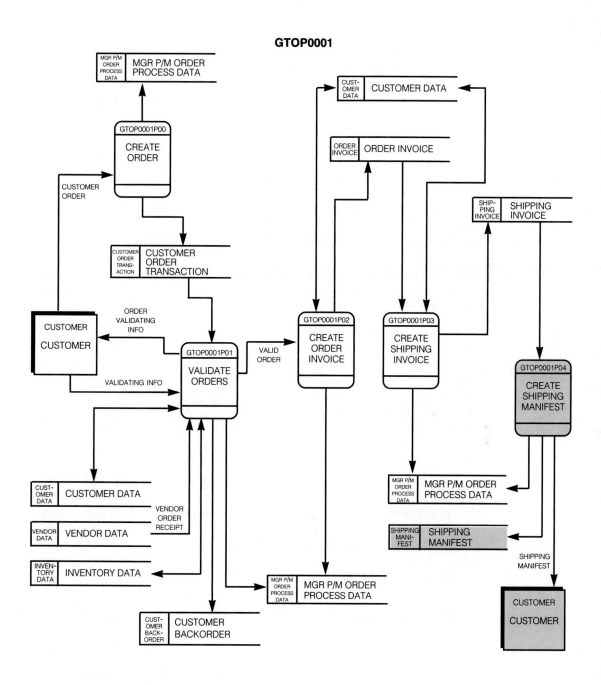

Figure 16-6. Changes to the level-2 DFD for exploding on the level-1 COMPLETE PHONE/MAIL INVOICES process

By now, you should be able to make changes to the STC created for this DFD process model to carry the changes forward into operational program procedures.

The changes reflected in the E/RD and DFD in Figures 16-5 and 16-6 constitute changes to the business model induced by NG&T's decision to perform all of its own delivery services. Notice that the business relationship between the CLERICAL PERSONNEL and CARRIER entities no longer appears on the top E/RD in Figure 16-5. You should compare the E/RD in Figure 16-5 with the E/RD in Figure 5-36 of Chapter 5. The replacement for this interaction now appears as a business relationship between the CUSTOMER and DELIVERY CLERK entities, a new E/R expression on the E/RD to which the first E/R expression in Figure 16-5 explodes.

Assuming delivery responsibility caused the DFD in Figure 8-25 of Chapter 8 to become the DFD in Figure 16-6, notice that the label for the process on the far right was changed to CREATE SHIPPING MANIFEST. Also notice that this process connects to the CUSTOMER entity, which reflects loading and delivering customer orders. These changes reflect that the NG&T delivery clerk/driver creates packing slips for order delivery, loads the delivery truck while filling in the load slip, and delivers the orders to the customers while retaining a delivery receipt notice.

REVIEW

After the system is implemented, a post-implementation formal review is conducted to determine how well the system functions. The key questions to answer are: (1) Were the expected benefits actually realized? (2) Was the project completed on time and within budget? (3) What was learned from this project that can be applied to the next project?

Once implemented, a system enters the period of its life known as maintenance. This period represents the greatest expenditures of effort and resources in its life. Generally speaking, maintenance is more important to most businesses than developing new systems.

Maintenance is needed because of the dynamic environment in which most firms operate. Both internal and external forces exert pressure for change that influences maintenance activities. A useful way to categorize the types of maintenance is as corrective, perfective, and adaptive maintenance.

Corrective maintenance involves actions to eliminate errors and failures. Perfective maintenance improves or maintains system performance. Adaptive maintenance changes the system to conform to new methods, functions, or technologies.

The goal of system development is to build maintainability into the system. A well-structured, top-down approach helps to achieve maintainability. A maintainable system is one that is easily understood, easily modified without loss of functionality, and easily transported to a new environment.

A system must be thoroughly retested and validated following a maintenance project. Since retesting takes time and costs the company money, IS managers make every effort to minimize the need for maintenance.

Many factors influence the maintenance activity for a particular project. Some of these factors are type of application, age of system, size of system, complexity of system, and quality of documentation.

IS managers must effectively and efficiently manage user requests for system change. A formal channel for requests must be established, including a specific request form to be completed by the user before any maintenance request is considered.

CASE tools and methods are normally thought to be best used in the analysis and design phases of a system development project. However, CASE may well be more important in the maintenance phase. Since the design of the system is stored on-line in a CASE environment, the design is always known and readily available. Also, minor changes in a system can be automatically applied when application generators are used.

QUESTIONS

1. What is a post-implementation review? Why is it necessary?

2. What are the main questions a post-implementation review is expected to answer?

3. For a company in your vicinity, obtain a copy of a report for a post-implementation review for one of its projects. Explain what happened at this review.

4. Why is maintenance frequently considered more important than system development?

5. Describe the three main maintenance activities.

6. Identify internal and external influences on maintenance.

7. For a company in your vicinity, identify some internal and external influences on maintenance. Explain how they influence the process.

8. List the main options available during maintenance.

9. Where should maintenance begin, and why is it important that it begin there?

10. What are the demands that frequently prevent maintenance from beginning at the proper place?

11. List and explain some of the firm's ongoing maintenance needs.

12. For a company in your vicinity, identify and explain some of its ongoing maintenance activities.

13. Describe each of the major categories of maintenance.

14. For a company in your vicinity, identify and explain a maintenance project of each type that it has completed.

15. Why is updating documentation an important maintenance function?

16. Explain why corrective maintenance usually occurs in the early stages of a system's life after implementation.

17. What types of maintenance dominate the latter portion of the life of a system? Why?

18. Clearly distinguish between perfective and adaptive maintenance.

19. When does perfective maintenance occur?

20. What factors cause adaptive maintenance to occur?

21. What are the ways to build maintainability into a system during system development?

22. What are the characteristics of maintainable systems?

23. What characteristic of programs contributes the most to making them modifiable?

24. Distinguish between the two main schemes of distributing IS personnel. Describe advantages of each.

25. Why is it advantageous for a development project team member to maintain the system after implementation?

26. Explain how scheduled maintenance should be managed within a firm.

27. How can the ripple effect be diminished?

28. Describe the characteristics and importance of each of the three types of documentation.

29. For a company in your vicinity, obtain a copy of each of the three types of documentation. Explain each one of these.

30. Identify and explain the maintenance controls that may be used by IS managers.

31. Identify the contents of effective maintenance requests.

32. For a company in your vicinity, obtain a copy of a maintenance request for one of its projects. Explain the request.

33. Identify the characteristics of a good maintenance policy.

34. For a company in your vicinity, explain its policy regarding maintenance.

35. Explain how a charge-back scheme assists in reducing maintenance.

36. Describe the major types of tools and techniques used during maintenance.

37. What purpose is served by program restructuring?

EXERCISES

Chapter 16 of the student workbook contains blank documentation forms to use in the following exercises.

1. Revise the E/RD in Figure 8-6 to reflect adding the business relationship between the DELIVERY CLERK/DRIVER entity and the CUSTOMER entity. This new E/R expression is supported by the following logical objects: (1) the

delivery manifest (order delivery objects), (2) the load slip (truck loading objects), and (3) the delivery receipt object. Create a lower E/RD for exploding on this new E/R expression. Show all entity, relationship, MLOG-DS, and LOG-DS dictionary entries for these two ER/Ds. Create a maintenance request form that would likely lead to this maintenance project.

2. Revise the first-cut STC in Figure 9-25 for changes to its DFD as reflected in Figure 16-6; also create its refined STC and accompanying dictionary entries for procedures and data flags or control flags. Create a maintenance request form that would likely lead to this maintenance project.

3. Revise the DFD completed for exercise 4 of Chapter 8, and the first-cut and refined STCs created for exercises 5 and 6 of Chapter 9, to reflect the change in having an NG&T delivery clerk for order deliveries. Create a maintenance request form that would likely lead to this maintenance project.

4. Revise the DFD completed for exercise 5 of Chapter 8, and the first-cut and refined STCs created for exercises 7 and 8 of Chapter 9, to reflect the change in having an NG&T delivery clerk for order deliveries. Create a maintenance request form that would likely lead to this maintenance project.

5. Suppliers of products sold by NG&T use order personnel equipped with hand-held bar code–reading computers. These persons, sometimes called *jobbers*, are independent from NG&T and from the manufacturers of the products they sell. The jobbers assume responsibility for all vendor product ordering by entering the count of the number of items on a shelf into the bar code–reading computer. Upon returning to their place of employment, the jobbers transfer the data from the bar code–reading computer to the product manufacturer's host computer. A program on that host computer then executes a procedure to create NG&T product orders, including charges to the jobbers for services rendered. A copy of these orders is then mailed to NG&T for partial payment (25 percent). Back orders created are now being mailed directly to the manufacturer by NG&T personnel. The back-ordered products are supposed to be treated as a special delivery with an extra charge by the manufacturer. These business changes cause the E/RDs, DFDs, and STCs for vendor order/receipt and accounts reconciling to change. Order receipts are unchanged except for comparing special-delivery orders with back orders that induced their delivery. Create a maintenance request form that would likely lead to this maintenance project.

   a. Revise the E/RD in Figure 16-5 to include the business relationship between the CLERICAL PERSONNEL and JOBBERS entities (also create a lower E/RD for exploding on this new E/R expression). Show all entity, relationship, MLOG-DS, and LOG-DS dictionary entries for these two ER/Ds.

   b. Create a revised DFD for exploding on the ORDER VENDOR ITEMS process of Figure 8-24 of Chapter 8 (exercise 3 of Chapter 8) to reflect the change of using jobbers for vendor order creation. Show all entity, data flow, data store, process, MLOG-DS, and LOG-DS dictionary entries for this DFD.

c. Create a revised first-cut and refined STC for the DFD created in exercise 5b. These STCs were initially created by completing exercises 3 and 4 of Chapter 9. Show all procedure, call, MLOG-DS, and LOG-DS dictionary entries for the refined STC.

d. Create a revised DFD for exploding on the RECONCILE CUSTOMER ACCOUNTS process of the DFD in Figure 8-24 of Chapter 8 (exercise 5 of Chapter 8) to reflect the change to reconciling customer accounts for using jobbers for vendor order creation. Show all entity, data flow, data store, process, MLOG-DS, and LOG-DS dictionary entries for this DFD.

e. Create a revised first-cut and refined STC for the DFD created in exercise 5d. These STCs were initially created by completing exercises 7 and 8 of Chapter 9. Show all procedure, call, MLOG-DS, and LOG-DS dictionary entries for the refined STC.

6. NG&T management decides to use an outside accounting firm to perform all customer billing and payment collection, as well as payment to manufacturers for products received by NG&T. This action is sometimes called *out-sourcing* billings and collections. This business decision causes the E/RD for the E/R expression between the CUSTOMER and ACCOUNTS CLERK to change, as well as the DFDs and STCs for accounts reconciling. Create a maintenance request form that would likely lead to this maintenance project.

a. Revise the E/RD in Figure 16-5 to include the business relationship between the CLERICAL PERSONNEL and the BILL/COLL FIRM entities (also create a lower E/RD for exploding on this new E/R expression). Show all entity, relationship, MLOG-DS, and LOG-DS dictionary entries for these two ER/Ds.

b. Revise the E/RD in Figure 8-6 of Chapter 8 to reflect the change to out-sourcing customer billings and collections. Show all entity, relationship, MLOG-DS, and LOG-DS dictionary entries for this ER/D.

c. Revise the DFD in Figure 8-24 of Chapter 8 to include a process labeled RECONCILE OUTSOURCED ACCOUNTS with entities and data stores for the out-sourcing firm attached to this process, as well as other entities and data stores that may need to be connected to this process.

d. Create a revised DFD for exploding on the ORDER VENDOR ITEMS process of Figure 8-24 of Chapter 8 (exercise 3 of Chapter 8) to reflect the change to out-sourcing billings and collections for products ordered from manufacturers. Show all entity, data flow, data store, process, MLOG-DS, and LOG-DS dictionary entries for this DFD.

e. Create a revised first-cut and refined STC for the DFD created in exercise 6d. These STCs were initially created by completing exercises 3 and 4 of Chapter 9. Show all procedure, call, MLOG-DS, and LOG-DS dictionary entries for the refined STC.

f. Create a revised DFD for exploding on the RECONCILE OUTSOURCED ACCOUNTS process of the DFD completed for exercise 6c to reflect the change to reconciling outsourcing customer accounts on jobbers for vendor order creation. Show all entity, data flow, data store, process, MLOG-DS, and LOG-DS dictionary entries for this DFD.

g. Create a revised first-cut and refined STC for the DFD created in exercise 6d. Show all procedure, call, MLOG-DS, and LOG-DS dictionary entries for the refined STC.

SELECTED REFERENCES

Boehm, B. 1978. *Characteristics of Software Quality*. Amsterdam: North Holland Publishing Co.

Gilb, T. 1980. "Maintainability Is More than Structured Coding." *Techniques of Programs and System Maintenance*. Lincoln, NB: Ethnotech.

Lientz, B., E. Swanson, and G. Thompkins. 1978. "Characteristics of Application Software Maintenance." *Communications of the ACM* 21, no. 6 (June).

Lietz, B. and E. Swanson. 1980. *Software Maintenance Management*. Reading, MA: Addison-Wesley.

Liu, C. 1976. "A Look at Software Maintenance." *Datamation* 22, no. 11 (November).

McClure, C. 1978. *Managing Software Development and Maintenance*. New York, NY: Van Nostrand Reinhold.

Martin, J. and C. McClure. 1983. *Software Maintenance: The Problem and Its Solution*. Englewood Cliffs, NJ: Prentice-Hall.

Reutter, J. 1981. "Maintenance Is a Management Problem and a Programmer's Opportunity." Conference Proceedings for the National AFIPS Conference. Volume 50 (May 4–7). Chicago, IL.

Swanson, E. 1976. "The Dimensions of Maintenance." Proceedings of the Second International Conference on Software Engineering. October 13–15. San Francisco, CA.

CHAPTER 17

Security
and Ethics

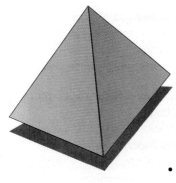

OVERVIEW

More and more, people interact directly with systems operations and management. As they do, problems increase regarding hardware, software, and data security. Security should be a major consideration in each phase of the system development life cycle, not an afterthought. The way the system is also used presents numerous ethical concerns. This chapter tells you how to properly secure a system, and how to use it ethically, by describing:

- The definitions of security-related terms
- Major types of security
- Special security issues in distributed environments
- Procedures used to track security breaches
- Special security issues in a CASE environment
- The definition of ethics
- How ethics differ from laws
- How computer technology can obscure ethical behavior
- Special areas of ethical concern
- Security measures at NG&T

KEY TERMS

Auditing

Backup

Computer abuse

Cryptographic algorithm

Data encryption standard (DES)

Data security

Dial-back program

Encryption

Ethic

Hardware security

Legal security

Logon procedure

Loss

Password

Recovery

Risks

Security

Security breach

Software security

Threat

User security

Virus

As computer system use grows in businesses of all sizes, problems such as security of hardware and software, privacy of information, and integrity of the system are dramatically increasing. Potential forms of computer abuse are major concerns in the development and maintenance of information systems. **Computer abuse** is any incident associated with computer technology in which perpetrators intentionally seek to gain something at the expense of their victims. What they seek to gain can take the form of financial gain or simple unauthorized use of computer resources. Using your employer's computer to play games is computer abuse unless you have specific permission to do so.

This chapter discusses four major types of security: legal, operational, data, and user security. It distinguishes between inadvertent and intentional breaches of security and discusses special security considerations in distributed and CASE environments. Protection against computer viruses has become almost routine, but given their unpredictability, analysts must remain alert to the potential security threat they pose. Finally, this chapter introduces the topic of ethical considerations in the use of information systems, which should be of concern to all those interested in the profession.

ASSESSING SECURITY NEEDS

Many terms have specific meanings in security that do not necessarily correspond to the standard usage of the terms. In the context of information systems, **security** means protecting data and computer systems from unauthorized access, modification, destruction, or misuse. This access, modification, destruction, or misuse may be either intentional or inadvertent. The term *intentional* implies malice, whereas *inadvertent* means accidental (without malice).

A **threat** is a danger that jeopardizes a system or data. Threats can take the form of activities associated with people or natural forces; they are either internal, external, or both. Threats from people usually occur because of ignorance, greed, or bad feelings. Natural threats include floods, earthquakes, storms, power failures, and equipment breakdowns. When analysts express threats statistically in terms of their probability of occurrence, they use the term **risks**.

Analysts must assess the costs associated with various risks. They perform a cost/benefit analysis to determine the feasibility of incorporating security measures in a developing system. A **loss** equals the adverse result of an event occurring for an associated risk. For example, the earthquake risks are much higher for firms in California than for those in Kansas, and the cost associated with the loss is much greater. On the other hand, firms in Kansas experience a much higher risk of loss resulting from a tornado than do those in California. As a result, these firms may incur security expenditures to prevent loss from earthquakes in California and from tornadoes in Kansas. The type of business also influences the levels and types of threats against which protection is needed. For example, a defense contractor will probably need much more security than a soup manufacturer.

To summarize, analysts should identify each possible threat to the firm, assign risk factors to the threats, and estimate the costs of possible losses. They should then compare those costs to the costs associated with acquiring and/or developing protection against the loss and deciding whether to implement the security measure, if this is the only measure used for comparison.

A simple example illustrates the risk analysis concept. Assume that a company expects employee theft to amount to $100,000 over a five-year period. Simple math tells you that on the average the firm can expect a $20,000 loss each year. If security measures to prevent this loss cost $50,000 per year, clearly it is not cost-effective to implement those security measures.

Security as an Auditing Function

Security also involves building in auditing functions regarding all aspects of the company. **Auditing** is a way of reviewing various aspects of a company to determine whether they are correct, that accountability exists regarding them, that factors regarding them can be traced, and that corrective actions exist for situations in which something outside the norm occurs.

Most companies include auditing measures in their activities, such as periodic counts of various company assets and identification of persons performing certain actions or using certain company assets. These auditing measures are built into the operational systems of the firm, and are often included as part of the firm's information systems. When recorded entries occur regarding aspects of the firm that require auditing, the measures that aid in auditing functions typically become part of the recording process. Some of the data recorded is by its nature a data value that aids in auditing. For example, an update of inventory that occurs as the inventory items are used by company personnel is by its nature a measure that can be used to audit inventory management. Some data is recorded explicitly for auditing purposes—for example, an employee ID number. If an ID number is always recorded when an employee performs some action that affects the firm (such as inventory use), the ID acts as a data value that can be used to trace various actions of employees for auditing purposes.

Outputs from information systems can also be used to audit various aspects of the firm and its information systems. Outputs should accurately depict what happens during various aspects of the operation of the firm. These data values can then be used to perform various auditing functions regarding the firm. Since this data supports auditing functions, the analyst should assess what data values might be included as output to aid in the auditing process.

The procedures and data used by information systems should also be capable of being audited. If the procedures are not performing actions as they should, are using incorrect data, or are producing improper output, a person known as an electronic data processing (EDP) auditor should be able to discern this. EDP auditing capabilities are especially important when legal or financial issues are involved. For example, an EDP auditor must be able to review the programs in banking systems that process financial information about bank customers.

Auditing functions also enter into the creation and maintenance of the information systems themselves. Each time someone creates or makes changes either in user requirements or in the firm's systems, audit data items should be recorded that document who performed the action, when it was performed, and what the action was. Encoding these actions with the ID numbers of IS personnel helps trace all of the actions that they perform over a given period. This is especially helpful when a company needs to investigate a possible vindictive act by a particular employee.

Information systems designed and developed using CASE systems aid the auditing function even more. The actual intent regarding certain actions a program performs can often be disguised in the ways those actions are performed. When the specifications for a system are entered into a CASE system, the intentions for many aspects of the system appear as explanations in dictionary entries for various parts of the business and system model. In the future, EDP auditors will review design/development specifications in addition to the code in the programs of the system. This way, audits will be able to probe even further into the company's information systems.

TYPES OF SECURITY

The many security concerns within an organization can be categorized under four major types: legal, operational, data, and user security. Table 17-1 lists the major types of security and areas of security considerations within them.

Table 17-1	Types of security and major areas of consideration

Type of Security	Major Protection Considerations
Legal	Rights of firm Rights of employees Rights of customers Rights of related firms
Operational	Hardware security Software security
Data	Destroyed data Improperly modified data Loss of data confidentiality Misuse of data
User	Identification of authorized user Background of user Security-consciousness of user Attitude of user

Legal Security

Failure to consider the legal issues in a particular system design often leads to lawsuits and/or fines for a company. **Legal security** protects customers, employees, and firms that enter into business agreements from violation of their legal rights. In addition, system design must include compliance with various local, state, national, and international laws as part of system security.

The Right to Privacy

One particularly important legal issue is invasion of privacy. Legislation regarding privacy continues to be revised. Many issues have not been decided by courts or addressed in laws passed by governments. For example, who should have the right to access the information in the customer accounts receivable file? Certainly the credit manager should have the right to confront overdue accounts, but should persons who sell goods to the customer or persons who produce those goods also be able to access these accounts? Should they have the right to access customer information? Do they have a legitimate need to know?

Another important issue in a person's right to privacy: when it is breached, who has the right to prosecute? For example, if a user in California illegally accesses a company's database in New York, is it a local, state, or federal violation? The matter becomes even more complex when data is transferred across international boundaries. Though not all of the details have been worked out, considerable progress has been made over the past ten years in defining and clarifying the legal issues of an individual's right to privacy, while extending the right to know to appropriate people.

Some well-known pieces of legislation on an individual's right to privacy are the Fair Credit Reporting Act, the Privacy Act, the Trade Secrets Act, and the Freedom of Information Act. The Fair Credit Reporting Act provides penalties for anyone who obtains information under false pretenses from a credit bureau about an individual. It also spells out the legal obligation for the accuracy and confidentiality of consumer information.

The Privacy Act governs distribution of information contained in federal records. The Trade Secrets Act makes it illegal for federal employees to disclose trade secret information regarding business processes, products, and/or services. Notice that these two laws apply only to federal records and employees; no comprehensive or uniform local, state, or federal laws cover nonfederal records or employees. The same holds true for the Freedom of Information Act—it governs only federal employees. Equivalent forms of these acts may exist in various states or cities; however, they are difficult to enforce because of the lack of uniformity from state to state and because of complications that arise involving interstate commerce.

The main benefit of many of these laws is the assignment of legal obligations and threats of lawsuits against private concerns, which encourages companies to comply with the laws. Regardless of the enforceability of a law by local, state, or federal authorities, companies generally want to avoid legal entanglements, particularly in areas that may get them involved in lawsuits.

Other Legal Restrictions

Looking at these laws, it might seem that few laws exist that govern private companies. This is not entirely true. Many such laws exist, but they are fragmented and often only locally applied. From this, should the systems analyst conclude that he or she can ignore legal issues when designing an information system? Not at all! Actually, it just makes the job more complex. The analyst must find ways to build the required legal security into the information system—not doing so invites lawsuits.

Adapting information systems to legal requirements is always a challenge. Fortunately, users in the application area affected by the system being designed often have a good understanding of legal restrictions. For example, a personnel manager may provide valuable insight into federal, state, and local laws regulating company personnel data. Likewise, a credit manager should understand many laws that affect collecting debts. The analyst should take advantage of user legal knowledge in functional areas.

Operational Security

Operational security protects hardware and software from either intentional or inadvertent threats. Inadvertent threats include fire, floods, earthquakes (and other natural disasters), power failures, computer operator error, and accidental modification of the database. Intentional threats include arson, theft, purposeful destruction of equipment, and fraudulent, unauthorized modifications of a program or file.

Regardless of whether the threat is intentional or inadvertent, analysts should install security measures to protect the hardware and software. Password security is a way to protect unwanted access to software, as opposed to unwanted physical harm to hardware.

Password Security

One form of operational security involves restricting access to a computer system over hard-wired terminals, telephone lines, or desktop computers. A user gains access to a computer system through a process called the **logon procedure**. During this procedure, system security measures use identification procedures and an accompanying password to identify users. A **password** is a special code assigned to a user that permits access to the computer system. Logon procedures and passwords are traditionally used to gain access to a host computer from either a terminal or a desktop computer, but they may also be used to secure files and programs that reside on a desktop computer.

Several different aspects of passwords need to be understood. First, security measures should check that a user initiates the logon procedure from an authorized terminal or desktop computer. For example, even if valid passwords are entered by a user, the terminal or desktop computer being used may not be valid for that type of access. Consider the case of personnel files. In most companies only a few terminals or desktop computers, physically located in the personnel department, are authorized to access certain portions of personnel files. If someone tries to gain access to these files via an unauthorized terminal or desktop computer, the system automatically disconnects the user and records information regarding the access attempt.

If a user attempts access over a telephone line, a dial-back program can verify that it is an authorized telephone line. A **dial-back program** causes communication contact to be initiated between a company's computer and a remote user who previously gained access to the company's computer systems. The dial-back program calls the remote user back after he or she accesses the company's computer, to verify that contact is being made by an authorized user on an authorized telephone line.

Second, security procedures should automatically disconnect a terminal or desktop computer after a small number of invalid logon attempts—say, three—have been made. The exact number of invalid attempts depends on the business and the particular application. The key concept is that repeated attempts should not be permitted. Access from that terminal or desktop computer should continue to be denied until someone discovers a reason for the invalid attempts.

Third, a system often provides multiple levels of password security. For instance, one password permits access to the computer facility, another permits access to particular application systems, a third allows access to confidential information within an application, a fourth restricts the actions that are permitted on particular data object properties, and a fifth restricts access to unsecured data only.

In a payroll application, for example, users enter a password to gain access to the computer system. After gaining access to the system, the user then needs a second-level password to access the personnel files within the system. Finally, within the personnel files, the user needs a third password to access monthly salaries. This multiple password level scheme may seem cumbersome until you realize that not everyone needs access to secured data, and not all data needs to be secured in this manner.

Finally, systems analysts must establish an appropriate system to assign and monitor passwords. The recognized guidelines for controlling passwords include these:

- Passwords must have a large number of possible combinations.
- Passwords should be generated randomly.
- Passwords must not appear on the screen as they are entered.
- Passwords must be changed periodically.
- Only trusted personnel should assign and monitor passwords.

Having a large combination of options for passwords reduces the chance that someone could try various combinations until the correct one is reached. A five- to six-digit alphanumeric password is recommended. For example, a five-digit alphanumeric password would have 36^5 (over 60 million) possible different combinations. Many firms have a computer program within their operating system that uses a random number generator to generate passwords. A responsible employee then distributes the passwords to users.

The danger of randomly generating passwords by a computer program is that users typically write them down somewhere near their computers in case they forget them. The problem is that others can also find these written passwords and use them for their own private purposes. To prevent this, many people recommend other schemes for assigning passwords. One suggestion is to use a phrase that is easy to remember and alter it to make it a password. For example, you could use the initial letters (TGIF) from the phrase "Thank God it's Friday" as a password.

Although it is common practice to let users choose their own passwords, many people believe that users should not be allowed to choose them at all. When users pick their own passwords, they may use combinations familiar to them, such as a spouse's name or a birth date. Such combinations make it easy for unauthorized users to guess passwords and gain access to the system. When users are permitted to select their own passwords, they should be advised to not use words, names, dates, or any other value that may appear in a dictionary or reference guide. Furthermore, passwords should be blanked out as users enter them, to prevent others from looking over their shoulders and stealing their passwords.

In larger organizations, the task of assigning passwords falls under the authority of the database administrator, who usually assigns this responsibility to a trusted member of their staff. Smaller firms may have only a single database administrator or some other systems professional, who assumes this and all other responsibilities regarding activities that affect the company's database.

When periodically changing passwords, those responsible for changing them should vary the exact time. However, when employees are terminated or resign, their passwords should become invalid immediately. Once an employee gives two weeks notice, he or she should not be allowed to access the system during that time.

Systems analysts must also establish controls to monitor access to the system. For example, a computer system should monitor and record each logon attempt, whether successful or not. Analysts should include specifications that create a log of all access attempts. Each log entry should contain the logon ID, the terminal used, the application accessed, the files accessed, and the changes made. The log should be reviewed daily to spot potential problems. Though these procedures may at first seem extreme, they are necessary to keep the system secure.

Hardware Security

Hardware security includes controlling physical access to the hardware as well as to the system. This control may exist in the form of locked doors, badge-reading locks, and restrictions on visitor access to rooms housing computer hardware. Another useful method consists of installing video recording cameras to film those who enter computer facilities. A network of these cameras may be strategically positioned, often placed at remote sites.

Both hardware and software security measures need to include procedures for ensuring the availability of the system. Downtime of hardware and software is a major concern for many businesses. To avoid or limit downtime, hardware and software security measures are put in place. These security measures typically involve backup versions for hardware and software at different sites.

Software Security

Software security goes hand-in-hand with hardware security. **Software security** protects systems and application programs from unauthorized access or modification. Analysts must concern themselves with software security throughout the entire system development life cycle, not just as an afterthought upon implementing an information system. Security measures should be part of the specifications used to develop and maintain the company's information systems. Some hardware security methods apply directly to software security: when access is restricted for computer hardware, it is also restricted for the software that resides on that hardware. However, several issues relate directly to software security. A payroll example helps illustrate the importance of software security during all life cycle phases.

A PAYROLL PROJECT EXAMPLE   In the analysis phase of a payroll project, the analyst should identify private data. Private data includes data concerning the status of employees; evaluations regarding them; work-related and nonwork-related incidents that reflect on them; other personal factors, such as financial characteristics; and any data retained on the computer that is not for public consumption, such as electronic mail (E-mail) files. Threats and risks should be evaluated to determine the costs associated with providing the necessary level of security.

In the logical design phase of a payroll application, the analyst should include control features as part of design: for instance, what data is involved, who gets it, and how it is used. The analyst establishes controls to keep incorrect and unauthorized payroll checks from being created.

In the physical design phase of the payroll application, the analyst must establish security features, such as levels of password protection, authorized user lists, and exception procedures to apply. The security features are then programmed into the system. If possible, different programmers should be assigned to creating the program and to inserting the security modules in the program. The reasons for this are readily apparent when you consider a bank programmer, for example, who designs and programs all the security features for a program she creates to process customer bank records. The temptation to enter intentionally incorrect code that may augment her own bank account may be too great. Assigning different programmers to create application and security programs is a good policy to establish for most of the programs that need additional security measures.

In the implementation phase, special tests are designed to verify that security features are working properly. This includes testing the various levels of passwords, testing application control features, and implementing a security training program. A security training program is especially important. Employees must be made aware and be constantly reminded of security issues and procedures to follow.

In the maintenance phase, the analyst must consider security for each change made in an application. In the payroll example, changes in any aspect of payroll processing require a detailed analysis of possible effects on current and future security.

Data Security

Recall that data integrity refers to the completeness, correctness, and consistency with which the data represents its real-world counterpart. Security measures that protect the integrity of the data fall under the category of **data security**. Three potentially harmful situations can occur: data may lose its confidentiality, it may be improperly modified or used, or it may drop completely out of sight. Any one, or a combination of these situations, can affect data integrity.

Loss of Data Confidentiality

When data is revealed to someone who does not have the "right or need to know," the data is no longer confidential. This type of security breach may be a simple case of allowing someone to access another employee's pay records or as serious as industrial espionage. Security measures already discussed in connection with hardware and software security, such as restricted access and password protection, help prevent loss of data confidentiality.

Improper Data Modification

Improper data modification can be more serious than the destruction of data. The problem is easier to identify when data is lost; incorrect data is difficult to catch. When managers need to make decisions based on certain misplaced data, an obvious problem exists. When these same managers decide on a course of action based on incorrect data values, the problem may never be known to them.

Instances of incorrect arithmetic formulas in spreadsheets are widely known in the business community. These incorrectly entered formulas provide faulty data on which business personnel might base important decisions. For example, a decision to purchase new capital equipment might be based on the calculation of current cash flows for a company; if the spreadsheet formula incorrectly calculates input and output cash flows, the decision as to when to purchase the new equipment may also be incorrect.

The same formula that may be entered into a spreadsheet can also become part of the computations performed within a program in the information system. A set of computations may be syntactically correct for that computer language, but logically incorrect, so that it produces incorrect output from the computations. Instances of entering the logical procedures of a program incorrectly relate to the well-known "GIGO" premise. GIGO stands for "garbage in—garbage out," which means that if you have bad procedures or data (garbage in), you will have bad output (garbage out). Bad code in program procedures or other software systems should be found during testing; however, it is naive to believe that people will always conduct all of the testing that is needed to identify and correct all problems of this type.

Security controls such as read-only access, restricting access to certain data items, and security logs of all changes made to data items also help eliminate the improperly modified data and/or identify when invalid modifications occur.

Destruction of Data

Data destruction happens for a variety of reasons: a computer operator may inadvertently load the wrong tape or disk and erase the data on it; a head crash on a disk device may wipe out all the data on a disk; a disgruntled employee may intentionally destroy certain data to "pay the company back;" or someone can infect a company's computer systems with a computer virus (discussed later in this chapter). To minimize data destruction risks, users and computer personnel should be properly trained, equipment regularly maintained, and access to data denied to disgruntled employees.

The best defense against the loss of data is to implement proper backup and recovery procedures. In this context, **backup** is defined as the periodic copying of data to other media or to the same media in a different storage area. **Recovery** is the process of restoring data to its original or prior form.

User Security

User security includes measures to ensure that only authorized users access data within their user view, but it also includes screening employees, educating them in security measures, and evaluating employee attitudes regarding the company and its systems. Many security measures we have discussed thus far ensure that users have both a need and a right to know. However, regardless of the quality of hardware and software security measures, firms that fail to screen and monitor employees are more likely to experience security breaches.

The best employee security method consists of a three-part approach. First, before hiring an applicant, company personnel should conduct a thorough background check on the prospective employee. Prospective employees with questionable backgrounds should be avoided. Even employees who pass background checks should not be assigned to work in sensitive areas before they demonstrate loyalty to the firm.

Second, security-consciousness should be encouraged in employees. Security programs sometimes fail simply because employees who do not understand the importance of security write down passwords in easily found places, give them to other employees, or give them out over the telephone. These instances are all common sources from which computer hackers can obtain a password. Alert employees often constitute the best possible security measure. If a data entry clerk who used to drive an old Chevy now drives a Porsche and takes weekend trips to Las Vegas, it may be time to review the company's security procedures.

Finally, consider employee attitudes as an aspect of security. Employees who are unhappy with their jobs or with the computer system are more likely to have thoughts of destroying the system or the data. At the very least, dissatisfied employees lose their alertness regarding security issues. Top management must promote the need to maintain security and make the entire organization aware of its importance. An organizational effort to educate personnel achieves greater security awareness; this is especially important in today's distributed environment.

SECURITY IN A DISTRIBUTED ENVIRONMENT

A distributed environment, illustrated in Figure 17-1, maintains systems and data at multiple locations, with separate processors for system execution. These processors are linked together via communication lines. Users in a distributed environment commonly have on-line access to one or more of the processors and databases. Challenges to security usually escalate with distributed processing simply because much more equipment and many more users need to be secured. In addition, problems associated with maintaining system integrity escalate because data is stored at different locations. Many of the security procedures we have already discussed apply equally well to a distributed environment.

Within a batch-oriented environment, physical control of the equipment is usually centralized. In a distributed environment, the issue changes from one of control to one of guidance or management. User departments typically provide their own physical control over much of the hardware and software. Therefore, major aspects of security in the distributed environment cover managing user hardware and software configura-

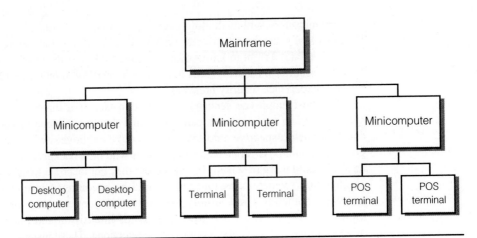

Figure 17-1. Example of a distributed system

tions, user involvement in data control, and user involvement with system operations.

The distributed environment permits many different users to access and/or change data stored in a system. This implies that users have the capacity, to some degree, to determine what data the system contains. Analysts must assemble proper control within a system to ensure that uncompromised data integrity continually exists.

Users often become system operators in a distributed environment, which requires that they be trained in proper system use. Since users have access through their workstations, analysts must emphasize security measures. Not only must users become aware of security for themselves, but their cautious behavior should extend to unauthorized users. For example, they should not allow another user to access the system using their password.

Inventory Management

A major issue in a distributed environment is how to manage the inventory of the various system components that are spread out in many different locations. Many companies are unaware of the magnitude of their monetary investment in hardware and software components. Proper inventory management requires a complete inventory control system. Even if departments maintain their own software and hardware, centralized inventory control is often desirable.

The tricky issue in distributed environments is convincing users that even though they may own individual hardware and software, centralized control, or at least guidance, is beneficial. Through assigning responsibility for inventory control to one department, benefits, such as volume discounts on purchases, may be experienced by all departments. One method for maintaining central control is to establish an approved hardware and software purchase list. An individual department may make the actual purchase, but anything purchased must be on the approved list. This list typically indicates standards for certain brands, models, and software packages.

In addition, making users responsible for disappearing property encourages them to become more security-conscious. Individual responsibility may also be assigned within departments.

Security of Transferred Data

Transferring data from one location to another in a distributed environment poses an even greater security problem. Companies should not transfer sensitive data in its original form. They should use some form of **encryption**, which is the process of encoding information to be deciphered only by persons with a decoding mechanism. Applying cryptographic algorithms and accompanying encryption keys makes text illegible to would-be security risks.

A **cryptographic algorithm** is a formula used to convert a stream of data to an unreadable form on one end of a transmission and then to convert it back to readable form on the other end. The simplest way to implement an encryption method is to place devices between the modem and data terminal at each end of the link, a method that does not require modifying software. Figure 17-2 illustrates this principle.

Another encryption method integrates the cryptographic algorithm into the central processing units of the computers on both sides of the transmission. Although it is the most secure approach, this method often requires modifying both software and hardware.

One of the most popular encryption methods in commercial use is the **data encryption standard (DES)** method of the National Bureau of Standards. DES mandates that a sequence of operations be imposed on a block of data, all determined by a user-specified secret key. Data coded in this way cannot be decoded without knowing *both* the cryptographic algorithm and the key used in coding the data. This key makes possible some 70 quadrillion combinations.

Two main disadvantages exist with encryption methods: (1) It is expensive to equip each location in the distributed environment with an encryption capability, and (2) the security measure is only as good as the management of the encryption key and cryptographic algorithm. Only data with appropriate sensitivity warrants the added expense of encryption. Here again, security only works if people make it work. Consequently, the need for security education and awareness on the part of employees is vital.

TRACKING SECURITY BREACHES

Various audit trails and procedures help identify and record security breaches. A **security breach** is an unauthorized access, modification, or destruction of data. Typically, detailed logs provide audit trails to track possible security breaches. These logs retain records of:

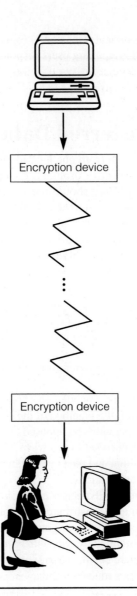

Figure 17-2. Data encryption

- Logons from all terminals or desktop computers, whether successful or not
- All accesses to files, including type of access
- All jobs processed by the system

These logs provide audit trails of who accessed the system or data, from where, making what changes, and running what jobs. The logs should be monitored daily for exception information: the type of data that is outside the norm and may point to conditions that need someone's attention. Audit trails can also aid auditing functions, as described earlier in this chapter.

Daily monitoring may seem relatively routine, but log sheets can hold important clues to help identify security breaches. Managers responsible for reviewing daily logs often have work piled on their desks for rush jobs. When system security runs smoothly for long periods of time, it is human nature to take care of the more pressing items first, neglecting many security measures. A company can prevent this by continually emphasizing the importance of reviewing security logs on a timely basis.

Once again, the human element is one of the most important and hardest resources to control. Training and overall corporate security emphasis may help impress each user with the importance of security.

COMPUTER VIRUSES

Computer viruses are a serious and increasing threat to computer-based information systems. A **virus** is a software program written inside another program intended for public or private distribution. It infects a computer system—called its *host*—by attaching itself to good code that resides on that computer or, in some cases, entirely replaces the good code when the publicly or privately distributed program is loaded onto that computer. A virus can do varying amounts of damage to the system software. Effects range from leaving harmless messages, such as "Legalize Marijuana," that periodically appear on the computer screen, to complete destruction of all programs and data on the computer. A harmless virus is called a *benign virus*; a virus that causes destruction is called a *malignant virus*. When a virus is passed to a computer, it is said that the computer is *infected*. The major problem with viruses is that once a single computer system is infected, all files and programs that it passes to other computer systems will carry the virus and infect the other systems.

Virus Protection

With hundreds of known viruses in existence, it is imperative that firms protect their computer systems against them. A protection plan includes access control, virus detection, and a recovery plan in case of infection.

- *Access control* means encouraging users to take precautions against virus infection. They should be encouraged to not transfer disks between home and office, not indiscriminately use bulletin boards, and never use a disk on a system until that disk has been checked for viruses.

- *Virus detection* means making sure that a virus is found before it can infect the computer system. This involves having a virus-checking program running on your system at all times. Each program file or data file is automatically scanned for viruses before it is made available to the system. Many of these virus-checking programs check for file size or program structure changes.

Antiviral programs come in three basic types: *preventers* that prevent viruses from getting into the system, *detectors* that find viruses that have already invaded the system, and *identifiers* that determine the type of virus that is present. Unfortunately, most of the software that prevents, detects, or identifies viruses works only for known viruses. If a new virus or one that has mutated turns up, the antiviral program may not find it. Thus, a recovery plan must be in place.

Recovery Plan

If a virus invades the system, it is often best to wipe the system clean and start all over. In order to do this, the firm must have backups of all of its programs and data. Of course, this recovery plan is part of the documentation that the project team has provided with each new system.

Virus protection often does not receive the attention it deserves. It is hard to justify virus protection as a tangible financial gain to the company. The success of any virus protection program depends in large part on convincing management of the importance of protecting information. All too often, virus protection only occurs after the fact, that is, after a system is infected.

SECURITY IN A CASE ENVIRONMENT

Most companies have source code repositories for mainframe programs that restrict changes to code and create audit trails of such changes. Repositories may also restrict the viewing of code to authorized users, though this is not often done. Such restrictions do not exist for systems analysis and design documentation. Many CASE tools are desktop computer-based, and few companies have anything beyond the most rudimentary security for this data.

Analysis and design specifications and requirements documentation provide information about the entire system. Access to this information should be greatly restricted, especially for sensitive data. Because CASE data often resides on easily accessed desktop computers, or in host computer files that can be accessed through a terminal or desktop computer, security poses a special problem. Furthermore, desktop computers often do not record changes, and changes must not go undetected. Company personnel should make sure that the CASE tool they are using has the capacity to track what changes are made, when they are made, and who makes them.

It may be necessary to keep analysis and design data on a special desktop computer that has an auditing system for changes. This desktop computer should also have security measures that restrict access to each system on it and to modules within particular systems.

Additional security issues emerge when all project work is done on-line with CASE tools accessible through a relational database management system (DBMS).

The DBMS must contain security measures that define different user views for each team member. For instance, the ability to upgrade system status from "submitted" to "approved" should only belong to the project leader.

Viruses constitute another potential security problem for CASE tools. It is possible for a programmer either to attach a virus to specific code generated by a CASE tool or to modify the CASE tool so that it always generates infected programs. A programmer familiar with a particular CASE tool may modify that tool to generate code that contains a virus. Very few people visually check all the code generated by a CASE tool.

Virus problems are bad enough when implanted in only one company's copy of a CASE tool. If a virus is placed in a CASE tool marketed to other companies, the damage and liability escalate. Firms must always be cautious regarding the possibility of a virus on both internal and external software.

In summary, any system may require security control measures. However, systems developed in a CASE environment are particularly vulnerable because of the centralized location of information about the system and the ease of changing the system. As CASE tools improve, aspiring analysts should expect additional and unexpected security issues to arise. This knowledge should, at the very least, keep systems personnel from falling into complacency.

You have seen how computerized systems gather, process, and disseminate information. When so many people have access to so much data, the way this information is used is not only a legal concern but an ethical concern as well. The next section covers some of the ethical concerns associated with the increased use of computerized systems.

ETHICS

Plato posed the issue of ethics in *The Republic*: "Suppose you had a ring which when you turned the stone made you invisible. Why then should you act justly?" The same question faces today's computer user who, with the aid of technology, can effectively become invisible.

Ethical Considerations

The need for special ethical considerations in the field of information systems arises from several unique characteristics of computers and of their use. Computers have become the primary repositories of negotiable assets, and of representations of many other assets, in the form of magnetic patterns and electronic pulses. These assets are no longer directly subject to manual handling and observation; they may be obtained and used only through technical and automated means. Because computer technology places a new power in the hands of the technologists who deal with processing and data storage, personal privacy and fair information practices have become major legislative issues.

The computer transforms the context in which ordinary ethical issues arise. For example, having information stored in a computer as opposed to a file cabinet changes the steps necessary to protect it. Thus, the standards for proper behavior and for what constitutes negligence change. In many cases, the computer so transforms the context that ordinary concepts and acknowledged moral rules are pulled into a *gray area* of unanswered legal and ethical questions.

Most sciences and professions have had hundreds of years in which to develop the ethical concepts that form the basis for dealing with new issues. On the other hand, computer information systems have only been in existence for thirty or forty years. Though the need for ethical standards in IS is equally critical, it is no wonder that serious problems arise in developing ethical concepts and practices in such a comparatively short time. This seems to be the case, for example, with liability for malfunctions in computer programs. Established laws assign liabilities differently when products rather than services are being bought and sold. With computer programs, it is difficult to figure out whether they are products or services. Questions like these draw ordinary moral rules into those gray areas.

What Are Ethics (Morals)?

Society relies on ethics or morals to prescribe generally accepted standards of proper behavior. An **ethic** is a standard of right and wrong based on an objective (or objectives). Ethical standards are often idealistic principles because they focus on one objective. In a given situation, however, several moral objectives may be involved, making it necessary for people to determine an appropriate action that takes all of the objectives into account. Even though various professional organizations and religious groups in society promote certain standards of ethical behavior, ultimately each individual is responsible for deciding what to do in a specific situation. Therefore, through choices, each person defines a personal set of ethical practices.

Ethics Versus Laws

Ethics differ from laws in several important ways. First, laws apply to everyone. You may disagree with the intent or the meaning of a law, but that is no excuse for disobeying the law. Second, if two laws conflict, the judicial process determines which law takes precedence. Third, the laws and the courts identify actions as being right or wrong. From the legal perspective, anything that is not illegal is considered right or just. Finally, laws are used to identify unlawful behavior.

In contrast to laws, ethics are personal. Different individuals have different frameworks for making moral judgments. What one individual thinks is perfectly justifiable, another might consider unthinkable. Second, when different ethical positions come into conflict, there is no arbiter. Thus, when two ethical positions collide, each person must decide which is dominant. Third, two people may assess ethical values differently; there is no universal standard of right and wrong. Finally, there is no enforcement for ethical choices as there is for laws. To summarize these two important concepts:

Laws	Ethics
Laws apply to everyone.	Ethics are personal.
If two laws conflict, judicial process determines which takes precedence.	If different ethical positions conflict, there is no arbiter.
Laws and courts identify actions as being right or wrong—anything that is not illegal is considered right or just.	There is no universal standard of right and wrong—two people may assess ethical values differently.
Laws can be enforced—there are ways to rectify wrongs done on the basis of ethical choices.	There is no enforcement for perceived unethical behavior.

The Good and Bad Influences of Computer Technology

Computer technology is the control technology of our time. The computer has become the symbol of an advanced technological society. In a relatively short period, computers have become fundamental to the operations of all industrial societies. Without computers and telecommunication systems, much of the manufacturing industry, transportation and distribution, the government, the military, health services, education, and research would cease to function. Computers are without a doubt the most important technology to emerge in this century. Dependence on computer technology will only continue to grow into the next century. Yet, as society becomes more dependent on computers, it also becomes more vulnerable to computer misuse.

The problems with computer technology can be viewed in terms of three areas: scope, pervasiveness, and complexity.

Scope of the Influence

Computer technology enables enormous quantities of information to be stored, retrieved, and transmitted at great speeds and on a scale not previously possible. This is good in one sense, but it has serious implications for data security and personal privacy, since computers are basically insecure.

Pervasiveness of the Influence

Computer technology is finding its way into almost every aspect of our lives, including many areas previously untouched by technology. However, unlike other encompassing technologies such as electricity and television, computers are on average less reliable and less predictable in their behavior.

Complexity of the Influence

Computer systems are often incredibly complex—so complex that they are not always understood even by their creators. This often makes them completely unmanageable from a technical as well as an ethical standpoint.

How Technology Obscures
Ethical Behavior

Computers pose new ethical problems, new versions of standard moral problems, moral dilemmas, and force us to apply ordinary moral norms in uncharted realms. The increasing use of computer technology has raised ethical questions that have never been posed in quite their present forms. For example, under what circumstances should copying of a computer program be considered stealing? Does accessing information stored in a computer about an individual constitute invasion of privacy? These are not new areas of ethical concern: the first question concerns property rights and the second one privacy. However, because of the new context—computers—ordinary moral concepts and rules must be reinterpreted. Should computer programs be considered private property? Should information stored in a computer be considered private?

Computer-specific ethical issues arise as the result of the unique roles of computers, such as these:

- *Repositories and processors of information.* Unauthorized use of otherwise unused computer services or of information stored in computers raises questions of appropriateness or fairness.

- *Producers of new forms and types of assets.* For example, computer programs are entirely new types of assets, possibly not subject to the same concepts of ownership as other assets.

- *Instruments of acts.* To what degree must computer services and users of computers, data, and programs be responsible for the integrity and appropriateness of computer output?

- *Symbols of intimidation and deception.* The images of computers as thinking machines, absolute truth producers, infallible, subject to blame, and as replacements for human errors should be considered carefully.

The mere appearance of computers on the technological scene reflects the goals and priorities held by society. Computers carry with them consequences that must be evaluated by something more than just a cost/benefit analysis: ethical questions must be answered before such an analysis can be made. This new technology demands a re-examination of what is of real value in society. Because it both reflects and shapes values, computer technology not only invites but compels ethical deliberation.

Ethics in the Organization

The likelihood of unethical computer conduct is increasing, in part because of the integration of computers and communications in information systems, the availability of software for distributed databases, the increasing use of desktop computers, and the development of end-user computing. The ethical principles of society are increasingly difficult to identify, and individuals' perceptions of unethical behavior vary.

Personal use of applications, illegal copying of software, and other thefts of computer services and information are common abuses in the easily accessible environments of most organizations. However, it is difficult to measure unethical behavior in organizations because many organizations conceal its occurrence. In addition, unethical conduct is more likely to occur if employees do not know what their organization considers unethical or criminal conduct. To set clear standards, some organizations have a code of conduct regarding computer use. For example, IBM's code specifies that all company computer systems are for business use only. IBM believes that any unauthorized use, whether for personal gain or not, is a misappropriation of IBM assets.

Codes of Ethics in Professional Organizations

One of the ethical questions faced by computer professionals and computer users is: Should computer professionals be bound by a code of conduct and, if so, what should it include? In answer to that question, many organizations have developed codes of ethics. The Data Processing Management Association (DPMA), the Association for Computing Machinery (ACM), the Institute of Electrical and Electronics Engineers (IEEE), and other associations have set up standards, and in some cases enforcement procedures, that begin to spell out the ethical responsibilities of computer professionals. These codes of ethics provide some general rules for practitioners to consider when faced with moral questions raised by the diverse applications and growing technological sophistication of computers.

Bruce E. Spiro (1983), Vice President of the DPMA Education Foundation, suggests that the time has come for all the professional societies in the computer/information business to get together and establish across-the-board ethical standards. He believes:

> . . . we, as individual organizations, have gone about as far as it is possible to go. The next step is to unify the various standards and ensure fair and equitable enforcement as a profession. If we can do this, we will take a giant step forward and provide a sorely needed base of understanding that the public can look to, and of which we, as a profession, can be extremely proud.

Although professional codes of ethics can set standards of behavior for computer professionals, many people with access to computers are beyond the reach of industry or organizational ethical codes. Computer resources, therefore, must be protected by the legal system. The United States is working toward a comprehensive federal statutory response to the problem of computer-related crime. These statutes are supplemented by state criminal statutes applicable to traditional crimes that are committed with the aid of a computer and by specific state computer crime statutes.

Areas of Ethical Concern

Computer usage, unlike other professions such as law or medicine, goes on extensively outside the profession. Directly or indirectly, practically everyone is a computer user these days, and consequently everyone faces the same ethical dilemmas and conflicts of loyalty. Many of these dilemmas, such as whether or not to copy software, fall into those gray areas for which no established case law and very few accepted rules or social conventions exist.

The following is just a sampling of the numerous ethical concerns faced by computer users and computer professionals:

- Is copying software a form of stealing? What sorts of property rights should software developers have?
- Are so-called "victimless" crimes (for example, those against banks) more acceptable than crimes against human victims?
- Should computer professionals be sued for lax computer security?
- Is hacking (any computer-related activity that is not sanctioned or approved of by an employer or owner of a system or network) merely harmless fun, or is it a crime equivalent to burglary, forgery, and theft?
- Should the creation of viruses, a class of computer programs that most often generate havoc and despair rather than increasing productivity, be considered deliberate sabotage and be punished accordingly?
- Does gaining access to information on individuals stored in a computer constitute an intolerable invasion of privacy? How much protection are individuals entitled to?
- Who is responsible for computer malfunctions or errors in computer programs? Should computer companies be required to provide warranties on software?
- Is artificial intelligence a realistic and proper goal for information systems personnel?
- Should the workplace be computerized if it means loss of skills and increased depersonalization, fatigue, and boredom?
- Is it acceptable for computer professionals to make false claims about the capabilities of computers when selling systems or representing computers to the general public?
- Should computer professionals be bound by a code of ethics?

Computer Ethics Education

Computer crime, including fraud, piracy, information destruction, and telecommunications abuse, is on the rise, creating serious problems for law enforcement officials. Prevention through education in the responsible use of computers is an important part of the effort to reduce computer crime. Specifically, computer education classes can provide role models of ethical and responsible conduct.

In order to have a significant impact on students, ethical issues regarding computer technology need to be addressed in classrooms and computer labs as part of the instruction process. Rules for ethical use of technology can become lifetime habits, especially if students understand and internalize the values behind the rules.

The prevalent theme of technology ethics instructions is that information technology, including software, hardware, and data, is an extension of human society. It is created and used by humans. It can be used to harm or benefit others. Some applications of this technology are ethical and others are unethical; still others fall in the gray area. Each individual has a moral responsibility for the way he or she uses computer technology.

It is not new for the educational system to teach ethics, but as the use of educational technology increases, so does the complexity of the task faced by educators. Although many of society's traditional values can be extended to the use of information technology, without educational intervention, some individuals will act unethically. The ultimate question is: What is the cost to society of not instilling a sense of ethical responsibility in those who will eventually be exposed to information technology?

SECURITY AT NATIONAL GOLF & TENNIS (NG&T)

Management at NG&T imposes security measures based on multiple levels of ID/password security. In addition, they provide functional security, meaning that each class of users has its own level of access authorization. NG&T establishes four functional security areas and assigns two transaction levels, "Display only" and "Update and display," to users in their respective areas. Each user must be identified by a logon ID and password for entry into the system. Table 17-2 lists NG&T users and their security status.

NG&T management also institutes procedures to back up software and data files. Company personnel make backups every day: one copy for on-site storage and one copy for off-site storage. Off-site storage should be backed up at least once a week; once a day is the recommended interval.

NG&T personnel also install an uninterruptible power supply and surge protectors to guard against electrical power surges and drops, and natural disasters that may affect electrical power to its computers. Management also decides to purchase several Halon fire extinguishers for the computing system to secure it from fire.

Management has investigated and purchased a maintenance contract to minimize losses due to downtime. This contract includes a clause that ensures that alternative computer equipment will be provided within six to twelve hours at an off-site location in the event of the destruction of its equipment. NG&T management also decides to obtain a computer insurance contract to protect the firm against losses due to downtime or physical disaster.

The security precautions at NG&T are not complete. They are examples of the various ways of securing all aspects of the firm, meant to spark your interest regarding further security issues that NG&T should address.

Table 17-2 System users and security levels

System User	Different Types of Security Status
Order entry clerks	Order entry and placement Update and display of order data Status inquiry of order data Display only
Managers	Report access Update and display of data
Purchasing and receiving personnel	Inventory update and inquiry Status inquiry and update Update/display of inventory data Update/display of shipping data Display of inventory/shipping data
Order-filling, warehouse, and shipping personnel	Inventory update and inquiry Update and display of shipping data Inventory inquiry Display only for particular data Display of output reports

Note: Each transaction has a display-only screen. Users are identified by logon ID and password entry into the system. Users are permitted access to transactions only in their functional area at their own security level.

REVIEW

With the advent of distributed processing and with more users wanting access to computer systems, the need for security planning and implementation increases. Computer abuse is a major concern. Security measures help prevent this abuse by protecting data and computer systems from unauthorized access, modification, or destruction. The four major types of security are legal, operational, user, and data security. Before implementing any one of these types of security, analysts must assess the costs associated with various risks by performing a cost/benefit analysis.

Legal security ensures against violation of the rights of customers and employees. The analyst must consider "invasion of privacy" issues in any system design. *Who* should have *what* information is a key concern. Operational security protects hardware and software from threats. Hardware security measures include limiting physical access to the system by means of locked doors, badge-reading locks, and video cameras.

Analysts usually maintain hardware and software security by using passwords and logon procedures. Guidelines for passwords include choosing a password with a large number of possible combinations, blanking out passwords on the screen as users enter them, changing them periodically, and making one person responsible for password control.

Data security maintains data integrity. Three harmful situations may occur: Data may lose its confidentiality, it may be improperly modified, or it may be entirely lost. User security consists of a three-part approach: thoroughly checking prospective employees before hiring them, making current employees more security-conscious, and changing the attitudes of employees concerning security.

Security problems in a distributed environment multiply along with the number of systems and users it services. Passwords must be closely controlled in order to prevent unauthorized access. Data encryption helps secure data passed between different locations.

Breaches of security are tracked using audit trails and procedures. Most installations maintain logs for computer access from all sources, accesses to all data items, and all jobs processed by the system.

As the use of information technology continues to expand, both in schools and society, the need to address the ethics of technology grows. The potential for criminal abuse is on the rise, and some applications of the technology challenge society's core values.

The important first step in determining ethics in a given situation is to obtain all the facts, ask about any uncertainties, and acquire any additional information that is needed. In simple terms, you must first understand the situation before judging it.

The second step is to identify the applicable ethical principles. Respect for privacy, proper compensation, honesty, and fair play are all ethical principles. Ethical principles often conflict, making it necessary to determine which principles are the most important in a given situation.

The third step is choosing a course of action that satisfies these ethical principles. Very often, making a decision and taking action are difficult, especially if the action may have negative consequences. However, taking action based on a personal ranking of principles is necessary. The fact that other equally sensible people may choose a different action does not excuse lack of action.

Finally, computer systems are by their nature insecure. Society has yet to come to terms with the consequences of this and has become more vulnerable to human misuse of computers in the form of computer crime, software theft, hacking, the creation of viruses, invasions of privacy, and so forth. Before there can be any "universal" code of ethics, some form of consensus must exist regarding the application of ethical principles to these sorts of situations.

QUESTIONS

1. Define *security*, *threats*, and *risk*.
2. List the major types of security.

3. Define *legal security*. What is invasion of privacy, and why is it an issue in information systems?

4. Define *operational security*. What is meant by intentional threats versus inadvertent threats?

5. For a company in your vicinity, describe the operational security measures it uses for its systems.

6. What is involved in hardware security?

7. What are the various aspects of passwords, and how are they related to maintaining effective security?

8. Explain five guidelines for controlling passwords.

9. For a company in your vicinity, describe the security measures it uses regarding password protection.

10. How does software security differ from hardware security? Describe how software security is built into the system at various stages of the system life cycle.

11. For a company in your vicinity, describe the security measures it builds into its software.

12. Define *data security* and describe the three major harmful situations that can occur with data.

13. For a company in your vicinity, describe its data security methods.

14. Define *user security*. Why is it important to be concerned with people outside of the IS department?

15. For a company in your vicinity, describe its user security methods.

16. Describe problems associated with maintaining security in a distributed environment.

17. Discuss three major aspects of security in a distributed environment.

18. Define *encryption*. Why is it important in a distributed environment?

19. For a company in your vicinity, describe how it uses encryption methods to secure its data and systems.

20. How are breaches of security tracked?

21. Name the three types of logs maintained for audit purposes.

22. For a company in your vicinity, describe the logs that it maintains for auditing purposes.

23. What is a computer virus? How is it spread?

24. What precautions should a firm take to protect itself from a computer virus?

25. For a company in your vicinity, describe how it protects against viruses.

26. Define *ethic*. How does an ethic differ from a law?

27. How does technology tend to obscure ethical behavior?

28. Name and discuss several ethical concerns in the information systems field.

29. For a company in your vicinity, describe the way it addresses ethical issues.

EXERCISES

Chapter 17 of the student workbook contains blank documentation forms to use in the following exercises.

1. Create a detailed plan for securing NG&T from viruses by identifying different types of viruses, a way to prevent infection, and a way to recover from infection if it occurs.

2. Create a detailed security plan for securing NG&T from a legal, operational, data, and user standpoint. Be sure to identify possible threats, methods of addressing them, ramifications of their detrimental effects, and recovery actions. You should also include measures for securing NG&T in a distributed environment.

3. Perform and document a cost/benefit analysis of the security measures recommended in exercise 2.

4. Design a questionnaire to determine the ethical beliefs of your classmates with regard to using pirated software, using computer systems for their own personal use, and stealing from a machine rather than from a person.

SELECTED REFERENCES

Blass, A. 1992. "Trade: Learning the Soft Way." *The Far Eastern Economic Review* 155, no. 48 (December 3): 54–56.

Brandt, R. 1992. "Bit by Bit, Software Protection is Eroding." *Business Week* (July 20): 86–88.

Brownstein, M. 1990. "Ashton-Tate's New CEO Faces His First Crisis." *InfoWorld* (December 24/31): 23.

Daly, J. 1992. "Court Dismisses Core of Apple GUI Suit." *Computerworld* (April 20): 1.

Ermann, M. D., M. B. Williams, and C. Gutierrez. 1990. *Computers, Ethics, and Society*. New York: Oxford University Press.

Fites, P., P. Johnston, and M. Kratz. 1989. *The Computer Virus Crisis*. New York: Van Nostrand Reinhold.

Forester, T. and P. Morrison. 1990. *Computer Ethics: Cautionary Tales and Ethical Dilemmas in Computing*. Cambridge, MA: The MIT Press.

Galen, M. 1989. "The Right to Privacy: There's More Loophole than Law." *Business Week* (September 4): 81.

Gardner, E. P., L. B. Samuels, B. Render, and R. L. Coffinberger. 1989. "The Importance of Ethical Standards and Computer Crime Laws for Data Security." *Journal of Information Systems Management* 6, no. 4: 42–50.

Hoffman, M. 1982. *Ethics and the Management of Computer Technology*. Cambridge, MA: Oelgeschlager, Gunn and Hain, Inc.

Hogan, M. 1988. "Try It, You'll Like It," *Forbes* 142, no. 12 (November 28): 227–228.

Johnson, D. G. 1985. *Computer Ethics*. Englewood Cliffs, NJ: Prentice-Hall.

Kirkpatrick, K. 1991. "Fox, Ashton-Tate Resolve Legal Disputes." *Computing Canada* (December 5): 25.

Mace, S. 1990. "Defending the dBase Turf." *InfoWorld* (January 8): 43–46.

Mayo, J. L. 1990. *Computer Viruses*. Blue Ridge Summit, PA: Windcrest/ McGraw-Hill.

Morris, W., ed. 1976. *The American Heritage Dictionary of the English Language:* 450.

Oppenheim, P. 1991. "Patent and Copyright Infringement—and You." *National Productivity Review* 10, no. 4 (Autumn): 533–535.

Paradice, D. and R. Dejoie. 1991. "The Ethical Decision-Making Processes of Information Systems Workers." *Journal of Business Ethics* (January): 1–20.

Parker, D. B. 1979. *Ethical Conflicts in Computer Science and Technology*. Menlo Park, CA: AFIPS Press.

Peak, M. 1992. "From Catchword to Content." *Management Review* 81 (November): 81.

Pfleeger, C. P. 1989. *Security in Computing*. Englewood Cliffs, NJ: Prentice-Hall.

Phillips, S. 1989. "Never Mind Your Number—They've Got Your Name." *Business Week* (September 4): 81.

Rothfeder, J., S. Phillips, et al. 1989. "Is Nothing Private?" *Business Week* (September 4): 74–80.

Scrogan, L. 1988. "The Online Underworld." *Classroom Computer Learning* 8, no. 5 (February): 58–60.

Sivin, J. P. and E. R. Bialo. 1992. "Ethical Use of Information Issues for Information Technologies in Education: Important Issues for America's Schools." *Issues and Practices in Criminal Justice*. Washington, DC: National Institute of Justice.

Spiro, B. E. 1983. "Ethics—The Next Step Is Crucial." *Data Management* (November): 32–33.

Vitell, S. and D. Davis. 1990. "The Relationship Between Ethics and Job Satisfaction: An Empirical Investigation." *Journal of Business Ethics* 9 (June): 489–494.

Weigner, K. and J. Heins. 1989. "Can Las Vegas Sue Atlantic City?" *Forbes* 143, no. 5 (March 6): 130–137.

PART VII

Appendixes

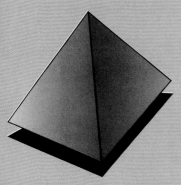

Appendix A provides a more technical description of database structures, including link list and inverted list. Appendix B reviews the concept of structured programming and provides specific structured programming rules for COBOL programs.

APPENDIX A

Database Data Structures

The creation of a database often involves using two methods that make data access more efficient. These two methods take the form of two database data structures, called link lists and inverted lists. These two database data structures make the data in a database more efficiently accessible by using either embedded data addresses in database records or separate files for indexing database records.

Correlating the logical and physical views of data is frequently accomplished by specifications in the schema and by the manner in which the database management system (DBMS) uses the schema to physically integrate the logically related data. Many DBMSs integrate related data items in a database by using structured relationship specifications called database data structures. The term *database data structure* should not be confused with the term *data structure*, which is commonly used to refer to logical or physical strings of actual data items for retrieval purposes. A data structure represents what data is to be structurally viewed as related to a specific data type. For example, the LOG-CUSTTRNS LDS depicted in Chapters 5, 6, 8, and 9 is such a data structure. A *database data structure* is a method for logically relating a set of physically independent data items to fulfill some information retrieval purpose. There are two database data structures:

- Link lists
- Inverted lists

These database data structures provide efficient ways to link related data items for accessing purposes.

LINK LISTS

A *link list* is a type of database data structure that provides a way to physically access logically related data. Linking logically related data using a link list involves embedding the address of the physical record containing the next data item in the *list* of logically related data items. Each physical record containing a data item in the list contains an additional *field*. The address of the physical record containing the next data item in the list of logically related data items is stored in this field.

For example, a link list supported database containing supplier and inventory item data types could include a field in the supplier record that indicates the address of the physical record containing the first inventory item the vendor supplies. The first inventory item record for that supplier subsequently would include a field containing the address of the physical record containing the next item the vendor supplies. Each succeeding inventory item record for a particular vendor would contain the address of the record containing the next item the vendor supplies. These embedded addresses are sometimes called *pointers*. Linking these related data items using a link list provides a way to physically access the logically related data items. Figure A-1 shows an illustration of the vendor/inventory item link list.

Figure A-1 contains supplier (vendor) records in record positions 01, 02, and 04. The remaining record positions contain item records for appropriate vendors. The data item in the last column contains pointer data values that are part of the specific data object. These data items are used to link vendor records with all of the items supplied by each vendor. For example, the pointer data item of the Black/Decker vendor data object contains an embedded pointer (03) to its first item data object (1/4 Drill). The

Record Position	Record ID	Vendor/Item	Record Pointer
01	1111	Black/Decker	03
02	5555	John Deere	05
03	101	1/4 Drill	08
04	3333	Stanley	06
05	205	Tractor	07
06	301	Hammer	10
07	275	Hay bailer	**
08	150	Drill press	09
09	175	Saber saw	**
10	305	Hand saw	**

Figure A-1. Example of vendor/item link list

1/4 Drill data object (Record Position 03) contains an embedded pointer (08) to the record position of the next inventory item (Drill press) supplied by Black/Decker. The Drill press data object (Record Position 08) contains an embedded pointer (09) pointing to the next inventory item (Saber saw) supplied by Black/Decker. The link list continues linking each related data object until all of them are linked for Black/Decker, or any other vendor.

The end of a particular set of related data objects in the link list is often identified by storing a special character combination in the embedded pointer data item for the last data object in the list of related data objects. The DBMS recognizes this special character combination as the end of a particular list of related data objects. For example, the data object in Record Position 09 contains the last data object (Saber saw) for the Black/Decker link list. This record contains ** as its pointer data item. This combination of characters *may* be a code that signifies the end of the list of logically related data items.

Two-Way Link Lists

Each different set of logically related data items requires a completely separate link list and accompanying embedded pointer data items. Data types linked together using link lists frequently contain two embedded pointer data items for each relationship, one pointing to the related data objects in ascending order and the other pointing to them in descending order. This is called a *two-way link list*. Furthermore, the last data object in a particular list may contain a pointer back to the first data object in the list. This is known as a *ring*, because it provides a continuous circle to access data objects for a particular list of data items. For example, Figure A-2 shows a two-way link list with a ring-type entry for the vendor/item database.

Notice that the data objects (Record Positions 07, 09, and 10) in Figure A-2, which contain the last inventory items in the link list for all three vendors, point back to the respective vendor in the first pointer, Record Pointer1. This constitutes a ring-type link list. Furthermore, notice that Record Pointer2 is a link list that links vendors and inventory items in reverse order, thus providing a two-way link list. For example, Record Pointer2 in the Black/Decker data object points to the Saber saw data object in Record Position 09, which in turn points to the next item data type, Drill press, in the descending list for Black/Decker, and so on.

The advantage of a two-way link list is that during updating actions, programs can more easily update pointers for data objects being added to or deleted from the database and the link list. For example, if the Drill press data object is being deleted from the vendor/item database, its Record Pointer1 and Record Pointer2 data items point to the other data objects in the list whose pointers need updating. In the first pointer for the Drill press is the record position of the next item in the ascending order list, the Saber saw, whose Record Pointer2 needs to point to the item before the Drill press: the 1/4 Drill in Record Position 03. Thus, Record Pointer2 of the Drill press data object is moved to Record Pointer2 of the Saber saw data object. Furthermore, the pointer value of Record Pointer1 for the Drill press data object needs to be moved to Record Pointer1 of the 1/4 Drill data object so that it now points past the Drill press data object

Record Position	Record ID	Vendor/Item	Record Pointer1	Record Pointer2
01	1111	Black/Decker	03	09
02	5555	John Deere	05	07
03	101	1/4 Drill	08	01
04	3333	Stanley	06	10
05	205	Tractor	07	02
06	301	Hammer	10	04
07	275	Hay bailer	02	05
08	150	Drill press	09	03
09	175	Saber saw	01	08
10	305	Hand saw	04	06

Figure A-2. Example of vendor/item two-way link list with a ring

to the Saber saw data object. The Drill press data object is now effectively deleted and all link list pointers are updated. The last action for the update would mark the Drill press storage as available space in which another data object can be added.

A two-way link list also makes adding a data object to the link list easier. If an additional item is being added to the list of items for a particular vendor, the item before and after the insertion item should have the next item (Record Pointer1) and previous item (Record Pointer2) updated, respectively. For example, if a Band saw item with Record ID 160 is added for Black/Decker in Figure A-2, it should be positioned in the link list between the Drill press and Saber saw data objects. Let's assume that the Band saw is placed in Record Position 11. Record Pointer1 for the Drill press should now point to Record Position 11, listing the Band saw as next in the list, while Record Pointer2 for the Saber saw should now point to Record Position 11 listing the Band saw as previous in the list. In addition, Record Pointer1 for the Band saw should contain 09 to point to the Saber saw as the next in the list, while Record Pointer2 for the Band saw should contain 08 to point to the Drill press as previous in the list. The record pointers in the Saber saw and Drill press data objects have the record position data values, next and previous, that aid in adding the Band saw data object and updating all pointers in the link list. Many different hierarchical and network DBMSs use the link list database data structure.

INVERTED LISTS

An *inverted list* is a database data structure in which a completely separate file is created to index related data items. The inverted list is a type of index file that contains data items that point to the physical addresses of actual data records containing data objects that have some logical relationship. For example, linking the vendor/inventory item data objects could also be accomplished by using an inverted list. A series of consecutive records in the inverted list (index file) represents the way to link all inventory items for a particular vendor. Figure A-3 contains the same vendor/item database as Figure A-1, but it uses an inverted list to link the related records.

When inverted lists are used, accesses to the database for a particular sequence of related records direct the DBMS to first read the inverted list to obtain the address of the actual data records to access. The DBMS then uses these addresses to obtain the actual data items requested.

Linking all of the inventory items for a particular vendor is accomplished by consecutively storing index records for each vendor. For example, all of the Black/Decker inventory item data objects are indexed first in the inverted list of Figure A-3. All of the John Deere inventory item data objects are indexed next in the inverted list. Finally, all of the Stanley inventory item data objects are indexed in the inverted list. Note that each index record contains the address and record position of the vendor data object, as well as the address of the inventory item data object associated with that vendor. For example, the first three index records in the inverted list have a Vendor pointer that points to the record position of the Black/Decker vendor. The Item pointers for these three index records have data values that point to the three inventory items supplied by Black/Decker in the same order as the link list pointed to them in Figure A-1: 1/4 Drill—Drill press—Saber saw.

The end of a list for a particular vendor in Figure A-3 is identified when the record position address value for the vendor changes in the list. For example, when the fourth index record in the inverted list is read by the DBMS, the change in record position from 01 to 02 for the Vendor pointer signifies the end of Black/Decker data objects and the start of John Deere data objects.

Record Position	Record ID	Vendor/Item	Inverted List Vendor	Item
01	1111	Black/Decker	01	03
02	5555	John Deere	01	08
03	101	1/4 Drill	01	09
04	3333	Stanley	02	05
05	205	Tractor	02	07
06	301	Hammer	04	06
07	275	Hay bailer	04	10
08	150	Drill press		
09	175	Saber saw		
10	305	Hand saw		

Figure A-3. Example of vendor/item inverted list

	Inverted List	
Vendor		**Items**
01		03,08,09
02		05,07
04		06,10

Figure A-4. Alternative inverted list format

An alternative format for the inverted list is to have a pointer for the vendor followed by all of its item pointers as separate pointer data items in the inverted list record. Figure A-4 illustrates this alternative form.

Each different logical relationship between data items requires creating a new inverted list for accessing the related records. Many hierarchical and network DBMSs, and some relational DBMSs, use inverted lists to physically access records that are logically related.

WHERE AND WHEN TO USE LINK AND INVERTED LISTS

Most commercially available hierarchical and network DBMSs use either link lists or inverted lists to provide a more efficient means of physically accessing logically related records. For some relational DBMSs, inverted lists can be used to make data retrieval easier. The database administrator (DBA) specifies in the schema which related data items need to be linked, and the DBMS accomplishes data linking using the type of database data structure designed for that DBMS.

The analyst provides the information to the DBA for defining relationships requiring either link lists or inverted lists. This information is the result of documenting user requirements and entering dictionary entries regarding relationships between data items. The entity/relationship model described in Chapters 5 and 8 for documenting user requirements often provides information to determine the necessity of physically providing for data linking using link lists or inverted lists.

Accommodating infinite combinations of logically related data items provides the basis for designing a database capable of being shared by a large number of applications in the firm's operations. Sharing of the database resource is accommodated by integrating related data for different business applications. Analysts provide the DBA with information regarding different applications for this purpose. The DBA then defines a schema that provides ways to integrate data relevant for those applications.

Two application design issues critical for this integration are:

- What data items carry a linking relationship?
- How frequently is the data going to be accessed using this linking relationship?

It must be remembered that a DBMS is always capable of using data values as the basis for searching the database to retrieve logically linked records. Therefore, the use of link lists and inverted lists is not always necessary or desirable. However, the use of these lists provides ways to more efficiently accomplish a linked data retrieval. For these instances, a link list or an inverted list may be created.

There is a cost associated with using link lists and inverted lists for more efficient access. This cost consists of the additional updating requirements needed when data is added to or deleted from the database. Adding and deleting data that has built-in linkages also requires updating the link or inverted lists. These added costs must be compared with the benefits attributed to quicker access to the data as provided by the use of link or inverted lists. The ideal situation in which to use link lists or inverted lists occurs for related data items that are frequently accessed for display purposes but are infrequently updated. When the data is frequently accessed and frequently updated, other influences, such as the functional importance of quick access, help to determine when to use a link list or an inverted list. When data is infrequently accessed by few users, the data should be accessed solely in regard to the comparative analysis already included in all DBMSs. However, it often occurs that political expedience for highly authoritarian supervisory personnel overrides this general guideline.

APPENDIX B

Structured Programming Rules for COBOL Programs

System development typically requires that programs be created in a structured programming format. A structured programming format can be used for programs in any computer language. To better understand what is meant by structured programming rules, this appendix lists the rules that might exist for structured programs using the COBOL language. COBOL was chosen as an example because of its wide use in business. The remainder of Appendix B lists a set of possible structured programming rules for COBOL programs.

- All divisional, sectional, and paragraph headings appear on a line by themselves and begin in column 8.

- The AUTHOR, DATE-WRITTEN, and REMARKS paragraphs must contain documentation entries concerning the program.

- All paragraph entries must begin on a separate line in column 12.

- Instructions requiring separate options appear with each option on a separate line following the initial specification, with succeeding like options indented to column 16.

- Instructions having additional options within the option of an instruction should have each option coded on a separate line, with the additional options indented to column 20.

- The options of FILE-CONTROL entries must appear on separate lines and be properly indented.

- Each FD entry must include the RECORD CONTAINS, BLOCK CONTAINS, LABEL RECORDS ARE, and DATA RECORD IS clauses.
- All FD clauses must appear on a separate line and begin in column 12.
- All names assigned to database objects or files, data types or records, and data items should completely define the data, with abbreviations and dashes included where necessary.
- Database objects or file names are assigned that describe the type of data being retained and include a prefix that designates the way it is used (input or output) within the program.
- Data type or record names and data item or field names are assigned that describe the type of data being retained and may include a prefix as an acronym to identify the database object or file of which the data is a part.
- All data type or record descriptions for input and output database objects or files are not subdivided in the FILE SECTION; separate WORKING-STORAGE section 01 entries are created for each different record description.
- PIC specifications begin with PIC starting in column 32 and the picture starting in column 36.
- The VALUE clause for a particular WORKING-STORAGE section entry should be on a separate line and begin with VALUE starting in column 32.
- All independent WORKING-STORAGE data items are defined as 05 entries under a 01 entry named WORK_AREA, with the 01 WORK_AREA appearing first in the WORKING-STORAGE section.
- All sequential access input files should be assigned end-of-file switches with an initial value of "N" and appear first within the 01 WORK_AREA (following the 01 WORK_AREA entry).
- All independent numeric WORKING-STORAGE data items are assigned an initial value of zero before program execution begins using the value clause.
- All table descriptions appear second in the WORKING-STORAGE section following all the 01 WORK_AREA entries.
- All input data type or record descriptions appear third in the WORKING-STORAGE section following table descriptions.
- All heading descriptions appear fourth in the WORKING-STORAGE section following input descriptions.
- All detail output descriptions appear fifth in the WORKING-STORAGE section following heading descriptions.
- All total output descriptions appear sixth in the WORKING-STORAGE section following detail output descriptions.
- The logic of the program should be segmented into modules that are short, easy to understand, and easy to maintain.
- Program modules should generally consist of fewer than fifty lines of code.

- The PROCEDURE DIVISION must be sectioned, with each section concluding with an EXIT paragraph.
- Overview documentation must be included at the start of the program and the start of each section of the procedure division to describe the purpose of that section. The description should include an explanation of how that section accomplishes its purpose.
- All PROCEDURE DIVISION section names must begin with a three-digit number, with succeeding sections having higher numbers starting with 000 and incremented by 50.
- The first section must be called CONTROL-SECTION, and it contains only PERFORM instructions providing overall program logic control for the remainder of the program.
- All performed sections must be positioned after the last section within which they are performed.
- The CONTROL-SECTION should primarily perform the INITIAL-SECTION, PROCESS-SECTION until end of program is detected, and CLOSE-SECTION.
- The INITIAL-SECTION should contain PERFORM instructions for the OPEN-SECTION, appropriate heading sections, appropriate data initialization sections, and appropriate read sections for "priming the pump" for input data processing.
- The PROCESS-SECTION should contain all conditional statements as close to the beginning of the section as possible.
- All required MOVE statements should appear next in the PROCESS-SECTION for moving input data items to output.
- All calculations should be expressed by using COMPUTE instructions.
- All required detail calculations should appear next in the PROCESS-SECTION.
- All required total calculations should appear next in the PROCESS-SECTION.
- Appropriate end-of-page or screen detection should appear next in the PROCESS-SECTION.
- Appropriate heading sections should be performed next in the PROCESS-SECTION if the end of page is detected.
- Appropriate detail output should be performed next in the PROCESS-SECTION.
- Appropriate data input sections should be performed last in the PROCESS-SECTION.
- The CLOSE-SECTION should perform all appropriate total sections first.
- The CLOSE-SECTION should contain all CLOSE instructions.

Index

READ statements, 542
Real-time systems, 542, 554-557
  in NG&T application, 556-557
Real value monetary costs, 673-675
Record counts, 637
Recovery. *See also* Crash recovery
  of data, 766
  from virus, 772
Recovery testing, 614
  in NG&T application, 620
Redundant data items, 502
Re-engineering, 453-454
  of system, 730
Refined user requirements, 351
Rehosting computer systems, 582
Relation, defined, 479
Relational models, 478-480
Relationship cardinality. *See*
  Cardinality relationship
Remote-driven interface, 313-314
Remote job entry systems (RJES),
  557-558
  in NG&T application, 558
Report conversion, 640
Reports, use of, 157
Repository support, 649, 654
  with CASE, 95-96
  for conversion and changeover,
    654-655
Resources for project, 694
Response checking
  routines/verification, 571-572
Reusable code, 123, 641-643
  benefits of, 642-643
  in fifth generation system, 589-590
Reverse engineering, 724
Review. *See also* Formal review
  post-implementation review, 718-723
Ripple effect, 27, 741-742
Risks, 758, 765
Rockard, John, 346
Rule, defined, 55

S

SA&D methodology. *See*
  Methodology
Schema of database. *See* Database
  schema
Scientific management, 112
Scope of problem, 148
Screen masks
  data manipulation commands
    (DMCs) and, 486
  interface, 313, 328
  for real-time system, 555, 556

reusability, 549
Scribes, 163
SDLC. *See* System development life
  cycle (SDLC)
Search argument, 730-731
Second normal form (2nd/NF), 501-503
Security
  assessing needs for, 757-759
  as auditing function, 758-759
  CASE environment, security in,
    772-773
  computer abuse, 757
  for database, 482-483
  data security, 765
  in distributed environment, 767-769
  electronic data processing (EDP)
    auditing, 759
  enciphering key, 483
  encryption procedures, 483
  for hardware, 764
  inventory management, 768-769
  legal security, 760-761
  in NG&T application, 779-780
  operational security, 762-765
  passwords, 762-764
  payroll project example, 764-765
  for software, 764-765
  tracking breaches in, 769-771
  of transferred data, 769
  types of, 759-767
  user security, 766-767
Selection, 52
Semantic data model (SDM), 60
Semantic functional primitive DFD, 256
Semantic objects
  associative semantic objects, 510
  categories of, 509-512
  composite semantic object, 510
  compound semantic objects, 510
  defined, 508-509
  generalized semantic objects,
    511-512
  hybrid semantic objects, 510
  normalized database design with
    OODD, 512-527
  simple semantic object, 509
Semistructured problem, 20
Sensitivity analysis, 552
Sensory approach to training, 630
Sequence, 52
  of STC procedure, 391-392
Sequential access files, 550-551, 604
Sequential file organization, 601
Sequential tasks, 407
Serial-access data objects, 391

Sign-off document for analysis phase,
  288
Simple network relationship
  models, 476-478
  normalizing, 520
Simple semantic objects, 509
  normalized database design and,
    512-513
Simulated test data, 616
Slack time in CPM, 698-700
Social orientation of company, 664-665
Soft copy, 316
Software
  acquisitions of, 566-567
  components, 12-13
  configuration by database
    administrator (DBA), 473-475
  converting existing formats, 566
  crash recovery routines, 573-574
  development, 543-546
  installation checklist for, 652-654
  for maintenance, 276
  project management software
    systems, 708-709
  security for, 764-765
  structured design, software
    produced through, 441
Software Magazine, 38
Source documents, use of, 156-157
Spanned system architecture, 30-31
Span of control for STCs, 432-433
Specifications for STCs, 449-451
Spiro, Bruce E., 777
SPQR/20, 116
SQL (Structured Query Language),
  486, 575
Standardized GUI, 314
Standardized programmer interface,
  579-580
Standards, 15, 57
Standard system architecture. *See*
  System architecture
Static testing tool, 616-618
Statistical time estimation methods,
  701-702
Stochastic determinations, 701-702
Storage testing, 614
  in NG&T application, 619
Strategic management, 24
Stress tests, 613
Structure charts (STCs), 56, 86-87,
  387-393. *See also* Boss module;
  GTOP0001 DFD; GTOP000101
  DFD
  cohesion in, 430-432